2004

SOCIAL WORK SERVICES IN SCHOOLS

FOURTH EDITION

PAULA ALLEN-MEARES, EDITOR
University of Michigan

Boston   New York   San Francisco
Mexico City   Montreal   Toronto   London   Madrid   Munich   Paris
Hong Kong   Singapore   Tokyo   Cape Town   Sydney

Executive Editor: Patricia Quinlin
Editor in Chief, Social Sciences: Karen Hanson
Editorial Assistant: Annemarie Kennedy
Marketing Manager: Taryn Wahlquist
Editorial-Production Service: Whitney Acres Editorial
Manufacturing Buyer: JoAnne Sweeney
Cover Administrator: Linda Knowles
Electronic Composition: Peggy Cabot, Cabot Computer Services

For related titles and support materials, visit our online catalog at www.ablongman.com

Between the time Website information is gathered and then published, it is not unusual for some sites to have closed. Also, the transcription of URLs can result in unintended typographical errors. The publisher would appreciate notification where these errors occur so that they may be corrected in subsequent editions.

Library of Congress Cataloging-in-Publication Data

Allen-Meares, Paula.
    Social work services in schools / Paula Allen-Meares—4th ed.
      p. cm.
    Includes bibliographical references and index.
    ISBN 0-205-38109-X
    1. School social work—United States. I. Title.
  LB3013.4.A45 2004
  371.7'0973—dc21   2003040430

Printed in the United States of America

10 9 8 7 6 5 4 3 2   08 07 06 05 04 03

CONTENTS

America has been turning its attention back to its children and schools, an effort with such compelling support and logic that the strong sociopolitical changes of our times will not change the course for long. This powerful fourth edition of *Social Work Services in Schools* offers a timely and important guide to developing the optimal use of social work in schools and the role of schools in delivering human services. The broadly expressed national concern for schools, children, and families has created many opportunities and challenges, and the authors address virtually all of them in crisp and telling treatments. Befitting their longstanding involvement in schools, communities, and with school social work, they cast the net broadly for topics that are critical to school social work practice, present and future. Several discussions address changes larger than the school (e.g., the impact of welfare reform and major initiatives in school financing), but most of them are focused on work with child, family, school, and community concerns.

Social Work Services in Schools continues to evolve to keep pace with the conceptual, empirical, practice, and program changes in social work. This volume has healthy roots in the 1986 first edition, written entirely by Paula Allen-Meares, Robert Washington, and Betty Welsh. The current volume continues to build on the undergirdings of that work and to offer the field an integrated view of school social work practice. By the third edition, the authors had added three chapters by social work practitioners with special expertise (Cynthia Franklin, David Dupper, and Sandra Kopels). The fourth edition builds on the same chapter structure while including content from several more of the nation's leading school social work scholars (including Ron Astor, Gary Bowen, and Siri Jayaratne) in order to reconceptualize and refresh earlier versions.

Taken together, this volume offers the best of a strong integrative framework provided by authored texts and the specialized content of edited volumes. It begins by examining recent education reforms, many of which were non-existent when earlier editions, even the last one in 1996, were penned. The role of public education is forcefully addressed, followed by pithy discussions of such issues as structural school reform, curricular reform, home schooling, charter schools, vouchers, the "achievement gap," and early intervention services. These issues are revisited in a variety of discussions later in the book. The writing is strong and sprinkled with insights that show that these authors have been actors in the evolution of school social work services, not just observers of its unfolding. The text draws strength and interest from the authors' participation in this rapidly changing field, which creates an inviting richness for the reader.

But this is not to suggest that the authors have taken the easier path and written a policy book or a book for middle managers. Although this text offers something for readers operating at each level, its centerpiece is clearly practice. The descriptions and analysis of practice are profoundly influenced by the ecological framework in which the child is at the intersection of complex, self-contained, yet interdependent systems. The authors continue to integrate new case study materials and recent research in order to breathe life into this ecological discussion. Bowen's contribution on the social organization of schools is one of several chapters that have been substantially reshaped by drawing on the most recent developments in theory and research.

Before moving from the larger scale trends in education to the specifics of practice, the authors review the history of school social work practice, a history that profoundly overlaps with the history of social work. This is the sole chapter that appears not to have had major changes since the last edition, as relatively modest strokes were needed on their 100-year-long canvas to sketch the changes in social work and education.

The practice chapters are many, well-textured, and attentive to the demands that school social work practice be evidence-based. This offers a precious tool for school social workers seeking to maximize their impact on schools and their ability to demonstrate the consequences to their colleagues and funding sources. In this intensely outcome-oriented era, the text's attention to examples of effective practice will be helpful to school social workers who are developing new positions or protecting old ones.

Articulating the influence of the social context on practice also requires a thorough understanding of specialized knowledge related to the educational setting. *Social Work Services in Schools* is especially competent in the areas of pupil rights and responsibilities, compulsory attendance, special education services, and zero tolerance policies. The chapter on groups of children with exceptional needs and the one on children with vulnerable social or behavioral profiles provide an abundance of new material that draws on the best practices across the profession and allied professions. These chapters yield illuminating discussions of implementing early intervention services; recent amendments to the school policy and special education policy; and services to adolescent parents, migrant children, homeless children, abused and neglected children, youth involved with gun violence and delinquent behavior, and youth with ADHD, to name just some of the well-covered topics.

Moving from the broad to the specific back to the broad, the volume propels the reader toward its conclusion with exciting and integrative chapters about the design and delivery of school social work services. These chapters consider issues related to the emergence of the school as a human service delivery system, school-linked services as a phenomenon distinguishable from school social work, and managed care.

Consistent with its message that the education world is becoming more accountable, the final chapter addresses the evaluation of school based practices and programs. The chapter has been largely rewritten by Jayaratne and takes a broader approach than the previous editions, addressing more of the evaluation strategies that school social workers might utilize. These include evaluability assessments, needs assessments, program evaluations, and single case evaluation.

Social Work Services in Schools is primarily designed for social work students and practitioners working in schools but could also be a key resource for child and family service providers working with schools and for other educators who want to know about school social work, its practice and promise. Public education has long been considered the great equalizer in American society. The challenge is becoming greater with the rise of private schools and the growing complexity of problems that make the school a less certain antidote to structural inequality as well as family problems and constraints. The authors, through their vast experience and clear vision, present an alternative that can help to reestablish the fundamental mission of both social work and the schools and provide equal access and opportunity for our youngest generation.

Richard P. Barth
Frank A. Daniels

We are excited about the fourth edition of *Social Work Services in Schools*. In this book we discuss historical and contemporary concepts, policies, and practices in the field of social work in schools. Along with these important concepts, new ones such as integrated service or full-service schools, violence in schools and preventive interventions, and issues of education and welfare reform are addressed. It is a basic book for persons specializing in social work services in schools as well as for those who are preparing to work in related agencies of the community and who find it necessary to understand school policies, educational practices, social services, and groups of pupils who are at risk of educational failure. Social workers who are now providing services will find the book a valuable resource about the state of this field and new forces shaping its future.

In recent years school social workers have grown in number and have become a well-organized and vocal group. Many have completed their professional education and are seeking to increase their competence by acquiring knowledge about new aspects of educational policy and practice and alternative models of social work services in schools.

The materials integrated in this book include empirical findings described in professional literature, case illustrations of social work practice in schools, and interviews. Social work practice is examined in relation to the present emphasis on improving the quality of education, charter schools, school reform, and full-service schools. Major educational policy issues, societal conditions that impact upon the quality of life of pupils and their families, and the strategic position of the school in attempting to solve critical problems of children and young people are also brought into focus. The chapter authors believe that social workers who are unfamiliar with major educational policies and practices and with the societal conditions that affect pupils cannot deliver responsive, quality social services in schools. A sound background and an understanding of the interdisciplinary nature of this field and how to collaborate are also required.

The major objectives of this textbook are: (1) to consider the conceptual framework of social work as currently developed by the professional and the application of those concepts to school social work; (2) to examine the roles and responsibilities of school personnel and of the children and parents served, as well as the legal framework for the establishment, financing, and governance of the school, and the unity and complexity of its interacting personalities and their functions; (3) to explain the major problem areas of public school education and to analyze the resultant sociological policy issues that affect the quality of education; (4) to identify target populations of school children for whom social work services are indicated at critical points of the life cycle; (5) to understand social work intervention and prevention in relation to the ecology of the school child; and (6) to present a basis for assuming the responsibility to design, deliver, and evaluate the effectiveness of school social work services within a multicultural context.

Although the order of the chapters lends itself to the construction of a coherent course and teaching outline, each chapter is written to stand alone so that, if desired, the chapters can be ordered to reflect individual preferences. Each chapter begins with a brief introduction that identifies the substantive content and provides unifying ideas.

Questions for study and discussion, suggestions for projects, and additional references for further study appear at the end of each chapter;

Internet Web sites are identified. The notes within each chapter are a source for additional exploration of ideas discussed in the text. Illustrations of school–community–pupil problems and appropriate interventions are intended to help the reader become familiar with the school setting within which social work takes place. Assessment instruments are discussed.

We continue to be grateful to Lela B. Costin, who, more than two decades ago, developed the original prospectus, which has been modified and expanded by chapter authors. This fourth edition is dedicated to her memory.

Paula Allen-Meares

Paula Allen-Meares, Ph.D., MSW, is currently dean and professor of the University of Michigan School of Social Work. Research interests include: the tasks and functions of social workers employed in educational settings and the organizational variables that influence service delivery; repeat births among adolescents and young adults; health care utilization, and social integration factors that influence sexual behavior and parenthood; and maternal psychiatric disorders and their direct and indirect effects on parenting skills and developmental outcomes of offspring. In addition, she has published on such topics as conceptual frameworks for social work, research methodologies, and racial/ethnic minority youths. Published books include: *Intervention with Children and Adolescents* (Longman Publishing), and *Social Work Services in Schools* (Allyn & Bacon). She is principal investigator of a W.K. Kellogg Foundation Grant, entitled "Global Program for Youth," and Co-Principal Investigator of the NIMH Center on Poverty, Risk, and Mental Health.

Ron Avi Astor, Ph.D., is an associate professor, who holds a joint appointment in the Schools of Social Work and Education at the University of Southern California. He is examining why some children are violent and how children's reasoning about justice affects their behavior.

Gary L. Bowen, Ph.D., MSW, is the William R. Kenan, Jr. Distinguished Professor, University of North Carolina at Chapel Hill, School of Social Work. His professional interests include social work with families, work and family linkages, the military family, research and evaluation, and family values.

Sally Atkins-Burnett, Ph.D., is an assistant professor of early childhood special education at the University of Toledo. She has taught elementary and special education in public and private schools and has provided early intervention and consultation support to families and programs that serve children with disabilities. Sally and her husband raised five children with special needs.

Anthony Derezinski, is the Director, Government Relations of the Michigan Association of School Boards. He is involved in legislative processes, state legislature and federal relations networks, lobbying and testimony on education issues, research and information on legislation and Department of Education issues.

Cynthia Franklin, Ph.D., LMSW-ACP, is a professor and coordinator of clinical social work concentration at the University of Texas, Austin, School of Social Work. Professor Franklin's professional interests are school social work, family therapy, clinical practice assessment and measurement, and integration of research and practice.

Siri Jayaratne, Ph.D., is associate dean and professor at the School of Social Work, University of Michigan. He has been studying the effects of work stress on the health and well-being of mental health practitioners, client violence towards social workers in the workplace, and conducting a survey of national practice standards.

Sandra Kopels, J.D., MSW, is an associate professor at the University of Illinois, Urbana-

Champaign, School of Social Work, where she teaches both law and social work policy courses. Professor Kopels has authored numerous articles, primarily focusing on the law's impact on the rights of vulnerable clients and the responsibilities of social workers who work on their behalf.

John W. Sipple, Ph.D., is an assistant professor of Education at Cornell University, where he teaches courses on American school reform, sociology of education, and administration of educational organizations.

CHAPTER 1

MAJOR ISSUES IN AMERICAN SCHOOLS

JOHN SIPPLE, CORNELL UNIVERSITY

INTRODUCTION

The American public educational system is a beleaguered public institution fraught with relentless criticism while also considered one of the most enduring and valued institutions in American society. Throughout its history, public education has been viewed as central to the survival of the democracy, individual opportunity, the production of a vibrant economy, the reproduction of society's economic and social strata, and the provision of equal opportunity. It is an extraordinary institution that is often praised as a solution to social, economic, and political problems while also branded as the cause of many of the same societal ills.

This chapter presents an introduction to the major issues—historical and current—in American education relevant to current and future school social workers. Beginning with a discussion of the broad and often competing purposes of public education, this section reviews the longstanding tension between public and private interests and how it is that most schools have configured themselves with staff and programming to serve both interests. Next, the social context of schooling is presented along with an examination of its role in the provision of equality of educational opportunity—especially in this time of unprecedented change in the demographics of American school children. Central to this discussion is the steady increase in the propor-

tion of minority students and the disturbingly consistent relationship between a child's race and social class and her school performance and outcomes. Next is a review of the major plans to "reform" schools to make them more excellent, equitable, and adequate, and discuss how different genres of reform are responding to different problems and promote different solutions. Such reforms include a greater academic press in schools, the effort to tighten the link between schools and other social service organizations, the push to allow market forces to drive school change, and the belief in the power of accountability and testing programs by both liberal and conservative critics alike. Inherent in this chapter is the opportunity and need for social work services in schools and communities, where such services have been called for and integrated, and where they have been overlooked.

Finally, this chapter is more representative than comprehensive. This is an attempt to illuminate major trends and practices that speak to the growing need for coordination among community- and school-based social workers, families, teachers, and administrators. This is increasingly important, as schools are facing ever-challenging and complex educational situations while at the same time an unprecedented inspection and expectation of practice and performance. From publicly reported test scores and increasing litigation to the recently institutionalized commitment to leave no child behind, educators, students, and school social workers find themselves under extraordinary scrutiny and pressure. Despite centuries of criticism, and with no let up in sight, public schools remain a central place in which to confront, question, and resolve the contradictions of American society and the current and future needs of American children.

PURPOSES OF PUBLIC EDUCATION

Posing a question to parents about what they want their local school to provide for their child will likely reveal an array of interests, needs, purposes, and goals for their local schools. Posing the question to community members (i.e., taxpayers) without a formal link to the local schools reveals a different though overlapping set of expectations, purposes and goals.[1] These multiple purposes are not new. There is much historical evidence that schools (public and private) have, from their inception, fulfilled multiple and competing purposes (Kaestle, 1983; Ravitch, 2000; Tyack & Cuban, 1995). These purposes encompass religious, social, political, economic, racial, and scientific interests. Remarkably, contemporary public schools attempt to provide for most of these interests through offering a range of academic subject area courses, remediation courses, Advanced Placement offerings, interscholastic athletics, art and music, student government, health and sex education, college advising, and—for too many children—the best nutrition and care they receive all day. The modern, comprehensive high school has even been compared to a shopping mall in that it caters to such a variety of interests and needs so that most consumers can find at least something they like (Powell, Farrar, & Cohen, 1985). Of

course, there is great variation across schools, school districts, and states in their ability or interest in providing what Kozol (1991) termed the "savage inequalities" between poor and wealthy schools, opportunities, and outcomes.

A central outcome of the socially determined purposes of public schools is the relative opportunity afforded each child. There is no debate that children arrive in kindergarten with very different levels of preparation and require a unique set of services in order to succeed.[2] What is debated are the nature of the educational services offered, how such services are provided, and who is responsible for the provision of such services. The history of American public schools provides a richly decorated canvas for further discovering and understanding the tensions and debates as to what social services are provided, by whom, and to whom.

David Labaree (1997) offers a set of alternative goals for American education and how these goals have been at the center of conflict since the founding of this nation. He writes that schools are in an "awkward position" between what "we hope society will become and what we think it really is" (p. 41). Labaree argues that the core problems with American schools are not pedagogical, organizational, social, or cultural, but rather "fundamentally political." The philosophical and pragmatic dilemma between Thomas Jefferson's political idealism and Alexander Hamilton's economic realism (Curti, 1935/1959, cited in Labaree, 1997) has outlasted two centuries of school reforms. Labaree suggests that schools promote equality while at the same time adapt to inequality; hence schools promote excellence for all children though are often organized to provide differential services to different students. In doing so, schools translate these contradictory purposes into three goals:

---

[1]See, for example, Rose & Gallup (2001), *The 33rd Annual Phi Delta Kappa/Gallup Poll of the Public's Attitudes Toward the Public Schools*, and U.S. Department of Education (1999), National Center for Education Statistics, Digest of Education Statistics, Table 23.

[2]The National Center for Education Statistics' *Early Childhood Longitudinal Study* (ECLS) is one of the first nationally representative studies to allow examination of early childhood and early educational experiences (see http://nces.ed.gov/ecls/).

1. *Democratic equality*—"A democratic society cannot persist unless it prepares all of its young with equal care to take on the full responsibilities of citizenship in a competent manner. . . . [S]chools must promote both effective citizenship and relative equality. . . . Education is seen as a public good, designed to prepare people for political roles."

2. *Social efficiency*—"[Society's] economic well-being depends on our ability to prepare the young to carry out useful economic roles with competence. . . . [S]ociety as a whole must see to it that we invest educationally in the productivity of the entire workforce. . . . Education is seen as a public good designed to prepare workers to fill structurally necessary market roles."

3. *Social mobility*—"Education is a commodity, the only purpose of which is to provide individual students with a competitive advantage. . . . [E]ducation is seen as a private good designed to prepare individuals for successful social competition for the more desirable social roles" (Labaree, 1997, p. 42).

How local, state, and federal policy and legal decisions impact these goals and how school personnel implement these goals should be of central interest to the reader of this book.

Over the course of the last 50 years, American schools have faced a variety of external pressures that have elicited responses embedded in one or more of the purposes of schooling. The pressures have come from the early industrialists (see Bowles & Gintis, 1976), the scientific managers of early corporate America (see Callahan, 1962), more contemporary business and political leaders (Chubb & Moe, 1990; National Commission on Excellence in Education, 1983), and research-based instructional methods and programs required by President Bush's Leave No Child Behind Act of 2001.

The *Brown v. Board of Education* decision in 1954 signaled a dramatic shift in how American society was to view and use its public schools. Stating that separate schools are inherently unequal, the Supreme Court overturned its 58-year-old doctrine affirmed in *Plessy v. Ferguson* (1896) of separate but equal. The implication of this decision was that de-jure segregation of schools was unconstitutional, though de-facto segregation continued and some argued has expanded (see Orfield 1978; Orfield and Eaton, 1996). Also, see Chapter 10 for a more comprehensive discussion of Brown and school desegregation.

After the launching of *Sputnik* in 1957 by the Soviet Union, Congress passed the National Defense Education Act (NDEA) to promote increased attention and scrutiny of math and science education. The law used schools as a central agent to increase the technical capacity of the country and counter the perceived scientific superiority of the Soviet Union. It was commonly perceived that the American way of life was being threatened and the schools were a major part of the solution to regain international superiority.

Robert Kennedy trekked with the media through Appalachia serving to bring the issue of rural poverty into the living rooms of middle class America. Furthermore, President Johnson's Great Society initiative included the passage of the Elementary and Secondary Education Act of 1965 (ESEA). For the first time, this act called for federal dollars to be given to public schools in an effort to improve the educational opportunities of economically and academically disadvantaged children. This began a new era of state support for academic opportunity for poor children and provided new resources for schools. Along with the new resources, however, came heightened expectations and broader obligations for local educators.

Whereas the ESEA began the flow of federal dollars into schools to enhance the education of poor and underperforming children, the passage of Public Law 94-142 (1975) marked a watershed moment in the education of handicapped children. While guaranteeing handicapped children a federal statutory right to an education, the law (in 1990 the law was renamed the Individuals with Disabilities Education Act, known as IDEA) provided guidelines, federal funding, and local accountability in promoting the education of handicapped children (see Chapter 8 for more on this).

A selection of other court cases has also dramatically shaped the purposes of public schools along with the opportunities and responsibilities of local educators and social workers. Among them are *Lau v. Nichols* (1974), in which the Supreme Court ruled that schools must provide native-language instruction to children whose native language is not English. This, like the inclusion of special education children, requires schools to provide a wide range of services to an increasing number of children. In light of the tremendous exodus of white families from inner cities that took place between the 1950s and 1970s, the *Milliken v. Bradley* (1974) decision had a profound effect on the ability of schools to provide an integrated educational experience for their students. Twenty years after *Brown,* and just three years after *Swann v. Charlotte-Mecklenburg* (1971), which allowed forced busing as a strategy to integrate schools, the *Milliken* decision disallowed the inclusion of suburban communities in city desegregation plans. The fallout from PL 94-142 and the *Brown, Lau,* and *Milliken* cases is that the public schools are required to educate all children, though typically do so in highly segregated communities (by race/ethnicity and wealth) and school buildings.

Less than a year after President Carter promoted the U.S. Office of Education to a department with cabinet-level status, newly elected President Ronald Reagan set out to abolish the Department of Education. The prevailing belief within the new Republican administration was that the federal role was unnecessary and that a return to more local control was what was needed to promote the improvement of public schools. To do so, the president established a blue-ribbon commission to report on the state of U.S. public education. The commission submitted their report (National Commission on Excellence in Education, 1983), and rather than reduce the federal role in education, they stated that the nation was at risk and stressed "the "imperative" for educational reform. This time the threat was economic, suggesting, "If an unfriendly foreign power had attempted to impose on America the mediocre educational performance that exists today, we might well have viewed it as an act of war" (p. 1). Rather than reducing the federal role in education, the report stirred so much interest that the federal government felt compelled to maintain its involvement.

The Goals 2000 Act, first promoted by President George H. Bush and then signed into law by President Clinton, exemplifies Labaree's statement that schools reflect what "we hope society will become and what we think it really is" (Labaree, 1997, p. 41). Among its many components, it called for the U.S. to be first in the world in math and science (reminiscent of the NDEA in 1958) and called for all children to be "ready to learn" by the time they entered kindergarten by the year 2000.

On January 3, 2002, President George W. Bush signed into law the No Child Left Behind Act of 2001 which reauthorized the ESEA. This 670-page bill is the most recent attempt to use the power and authority of the federal government to improve the performance of American public schools. This law, however, ties together many themes and reflects the confounding nature of the multiple and competing purposes of public schools. The full title of the act signals the attempt to promote each of the goals: "An act to close the achievement gap with accountability, flexibility, and choice, so that no child is left behind." This accentuates the need to reduce the achievement gap while also preserving the American commitment to liberty.

Each of these major events in the past 50 years promotes one or more of the aforementioned purposes of American schools. Some press for increased equality and the preservation of democracy while others promote competitiveness found in the free market and the gain of some at the expense of others. Later in this chapter, some major reform models are reviewed and highlight the goals they support or contradict and discuss the challenging position of educators and social workers.

THE SOCIAL CONTEXT OF SCHOOLING

The seemingly ubiquitous relationship between students' social class or race/ethnicity and school performance is a continual challenge for educators, policymakers, and communities. Whether measuring SATs, reading aptitude, or science achievement, the relationship holds. This relationship is not new, however, nor has it been ignored. Researchers have documented the relationship for nearly 40 years, while schools, communities, and governments have undergone multiple attempts to reform; at least some of which have targeted the achievement gap.

The Inexorable Link Between Poverty and School Performance

On Saturday, July 2, 1966,[3] then U.S. Commissioner of Education Harold Howe held a press conference to release a report in response to Section 402 of the Civil Rights Act of 1964.[4] The act called for the commissioner to conduct a survey "concerning the lack of availability of equal opportunities for individuals by reason of race, color, religion, or national origin in public educational institutions at all levels in the United States." This report intended to document the unequal opportunities afforded minority students in the segregated and underfunded schools that existed at that time. Specifically, the report addressed four questions: 1) To what extent are racial and ethnic groups segregated from one another in public schools? 2) Do schools offer "equal educational opportunities" to students of different races? 3) How much do students learn in different schools as measured by standardized exams? 4) What is the relationship between stu-

dents' achievement and the kinds of schools they attend? In conducting the study, Coleman and his colleagues surveyed approximately 600,000 students (roughly half white and half minority), 67,000 teachers, and 4,000 principals. This study, entitled *Equality of Educational Opportunity* (Coleman, 1966), later came to be known as the Coleman Report.

The report itself was lengthy, more than 700 pages, and exceedingly complex in its design, conclusions, and politics (Grant, 1973). The danger with such complexity lies in its interpretation by the media, policymakers, citizens, and educators. The desire for a simple message is natural, and yet this study did not lend itself to such simple messages and conclusions.

To the surprise of most, the results of the massive Coleman Report did not support the conventional wisdom that minority students were at a significant disadvantage, compared with white students, because of the "kind" of schools they attended. The summary report attempted to capture the essence of the study's findings.

— *Segregation:* Four in five white students attended schools that were at least 90% white. Sixty-five percent of Negro[5] students attended schools that were at least 90% Negro. In the South, most students attended schools that were either 100% Negro or white.

— *Teachers:* 65% of the teachers in the average Negro elementary school were Negro. In the South this was close to 100%.

— *Facilities:* "There is not a wholly consistent pattern—that is, minorities are not at a disadvantage in every item listed" (p. 9; e.g., age of building, class size, librarian, free textbooks, textbooks under four years old, chemistry laboratory), though the disadvantage exists most consistently with facilities more closely

---

[3]The report was released on the Saturday of July 4th weekend with the hope of minimizing media coverage.
[4]See Grant (1973) for the "best treatment" of the Coleman Report (personal communication with Harold Howe, Hanover, NH, February 1998).
[5]"Negro" is the term used in this 1966 report.

related to student learning (e.g., laboratories and numbers of books in libraries). This relationship is stronger in the South than in other regions of the country.

— *Programs:* Children attending Negro schools had slightly less access to curricular and extracurricular programs more related to academic learning (e.g., college preparatory curriculum, debate teams), though, again, the inequality is much greater in the South than elsewhere.

— *Achievement:* "The minority pupils' scores are as much as one standard deviation below the majority pupils' scores in the first grade. By 12th grade, the gap of average test scores between races is larger."

Finally, in what may be the most important and talked about finding from the study:

— "It appears that a pupil's achievement is strongly related to the educational backgrounds and aspirations of the other students in the school" (p. 22). Further analyses suggest "if a white pupil from a home that is strongly and effectively supportive of education is put in a school where most do not come from such homes, his achievement will be little different than if he were in a school composed of others like himself. But if a minority pupil from a home without much educational strength is put with schoolmates with strong educational backgrounds, his achievement is likely to increase" (p. 22).

The repercussions from this study were felt across the country and still reverberate today. The study had a profound impact on policy decisions on matters of school reform, racial desegregation and busing plans, and school finance litigation. The most common interpretations from the Coleman Report were that "money doesn't matter" and that "schools don't matter." Coleman and his associates refuted these claims, but, in part due to the complexity of the study and its complicated and contextualized findings, the simple interpretations held. One immediate

implication was that there was no tangible infusion of funds into minority schools as was anticipated with the passage of the Civil Rights Act. Rather, attention turned toward efforts at racial integration programs; typically through voluntary or forced busing of minority children into predominantly white schools (see *Swann v. Charlotte-Mecklenberg*, 1971, and Chapter 10 in this volume).

Despite many attempts to refute the findings (e.g., Jencks, 1972; Jencks & Phillips, 1998), the consistent relationship between student background and academic performance is inescapable. While billions of federal dollars have been spent through the ESEA and Head Start programs and many other major efforts at local, state, and national levels, current academic assessments reveal a similarly strong and consistent achievement gap. Whether it is educational attainment, dropout rates, or SAT scores, the disparities hold (e.g., see Figure 1.1). Some measures suggest a closing of the gap between Black Americans and whites, particularly in dropout rates, though disparities between Hispanics and whites remain great. The so-called "Nation's Report Card," the National Assessment of Educational Progress (NAEP), provides the best measure of state and national progress in increasing educational performance. In a 2002 report on *Raising Achievement and Reducing Gaps* (Barton, 2002) using NAEP data, the author states:

> No significant progress has been made [since 1994] in reducing the performance gaps experienced by minority and economically disadvantaged children. This is the *fundamental challenge* that must be the focus of the next phase of the education reform and improvement (p. 7, emphasis added).

Schools, Their Students, and Their Communities

Given what we know about the link between race, ethnicity, poverty, and student achievement and academic outcomes, it is especially im-

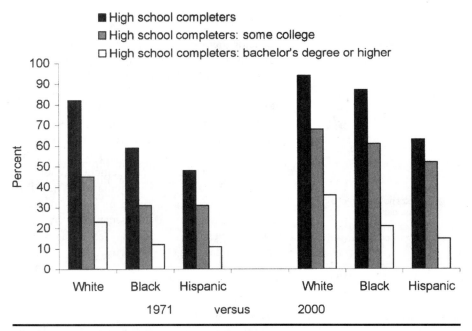

High school completers
High school completers: some college
□ High school completers: bachelor's degree or higher

FIGURE 1.1   Educational Attainment by Race, 1971–2000

Source: U.S. Department of Education (1999), National Center for Education Statistics, Current Population Survey.

portant to examine the changing demographic makeup of the school-age population. As a result of recent immigration, migration, and fertility patterns, an increasing proportion of school-aged children are African American, Asian American, and Hispanic American.

Demographic and Population Changes. The population of school-age children closely reflects the changes in the U.S. population and is becoming increasingly diverse in terms of race, ethnicity, language, and religion. The number of children in elementary and secondary schools increased from 35 million children in 1960 to 45 million in 1970. This number fell back to less than 40 million by 1985, but then increased steadily through 2000 returning to approximately 45 million students. Despite the fluctuations in the overall population, there has been a steady increase in pre-primary (preschool and kindergar-

ten) education. The number of children enrolled in such formal programs has doubled since 1965, topping out at eight million children by the mid-1990s (Digest of Education Statistics, 2001) (see Figure 1.2).

The national trends, however, mask important state-level differences in K–8 enrollments. Ten states, mainly in the Southwest and Rocky Mountain regions, are forecast to increase their enrollments by more than 5%, while 12 states, predominantly in the Northeast, will likely experience a decrease of at least 5% (Digest of Education Statistics, 2001). The population growth is overrepresented by increases in minority populations, in particular growth in the number of Hispanic children.

Such demographic changes create both an opportunity and demand for the provision of additional social work services. Given the achievement gap and the disproportionate growth of

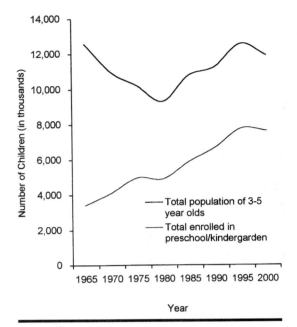

FIGURE 1.2   Growth in Pre-Primary Education, 1965–2000

Source: National Center for Education Statistics (2002), *Digest of Education Statistics, 2001*, Table 43.

minority children, it is particularly important that greater numbers of children receive appropriate educational, social work, and health care services before and during their formal schooling. The integration of children and family services, economic development, and educational opportunities, all of which are sensitive to the particular needs of greater proportions of minority children and families, is critical.

SCHOOL REFORM

Among the myriad efforts at improving school performance, reducing the achievement gap, and increasing the "school effect,"[6] are a number of reforms that warrant further attention. Structural, technical, and free market approaches are prevalent and receive much publicity.

Structural Reform

A major focus of reforming schools in the 1980s and 1990s targeted the traditional structural arrangements of schools. Among the chief concerns were the traditional top-down decision making and the arrangement of students. A common and highly visible strategy to reconfigure the locus of decision making and to increase community involvement in schools was a strategy called site-based management (sometimes termed school-based management). While this reform strategy was adopted by school districts across the nation, and even mandated by some state policies (e.g., NY), analyses of the reform described it as largely ineffective. The value was at best symbolic, and at worst served to create a false sense of empowerment and community involvement (Ogawa, 1994). Whereas most districts that adopted the practice continue to use it, the practice is largely ineffectual, as it serves to alter the structural arrangement of schools, though it usually does little to alter the locus of power and decision making.

Another such structural reform was the practice of altering the school schedule from one that includes eight 40-minute class periods to one which includes four 90-minute class sessions. The goal of such change is to allow for a different set of instructional strategies and learning activities, namely those that would allow for more in-depth study and exploration. Unfortunately, simply providing longer instructional periods does not, in itself, translate into different forms of instruction, let alone more effective forms of instruction. An example of the effect on instruction of the switch to block scheduling was when a teacher stated, "Good, now I can show the whole movie in one day" (cited in Elmore, 1995).

A third example of structural change that has received much attention since the mid-1980s is the reform practice of abolishing homogeneous "tracked" classes in favor of heterogeneously grouped classes. Arguing that low-tracked

---

[6]In contrast to a non-school or home effect by which school performance is more impacted by home influences than school experiences.

classes limit the learning opportunities for students and are disproportionately filled with poor and minority children, traditional segregation by academic tracks is unfair and provides fundamentally different learning opportunities for children in the different tracks (Hallinan, 1995; Oakes, 1985). Fueling this reform is the long-standing finding dating back to the Coleman Report (1966) that less than one-fourth of the variance in student achievement is attributable to between-school differences. This, of course, suggests that three-quarters of the variance is attributable to non-school and within-school differences in students and programs.

The development and institutionalization of the honors, college preparatory, general, and vocational tracks have taken place since the expansion of the American comprehensive high school in the 1940s and 1950s. Powell, Farrar, and Cohen (1985) referred to these as "shopping mall high schools" because the modern high school has tried to adapt to the need to offer programming for everyone. Many such programs, however, have little resemblance to academic schooling and do little to prepare the students for future academic work or employment.

Critics of tracking argue that teacher and student expectations are reduced and the curriculum less meaningful and useful in low-tracked classes than in the high-tracked courses (Oakes, 1985). *Detracking,* the removal of academic tracks, results in all classes being a mix of low- and high-ability students (i.e., heterogeneous grouping). Schools, and the communities they serve, often resist such changes to the school structure, particularly the parents of the more traditionally successful students (Welner, 2001). Oakes et al. (1997) suggest that communities often resist the changes on ideological and political grounds.

Structural reforms such as site-based decision making, block scheduling, and detracking—in and of themselves—are unlikely to stimulate measurable improvement in the education of children. Elmore, Peterson, & McCarthey (1996) suggest that school restructuring may very well be a necessary first step to real school improvement, though such changes are too often viewed as the end product. Efforts at school restructuring are rarely followed by the hard work of additional teacher learning and the provision of additional and adequate services to take advantage of opportunities provided by the changes in structure.

Systemic Reform

In an attempt to learn from the lessons of failed school reform in previous decades, some pushed for what became known as *systemic reform.* Rather than falling into the same trap as previous reforms as either being too top-down and prescriptive (i.e., not allowing enough flexibility for local needs and circumstances) or being too loosely coupled and unique to enable the scaling up of successful local reforms, researchers began calling for a blend of mutually supportive pressures and strategies for reform (O'Day & Smith, 1993; Smith & O'Day, 1991). The mutually reinforcing policies must also be more comprehensive in that they must take into account state, community, and individual needs and strengths. Simply altering the school schedule, adding an additional advisory group, or adding additional days or courses to the school year, most previous reforms have been too narrowly defined to impact the broader school system and the exceedingly complicated and interrelated set of issues and programs that encompass the instruction of children in public schools.

The new emphasis on systemic reform emphasizes the concurrent and interrelated set of curricular, instructional, medical, political, and structural changes. This broad set of mutually reinforcing reforms is thought to ensure coherence, consistency, and buy in from both local educators and state policymakers (See Fuhrman, 1993, 2001; Fuhrman & O'Day, 1996; Vinovskis, 1996). Among the multiple components to the systemic reform movement are those aimed at improving the 1) *knowledge base* of pre- and inservice teachers, administrators, social workers, and health care providers, 2) *curriculum* to make it more rigorous and content-based, and 3) *accountability* mechanisms in the form of uniform testing and the public reporting of results (Elmore, Peterson, & McCarthey, 1996).

The standardization of content-based curricula serves two purposes. First the standardization of curricula ensures that more students are exposed to high(er)-quality curricula. This coupled with a reform such as detracking pushes an academic curriculum into more classrooms, thus overcoming the culture of low expectations in the traditionally non-academic track classrooms. The content-based aspect of this curricular reform allows, and in fact encourages, teachers to teach what will be measured on the assessment exams. This reform receives some support from conservatives because it sets up an accountability system for how well teachers can teach and students can learn a common curriculum. Many liberals, on the other hand, support a common curriculum to reduce the negative impact of low expectations on poor and minority students. If all students are exposed to the same enriched curriculum, then more students will have the opportunity to perform at high levels.

Another aspect of curricular reform is the switch away from a basic skills curriculum and toward one more focused on higher order skills thinking and performance. This is in response to the "back to basics" push of the 1980s and 1990s. Many believed the schools had lost their focus and were offering too many non-academic offerings. The back to basics movement, however, resulted in a greater emphasis on low-level memorization and recitation. The current curriculum reform movement attempts to push beyond such an emphasis on basic skills, and toward more content-based and higher-order knowledge skills for a wider variety of students. At the other end of the academic spectrum, a recent report from the National Research Council (2002), criticized the Advanced Placement (AP) exams as requiring a wide range of very thin knowledge. Some refer to such a curricular focus as a mile wide and an inch deep. The degree to which new and revised state curriculum frameworks and assessments are of high quality is being debated and compared (American Federation of Teachers, 2001; Education Week, 2002; Kendall & Marzano, 2000).

The rise and scope of accountability programs have captured many headlines in the last decade. At the forefront of this movement has been the unprecedented adoption of assessment instruments by nearly all states. Beginning with the first state-wide testing program (though not for all students) in New York State during the nineteenth century up to the present, when 49 states have adopted some form of standards and accountability program, state supported exams aim to gauge the relative levels of learning and gains over time for elementary through high school students (Education Week, 2002).

Walking the tightrope between a national system of education and true local control is the federal government. It is clear that the growth in state involvement has eroded much of the traditional local control that had become the trademark of American public education. The federal government has straddled this tension by at times impressing a national influence and at other times using the bully pulpit to call for a return to more local control. Within this debate is identifying an appropriate and effective role for the federal government to be involved in American education. The Center for Education Policy sponsored a meeting in 2000 and published a set of papers on the future of the federal role in public education. The recommendations for a revised federal role in elementary and secondary education include:

— Encourage high academic standards, demand "meaningful accountability" for improved student achievement, and accept "national responsibility" to assist in the "proper use of tests."
— Double Title 1 funding.
— Consolidate federal programs based on criteria that there is a clear purpose and accountability, assurance of increased appropriations, and

allocate funds based on the number of low-income children the schools are serving (Jennings, 2001).

Early Childhood Intervention. The 1990s witnessed a dramatic increase in attention paid and resources directed toward pre-kindergarten programming. Prior to this time period, the most extensive attention to the pre-primary (ages 3–5 years) population had been the longstanding federal Head Start program—a health and nutrition program that targeted underprivileged children. In recent years, however, there has been a new interest in the preparation of young children for school. Nearly all states now offer, and most require, kindergarten, with an increasing number of states and districts offering full-day kindergarten. Another important factor in the provision of preschool services for children is the requirement set forth by the federal special education law which requires public schools to provide diagnostic and educational services to qualified 3-year-olds. See Chapter 8 for a more complete discussion of special education services.

Community-School Integration. The horrific events at Columbine (CO) and Paducah (KY) high schools sent shock waves through the public school system and American society. Much of the public was stunned that such violent acts were intruding into what were generally considered to be successful and safe suburban schools. Inherent in the public outrage that followed was a seeming admission that violence was a regrettable, though acceptable, part of urban school life, though a completely new and unacceptable phenomenon in rural or suburban communities (e.g., How could this happen in a school like that?). Nevertheless, the response of the public, policymakers, and educators was swift and highly visible.

There is no accounting for the number of dollars or hours spent in reviewing school policies and procedures because of the mass shootings; no accounting for the number of metal detectors purchased, suspensions handed out, or instructional hours lost. There is also no accounting for the effectiveness of such measures. The rate of major acts of school violence across the country had already undergone a decade of consistent decline when these deadly acts of violence took place (National Center for Education Statistics, 2001). An important question, however, is how many school, community, and state leaders reacted to real threats of violence in their own schools, and how many school, community, and state leaders acted because they would look negligent if they didn't?

Market-Based Reforms

Allowing market forces to enter the environment of public education is not a new idea. In fact, in the early decades of the republic, that is all there was. But with the growth of the bureaucratic educational system throughout the last century (see Meyer et al., 1988; Tyack, 1974), market-based reforms have taken a prominent position amongst some school reformers (see Chubb & Moe, 1990). An interesting mix of conservative and liberal reformers has called for the break-up of the public school "monopoly." Conservatives, because of their inherent beliefs in the efficiency and productivity of free markets, and liberals, because of the need to provide any kind of choice alternatives for those parents and children left with no options other than the local school infested with academic apathy and violence. Those with economic means have choices for their children. These choices may take the form of paying private school tuition or, in growing numbers, the decision to homeschool their children. Poor families have no such choice given their inability to pay tuition, transportation, or afford the opportunity cost of forgoing work to homeschool their children.

Vouchers. This issue is at the heart of a voucher program upheld by the U.S. Supreme Court in 2002 (*Zelman v. Simmons-Harris*, No.

00-1751). In what may be the most important education-related case argued before the high court in decades, the Court decided 5-4 that the Cleveland (OH) voucher plan is constitutional. The plan offers a voucher worth $2,500 toward the tuition at any public or private school to students living in the city of Cleveland. The vouchers presumably offer choice options for children and parents who are not satisfied with their assigned public school in the city of Cleveland. In practice, however, the plan is restricted by the fact that not a single suburban district chose to participate in the voucher program. The result is that 97% of the students taking advantage of the vouchers are attending private or religious schools in and around Cleveland.

The Court's decision rested on whether the program violates the establishment clause of the Constitution. This clause prohibits the state from promoting or inhibiting the establishment of religion and thus violating the separation of church and state. There was precedent for state money to be given to religious schools, however, but these funds were typically restricted to textbooks and transportation. The argument is that government payments for books and buses narrowly assists the education of children thus benefiting the child and does not more broadly benefit the religion or church. In *Lemon v. Kurtzman* (1971) the Court established guidelines for such state involvement in religious schools in the form of a three-part "Lemon" test: "a statute or other government policy 1) must have a secular legislative purpose, 2) must have a principal effect of that neither advances nor inhibits religion, 3) and must not foster 'an excessive government entanglement with religion'" (*Lemon v. Kurtzman*, cited in Zirkel, Richardson, & Goldberg, 1995).

Two other voucher plans have also received much attention. The Milwaukee plan is the oldest, having begun in 1991 and hence receiving the most study and scrutiny. This plan differs from Cleveland's in that it offers vouchers only to poor families. There is no widespread agreement as to whether this program is effective, as

both proponents and opponents find data to support their positions.

A more recent plan in Florida uses school performance to determine who qualifies for participation. Each school in the state is assigned a grade (A, B, C, D, F) based on the achievement of its students on state exams. If a school receives a grade of an F twice in a four-year period, the students attending that school are given a voucher to use toward the cost of enrolling in another public or private school. Given the tremendous growth in the school-age population in recent years, the elasticity of the market in Florida is in question. In other words, as more schools receive Fs, will other public and private schools have enough available seats to enroll the students from the failing schools? Preliminary analyses are skeptical as to how much of a market is available in south Florida (Diaz de La Portilla, 2003).

Charters.   A second type of school reform founded on free market principles, though avoiding the litigious nature of voucher programs, is charter schools. Charter schools are publicly funded schools without attendance boundaries and free of at least some state regulation or local work rules. Depending on the strength of the authorizing state statute, some charter schools are free of most regulation that governs the public schools while others are constrained in their effort to be different from the public schools.

The first charter school law was passed in 1991 in Minnesota and since that time the numbers have grown exponentially (see Figure 1.3). As of July 2001, 38 states had passed a law allowing the creation of charter schools, within which the number of charter schools varies widely. Arizona and Michigan are the states where charter schools are most prevalent.

The Center for Education Reform (CER), an organization that publicly supports the charter school movement, categorizes state charter school legislation into strong and weak laws. Strong laws "foster the development of numerous, genuinely independent charter schools . . .

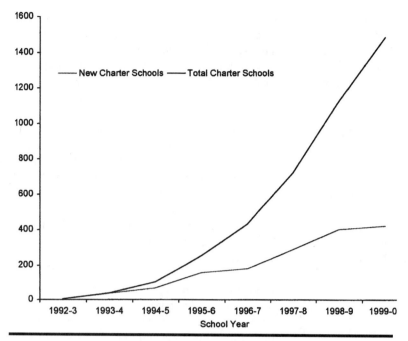

FIGURE 1.3   Estimated Number of Operational Charter Schools, by Year

Source: US DOE (2000, January). The State of Charter Schools 2000: Fourth-Year Report. Washington, DC: Office of Educational Research and Improvement, U.S. Department of Education. Available at http://www.ed.gov/pubs/charter4thyear/.

available to a wide array of children and families" (p. 1). Weak laws are described as those that "provide fewer opportunities for charter school development." More specifically, CER assesses the strength of charter school laws in ten major categories including the number of charter schools allowed, whether there are multiple chartering authorities, whether schools may be started without evidence of local support, whether there is an automatic waiver from state/local laws, the degree of fiscal autonomy, and whether the schools are exempt from collective bargaining agreements. According to the CER (2001), Arizona, Delaware, Minnesota, the District of Columbia, Michigan, Indiana, and Massachusetts have enacted the strongest laws. On the other end of the continuum are Arkansas, Hawaii, Rhode Island, Virginia, and Mississippi, which received a grade of "D" or "F."

Key questions abound for voucher and charter-school programs. For whom are they created? Whom do they serve? Are they effective? No doubt it is easier to document whom they serve than how effective they are. Charter schools, on average, serve students that closely mirror the populations that attend the surrounding traditional public schools. The fear that charter schools will promote additional white flight from the public schools is largely unfounded. A proportional number of poor and minority children are attending charter schools and using vouchers (Gill et al., 2001). Concerning the effectiveness of voucher programs or charter schools, the research is still inconclusive. A recent Rand study attempting to measure the effectiveness of vouchers and charters concluded that there is simply not yet enough evidence to make a clear determination as to whether vouchers or charters are more or less effective than the traditional public schools (Gill et al., 2001).[7]

One obstacle to the growth in the number of charter schools (beyond the authorizing legislation) is the start-up cost of opening a charter school. Building the infrastructure for charter schools requires a great amount of capital. A Government Accounting Office report (GAO, 2000b) identified three major issues in charter school development: 1) the degree to which charter schools have access to traditional public school facility financing, 2) whether alternative sources of facility financing are available to charter schools, and 3) potential options available to the federal government if it were to assume a larger role in character school facility financing.

Homeschooling.   *Time* magazine featured a question on its cover: "Is homeschooling good for America?" (August 27, 2001). This is a new wrinkle on the typical question as to whether homeschooling is good for the homeschooled child or the local school. Nevertheless, homeschooling has come of age in the last decade. It is now more publicly acknowledged, in many circles acceptable, and exhibiting significant growth in the numbers of homeschooled children. Researchers have begun to study the phenomenon, policymakers are paying attention, and educators are beginning to feel the effects of greater numbers of children staying at home to go to school.

A report published by the National Center for Education Statistics using data collected from the Parent Survey of the *National Household Education Surveys Program, 1999* (Parent-NHES:1999) provides a comprehensive portrait of the extent of homeschooling, by whom, and for what reasons. NCES (U.S. Dept. of Education, 2001d) summarized the major findings:

— In the spring of 1999, an estimated 850,000 students nationwide were being homeschooled. This amounts to 1.7% of U.S. students, ages 5 to 17, with a grade equivalent of kindergarten through grade 12. Four out of five homeschoolers were homeschooled only (82%) and one out of five homeschoolers were enrolled in public or private schools part-time (18%).

— A greater percentage of homeschoolers compared to non-homeschoolers were white, non-Hispanic in 1999—75% compared to 65%. At the same time, a smaller percentage of homeschoolers were black, non-Hispanic students and a smaller percentage were Hispanic students.

— The household income of homeschoolers in 1999 was no different than non-homeschoolers. However, parents of homeschoolers had higher levels of educational attainment than did parents of non-homeschoolers.

— Parents gave a wide variety of reasons for homeschooling their children. These reasons included being able to give their child a better education at home, for religious reasons, and because of a poor learning environment at school.

These data (see Table 1.1) clarify some of the assumptions surrounding who is being homeschooled. What remains unclear is whether children in need of special education services or other social services are disproportionately kept in schools to receive the services, or whether schools must provide such services for homeschooled children. A clear concern with at-risk children being homeschooled is the separation or isolation from the school and services provided therein. Just how social service agencies can find and track at-risk children if they are homeschooled remains to be seen.

Despite the notion that homeschoolers are not part of the public school system, schools are sometimes required, or offer, to provide additional services for homeschoolers. Public school

---

[7]See a special report in *Education Week,* "Changed by charters." This three-part report can be found at http://www.edweek.org/sreports/special_reports_article.cfm?slug=charters.htm.

TABLE 1.1 Characteristics of Homeschooled and Non-homeschooled Students

	HOMESCHOOLERS[1]	NON-HOMESCHOOLERS
Grade level		
Grades K–5	50.4	48.7
Grades 6–8	21.9	23.5
Grades 9–12	27.7	27.8
Race/ethnicity		
White, non-Hispanic	75.3	64.5
Black, non-Hispanic	9.9	16.1
Hispanic	9.1	14.1
Other	5.8	5.2
Number of siblings		
One	14.1	16.4
Two	24.4	39.9
Three or more	61.6	43.7
Number of parents		
Two	80.4	65.5
One	16.7	31.0
Nonparental guardians	2.9	3.5
Parents' participation in labor force		
Two parents—one in labor force	52.2	18.6
Two parents—both in labor force	27.9	45.9
One parent in labor force	11.6	28.0
No parent in labor force	8.3	7.5
Household income		
$25,000 or less	30.9	33.5
$25,001–50,000	32.7	30.3
$50,001–75,000	19.1	17.1
$75,001 or more	17.4	19.2
Parents' highest educational level		
High school diploma or less	18.9	36.8
Vo-tech degree or some college	33.7	30.2
Bachelor's degree	25.1	16.3
Graduate/professional school	22.3	16.7
Urbanicity		
City	53.5	62.3
Town	14.2	12.4
Rural	32.4	25.3

Source: U.S. Department of Education, National Center for Education Statistics, Parent Survey of the National Household Education Surveys Program, 1999.

Note: Numbers may not add to 100 due to rounding.

[1]Excludes students who were enrolled in school for more than 25 hours and students who were homeschooled due to a temporary illness.

services most frequently offered and/or used by parents of homeschooled students include the use of curriculum, books, and instructional materials, and extracurricular activities (National Center for Education Statistics, 2001d). Beyond the provision of artifacts (books) and opportunities in public schools (sports), it is unclear just what services are being provided to homeschooled children, who decides what services are provided (parent, school, social worker), and what impact the relative isolation of homeschoolers has on their well-being when services are needed.

Finally, public support for homeschooling has grown in the last decade. In 1985, only 16% of the general public agreed that homeschooling was a "good thing for the nation." By 2001, the percent increased to 41%. While still not a majority, the trend is clear. Public support is similar for the notion that homeschooling raises the nation's academic standards (43%) and promotes good citizenship (46%) (Rose & Gallup, 2001).

Finance

By any measure, Americans spend a great deal of money educating their children. While debate continues as to whether we spend too much or too little, there is also much debate about how current education revenues are raised and how the money is spent. At the heart of the issue are issues of equity, equality, excellence, and accountability. The financing of American education is derived from local, state, and federal sources with expenditures for the 2001–2002 school year totaling approximately $350 billion (National Center for Education Statistics, 2001b). Given the total current student enrollment of approximately 47 million elementary and secondary students this amounts to more than $7,000 per pupil, up from $137 billion (or $213 billion adjusted for 2000 dollars) and $5,400 per student ($3,400 in current dollars) in 1986 (Digest of Education Statistics, 2001, Table 167).

Given that there is no mention of education in the U.S. Constitution and that the Tenth Amend-

ment delegates all rights and privileges not included in the Constitution to the states or to the people, states are granted the plenary authority for the provision of public education. Following *Rodriguez v. San Antonio* (1973) in which the U.S. Supreme Court declared that there is no federal right to a public education, the state courts have been the locus of the debate on the equality, equity, and adequacy of school finance practices. The debates involve the distribution of local and state resources to school districts within each state. Specifically, the debates involve the degree to which state funding formulas *equitably* redistribute dollars from wealthy to poor communities and whether the absolute number of dollars spent on public education is *adequate*. Since the first state-court (CA) school finance case was decided in 1975 (*Serrano v. Priest*), at least 38 states have had their funding formulas reviewed by their state supreme court with about one-half being found unconstitutional. Muddying this fiscal debate is the lack of agreement among policymakers and researchers as to how important additional dollars are to improving school performance (see e.g., Ladd, Chalk, & Hansen, 1999).

Federal Priorities.   The federal government has long had a minor role in the financing of public education. The federal role has hovered around 5% of local district revenue for nearly three decades (National Center for Education Statistics, 2001b). The largest source of federal money is the ESEA. While the IDEA and the free and reduced price lunch/breakfast programs also contribute to local revenues, the bulk of federal funding for most school districts, particularly those serving a greater percentage of poor students, is found within the ESEA. With the 2002 reauthorization of the ESEA, federal funding is less restrictive and hence less targeted than it has been since the early years of the Reagan Administration when the Education Consolidation and Improvement Act of 1981 consolidated dozens of categorical programs into a block grant. Unfortunately, for many schools this meant a reduction in the absolute number of federal dollars received. How the new act will support schools is at this time unclear.

In further trying to promote equity, excellence, and adequacy, the federal government began requiring states to collect and report assessment data by disaggregated groups of students. According to a 2000 GAO report, only one-third of the states were collecting disaggregated data. Not reporting disaggregated results "can mask the results of disadvantaged students and prevent the states and the districts from identifying schools that may not be meeting the educational needs of disadvantaged students" (GAO, 2000a). It remains to be seen what happens to the flow of dollars and federal commitment to reducing the achievement gap.

Local Effort.   While the local proportion of the cost of public education has diminished since the 1970s, the absolute number of local dollars being spent on local schools has steadily increased. Targeted state and federal programs supplement local funds, but often are not allowed to supplant local effort. Therefore, as the expectations for public schools continue to increase (e.g., educate all children to high levels, provide additional social services, provide more meals, ensure a safe environment, provide extracurricular activities and character/citizenship education), the money to provide such services is stretched thin and often requires additional local effort. This leaves local community and school leaders few choices. Options include increasing local property taxes, reducing services, and sometimes consolidation with other school districts. Each of these options is likely to improve the short term fiscal picture, though the resultant effect on at-risk children can be harsh. It is these decisions, however, that must be weighed carefully if children are to be adequately and equitably served by their public schools.

CONCLUSION

In reviewing the major issues in American schools, one is struck by the remarkable successes and failures of the American public educational system; success in that we have achieved universal participation for school-age children and continue to increase the number of very young children who are now provided with social and educational services. We have come to some sort of agreement that schools must serve all children in various ways, that no child should be left behind. There are consistent efforts at altering structural arrangements in schools in the name of improving the social and educational services. Schools are becoming a hub for a wide range of services for children. There are steady increases in funding to pay for at least part of the cost for the additional services.

The public educational system is also fraught with failure. The achievement gap documented so starkly in the mid-1960s remains. Early childhood programs are estimated to serve only one-half of eligible children. While there has been much effort to "reform" schools, much of the change has been superficial or fallen short of the true investment in time, expertise, and resources to fundamentally improve the educational and social services provided. Finally, beneficial coordination of services between schools and communities has been spotty, with the highest-need children in low-wealth communities and schools most often coming up short. Efforts are often hampered by the overburdened agencies and educators due to two distinct, though related issues: lack of sufficient resources and the ever-increasing need for schools to provide more and better services for all children.

FOR STUDY AND DISCUSSION

The challenge for social workers, whether they work in schools or in community agencies that interface with schools, is to build on past successes and learn from the failures. Thoughtful provision of services that meet the individual needs of children is more likely when social workers have an enriched understanding of the broader issues at play in schools. This chapter, coupled with the more detailed chapters that follow, should provide the reader with knowledge necessary for improved practice and understanding of school social work and the remarkable organizations in which the work takes place.

1. Interview several teachers, administrators, parents, and policymakers, inquiring about their expectations for their local school and the purposes of the broader public educational system. How (dis)similar are the responses, and what are the implications for practice?

2. Given the growth in homeschooling and market-based reforms (e.g., voucher programs and charter schools), how might the practice of social workers need to change? What new services must be provided?

3. Labaree (1997) argues that the core problems with schools are political and not technical. Do you agree? How do local and national politics impact the services provided to different children? What technical services can be provided regardless of politics?

4. Researchers have documented the differential levels of school success for different groups of children for more than 40 years. What can be done to interrupt the reproduction of society's social and economic strata?

5. Discuss the concept of equality of educational opportunity. How do the different types of school reform enhance or inhibit educational opportunity for poor or minority children? For wealthy or majority children? What role does the current financing of public education play in the provision of equal educational opportunity?

ADDITIONAL READING

Brewer, C. A., & Suchman, T. A. (2001). *Mapping census 2000: The geography of U.S. diversity* (CENSR/01-1). Washington, DC: U.S. Census Bureau.

Coleman, J. (1968). The concept of equality of educational opportunity. *Harvard Educational Review, 38*(1), 7–22.

Collins, R. (1979). *The credential society: An historical sociology of education and stratification.* New York: Academic Press.

Conant, J. B. (1959). *The American high school today.* New York: McGraw-Hill.

Cuban, L. (1993). *How teachers taught: Constancy and change in American classrooms, 1890–1990* (2nd ed.). New York: Teachers College Press.

Cuban, L. (1998). How schools change reforms: Redefining reform success and failure. *Teachers College Record, 99*(3), 453–477.

Dewey, J. (1938). *Experience and education.* New York: Collier.

Dewey, J. (1943). *The school and society* (Rev. ed.). Chicago: University of Chicago.

Engel, M. (2000). *The struggle for control of public education: Market ideology vs. democratic values.* Philadelphia: Temple University Press.

Epstein, J. L. (2001). *School, family, and community partnerships: Preparing educators and improving schools.* Boulder, CO: Westview Press.

Jencks, C. (1992). *Rethinking social policy: Race, poverty, and the underclass.* Cambridge, MA: Harvard University Press.

Lareau, A., & Horvat, E. M. (1999). Moments of social inclusion and exclusion: Race, class, and cultural capital in family-school relationships. *Sociology of Education, 72,* 37–53.

Louis, K. S., & Smith, B. A. (1992). Cultivating teacher engagement: Breaking the iron law of social class. In F. M. Newmann (Ed.), *Student engagement in American secondary schools.* New York: Teachers College Press.

Ogbu, J. U., & Simons, H. D. (1998). Voluntary and involuntary minorities: A cultural-ecological theory of school performance with some implications for education. *Anthropology and Education Quarterly, 29*(2), 155–188.

Orfield, G., & Kornhaber, M. L. (2001). *Raising standards or raising barriers? Inequality and high-stakes testing in public education.* New York: Century Foundation Press.

Ravitch, D., & Viteritti, J. P. (2001). *Making good citizens: Education and civil society.* New Haven CT: Yale University Press.

Ravitch, D., & Viteritti, J. P. (2000). *City schools:*

Lessons from New York. Baltimore: Johns Hopkins University Press.

Sapon-Shevin, M. (1993). Gifted education and the protection of privilege. In L. Weiss & M. Fine (Eds.), *Beyond silenced voices* (pp. 25–44). Albany, NY: State University of New York Press.

Tyack, D. B., & Hansot, E. (1982). *Managers of virtue: Public school leadership in America, 1820–1980.* New York: Basic Books.

Valenzuela, A. (1999). *Subtractive schooling: U.S.-Mexican youth and the politics of caring.* Albany, NY: State University of New York Press.

REFERENCES

American Federation of Teachers (2001). *Making standards matter.* Washington, DC: Author. Available at http://www.aft.org/edissues/standards/MSM2001/Index.htm.

Barton, P. E. (2002). *Raising achievement and reducing gaps: Reporting progress toward goals for academic achievement in mathematics.* Washington, DC: National Education Goals Panel.

Bowles, S., & Gintis, H. (1976). *Schooling in capitalist America: Educational reform and the contradictions of economic life.* New York: Basic Books.

Business Roundtable (1992). *The essential components of a successful education: Putting policy into practice.* Washington, DC: Author.

Callahan, R. E. (1962). *Education and the cult of efficiency; a study of the social forces that have shaped the administration of the public schools.* Chicago: University of Chicago Press.

Center for Education Reform (2001). *Charter school laws across the states.* Washington, DC: Author.

Chubb, J. E., & Moe, T. M. (1990). *Politics, markets, and America's schools.* Washington, DC: Brookings Institution.

Cohen, D. K. (1995). What is the system in systemic reform? *Educational Researcher, 24*(9), 11–17, 31.

Coleman, J. S. (1966). *Equality of educational opportunity* (Report to the President and Congress). Washington, DC: U.S. Office of Education.

Comer, J. P., & Haynes, N. M. (1992). *Summary of school development program effects.* New Haven, CT: Yale Child Study Center.

Diaz de la Portilla, R. (2003). *The effect of Florida's tuition credits on public schools: Competition or convolution?* Unpublished master's thesis, Cornell University, Ithaca, NY.

Education Week (2002). *Quality counts, 2002.* Washington, DC: Author. Available at http://www.edweek.org/sreports/qc02/.

Elmore, R. F. (1995). Structural reform in educational practice. *Educational Researcher, 24*(9), 23–26.

Elmore, R. F., Peterson, P. L., & McCarthey, S. J. (1996). *Restructuring in the classroom: Teaching, learning, and school organization* (1st ed.). San Francisco: Jossey-Bass.

Firestone, W. A., Bader, B. D., Massel, D., & Rosenblum, S. (1992). Recent trends in state educational-reform: Assessment and prospects. *Teachers College Record, 94*(2), 254–277.

Fuhrman, S. H. (Ed.). (1993). *Designing coherent educational policy: Improving the system.* San Francisco: Jossey-Bass.

Fuhrman, S. (Ed.). (2001). *From the capital to the classroom: Standards-based reform in the states.* Chicago: University of Chicago Press.

Fuhrman, S., & O'Day, J. A. (1996). *Rewards and reform: Creating educational incentives that work* (1st ed.). San Francisco: Jossey-Bass.

Gill, B. P., Timpane, P. M., Ross, K. E., & Brewer, D. J. (2001). *Rhetoric versus reality: What we know and what we need to know about vouchers and charter schools.* Santa Monica, CA: Rand.

Government Accounting Office. (2000a). *Title I program: Stronger accountability needed for performance of disadvantaged students* (HEHS-00-89). Washington, DC: U.S. Government Printing Office. June 1.

Government Accounting Office. (2000b). *Charter schools: Limited access to facility financing* (HEHS-00-163). Washington, DC: US Government Printing Office. September 12.

Grant, G. (1973). Shaping social policy: The politics of the Coleman Report. *Teachers College Record, 75*(1), 17–54.

Hallinan, M. T. (1995). Tracking and detracking practices: Relevance for learning. In P. W. Cookson & B. Schneider (Eds.), *Transforming schools* (pp. 35–55). New York: Garland.

Jencks, C. (1972). *Inequality; A reassessment of the effect of family and schooling in America.* New York: Basic Books.

Jencks, C., & Phillips, M. (1998). *The black-white*

test score gap. Washington, DC: Brookings Institution Press.

Jennings, J. (2001). An education agenda for the congress and the new administration, *The future of the federal role in elementary and secondary education* (pp. 5–12). Washington, DC: Center on Education Policy.

Kaestle, C. (1983). *Pillars of the republic: Common schools and American society*. New York: Hill & Wang.

Kendall, J. S., & Marzano, R. J. (2000). *A Compendium of Standards and Benchmarks for K–12 Education* (3rd ed.). Aurora, CO: MCREL. Also see http://www.mcrel.org/standards-benchmarks/

Kozol, J. (1991). *Savage inequalities: Children in American schools*. New York: Crown.

Kozol, J. (1995). *Amazing grace: The lives of children and the conscience of a nation*. New York: Crown.

Labaree, D. (1997). Public goods, private goods: The American struggle over educational goals. *American Educational Research Association, 34*(1), 39–81.

Ladd, H. F, Chalk, R., & Hansen, J. S. (1999). *Equity and Adequacy in Education Finance: Issues and Perspectives*. Washington, DC: National Academy Press.

Lemon v. Kurtzman, 403 U.S. 602, 1971

Meyer, J. W., Scott, W. R., Strang, D., & Creighton, A. L. (1988). Bureaucratization without centralization: Changes in the organizational system of U.S. public education, 1940–80. In L. G. Zucker (Ed.), *Institutional patterns in organizations: Culture and environments* (pp. 139–168). Cambridge, MA: Ballinger.

National Center for Education Statistics. (1999a). *Parent survey of the National Household Education Surveys Program, 1999*. Washington, DC: National Center for Education Statistics.

National Center for Education Statistics. (1999b). Current Population Survey. Washington, DC: U.S. Government Printing Office.

National Center for Education Statistics. (2001a). Digest of Education Statistics, Table 43. Washington, DC: U.S. Government Printing Office.

National Center for Education Statistics. (2001b). Digest of Education Statistics, Table 157. Washington, DC: U.S. Government Printing Office.

National Center for Education Statistics. (2001c). Digest of Education Statistics, Table 167. Washington, DC: U.S. Government Printing Office.

National Center for Education Statistics. (2001d). *Homeschooling in the United States: 1999* (NCES 2001033). Washington, DC: U.S. Government Printing Office. http://nces.ed.gov/pubs2001/HomeSchool/index.asp.

National Center for Education Statistics. *Early Childhood Longitudinal Study*. On-going study. Available at http://nces.ed.gov/ecls.

National Commission on Excellence in Education. (1983). *A nation at risk: The imperative for educational reform*. Washington, DC: U.S. Dept. of Education.

National Research Council. (2002). *Learning and understanding: Improving advanced study of mathematics and science in U.S. high schools*. Washington, DC: National Academy Press.

Oakes, J. (1985). *Keeping track: How schools structure inequality*. New Haven, CT: Yale University Press.

Oakes, J., Wells, A. S., Jones, M., & Datmow, A. (1997). Detracking: The social construction of ability, cultural politics, and resistance to reform. *Teachers College Record, 98*(3), 482–510.

O'Day, J. A., & Smith, M. S. (1993). Systemic reform and educational opportunity. In S. H. Fuhrman (Ed.), *Designing coherent education policy* (pp. 250–312). San Francisco: Jossey-Bass.

Ogawa, R. T. (1994). The institutional sources of educational reform: The case of school-based management. *American Educational Research Journal, 31*(3), 519–548.

Orfield, G. (1978). *Must we bus? Segregation and national policy*. Washington: Brookings Institution.

Orfield, G., & Eaton, S. E. (1996). *Dismantling desegregation: The quiet reversal of Brown v. Board of Education*. New York: New Press.

Powell, A. G., Farrar, E., & Cohen, D. K. (1985). *The shopping mall high school: Winners and losers in the educational marketplace*. Boston: Houghton Mifflin.

Ravitch, D. (1974). *The great school wars, New York City, 1805–1973; A history of the public schools as battlefield of societal change*. New York: Basic Books.

Ravitch, D. (2000). *Left back: A century of failed school reforms*. New York: Simon & Schuster.

Rose, L. C., & A. M. Gallup (2001). The 33rd Annual

Phi Delta Kappa/Gallup Poll of the Public's Attitudes Toward the Public Schools. *Phi Delta Kappan, 83*(1), 41–58.

San Antonio Independent School District v. Rodriguez, 411 U.S. 1 (1973).

Serrano v. Priest, 5 Cal. 3d 584 (1971).

Smith, M. S., & O'Day, J. A. (1991). Systemic School Reform. In S. H. Fuhrman & B. Malen (Eds.), *The politics of curriculum and testing.* Bristol, PA: Falmer Press.

Time (2001). Is homeschooling good for America? August 27, 2001.

Tyack, D. B. (1974). *The one best system: A history of American urban education.* Cambridge, MA: Harvard University Press.

Tyack, D. B., & Cuban, L. (1995). *Tinkering toward utopia: A century of public school reform.* Cambridge, MA: Harvard University Press.

U.S. Department of Education (2000). *The State of Charter Schools 2000: Fourth-Year Report.* Washington, DC: Office of Educational Research and Improvement, U.S. Department of Education. Available at http://www.ed.gov/pubs/charter4thyear/.

Vinovskis, M. A. (1996). Analysis of the concept and uses of systemic educational reform. *American Educational Research Association, 33*(1), 53–85.

Welner, Kevin G. (2001). *Legal rights, local wrongs: When community control collides with educational equity.* Albany, NY: State University of New York Press.

Zelman v. Simmons-Harris, No. 00-1751.

Zirkel, Perry A., Richardson, Sharon N., & Goldberg, Steven S. (1995). *A digest of Supreme Court decisions affecting education.* Bloomington, IN: Phi Delta Kappa Educational Foundation.

CHAPTER 2

SCHOOL SOCIAL WORK: HISTORICAL DEVELOPMENT, INFLUENCES, AND PRACTICES

Children are important. Education and schools are important. The child who comes to school must be accepted as he is. School social work has a philosophy, a discipline, and a service to offer that is good in meeting the needs of children.[*]

—Ray Graham

INTRODUCTION

The history of school social work is interesting and rich. In 1906 social conditions, life struggles, and a growing immigrant population were forceful factors that supported the development and expansion of education and, in turn, school social work. As education became increasingly regarded as a right for every child, the importance of linking school and community took on more significance. It was during this period that school social workers (known as visiting teachers) recognized that their role should be more in tune with social conditions and social movements and sought changes in school policies that adversely affected the lives of children. Essentially, they served as the link between the school and the home.

Unfortunately, as this field of practice grew, the role of liaison received less emphasis. School social workers, concerned about their identity, sought a more specialized role, one that they believed would link their efforts more closely to the central purpose of education. The 1940s and 1950s were primarily dominated by the social casework approach. The emphasis upon establishing a liaison between home and school was not considered as important. However, by the late 1960s and 1970s the literature once more demanded a broader, more responsive role definition and approach to practice.

Presently, legislation and mandates to a large degree determine role definitions. Reactions from school social workers have been mixed.

---

[*]Copyright 1952, National Association of Social Workers, Inc. Reprinted with permission. Ray Graham, "The Development of School Social Work Practice: Trends toward the Integration of a Social Work Function within an Educational Setting," in *Bulletin of the National Association of School Social Workers* 28, no. 1 (September 1952): 8.

Some fear that mandates may cripple the search for different approaches that began during the 1970s. Others feel that what school social workers should contribute to the educational process is clear for the first time in the history of education.

THE ESTABLISHMENT OF SCHOOL SOCIAL WORK

School social work began at about the same time (during the school year 1906–1907), although independently, in three cities: New York, Boston, and Hartford. The development originated outside of the school system; private agencies and civic organizations in these three localities supported the work (Costin, 1969). It is important to note that at this same time a similar program was being established in London, the outcome of which today forms a striking contrast to U.S. school social work services (Lide, 1959).

As in the development of social work generally, school social work was first intended to benefit the so-called underprivileged. In New York City, settlement workers from the Hartley House and Greenich House thought that it was necessary to know the teachers of children who came to the settlements, and they assigned two workers to visit schools and homes to work more closely with schools and community groups, for the purpose of promoting understanding and communication (Lide, 1959).

In Boston, a similar development was taking place. The Women's Education Association placed visiting teachers in the schools for the purpose of bringing about more harmony between school and home, to make the child's education more effective.

The director of the Psychological Clinic in Hartford initiated the first visiting teachers' program in that area. The director of the clinic recognized the help that could be derived from such a program. This person would assist the psychologist in securing histories of children and implementing the clinic's treatment plans and recommendations.

It was not until 1913, in Rochester, New York, that the first board of education initiated and financed a "visiting teacher program." The board of education stated:

> This is the first step in an attempt to meet a need of which the school system has been conscious for some time. It is an undisputed fact that in the environment of the child outside of school are to be found forces which will often thwart the school in its endeavors. The appointment of visiting teachers is an attempt on the part of the school to meet its responsibility for the whole welfare of the child . . . and to maximize cooperation between the home and the school. (Oppenheimer, 1925, p. 5)

The Rochester Board of Education took an active role in the development of the service. The board placed visiting teachers in special departments of the school, under the administration and direction of the superintendent of schools. This arrangement pointed up the necessity of avoiding separation of the school social worker from the whole school system and the community.

A national professional association had emerged—the National Association of Visiting Teachers. It held its first meeting in New York City, where concern was expressed about the organization, administration, and role definition of visiting teachers.

Early Influences

The early twentieth century was a fertile period for the development of school social work. Important influences in its early development were:

1. *Passage of compulsory school attendance laws.* A concern for the illiteracy of immigrant children and then the illiteracy of American-born children brought attention to the child's right to at least a minimum education and the states' responsibility for securing this for all children and gave support to the enactment of compulsory attendance statutes in some states. However, statutes were often circumvented both by parents who wished their children to work to supplement inadequate adult wages and by factory owners who wished to use the cheap labor of children. Without compulsory birth registration to make a child's age a matter of public record, it was easy for children to secure working papers before they were legally of age. This situation was aggravated by the failure of school districts to provide facilities for children who were ready and willing to attend school.

The lack of effective enforcement of school attendance laws led to such studies as that of Abbott and Breckinridge (1917) on the nonattendance problem in the Chicago schools. The findings of this study supported the need for school attendance officers who understood the social ills of the community—such as poverty, ill health, and lack of secure family income—and their effects on attendance (Abbott & Breckinridge, 1917). Abbott and Breckinridge held that this responsibility should be assigned to the school social worker, someone knowledgeable about the needs of children and the effects of such conditions. Further, they indicated that some poverty-stricken families had not come to the attention of community social service agencies, implying that the school was an important institution in the lives of these families.

The first compulsory attendance laws in the United States were those of Connecticut and Massachusetts during the colonial period. By 1918 each state had passed its own compulsory attendance law, a situation that in effect proclaimed that each child had not only the *right* to benefit from what the school had to offer but an *obligation* to secure these advantages. This marked a new era in education, especially for parents, who were now forced to send their children to school.

As legislatures in various states extended the scope of compulsory education laws, schools were required to expand their facilities in order to provide for larger numbers of children with a greater range of individual abilities and backgrounds. School social workers played an important role—one of clarifying and sensitizing school personnel to the out-of-school lives of children and how they are affected.

2. *Knowledge of individual differences.* As the scope of compulsory education laws expanded, states were forced to provide an educational experience for a variety of children. Simultaneously, new knowledge about individual differences among children and their capacity to respond to improved conditions compelled school personnel to look to other fields for an understanding of these differences.

Previously there had been no real concern about whether children had different learning needs; those who presented a challenge were not enrolled. Compulsory attendance laws changed this situation very quickly. Teachers concerned about these "different and/or excluded" children sought knowledge about individual differences so that they would be better prepared to address the educational needs of such children.

Again, the role of school social workers was one of sensitizing both teachers and other school personnel to the life conditions and forces that affect learning. Some social workers sought adaptations in the school program. The Henry Street Settlement, under the auspices of the New York City Board of Education and with social work leadership, formed the first class for upgraded pupils (children who suffered from mental defects). This settlement provided the necessary equipment and instructional resources so that these children could be educated. This was one of the first attempts to adapt instructional materials and resources to meet the special needs of students (Wald, 1915).

3. *Realization of the strategic position of education.* Social workers of the early twentieth century were keenly aware of the strategic place of school and education in the lives of children and youths and were impressed by the opportunities presented to the school. S. P. Breckinridge, addressing the National Education Association in 1914, stated:

> To the social worker the school appears as an instrument of almost unlimited possibilities, not only for passing on to the next generation the culture and wisdom of the past, but for testing present

social relationships and for securing improvement in social conditions. (Breckinridge, 1914)

She begged for a closer inspection and study of failures of the school and of the consequent loss in social well-being for children and their future happiness.

4. *Concern for the relevance of education.* Simultaneously, social workers in the settlement houses were expressing the need for the school to relate itself more closely to the present and future lives of the children. Oppenheimer (1925) noted that during the early twentieth century the influence of the social settlement upon the development of school social work was very strong, "both in respect to the type of methods used and in respect to the development of [the] social center in the schools" (Oppenheimer, 1925, p. 2). Social workers in the settlements expressed concern about "the insufficient number of visiting teachers to bring the school and home together" (Lide, 1959, p. 109).

Early Definitions

In 1916, Jane Culbert defined the role of school social worker as follows:

Interpreting to the school the child's out-of-school life; supplementing the teacher's knowledge of the child . . . so that she may be able to teach the whole child . . . assisting the school to know the life of a neighborhood, in order that it may train the children for the life to which they look forward. Secondly, the visiting teacher interprets to the parents the demands of the school and explains the particular difficulties and needs of the child. (Culbert, 1916, p. 595)

The principal activity in school social work continued to be as a home-school-community liaison. In 1925, Julius Oppenheimer carried out a study to obtain a more detailed list of tasks than had been delineated in the 1916 definition of function. The study involved the analysis of 300 case reports; it resulted in a list of 32 core functions of the visiting teacher service. An appraisal

of the nature of these tasks affirmed the emphasis on school-family-community liaison as the main body of school social work activity. Not found in the study were tasks involving a one-to-one, ongoing relationship of a visiting teacher with individual children to help them with their personal problems. One of the most important functions of the school social worker, Oppenheimer stated, "was to aid in the reorganization of school administration and of school practice by supplying evidence of unfavorable conditions that underlie children's school difficulties and by pointing out needed change" (Oppenheimer, 1925). According to Oppenheimer, the visiting teacher was the one person in the school who was knowledgeable about the outside life and social environment of children.

Expansion in the 1920s

The number of school social workers increased, largely as a result of a series of three-year demonstrations, under the auspices of the Commonwealth Fund of New York, which were aimed at the prevention of juvenile delinquency (Oppenheimer, 1925).

The Commonwealth Fund gave the National Committee of Visiting Teachers financial support for a countrywide demonstration and for experimentation in the field of school social work. Thirty school social workers were placed in 30 different communities, both rural and urban, throughout the country for a demonstration project.

Each local community shared in the payment of the salaries of these visiting teachers. When the Fund withdrew its support in 1930, 21 of the communities that had served as demonstration sites continued the programs. Meanwhile, other cities were busily implementing their visiting teacher programs. By this time, there were about 244 school social workers in 31 states.

It was the massive demonstration project initiated by the Commonwealth Fund that gave social service in school its visibility. Boards of education, noting the value of the service, responded by establishing visiting teacher programs in other communities. In turn, the National Association of Visiting Teachers grew and focused its efforts on establishing professional standards and direction for its membership.

The school was viewed as a strategic center of child welfare work, linking children and their families with resources, so that learning and growth would not be hindered.

Influence of the Mental Hygiene Movement

The literature of the 1920s reflects the beginning of a therapeutic role for school social workers in the public schools. The mental hygiene movement brought about an increasing emphasis on treating the individual child. According to Lela Costin,

> the increasing recognition of individual differences among children and interest on the part of the mental hygienists in understanding behavior problems led to an effort on the part of visiting teachers to develop techniques for the prevention of social maladjustment. (Costin, 1978, p. 4)

Mental hygiene clinics sprang up in almost every community. Their central purpose was to diagnose and treat nervous and difficult children. Such questions as "How can we help the emotionally disturbed child through the school experience?" and "How can we help all children to find in their lives at school an emotionally enriching and stabilizing experience?" guided both school social workers and mental hygienists at this time.

Jessie Taft wrote:

> The only practical and effective way to increase the mental health of a nation is through its school system. Homes are too inaccessible. The school has the time of the child and the power to do the job. It is for us who represent mental hygiene and its application through social casework to help the school and teacher to see their vital responsibility for an education which shall mean the personal ad-

justment of the individual through the activities of the group. (Taft, 1923, p. 398)

Shifting Goals of the 1930s

The development of social work service in the schools was greatly retarded during the depression of the 1930s, as were other social service programs for children. Services provided by visiting teachers were either abolished or seriously cut back in volume (Areson, 1923, p. 398). The provision of food, shelter, and clothing preoccupied much of what activity there was. As the depression worsened, federal aid was made available to hard-pressed families. At this time visiting teachers began to view their role differently. The early image of law enforcer and attendance officer was essentially replaced by the role of social caseworker. Abandoning their earlier commitment to change adverse conditions in the schools and linking home, school, and community, school social workers sought a more specialized role—providing emotional support for troubled children (Hall, 1936).

Many of these workers were anxious to improve their image. The role of attendance officer was not viewed as "professional." Further, because some were being used as "errand boys," school social workers were eager to have a more well-defined role—one with more specialized skills and less stigma.

Gladys Hall and Edith Everett saw the primary role of visiting teachers as supporting "wholesome childhood." Hall noted that the role of the school social worker was changing from one of school-community liaison to preventing poor mental health among children, a duty that later became associated with social casework. Everett stated:

> My own feeling as a result of a good many years of experience in connection with a city school system is that we can be most helpful by limiting our professional responsibility to doing as well as we humanly can our casework job within the school itself. (Everett, 1938, p. 58)

Everett further spoke against the practice of some visiting teachers who took on a community responsibility outside the field of casework.

On the other side, Bertha Reynolds was one of the first to recognize that not all problems experienced by the "troubled child" were inherent in his or her personality or background and that the school could be the source of the child's problem.

> It is clear that the contribution of social casework is to supplement the basic public administrator, not to struggle to make up for mistakes of a poor one. If a faculty school curriculum is causing every year thousands of school failures, it would be stupid to engage visiting teachers to work individually with the unsuccessful children. Why not change the curriculum and do away with that particular problem at one stroke? (Reynolds, 1935, p. 238)

Others, such as Charlotte Towle, raised similar concerns, urging school social workers to see the potential of social casework from a broad social perspective. She wrote:

> We are coming not only to recognize the futility of persisting in situations which are beyond the scope of casework help, but to realize also our social responsibility for revealing the inadequacy of social work in these instances, in order that interest and effort may be directed toward social action. (Towle, 1936)

Emphasis on Social Casework 1940–1960

By 1940, school social workers' roles as home-school liaisons and attendance officers had been virtually forsaken for a more specialized role. The literature, which had grown markedly during this period, called attention to "an appropriate function" of school social work: social casework. No longer were social change and neighborhood conditions seen as targets of intervention. Instead, the profession now had a clinical orientation. The personality needs of the individual child took on primary attention.

Ruth Smalley described the role of the school social worker as being a "specialized form of social casework, a method of helping children use what the school offers" (Smalley, 1947, p. 22). Swithun Bowers described social casework as "an art in which knowledge of the science of human relations and skill in relationship are used to mobilize capacities in the individual" (Bowers, 1949, p. 417). Joseph Hourihan, in a study of the duties and responsibilities of the visiting teachers in Michigan, recommended limiting work to those duties and responsibilities which are related to assisting individual emotionally maladjusted children (Hourihan, 1952).

A book entitled *Helping the Troubled School Child: Selected Readings in School Social Work, 1935–1955,* dealt extensively with the provision of social casework services to different groups of children. "Casework Method: An Elementary School Child" and "The Child and the Social Caseworker in the Schools" are typical titles of the chapters contained in this volume. The introduction to the chapter on the practice of school social work begins:

> More and more state and local systems of education are providing specialized casework services for children who are showing by their failure to use the school experience effectively that they have social and emotional difficulties. This is a skilled method of working with individual children and their families. . . . The school social worker is responsible for individual children who show that they need an additional and different kind of help from that provided in the classroom. . . . Through casework skills the worker develops a relationship with an individual child through which he may be enabled to gain a better understanding of himself, the school situation, and the problem that is hindering his use of the school experience to his potential capacity. (Lee, 1959, p. 231)

In the same volume, Poole (1949) wrote:

> Social casework with the child in school has certain characteristics that are specific to the setting and that must be understood and related to the ge-

neric principles of the social casework process. The school is a setting which, to the child, is very much his own and one in which he is very much on his own. He assumes a major part of the responsibility for the use which he will make of his school experience. When he encounters some difficulty in this setting, the worker helps him to take responsibility for solving it. She helps him to understand the difficulty as it appears to the school and to clarify the problem as it exists for him. (Poole, 1949, p. 456)

Ruth Smalley wrote:

The psychological base for social work is found in the social worker's appreciation of the psycho-biological organizing force which characterizes and is the essence of every living being. . . . The method which social work has developed to discharge its responsibility is a casework method, which comes alive as skill, and is made available and used, within an individual-to-individual relationship. (Smalley, 1955)

Mildred Sikkema's study of types of referrals made to school social workers confirmed that, in all community studies, behavior or personality problems far outnumbered any other type of referral (Sikkema, 1953). In contrast, Jane Culbert found that the largest number of referrals stemmed from maladjustment in scholarship and deficiency in lessons (Culbert, 1923, p. 28). The literature of the 1950s also confirmed that indeed a transition had taken place. Descriptions of casework practice led the reader to believe that the transition was fully completed and that a new era had emerged.

In addition to the casework method, another social work method used in the schools was group therapy. Paul Simon undertook a study on the assumption

that although school social work consisted primarily of casework with children and parents, with concomitant relationships with teachers and others, children might also be helped to resolve some of their problems in interpersonal relationships through the use of selected group experience. The primary objective was to help the child in his relationship to his peers and teachers. (Simon, 1955, p. 26)

Work with Others to Promote Social Casework Goals. The social worker recognized that the casework approach relied upon communication with the parents of troubled children. A varying amount of casework was spent with parents, with the intent of helping the parent to perceive and share the school's concern and to support the child's casework relationship. Anna Braunstein stated that "the social worker's objective in interviewing the parent is to understand the child and his behavior in order to learn the probable cause of it. She can then offer assistance in providing better conditions for the child" (Braunstein, 1959, p. 268). Also, the potentiality of working with parent groups was acknowledged by Aline Auerbach (Auerbach, 1955). The goal of these group sessions was to educate parents about their children, the school, and various developmental behaviors.

In the 1940s and 1950s, social workers consulted with teachers frequently to interpret the child's emotional difficulties and to aid them in an early recognition of personality difficulty (Alderson, 1952). Social workers' collaboration with other school personnel concerning changes in the educational program received minimal attention in the literature; the importance of differentiating the casework relationship from the interprofessional relationship was stressed to some degree. Sikkema attempted to broaden the bases of collaboration by stressing the point that the school social worker could aid other school personnel in understanding human behavior and then translating it into practice in curriculum planning (Sikkema, 1949). John Nebo cited one instance in which school social workers, after two years of conferences, were instrumental in changing the unsound administrative practice of allowing uniformed police officers to come to the school and take children to the police station for questioning without the consent of their parents. However, it should be understood that social work influence in changing school policies was not a "typical professional activity" (Nebo, 1955).

Still we find concern expressed about who the school social worker was.

> Who is the school social worker? . . . He may be "visiting teacher," "visiting counselor," "school counselor," "school social worker," or any of the other several titles. This lack of uniformity seems to reflect to some extent the confusion as to the purpose and function of service. (Kozol, 1967; National Advisory Committee on Civil Disorders, 1968; Silberman, 1970; Task Force on Children Out of School, 1970)

Changing Goals and Methods in the 1960s

Public schools were under attack from all quarters during the 1960s. There were those who argued that public education was not educating the pupils. Further, there was considerable discussion about the need for change in the public school as well as change in the practices of various pupil personnel staff: social workers and guidance counselors. Several studies of public education documented adverse school policies. It was claimed that inequality in educational opportunity existed as a result of segregation; that public schools were reinforcing the myth that minority children and those youths from low-income backgrounds could not perform as well as their middle-class white counterparts, with the result that the educational staff expected poor performance from these students; that the school was essentially a repressive institution, hindering the development of creativity and the desire on the part of some pupils to learn. Some parents claimed that they felt alienated from the school and that they wanted more voice in the education of their children (Lide, 1959).

In the midst of all of these critical issues confronting public education, many school social workers remained somewhat entrenched in their emphasis of individual work with emotionally disturbed children, even though the literature at this time was calling for a broader view of the role of the school, and of social work services: the school as a "social system" was widely discussed in the writings of educators as well as in those of some social workers (Wessenich, 1972; Willis, 1969).

Some experimentation with different methods of social work was also cited in the literature. Virginia Crowthers spoke strongly in support of "school social workers using group work for parents and students, stressing the importance of understanding the individual and his behavior in relationship to the group" (Crowthers, 1963). In a research progress report, Robert Vinter and Rosemary Sarri described the effective use of group work in dealing with such school problems as high school dropouts, underachievement, and academic failure. According to these authors, pupil malperformance was a result of both pupil characteristics and school conditions. This report led the researchers to conclude that school social workers should address themselves more to the conditions of the school and not limit their efforts to contact with pupils; that school social workers are in a strategic position to identify school policies and arrangements that adversely affect children; and that social workers in the schools should have a dual function—they should assist specific individuals and simultaneously deal with the sources of pupil difficulties within the school (Vinter & Sarri, 1965).

Accompanying a growing interest in the use of group work in the schools was attention to new ways of working with the community. A broader kind of community work was recognized, aimed at bringing the school community and geographical community closer together. Hourihan, in describing community work in Detroit, emphasized "the two-way communication established by such a relationship in helping troubled children" (Hourihan, 1965). A project in the Detroit public schools, sponsored by the Ford Foundation, also provided evidence that the community was taking on more importance. The thrust of this project was to bring the inner-city community and school closer together. Because inner-city children were not achieving, and in fact were far behind other students, school-community agents were appointed whose job was to connect school and community as partners in education (Deshler & Erlich, 1972).

Confusion of Roles. As school social workers began to use different methods to deal with problems in the public schools, there were those who were systematically investigating how others viewed the social work role and the role of related disciplines. The school social worker generally operates as a team member, working in collaboration with other school personnel—principal, psychologist, nurse, special educator, and so forth. Robert Rowen conducted a study in New Jersey to determine the differences in the perceptions of the function of school social workers by school superintendents and school social workers, respectively. He found significant disagreement or confusion existed in about one out of every four tasks performed by the school social worker. The superintendent saw the school social worker's role as encompassing more tasks than most of the workers actually performed. These tasks included investigation of the child's home, neighborhood, and environment; assistance in the collection of background materials on the child and family for the psychologist when mental retardation was suspected; and service on community committees and other social agencies (Rowen, 1965).

John Fisher's study of role perception of various school specialists (attendance coordinators, psychologists, and social workers) found that each specialist group believed that its members were more highly involved in various sample situations presented than anyone else thought they were (Fisher, 1966).

Merville Shaw, in a study of role delineation among the guidance professionals, found that their functions overlapped significantly with those that the school counselors, school social workers, and school psychologist wanted to carry out (Shaw, 1967). Richard J. Anderson found that the confusion among roles was not confined to the school, but that it was reflected in ineffec-tive working relationships of school personnel with community agencies. He studied the process and problems of referring maladjusted school children to mental health clinics in Illinois and concluded that troubled children suffer because of the inability of professional personnel working in clinics and school personnel to cooperate with each other. Only the highly motivated child and parent would be willing to blunder through the lack of communication and coordination (Anderson, 1968). In 1969, Costin assessed the importance that a national sample of school social workers attached to specific tasks and sought to determine whether their practice was in tune with changes in social conditions and problems affecting public schools and youths (Costin, 1969). Her findings revealed that the social workers' description of social work reflected the clinical orientation of the social work literature of the 1940s and 1950s, showed little response to the concerns expressed in both education and social work literature, and ranked leadership/policymaking tasks least important. Furthermore, these practitioners were not willing to delegate school social work tasks to individuals with less and/or different levels of education and training than their own. Based on these data and a review of issues in education, Costin later stated:

> It is apparent that if social workers in the schools are to meet their professional obligations and account for their claim on education resources, then they must move with speed to provide part of the remedy for problems of the school and its pupils. The first step is to reassess the objectives of a school social work service. . . . In today's world the focus of social work with pupils must be shifted away from a major emphasis on emotion, motivation, and personality and toward such cognitive areas as learning, thinking, and problem solving. Goals should center upon helping pupils acquire a sense of competence, a readiness for continued learning, and a capacity to adapt to change. (Costin, 1972, p. 350)

John Alderson and Curtis Kirshef undertook a partial replication of Costin's study, asking a population of Florida school social workers who had varying levels of professional training and preparation to indicate the importance of social work tasks and their willingness to delegate them (Alderson & Kirshef, 1973). This population ranked leadership and policymaking as either first or second. In Costin's study it had been ranked least important. Also, this group demonstrated greater readiness to experiment with different staffing patterns, suggesting a positive move not evidenced in Costin's study. However, caution should be used in comparing these studies: Costin analyzed a national random sample of social workers with master's degrees; Alderson and Kirshef analyzed professionals with different backgrounds and levels of training in one state.

Robert Bruce Williams investigated the extent to which the behavior of the school social worker reflected the climate of the individual school and the professional acts of the school social worker in compatible (receptive school social work) and incompatible (not very receptive) schools (Williams, 1970). This research was based on the assumption that the principal primarily determined the administrative policies and practices of each school and thus played a key role in determining social work practice. The results of this study suggested that the performance or nonperformance of the social worker was attributed to attitudinal and behavioral aspects of the principal–social worker relationship.

John P. Flynn studied how other school personnel perceive social work tasks (Flynn, 1976). Pupil personnel service workers, teachers, principals, and instructional specialists were asked to rate the importance and performance of 107 school social work tasks. The results were: (1) Each professional group differed in its perception of task importance and task performance. (2) Only a few of the tasks were viewed as shared with other groups, either in terms of task importance or task performance. (3) These groups also ranked casework and clinical service as most important and a policymaking role as least important.

Expansion in the 1970s: The Call for Leadership

The 1970s were a time of great expansion. The number of school social workers increased and more emphasis was placed on family, community, teaming with workers in other school-related disciplines, and handicapped pupils. Social conditions were also changing rapidly.

A document that significantly influenced public education during this time was the Kerner Report (National Advisory Committee on Civil Disorders, 1968). It analyzed the racial violence of the 1960s and placed much of the blame on public schools and their failure to educate minority children. The report recommended that racial segregation in the nation's schools be eliminated and that opportunities for parental and community participation in the public schools be expanded. Sarri and Maple believe that school social work was greatly influenced by the Kerner Report:

> The report virtually placed on the doorsteps of the school much of the responsibility for the race riots of the 60's. In reaction to the report, as well as being aware of the needs to strengthen school social work's contribution to American Education, the NASW [National Association of Social Workers] Council on Social Work in the Schools undertook a three-year project to expand the school-community linkage role. Jointly funded by the National Institute of Mental Health and NASW, the project produced a national workshop and twelve regional institutes. (Sarri & Maple, 1972)

"Social Change and School Social Work" in the 1970s was the theme of the national workshop held at the University of Pennsylvania in June 1969. The thrust of the workshop was to "stimulate innovation and change in school social work throughout the United States and to encourage school social workers to assume leadership roles" (Sarri & Maple, 1972). Proceedings of these national and regional meetings were later incorporated in a book entitled *The School in the Community*.

Linda Wessenich, Helen Nieberl, and Betty Deshler and John Erlich were among the contributors to *The School in the Community*. Wessenich studied systems analysis, proposing that systems theory be used as a basis for school social work problem-solving (Wessenich, 1972). Nieberl urged focusing away from the microcosm of the individual child to the wider world of the school and community (Nieberl, 1972). This approach required the collection of data about the school and its community in order to determine the various factors that affect student learning. Deshler and Erlich reported on a demonstration project in Detroit in which social workers were used as agents to extend the links between school and community (Deshler & Erlich, 1972).

Other writers also denounced the stagnation gripping the field. K. Spitzer and Betty Welsh called for a problem-focused practice approach rather than method orientation, delineating specific steps to be included in the problem-solving process (Spitzer & Welsh, 1969). Benjamin Gottlieb and Lois Gottlieb concluded that there were essentially three constraints inhibiting a more responsive approach to practice: (1) The educational preparation of school social workers focused too much on individual casework and a method orientation. (2) This training was based on a medical orientation, which focused on intrapsychic factors rather than environmental conditions. (3) The traditional expectations held by educational administrators encouraged practitioners to be caretakers of deviants (Gottlieb & Gottlieb, 1971).

Models of Practice. As school social work practice has evolved, so have different practice models. A practice model can be defined as the "representation or statement of essential facts, central ideas and concepts and their interrelationships within the domain established for the expository model. Constructed simplification of a complex of phenomena which can be perceived" (Johnson, 1972). William Reid and Laura Epstein state that a model is "a coherent set of directives which state how a given kind of treatment is to be carried out. A model is basically definitional and descriptive. It usually states what a practitioner is expected to do or what practitioners customarily do under given conditions" (Reid & Epstein, 1972). Peter Kettner identified several components for analyzing and comparing models: theoretical underpinning, level of intervention, target group or system, roles and responsibilities of the worker, goals and objectives, methods of assessment, strategies employed, to name a few (Kettner, 1975). Models are developed to fit a particular practice need, which, of course, is designed in context to environmental conditions of the time.

Alderson has done considerable work in this area and has offered four models of school social work practice: the traditional clinical model, the school change model, the social interaction model, and the community school model (see Table 2.1) (Alderson, 1972).

The best-known and most widely used model described by Alderson is the traditional clinical model, which focuses on individual students with social and emotional problems that interfere with their potential to learn. This model uses psychoanalytic and ego psychology as its primary theoretical base. A major assumption of the model is that the individual child (and/or the child's family) is dysfunctional and is experiencing difficulty. Thus, the school social worker provides casework services to the child and/or the child's family. The school system itself is not the focus of the worker's activity. School personnel become involved in the assessment process only to share their perspectives and insights on how the child operates in school.

A second model identified by Alderson is the school change model. The target for this model is the school and its institutional policies and practices; the school in its entirety—all persons and subgroups—is viewed as the client. This model encourages changes in institutional poli-

TABLE 2.1 Alderson's Practice Models for School Social Work

	TRADITIONAL CLINICAL MODEL	SCHOOL CHANGE MODEL	COMMUNITY SCHOOL MODEL	SOCIAL INTERACTION MODEL
Focus	Pupils identified as having social or emotional difficulties	The milieu of the school (especially school norms and conditions)	Deprived and disadvantaged communities that misunderstand and mistrust the school	Reciprocal interaction between pupils and the school; identify problems in interaction
Goals	Enable the pupil identified as having a school-related social or emotional difficulty to function more effectively	Alter dysfunctional school norms and conditions	Develop community understanding and support; develop school programs to assist pupils who are poverty victims to reciprocal interaction	Foster development of mutual aid system; remove barriers to reciprocal interaction
Target system	Pupil-clients and their parents	Entire school	Community and school become targets as well as other systems	Interactional field
View of sources of difficulty	Child's emotional or psychic difficulty, stemming primarily from family, especially parent-child problems	Dysfunctional school norms and conditions	Poverty and other social conditions; school personnel lack full understanding of cultural differences and effects of poverty	Difficulty of pupil-clients, and the various systems within which social interaction occurs, to communicate and to mutually assist
Worker tasks and activities	Casework, primarily with pupils and parents; some work with groups and with family as a group; liaison functions between and among pupils, parents, and educational staff, including teachers	Identify school norms and conditions which are dysfunctional; some direct work with pupils, especially group work; consult with teachers and administrators, individually and in groups	Involve self in activities of community; enable community to ask questions and raise issues; assist community in understanding school and vice versa; encourage community involvement in school programs	Identify and highlight commonalities; establish mutual goals; improve and assist communication; establish mutual aid system; direct work with individuals, groups, and community
Major workers' roles	Enabling supportive collaboration and consultation	Advocacy, negotiation, consultation, mediation	Mediation, advocacy, and outreach	Mediation, consultation, enabling
Conceptual and theoretical base	Psychoanalysis, psychosocial, ego psychology, and casework theory and methodology	Social science theory, especially theories of deviance; organizational theory	Community-school concept, communication theory	Systems theory, social science theory, communication theory

Source: Copyright 1972, National Association of Social Workers, Inc. Reprinted with permission, from John Alderson in Rosemary Sarri and Frank F. Maple, eds., *The School in the Community*, pp. 57–74, excerpts; Fig. 1.

cies that are seen as causing student malperformance.

The third model, the community school model, focuses primarily on deprived or disadvantaged communities. Its thrust is to educate these communities about what the school has to offer, to organize support for the school and its programs, and to explain to school officials the dynamics of the community and the operant societal factors.

A fourth model, the social interaction model, has as its emphasis reciprocal influences of the acts of individuals and groups. The target of intervention is the kind and quality of exchanges between parties (the child, groups of children, families, the school, and the community). The social worker is a mediator, a clarifier, and a facilitator of better understanding between and among the parties. This mediation involves identifying "common and shared ground": The worker points out the mutual interests of the parties to help them define a specific goal or objective.

Costin's Model. An important model that grew out of a demonstration project of a multiuniversity consortium for planned change in pupil personnel services is Costin's school-community-pupil relations model (Anderson, 1974; Costin, 1975; Vargus, 1976). This model emphasizes the complexity of the interactions among students, the school, and the community (see Table 2.2). Its primary goal is to bring about change in the interaction of this triad and thus to modify to some extent harmful institutional practices and policies of the school. Attention is given to the characteristics of groups of pupils and of their school. The focus is on the situation of student groups, not on the personality development of individual group members.

Each problem involves groups of students who are similarly situated (truants, pregnant teenagers, or children with similar learning needs) and who form a dysfunctional unit as their unique characteristics interact with conditions in the school and community. The problem is not viewed as springing entirely from the

group; the school and the community are viewed as contributors.

Frequently, the school social worker may provide casework, group work, and crisis intervention on behalf of individual children who are members of a particular target group. However, social casework is not the major social work task according to this model. Instead, the school social worker may assist in the development of new programs, consult and collaborate with school officials regarding policies and practices that contribute to malperformance, and work with community agencies to provide services for the pupils and their families. Interdisciplinary teamwork and cooperation between school social workers and auxiliary school personnel are necessary components of this model.

Replication of Costin's Study: 1970s. In the late 1970s, Allen-Meares replicated Costin's 1969 study to assess the status of social work practice in schools (Allen-Meares, 1977). Stimuli for this investigation were the social work literature calling for new roles and models of practice; the *NASW Manpower Policy Statement* (Costin, 1973; Willis & Willis, 1972), which brought renewed attention to teaming; the unfavorable social conditions and rapid social change (inflation, drug abuse, child abuse and neglect, poverty, and high dropout rates) confronting public schools; and support for a new, humanistic approach to education, which had positive implications for school social work.

Allen-Meares modified Costin's original questionnaire to incorporate activities then being described in the literature. The final questionnaire was mailed to a randomly selected national sample of school social workers. As in Costin's study, respondents rated task importance and indicated their willingness to delegate tasks to persons with less and/or different educational preparation than their own.

Factor analysis of the data yielded seven factors. In rank order of importance, these are: clarifying the child's problem with others; tasks preliminary to the provision of social work ser-

TABLE 2.2 Costin's School-Community-Pupil Relations Model

Focus: On school and community deficiencies and specific system characteristics as these interact with characteristics of pupils at various stress points in their life cycles

Goal: To bring about change in school-community-pupil relations that will alleviate stress upon target groups of pupils

Assessment Procedures: Study and evaluate pupil characteristics and school and community conditions that affect equality of educational opportunity for target groups of pupils; assess needs and identify problem situations that form a problem complex; consult with administrators, teachers, other school personnel, and the affected group—pupils and their parents

Development of a Service Plan: Requires continuing consultation with administrators, teachers, and other school personnel, and with concerned individuals; submission of written plan to administrators and others whose participation and support are essential; agreement on time-limited contract for service; and control of the workload of those who have responsibility for carrying out the service plan

Worker Tasks and Activities: Help student groups diagnose and articulate the problems they see as critical in their school; serve as ombudsman, as individual or group, for student grievances; set up informal groups of teachers, students, and administrators to voice concerns and settle conflicts; form change-agent or problem-solving teams; act as an advocate, consultant, mediator, and negotiator with teachers, administrators, families, and agencies; address the conditions of the school rather than limiting efforts to contacts with students; assist teachers and administrators in identifying those school practices and arrangements that inadvertently hinder learning and adjustment; assess the functioning of target groups of children in relation to the general characteristics of the school

Development of Personnel: Establish a member of a pupil specialist team that is optionally interdisciplinary; maintain maximum flexibility within the team to allow for differentiation of skills, but implement a unified approach to problem-solving and team authority; emphasize open sharing of information and ideas among team members and other persons who can help

Supporting Theories: Social learning theory; systems theory and some of its derivatives (organization development, situation theory, classification of role, and system problems)

vices; assessing the child's problem; facilitating school-community-pupil relations; educational counseling with the child and parents; facilitating the utilization of community resources; and leadership and policymaking. The five highest-ranked factors led to the conclusion that school social work practice was in transition, away from the predominantly clinical casework approach found in Costin's study to one of home-school-community liaison and educational counseling with children and their parents. However, leadership and policymaking was still considered least important. These conclusions fell between the traditional casework approach and the systems-change models or those involving school-

community relations. They did not indicate a strong emphasis on identifying target groups of children, changing adverse conditions of school and community, or responding to the crises in schools. These practitioners also remained reluctant to delegate and assign tasks, apparently maintaining that they were the only professionals within the school system who could perform these functions—a result that conflicted with literature findings that supported experimentation with teaming.

The NASW Study. The NASW Council on Social Work in Schools met for the first time in the fall of 1973 and identified numerous issues facing school social workers. Since inflation and budget cuts were threatening public education and other school personnel were claiming roles similar to those provided by school social workers, it became imperative for the council to assess the current status of practice. To bring attention to these issues and to secure the opinions of practitioners, the council published an open letter in an issue of the *NASW News,* inviting school social workers to share their perceptions (Watson, 1975). The response was overwhelming; letters from all over the United States reinforced the council's concerns. Later in 1974 the council made a report to the Midwest Conference on School Social Work. At this meeting it became clear that national standards were needed to clarify the nature of services and to explain the parameters of the services to other personnel in the school setting.

Before embarking on this task, the council sought additional information on the status of practice, the educational preparation of school social workers, and the structure of school social work systems throughout the United States. The survey was done in the summer of 1975. Representatives of each of the 50 state departments of education were interviewed; questionnaires were mailed to a sample of school social workers and to graduate and undergraduate departments in schools of social work.

Almost all of the school social workers surveyed at the time (88.4 percent) were employed by a local school district, and their positions were funded by state or local agencies or a combination of both (*Summary of the Preliminary Report on the Survey of Social Workers in the Schools,* 1978). Most (88.8 percent) had a master's degree in social work (MSW) and were eligible for tenure and collective bargaining. One-fifth reported that they were directly responsible to a social work supervisor, and about 90 percent were members of an interdisciplinary team. Professional practice was defined primarily as direct service. Typical problems were those of parent-child relationships involving emotionally disturbed pupils. Almost half of these children came from low-income areas, and two-thirds were white. The most often identified work-related problems were too many referrals, excessive case loads, and school personnel who did not understand the social workers' role and functions.

Fifty states reported that school social workers were employed by school districts, but only six states required the employment of school social workers. About two-thirds of the states required that school social workers have an MSW degree.

At the undergraduate level (230 schools) less than one-third of the schools offered a specialized curriculum in school social work, but the school setting was frequently used as a fieldwork placement. Almost all reported that there was little collaboration between them and the department of education on the same campus.

At the master's degree level, only eight graduate schools (of 82 contacted) reported a special curriculum in school social work, and 19 offered some graduate courses in school social work. As at the undergraduate level, the departments of education and the schools of social work had minimal, if any, collaborative arrangements.

When the findings of the NASW study were compared to Allen-Meares' study, several similarities became apparent. Both found that the practice was described as focusing on the individual child and his or her parents rather than on helping target groups of children or changing adverse educational policies and practices, although Allen-Meares did find that practice was in transition.

1980s—The Interface of Social Work and Education

School Social Work: Practice and Research Perspectives (Constable & Flynn, 1982) captures the thrust of the service in the 1980s and some of the important research endeavors and educational issues of the future. Representative topics are: "An Ecological Perspective on Social Work in the Schools"; "School Social Work Practice and P.L. 94-142"; "Implications of Legal Mandates for

Schools and School Policy"; "Social Work in Regular and Special Education"; "The School as an Organization"; "Research Processes for System Change"; "Practical Approaches to Conducting and Using Research in the Schools"; and "Program Evaluation and School Social Work."

A content analysis of school social work literature over the period 1968–1978 indicated several important shifts in practice. School social work focused on pupil groups (specifically handicapped children) and on work with other school personnel. The liaison role was emphasized, as was the role of promoting change in the school policies (Allen-Meares & Lane, 1982). Another research project confirmed these findings. This project sought information about school social workers' perceptions of P.L. 94-142 and its impact on their practice. Consultation, learning, diagnosing handicapped conditions, a move away from long-term clinical treatment, and an organizational role that assisted the school in its primary function were found (Timberlake, Sabantino, & Hooper, 1982).

Interestingly, this book reflects the impact of changes both in social work and in education. Presently in social work there is a strong push for adopting an ecological perspective of practice. And the evaluation of practice is advocated (Constable & Flynn, 1982; Germain, 1979; Tripodi & Epstein, 1980; Winters & Easton, 1983). During the 1980s, school social workers grew in number, and so did their state associations. In response to this growth, NASW had a number of special conferences to address the needs of this group. For example, in 1988 the school social work conference was held in Philadelphia, and in 1990 a special school social work track was held as a part of the NASW annual meeting. These special conferences primarily focused on expanded roles (e.g., work with infants, the role of the school social worker in early childhood special education, school reform and how the school social worker could enhance cultural diversity, and mainstreaming children with learning disabilities), new populations (e.g.,

chemically exposed infants and youth infected with AIDS), and how to respond to the increasing number of homeless children and their families. In response, the need for literature about the practice escalated. *Social Work Services in Schools,* published in 1986, was the first comprehensive text that dealt with this subject matter (Allen-Meares, Washington, & Welsh, 1986). Some state associations of school social workers published their own journals and newsletters.

Educational legislation continued to play a major role in shaping and expanding school and social work services. For example, school social workers were included as "qualified personnel" in Part H of the Education of the Handicapped Act Amendments of 1986, P.L. 99-457, Early Intervention for Handicapped Infants and Toddlers; in P.L. 100-297, the Elementary and Secondary School Improvement Amendments of 1988; and in P.L. 101-476, known as the Individual with Disabilities Education Act.

The debate about the quality of education and the challenge to reform the system led to a national study of state offices of education to ascertain reform initiatives and conditions that were barriers to excellence. Allen-Meares (1987) maintained that the impetus for the study also evolved from concern about the erosion of federal support for social welfare programs for children and their families (Allen-Meares, 1987). The call for excellence in education ignored such barriers as poverty, inadequate health care, race and gender discrimination, and their interaction with schooling. Her study found that excellence was defined by having an effective school administrator, maintaining high expectations for students and staff, involving students in learning, and eradicating school problems. Reform initiatives were: appoint blue ribbon committees; pressure the legislature to increase funding; increase the scholastic requirements for teachers and pupils; and give attention to math and science. Barriers to excellence in education were: parental apathy, poverty, child abuse and neglect, family crisis; poor parenting skills; economic deprivation; poor parent-teacher relationships; lack of dropout prevention programs and teamwork among school personnel; and lack of financial resources.

1990s–Present

In 1994 (known as the Year of Education Reform) school social workers were once more included in a major piece of legislation—the American Education Act, P.L. 103-227. This act was signed into law on March 31, 1994. Eight national goals were included (see Chapter 1). The major objectives of the act were to promote research, consensus building, and systemic change to ensure equality of educational opportunities for all students.

Though this major piece of legislation targets reform initiatives particular to schools, major social, technological, and economic changes in the broader society may prevent it from achieving equity in educational opportunity. For example, an increasing number of children and female-headed households live in poverty (Danziger & Gottschalk [eds.], 1993), technological advancements require a more sophisticated labor force, reform in welfare and healthcare are still topics of debate without firm proposals for real change, there is a call for more community control of schools, and violence in the community and in schools is at an all-time high. It is important to relate this state of affairs to the conceptual framework of this book. The school is impacted upon by its larger community and societal context. If social supports are not present for children and their families to buffer the consequence of poverty and other problems, even with the implementation of school reform proposals, educational success is highly unlikely.

The Growth of State Associations of School Social Workers and a New National Organization. Since the early 1970s, the number of state associations of school social workers has risen. Many NASW chapters now have school social

work committees. There are four regional councils: Midwest School Social Work Council, formed almost three decades ago; the Southern School Social Work Conference; the Western Alliance; and the Northeastern Alliance. In 1994, spearheaded by the school social work leadership, a National Association of School Social Workers was formed independent of the NASW (National Association of Social Workers Commission on Education, 1991).

In many state offices of education there are persons who assume administrative responsibility for school social work services. These individuals are known as school social work state consultants. There is a National Council of State Consultants in school social work.

These state, regional, and national organizations are providing their members with educational opportunities for professional growth, yearly workshops, job networks, continuing education credit, and legislative advocacy. As state associations increase and develop, it will be essential for them to form linkages with NASW and other related school-based progressive groups. It would be detrimental to the profession if these independent membership groups isolated themselves from the national organization. In 1994, NASW identified school social work as the first section under its then newly organized structure. The NASW School Social Work Section has celebrated several anniversaries. The section provides members with national leadership for school social workers, a newsletter, professional development opportunities at the national conference, lobbying at the national level and comment on federal education legislation and regulations, and advocacy to influence relevant policies. The section is producing a series of minipublications on school social work effectiveness (NASW Steering Committee, 1997).

School Social Work Credential. States are now taking a more active role in specifying education requirements for practice in the school. For example, in Illinois, practitioners seeking certification must complete an approved graduate social work program that includes special coursework on school social work (e.g., educational legislation; exceptional children; models of practice; and state and school laws) and take the two special exams (a test of knowledge specific to school social work and a test of basic skills in math, reading, etc.). For those practitioners who completed their coursework prior to the implementation of these requirements, procedures are in place to certify them. Since so many states are adopting credentialing procedures for all school employees as a way to upgrade the quality of personnel, NASW, in consultation with Allen-Meares and the Education Testing Service, Princeton, New Jersey, developed the first School Social Work Credential Exam. This exam was first administered in 1992.

The School Social Work Specialist (SSWS) credential is voluntary and not yet required for state social work certification (NASW School Social Work Section Committee, 1996). This credential recognizes school social workers who have:

— met nationally established standards of knowledge and practice by achieving a passing score on the National Teachers Exam's (NTE) School Social Worker Specialty Area Test
— demonstrated two years of paid post-MSW social work experience and professional supervision in a school setting
— provided a professional evaluation from a social work supervisor and a reference from a colleague

What makes this credential important is that holders of it agree to adhere to the NASW code of ethics and the NASW standards for school social work services; it provides specialty standards; the likelihood of creating additional reciprocity arrangements between states is enhanced; it strengthens and makes the case that there is unique knowledge in this specialized field; and it contains a continuing education requirement so that practitioners can stay abreast of current knowledge.

The move to test and review the credentials of those seeking employment as school social workers holds important implications for the educational preparation offered by schools of social work.

Standards for Social Work Services in Schools. In 1976 the first standards for school social work services were developed. These standards were grouped into three areas: (1) attainment of competence, (2) organization and administration, and (3) professional practice. The standards included a taxonomy of school social work tasks. An important theme running throughout the standards was prevention.

In 1992 the standards for social work services in schools were revised by the Education Task Force (Education Commission Task Force, 1992). The standards were divided into three sections: (1) competence and professional practice, (2) professional preparation and development, and (3) administrative structure and support. Appropriate ratios for social worker–student populations are determined by the populations of the student body and its needs. For example, a school consisting of a large number of handicapped pupils would need more workers.

Future Directions and Challenges. Questions about the quality of schooling, reduced tax base, increased demand to serve a more diverse student population, increased poverty among children and families, and increased violence will challenge the profession to think creatively and differently about their services. The capacity of the community to devote its resources to enhance the availability and scope of social and economic supports will be a decisive factor. Building integrated school and community service models will be important if we are to achieve success.

What does this mean for school social work services? With the new emphasis on developing integrated service-delivery systems (or full-service schools) involving collaboration between schools and community agencies, the challenge will be to redefine school social work to meet this paradigm shift.

CONCLUSION

Since the early twentieth century, school social work has been preoccupied with essentially three questions: Who are the school social workers? What services can such individuals provide? To

whom must they relate? In order to do full justice to the historical development of the service, we should trace the history of education in the United States. Table 2.3 summarizes some of the key forces in society and education that have shaped social work services in schools. School social workers should be conscious of the changes in approaches to education and in those social conditions that education responds to. By doing so, school social workers can be proactive rather than reactive in the determination of their role.

FOR STUDY AND DISCUSSION

1. Identify positive and negative vestiges of the historical development of social work services that exist in schools today.

2. Identify and discuss reasons why social workers in schools have been so preoccupied with role definition.

3. Visit a local school and talk with administrators, other school personnel, and the social worker about their roles and tasks. Find out how they "team" and what factors undermine teaming. Also obtain their opinions about what each discipline contributes to the education of children. Is there overlap?

4. Identify several social forces or conditions that presently have a direct bearing on education in the United States. What are the implications for social work practice in schools? What are the implications for the educational preparation of social workers?

5. Obtain a copy of *NASW Standards for Social Services in Schools.* Evaluate these standards in light of contemporary educational issues and concerns. What targets of service would you give most attention to? Why?

ADDITIONAL READING

Allen-Meares, P. (1992). International and multicultural themes relevant to school social work [Special issue]. *Social Work in Education, 14*(3).

Allen-Meares, P. (1993). The new federal role in education and family services: Goal setting without responsibility. *Social Work, 41,* 533–540.

Barth, R. (1987). Social promotion and nonpromotion: Nonsolutions to underachievement. *Social Work in Education, 9,* 26–33.

Burt, M. R., Risnick, G., & Matheson, N. (1992). *Comprehensive service integration programs for at risk youth: Final report.* Washington, DC: Urban Institute.

Campbell, D., & Green, D. (1994). Defining the leadership role of school boards in the 21st century. *Phi Delta Kappa, 75*(5), 391–395.

Chavkin, N. (1985). School social work practice: A reappraisal. *Social Work in Education, 8,* 3–13.

Constable, R. (1992). The new school reform and the school social worker. *Social Work in Education, 14*(2), 106–108.

Ford Foundation (1989). *The common good: Social welfare and the American future.* New York: Author.

Hare, I. (1994). School social work in transition. *Social Work in Education, 16*(1), 64–68.

Hill, P. (1994). Reinventing urban public education. *Phi Delta Kappa, 75*(5), 396–401.

Kozal, J. (1995). *Amazing grace: The lives of children and the conscience of a nation.* New York: Crown.

Radin, N. (1989). School social work services: Past,

TABLE 2.3 Historical Development of and Influences on School Social Work, 1800–21st Century

SOCIAL TRENDS AND MOVEMENTS	PUBLIC EDUCATION	SOCIAL WORK	SCHOOL SOCIAL WORK
1800–1919			
Immigrant population increase.	Crusade for public education; expansion of public education at elementary, secondary, and college levels (1875–1900) in northern and western states.	Movement from volunteer to paid employment.	Outside agencies provided social work services to students in schools in Hartford, Boston, and New York City, 1906–1907.
Age of progressiveness: liberalism, social Darwinism.		Growth in immigrant population and thus the first settlement house in the United States, 1887.	First school system to finance school social work service: Rochester, New York, 1913.
Development of social science as a body of knowledge.	Influence of John Dewey and "progressive education."	Beginning of social work education with an emphasis on method of practice; social science theory predominant.	
Growth of labor movement; concern for working conditions.	Concern for the development of the individual child.		
Child labor movement.	Compulsory attendance required in all 48 states (first: Mass., 1852; last: Miss., 1918).	Beginnings of establishing practice theory with publication of Mary Richmond's *Social Diagnosis* (1917).	
Establishment of juvenile courts.	Smith-Hughes Act for the support of vocational education.	Development of practice in specialty areas.	
World War I ("Make the world safe for democracy").	Emergence of nonpublic schools.		
Nativists believed that the new wave of immigrants from Europe were destroying the "fabric of society and the race."			
Development and influence of psychology and Freudian theory.			
1919–1929			
Prosperity: national income high, unemployment low.	Established that nonpublic schools may be an acceptable alternative to public schools, 1925.	Marked increase in philanthropic foundations.	Commonwealth Fund, a private fund, a private foundation, supported 30 school social workers in 20 different communities.
Reduction in immigration; deportation of alien radicals.	Increase in student population and growth of school programs reflective of prosperity.	Formation of community chests and reorganization of private charities.	Increase in number of visiting teachers.
Increase in racial intolerance; upsurge of Ku Klux Klan.		Rise of "child guidance," "mental hygiene," and character-	

TABLE 2.3 *(Continued)*

SOCIAL TRENDS AND MOVEMENTS	PUBLIC EDUCATION	SOCIAL WORK	SCHOOL SOCIAL WORK
			1919: National Association of Visiting Teachers established.
		building agencies; concern for the prevention of delinquency.	
		Emphasis on function of social work rather than on social cause; emphasis on the adjustment of individuals.	
1930–1945			
Great Depression; solutions sought for economic and social ills in action by the federal government.	Development of the Civilian Conservation Corps (CCC); educational programs were developed in each CCC camp (significant influence on youth).	Federal government became involved in social welfare, relief programs, and public works programs.	Services provided by visiting teachers either abolished or seriously cut back in 1930s.
New Deal: entrance of federal government into relief program.	National Youth Administration (NYA) provided employment for students in high schools and colleges.	Federal funding; state administration of assistance for children, the aged, and the disabled.	Movement to a more specialized role in social casework.
Mass movement from rural to urban settings.		Group work became a part of social work; formation of the National Association of the Study of Groups, 1936.	1944: Michigan first state to pass legislation for State Department of Education reimbursement of social work services in schools.
Fair labor standards, continued development of labor unions.		Lane Report on Community Organization as a method; fewer settlement houses established.	
World War II: Revolt against totalitarianism and emphasis on nation unity.			
Social Security Act of 1935.			
1946–1960			
Postwar prosperity.	Expansion of schools; crowded schools; half-day sessions.	Growth of National Institute of Health.	Emphasis on collaboration with other school personnel; development of pupil personnel services.
Population explosion.	*Brown v. Board of Education* (1954): "Separate but not equal education."	Concern about juvenile correctional institutions and delinquency.	Increase in visiting teacher programs.
Growth of metropolitan communities; migration of minorities from cities.			

(continued)

43

TABLE 2.3 (Continued)

SOCIAL TRENDS AND MOVEMENTS	PUBLIC EDUCATION	SOCIAL WORK	SCHOOL SOCIAL WORK
Television promoting image of happy home.	National Science Foundation developed (1950) to promote basic research and education in the sciences.	Growth in community chests and councils; establishment of United Foundation.	1955: NASW by-laws provide for the establishment of school social work.
	Establishment of the U.S. Department of Health, Education, and Welfare, 1954.	National Mental Health Act, 1946.	
	Passage of bill creating and funding position of elementary school counselor.	Establishment of the U.S. Department of Health, Education, and Welfare, 1954.	
1961–1970	Vocational Education Act of 1963.	War on poverty; Great Society.	Great Cities Project, funded by Ford Foundation—developed community-school programs in 13 urban cities to bridge the gap between school and community; social workers employed as "community agents."
High employment.	Elementary and Secondary Education Act of 1965 and title program.	Growing ADC roles; AFDC (1962).	
From civil rights to black power-minority rights issues.	Civil Rights Act of 1964 and the Coleman Report.	Development of community social work with an emphasis on politics, social planning, and advocacy.	
Women's liberation movement.	National assessment of educational progress, 1963.	Concern with manpower issues.	Move to change name from visiting teachers to school social workers.
Report of the National Advisory Commission on Civil Disorders, 1968.	Supreme Court call for immediate termination of dual school systems.	Growth of social workers in many new agency settings created by the Great Society programs.	Recognition in literature that the school environment contributes to student learning.
Space program.	Increased federal support for education.	Increased emphasis upon "social system" theory.	Integration of group work method in school social work casework practice.
Kennedy assassination.	Child abuse legislation in many states making school personnel	National Institute of Mental Health and NASW funded project entitled "Social Change	
Vietnam War and student demonstrations and protests.			
Gault decision (1965), right of juveniles to legal representation.			

TABLE 2.3 *(Continued)*

SOCIAL TRENDS AND MOVEMENTS	PUBLIC EDUCATION	SOCIAL WORK	SCHOOL SOCIAL WORK
	and school social workers responsible for reporting.	and School Social Work in the '70s.	
	Move toward community control of schools.		
1971–1989			
Inflation; fiscal retrenchment.	Section 504, Vocational Rehabilitation Act of 1973.	Accreditation of Bachelor of Social Work programs; development of doctoral programs; diversity of educational programs.	Increase in number of school social workers and development of new programs.
Concern for law and order; Watergate; consumerism; conservative trend.	P.L. 94-142, Education for All Handicapped Children Act.		Shift of service to handicapped students.
Unemployment climbs.	Family Rights and Privacy Act.	NASW accepts BSW for membership; new NASW Code of Ethics, 1979.	Evaluation and accountability stressed.
Rights of the handicapped recognized.	Drop in student enrollment; closing of school buildings.	Proliferation of new practice modalities.	Emergence of ecological approach to practice.
Influence of computer in business and education; scientific advances in all areas.	Dismissal of school personnel, including some tenured persons.	Emphasis on research and theory development.	NASW task force on social work.
Continued recession with high unemployment at all levels of society.	Emphasis on accountability.	Growing emphasis on the ecological perspective.	*School Social Work Journal* (NASW).
Reduction in social programs and aid to the poor.	Development of student codes of conduct.	Development of integrated or generalist methods.	First National Conference on School Social Work.
Conservative national policies.	Violence in schools.	Growth of state licensing laws.	NASW Committee on Social Work in Schools (1976).
The age of the computer and other technological advances.	Concern about illiteracy at graduation.	Increases in number of social work journals.	1979: Provisional Council on Social Work Services in Schools created.
	Bilingual education programs.	Development of specializations in graduate social work programs.	Second National Conference on School Social Work.
	Development of preschool public education.		NASW Board creates Practice Advancement Council on Social Work Services in Schools.
	Increased number of private schools.		
	Continued reduction of school programs.		

(continued)

TABLE 2.3 *(Continued)*

SOCIAL TRENDS AND MOVEMENTS	PUBLIC EDUCATION	SOCIAL WORK	SCHOOL SOCIAL WORK
	Reduced federal support to education. Development of the Office of Education. Threat to eliminate the Office of Education. Increased development of vocational education. Evaluations of education urge an overhaul of the system.	Emphasis on prevention of social and mental health problems. Continued rise of "clinical social work" movement and private practice. Increased emphasis on the evaluation of practice and accountability. Integration of research and practice.	1985: Commission on Education created by NASW. 1986: First comprehensive book published on school social work. Decrease in number of social workers in schools because of economic situation and decrease in enrollment. Third National Conference on School Social Work. School Social Work track in NASW conference (1988 and 1990). 1989: National Survey of School Social Workers in collaboration with Allen-Meares, ETS, and NASW. Links with related national organizations take on more importance (e.g., National Association of School Psychologists, Council on Exceptional Children, National Association of School Nurses, etc.).
1990s–21st Century Increasing numbers of children and families living in poverty, particularly in single-parent and minority homes. Continuing concerns re: substance abuse, the homeless, domestic violence, unemployment, and underemployment.	Increased pressure for choice and alternative schools as a result of a decrease in confidence in the public schools. Many states move towards statewide academic standards and assessments in an attempt to increase performance standards of students and schools.	In 1993, a new structure was adopted by the NASW Board of Directors, which created optional specialty practice sessions. The first section is School Social Work. Increased community-based vs. residential-based services.	A trend exists which creates integrated collaborative services in which schools and community agencies provide health and social services to children and families in or near schools. School social workers are the "glue-factor" for the collaboratives. School-based link services.

TABLE 2.3 (Continued)

SOCIAL TRENDS AND MOVEMENTS	PUBLIC EDUCATION	SOCIAL WORK	SCHOOL SOCIAL WORK
Continuing transition from Industrial to Technological Age. Political emphasis on welfare and healthcare reform.	Increase in public preschool, day care programs, and after school care.	Call for a better understanding of the influence of chronic urban violence on teens.	School social workers serve more populations (e.g., preschool, Head Start, autistic, alternative education).
Increasingly diverse U.S. population. Highest immigration rates since the 1920s.	Increase in violence in schools.	Continued increase in private practice.	Some states adopt competency requirements for practice. New standards for School Social Work Services, 1992.
Attention to new immigrants.	Call for more school-community partnerships to improve school and student performance.	Increased development of social work services in business and industry.	Increased emphasis on coordination of family, school, and community.
Increase in violence as a means of resolving conflict. Teens are five times more likely to be a victim of violent crime than any other age group.	Continued debate on public vs. private education.	A call for more political action.	Provides services to reduce/eliminate substance abuse, violence, and so forth, as well as special education.
Debates on gay and lesbian issues.	Increased pressure to fully include special education students.	More emphasis on research to undergird interventions.	Increased emphasis on multidisciplinary teamwork.
Efforts to stabilize the economy.	Pressure comes from the courts, statutes, and advocacy groups.	NIMH research centers focus on mental health of children and families.	Position statement on the School Social Worker and confidentiality.
Awareness of precarious economy in light of deficit.	Extension of school services to at-risk and disabled children prior to them beginning kindergarten. This was begun in 1986 by the EHA (P.L. 99-457) and served to extend the provisions of P.L. 99-142 to children from birth through 5 years old.	Emphasis on family preservation.	Elimination of NASW Commission on Education.
Increased U.N. and U.S. involvement in international conflicts and issues.		Increase in number of specializations.	School social workers must play an active role in early childhood special education and with infants and toddlers with disabilities.
AIDS reaching epidemic proportions.	Comprehensive health education which includes sex education and other concerns such as AIDS.	Move toward solution-focused, short-term interventions.	Development of National School Social Work Association.
Passage of Americans with Disabilities Act (ADA).	Debates on teaching human sexuality.		National NASW School Social Work Specialist credential.
Increase in school-age population—"Baby Boom Revisited."	1994: American Education Act passes.		Guidelines for HIV and AIDS student support services.
Increase in self-advocacy and empowerment among varied			

(continued)

47

TABLE 2.3 (Continued)

SOCIAL TRENDS AND MOVEMENTS	PUBLIC EDUCATION	SOCIAL WORK	SCHOOL SOCIAL WORK
groups. An increased move toward inclusion in all sectors.	Increased emphasis on technology.		School Social Work becomes NASW's First Section—more than 16,000 signed the petition.
People first language (i.e., child with disabilities not disabled child).	Charter schools.		Social work is the lead agency in the delivery of Part C (formerly called Part H) service in the Individual with Disabilities Education Act (IDEA) in some states.
Elimination of entitlements to welfare; passage of welfare reform.	Wraparound services for children with complex needs.		Transition planning for special education students.
Research on brain development focuses new emphasis on importance of early development.	Increased recognition of need for developing community in schools.		Functional behavioral assessment for special education students.
More grandparents parenting children.	Growing home school movement.		In some states the social worker acts as advocate/parent surrogate for children in residential facilities.
Increased homelessness as housing represents a larger percentage of income.			

Source for the discussion on education comes largely from Ronald F. Campbell et al., *The Organization and Control of American Schools*, 3d ed. (Columbus, OH: Charles E. Merrill, 1975); the source for the discussion on social work and societal trends in Louise C. Johnson, *Social Work Practice: A Generalist Approach*. Published by Allyn & Bacon, Boston, MA. Copyright © 1983 by Pearson Education, Inc. Both reprinted with permission.

present, and future trends. *Social Work in Education, 11,* 213–225.

Rubin, L., & Borgers, S. (1991). The changing family: Implications for education. *Principal, 71*(1), 11–13.

Washington, V., & Bailey, V. (1995). *Project Head Start: Models and strategies for the twenty-first century.* New York: Garland.

REFERENCES

Abbott, E., & Breckinridge, S. (1917). *Truancy and non-attendance in the Chicago schools: A study of the social aspects of the compulsory education and child labor legislation of Illinois.* Chicago: University of Chicago Press.

Alderson, J. J. (1952). The specific content of school social work. *Bulletin of the National Association of School Social Workers, 27.*

Alderson, J. (1972). Models of school social work practice. In R. Sarri and F. Maple (Eds.). *The school in the community* (pp. 151–160). Washington, DC: NASW.

Alderson, J., & Kirshef, C. (1973). Another perspective on tasks in school social work. *Social Casework, 54,* 591–600.

Allen-Meares, P. (1977). Analysis of tasks in school social work. *Social Work, 22,* 196–201.

Allen-Meares, P. (1987). A national study of educational reform: Implications for social work services in schools. *Children and Youth Services Review, 19,* 207–219.

Allen-Meares, P., & Lane, B. A. (1982). A content analysis of school social work literature, 1968–1978. In R. Constable and J. Flynn (Eds.), *School social work: Practice and research perspectives* (pp. 49–72). Homewood, IL.: Dorsey Press.

Allen-Meares, P., Washington, R. O., & Welsh, B. (1986). *Social work services in schools.* Engelwood Cliffs, NJ: Prentice Hall.

Anderson, J. J. (1974). Introducing change in school community-pupil relationships: Maintaining credibility and accountability. *Journal of Education for Social Work, 19,* 3–8.

Anderson, R. J. (1968). *Procedures and problems in referring school children to mental health clinics.* Unpublished doctoral dissertation, Illinois State University.

Areson, C. W. (1923). Status of children's work in the United States. *Proceedings of the national conference of social work* (p. 398). Chicago: University of Chicago Press.

Auerbach, A. B. (1955). The special contribution of school social work in work with parent groups. *Bulletin of the National Association of School Social Workers, 30,* 10–19.

Bowers, S. (1949). Nature and definition of social casework. *Social Casework, 30,* 417.

Braunstein, A. (1959). The social worker and the parents. In G. Lee (Ed.), *Helping the troubled school child. Selected readings in school social work, 1935–1955* (p. 268). Washington, DC: National Association of Social Workers.

Breckinridge, S. (1914). Some aspects of the public school from a social worker's point of view. *Journal of Proceedings and Addresses of the National Education Association.*

Constable, R., & Flynn, J. (Eds.). (1982). *School social work: Practice and research perspectives.* Homewood, IL: Dorsey Press.

Costin, L. B. (1969a). An analysis of the tasks in school social work. *Social Service Review, 43,* 274–285.

Costin, L. B. (1969b). A historical review of school social work. *Social Casework, 50,* 439–453.

Costin, L. B. (1972). Adaptations in the delivery of school social work services. *Social Casework, 53,* 350.

Costin, L. B. (1973). School social work practice: A new model. *Social Work, 20,* 135–139.

Costin, L. B. (1978). *Social work services in schools: Historical perspectives and current directions. Continuing education series #8* (pp. 1–34). Washington, DC: NASW.

Crowthers, V. L. (1963). The school as a group setting. *Social work practice 1963. Selected papers, 90th annual forum, National Conference on Social Welfare* (pp. 70–83). New York: Columbia University Press.

Culbert, J. (1916). *Visiting teachers and their activities: Proceedings of the National Conference of Charities and Correction* (p. 595). Chicago: Hildman Printing Co.

Culbert, J. (1923). *Visiting teachers in the United States* (p. 28). New York: Public Education Association of the City of New York.

Danziger, S., & Gottschalk, P. (Eds.). (1993). *Uneven tides: Rising unequality in America.* New York: Russell Sage Foundation.

Deshler, B., & Erlich, J. L. (1972). Changing school/community relations. In R. Sarri & F. Maple (Eds.), *The school in the community* (pp. 233–253). Washington, DC: NASW.

Education Commission Task Force. (1992). *NASW standards for school social work services* (pp. 1–23). Washington, DC: NASW.

Everett, E. M. (1938). The importance of social work in a school program. *The Family, 19,* 58.

Fisher, J. K. (1966). Role perceptions and characteristics of attendance coordinators, psychologists, and social workers. *Journal of the International Association of Pupil Personnel Workers, 10,* 1–8.

Flynn, J. P. (1976). Congruence in perception of social work–related tasks in a school system. *Social Service Review, 59,* 471–481.

Germain, C. (Ed.). (1979). *Social work practice: People and environments.* New York: Columbia University Press.

Gottlieb, B. H., & Gottlieb, L. J. (1971). An expanded role for the school social workers. *Social Work, 16,* 12–21.

Hall, G. E. (1936). Changing concepts in visiting teacher work. *Visiting Teachers Bulletin, 12.*

Hourihan, J. (1952). *The duties and responsibilities of the visiting teacher.* Unpublished doctoral dissertation, Wayne State University, Detroit, Michigan.

Hourihan, J. P. (1965, May). *Social work in the schools: New developments in theory, knowledge, and practice.* Paper presented at the NASW Tenth Anniversary Symposium on Social Work Practice and Knowledge, Atlantic City, New Jersey.

Johnson, L. (1972). *Definition of model social work practice: A syllabus and book of readings* (pp. 95–96). Iowa City: University of Iowa Press.

Kettner, P. M. (1975). A framework for comparing practice models. *Social Service Review, 49,* 629–642.

Kozol, J. (1967). *Death at an early age.* Boston: Houghton Mifflin.

Lee, G. (Ed.). (1959). *Helping the troubled school child. Selected readings in school social work, 1935–1955* (p. 231). Washington, DC: NASW.

Lide, P. (1959). Historical influences on function of school social workers. In G. Lee (Ed.), *Helping the troubled school child. Selected readings in school social work, 1935–1955* (pp. 18–33). Washington, DC: NASW.

Lide, P. (1959). Study of the historical influences of major importance in determining the present function of the school social workers. In G. Lee (Ed.), *Helping the troubled school child. Selected readings in school social work, 1935–1955* (pp. 107–129). Washington, DC: National Association of Social Workers.

NASW manpower policy statement. (1973). Washington, DC: NASW.

National Advisory Committee on Civil Disorders. *The Kerner Report.* (1968). Washington, DC: Government Printing Office.

National Association of Social Workers Commission on Education. (1991). *Fact sheet—School social work and NASW* (pp. 1–7). Washington, DC: NASW.

National Association of Social Workers Steering Committee. (1996). *The section connection* (pp. 1–12). Washington, DC: NASW Press.

National Association of Social Workers Steering Committee. (1997). *The section correction.* (pp. 1–23). Washington, DC: NASW Press.

Nebo, J. C. (1955). Interpretation of school social welfare services to educators and other professionals who serve the schools. *Bulletin of the National Association of School Social Workers, 30,* 1–55.

Nieberl, H. R. (1972). Breaking out of the bind in school social work practice. In R. Sarri and F. Maple (Eds.), *School in the community* (pp. 151–160). Washington, DC: NASW.

Oppenheimer, J. (1925). *The visiting teacher movement, with special reference to administrative relationships,* 2nd ed. (p. 5). New York: Joint Committee on Methods of Preventing Delinquency.

Poole, F. (1949). An analysis of the structure and practice of school social work today. *Social Service Review, 23,* 456.

Reid, W., & Epstein, L. (1972). *Task-centered casework* (pp. 7–8). New York: Columbia University Press.

Reynolds, B. C. (1935). Social casework: What is it? What is its place in the world today? *The Family, 16,* 238.

Rowen, R. (1965). The function of the visiting teacher in the school. *Journal of the International Association of Pupil Personnel Workers, 9,* 3–9.

Sarri, R., & Maple, F. (Eds.). (1972). *School in the community.* Washington, DC: NASW.

Shaw, M. C. (1967). Role delineation among the guidance professions. *Psychology in the Schools, 4.*

Sikkema, M. (1949). An analysis of the structure and practice of school social work today. *Social Service Review, 23,* 447–453.

Sikkema, M. (1953). *Report of a study of school social work practice in twelve communities.* New York: American Association of Social Workers.

Silberman, C. (1970). *Crisis in the classroom.* New York: Random House.

Simon, P. (1955). Social group work in the schools. *Bulletin of the National Association of School Social Workers, 27.*

Smalley, R. (1955). School counseling as social work. *Bulletin of the National Association of School Social Workers, 30,* 21–34.

Smalley, R. E. (1947). School social work as a part of the school program. *Bulletin of the National Association of School Social Workers, 22.*

Spitzer, K., & Welsh, B. (1969). A problem-focused model of practice. *Social Casework, 50,* 323–329.

Summary of the preliminary report on the survey of social workers in the schools (1978) (pp. 1–11). Washington, DC: NASW.

Taft, J. (1923). The relation of the school of mental health of the average child. *Proceedings of the National Conference of Social Work* (p. 398). Chicago: University of Chicago Press.

Task Force on Children Out of School (1970). *The way we go to school.* Boston: Beacon Press.

Timberlake, E. M., Sabantino, C. A., & Hooper, S. N. (1982). School social work practice and P.L. 94-142. In R. Constable and J. Flynn (Eds.), *School social work: Practice and research perspectives* (pp. 49–72). Homewood, IL: Dorsey Press.

Towle, C. (1936). Discussion of "Changing concepts in visiting teacher work." *Visiting Teachers Bulletin, 12,* 15–16.

Tripodi, T., & Epstein, I. (1980). *Research techniques for clinical social workers.* New York: Columbia University Press.

Vargus, I. (1976). Developing, launching and maintaining the school-community-pupil program. In D. J. Kurpiur and I. Thomas (Eds.), *Social services and the public schools* (pp. 61–73). Bloomington, IN: Midwest Center Satellite Consortium for Planned Change in Pupil Personnel Programs for Urban Schools.

Vinter, R., & Sarri, R. (1965). Malperformance in the public school: A group work approach. *Social Work, 10,* 38–48.

Wald, L. (1915). *The house on Henry Street.* New York: Henry Holt and Co.

Watson, T. F. (1975). An open letter to social workers in schools. *NASW News, 19.*

Wessenich, L. P. (1972). Systems analysis applied to school social work. In R. Sarri and F. Maple (Eds.), *The school in the community* (pp. 196–210). Washington, DC: NASW.

Williams, R. B. (1970). School compatibility and social work role. *Social Service Review, 44,* 169–174.

Willis, J. (1969). The mental health worker as a systems engineer. In R. Sarri & F. F. Maple (Eds.), *The general systems approach: Contribution toward an holistic conception of social work.* New York: Council on Social Work Education.

Willis, J. W., & Willis, J. S. (1972). The mental health worker as a systems behavioral engineer. In R. Sarri and F. Maple (Eds.), *The school in the community* (pp. 151–160). Washington, DC: NASW.

Winters, W., & Easton, F. (1983). *The practice of social work in schools: An ecological perspective.* New York: Free Press.

CHAPTER 3

SOCIAL ORGANIZATION AND SCHOOLS: A GENERAL SYSTEMS THEORY PERSPECTIVE

GARY L. BOWEN, THE UNIVERSITY OF NORTH CAROLINA AT CHAPEL HILL

All growth in nature arises out of an interplay between reinforcing growth processes and limiting processes. The seed contains the possibility for a tree, but it realizes that possibility through an emergent reinforcing growth process. [*]

—Peter Senge

INTRODUCTION

School social workers practice in settings where the focus of service is on education rather than social work. Social workers must cooperate with school personnel to achieve the goals of education. The holistic philosophy of education recognizes the value of social work expertise in the design of preventive and remedial measures to promote the social functioning of students and their families, support teachers and school administrators in performing their duties, and ameliorate environmental conditions that impede the learning process. Although employed by the school, they are hired, in part, to represent and advocate for children and parents who cannot express special needs effectively and who are unable to assert their educational rights.

Social workers bring a perspective to practice in schools that focuses on the transactions between people and their social environments as the primary unit of analysis in planning and implementing social interventions (Richman & Bowen, 1997). This transactional or person-environment fit perspective emphasizes the environments forming children's ecosystem (e.g., school, community, family), the system-level interfaces between the environments in which children live and function (e.g., schools and neighborhoods, schools and families), and the larger institutional forces that frame and shape environments for children and youth at all levels (e.g., funding for social work services in schools). Social work interventions should and

[*]From "The Life Cycle of Typical Change Initiatives," in *The Dance of Change: The Challenges to Sustaining Momentum in Learning Organizations* by Peter Senge, Art Kleiner, Charlotte Roberts, Richard Ross, George Roth, and Bryan Smith, copyright 1999, by Doubleday/Currency, p. 7. Reprinted by permission of the publisher.

can occur within any system, or any combination of systems, that impinge negatively upon students' functioning at the micro level or the performance of schools at the macro level.

School social workers must have a working understanding of the collective processes that influence student functioning and learning outcomes. For example, if the social climate of the school lacks warmth, support, and incentives, then learning and teaching become difficult. If the neighborhood in which the student lives is unsafe and lacks supportive adults to monitor the behavior of children and youth who live there, the student may not have a safe route between home and school. Consequently, the student may be less prepared to learn when they arrive at school. The school social worker is in the position to intervene directly or to collaborate with others to change the quality of this environment.

This chapter focuses on the school as a social system. In particular, I focus on social organizational processes in schools that distinguish high performing from low performing schools. Also, I examine the functioning of schools in the broader community, and how the local environments in which students are embedded influence their school performance. General systems theory provides concepts that are useful for understanding and analyzing the functioning of schools and the broader context in which they function. I focus specific attention on the general systems theory concept of social organization, and the application of this concept to the schools that students attend and the neighborhoods in which they reside.

Schools are a specific type of social system that sociologists label *formal organization*. Unlike informal organizations that are more voluntaristic and typically less organized networks of personal and collective relationships, formal organizations are social systems that have been "planfully instituted" to accomplish specific objectives and typically have more rigidly enforced rules and norms that govern social interaction and performance (Bertalanffy, 1968, p. 9). As stated in Chapter 1, schools in America exist to prepare children and youth to participate as citizens in a democratic society and to develop specialized abilities to function successfully as workers in the economy.

A GENERAL SYSTEMS THEORY PERSPECTIVE

General systems theory, which has been used as an integrative perspective in social work education since the mid-1950s, provides an organized means for studying schools as dynamic environments and for studying the multifaceted interactions between schools and other segments of society. General systems theory uses assumptions and concepts from the systems paradigm to study living beings and their interrelationships at multiple levels (Barker, 1999).

Using an organismic metaphor to describe formal organizations (e.g., schools) with the same principles and concepts used to describe biological organisms, general systems theory is most closely associated with Ludwig von Bertalanffy (1968), whose work in the 1920s and 1930s captured the dynamic relationship between biological organisms and their environment. A Viennese biologist, Bertalanffy brought together the common principles of an evolving "systems" approach in such diverse disciplines as biology, the social sciences and economics under the rubric of general systems theory. Bertalanffy defined a system as "sets of elements standing in interrelation" (p. 38). Social systems theory applies a general systems perspective to humans, individuals, or groups of individuals standing in interrelation (Bausch, 2001).

General systems theory shares a close kinship with Lewin's (1951) psychological field theory and ecological theories (Bronfenbrenner, 1979; Lerner, 1995). Structural concepts from ecological theory (microsystems), which are reviewed in Chapter 4, may be combined with dynamic concepts from general systems theory (e.g., positive and negative feedback) to create an ecosystems perspective for social work practice (Greif & Lynch, 1983).

As a core perspective in the knowledge base of school social work (Freeman, 1995), general systems theory helps the school social worker to understand that schools are social systems with complex properties and subsystems (parts of the larger whole) and suprasystems (environmental contexts). As open systems with permeable boundaries, schools function in dynamic equilibrium with their environments; that is, they have both internal and external inputs and outputs. Open systems tend to maintain themselves in steady states through feedback processes (positive and negative feedback loops) that operate through the dynamic interplay of subsystems and suprasystems.

A major assumption of general systems theory is that all systems are purposeful and goal-directed. Human or social systems are self-aware in their purposefulness, while other types of living systems are simply self-monitoring (Whitchurch & Constantine, 1993). As a social system, a school exists to achieve objectives through the collective effort of individuals and groups in the system. For example, student achievement as reflected in grades and end-of-the-year performance evaluations are major purposeful goals of schools as social systems.

Schools as Goal Oriented

The simplest example of a school as a social system is a single school with a student body, teachers, and an administration. Edgar Schein (1985) has described two major goals of social systems, such as schools, that interact in a highly interdependent state: (1) external adaptation, which addresses the mission and purpose of the system, and (2) internal integration, which addresses the internal functioning of the system. Although it is possible that a school could evidence high levels of internal integration without achieving a similar level of external adaptation, the converse is unlikely. A school without internal bonds of commitment, supportive cohesion, and a sense of caring and support is unlikely to achieve its mission. Yet, according to Schein, internal integration is promoted by successful performance or by high levels of external adaptation. We have all perhaps felt the highly positive charge of be-

ing part of a winning team. In addition, schools may achieve similar levels of external adaptation and internal integration in different ways. General systems theory uses the concept of *equifinality* to describe the ability of social systems to arrive at the same end point from different starting points and from the use of different strategies and combinations of strategies.

In the context of managing the problems of external adaptation and internal integration, social systems develop group boundaries that define insiders and outsiders and rules for behavior that regulate interactions and exchanges. Over time, they also develop cultures, which Schein (1985) defines as "a pattern of basic assumptions—invented, discovered, or developed by a given group as it learns to cope with its problems of external adaptation and internal integration—that has worked well enough to be considered valid and, therefore, to be taught to new members as the correct way to perceive, think, and feel in relation to those problems" (p. 9). A less complex description of culture is simply "how we do things around here." Cultures may be overt or covert, positive or negative, and supportive or unsupportive to achieving the system-level goals of external adaptation and internal integration.

Subsystems

The success of a school in achieving its goals depends in large part upon the facilitating effects of several subsystems within the system. Subsystems, which include classrooms, teachers, and social workers, are designed to achieve order and organization in the face of environmental demands. Subsystems represent a division of labor and are designed to promote the external adaptation and internal integration of social systems. The classroom, and the functioning of teachers within the classroom, is one of the most defining subsystems in schools.

Component subsystems do not usually all have equal power—some individuals and subgroups have greater power than others. By *power,* we mean the ability to make decisions and to influence the actions and behavior of others. Like businesses, schools are typically hierarchical social systems. The principal and his and her management team are the sanctioned leaders in a school. Teachers and other professional staff members, such as school social workers, operate under the authority of the principal and his or her management team, and students are at the bottom of the hierarchy (see Figure 3.1). Student groups may be more or less organized in schools to exercise more influence and control over decisions and to gain access to scarce resources (see Waller, 1965).

James Coleman (1997) described schools as an example of an "administratively-driven organization" (p. 16). These highly centralized organizations have long feedback loops from the top of the organization (e.g., the principal) to each component subsystem (e.g., teachers, students). Coleman contrasted "administratively-driven organizations" with "output-driven organizations,"

which he described as allocating power and decision-making authority at multiple levels (p. 16). Coleman considered schools with decentralized authority structures and norms of accountability and social support as having more promise than ones with traditional bureaucratic forms for increasing teacher and student performance.

Subsystems may be examined as either parts of a larger system or as social systems in their own right. Central to understanding this idea is that any system is by definition both part and whole. General systems theory uses the concept, *holon,* to describe this ability to see the same entity from either perspective. For example, a single classroom may also be studied as a social system. Its inputs and processes, however, are tied to the operating processes of the entire school. Pupils and teachers leave and enter the classrooms; materials and physical facilities are provided; even social relationships are regulated in terms of classroom norms as well as products

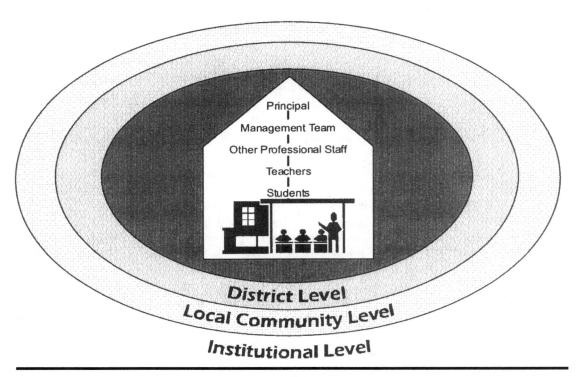

FIGURE 3.1   The Organizational Structure of Schools: Subsystems and Suprasystems

of the larger school, the school district, and educational establishment. Conversely, the social system of the classroom is composed of an intricate network of interactions and relationships composed of physical seating arrangements, status hierarchies, racial differences, authority structures, and differences in learning histories, ability, sex, and age. Members of the class may alternately be studied as systems based on dyads, small groups, or as a holon.

Suprasystems

Schools are open systems; they operate within a larger context with which they exchange matter, energy, and information through formal and informal feedback processes. In general systems terminology, *environment* is defined as the totality of physical and social factors that are external to a system's boundaries and exert an influence on the system. Three levels of external influence are discussed below as providing a context for school performance: (a) the district level, (b) the local community level, and (c) the institutional level. From a general systems theory perspective, a school functions in dynamic interaction with its larger context.

The District Level. Typically, schools operate in a larger complex of school units, both elementary and secondary, each with its own administrator and teaching staff, overlaid with a system-wide administrative cadre. In moderately complex systems, this administrative cadre consists of a chief administrator (superintendent), who is responsible for the direction of all system activities, and his or her immediate staff. In more complex systems, there may also be administrative echelons for directing instructional activities (e.g., directors of elementary or secondary education), multiple hierarchies for providing supportive professional and nonprofessional services (e.g., a director of personnel), and a large number of individuals holding staff positions in agencies attached to the superintendent's office. School reform at the district level may focus on policies

about the allocation of scarce resources to individual schools, including decisions about teacher-student ratios and about the employment of school social workers.

The Local Community Level. Schools also operate in a local community context, which includes community structure and processes. *Community* is defined as "the proximate spatial setting in which schools are located and in which students reside" (Bowen & Richman, 2002, p. 68). This local setting includes a physical infrastructure; the quality and kind of community resources; the demographic and social profile of the community, which varies according to social class, age, and racial and ethnic composition; the community power structure; and community norms that influence the organizational structure and functioning of the school (Arum, 2000; Furstenberg & Hughes, 1997). Employers, places of worship, neighbors, families, peer groups, and public and private community agencies are all part of this local community ecosystem, which includes schools. Many of the entities at the local community level may be classified as *constituencies* of the school system—people and organizations with a vested interest in school- and student-level performance.

An important focus of research from a general systems theory perspective is the effects of structural features (e.g., availability and access to support services and programs) and collective processes (e.g., behavioral patterns) in both communities and schools on school-related outcomes. School reform at the local community level may focus attention on building and strengthening the networks of relationships among institutions and community members that support student achievement (Timpane & Reich, 1997).

The Institutional Level. Schools also are situated in larger, nonlocal, institutional contexts—a focus that will resonate well with many social workers involved in management and community practice. Arum (2000), who distinguished these broader contexts from local community structures and processes, defined these contexts as "organizational fields" (p. 395). These organizational fields, which influence policies and practices at the local community and school levels, include federal and state public welfare policies, mechanisms for financing and administering health and social services, court decisions, policies from state boards of education, the functioning of labor unions and teacher associations, training curriculums in schools of education, and marketplace dynamics.

Research by Orthner, Cook, Rose, and Randolph (2002) demonstrated the value of assuming such a broad perspective in examining school-related outcomes. Combining administrative data from school and public agency sources on both adults and children who received public welfare, the authors examined the relationship between children's performance in school and the recent implementation of more aggressive welfare reform strategies. The results suggested higher rates of school dropout for successive ninth-grade entry cohorts of children (1993–94 to 1999–2000) living in poverty whose families received cash assistance through Temporary Assistance to Needy Families (TANF). Although the authors were careful to assert the limitations of their data, the findings suggest that the goals of welfare reform and the goal of school success for children from poor families may need some reconsideration. The authors recommended that welfare reform legislation reflect more of a family perspective—strategies that are attentive to the needs of both parents and children.

School reform from a neoinstitutional perspective addresses these larger political, social, and professional forces. Such forces shape the opportunity structure and the normative environment for school success either directly or indirectly through local community structure and processes.

SOCIAL ORGANIZATION

Schools and communities across this nation generally consider students' academic performance as the primary indicator of school success. However, the latest statistics about educational outcomes are not encouraging. In the context of structural shifts in the American economy that have increased the importance of educational success and postsecondary education (Vernez, Krop, & Rydell, 1999), many students are failing to complete high school; many others are finishing school with limited skills in reading and mathematics and without the academic qualifications to further their education. Generally, American students perform lower in math and science than their counterparts in other developed nations, and the relative performance standing of American students falls significantly from grade 4 to grade 12 (Haycock & Huang, 2001). Students from low-income homes and African-American and Hispanic/Latino students are particularly likely to face challenges in meeting performance standards at each grade level, demonstrating the requisite academic skills for promotion from one grade to the next, completing high school, graduating from high school with the qualifications necessary to attend a four-year college, and pursuing and completing some form of postsecondary education (Gladieux & Swail, 1998; Haycock & Huang, 2001; Richman, Bowen, & Woolley, in press). The academic gap between income and racial/ethnic groups looms large, and trends in low achievement and school failure start early.

This chapter is based on the premise that social organizational processes in school and community systems can be understood and controlled in the interest of promoting outcomes associated with successful school performance and that the primary function of school social work is to help in that process. Social organization is a dimension of social systems that refers to networks of relationships among people, their patterns of exchange and levels of reciprocity, and the degree to which they provide instrumental and expressive support to one another in achieving their individual and collective goals (Mancini, Martin, & Bowen, in press). Social organization also includes accepted standards and norms that inform and regulate individual and collective behavior, such as expectations for social responsibility and mutual support for one another, and the content and extent of shared values that support these standards and norms (Furstenberg & Hughes, 1997; Sampson, 2001).

It is important to note several caveats in my definition of social organization. First, social organization is not a property of an individual; it is an emergent and collective property of a social system that is associated with individual and collective outcomes. The emergent property of social organization is captured in the concept of *wholeness* from general systems theory.

Second, as defined above, the concept of social organization is closely related to the concept of internal integration that was defined earlier as a critical goal of social systems. In discussing the concept of internal integration, Schein (1985) makes the following statement: "What keeps a group together, its 'reason to be,' or what I have called the 'external adaptation function,' is quite different from the processes of creating that togetherness, processes that make groups capable of accomplishing things that individuals alone cannot accomplish" (p. 65). The internal integration or the cohesion of a group is considered a component of social organization, which is a broader and more encompassing concept. Social organizational processes may also include dimensions of external adaptation or performance expectations, which we will see below in our discussion of academic press in school environments.

Third, it is important to distinguish social structure from social process. In their review of neighborhoods as a context for child development, Furstenberg and Hughes (1997) distinguish social organization from structural features of social systems, which they describe with regard to their physical infrastructure, social and demographic features, and institutional resources. These structural features operate as a context for social organizational processes in schools and communities; they influence outcomes for children and youth indirectly through

their direct influence on these collective processes (Lee, Dedrick, & Smith, 1991; Sampson, 2001).

In the sections below, I provide examples of social organizational processes in schools and communities that are associated with student achievement. In schools, we look at the research that examines the influence of *academic press* and *sense of community* on student achievement. In communities, we limit our attention to the burgeoning research related to influence of neighborhoods on school-related outcomes. We focus our attention on two key social organizational processes in neighborhoods: *social control* and *social support*.

Our discussion of social organizational processes in schools and communities is informed by the work of a number of behavioral and social scientists who have examined how dimensions of social organization influence outcomes for children and youth (Croninger & Lee, 2001; Furstenberg, Cook, Eccles, Elder, & Sameroff, 1999; Leventhal & Brooks-Gunn, 2000). The seminal research of James Coleman (1997) in examining schools as social institutions anchors our analysis. Coleman's (1988) concept of social capital is a theoretical cornerstone in our analysis of social organizational processes in schools and communities. As discussed by Coleman (1988), social capital is an enabling resource emanating from social relations that allows individuals to achieve otherwise unattainable outcomes. Coleman identified three forms of social capital that are consistent with our conceptualization of social organization: reciprocal obligations, information sharing, and social norms. Framed by this social capital perspective, we first turn our attention to social organizational processes in schools.

Schools

The Coleman Report (1966), *Equality of Educational Opportunity,* which was published by Coleman and his associates more than 35 years ago, is a useful starting point in discussing social organizational processes in schools that are associated with student outcomes (see Shouse, 2002 for a brief overview of this report and its major findings). In examining gaps in academic achievement across racial/ethnic and socioeconomic groups, Coleman and his associates included in their investigation a focus on the influence of school-level factors on student-level achievement. A number of important findings emerged from the analysis. Perhaps the most surprising finding in the context of this review was the general weak effect of teacher characteristics (e.g., education and experience) and school resource factors (physical facilities, curricula, per-pupil spending) on student achievement. Although the findings of Coleman and his associates have been the target of numerous methodological critiques, their findings have prompted researchers to look beyond structural correlates of student achievement to examine social organizational processes within schools that may help account for differences in achievement across racial/ethnic and socioeconomic groups. From a general systems theory perspective, researchers are attempting to identify the *throughputs* that connect *educational inputs,* such as average pupils per class, to *educational outputs,* such as student achievement (Shouse, 2002, p. 520).

Academic Press and Sense of Community.   A significant body of research has established two key social organizational processes in schools as important correlates of student achievement: academic press and sense of community (Bryk & Driscoll, 1988; Bryk, Lee, & Holland, 1993; Lee & Smith, 1999; Phillips, 1997; Royal & Rossi, 1996; Shouse, 1997). Shouse defined the first, academic press, as "the degree to which school organizations are driven by achievement oriented values, goals, and norms" (p. 61). According to Shouse, schools with high academic press provide students with diverse and challenging courses, recognize and reward high performance, expect students to attend school and complete homework, provide an attractive and safe envi-

ronment for students, and have teachers that use innovative teaching strategies, make assignments meaningful and challenging, and have high expectations for student learning and performance.

Sense of community is the second key social organizational feature associated with student achievement. While definitions of sense of community are often fairly abstract and elusive, the most central feature of schools with a strong sense of community is a spirit of caring that governs social interactions within and between all levels of the school organization. A central feature of communality is the nature of the relationship between teachers and students, such as the degree to which students perceive teachers as caring about them and respecting and appreciating them as individuals (Bowen & Richman, 2001).

As described by Bryk, Lee, and Holland (1993), this *ethic of caring* is reinforced by two additional components of sense of community: *shared values* that promote a common agenda and encourage social responsibility and *shared activities* that offer opportunities for social interaction and reinforce communal norms (pp. 277–278). In schools that evidence these two additional components of communality, there is a crystallization of values and norms among adults at school about academic goals and school priorities, and all students are encouraged and afforded opportunities to participate fully in school-related activities. Royal and Rossi (1997) see respect for diversity as an additional component of sense of community.

Research Findings.   From this discussion, we would assume that student achievement would be highest in schools with both high academic press and a high sense of community. On the other hand, we would assume that student achievement would be lowest in schools in which academic press and sense of community are both low. School-level research by Shouse (1997) suggests a more complex relationship between these two features of social organization. First, in examining the mathematics test scores of a national sample of high-school students, Shouse reported that academic press had a positive and significant effect on student mathematics achievement. On the other hand, the positive influence of sense of community was virtually eliminated once academic press was entered into the predictive equation. In other words, in the context of academic press, school sense of community did not have a statistically significant influence on student math achievement. In an examination of the mathematics achievement and attendance of middle school students, Phillips (1997) reported a similar finding.

In combination, these findings might bring into question the impact of sense of community on student achievement. However, Shouse (1997) pushed his analysis a step further by examining the influence of academic press and sense of community by the average socioeconomic status (SES) of students attending schools in the sample (low, mid, and high). He also subdivided both school-level academic press and sense of community into low, mid, and high categories for purposes of this interactive analysis. His findings revealed that the influence of sense of community on student achievement must be considered in the context of both academic press and the school's socioeconomic level.

Academic press had its strongest effect on student achievement in low-SES schools. In low-SES schools, sense of community enhanced student achievement when academic press was high. However, at low-SES schools with a low level of academic press, higher levels of sense of community actually lowered student achievement. Math achievement was lowest for those students who attended schools with low academic press and a high sense of community. In a subsequent publication, Boyd and Shouse (1997) described the paradigmatic motto of these schools as "No one fails here who shows up" (p. 149). In examining these findings, Shouse drew the following conclusion: "For low-SES schools, a strong academic context serves as a prerequisite for communality's positive achievement effects" (p. 73).

In middle-SES schools, sense of community enhanced student achievement at all three levels of academic press (low, mid, and high). The combined effects were particularly pronounced at those schools with both high academic press and high sense of community. Sense of community played an even more important role in high-SES schools. In these schools, student achievement was more dependent on sense of community than academic press. Academic press had little influence at high-SES schools with a high sense of community. Shouse (1997) argues that students from more affluent families are more likely than students from lower-income families to have ties with adults outside the school who stress academic achievement. Consequently, they have less dependence on the school as a source of academic press.

Discussion. These findings are perhaps both illuminating and frustrating for school social workers. On one hand, they reinforce what many school social workers already know: social interventions must be tailored to reflect the uniqueness of each school. On the other hand, they indicate the power of research to identify social organizational processes that are leverage points in promoting student achievement. The findings have particular relevance for schools in which school social workers are most likely to be employed—schools with a high proportion of low-income students. In these schools, the development of a caring and nurturing school environment is likely to have greater positive consequences on student achievement when academic press is high. Promoting a high sense of community in low-SES schools with low academic press may actually have a counterproductive effect on student achievement. As Shouse (1997) states, the educational experiences of students in these schools may be more "socially therapeutic" than "academically challenging" (pp. 64–65).

The challenge for social work practitioners is to develop empirically based intervention strategies for influencing these outcomes. School-based interventions, such as Project Peace (de Anda, 1999), are a case in point. Project Peace works to promote a safer and more supportive school climate, greater student confidence in adults at school, and more affirming peer interaction. However, as noted earlier, schools do not exist in isolation from the broader community in which they are situated. Successful interventions to promote students' academic outcomes require not only an understanding of the school environment, but also the community environment in which the school is located. We now shift our attention from the school to the community social environment.

Communities

As in schools, it is also possible to examine social organizational processes in the communities in which schools are located. For our purpose, we are interested in how these processes spill over to influence both student outcomes and social organizational processes at the school level. Durkheim was one of the first scholars to discuss the interdependency between schools and the surrounding community (Boocock, 1973).

Although schools mirror the larger community of which they are a part, researchers and practitioners often treat schools as if they were insular. However, relatively few students attend boarding schools where they live on campus and where faculty function as surrogate parents. (And even these students are not captives in school-based enclaves with no contact with the external world.) Most students live in family households, and these households are located in residential communities or neighborhoods. The distance of the school from the students' residences may vary from a few blocks to many miles, and students at a school may be drawn from multiple locations in the community. Irrespective of the distance traveled from home to school and the number of locations from which students are drawn, from a general systems theory perspective, students transport matter, information, and energy across the boundaries of systems in which they participate. Events and situations in one setting have implications for events and situations in other settings.

Both researchers and practitioners increasingly recognize the local community as an important setting for child and youth development (Booth & Crouter, 2001). This attention has been spurred in part by Coleman's (1988) work on social capital as a resource that exists within and between multiple microsystems, social work's adoption of the ecological theory as a guiding framework for practice (see Chapter 4), and a renewed emphasis on community practice in social work (Bowen, Martin, Mancini, & Nelson, 2000; Johnson, 1998; Sviridoff & Ryan, 1997; Weil, 1996). Social workers today realize that schools cannot solve the complex challenges faced by many students in succeeding academically at school (Bowen & Richman, 2002). As concluded by Turner (1998), human service professionals today increasingly search for "the holy grail of community and neighborhood" in an attempt to strengthen the effectiveness of their interventions (p. ix).

Social Control and Social Support. I focus in this section on two interrelated social organizational processes in neighborhoods: social control and social support. I highlight several recent studies as illustrative of neighborhood effects that demonstrate the negative influence of crime and disorder (lack of social control) and the positive influence of support from neighbors (presence of social support) on the educational behavior and academic achievement of middle- and high-school students. Neighborhoods are defined from a geographical perspective as the spatial settings in which children and youth reside. This definition is conceptually similar to the one proposed by Sampson, Raudenbush, and Earls

(1997): "a collection of people and institutions occupying a subsection of a larger community" (p. 919).

Researchers have used the level of crime and violence reported by residents as an indicator of neighborhood social control. Crime and violence are likely to be higher in neighborhoods where residents have little influence over the behavior of others and where norms for looking out for one's neighbors and for children in the neighborhood are low. Research by Bowen, Bowen, & Cook (2000) and Brodsky (1996) suggests that living in neighborhoods with threatening characteristics, like crime and violence and negative youth behavior, may increase the level of social isolation among residents and decrease supportive patterns of exchange and reciprocity.

High rates of community crime and violence may not only spill over directly into the school and increase the probability of school crime and violence (Bowen & Van Dorn, 2002), but also may negatively influence the educational engagement and academic performance of students who live in these communities. Only recently have researchers begun to examine the influence of indicators of social control in the neighborhood, such as crime and violence, on school-related outcomes. The work of Bowen and Bowen (1999) is a case in point, which will be used to focus our discussion below.

Research Findings. Using a nationally representative sample of middle- and high-school students, Bowen and Bowen (1999) examined the effects of crime and violence in neighborhoods and schools on the school behavior and performance of adolescents. Bowen and Bowen's analysis was preceded by earlier work that indicated that more than one-third of the students in their national sample reported one or more than one personal experience with neighborhood crime and violence in the past 30 days (Bowen, Bowen, & Richman, 1998). In addition, almost one in three teens in the earlier analysis reported either feeling unsafe in their neighborhood, afraid on the way to school, or both. As expected, Bowen and Bowen found that the greater students' confrontation with personal threats to their safety in the neighborhood, the lower their attendance at school, the greater their involvement in problem behaviors, and the lower their academic performance. Not surprisingly, students who experienced personal threats in the neighborhood were also more likely to face threatening situations at school. This finding indicates that some students may not have any place that they can consider a safe zone.

In a study of 4,772 middle- and high-school students who had been identified by school personnel as at risk of school failure, Nash (2002) provided further support for the link between students' exposure to crime and violence in the neighborhood and school outcomes. Nash reported that students' reports of crime not only directly and negatively influenced their educational behavior (e.g., attendance, avoidance of problem behavior, and grades) but also indirectly influenced these outcomes by decreasing the likelihood that they find school meaningful, manageable, and comprehensible. Nash labeled this last domain "sense of school coherence."

When neighborhoods evidence high social control, as indicated by low rates of crime and violence, they are also likely to evidence positive relationships among neighbors. Personal relationships among neighbors operate as a lubricant for their willingness to get involved on each other's behalf and to monitor the behavior of children and youth (Sampson et al., 1997). These positive relationships help explain why communities with stable populations often have low crime rates. Consequently, researchers have combined measures of social control and social support, like neighbor support, into a single construct. Sampson et al. used the term *collective efficacy* to describe neighborhoods with high social control and high social support, which they defined as "social cohesion among neighbors combined with the willingness to intervene on behalf of the common good" (p. 918). Bowen,

Bowen, and Ware (2002) described the flip side of this situation, neighborhoods with low social control and low social support, as socially disorganized neighborhoods.

In a recent analysis, N. K. Bowen et al. (2002) reported that neighborhood social disorganization (i.e., lack of neighbor support, negative peer behavior, and crime and violence) exerted a strong and negative effect on middle- and high-school students' reports of positive education behavior, including grades. Neighborhood social disorganization not only had a direct effect on students' education behavior but also an indirect effect through its negative effect on supportive family behaviors. These findings, based on a national sample of middle- and high-school students, are consistent with other studies that show how social control and social support components in neighborhoods directly and indirectly spill over to influence child and adolescent adjustment and their experiences and outcomes at school (Bowen & Chapman, 1996; Nash, 2002). Darling and Steinberg (1997) surmised that students in well-functioning neighborhoods might benefit less from their experiences with adults as agents of social control and social support and more from their peer relationships that are more likely to be affirming and supportive in such neighborhoods.

Discussion.   These findings suggest the importance of building bridges between schools and the neighborhoods in which students and their families reside. From a general systems theory perspective, the success of schools in educating our children and youth requires interventions that target the multiple environments in which students and their families live and work. School social workers can work as partners with law enforcement agencies and neighborhood groups to develop strategies for increasing neighborhood safety. For example, community involvement in a neighborhood block watch program may decrease some types of crime (Williams, Ayers, & Arthur, 1997). Consistent with central assumptions from Maslow's (1954) hierarchy of needs theory, it will be difficult to develop connections between neighbors without first attending to their safety needs. Bowen and Van Dorn (2002) stress the importance of involving parents and youths in discussions about community-based interventions. As concluded by Daniel Yankelovich ("An Interview," 1992), "If you include people in the dialogue, they will struggle with the hard issues. They will take the responsible positions. If you exclude them, the opposite happens" (p. 14). The work of Nelson (2000) in facilitating community "self-governance" dialogues demonstrates the willingness of citizens to come together and tackle the tough problems like crime and violence. School social workers can work as catalysts in supporting school and community stakeholders to sponsor community dialogues for purposes of strengthening community ties and mobilizing community efforts on behalf of children and youth.

CONCLUSION

General systems theory offers school social workers a familiar perspective. From this perspective, schools must be understood as dynamic systems that are embedded in larger community and institutional settings. The concept of social organization brings social workers to a touchstone of practice—a focus on people and collective processes. Findings presented in this chapter clearly note that collective processes in schools and communities can overpower the detrimental effects of place.

This chapter has offered a broad perspective, and we have been judicious in discussing only a few of the many social organizational processes in schools and communities that may influence student achievement. For example, the influence of parent involvement in schools on student achievement (e.g., Bowen & Bowen, 1998), the powerful effect of prosocial and academically engaged peers on the school-related attitudes and behavior of middle- and high-school students (e.g., Darling & Steinberg, 1997), and the role of school-linked services in schools on the coordination and delivery of support services to students (e.g., Jozefowicz-Simbeni & Allen-Meares, 2002) are also important topics of discussion. The aim of this chapter has been illustrative with regard to the application of general systems theory rather than either comprehensive or definitive.

General systems theory provides school social workers with a broad lens through which to view schools as organized, complex, and dynamic entities. A body of highly integrated concepts helps them to address the school's effectiveness as a social system committed to achieving the optimal development of children. One of this theory's greatest contributions lies in translating the participation of many scientific disciplines into a common theoretical formulation or set of constructs that allows communication across disciplines. Such communication has done much to broaden the conceptual and empirical foundation for effective social work practice in schools.

IMPLICATIONS FOR SOCIAL WORK PRACTICE IN SCHOOLS

Since the publication of the Coleman Report in 1966, researchers have made significant progress in identifying social organizational processes in schools and communities that separate effective schools from ineffective ones. This chapter has addressed a few of these influential processes, using the concept of social organization as a conceptual umbrella. Yet, schools continue to struggle to meet academic goals and too many students remain unprepared and ill equipped to meet the economic and social realities of the twenty-first century. If social work is to contribute to solving the challenges faced by our nation's schools, social interventions are needed that target social organizational leverage points in schools and communities.

What is the *science* of social work practice in schools? A great deal of discussion in social work today centers around the issue of evidence-based practice (Gambrill, 1999). What do we know as social workers, for example, about how to promote academic press and sense of community in schools and social control and social support in neighborhoods?

In a recent book, *Community Programs to Promote Youth Development,* which was published under the auspices of the National Research Council and the Institute of Medicine (2002), the interdisciplinary committee identified the role of "supportive relationships" as a key feature of effective programs to promote youth development. Programs, such as Teen Outreach, Quantum Opportunities, and Big Brothers and Big Sisters, were included as examples of programs where social relationships are a key focus of social intervention and as examples of promising initiatives on the basis of the evidence reviewed. School social workers can play an important role in working with both school-based partners and community agencies to offer such evidence-based program initiatives in schools and local communities.

A special challenge for school social workers is to develop the knowledge, attitudes, and skills for working effectively as change agents within a highly centralized bureaucracy to develop the types of administrative and support structures that optimize the preparation of students for adult roles. Effectiveness in their roles as change agents also requires that school social workers practice in the context of broader community, including the neighborhoods in which students and their families reside. School social workers must understand that like individuals and families, schools and communities vary in their demographic and social profiles and have developmental rhythms that must be appreciated in designing interventions (The Harwood Group, 1999).

From a general systems theory perspective, social organizational processes in schools and communities do not exist independently of their structural and institutional context. For example, Shouse's (1997) research described how the impact of academic press and sense of community on student achievement varied depending on the average socioeconomic status of students attending the school. Research by Sampson et al. (1997) depicts how structural conditions in neighborhoods, such as concentrated disadvantage and residential instability, may adversely influence the probability of collective efficacy among residents. Many other structural variables influence social organizational processes in schools and neighborhoods. For example, the research on school size suggests the challenge of developing academic press and sense of community in large schools (Bowen, Bowen, & Richman, 2000). Other research suggests how social relations for school-age youth may be especially restricted in neighborhoods in which socioeconomic inequality is race-linked (Blau, Lamb, Stearns, & Pellerin, 2001). School social workers may influence social organizational processes through structural interventions, such as advocating for smaller schools or for the start-up of community development corporations in neighborhoods that are ecologically disadvantaged.

Some policymakers and researchers believe that nothing less than a fundamental shift in the way schools are organized and governed will result in significant educational progress for students (see Boyd & Shouse, 1997, for a discussion of this point). In the absence of such changes, serious attempts at school reform to promote student achievement are likely to be thwarted or limited at best (Willower, 1991). Others believe that the answer to American students' poor performance lies less in the institutional and organizational structure of schooling and more in the nature of their personal, family, and community lives outside of schools (Steinberg, 1996). As employees of the school and as advocates on behalf of students and their families, school social workers have an important voice in debates about school reform and about the design and implementation of interventions to address the support needs of students and their families.

In a recent review, Cynthia Franklin (2000), editor of *Children & Schools,* discussed the future of school social work as involving more attention to community networking and coordination of services between schools and local community agencies. Winters and Gourdine (2000) added the role of community organizer to the expanding job description of school social workers in the new millennium, a role that is consistent with promoting a more positive interface between the neighborhood and the school. A special focus of this expanded role for school social workers is increasing the community connections between racial and ethnic groups in an attempt to promote more cultural appreciation and to reduce the cultural disconnect that minority students and their parents may feel in schools where the majority of administrators and teachers are white (Ogbu, 1978).

In their recent book, *The Dance of Change: The Challenges to Sustaining Momentum in Learning Organizations,* Peter Senge and associates (1999) encouraged managers to stop thinking of themselves as *mechanics* whose role is to fix something and to begin thinking of themselves as *gardeners* whose role is to grow something. We think that this metaphor is as pertinent for school social workers as it is for managers. As stated by Senge in a subsequent interview, "the most universal challenge that we face is the transition from seeing our human institutions as machines to seeing them as embodiments of nature" (Webber, 1999, p. 179). The view of schools as living entities in broader context is undergirded by general systems theory, consistent with a focus on social organization in schools and communities, and supportive of the expanded practice roles and responsibilities of school social workers.

FOR STUDY AND DISCUSSION

1. This chapter begins with a quote from Peter Senge, a senior lecturer at the Massachusetts Institute of Technology and an expert in management innovation. What is the relevance of this statement in the context of the chapter's focus?

2. The statement *the whole is greater than the sum of its parts* is associated with the systems paradigm. Although we did not discuss this statement explicitly in the chapter, explain why this statement is consistent with a general systems theory perspective, and identify an example of this phenomenon in schools and in neighborhoods.

3. Of all the concepts that were introduced and discussed in this chapter, what single concept had the most influence on your thinking about school social work practice? Please discuss the implications of this concept for social work practice with a colleague.

4. What are some strategies that school social workers may use to gain entry to working with neighborhoods as a context for practice?

ADDITIONAL READING

Arum, R., & Beattie, I. R. (2000). *The structure of schooling: Readings in the sociology of education.* Mountain View, CA: Mayfield Publishing Company.

Bidwell, C. E. (2001). Analyzing schools as organizations: Long-term permanence and short-term change. *Sociology of Education Extra Issue,* 100–114.

Blum, R. W., McNeely, C. A., & Rinehart, P. M. (2002). *Improving the odds: The untapped power of schools to improve the health of teens.* Minneapolis, MN: Center for Adolescent Health and Development, University of Minnesota.

Coleman, J. S., & Hoffer, T. (1988). *Public and private high schools: The impact of communities.* New York: Basic Books.

Dornbusch, S. M., Glasgow, K. L., & Lin, I-C. (1996). The social structure of schooling. *Annual Review of Psychology, 47,* 401–429.

Kozol, J. (1991). *Savage inequalities: Children in America's schools.* New York: Crown Publishing.

Miller, J. (1978). *Living systems.* New York: McGraw-Hill.

National Association of Secondary School Principals (2002). *What the research shows: Breaking ranks in action.* Reston, VA: Author.

Putnam, R. D. (2000). *Bowling alone.* New York: Simon & Schuster.

Skyttner, L. (2001). *General systems theory: Ideas and applications.* Singapore: World Scientific.

Traub, J. (2000, January 16). What no school can do. *New York Times Magazine,* pp. 52–67.

Waller, W. (1932). *The sociology of teaching.* New York: Wiley.

Wehlage, G. G., Rutter, R. A., Smith, G. A., Lesko, N., & Fernandez, R. R. (1989). *Reducing the risk: Schools as communities of support.* Philadelphia: Falmer Press.

REFERENCES

An interview with Daniel Yankelovich (1992, Summer). *Family Affairs, 5*(1–2), New York: Institute for American Values.

Arum, R. (2000). Schools and communities: Ecological and institutional dimensions. *Annual Review of Sociology, 26,* 395–418.

Barker, R. L. (1999). *The social work dictionary* (4th ed.). Washington, DC: NASW.

Bausch, K. C. (2001). *The emerging consensus in so-cial systems theory.* New York: Kluwer Academic/Plenum.

Bertalanffy, L. von. (1968). *General systems theory.* New York: Braziller.

Blau, J. R., Lamb, V. L., Stearns, E., & Pellerin, L. (2001). Cosmopolitan environments and adolescents' gains in social studies. *Sociology of Education, 74,* 121–138.

Boocock, S. S. (1973). The school as a social environment for learning: Social organization and microsocial process in education. *Sociology of Education, 46*(1), 15–50.

Booth, A., & Crouter, A. C. (Eds.). (2001). *Does it take a village? Community effects on children, adolescents, & families.* New York: Lawrence Erlbaum.

Bowen, G. L., Bowen, N. K., & Cook, P. G. (2000). Neighborhood characteristics and supportive parenting among single mothers. In G. L. Fox & M. L. Benson (Eds.), *Families, crime and criminal justice* (pp. 183–206). New York: Elsevier Science.

Bowen, G. L., Bowen, N. K., & Richman, J. M. (1998). *Students in peril: Crime and violence in neighborhoods and schools.* Chapel Hill, NC: Jordan Institute for Families, School of Social Work, The University of North Carolina at Chapel Hill.

Bowen, G. L., Bowen, N. K., & Richman, J. M. (2000). School size and middle school students' perceptions of the school environment. *Children & Schools, 22,* 69–82.

Bowen, G. L., & Chapman, M. V. (1996). Poverty, neighborhood danger, social support, and the individual adaptation among at-risk youth in urban areas. *Journal of Family Issues, 17,* 641–666.

Bowen, G. L., Martin, J. A., Mancini, J. A., & Nelson, J. P. (2000). Community capacity: Antecedents and consequences. *Journal of Community Practice, 8*(2), 1–21.

Bowen, G. L., & Richman, J. M. (2001). *School Success Profile.* Chapel Hill, NC: Jordan Institute for Families, School of Social Work, The University of North Carolina at Chapel Hill.

Bowen, G. L., & Richman, J. M. (2002). Schools in the context of communities. *Children & Schools, 24,* 67–71.

Bowen, G. L., Richman, J. M., & Bowen, N. K. (2000). Families in the context of communities across time. In S. J. Price, P. C. McKenry, & M. J. Murphy (Eds.), *Families across time: A life course perspective* (pp. 117–128). Los Angeles: Roxbury.

Bowen, G. L., & Van Dorn, R. A. (2002). Community violent crime rates and school danger. *Children & Schools, 24,* 90–104.

Bowen, N. K., & Bowen, G. L. (1998). The mediating role of educational meaning in the relationship between home academic culture and academic performance. *Family Relations, 47,* 45–51.

Bowen, N. K., & Bowen, G. L. (1999). Effects of crime and violence in neighborhoods and schools on the school behavior and performance of adolescents. *Journal of Adolescent Research, 14,* 319–342.

Bowen, N. K., Bowen, G. L., & Ware, W. B. (2002). Neighborhood social disorganization, families, and the educational behavior of adolescents. *Journal of Adolescent Research, 17,* 468–490.

Boyd, W. L., & Shouse, R. C. (1997). The problems and promise of urban schools. In H. J. Walberg, O. Reyes, & R. P. Weissberg (Eds.), *Children and youth: Interdisciplinary perspectives* (pp. 141–165). Newbury Park, CA: Sage.

Brodsky, A. E. (1996). Resilient single mothers in risky neighborhoods. *Journal of Community Psychology, 24,* 347–363.

Bronfenbrenner, U. (1979). *The ecology of human development.* Cambridge, MA: Harvard University Press.

Bryk, A. S., & Driscoll, M. E. (1988). *The school as community: Theoretical foundations, contextual influences, and consequences for students and teachers.* Chicago: The University of Chicago Benton Center for Curriculum and Instruction.

Bryk, A. S., Lee, V. E., & Holland, P. B. (1993). *Catholic schools and the common good.* Cambridge, MA: Harvard University Press.

Coleman, J. S., Campbell, E. Q., Hobson, C. J., McPartland, J., Mood, A. M., Weinfeld, F. D., & York, R. L. (1966). *Equality of educational opportunity.* Washington, DC: U.S. Government Printing Office.

Coleman, J. S. (1997). Output-driven schools: Principles of design. In J. S. Coleman, B. Schneider, S. Plank, K. S. Schiller, R. Shouse, & H. Wang with S. A. Lee (Eds.), *Redesigning American education* (pp. 13–38). Boulder, CO: Westview Press.

Coleman, J. S. (1988). Social capital in the creation of human capital. *American Journal of Sociology, 94,* S95–S120.

Croninger, R. G., & Lee, V. E. (2001). Social capital and dropping out of high school: Benefits to at-risk students of teachers' support and guidance. *Teachers College Record, 103,* 548–581.

Darling, N., & Steinberg, L. (1997). Community influences on adolescent achievement and deviance. In J. Brooks-Gunn, G. J. Duncan, & J. L. Aber (Eds.), *Neighborhood poverty* (Vol. II, 120–131). New York: Russell Sage Foundation.

de Anda, D. (1999). Project Peace: The evaluation of a skills-based violence prevention program for high school adolescents. *Social Work in Education, 21,* 137–149.

Franklin, C. (2000). Predicting the future of school social work practice in the new millennium [Editorial]. *Social Work in Education, 22,* 3–7.

Freeman, E. M. (1995). School social work overview. In R. L. Edwards (Ed.), *Encyclopedia of social work* (19th ed., Vol. 3, pp. 2087–2099). Washington, DC: NASW.

Furstenburg, F. F., Jr., Cook, T. D., Eccles, J., Elder, G. H., Jr., & Sameroff, A. (1999). *Managing to make it: Urban families and adolescent success.* Chicago: University of Chicago Press.

Furstenberg, F. F., Jr. & Hughes, M. E. (1997). The influence of neighborhoods on children's development: A theoretical perspective and a research agenda. In J. Brooks-Gunn, G. J. Duncan, & J. L. Aber (Eds.), *Neighborhood poverty* (Vol. II, pp. 23–47). New York: Russell Sage Foundation.

Gambrill, E. (1999). Evidence-based practice: An alternative to authority-based practice. *Families in Society: The Journal of Contemporary Human Services, 80,* 341–350.

Gladieux, L. E., & Swail, W. S. (1998). Financial aid is not enough: Improving the odds of college success. Reprinted from *The College Board Review, 185,* 1–11.

Greif, G. L., & Lynch, A. A. (1983). The eco-systems perspective. In C. H. Meyer (Ed.), *Clinical social work in the eco-systems perspective* (pp. 35–71). New York: Columbia University Press.

The Harwood Group (1999). *Community rhythms: Five stages of community life.* Washington, DC: The Harwood Group and the Charles Stewart Mott Foundation.

Haycock, K., & Huang, S. (2001, Winter). Are today's high school graduates ready? *Thinking K–16, 5*(1), 3–17.

Johnson, A. K. (1998). The revitalization of community practice: Characteristics, competencies, and curricula for community-based services. *Journal of Community Practice, 5*(3), 37–62.

Jozefowicz-Simbeni, D. M. H., & Allen-Meares, P. (2002). Poverty and schools: Intervention and resource building through school-linked services. *Children & Schools, 24,* 123–136.

Lee, V. E., Dedrick, R. F., & Smith, J. B. (1991). The effect of the social organization of schools on teachers' efficacy and satisfaction. *Sociology of Education, 64,* 190–208.

Lee, V. E., & Smith, J. B. (1999). Social support and achievement for young adolescents in Chicago: The role of school academic press. *American Educational Research Journal, 36,* 907–945.

Lerner, R. M. (1995). *America's youth in crisis: Challenges and options for programs and policies.* Thousand Oaks, CA: Sage.

Leventhal, T., & Brooks-Gunn, J. (2000). The neighborhoods they live in: The effects of neighborhood residence on child and adolescent outcomes. *Psychological Bulletin, 126,* 309–337.

Lewin, K. (1951). *Field theory in social science.* New York: Harper & Brothers.

Mancini, J. A., Martin, J. A., & Bowen, G. L. (in press). Community capacity and social organization: The role of community in the promotion of health and the prevention of illness. In T. Gullotta & M. Bloom (Eds.), *Encyclopedia of primary prevention and health promotion.* New York: Kluwer Academic/Plenum.

Maslow, A. (1954). *Motivation and personality.* New York: Harper Collins.

Nash, J. K. (2002). Neighborhood effects on sense of school coherence and educational behavior in students at risk of school failure. *Children & Schools, 24,* 73–89.

National Research Council and Institute of Medicine (2002). *Community programs to promote youth development.* J. Eccles & J. A. Gootman (Eds.), Board on Children, Youth, and Families, Division of Behavioral and Social Sciences and Education. Washington, DC: National Academy Press.

Nelson, G. M. (2000). *Self-governance in communities and families.* San Francisco: Berrett-Koehler.

Ogbu, J. U. (1978). *Minority education and caste: The American system in cross-cultural perspective.* New York: Academic Press.

Orthner, D. K., Cook, P. G., Rose, R. A., & Randolph, K. (2002). Welfare reform, poverty, and children's performance in school: Challenges for the school community. *Children & Schools, 24,* 105–121.

Philips, M. (1997). What makes schools effective? A comparison of the relationships of communitarian climate and academic achievement and attendance during middle school. *American Educational Research Journal, 34,* 633–662.

Richman, J. M., & Bowen, G. L. (1997). School failure: An ecological-interactional-developmental perspective. In M.W. Fraser (Ed.), *Risk and resilience in childhood: An ecological perspective* (pp. 95–116). Washington, DC: NASW Press.

Richman, J. M., & Bowen, G. L., & Woolley, M. E. (in press). School failure: An eco-interactional-developmental perspective. In M.W. Fraser (Ed.), *Risk and resilience in childhood: An ecological perspective* (2nd ed.). Washington, DC: NASW Press.

Rosenfeld, L. B., Richman, J. M., & Bowen, G. L. (2000). Social support networks and school outcomes: The centrality of the teacher. *Child and Adolescent Social Work Journal, 17,* 205–226.

Royal, M. A., & Rossi, R. J. (1996). Individual-level correlates of sense of community: Findings from workplace and school. *Journal of Community Psychology, 24,* 395–416.

Royal, M. A., & Rossi, R. J. (1997). *Schools as communities* (ED405641). Eugene, OR: ERIC Clearinghouse on Educational Management.

Sampson, R. J. (2001). How do communities undergird or undermine human development? Relevant contexts and social mechanisms. In A. Booth & A. C. Crouter (Eds.), *Does it take a village? Community effects on children, adolescents, & families* (pp. 3–30). New York: Lawrence Erlbaum.

Sampson, R. J., Raudenbush, S., & Earls, F. (1997). Neighborhoods and violent crime: A multilevel study of collective efficacy. *Science, 277,* 918–924.

Schein, E. H. (1985). *Organizational culture and leadership*. San Francisco: Jossey-Bass Publishers.

Senge, P., Kleiner, A., Roberts, C., Ross, R., Roth, G., & Smith, B. (1999). *The dance of change: The challenges to sustaining momentum in learning organizations*. New York: Doubleday/Currency.

Shouse, R. (1997). Academic press, sense of community, and student achievement. In J. S. Coleman, B. Schneider, S. Plank, K. S. Schiller, R. Shouse, & H. Wang with S. A. Lee (Eds.), *Redesigning American education* (pp. 60–86). Boulder, CO: Westview Press.

Shouse, R. C. (2002). School effects. In D. L. Levinson, P.W. Cookson, & A. Sadovnik (Eds.), *Education and sociology: An encyclopedia* (pp. 519–524). New York: Routledge Falmer.

Steinberg, L. (1996). *Beyond the classroom: Why school reform has failed and what parents need to do*. New York: Simon & Schuster.

Sviridoff, M., & Ryan, W. (1997). Community-centered family service. *Families in Society: The Journal of Contemporary Human Services, 78,* 128–139.

Timpane, M., & Reich, B. (1997, February). Revitalizing the ecosystem for youth: A new perspective for school reform. *Phi Delta Kappan,* 464–470.

Turner, J. B. (1998). Foreword. In P. L. Ewalt, E. M. Freeman, & D. L. Poole (Eds.), *Community building: Renewal, well-being, and shared responsibility* (pp. ix–x). Washington, DC: NASW Press.

Vernez, G., Krop, R. A., & Rydell, C. P. (1999). *Closing the education gap: Benefits and costs*. Santa Monica, CA: RAND.

Waller, W. (1965). *The sociology of teaching*. New York: John Wiley & Sons.

Webber, A. M. (1999, May). Learning for a change. *Fast Company.com*, pp. 178–188. (http://fastcompany.com/online/24/senge.html)

Weil, M. O. (1996). Community building: Building community practice. *Social Work, 41,* 481–499.

Whitchurch, G. G., & Constantine, L. L. (1993). Systems theory. In P. G. Boss, W. J. Doherty, R. LaRossa, W. R. Schumm, & S. K. Steinmetz (Eds.), *Sourcebook of family theories and methods: A contextual approach* (pp. 325–352). New York: Plenum.

Williams, J. H., Ayers, C. D., & Arthur, M. W. (1997). Risk and protective factors in the development of delinquency and conduct disorder. In M. W. Fraser (Ed.), *Risk and resilience in childhood: An ecological perspective* (pp. 140–170). Washington, DC: NASW Press.

Willower, D. J. (1991). School reform and schools as organizations. *Journal of School Leadership, 1,* 305–315.

Winters, W. G., & Gourdine, R. M. (2000). School reform: A viable domain for school social work practice. In J. G. Hopps & R. Morris (Eds.), *Social work at the millennium* (pp. 138–174). New York: Free Press.

CHAPTER 4

AN ECOLOGICAL PERSPECTIVE OF SOCIAL WORK SERVICES IN SCHOOLS

*An ecological metaphor for practice can respond to the dual function in
a way that the traditional medical or disease metaphor cannot do.*[*]
—Carol Germain

INTRODUCTION

An important theme in most of the social work literature has been the search for a unifying conceptual framework useful for guiding practice. In recent years considerable progress has been made in this regard, and some agreement has been reached. As indicated in Chapter 2, the literature seems to recommend that the social work profession adopt an ecological perspective of practice. Such a perspective is most useful for attaining social work goals and for directing practice. This chapter is concerned with this perspective, the concepts and elements that distinguish social work from other professional practices, and its application to social work in schools. We view social work in schools as a specialized field of practice within the profession. In this chapter we present examples and illustrations of professional social work values and their special relevance for school social work.

THE PROFESSION OF SOCIAL WORK

Throughout its history and development, the social work profession has sought a schema that conceptualizes its practice. But how do we conceptualize practice when social work is so diverse in methods, clients, settings, funding sources, and focus? What is the common base? The profession has spent considerable time and energy studying these questions. Some of the milestones in this process have included (1) the 1929 Milford conference, which confirmed that the various specialty interests had enough in common to validate the idea that all social workers are part of one profession; (2) the 1951 Hollis-Taylor report, which attempted to define what social work was and what it was not; (3) the 1958 meeting of a subcommittee of the National Association of Social Workers Commission on Practice, which devised a definition of social work practice that included an explanation of

---

[*]Carol Germain, "An Ecological Perspective on Social Work in the Schools," in R. Constable et al., eds., *School Social Work: Practice and Research Perspectives,* 2d ed. Chicago: Lyceum, 1991, p. 19.

social work value, purpose, sanction, knowledge, and method; and (4) the 1959 curriculum study of the Council on Social Work Education (CSWE) (Special Issue on Conceptual Frameworks, 1977; Brieland, 1977). The curriculum study offered the following definition of social work:

> Social work seeks to enhance the social functioning of individuals, singly, and in groups, by activities focused upon their social relationship which constitute the interaction between man and his environment. These activities can be grouped into three functions: restoration of impaired capacity, provision of individual and social resources, and prevention of dysfunction. (Werner, 1959, p. 54)

This definition is consistent with the report issued by the NASW Task Force on Specialization:

> Social work focus is on the interaction between people and their environments. . . . The fundamental zone of social work is where people and their environments are in exchange with each other. Social work intervention aims at the coping capabilities of people and the demands and resources of their environments so that the transactions between them are helpful to both. Social work's concern extends to both the dysfunctional or deficient conditions at the juncture between people and their environments, and the opportunities there for producing growth and improving the environment. It is the duality of focus on people and their environments that distinguishes social work from other professions. (NASW Task Force on Specialization, 1978, p. 3)

A fifth milestone in this process was the publication in 1977 of a special "conceptual frameworks" issue of the NASW journal, *Social Work* (Special Issue on Conceptual Frameworks, 1977), in which such scholars as A. Minahan, A. Pincus, W. Reid, W. Gordon, and S. Cooper examined existing perspectives and raised some serious but crucial questions concerning the context of contemporary problems: What is the mission of social work practice? What are the skills, values, and commonalities of the profession? What are the practical and educational implications of these dynamics? The same types of

questions were considered more fully in a second special issue of *Social Work* (Conceptual Frameworks II: Second Special Issue on Conceptual Frameworks, 1981).

We have learned from these efforts that certain concepts or elements distinguish the various specializations of social work from other professional practices. These include values, purpose, knowledge, sanction, and interventive methods.

Values

In general, the profession of social work has a unique value system. Values can be defined as ethical concepts or principles that provide a philosophical foundation for a profession. It is values that determine how social workers relate to people and provide services to them. According to Harriett Bartlett, values are frequently divided into ultimate (or ideal) values and instrumental values (the means to achieve ultimate values). That every human being is entitled to liberty and self-realization is an example of an ultimate value. An example of an instrumental value, which is more specific, is that every individual has a right to self-determination and equal educational opportunity. The second level of values refers to the valued qualities of a well-functioning person; and the third level focuses on operational values, which are the means to achieve the higher value (Bartlett, 1970). Ultimate and instrumental values are to be distinguished from cultural values, which are concerned with societal mores and expectations for social behavior in society.

Some primary social work values and examples of applications in school social work follow:

Social Work Values

1. Recognition of the worth and dignity of each human being
2. The right to self-determination or self-realization

3. Respect for individual potential and support for an individual's aspirations to attain it
4. The right of each individual to be different from every other and to be accorded respect for those differences

Applications to Social Work in Schools

1. Each pupil is valued as an individual regardless of any unique characteristic
2. Each pupil should be allowed to share in the learning process and to learn
3. Individual differences (including differences in rates of learning) should be recognized; intervention should be aimed at supporting pupils' educational goals
4. Each child, regardless of race and socioeconomic characteristics, has a right to equal treatment in the school

Examples of other values compatible with those of the profession as a whole but having special relevance to school social work are (1) that children are entitled to equal educational opportunities and to learning experiences adapted to their individual needs; and (2) that the process of education should not only provide the child with tools for future learning and skills to use in earning a living, but be an essential ingredient of the child's mental health.

These social work values highlight the central position of the individual pupil in social work. This does not mean that casework or work with the individual is the only preferred way of offering school social work services. Other forms of intervention can also contribute to the realization of these values. The practitioner should keep in mind that although the child may be the identified client, that child may actually be signaling for help for the family or the class or bringing attention to an area of injustice in some other system. However, the focus on the individual reflects the democratic commitment to the welfare of each individual in society and to the assumption of social responsibility by citizens.

In situations involving one or more persons, some values appear to weigh more heavily or even to conflict. When this is so, school social workers must then search for an acceptable balance. The "best interest of the child" should guide these deliberations. One example of conflicting values, taken from school social work practice, is a gifted child whom the father wants to be just average because the child, who is showing signs of stress from underachievement, "will be happier that way." Another example is secondary-school students whose excessive absenteeism shows that alternative forms of education are needed, even though the community and school do not recognize such need. Ultimate value should guide practice. The school social worker's course of action should profit the client(s) but not at the expense of another person.

Purpose

School social workers contribute to improving the quality of life by adding their efforts to the school's attempt to achieve its central purpose—to provide a setting for teaching and learning in which children and young persons can acquire a sense of competence, a capacity for problem solving and decision making, and a readiness to adapt to change and to take responsibility for their own continued learning.

Just as the values of the profession determine its purpose, knowledge makes some purposes and goals more practical and attainable than others. Thus, values and knowledge interact to determine the dominant goals (purposes) of social work.

Knowledge

According to Bartlett, a profession's strongest foundation is its body of knowledge (Bartlett, 1970; Gordon, 1962). Newly attained knowledge drawn from research and study results in verifiable propositions that can be confirmed. Knowledge can be distinguished from value assumptions—propositions that do not appear confirmable, although they may become so later. Most importantly, all knowledge building is guided by the ultimate values of the profession.

The knowledge base of social work and school social work is as broad as human behavior. This characteristic has led social workers to borrow knowledge from other fields such as education, behavioral and biological sciences, psychiatry, medicine, law, and political science. The borrowed knowledge includes concepts and principles selected for relevance to social work, then tested in practice, and sometimes reformulated in social work terms. Such clusters of borrowed knowledge are useful and legitimate if appropriately integrated with social work purpose. Essentially, the concepts of the social work profession guide in the selection of knowledge.

Examples of Knowledge Applicable to School Social Work. School social workers can find support for their purpose and concerns in new knowledge about the development of an individual's intelligence. As a result of research conducted by educators and child psychologists, we now know that the belief in fixed intelligence is not tenable. Development can no longer be viewed as predetermined, and the brain's intellectual processes may be viewed as comparable to the active information processes programmed into electronic computers for problem solving. Because experience is the "programmer" of the human brain, the early experiences of young children are highly important for perceptual, cognitive, and intellectual functions. Learning is motivated by the intrinsic motivation inherent in information processing, among other factors.

Further, we now know that the home environment affects the level of a child's measured intelligence and success in school. Important characteristics of the home conducive to school learning are learning materials, models and help in language development, and parental stimulation and concern for achievement.

As a result of the historic research of the educator Benjamin Bloom, we have learned that differences found among racial and socioeconomic groups of children are not inherent or fixed, but can be explained by widely differing amounts and kinds of environmental stimulation. Also, early school achievement is essential for later school achievement or for obtaining a job and being successful in that job. Further, although family and social factors are critical, most pupil failures can be overcome through adjustment of the learning conditions in schools. According to Bloom, most children can learn; it is important to analyze the entry-level skills and motivation of each child and to make certain that appropriate instruction is given (Bloom, 1976).

Sanction

The authority to act is granted to school social workers by the state (in many instances), the community, the school, the profession of social work, and by the record of competent performance of individual professional social workers. Sanction does not define school social work in the same sense that value, purpose, and knowledge do; nevertheless, sanction is a necessary condition for professional practice.

Sanction from the community comes through federal and state legislation that provides for social work services in schools, systems of licensure and certification, and allocation of resources. The sanction of the school is indicated by the hiring policies of the school board and by consultations and negotiations with school administrators.

The *NASW Code of Ethics and Professional Standards* (1999) provides professional sanctioning for certain kinds of ethical behaviors and the basic values and principles undergirding social work. A unique characteristic of social work is the focus on the empowerment of people who are vulnerable, oppressed, and living in poverty. It is the focus on individual well-being in a social context, and environmental forces that create/ contribute to problems in living that also distinguishes social work from other professions. The core professional values are: service, social justice, dignity and worth of the person, importance of human relationships, integrity and competence. It is truly this constellation of values from which concern about balance between context and the complexity/struggle of everyday living or the human experience is derived (NASW Code of Ethics). Clients are individuals, families, communities, groups, and organizations, which exist in culturally diverse contexts. Social workers are sensitive to cultural and ethnic diversity and strive to end discrimination, oppression, poverty and other forms of social injustices.

The *NASW Standards for Social Work Services in Schools* (1992) has served as the guide for the development of school social work. The Standards have been revised to reflect changes within the profession and current social work policies and practices. These Standards are currently under revision. Overall, past and current Standards reinforce the traditions and current practices of this field of practice and the goals and objectives of the school systems. However, for some school systems these Standards provide a challenge, or goals, to be achieved in the best interest of pupils, the educational process, and the desired outcomes. The Standards underscore the importance of interdisciplinary team work, ethics and how the service is to be organized to accomplish its objectives (*NASW School Social Work Standards* [in press]).

School social workers obtain sanction from the clients they serve. One illustration is parental permission to provide social services to young children and participation by parents in determining appropriate intervention. Also important is the sanction acquired through competence in the performance of school social work tasks, which brings respect for the profession and for the individual social worker. However, school social workers should be alert to hazards to school children and young persons when ser-

vices become involuntary and limits of authority are exceeded.

Intervention Methods

Professional intervention refers to the action of the practitioner that is directed to some part of a social system or process with the intention of inducing a change in it. Such a professional act is guided and carried out through the unconscious use of social work knowledge and values and thus is consonant with the idea of their priority (Bartlett, 1970, p. 76). Intervention is an umbrella term comprising a variety of acts to select from according to their pertinence to various situations.

"Intervention—1. Interceding or coming between groups of people, events, planning activities, or an individual's internal conflicts. 2. In social work, the term is analogous to the physician's term 'treatment.' Many social workers prefer using 'intervention' because it includes 'treatment' and also encompasses other activities social workers use to solve or prevent problems, or achieve goals for social betterment. Thus, it refers to psychotherapy, social planning, group work, community organization, finding and developing resources, and many other activities" (Barker, 1999, p. 252).

THE ECOLOGICAL PERSPECTIVE

Social workers must be aware of the effect many institutions have on the social functioning of the child. One perspective for examining the transactions between and among the child and various institutions and systems is the ecological perspective. As discussed in Chapter 3, general systems theory provides tools to help social workers examine and understand the organization of the public school and its subsystems. This theory maintains that environments do have boundaries, structures, and maintenance systems. The concepts of this theory are useful for conceptualizing, gathering, and organizing data about and from the various institutions and systems in which the child functions (the school, family, and community). An ecological perspective provides the framework for understanding the nature of the transactions between the person and different institutions and/or systems. It helps the social worker to identify and consider all systems contributing to the pupil's situation or difficulty. Further, it recognizes that resolution may be more effective when intervention takes place within more than one system. Ecological theory is a theory of interaction and/or transaction. It deals with the broad, complex reciprocal transactions between organisms and their environments. It is not based on static units of pupil behavior encompassed in the labels "dropout," "emotionally disturbed," or "slow learner." It is concerned with dynamic transactions of which the child's behavior is but one part.

Swartz and Martin (1999) identify several assumptions undergirding the perspective (pp. 97–105). They are:

— Behavior has a value specific to the setting. In other words, a pupil's behavior is defined within the setting. Behavior of a pupil that may be culturally appropriate in his/her home and community could be viewed as deviant in the classroom.
— Deviancy refers to behavior that is discordant with the values of its setting.
— It is important to consider the fit of the person to the setting.
— People within the setting make the value judgement.
— There is bi-directionality to interactions within a setting. In other words, there are two transactions between the teacher and the student. The teacher responds positively to a child who adapts positively to the classroom which in turn reinforces the child's behavior.
— Ecological-systems, rather than people, may need to be changed. In other words, altering the environment/ecosystem could be one target of intervention. Changing the expectations/belief systems/behaviors of teachers, parents, and peer groups could result in a better fit for the pupil.

— Ecological interventions are heuristic and eclectic. There is no prescribed intervention or set of ascribed assumptions about a specific situation.

The ecological perspective is the most appropriate perspective for viewing social work practice in schools and for locating the target(s) of intervention. It is appropriate in that it directs attention to the whole and not to any one part, system, or aspect of the client's situation (see Appendixes I and II). The focus is on the social process of interaction and the transactions between a child and that child's environment. The environment is defined as the aggregate of external conditions and influences that affect and determine a child's life and development. In addition to the family, some of these determinants are schools, courts, neighborhood, hospitals, clinics, and the mass media. As Carol B. Germain states, "actually the school social worker stands at the interface not only to the child and school, but family and school, and community and school. . . . Thus, he/she is in a position to help child, parents, and community develop social competence and, at the same time, to help the school's responsiveness to the needs and aspirations of children, parents, and community" (Germain, 1982, p. 6).

The social worker's function is to work at the interface of the person and the environment to bring about a fit between the client's needs (indicated by coping behaviors) and environmental resources. Person–environment fit is the actual fit between an individual's or a collective group's needs, rights, goals, and capacities and the qualities and operations of their physical and social environments within particular cultural and historical contexts. The fit can be favorable, somewhat adequate, or dysfunctional (Germain & Gitterman, 1995, p. 817). In a book entitled *The Bell Curve,* the authors argue that persons are genetically different at birth and that it is this variable that determines intellectual growth and thus achievement. These authors virtually ignore the role of environment in the determination of coping behaviors for growing and achieving (Monkman, 1978; Monkman, 1982a; Monkman, 1982b; Herrnstein & Murray, 1994). Social workers can achieve a good match only if they have fully assessed each side of the interface. An analysis of the components of each side of the interface begins with an analysis of the coping behaviors of the individual (see Figure 4.1). Coping

behaviors are defined as behaviors that are directed toward the environment, including the efforts of the individual to exert some control over his or her own behavior—to use the "self" purposefully. Social workers deal with three categories of coping behaviors. *Coping behaviors for surviving* enable the person to obtain and use resources and make it possible to continue life

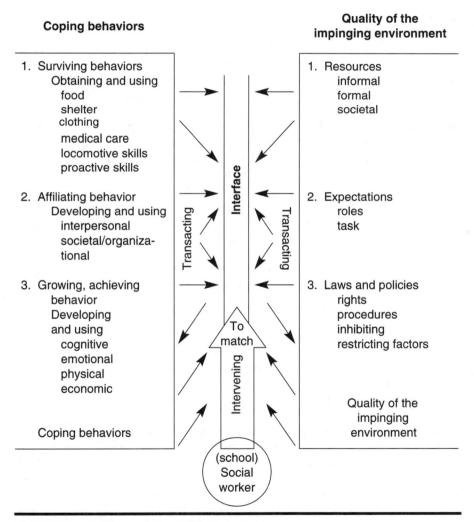

FIGURE 4.1 A Framework for Social Work Practice

Source: Marjorie McQueen Monkman, "The Specialization of the School Social Worker and a Model for Differential Levels of Practice," in *Differential Levels of Student Support Services,* Minnesota Department of Education, 1982, p. 139. Reprinted with permission.

activity—for example, the effort to obtain food, shelter, and medical treatment. In school social work practice, we often assess the pupils, their families, and significant others in terms of their capability to provide essential life needs. A child cannot survive in an environment that is physically and emotionally abusive. *Coping behaviors for affiliating* enable individuals to unite in close connection with others in their significant environments. Subcategories of affiliating behavior are the capacity to develop and maintain intimate personal relationships (social skill functioning) and the ability to use organizations and organizational structures (such as clubs, school, family, and social services). *Coping behaviors for growing and achieving* enable the person to pursue intellectual and social activities useful for self and others. Subcategories of coping behaviors for growing and developing are cognitive functioning, and development of physical, economic, and emotional capacities.

The coping behaviors of individuals develop over a lifetime. Often, behaviors displayed by an individual or group of individuals are related to an accumulation of information that individuals have about themselves or to feedback from significant environments.

In the ecological perspective the child is viewed as a member of a social system. There is equal emphasis on the pupil and the social systems/environments. Rosenberg and Reppucci (1985) identify four target levels of intervention: individual, family, community, and societal. Intervention planning is grounded in information about the aspects of the ecosystem in terms of culture and social class. These ecosystems contain both supporting and inhibiting factors. They place demands on the pupil in terms of expectations and/or ways of behaving.

Some environments may be stressful for children. Stress is the internal response to life stressors and is characterized by troubled emotional or psychological states, or both (Germain & Gitterman, 1995, p. 817). Life stressors are generated by critical life issues that people perceive as exceeding their personal and environmental

resources for managing them. Life stressors include difficult social or developmental transitions, traumatic life events, and any other life issues that disturb the existing fit (Germain & Gitterman, 1995, p. 817). For example, consistent negative information and feedback from family and school to a child about that child's academic abilities could result in and maintain poor academic performance. Monkman defines the environment as those qualities and characteristics of the situation with which the individual is in direct contact. Environments in which children of poverty-level urban families function could be characterized as dense and often lacking appropriate cognitive stimuli. In practice, social workers assess the individual's capacities to obtain what is needed from the environment for surviving, affiliating, and growing or achieving. If they discover that what the individual needs in order to improve social functioning is not available from the environment and the expectations of significant others or that there is a mismatch in the transactions, the environment becomes the target of change. The social worker may attempt to restructure the environment in such a way that the child or groups of children receive positive feedback to encourage self-worth and academic performance.

Case Illustration

A number of children who lived in a multifamily dwelling in an inner-city neighborhood were not turning in homework, an expectation of the fifth- and sixth-grade teachers. Further exploration of the situation by the social worker revealed that the apartments (the living environment) were small and there were no areas where the children could study quietly. A meeting with the manager and interested residents resulted in formulation of a plan to provide a quiet place. The manager of the building offered use of the community room evenings from 6:00–8:00, when it was not used much by the residents. Volunteers were found in the building who would supervise the "study hour" on Tuesdays and Wednesdays. Teachers agreed to give homework only on those nights. Students were involved in each phase of the plan.

In the attempt to change the environment, the emphasis is on determining quality (availability of assistance, degree of stress, and responsiveness). Additional dimensions of the environment include resources, expectations, and laws and policies. *Resources* are defined as people, family, organizations, or institutions that can be turned to for support or help, as needed or desired. Resources may be available supplies. Informal resources may provide support, affection, advice, and concrete services. Formal resources include membership organizations, businesses, schools, and social service agencies. These resources are drawn into the development of social service plans and often are coordinated to assist pupils and families. *Expectations* are defined as the patterned performances and normative obligations that are grounded in established societal structures (see Figure 4.1). Expectations can involve roles and tasks. For example, a child may have several roles—class member, student-learner, family member, and member of organizations such as boys' clubs and Boy Scouts. The pupil performs specific tasks in meeting the expectations of persons in the environment and fulfilling role requirements. *Laws and policies* are defined as binding rules of conduct created by controlling authorities at national, state, and local levels. Laws and policies dictate institutional policies and practices and govern individual behaviors. P.L. 94-142 (the Education for All Handicapped Children Act), the forerunner of today's Individual with Disabilities Education Act, discussed in Chapter 2, changed the role, tasks, and functions of school staff and parents and has to some degree restructured the educational process (by emphasizing individual educational programs, due process, and nondiscriminatory testing) and the learning environment of handicapped pupils (by emphasizing the least restrictive environment).

Social work intervention can seek change in either the coping behaviors of the individual (surviving, affiliating, growing, and achieving), the quality of the environments (policies and practices, resources, and expectations), or both. For example, crack babies and pupils classified as attention deficit disordered, may need one-on-one intervention. If a local school policy discriminates against one pupil group because of the pupils' inability to pay a certain fee, and the activity is identified as an important educational experience, the school social worker should seek to change the policy.

Since school social workers are located at the interface, they are in an excellent position to prevent problems before they arise. Prevention is frequently advocated by social workers. Felner, Phillips, DuBois, and Lease (1991) have developed preventive intervention efforts that wed ecological theory and research in the school setting to assist at-risk pupils. They adopt a developmentally ecological model to maximize school achievement and healthy developmental outcome.

DeMar (1997) reports on school-based preventive intervention that strengthens personal and social competence, and resilience, in children, and prevents future chemical dependency. Structured group work combined with social and cognitive elements was the primary intervention. The sample included fourth- and fifth-grade students, of whom 69 percent were black, Latino, or Asian. The experimental groups performed significantly better than the control groups in cognitive and behavioral areas. Significant increases in internal locus of control and assertive social skills were revealed, and there was a significant decrease in acting-out behavior. Assertive social skills are needed in life-compromising situations (e.g., when one is being coaxed to use drugs). To employ a preventive approach, practitioners must be aware of and understand the role of the significant ecological environment (the school, community, relevant resources, and the unique needs of different pupil groups). Then, and only then, can they have the foresight and insight to prevent problems through collaborative efforts and advocacy. Collaboration and consultation with the school's significant others are fundamental tasks of school social workers.

To attain the objectives of school social work, intervention tasks must be defined in terms of dysfunctional transactions or discord: such tasks are generated by the interaction and transactions between school children and their environments. School children and their family-neighborhood-school-community environment make up a complex system. A first task of the practitioner is to try to locate children's difficulty at the point of "misfit" between their needs and the qualities of their environment, and to recognize the difficulty in the transactions. In locating the point of misfit, the practitioner must examine the structure of the school and community. Which ones are detrimentally affecting large numbers of pupils? Norma Radin, an advocate of structural assessment, suggests that one course of action is to develop in-school alternatives and community services, and to modify policies that reinforce the misfit. According to Radin, optimum effectiveness and efficiency can be achieved by school social workers if they analyze the variables that hinder the development of many children rather than those that hinder a single child. By doing so, practitioners can pin an understanding of some of the blocks to children's growth and increase their own visibility and credibility, while simultaneously developing healthy environments (Radin, 1975).

Case Illustration

School and Community Interface. A school social worker, concerned about the poor attendance and lack of interest in school in one geographical area, decided to collect additional information about the situation. The worker held informal discussions with the pupils and their parents and learned that they felt isolated and ignored by the school's officials. The area, characterized as low income and racially mixed, with

municipal housing, had a community center that was rarely used by the residents. The worker secured permission from the management of the housing project to utilize the center for parent-school meetings.

The worker then described the parents' and pupils' sentiments regarding the school to key school administrators and found that they were very concerned about these residents' apathy and lack of involvement in school activities. They had assumed that these parents were just not interested in the school that served their children.

After considerable discussion with the parents and school administrators, agreement was reached that a meeting of parents, pupils, and school officials to exchange information would benefit all parties. The worker then contacted parents and administrators to discuss the possibility of meeting at the community center (as part of a plan to develop an outreach program to promote communication). The meeting was well attended and parents freely shared their impressions, criticisms, and concerns. Specific concerns were that their children had to cross a dangerous intersection on the way to and from school without supervision, and that there was no bus service. Administrators, unaware of these concerns, responded positively and promised to investigate. They explained some of the changes in curriculum that they were developing and described the opportunities for parents and pupil involvement that existed in the school. This effort opened up lines of communication between the school and a section of the community it served. Results of the project included improved attendance and a significant increase in the number of parent-school contacts (Midwest Center Satellite Consortium for Planned Change in Pupil Personnel Programs for Urban Schools in Indiana, 1974, p. 7).

Family/school relations and connections are essentially the cornerstone of school social work practice. The characterization of family/school relations is described in a variety of ways in the literature: family/school collaboration/partnership/alliance and/or family-centered priorities. If you consider the family and the school as two nurturing systems in the lives of children, their importance takes on considerable significance as targets of intervention. These relationships are indeed very complex. Building functional relations, helping each to problem-solve, finding a common ground between the two when there are differences, linking each with other community/statewide resources is all about building mutual support that advances the development and education success of the youth. When there are inconsistencies and poor communications between the family and school, the consequences can be devastating.

In a recent issue of *Phi Delta Kappan* (January, 2002), Davis indicates that for the most part schools have hardly caught up with the flourishing rhetoric that schools should reach out to parents and form partnerships to promote and support the academic success of pupils. According to Davis, the culture of school still remains at arm's length in terms of parent involvement: too few parents are truly involved in meaningful ways though there is rhetoric calling for their involvement. In reality we see "the tried-and-true" forms of parent involvement: an open house in the fall, two or three short parent conferences a year, and parents attending sports events, fairs, and as partners in fundraising, etc. Too few parents are involved in efforts to change the school curriculum, school policies, and innovations. The traditional separateness remains, and even when partnerships are developed with families and community groups, input is too limited. Yet, the literature suggests that school success and reform is linked to community success and vice versa. In other words, school and community success are linked, and parents are indeed significant stakeholders and components of the community. Davis urges that schools change their culture to make way for new opportunities to truly involve parents and communities.

Dryfoos (2002) offers a note of optimism regarding school-community partnerships. Involvement of community agencies in the schools can provide numerous opportunities for addressing barriers to learning. Though hard core empirical evidence is still in its formative stage, a review of existing partnerships indicates such findings as: these partnerships are complex, and community schools are beginning to demonstrate "positive effects on students, families, and communities" (Dryfoos, p. 398).

Pupil and School Interface. A social worker in a small Midwest school district, concerned about the large number of high-school students who were spending their days in a local park and shopping center, sought to understand their lack of interest in schooling. The worker held discussions with these youths and found that they were bored and restless, they cut classes regularly, and they felt that the school offered neither challenge nor satisfaction. Although many of them had some of the cognitive skills necessary for success in school, they were not committed to learning, given the school environment.

The worker took this information to the superintendent and other school officials. After much discussion with them and with the pupils, the worker developed a proposal for an alternative educational program for that high school. This proposal was submitted to the school board and was approved. The cost of starting the program was low because the new school would be held in a frame building already owned by the school district. Twenty-five students enrolled in the nine-week pilot program. Students, volunteers, parents, and administrators who were interested in the program held a retreat to discuss the new school—its educational program, policies, and procedures. The students described how thoroughly disillusioned they were with the existing school framework.

The school social worker asked such questions as: What do you see in your school now? What would you like to see? What are our mission objectives? The school met the requirements of the *Illinois School Code,* including the course requirements. The students established the goals, assisted in the design of the curriculum, and interviewed prospective teachers.

The program was a great success. Students' attendance increased 48 percent, their self-esteem increased, and academically they were achieving. Encouraged by the success of the alternative educational program, the school district voted to continue it, to expand it to 75 students, and to increase the budget.

The creation of this program is an excellent illustration of how to bring about change in transactions between a pupil group and the school. The identification and analysis of an imbalance, followed by implementation of a carefully thought-out plan of intervention that facilitates healthy exchange, exemplifies an ecological approach to school social work practice.

According to J. Rappaport,

> the ecological viewpoint should be regarded as an orientation emphasizing relationships among persons and their social and physical environment. Conceptually the term implies that there are neither inadequate persons nor inadequate environment, but rather the fit between persons and environment may be in relative accord and/or discord. (Rappaport, 1977, p. 7)

The ecological perspective also makes one aware of relationships existing among systems—for example, relationships between family and school and between peer group and community. According to Carel Germain, one major advantage of the ecological perspective of social work is that it

> contributes scientific knowledge concerning the delicate relationships of human beings to the rapidly changing physical and social environment. At the same time, it fosters a passionate concern for human aspirations and for the development of milieus to promote them. An ecological perspective enables us to reach toward a complementarity between our scientific and humanistic concerns, between cause and function. (Germain, 1979, p. 326)

Risk and Resiliency

According to Werner (1986), Bernard (1992), and Fraser (1997), a pupil's risk when viewed from a developmental perspective changes with the social context (environments) in which he or she lives. Risk can be defined as the likelihood of an individual's developing a certain problem or difficulty in functioning, over a specific period of time. For example, infants and toddlers deprived of early cognitive and physical stimuli may be at risk of various developmental delays. There is a set of predisposing factors (in this case the lack of stimuli) that place the child at risk. Risks can be buffered or minimized if the appropriate resources and protective factors are provided at critical stages of development. These protective factors reduce and/or eliminate risk and in some instances promote competence. In the literature there is mention of children who appear to triumph over adversity. They are beset with problems (e.g., poverty, dysfunctional homes, parents who may suffer from mental illness), yet they appear to be resilient or invulnerable. Perhaps informal environmental factors, caregiving, and social relations act as protective factors/buffers for these children and increase their stress resistance.

Resilience is defined as a set of behaviors and, as internalized capacities, resilience represents positive outcomes when risks are present. Behaviorally, resilience means coping with, recovering from, or overcoming adversity. Persons who are resilient cope through flexible, problem-solving, and help-seeking behaviors rather than with rigid and brittle responses to stress and other adversities (Gilgun, 1996, p. 398).

Protective factors are assets that individuals use to cope with, adapt to, or overcome vulnerability or risks. Protective factors can include residence within a family, social group, or community; peer applications and a healthy relationship with parents; adequate financial resources to provide a decent standard of living; external social supports (e.g., relatives and friends); and positive social competencies (Gilgun, 1996, p. 397).

Ecological Environments

Figure 4.2 shows the significant environments and/or systems in which the child interacts and

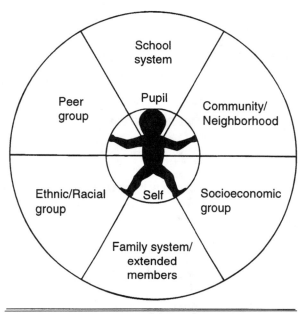

FIGURE 4.2   A Child's Natural Habitat

Source: Allen-Meares, Lane, and Oppenheimer, 1981, and updated 2002.

with which the child transacts (Allen-Meares, Lane, & Oppenheimer, 1981, and modified in 2002).

The ecological environment is a nested arrangement of structures, each of which is contained within the next. The definitions of each structure are as follows (see Figure 4.3 [Apter & Bronfenbrenner, 1977; Swap, 1978]):

Microsystem—the complex of relations between the developing person and the environment, which is an immediate setting containing that person (home, school, work)

Mesosystem—the interrelations among major settings containing that person (home, school, work)

Exosystem—an extension of the mesosystem, comprising other specific social structures, both formal and informal, that do not themselves contain the developing person but affect or encompass the immediate settings in which that person is found and thereby influence, delimit, or even determine what goes on there. (These structures include the major institutions of the society, both deliberately struc-

tured and spontaneously evolving, as they operate at the local level.)

Macrosystem—the overarching institutional patterns of the culture or subculture, such as the economic, social, educational, legal, and political systems, of which micro-, meso-, and exosystems are the concrete manifestations. (Apter, 1982, p. 60)

One can apply this four-level ecological systems perspective to design gang prevention programs. However, all four levels must be addressed if the intervention is to be effective at reducing the impact such groups have on society (Phillips & Straussner, 1997). At the micro level, each gang member's personality, academic skills, cognitive ability, physical characteristics, and family relationships must be addressed. At the mesosystem level, various systems in the environment of gang members must be addressed (e.g., schools, neighborhood programs, and recreational centers). At the exosystem level, the attitudes, practices, and actions of leaders could

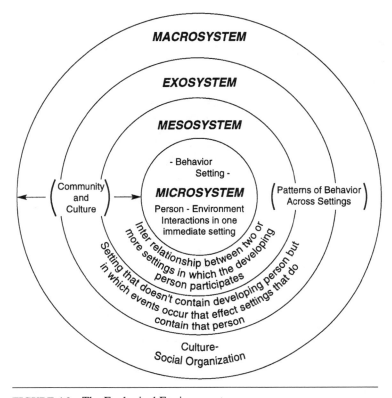

FIGURE 4.3   The Ecological Environment
Source: Developed by Apter, 1982 after Bronfenbrenner, 1977 and Swap, 1978.
Reprinted with permission.

influence gang members' access to mental health and youth services. Community business leaders, the police department, and neighborhood constituencies must work together to provide support where needed. The outermost level—the macrosystem—which represents values, laws, and policies of society, impacts the other three levels. Legislative action resulting in programs and policies has a bearing on opportunities to reintegrate gang members into society, as well as developing programs to prevent delinquency. All too often gang members have lost their connections with constructive relationships, and the gang itself has become a closed mesosystem in which antisocial behaviors are reinforced. Clearly schools, civic leaders, religious institutions, concerned citizens, social and human service agencies, and the justice system will need to work together to address this problem.

The nested arrangement that characterizes the ecological environment is described as:

> It seems useful to picture the ecological network as consisting of three nested systems or levels. The first level and the most basic environmental unit or system is the behavior setting. . . . The behavior setting consists of a physical milieu, a program of activities, inhabitants, and a location in time and space. A child in a behavior setting (such as a classroom) is a component of the setting and is also significantly influenced by the expectations, constraints and opportunities available in that setting. Behavior settings can be described with various degrees of inclusiveness: the kindergarten class or the whole school; the family at breakfast or the home.
>
> The second level of analysis in this nested model is patterns of behavior across settings. At this level, behavior settings comprise the building blocks for studies of more complex child-

environment interactions, including, for example, the behavior of the same child at home and school or the behaviors of children labeled disturbed and nondisturbed in different settings.

The community and culture influence the design and meaning of simple behavior settings and the relationships among them. Community and culture as the third and most complex level of analysis includes formal and informal structures at local and supra-local levels as well as characteristics of the physical environment. (Swap, 1978, p. 186–196)

Components of the ecological system of the school and the place of the learner in it are depicted in Figure 4.4. Every pupil or learner is considered unique, and thus his or her transactions and interactions with the school and its subsystems are unique.

Ecological Assessment. There is an excellent book that describes assessment and interventions in the primary microsystems in which pupils live: home, community and school (Swartz & Martin, 1997). The authors provide a useful framework for assessment that is consistent with the perspective advocated in this book. Specifically, assessment must include attention to individual, physiological factors and aspects of environment. A poor fit between pupil characteristics and demands of the environment can result in a disturbance of child adjustment. For example, a pupil may not be capable of performing certain academic and behavioral tasks considered to be normative for his/her age group, and thus perceived to be deviant by his/her teacher. This is known as the ecological perspective of deviance. Allen-Meares and Lane (1987) offer a

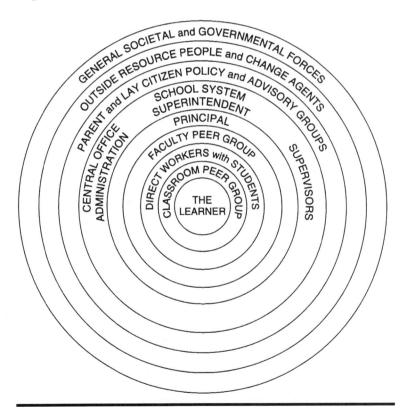

FIGURE 4.4 Components of the Ecological System

Source: From Steven Apter, *Troubled Children—Troubled Systems;* and Fox, Robert et al., *Diagnosing Professional Climates of Schools,* 1975, p. 4. Copyright 1973, NTL Learning Resources Corp., Inc. Reprinted with permission.

framework for ecological assessment. Rooted in the ecological perspective and systems concepts, it facilitates the isolation of three major dimensions of assessment as well as relevant data sources (see Figure 4.5). By breaking the three-dimensional block into its component cells, one can begin to identify the assessment components represented by each cell. Figure 4.5 represents an ideal framework. In our daily practice it may be impossible to address every cell, and in some cases perhaps there is no need to do so. There are many constraints that prevent practitioners from conducting comprehensive assessments (e.g., agency policy, time, large case loads, client/family resistance).

Six practice principles are derived from this framework:

1. A comprehensive ecosystems assessment requires that data be collected about multiple

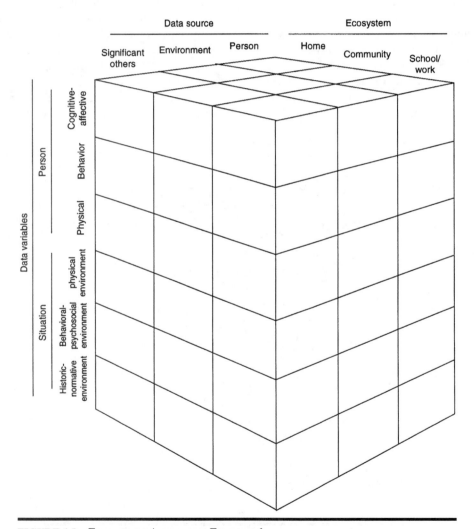

FIGURE 4.5   Ecosystems Assessment Framework

Source: Allen-Meares, P., and Lane, B., "Grounding Social Work Practice in Theory: Ecosystems," *Social Casework,* 68, no. 9 (November, 1987), p. 519. (Reprinted with permission.)

ecosystems (e.g., school, home, and community). Questions to consider include: What are the educational opportunities of the community/family? Are there unique ethnic and cultural characteristics?

2. Assessment should include data from all three data sources (person, significant others, and direct observations of the pupil in his or her environment). The school social worker may want to observe a pupil in the home, classroom, and an informal setting. The practitioners may want to speak with different persons about the pupil's behavior in different contexts and at different times of the day.

3. The third principle advocates for assessment data on all of the critical data variables that describe the person (cognitive, affective, behavior, physical attributes) and the situational context. For example, a pupil's intellectual functioning on standardized tests suggests above normal capacity, but the teacher reports underachievement and sleeping in the classroom (even though there is no special illness).

4. A comprehensive assessment should include as many components as is possible. For example, to understand a pupil's inability to make friends, a school social worker would also want to assess the child's social skills across settings, obtain information from a number of persons, and perhaps draw upon objective techniques such as sociometric ratings from peers.

5. The assessment data must be integrated into a comprehensive picture of the pupil's situation. Each variable is one piece of a total picture. It also helps the practitioner to locate the source of difficulty (in the pupil, the environment(s), or both).

6. The sixth principle deals with connecting the assessment with an elective and effective repertoire of intervention strategies. The school social worker would need to know about interventions that target the person and the environment(s).

In an article on the assessment of adaptive behavior of pupils for possible placement in special education classes, a case is made for the inclusion of standardized assessment measures (Allen-Meares & Lane, 1983). This article draws upon the same perspective and theoretical constructs presented in this chapter.

Standardized measures have an important role to play in our practice; however, their use should be based upon a set of criteria consistent with our theory, values, and what we know about the empirical validation of assessment measures.

Chung and Pardeck (1997) speak to the overwhelming perception about one minority group that is perceived as a "model minority"—successful, well adaptive emotionally and socially. Asian American youth and their friends do experience social isolation, discrimination, and family dysfunction. Chung and Pardeck make the case for this group's empowerment through an ecosystem approach.

There are a number of ecologically sensitive assessment instruments and techniques (Swartz & Martin, 1999). Though it is beyond the scope of this book to elaborate on each of these instruments, a few will be described. The Eyberg Child Behavior Inventory (a rating scale that measures the interaction of the parent-child, which indicates conduct disorder and social emotional behaviors), the Temperament Assessment Battery for Children (three rating scales which allow for the comparison of viewpoints of parents, teachers, and practitioners, measures emotional intensity, adaptability to changing social circumstances, etc.), the Instructional Environment Scale (determines the extent to which a student's academic and behavioral processes are a function of factors in the instructional environment and identifies points for instructional intervention), the student observation system, a portion of the Behavior System for Children (lends itself well to ecological assessment of a pupil within a classroom, and provides a multi-dimensional system for recording classroom behavior), and the Maslach Burnout Inventory Form (provides insight into teacher characteristics which may affect student functioning). These instruments focus on the intersection/transactions of the child with his parents, the child in the classroom, the characteristics of the classroom, and the characteristics/competencies of the teacher. The psychometric properties of these instruments are well documented. Of course, school social workers rely on informal sources of data to complement data gathered from standardized instruments. For example, a review of pupil records, teacher and parent interviews, observational data, and various rating scales provide useful information for ascertaining a comprehensive ecological perspective of the pupil.

Ecological Intervention.   School social workers intervene in transactions. Their intervention can be aimed at a perceived cause of imbalance existing outside the school environment or within the school system, at the child, or at a combination of these. Targeting intervention at the pupil or at groups of pupils is just one strategy that the school social worker can employ. To promote change in the various transactions, Apter suggests that school social workers build strong ecosystems and link the various aspects of each child's world. A school social worker might seek to achieve the following goals:

To build new social skills or competencies on the part of adults, parents, and children

To identify new resources and social service agencies that will assist children and their families and to develop new programs in the school and community

To change the perceptions of adults (such as teachers who may have a negative view of a pupil)

To increase knowledge and understanding (for example, provide in-service training to educators about child abuse and neglect)

To restructure activities (for example, develop modified educational schedules for children who have difficulty functioning in an all-day setting)

To develop new ties with relevant community agencies (such as mental health and adolescent services) and school-based services

To develop new roles for teachers, parents, and community agency personnel (for example, teacher as group work leader, parent as volunteer, agency personnel as a school resource)

To develop new and innovative programs where a need exists (such as alternative programs, flexible scheduling, in-school programs for pregnant girls, after-school programs for children whose parents are employed, modified physical education programs for those with physical handicaps) (Apter, 1982, pp. 70–71).

The case or need for environmental and/or school change is highlighted by research which suggests that children with behavior disorders are more likely to be rejected by their non-disabled peers than are pupils with other disabilities (Van Hook, 1992). School social workers must work to change the attitudes of peers and teachers as well as the overall climate of the school. Too often social workers will focus on the individual pupil, perhaps by enhancing his or her social skills, while ignoring the need to change the climate of the classroom and the attitude of peers.

We know that a pupil's school experiences are shaped not only by the classroom setting but also by the larger school environment. In order to prevent problems and stress for pupils, school social workers must understand what the social environment is like and its influence on those who occupy it (Vincent & Trikett, 1993).

The organizational climate of the school has been the subject of considerable empirical investigation. Though there is no standard definition of organizational climate and some use the terms climate and culture interchangeably, attempts to measure it continue. The notion of organizational health and/or healthy environments focuses attention on how schools conduct their business and on the nature and quality of the interactions among those within the system. In the literature, we find discussion of climate assessment tools such as the Organizational Climate Descriptions Questionnaire and the Organizational Health Inventory (Hoy, Taiter, & Bliss, 1983).

There is a growing body of literature on systemic interventions for promoting safe schools that is congruent with the theoretical framework espoused in this chapter (Conoley & Conoley, 2001). Schools are located within a context that makes them an important location for mounting preventive interventions to reduce violence (see Chapter 7) and for linking with important service providers. Approaches that change the systems and relationships of the school, community and classrooms are important for effective interventions to reduce violence. Whatever approach is adopted for prevention, a critical variable is early and comprehensive intervention. Interventions such as parent training (that focuses on how to handle early childhood oppositional behavior), social cognitive skills training (which focuses on the promotion of functional social skills, anger management and conflict resolution), and multisystemic therapy (which focuses on highly structured, intensive family and community-based treatment that targets inappropriate and violent behaviors) are promising. The promotion of positive identification with the social context or one's community also acts as a buffer against violence (which means that there must be a good fit between the child and the school's culture/policies/practices). And there must be in place, within the school, ways for assisting pupils with academic performance (e.g., tutoring, self-monitoring, and time delay procedures, the method of transferring stimulus control by changing the temporal interval between the natural cue and the teachers prompt). Singularly, and/or in combination, the aforementioned interventions offer promising approaches for responding to different graduations of violence.

One role that practitioners can play as they promote change in linkages and ecosystems is the role of advocate. Advocacy on behalf of pupil groups can take place on several levels: in school and community committees organized to develop and plan programs for pupils; at the state and national levels (supporting the rights of high-risk pupil groups); and within the school and community systems (identifying adequate services and unfair policies and practices). Examples of those skills that are relevant include:

1. Collecting appropriate information to document aspects of the biological, medical, psychological, cultural, sociological, emotional, legal, and environmental factors that affect the learning process of school pupils
2. Collaborating with community agencies in school-linked service projects or other programs to solve specific problem situations, or develop new resources for children and their families
3. Identifying and developing resources within and outside the local education agency and the community
4. Making systematic observation and assessment of needs and characteristics of pupils, parents, school system, neighborhood, and community, and evaluating the effects of the interaction of these characteristics with pupil characteristics
5. Analyzing and influencing policy at local, county, state, and national levels
6. Consulting with persons in the client system in order to clarify situations, give or receive information, monitor progress in an intervention plan, or mediate among points of view
7. Assessing the influences operating in school-community-pupil-parent relations and interpreting these influences (*NASW Standards for Social Work Services in Schools,* in press).

A FRAMEWORK FOR SPECIALIZATION IN SCHOOL SOCIAL WORK

Essentially, school social work is one of the specialized fields of social work practice. According to Bartlett, defining the characteristics of a field of practice makes it possible to define desirable educational input. Bartlett specifies five characteristics of social work practice: (1) a central problem, (2) a system of organized services, (3) a body of knowledge, (4) sociocultural attitudes, and (5) characteristic responses and behavior of the persons served (Bartlett, 1970). We would add a sixth characteristic: contemporary forces of change, both inside and outside the field of practice.

1. *Central problem.* The primary function of the public schools is education. When the interaction between the school and the child results in a dysfunctional relationship for both—in particular, when pupils are not learning and adapting and the school is experiencing difficulty in helping them to achieve—then there is a problem.

2. *System of organized services.* The school is a highly departmentalized bureaucracy. It has levels of achievement and advancement that operate to categorize children; it has specialized personnel such as regular classroom teachers, psychologists, reading teachers, counselors, social workers, and administrators at various levels to oversee specific areas. The school's rules of operation are intricate and well established to enhance performance and conformity.

3. *Body of knowledge.* The field of education contains a variety of teaching materials and methods as well as ideologies concerning how and under what conditions children learn best. Differences in opinion range from the humanistic approach to the more structured behavioral approach. The fundamental knowledge base and the methodologies for preparing educators are different from those used in the preparation and training of social workers. The educator focuses on mastery of cognitive and affective skills and on the child's in-school performance. The social work profession also values these dynamics, but its focus is broader in that it includes the "total child" (family, school, community, and culture) and the quality of interaction among these components. Skills and other elements of competen-

cies for working with this population of school children have been identified in the *NASW Standards for Social Work Services in Schools.* These skills emerge from a substantial body of knowledge. This knowledge is translatable into social work intervention in the transactions between school children and their home-school-community environment.

4. *Sociocultural attitudes.* Our society highly values the function of the public schools. It gives the schools responsibility for developing the population's functional skills and preparing children for career opportunities and citizenship—all of which enhances and perpetuates the society. Academic success in our society is often considered to be one of the keys to upward mobility and self-respect.

5. *Characteristic responses of the person served.* The general response of the majority of children to the school setting is one of adaptation. However, there are children who are anxious and whose fear of failure undermines their potential for learning. There are also children who do not adapt to the structure of the institution and its environmental, social, and psychological demands, and thus are rejected or assigned to various specialized or remedial programs.

6. *Forces of change.* Because of innovations, laws, and community pressure, the public school system has periodically changed its methodology and has frequently altered its theories of how children learn. Historically, legislation has played a significant role in shaping our educational system, and it still does. The interplay among legislation, innovations in education, and developments related to social work services in the schools should be analyzed periodically (Allen-Meares, 1981).

CONCLUSION

In this chapter the reader was introduced to the profession of social work: its values, purposes, goals, and sanctions; the search for a conceptual framework; and the application of social work in the school setting. An ecological perspective of practice was advocated, for it offers a comprehensive view of pupils, school, community, and parents, and of the transactions and interactions among them that can cause pupil malperformance. The goal of school social workers is to change either the pupil, the environment, or both—in order to promote the healthy social functioning of pupils. This chapter also made clear the unique contribution of the social work profession to schools and the profession's dual perspective of person and environment. No other discipline in the school works at the interface. The school social worker recognizes that the quality of pupils' transactions with environments outside of the school as well as those within the school system has much to do with the pupils' academic performance and the development of competencies required for successful societal adjustment. As Bernard states, "The challenge . . . is the implementation of prevention strategies that strengthen protective factors in our families, schools, and communities" (Bernard, 1992, p. 3).

FOR STUDY AND DISCUSSION

1. List several positive aspects of an ecological perspective of social work practice in schools. Why do you think this perspective is advocated? Some have questioned whether the ecological perspective is sufficient to inform and direct social work practice. Can the ecological model guide social work practice? What is your opinion?

2. In the school we often find school psychologists, counselors, and other supportive service staff. Describe some of the tasks that might be shared by these individuals and that they might share with the school social worker. Then describe the unique contributions of, and tasks performed by, the social worker.

3. Why has it been so difficult for the profession of social work to define and adopt a conceptual framework? Identify several factors unique to the profession that may contribute to this situation.

4. Write your state department of education and request the certification requirements for school social workers.

5. Cite several hypothetical case illustrations of a poor "fit" or "match" between any of the following combinations: school, community, pupil group, and parents. (Note the case illustrations in this chapter.) What would be the role or service plan of the practitioner? How should the practitioner proceed to achieve a better match?

6. Secure a copy of the *NASW Standards for Social Work Services in Schools.* Why is this document important to school social workers? What standard(s) would you add and why?

7. Why is the study of risk, resiliency, and protective factors so important for social work practice in schools? Identify and discuss a list of protective factors for pupils in an urban setting.

ADDITIONAL READING

Baker, J. A. (1998). Are we missing the forest for the trees? Considering the social contexts of school violence. *Journal of School Psychology, 36,* 29–44.

Beck, B. M. (1959). School social work: An instrument of education. *Social Work, 4*(4), 87–91.

Begun, A. L. (1993). Human behavior and the social enviornment: The vulnerability, risk, and resilience model. *Journal of Social Work Education, 29,* 26–35.

Bernard, B. (1993). Fostering resiliency in kids. *Educational Leadership, 51*(3), 44–49.

Borgelt, C., & Conoley, J. D. (1998). Psychology in schools: Systems intervention cases. In T. Gretkin & C. R. Reynolds (Eds.), *The handbook of school psychology* (3rd ed., pp.1056–1076). New York: Wiley.

Brooks, R. B. (1994). Children at risk: Fostering resilience and hope. *American Journal of Orthopsychiatry, 64,* 545–553.

Cicchetti, D., & Garmezy, N. (1993). Editorial: Prospects and promises in the study of resilience. *Development & Psychopathology, 5,* 497–502.

Clancy, J. (1995). Ecological school social work: The reality and the vision. *Social Work in Education, 17*(1), 40–47.

Comer, J. (1984, May). Home-school relationships as they affect the academic success. *Education & Urban Society,* 323–327.

Dryfoos, J. (1993, Spring). Schools as places for health, mental health, and social services. *Teachers College Record, 94*(3), 541–567.

Early, B. (1992, October). An ecological exchange model of social work consultation within the work group of the school. *Social Work in Education, 14*(4), 207–214.

Ellis, J. A. N., & Bryant, E. (1976). Competency-based certification for school social workers. *Social Work, 21,* 381–385.

Ezeland, B., Carlson, E., & Stroufe, L. A. (1993). Resilience as process. *Development & Psychopathology, 5,* 517–528.

Felix-Ortiz, M., & Newcomb, M. D. (1992). Risk and protective factors for drug use among Latino and white adolescents. *Hispanic Journal of Behavioral Sciences, 14,* 291–309.

Fraser, M. (1996, July). Aggressive behavior in childhood and early adolescence: An ecological-developmental perspective on youth violence. *Social Work, 41*(4), 347–361.

Garmezy, N. (1990). Children in poverty: Resilience despite risk. *Psychiatry, 56,* 127–136.

Goldstein, H. (1990). Strength or pathology: Ethical and rhetorical contrasts in approaches to practice. *Families in Society, 71,* 267–275.

Helper, J. (1994, July). Mainstreaming children with learning disabilities: Have we improved their social environment? *Social Work in Education, 16*(3), 143–151.

Hensseler, S. W., Schoenwald, S. K., & Pickrel, S. G. (1995). Multi-systemic therapy: Bridging the gap between university and community-based treatment. *Journal of Consulting and Clinical Psychology, 63*(5), 709–717.

Hensseler, S. W., Schoenwald, S. K., Borduin, C. M., Rowland, M. D., & Cummingham, P. B. (1998). *Multisystemic treatment of antisocial behavior in children and adolescents.* New York: Guilford Press.

Hyman, I. A., & Perone, D. C. (1998). The other side of school violence. Educational policies and practices that may contribute to student misbehavior. *Journal of School Psychology, 36,* 7–27.

Kochanek, T., & Buka, S. (1992, July). Using biologic and ecologic factors to identify vulnerable infants and toddlers. *Infants & Young Children, 4,* 11–25.

Lee, Laura. (1977, May). The school social workers in the political environment. *Social Work, 22*(3), 196–201.

McCubbin, H. I. T., Thompson, E. A., Thompson, A. I., & Fromer, J. E. (1995). *Resiliency in ethnic minority families: Native and immigrant American families, I.* Madison: University of Wisconsin Press.

Michals, A. P., Counroyer, D. E., & Pinner, E. E. (1979). School social work and educational goals. *Social Work, 24*(2), 138–144.

Oestmann, J., & Walker, M. B. (1997). Intervention for aggressive students in a public school-based day treatment program. In A. P. Goldstein & J. C. Connolly (Eds.), *School violence intervention: A practical handbook* (pp. 160–188).

O'Keefe, M. (1994). Adjustment of children from maritally violent homes. *Families in Society, 75,* 403–415.

Pardeck, J. (1996). *Social work practice: An ecological approach.* Westport, CT: Auburn House.

Peoples, F., & Loeber, R. (1994). Do individual factors and neighborhood context explain ethnic differences in juvenile delinquency? *Journal of Quantitative Criminology, 10*(2), 141–157.

Plomin, R. (1989). Environment and genes: Determinants of behavior. *American Psychologist, 44,* 105–111.

Popham, W. J. (1995). *Classroom assessment: What teachers need to know.* Boston: Allyn & Bacon.

Sarason, S. B. (1971). *The culture of the school and the problem of change.* Boston: Allyn & Bacon.

Sosin, M., & Caulum, S. (1983, January–February). Advocacy: A conceptualization for social work practice. *Social Work, 28*(1), 3–13.

Vinter, R., & Sarri, R. (1965, January). Malperformance in the public schools: A groupwork approach. *Social Work, 10*(1), 3–13.

Welch, M. (1994). Ecological assessment: A collaborative approach to planning instructional interventions. *Intervention in School & Clinic, 29,* 160–164.

Wolin, S., & Wolin, S. (1995). Resilience among youth growing up in substance-abusing families. *Pediatric Clinics of North America, 42,* 415–429.

Zigler, E., Toussig, C., & Block, K. (1992). Early childhood intervention: A promising preventive for juvenile delinquency. *American Psychologist, 47,* 997–1006.

REFERENCES

Allen-Meares, P. (1981). Educating social workers for specialization. *Social Work in Education, 3,* 36–51.

Allen-Meares, P., & Lane, B. (1983). Assessing the adaptive behavior of children and youths. *Social Work, 28,* 297–301.

Allen-Meares, P., & Lane, B. (1987). Grounding social work practice in theory: Ecosystems. *Social Casework, 68*(9), 519.

Allen-Meares, P., Lane, B., & Oppenheimer, M. (1981, May). *Assessing the adaptive behavior of children and youth.* Paper presented at the Second National Conference on School Social Work, Washington, DC.

Apter, S. J. (1982). *Troubled children—Troubled systems* (Rev. ed.). Elmsford, NY: Pergamon Press.

Apter, S., & Bronfenbrenner, V. (1977). Toward an experimental ecology of human development. *American Psychologist, 32,* 513–531.

Barker, R. (1999). *The social work dictionary* (4th ed.). Washington, DC: NASW.

Bartlett, H. M. (1970). *The common base of social work practice.* Washington, DC: NASW.

Bernard, B. (1992). Fostering resiliency in kids: Protective factors in the family, school and community. *Prevention Forum, 12,* 1–16.

Bloom, B. (1976). *Human characteristics and school learning.* New York: McGraw-Hill.

Brieland, D. (1977). Historical overview. *Special Issue on Conceptual Frameworks. Social Work, 22,* 338–433.

Chung, W., & Pardeck, J. (1997). Treating powerless minorities through an ecosystem approach. *Adolescence, 32,* 624–638.

Conceptual Frameworks II: Second Special Issue on Conceptual Frameworks. (1981). *Social Work, 2.*

Conoley, J., & Conoley, C. (2001). Systemic interventions for safe schools. In J. Hughes, A. Greca, & J. Conoley (Eds.), *Handbook of psychological services for children and adolescents* (pp. 439–455). New York: Oxford Press.

Davis, D. (2002, January). The 10th school revisited: Are school/family/community partnerships on the reform agenda now? *Phi Delta Kappan, 83*(5), 388–392.

DeMar, J. (1997). A school-based group intervention to strengthen personal and social competencies in latency-age children. *Social Work in Education, 19,* 219–229.

Dryfoos, J. (2002, January). Full-service community schools: Creating new institutions. *Phi Delta Kappan 83*(5), 393–399.

Felner, R., Phillips, R., DuBois, D., & Lease, M. (1991). Ecological interventions and the process of change for prevention: Wedding theory and research to implementation in real world settings. *American Journal of Community Psychology, 19*(3), 379–387.

Fraser, M. (Ed.). (1997). *Risk and resilience in childhood.* Washington, DC: NASW Press.

Germain, C. (1979). Ecology and social work. In C. B. Germain (Ed.), *Social work practice: People and environment.* New York: Columbia University Press.

Germain, C. B. (1982). An ecological perspective on social work in the schools. In R. Constable and J. Flynn (Eds.), *School social work: Practice and research perspectives.* Homewood, IL: Dorsey Press.

Germain, C., & Gitterman, A. (1995). Ecological perspective. In R. Edwards (Ed.), *Encyclopedia of social work* (19th ed., pp. 817–825). Washington, DC: NASW.

Gilgun, J. (1996, September). Human development and adversity in ecological perspective, Part I: A conceptual framework. Families in society: *The Journal of Contemporary Human Services, 77*(7), 395–402.

Gordon, W. (1962). A critique of the working definition. *Social Work, 7,* 3–13.

Herrnstein, R., & Murray, C. (1994). *The bell curve: Intelligence and class structure in American life.* New York: Free Press.

Hoy, W., Taiter, J., & Bliss, J. (1983). Organizational climate, school health, and effectiveness: A comparative analysis. *Educational Administration, 26,* 260–279.

Midwest Center Satellite Consortium for Planned Change in Pupil Personnel Programs for Urban Schools in Indiana. (1974). *A final report from the Jane Addams School of Social Work.* Urbana, IL: University of Illinois, School–Community Pupil Training Programs.

Monkman, M. M. (1978). A broader, more comprehensive view of social work practice. *School Social Work Journal*, 2–7.

Monkman, M. M. (1982a). The contribution of the social workers to the public schools. In R. Constable (Ed.), *School social work: Research and practice perspectives*. Homewood, IL: Dorsey Press.

Monkman, M. M. (1982b). The specialization of school social work and a model for differential levels of practice. In *Differential levels of student support services*. St. Paul: Minnesota Department of Education.

NASW Code of Ethics and Professional Standards, Policy Statement no. 1. (1980). Washington, DC: NASW.

NASW Standards for Social Work Services in Schools. (1978). Washington, DC: NASW.

NASW Task Force on Specialization. (1978). *Specialization in the social work profession*. Washington, DC: NASW.

Phillips, N., & Straussner, S. (1997). *Children in the urban environment: Linking social policy and clinical practice*. Springfield, IL: Charles C. Thomas Publisher.

Radin, N. (1975). A personal perspective on school social work. *Social Casework, 56*, 605–613.

Rappaport, J. (1977). *Community psychology: Values, research, and action*. New York: Holt, Rinehart, and Winston.

Rosenberg, M. S., & Reppucci, N. D. (1985). Primary prevention of child abuse. *Journal of Consulting and Clinical Psychology, 53*, 576–585.

Special Issue on Conceptual Frameworks. (1977). *Social Work, 22*.

Swap, S. (1978). The ecological model of emotional disturbance in children: A status report and proposed synthesis. *Behavioral Disorders, 3*, 186–196.

Swartz, J., & Martin, W. (1997). (Eds.). *Applied Ecological Psychology for Schools within Communities: Assessment and Intervention*. Mahwak, New Jersey: Laurence Earlbaum Associates.

Van Hook, M. (1992). Integrating children with disabilities: An ongoing challenge. *Social Work in Education, 14*, 25–35.

Vincent, T., & Trikett, E. (1993). Preventive interventions and the human context: Ecological approaches to environmental assessment and change. In R. Feldner, L. Jason, J. Mortisqu, & S. Farber (Eds.), *Preventive psychology: Theory, research and practice* (pp. 67–85). New York: Pergamon Press.

Werner, B. (1959). *Objectives of the social work curriculum of the future* (p. 54). New York: Council on Social Work Education.

Werner, E. (1986). The concept of risk from a developmental perspective. *Advances in Special Education, 5*, 1–23.

CHAPTER 5

SCHOOL ATTENDANCE

TONY DEREZINSKI, MICHIGAN ASSOCIATION OF SCHOOL BOARDS

Truancy and excessive absenteeism influence an entire spectrum, from pupils whose education is affected, to teachers whose instruction is disrupted, principals who must account for empty desks, superintendents who must rely on attendance for state aid, attendance officers, home-school counselors and law enforcement officials who must contact the parents and locate absent students, judges who occasionally rule on truancy cases, and merchants who complained of daytime financial losses due to adolescent loitering and misbehavior. *

—Paul J. Porwall

INTRODUCTION

Since the 1960s, educational legislation and a re-interpretation of previous court decisions have reshaped school policies and practices. Chapters 5 through 10 are concerned with educational policies and court decisions that are relevant to social workers in the school. Some readers may question the emphasis on school attendance, pupil rights, control of pupil behavior, special educational legislation, and issues surrounding bilingual education, racism, and sexism. Social workers cannot function effectively in the school if they are unfamiliar with the issues that have been raised in these important policy areas. Educational policies and court decisions affect how schools operate, how children are educated, and what roles school personnel play. With changes in such policies and reinterpretation by the

courts, school social workers must be ready to reinterpret their contributions in terms of implementation. If policies seem unfair and detrimental to any particular pupil group, they must organize and advocate change at the appropriate governmental or court levels. Advocacy is a fundamental aspect of the school social workers' job definition.

If children do not attend school, they will be ill-prepared to handle life tasks. If subjected to physical punishment for misbehavior in the school, children will quickly use force to achieve their ends. If special education students are denied their right to obtain an appropriate education and to achieve their maximum potential, they lose and so does society. Equal educational opportunity should be guaranteed to every pupil

---

*Paul J. Porwall, *Student Absenteeism* (Arlington, VA: Educational Research Service, 1977). Reprinted with permission.

regardless of language, race, or sex. Knowledge of the policies and laws that protect these vulnerable school populations is a requirement for every social worker in the school.

It goes without saying that the success of the school in performing its primary function of educating and socializing the young is predicated on regular school attendance by pupils. Although poor attendance (including truancy or unexcused absence from school, cutting classes, tardiness, and leaving school without permission) is seen as an important problem, the limited research data available on the subject seem to reveal that schools are poorly organized to deal with such problems. Most problems of attendance are related to a combination of problems associated with the child, home, school, and community. For example, almost eight percent of urban middle school and senior high pupils miss at least one day of school a month. They are absent because they are afraid to go to school, faced with inadequate food or clothing, or suffering from some other problem associated with their environment.

Social workers are particularly equipped to help teachers understand the environmental forces that impinge upon regular attendance in school. Since Bronfenbrenner published his comprehensive model for portraying the environment's role in child and adolescent development, social workers have had at their disposal a rich body of ecological theories and strong empirical data from which to draw (see Chapter 4). Empirical evidence substantiates the influence of family background, peer-group pressure, social support and community resources, neighborhood safety, and the general quality of life as dynamic forces affecting the pupil's school attendance. In other words, we need teachers and school officials who are trained not just in pedagogy but also in child development and different cultural perspectives if they are to deal successfully with psychological and cultural factors that are reflected in absenteeism and poor performance in schools.

Moreover, school and community leaders must acknowledge that early intervention and tying the improvement of school attendance to dropout prevention programs may be the key. More often than not, truancy and dropping out of high school are decisions teenagers made about school attendance and performance much earlier, perhaps during the pre-adolescent stage. Their decisions may have been influenced by similar decisions made by family members, peer groups, and neighborhood residents.

THE CONCEPT OF COMPULSORY EDUCATION

The notion of compulsory school attendance derived from the belief that democracy requires an educated citizenry and that it is inefficient and impractical to leave the education of the future citizens of the United States to the family. Nolte (1982) suggested that the concept of mass education was intended to be the "leveler and equalizer" of the political invention called "democracy." The notion that education for all, paid for out of the coffer of a grateful government on the grounds that every child, no matter what his or her race, religion, or economic condition, is entitled to at least enough formal training to permit him or her to function as a productive citizen, has now become what the late Justice William O. Douglas called a "Constitutionally protectible interest."

Education is not provided for directly in the United States Constitution and, while there is an increasing role being played by the federal government, it is essentially a function of the states. In perhaps one of the most important cases ever decided by the United States Supreme Court, *Brown* v. *Board of Education,* 1954, deciding that racially segregated, "separate but equal" school facilities were a violation of equal protection, the Court stated as follows:

> Today, education is perhaps the most important function of state and local governments. Compulsory school attendance laws and the great expenditures for education both demonstrate our recognition of the importance of education to our

democratic society. It is required in the performance of our most basic public responsibilities, even service in the armed forces. It is the very foundation of good citizenship. Today it is a principal instrument in awakening the child to cultural values, in preparing him for later professional training, and in helping him to adjust normally to his environment. In these days, it is doubtful that any child may reasonably be expected to succeed in life if he is denied the opportunity of an education. Such an opportunity, where the state has undertaken to provide it, is a right which must be made available to all on equal terms.

States derive their authority to require that all pupils be educated from the implied powers in the Bill of Rights, and this authority is bolstered by the doctrine of *parens patriae,* which means that the state is the father or guardian for minors or others "to the end that the health, patriotism, morality, efficiency, industry, and integrity of its citizenship may be preserved and protected" (*Strangway* v. *Allen,* 1922).

Consistent with the idea of a productive citizen is the belief that the social order must be secured and preserved and that children must be inducted into society's culture and trained in society's value system and skills. As citizens they are expected to obey the law, to vote, to pay taxes, and to serve on juries and in the armed forces when called on to do so. The prevailing ethos is that only individuals with at least a grade-school education can adequately perform all these responsibilities.

By 1918, all 48 states then in the Union had compulsory school attendance laws. The original Compulsory School Attendance Act of 1852, passed in Massachusetts, became the model for most states. It required public school attendance of all able bodied children of a certain age, unless the parent could demonstrate that the child was receiving equivalent instruction elsewhere. The equivalency clause recognized the right of parents to educate their children in private schools if they so desired, but it nonetheless established the right of the state to judge the adequacy of the education of all youths within its borders.

Over the years, parents have been subjected to criminal prosecution, charged with committing a misdemeanor, convicted on the charge that their negligence led to their children's delinquency, and have even had their children taken away from them for failing to comply with state education laws.

Attention is invited to the provisions of the Michigan Revised School Code, Part 24, "Compulsory School Attendance," Michigan Compiled Laws, MCL Sections 380. 156 1-1599 as an example, with its general provisions, exceptions, and enforcement provisions. As to enforcement, see *Eukers* v. *State* (2000), in which the Indiana Court of Appeals upheld the criminal conviction of the mother of a student who accumulated 23 absences in four months. She was sentenced to 180 days in jail, suspended, and to one year's probation. She challenged her conviction unsuccessfully in part on the basis that it was unconstitutional for the Indiana General Assembly to delegate the power to set the number of absences that could result in criminal penalties to the local school board—which the Court of Appeals upheld. Finally, see *Ventura* v. *Hardge* 2000, in which the United States District Court for the Northern District of Texas threw out a civil case by an irate parent who was criminally charged, arrested, and briefly jailed for violation of that state's compulsory attendance law—on the basis of mistaken identity with a parent with the same last name. In holding that there were no damages for what was termed "an honest mistake," the judge in a footnote added: "Nonetheless, the Court strongly advises DISD (Dallas Intermediate School District) to review its preprinted arrest warrant affidavit form in light of Fourth and Fourteenth Amendment case law. DISD may not get so lucky next time!"

Historically, the overriding interest of the state in the education of the child has been not so much the welfare of the child as the welfare of the state. Parents have the duty to educate the child not just because to do so will lead to individual advancement, but more importantly because the child is a citizen of the state and indeed may someday be one of its leaders. (If not a leader, the child still has the obligation to be a responsible citizen.) The prevailing rationale for state control of education is that the state must, as a means of self-protection, require that all children be educated to be good citizens. State courts have defended this position in many compulsory attendance cases, holding that an education is not so much a right guaranteed to individuals as a duty imposed on them, for the public good.

THE FUNCTION OF THE STATE IN ENFORCING COMPULSORY EDUCATION

The concept of education for the public good permits the state to assume that: (1) state legislatures have the power to tax everyone, including the childless and those whose children attend private schools, in order to provide free public education for all; (2) state legislatures have the power to require every parent or guardian to provide for his or her child or ward a basic education in secular subjects; and (3) free education must be secular. States take seriously the idea that the child must be educated; unless the parent can demonstrate alternative means to the satisfaction of the court, the state may insist on educating the child the state's way. For example, a mother in Maryland who was home-schooling her children filed a section 1983 action alleging that monitoring provisions in the Maryland compulsory education law violated the free exercise clause of the First Amendment and the Religious Freedom Restoration Act. The mother claimed that since public schools indoctrinate children in atheistic views, they place a substantial burden on their right to free exercise of religion. The mother refused to fill out a consent form, prepare a portfolio, or allow observation of her teaching. The federal trial court dismissed in favor of the district (*Battles* v. *Anne Arundel,* 1995). The court noted that if the district had tailored the home school curriculum to every parent's demand, it would have involved a greater entanglement with religion.

Operating within constitutional provisions, state legislatures may prescribe admissions and residence requirements for attendance in public schools. Where state constrictions have established the age span within which all have a right to attend public schools, legislatures must also provide at least the specified minimum education; but they are not restricted from creating additional educational opportunities. For example, the constitutional requirement that a state provide schools for all children between the ages of five and twenty years does not prevent the legislature from establishing a nursery school for four-year-olds. Neither does such a provision prohibit the establishment of institutions for higher education (Alexander & Alexander, 1992).

When a state establishes a system of public education, it cannot withhold services arbitrarily from a particular class of persons. Although a state is not required by the federal constitution to provide public education, when it does so, education must be open and available to all (*Griffin* v. *County School Board of Prince Edward County,* 1964). In this regard, children whose parents are illegal aliens are entitled to attend public schools so long as they reside in the United States. The United States Supreme Court has said that if a state is to deny the child of illegal alien parents a free public education, then the state must demonstrate that the denial advances a substantial state interest. It is insufficient for the state to claim that the denial of a free education is justified on the grounds that the education of undocumented children requires the state to spread scarce fiscal resources among greater numbers of children (*Plyler* v. *Doe,* 1982).

States may, however, impose restrictions on school attendance provided they are reasonable. Reasonableness may relate to the health, safety, and welfare of other children or may have to do with the orderly organization and administration of school systems. Residency requirements based on geographical boundaries drawn within and between school districts have been upheld provided there is no intent to discriminate against a certain class of children. For example, the drawing of attendance zones has been upheld as a valid exercise of state prerogative where boundaries were drawn to promote integration.

Most state laws require that children be residents of the school district in which they attend school. A school district has the legal authority to challenge the residence of a pupil. If a pupil changes guardianship solely for the purposes of attending a particular school, he or she may be denied attendance (*In the Matter of Proios* (N.Y. sur. 1981)). The United States Supreme Court has held that an appropriately defined and uniformly applied residence law is constitutionally valid. The state's interest in assuring appropriate educational services to be enjoyed by the residents is rationale enough to support such a requirement (*Martinez* v. *Bynum,* 1983).

A developing trend relating to school district residency is the so-called School Choice movement that intends to provide children and parents with alternatives as to where to attend, and thus introduce competition into elementary and secondary education. In addition to home schooling, charter schools, and vouchers, choice is being provided, or mandated, within and among school districts by law. In Michigan, changes in the State School Aid Act now allow parents to send their children to certain schools outside their home districts if they believe it will benefit their education. Thus, under Section 105 of the act, a student can transfer from his or her home district to a school in the same county or intermediate school district if that other district has elected to be open to other students as a "Section 105 School of Choice." In addition, under Section 105c, a student can also transfer from his or her district to one in another district that has designated itself as a "Section 105 School of Choice" that is in a contiguous intermediate school district. In either case, the student does not need the permission of the home district to transfer, and that student takes the state per pupil "Foundation Allowance" along, which is an average of $6,700 in state funding. The new enrolling school district, however, is not required to provide transportation to the new, nonresident student, with the exception of certain special education students, but only to provide information as to options.

EXEMPTIONS FROM COMPULSORY SCHOOL ATTENDANCE

Compulsory attendance laws are found in all 50 states, the District of Columbia, and Puerto Rico. The general trend among states appears to be toward requiring school attendance at an earlier age and for more years.

States and courts have established conditions under which children are exempt from compulsory public school attendance. Forty-seven states specify exemptions from compulsory attendance because of mental, emotional, or physical disability. Twenty-nine states exempt pupils from compulsory attendance if they have satisfactorily completed a program of prescribed minimum requirements. Completion of the twelfth grade is required in 19 states. The statutes of 24 states specifically mention attendance at a nonpublic school as sufficient reason for exemption from the compulsory attendance provisions. In 14 states a child can be exempted if he or she is receiving instruction from a private tutor.

The absence of pupil transportation is grounds for exemption from compulsory attendance in 15 states, provided the child resides a specific distance from the school to which he or she is assigned. In all but two of those 15 states, the statutes specify the distance the child has to live from school in order to be exempted, the most common distance being 2.5 miles, with different requirements for children of varying ages in several of the 15 states. Exemptions are permitted for legal employment in 23 states. To qualify for this exemption, pupils are required to have a work permit and to have reached a certain age, typically 14 years. In many states, statutes empower the school board, superintendent of schools, or two judicial officials to approve exemptions from compulsory school attendance for reasons other than employment.

The compulsory school attendance requirements for married students vary among the states but there appear to be three patterns. First, married pupils may be exempt from compulsory attendance provisions and may choose not to attend school. Florida statutes allow pupils this option. In Idaho, an official opinion by the attorney general can exempt married pupils. Court decisions in Louisiana and Missouri have established that a married woman is not subject to compulsory attendance provisions. The second pattern, observed in Wisconsin, is that a married pupil can be compelled to attend school. The third pattern has been observed in seven states, where local school authorities have sought to exempt pupils solely on the basis of marriage but were prevented from doing so. Attorneys general in Colorado, Kansas, Kentucky, Minnesota, Arizona, Louisiana, and New Mexico have ruled that marriage alone is not sufficient grounds to justify exemption. The Kentucky opinion invalidated the local school board's authority to exclude the married pupil even when she is pregnant. In Georgia, however, the compulsory attendance statutes empowered the local school board to set rules concerning the rights of married pupils to attend schools.

Religious Grounds

The attempt to use religion or religious beliefs as a basis for seeking exemption from attending any school at all has generally failed. Since the decision in *Pierce* v. *Society of Sisters* (1925), it has generally been assumed that children can be compelled to attend a public, private, or parochial school, but that no child has a right not to attend any school at all.

Other early cases established that the child's and the parent's rights of religious freedom, as protected by the First Amendment of the United States Constitution, were not sufficient to diminish the state's power to compel compulsory attendance. Justice Benjamin Cardozo, in a concurring opinion in *Hamilton* v. *Regents* (1934), maintained that there may be undesirable results when religious scruples predominate over reasonable state laws. In delivering the opinion, Cardozo said:

> Manifestly a different doctrine would carry us to lengths that have never yet been dreamed of. The [defendant], if his liberties were to be thus extended, might refuse to contribute taxes in furtherance of any other end condemned by his conscience as irreligious or immoral. The right of private judgment has never yet been so exalted above the powers and the compulsion of the agencies of government. One who is a martyr to a principle—which may turn out in the end to be a delusion or an error—does not prove by his martyrdom that he has kept within the law.

Following this rationale, other courts have concluded that the individual cannot be permitted, on religious grounds, to decide whether he or she has a duty to obey reasonable civil requirements enacted in the interest of public welfare.

In a 1948 Virginia case, three sets of parents sought to prevent enforcement of compulsory attendance laws on religious grounds. They interpreted the Bible as commanding parents to teach and train their own children and believed that sending their children to public schools was incompatible with the primary religious obligation they felt they owed their Maker. Their willful intent to violate the law was based solely on sincere religious convictions. The court, in deciding against the parents, declared:

> No amount of religious fervor he [parent] may entertain in opposition to adequate instruction should be allowed to work a lifelong injury to his child. Nor should he, for this religious reason, be suffered to inflict another illiterate citizen on his community or his state. (*Rice* v. *Commonwealth*, 1948)

According to the court, religious grounds did not permit individuals to decide whether it was their duty to obey reasonable laws. Although the religious issue was the *ratio decidendi* in this case, the court ruled that the parents were not capable of adequately educating the children themselves.

Until the early 1970s, the prevailing view of the courts had been that religious beliefs cannot interfere with the state's objective of universal compulsory education. The precedent-setting case that radically altered this view was *Wisconsin* v. *Yoder* (1972). Yoder contested the power of the state to require school attendance of Amish children after the eighth grade. Although the issue in this case was limited to the compulsory attendance of Amish children between the time they complete the eighth grade and the time they reach 16 years of age, the case nevertheless had profound implications for all future cases involving compulsory attendance.

The decision of the Supreme Court in this case can be summarized as follows. First, although the state has power to impose reasonable regulations, this power must be balanced against the fundamental rights and interests of individuals. Second, beliefs that are philosophical rather than personal are not sufficient to evoke free exercise of religion. Third, when parents show that enforcement of compulsory education will endanger their religious beliefs, the *parens patriae* power of the state must give way to the free exercise of religion clause of the First Amendment.

The Court acknowledged that the state, having the final responsibility for the education of its citizens, possessed the power to impose reasonable regulations for the "control and duration" of basic education. But it noted:

> This power is not free from a balancing process, however, when it impinges on a basic freedom. . . . The essence of all that has been said and written on the subject is that only those interests of the highest order and those not otherwise served over-balance legitimate claims of free exercise of religion.

The power of the state is not absolute to the exclusion or subordination of other interests, even when the issue is one as legitimate as compulsory attendance.

Almost 20 years later, a Minnesota court found that education constitutes a "compelling interest" (*in the Matter of Welfare of T.K. &*

W.K., 1991). The court noted that the fact that education is a compelling "public interest" gives the state, in its sovereign power, the right to make reasonable laws with regard to education even though some parents may believe that such laws encroach on their religious freedom.

In a Maine case, the state required that information be submitted to the school board for prior approval before allowing home instruction. The parents refused for religious reasons. The court found that providing information to the local school board prior to approval of home instruction was reasonable. It noted that even though the parents were motivated by sincerely held religious beliefs, they still had to fulfill the state's prior approval requirements because the state's "public interest in education" outweighed the parents' private religious beliefs. The state's insistence that parents supply the local school committee with information was not unduly restrictive of religious freedom, given the state's vital interests in education (*Blount* v. *Department of Education and Cultural Services,* 1988).

See also the more recent case of *Francis* v. *Barnes* (1999), in which a federal district court in Virginia upheld the denial of a religious exemption from school attendance based on lack of sufficient information, and also dismissed a civil rights case the aggrieved parents brought against the school growing out of the matter. For an interesting review of case law and developments in this area, see the articles contained in Colloquium: "75 Years After *Pierce* v. *Society of Sisters,*" 78 University of Detroit Mercy Law Review 373 *et. Seq.* (Spring 2001).

Vaccination.   To protect the health and welfare of citizens, states have required that pupils be vaccinated. Courts have generally held that if a parent violates a statute requiring vaccination, the parent is subject to arrest or fine. Religious, conscientious, or scientific objections are not generally accepted as valid reasons for failure to vaccinate children. In the leading cases involving objections to vaccination as a requirement for school attendance, the courts have generally held that: (1) the legislature has the power to enact a statute providing for vaccination and to penalize parents for noncompliance; (2) neither the parent nor the child has a constitutional right to schooling without complying with the statutory requirement of vaccination; (3) a parent cannot escape conviction for failing to have the child vaccinated by demanding that the child be admitted to school unvaccinated; (4) religious objection is not a valid ground for attempting to prevent enforcement of compulsory vaccination and attendance requirements.

Home Schooling and Private Instruction

The state's interest in public education may be stated in terms of two goals: (1) the attainment of knowledge, and (2) socialization. Thus, states usually defend compulsory attendance laws by requiring some assurance of quality of education and by maintaining that attending public schools with other children from various walks of life promotes tolerance and understanding of others. Alexander and Alexander bemoan,

> The value of the public schools as an engine to promote commonality and community interest, as opposed to individual egoism or selfish group interest, has largely fallen by the wayside as legislatures have allowed much greater parental option in permitting children to opt out of public schools and avail themselves of only home or private schooling (1995, p. 24).

In addition to the impact of home and private schooling on the two goals of public education as noted above, there is growing concern regarding the impact of private, for profit providers that contract to run public schools and particularly charter schools (See Note: "The Hazards of Making Public Schooling A Private Business," 112 *Harvard Law Review* 695-712 [Spring 1999]).

There is, however, a growing interest in alternatives to traditional public schools across the country, particularly with charter schools, the traditional sectarian or faith-based private schools,

and also home schooling. The National Home Education Research Institute estimated that there were between 1,300,000 and 1,700,000 children in the K–12 age range being home schooled during 1999–2000, and growing at a rate from 7 percent to 15 percent per year (2002). Religion is the primary stated reason why parents do not want their children to attend public schools. They generally object that their particular sectarian brand of religion is not taught and/or that the public schools are secular. And inevitably, numerous clashes have occurred between home schoolers and those who enforce the compulsory attendance laws of the states. Thus, a group of Texas parents filed suit to make home schooling exempt from that state's compulsory attendance statute and won, arguing that home schooling should be viewed as private schooling (*Texas Education Agency* v. *Leeper,* 1991). Most courts have held that in order to be recognized, a private school must provide instruction equivalent to the free instruction furnished in public schools and must comply with the statutory period of attendance (*State* v. *Garber,* 1966).

Equivalency

The state has the prerogative to define what constitutes equivalent instruction, and the private school must accommodate the state. Although vaguely defining the term "equivalent" as meaning "equal," the courts generally refer to the qualifications of the instructor and the available teaching materials as the primary criteria for determining equivalency of instruction. Should the state require that students be tested, it makes no difference that the private school would rather opt for some other measures of equivalency (*Murphy* v. *State of Arkansas,* 1988). In general courts will uphold the state standards so long as they are reasonable and are not too vague for proper implementation. State equivalency regulations may require that children (a) be taught by a certified teacher; (b) be taught a minimum specified, listed curriculum; (c) fulfill specified minimum attendance standards that are appropriate and will be upheld by the courts; (d) or pass tests as specified by the state (*State* v. *Melin,* 1988; *State* v. *Patzer,* 1986).

Two years after its decision in *Patzer,* the North Dakota Supreme Court declined to reverse its earlier holding that teacher certification requirements did not violate the establishment clause. However, in *State* v. *Anderson* (1988), while affirming the convictions of the parents involved, the court did rule that home schools relying on the private school exception to the compulsory attendance law did not have to comply with all municipal and state health, fire, and safety laws. Subsequent to that case, the North Dakota Legislature amended the law to add a home-based instruction exception. Once again, its meaning and relationship to the private school exception came before the North Dakota Supreme Court which held, in *Birst* v. *Sanstead* (1992) that as the two exceptions were not inconsistent or incompatible, parents were free to elect between them and, if they chose to follow the private school route, they still did not need to comply with all the aforementioned health and safety codes. The court relied substantially on the legislative history of the amendment, finding its intent "to ease the home school situation in North Dakota at that time."

The trend across the country is toward relaxation of rules applying to home schooling in particular. The Michigan Supreme Court, in *People* v. *DeJonge* (1993) dealt with a teacher certification requirement and stated that: "The nearly universal consensus of our sister states is to permit home schooling without demanding teacher certified instruction. Within the last decade, over twenty states have repealed teacher certification requirements for home schools." The *DeJonge* decision held that Michigan's certification requirement for home tutors could not be applied to families who held a sincere religious belief against such certification, as it would constitute a denial of their free exercise of those religious beliefs.

The Demand to Attend

After establishing the right to educate children at home through court challenges and aggressive lobbying for changes in state law over the past few decades, parents favoring home schooling in general are turning their attention back to the public schools. They are asserting the right to have their children participate in public school activities, as well as attend some of the classes being offered, which they cannot provide, or provide as well, at home. In addition to changes in state laws that provide for part-time attendance by nonpublic school children, or attendance in specified activities or classes, the right to do so has also been the subject of litigation. For example, in *Snyder* v. *Charlotte Public Schools,* 421 Mich 517 (1985), the Michigan Supreme Court dealt with the request of a student attending a local Christian school to enroll in the sixth grade band course at the local public school. It was denied because school policy limited enrollment to full time students. When challenged in court, the school relied on numerous statutory provisions authorizing local boards to determine local operating policies and setting curriculum and requirements. In addition, it pointed out that such part time attendance would dilute the school programs for full time students, taking a disproportionate amount of scarce resources, and may cause many administrative and financial problems. The Michigan Supreme Court, however, found differently, relying primarily on a state statute (MCL 380.1147) that provides: "[a] person, resident of a school district [and] . . . at least 5 years of age on the first day of enrollment of the school year, *shall have a right to attend school in the district.*" It held that Section 1147 requires public schools to allow students who reside in the school district to access non-core programs offered by the schools. The court went on to state that as to "nonessential elective courses," such as band, art, domestic science, shop, advanced math and science classes, once they are "offered to public school students in the district, they must also be offered to resident nonpublic school students." Not only in Michigan, but also in other states, another major battleground is over extra-curricular activities, and sports in particular. Those home schooling their children see the benefit of such programs, and since they pay taxes to support them, believe they should be able to participate in them. This issue was tried recently in Michigan in *Reid* v. *Kenowa Hills Public Schools,* Case No 99-10536 CZ (Circuit Court for the County of Washtenaw). Plaintiffs who home schooled their children also wanted them to participate in public school interscholastic athletic programs, but could not because of a rule established by the Michigan High School Athletic Association which required enrollment for at least 20 hours a semester to participate. The parents challenged the rule on numerous constitutional and statutory grounds, and also asserted that athletics were "non-core" programs and came under the ambit of the ruling in *Snyder.* The court, noting that the real distinction was between "curricular" and "non-curricular," stated that interscholastic sports "are non-classroom, competitive, emotionally charged and in part loyalty-driven; non-core courses are classroom activities, only incidentally competitive, generally more objective or intellectual endeavors that do not involve the feelings of loyalty or the privilege of representing the school." Thus, the court granted the defendant school's motion for summary disposition on the *Snyder* claim and on all other bases, and dismissed the case. The plaintiffs have appealed to the Michigan Court of Appeals. In its opinion, the Washtenaw Circuit Court cited a number of bills that had been introduced in the Michigan Legislature, but not passed, that would have explicitly expanded the holding in *Snyder.* This pattern of litigation and legislative changes to provide more attendance in public school curricula by nonpublic students, while encountering resistance by more traditional members on both sides, is nonetheless changing the pattern. Indeed, as a recent set of articles in the *American School Board Journal* (Hardy, "Learning without School," 2001; Talluto, "Ac-

countability for Home Schoolers," 2001) point out, even though there are major concerns with accountability regarding the nonpublic school students, and the "socialization" goal of education, public school districts, such as the Des Moines Public Schools, are making accommodations and providing special assistance to the home schooled students who join them in classes.

Major Problems Associated with Attendance

The most serious problems associated with attendance fall into three categories: (1) absenteeism and tardiness, (2) truancy, and (3) school phobia.

Absenteeism and Tardiness.   Student absenteeism is a major concern for elementary and secondary school principals. The 1998 NCES study found that for elementary and high schools, principals reported that pupil tardiness and pupil absenteeism or class cutting during the 1996–97 school term were among the three most often cited serious or moderate discipline problems (32 percent and 67 percent, respectively, for pupil tardiness; and 17 percent and 52 percent, respectively, for pupil absenteeism/class cutting). Principals in large schools (more than 1,000 pupils) report pupil tardiness as a serious or moderate problem more than those in medium-sized (300–999 pupils) and small schools (fewer than 300 pupils) (64 percent compared with 42 percent and 29 percent, respectively).

Student absenteeism/class cutting was also more of an issue in large schools, with 53 percent of those schools—compared with 24 percent of medium schools and 19 percent of small schools—considering it a serious or moderate problem.

A recent digest of statistics on nonattendance and current literature underscores these high absentee rates and their consequences on delinquency and crime rates, on student achievement, and on dropout rates and later earning potential (DeKalb, 1999). The compulsory attendance laws of most states do not specify the number of absences needed to invoke various possible sanctions, but delegate that function to local school boards to do so in their policies. However, a number of states have mandated such a limit. See a recent compilation in ECS StateNotes, "Attendance," (2001). According to the Education Commission of the States, since 1999 at least 30 states have seen legislation passed amending their truancy laws ("Recent State Legislation: Attendance," ECS Selected State Policies [2002]). Under current laws, parents can face criminal charges for failing to have their children attend school, or civil actions to have them placed under court jurisdiction as wards of the court, and the students can be expelled or placed in detention facilities (McCarthy, McCabe, & Thomas, 1998).

In a Maryland case where two women, each with two children, allowed the children to miss a total of 70 school days, the state sought conviction of the women for violation of the compulsory attendance laws. The women claimed that their constitutional rights of due process were violated because the law imposed "strict liability" by prosecuting parents for actions of their children. The court held that the law, on the contrary, did not prosecute parents for the failure of their children; but prosecuted them for their own failure to see that their children attended school. Performance of such an affirmative duty as imposed by the law is offended by "passive acquiescence (by the parent) in the child's nonattendance of school" (*In re Jeannette L,* 1987).

Truancy. When a child is declared a chronic or habitual truant, the school may institute legal proceedings that may include criminal penalty of the parent. "A 'truant' is defined as a child subject to compulsory school attendance and who is absent without valid excuse from such attendance for a school day or portion thereof" (Ill.—S.H.A. 105 ILCS 5/27-2a).

Truancy charges, however, must be sustained by evidence, and the school must be able to present the factual information necessary to enforce a conviction of parents. In a Minnesota case where the evidence failed, an appellate court ruled that (1) truancy must be proved beyond a reasonable doubt, and (2) the pupil had a right to confront and cross-examine witnesses against him. This court ruled that school attendance records were hearsay and could not be used in court in lieu of a school attendance officer's testimony. Moreover, in truancy cases, the burden of proof is on the state to prove beyond a reasonable doubt that no valid excuse existed for the pupil's absence from school. Pupils are not required to prove that their absences were excused; the state must prove that the absences were unexcused (*In the Matter of Welfare of L.Z.,* 1986). Valid causes for absences may be variously defined by statute as illness, death in the family, family emergency, or situations beyond the control of the student.

School Phobia. School phobia manifests itself in many ways and may occur in varying degrees. It differs from truancy in that a child's truancy is more related to antisocial behavior and rebellion against authority. School phobia, on the other hand, is more related to emotional disturbances in the child and is manifested by separation anxiety among young children, fear of bullies, lack of skills needed to handle social interactions, lack of self-esteem, and sheer fright from the stress of being away from the security of the home (exaggerated parent-child dependency).

Displays and behavior that may be signs of school phobia are throwing tantrums, complaining of stomachaches, headaches, or nausea. Experts say that about 10 percent of U.S. school children suffer from this illness in its mildest form and about one percent in its severest condition. Several other warning signs can alert teachers and social workers that a child is school phobic, including crying fits in class, withdrawn behavior, and excessive time spent in the nurse's office. Helping a child to overcome school phobia requires a team effort that includes the parents, teacher, school social workers, and perhaps significant others.

One approach to dealing with school phobia is the behavioral intervention approach developed by Blagg (1981), which incorporates the following steps.

1. A detailed clarification of the problems involving elimination of possible medical causes and identification and investigation of precipitating and maintaining factors
2. Desensitization of child and parent worries
3. Elimination of maintaining factors through contingency management (parent education is important in this phase)
4. Return to full-time attendance even if it must be forced
5. Follow-up to monitor subsequent absences

STRATEGIES TO DEAL WITH ABSENTEEISM

Howard and Anderson (1978) conducted an extensive review of the literature on absenteeism and school dropouts and discovered that the decrease in pupil motivation leading to attendance problems is part of a fairly predictable sequence. First the pupil's interest lags, which leads to poor achievement and lower grades and encourages the skipping of classes. The pupil, who is then in trouble with school authorities, becomes disruptive and is expelled from class. When his or her parents become involved, the pupil becomes increasingly negative and defensive and eventually decides to flee. Pupils' reasons for leaving range from employment, marriage, bad health, and a desire to be with friends who are not in school, to the inability to achieve, dislike of school, and rebellion against parents. These reasons may reflect deeper underlying factors deriving from two sources: family history and academic difficulties.

The important factor in family history is socioeconomic status. Typically, pupils who become chronic truants and poor achievers are members of families of low socioeconomic status. Their learning environment is both generally inferior and specifically inadequate when compared with that of pupils from middle-class homes. A number of studies reveal that the relationship between poor-achieving pupils and family members is less affectionate than among high-achieving pupils and their families. As might be expected, the parents of poor achievers tend to have less education than the parents of achievers. In addition, their parents' values tend to be either neutral or negative with respect to education, whereas the parents of achievers tend to place a value on education. It has also been shown that the relationship between poor achievers and their parents tends to be more distant than that which exists between achievers and their parents. Parents of achievers also show a greater inclination to push their children toward achievement, not only in school but in other areas as well; the parents of poor achievers appear to demand less in the way of specific performance from their children. Broken homes, working parents, and other forms of family disorganization are found in a much higher proportion among poor achievers.

Social workers can play a leading role in helping educators to understand that the poor achiever's alienation from school is not so much a result of discriminatory or rejecting attitudes of teachers and other school personnel (although the importance of this factor should not be underestimated); it is in greater measure a reflection of a curriculum that is too demanding of the poor achiever. Too often the result is confusion, demoralization, resentment, and low self-esteem. The pupil frequently feels frustrated, and this frustration is often manifested by hostile, aggressive behavior. Under many circumstances, then, the school setting is a battleground where the pupil settles his or her personal problems.

More often than not, poorly achieving truants do not have just one problem; their problems are frequently multidimensional. They may be skipping school to be with accepting peers. There may be a classroom situation to which they have not learned to adjust, or they may feel that the school situation is life-threatening. Truancy may be their method of getting back at parents. From the point of view of the teacher, these pupils' behavior is frequently seen as maladjustment. But from the pupils' point of view, this behavior may be a means of adapting or adjusting in accordance with their own frame of reference. Occasionally, these pupils may be solving a serious problem that they may have had for a long time, in the best and only way they know how.

A contributing factor to truancy and to lack of achievement in school may be a conflict in value systems. These lower-class pupils are being forced to conform to middle-class standards, which in most cases do not have any substantial meaning for them. For many of these pupils, personal contacts with the school and teachers may be their only intimate, effective interaction with middle-class values.

Another factor related to student achievement, truancy, and poverty is the mobility or transiency of some students. Biernat and Jax (1999) note that the fairly well accepted link between poverty and student achievement needs finer scrutiny to define the factors that tie them together. One of those factors is the high mobility of the students; frequent moves are much more prevalent in poor families, and are caused by a variety of socio-economic and practical reasons; and the moves between schools compromise student achievement. There are, however, many limits on what states can do to limit this mobility, and the chief tools have been, as described earlier, truancy and child neglect proceedings, which do not get to root causes.

The only logical response of educators to truancy, according to Hoback (1976), is to adapt to the new legal and social milieu. He suggests that administrators begin by accepting the reality that there is today little power inherent in the positions of principal or teacher. The power must come from the performance of the individual occupying the position and from purposeful planning and organization. Hoback says that "we must have a clear rationale for what we do, especially in matters of compulsory attendance. Rather than attendance being an end in itself, the alternate philosophy that it should be a means to serving educational ends seems more fitting for coping with today's problems." He suggests four goals for a new attendance policy: (1) Pupils should be made to feel a sense of responsibility. They should be made to feel that their presence is important. They should also learn the courtesy of seeking to negotiate solutions to problems. Allowing them to remain dependent on parents and educators is a disservice to all concerned. (2) Truancy should be treated as a symptom of a problem that needs to be dealt with. It may indicate an emotional problem, a family problem, a learning disability, or ineffective teaching. Making pupils feel that they are losers just because they are truants merely compounds the problem. (3) Out-of-building educational opportunities must be taken advantage of. (4) Pupils should relate attendance to the total pattern of their learning needs. The components of learning are: identifying a problem, planning the solution to the problem, carrying out the solution, and evaluating the results and the process. If pupils are just passive observers while the teacher does all this for them, they will not feel a need to be present. In Chapter 8 we describe the programmatic components necessary to improve the schools' milieu.

Grade Reduction

School systems have used a variety of strategies to reduce truancy. These include alternative individualized programs, punishment (such as lowered grades) for absences, and rewards (such as parties or higher grades) for good attendance. Some school districts also use pupil aides, counselors, welfare caseworkers, and "buddies" to improve pupil attendance. James Mervilde (1981) divides strategies to deal with absenteeism into six categories: (1) plans that are primarily punitive and restrictive in nature; (2) plans that have parental involvement as a primary ingredient; (3) plans that are pupil-centered, that is, place the burden for change on the pupil; (4) plans that are based upon counseling approaches; (5) plans that stress the involvement of community and social service agencies; and (6) alternatives that are not normally employed in a traditional school setting.

For many years, educators in the United States considered grade reduction to be one of the best means to combat truancy. Researchers now argue against such practices. They contend that there is very little evidence that such practices motivate pupils to attend school regularly. Grade point reduction can instead serve to alienate pupils and to drive them further from school. State statutes generally provide the authority for schools to use grade reduction as an enforcement device, and often rely on the local school districts to develop policies to do so within their discretion. In Michigan, this authority was discussed in an opinion of the attorney general, OAG No. 5414 (December 20, 1978), in which he concluded that "School authorities may determine that attendance, class participation and similar factors are proper educational values bearing on a student's academic achievement; therefore, a school district may consider attendance in determining a student's grade in a class." The devil, however, is in the details, and how the local policy is drafted.

In Harrison, Michigan, school authorities adopted an attendance policy for the high school that denied academic credit for each subject in which the pupil missed more than seven days of class during the term. Specifically, the policy provided three options for such a pupil: (1) the pupil could attend the class for the rest of the term with no hope of credit in that class; (2) the pupil could take a "home pass," an agreement to stay off school grounds during the class; (3) the pupil could appeal to an attendance appeal board for an opportunity to obtain credit for the class. One pupil who had been denied credit brought a class action suit on behalf of all past, present, and future pupils, challenging the attendance policy on both statutory and constitutional grounds. In *Sprague* v. *Harrison Community Schools* (1980), the Circuit Court of Clare County granted the plaintiffs motion for summary judgment, invalidating the attendance policy, reinstating academic credit of the pupils who would have

completed the courses had the policy not been enforced, and providing opportunity for remedial and tutoring services to those pupils who had accepted a home pass.

The court argued that by creating the attendance board in the absence of express authority to issue penalties for attendance, the school board illegally displaced the attendance officer, who had this function under Michigan's truancy statute. The court further ruled that by failing to distinguish between excused and unexcused absences, the attendance policy also violated the purposes of the state's compulsory education laws. Thus deciding the matter on statutory grounds, the court did not consider the plaintiff's constitutional claims. Earlier, an appellate court in Colorado had invalidated on statutory grounds an almost identical local attendance policy in *Gutierrez* v. *School District* (1978). In adjudicating complaints against schools that impose academic penalties for absences, the courts and other tribunals have been mixed in their reasoning. For example, the New Jersey Commissioner of Education in the case of *Minorities* v. *Phillipsburg Board of Education,* decided against a school policy that gave a pupil a zero for every day of unexcused absence and a failing quarterly grade if a test was given on the missed day, because he considered the penalty too harsh (Zirkel & Gluckman, 1982). In the first reported court decision concerning grade reduction (*Dorsey* v. *Bale,* 1975), a Kentucky appellate court invalidated a policy that reduced grades for unexcused absences. It reasoned that since the definition of excused absences included suspensions, the policy imposed an additional punishment for the suspension-causing conduct that was not expressly authorized by state statutes.

Case Illustration: *Knight* v. *Board of Education* (1976)

Knight, a senior at the defendant district high school, did not attend classes during two days of the spring semester. The school administration did not excuse the absences, and as a result and in consideration of the school board's policy that grades would be lowered by one letter grade per class absence, the plaintiff's grades were lowered. Knight alleged that the consequences imposed upon him as the result of the refusal of the school administration to excuse the absences deprived him of substantive due process of law. In another early landmark decision, an Illinois appellate court described its substantive due process test with regard to an attendance policy that called for a reduction of one letter grade for each day of unexcused absence: "to weigh the severity of the punitive effect of this sanction against the severity of the conduct sanctioned."

The court hearing the *Knight* case referred to *Goss* v. *Lopez* (discussed at length in Chapter 6) and acknowledged that the Illinois Constitution, like that of Ohio, provided that all youths of a certain age were entitled to a free public school education. Therefore, the rights incident to the receipt of an education as granted by the State of Illinois to its youths would, as in *Goss,* entitle those youths to the protection of procedural due process. However, in *Knight* the right incident to the receipt of an education that was claimed to be impaired was not the opportunity to attend class but the receipt of grades. In *Goss,* the court acknowledged the impairment of employment opportunities caused by a permanent school record containing derogatory information about a pupil. Despite the analogy that can be drawn between the effects of pupil expulsion and of reduction of a pupil's grades, the court in *Knight* held that when a grade was dispensed by a teacher within that teacher's subjective discretion, "we can see no justification for court intervention."

Although the court in *Knight* drew heavily on *Goss* v. *Lopez* in determining whether the student's rights were entitled to the protection of procedural due process, the court referred to two related court opinions to arrive at a test by which to determine if the violation of Knight's rights amounted to a deprivation of due process. The test articulated by the court was to weigh the severity of the punitive effect of the sanction against the severity of the conduct being pun-

ished. The court held that the reduction in plaintiff's grades by one letter grade for a period of one quarter of the year in three subjects in consequence of two days of truancy was not so harsh as to deprive him of substantive due process.

Knight's counsel also claimed, basing his charge on the decision in *Jacobs* v. *Benedict* (1973), that he had been deprived of substantive due process and equal protection of the law because there was no rationale between grades and the misconduct of truancy. As in all cases concerning the subject of grading prior to *Knight,* the court found that most grading systems commingle factors of pupil conduct with scholastic attainment in rendering grades, and that it is difficult to see how grading can be undertaken sensibly without consideration being given to the pupil's conduct and effort. "Particularly among inept pupils, it is common to give a higher grade to those who attend class and try than to the laggard truant. Truancy is a lack of effort and plaintiff here exhibited a lack of effort. There was, therefore, a sufficiently rational connection between the grade reduction he was given and his truancy to satisfy the requirements of both equal protection and substantive due process."

Federal appeals courts seem to be in conflict with the United States Supreme Court's ruling in *Goss.* In that case, the Supreme Court held that it made no difference how severe the deprivation; what was important was that a deprivation of a property or liberty interest had occurred. In the Illinois appellate court, as articulated in *Knight,* the test was one of the severity of the deprivation.

Two years after the *Knight* case, in *Hamer* v. *Board of Education* (1978), another Illinois appellate court similarly rejected a variety of other constitutional and statutory challenges to a high school rule that called for a grade reduction of three percent for each unauthorized absence. *Hamer* concerned a pupil at one of the district's high schools who had left the campus during a school day without proper permission. The resulting absences from her remaining classes for the day were unexcused. Hamer received a three percent reduction in the total grade for each class missed as a result of the unauthorized absences. The plaintiff was advised by the assistant superintendent of schools that the grade reduction was board policy and that regulations had been adopted by the high school pursuant to said policy. Although plaintiff's parents exchanged correspondence with school authorities and met with the principal, they were advised that such absences without notification were unauthorized under the rules and that she was thus subject to punishment. No hearing before the school board was allowed.

Board policy provided that each principal was allowed to adopt rules and regulations that would remain in effect so long as they were permitted by law and by the policies of the board. In other words, the board had delegated its authority to impose attendance-related discipline of the school districts' pupils, as provided by the appropriate state statutes, to the individual principals. There was no indication in any school board policy that a grade reduction should or could be imposed upon a pupil as a disciplinary measure unrelated to the scholastic attainments of the pupil. Thus, the plaintiff contended that the sanction was not authorized either by statute or by regulation of the board and that it offended constitutional guarantees.

In *Hamer* the court reaffirmed the *Knight* decision by acknowledging that it had been established that rights incident to a public education are property rights that are entitled to both substantive and procedural due process. The court in *Hamer* also accepted the *Goss* v. *Lopez* theory that educational and employment opportunities can be impaired by a poor school record. Although it acknowledged that *Knight* had established that a pupil was not deprived of substantive due process as a result of a grade reduction imposed for an unexcused absence, the court in *Hamer* believed the plaintiff was entitled to be heard on the question of whether the grade reduction sanctioned for unauthorized absence was the approved policy of the board. Further, the plaintiff was entitled to be advised what, if any, procedural remedies were available

to her before such a sanction could be imposed and whether the application of such a rule arbitrarily and capriciously resulted in a grade reduction without the subjective determination of the classroom teacher.

In the early 1980s, the grade reduction issue began to surface in federal courts. In *Raymon* v. *Alvord Independent School District* (1981), a federal circuit court of appeals held that the minor decrease of a pupil's grade point average due to an unexcused absence was so insignificant that no substantial federal question was presented. In *Church of God* v. *Amarillo Independent School District* (1981), a federal district court also held that a school board policy limiting the number of excused absences for religious holidays was a violation of the pupil's First Amendment right to free exercise of religion.

Restricting Extracurricular Activities

Restricting truants from extracurricular activities may make things worse. It often isolates pupils from the positive influences of teachers, counselors, and coaches, thereby reinforcing feelings of failure and rejection. Truants should be encouraged to participate in both school extracurricular activities and community-based programs. These programs may range from YMCA or YWCA programs to sand-lot football. Wynn et al. developed a typology of community supports that delineate their range and purpose: (1) opportunities to participate in organized groups, (2) avenues for contributing to the well-being of others, (3) sources of personal support, and (4) access to and use of community facilities and events (1988).

Curtailing Driving Privileges

Some states are trying to enhance attendance by applying penalties for truancy that strike at something very coveted by students, especially in high school: the right to obtain, and retain, their drivers' licenses. In California, a student who is reported for a fourth time as a truant in the same school year will be placed under the jurisdiction of the juvenile court which may, among other actions, suspend or revoke the student's driving privileges (Annotated California Code, Section 13202.7). In Tennessee, a statute passed in 2000 provides that a student will be denied a driver's license or permit if he or she has withdrawn from secondary school or has more than 10 consecutive or 15 total unexcused absences while attending a course leading to a GED. A student will be considered "withdrawn" if he or she has more then 10 consecutive or 15 days total unexcused absences (Tennessee Code Annotated, Section 49-6-30 17, see also Florida Statutes Annotated, Section 322.09 1). Finally, a "truancy package" of bills was introduced in the Michigan House of Representatives in 2001. House Bill 4845, among other things, provides that the probate court, upon obtaining jurisdiction over a juvenile for truancy, and within five days after a hearing, must enter an order requiring the juvenile to attend school, and also requires the secretary of state to suspend the juvenile's driver's license for not more than two years under certain conditions. And if his or her license had already been suspended for truancy, then the new suspension would begin to run at the end of the suspension then in effect. The court could also shorten the suspension if the student later satisfied attendance requirements (HB 4845, House Legislative Analysis of House Bills 4842, 4844 and 4845, 2001).

Providing Incentives

The point is that strategies to reduce absenteeism should be built around incentives. Some schools employ grade promotion, modification of previously earned failing grades (through extra assignments), or access to summer employment as inducements to improving attendance. A few teen-parent programs have successfully used onsite, subsidized, or specially arranged daycare as an incentive for continued school attendance by adolescent mothers. More publicized are several recent initiatives that guarantee college scholarships, access to vocational training, or full-time jobs to targeted at-risk pupils who successfully complete high school requirements and graduate. The most well-known of these is perhaps the "I Have A Dream" program, in which a wealthy businessman returned to his elementary school in East Harlem and offered students in the sixth-grade class college scholarships if they graduated from high school. What is perhaps less well known is that the businessman also hired a full-time social worker to follow the class through its school years, providing encouragement and individual attention and helping the students to solve problems that arose along the way.

Another example of a community-supported incentive program is one run by a national food chain in Cincinnati, which provides free groceries and monetary incentives to disadvantaged elementary school pupils for good attendance, good grades, and positive attitudes. Pupils can earn up to $1,000 per year toward college tuition. Another program, developed in the Los Angeles Unified School District, is directed specifically at improving attendance. Persons acting as "mediators" between school counselors and students, teachers, parents, or friends provide rewards to students who improve their attendance at school. In each of these examples, school districts have recognized the powerful role incentives can play in motivating student performance. Social workers can bring many insights to these efforts in order to make them more successful.

The Wisconsin Legislative Audit Bureau recently undertook a comprehensive study to examine that state's truancy laws, how they were implemented by schools and local governments, and how effective they were in reducing nonattendance. It issued a report entitled "Truancy Reduction Efforts" in August of 2000, which contains a comprehensive review of that state's truancy laws, a comparison to those of certain other Midwestern states, statistics on truancy from 23 Wisconsin school districts, and the results of interviews with school personnel, law enforcement officials, and municipal judges. It provides an excellent, comprehensive review of the efforts of one state and its subdivisions in addressing the truancy problem, and whether, and which, are effective.

Nontraditional Alternatives

Many critics of U.S. public schools question whether there should be compulsory attendance. They argue that a pluralistic society requires that the equivalency or adequacy clauses in compulsory school attendance laws be eliminated so that there is legal provision for that which is unique or different. Some critics believe that the twentieth century trend of extending the school-leaving age has been a bane rather than a blessing. They argue that the extension of compulsory attendance to the later teen-age years has largely been a byproduct of the economic depression of the 1930s and the increasing power of labor unions, whose main interest was to keep youths out of the labor market. The results, they say, have brought little benefit to the laboring man, a loss to the general public, and damage to the schools (the last as a result of the unwise attempt to force inappropriate schooling upon rebellious youths). Underlying this criticism is the notion that formal schooling is not the only path to success. What is needed, critics contend, is a massive effort to devise alternative means of education appropriate to various talents, conditions, and careers. "We should be experimenting," writes Paul Goodman, "with different kinds of schools, no school at all, the real city as school, farm schools, practical apprenticeships, guided travel, work camps, little theatre, and local newspapers, [and] community service. . . . Probably more than anything, we need a community . . . spirit, in which many adults who know anything, and not just professional teachers, will pay attention to the young" (1964).

Another commentator writing in *National Review* (Toby, 1999), discussed the futility of compulsory attendance, noting that those students that are not getting or cannot get what is being taught are wasting their time and can adversely affect those around them, including their teach-

ers who get discouraged and, in many instances, burn out and leave the profession.

Building Support Systems and Networks

Most research emphasizes the broker role and the need to build systems of social support for at-risk youth. Such systems include "mainstreaming" them into existing community-based programs as well as regular educational activities at school. Social support has also been defined as the provision of aid, affirmation, and affect. By *aid* we refer to practical services and material benefits. *Affirmation* refers to feedback that raises self-esteem and strengthens identity. *Affect* refers to the showing of affection, caring, and nurturance. More recently, Heller (1991) and colleagues suggested that social support should also include social structures such as the school, and caring relationships should foster the development of competence, esteem, and belonging.

To understand the role of social support more clearly, we need to understand better the nature of networks of social support and how such networks can be strengthened through the understandings that school social workers bring to them. Social workers are in the position to be the focal point of such networks on behalf of pupils. Using Bronfenbrenner's conception of ecology, social workers as brokers, mediators, advocates, or conferees seek to adjust the environment to the needs of the pupil and his/her family by connecting them to needed resources, negotiating problematic situations, and changing existing social structures that limit the pupils' ability to function independently and with confidence. For example, the social worker can play a leading role in negotiating on behalf of the pupil whose attendance is affected by lack of nutrition or clothing and abuse or neglect. The social worker is reminded, as we pointed out in Chapter 3, that the pupil and the family are part of a social system—a complex of elements in mutual interaction—and the worker is guided by the principle that any change effected will result in a multitude of interrelated changes, because no one part of the system can change without changes taking place in other parts. This affords social workers great influence in motivating the pupil. Social workers have a unique opportunity as facilitators and enablers to influence all components of the network to create a climate and outcomes that are sensitive (empathetic) to the needs of the pupil. For example, activities and goals that are developed in partnership with the pupil on behalf of the pupil are much more likely to motivate school attendance than those that offer support or direction primarily aimed at the control of behavior.

CONCLUSION

In this chapter we have explored why poor attendance has become an increasingly serious problem in the schools, particularly in the secondary schools. Schools in some large cites have reported absenteeism rates as high as 50 percent per day. Teachers, counselors, and administrators have been forced to spend inordinate amounts of time on the details of managing attendance. It goes without saying that when time is taken away from the primary instructional duties for which school personnel are employed, the quality of teaching and learning in the schools eventually suffers. "Blue ribbon" studies have spelled out in detail where the deficiencies in public school education lie. Clearly, pupils cannot be taught if they do not attend school. The challenge for schools, therefore, is to create workable solutions based on the needs of pupils as well as the mission of the school.

The typical chronic truant is a youngster whose problems can be traced to the home, the school, and the community. The child is unhappy at home for myriad reasons and is not likely to be living with both parents or to be enrolled in a college preparatory program, or to have a high IQ and high class rank. He or she is likely to be a member of a minority group living in an urban setting. The system of rewards and sanctions for teachers who do or do not enforce attendance

policies appears weak; also, pupils are not provided with very strong incentives to stay in school on a regular basis (there are inflexible academic standards, inappropriate curricula, and teachers who lack the necessary skills to deal with problem pupils).

In his study of relationships between attendance, curriculum, school organization, and staff characteristics, Wright (1978), found that there was a strong statistical correlation between attendance and age of the staff in urban schools. Urban schools with younger staffs had a high rate of attendance. In addition, urban schools with work programs offering credit without classroom requirements had high attendance averages. Urban schools with low pupil-to-teacher ratios tended to have good attendance. In suburban schools, work programs and health and physical education classes were found to be related to good attendance. Large suburban schools had poorer attendance records than small suburban schools. Suburban schools with open campuses had better attendance records than those with closed campuses.

What does this mean for the school social worker? First, the social worker must appreciate the fact that poor attendance by pupils has negative consequences for all concerned; therefore, to be viable, a solution must protect all interests. Absenteeism may be a result of organizational inertia and curriculum inadequacy, but these may be only two of many causes. Many schools that operate as open systems, with broad and flexible programs, continue to face severe attendance problems. Obviously, increasing absenteeism has deep roots leading in many directions. Social workers can help school officials, parents, and pupils to understand the ecological dimensions of these various forces. Chapter 12 is devoted to a discussion of the various roles social workers may play in assisting their clients to overcome these forces.

There are four sets of behaviors social workers in schools may exhibit in helping pupils to improve their attendance and school performance. Social workers may act as (1) brokers; (2) mediators; (3) advocates; and (4) conferees. The broker stands at the interface between the pupil's need and the resources in the school and community, creating a support system that connects needs with resources. But brokerage is not enough, because each (the pupil and the school) does not recognize their complementary of interest. Thus through the role of mediator, the social worker tries to help the pupil and the school to recognize their complementary of interest and perform accordingly. As an advocate, the social worker demands that the school provide the pupil with the benefits to which he/she is entitled.

In the fourth role, the social worker determines with the pupil, the family, and the school (1) the tasks to be accomplished to improve attendance and school performance, and (2) a course of action to be pursued. The social worker confers with the pupil, his/her family, and school officials, providing information on alternative courses of action and the possible consequences of each. The social worker encourages the pupil to actively participate in the decision to be made.

Drawing upon general systems theory and the ecological perspective, social workers have a solid foundation from which to help school personnel understand the problems of absenteeism and the effect of the environment on the truant— that is, to view the pupil and the environment not as two separate entities but as an interactional field. The truant may thus be viewed less as a recalcitrant than as an individual responding to impinging forces.

The social worker's goal is to enhance individual social functioning wherever the need for such enhancement is either socially or individually perceived. Social workers, in helping pupils with their school adjustment and/or attendance problems, may be required to assist school personnel in exploring and identifying nonschool factors that contribute to adjustment and/or attendance problems, to assist officials in determining the severity of these problems, and to refer pupils to appropriate social services outside of the school.

When schools are viewed as social systems, school social workers often operate as one of the human feedback mechanisms that assess the activities of the school. Such assessment data are then used formatively to improve the operation of the school. Social workers, far more than teachers, counselors, or administrators, have an opportunity to hear from pupils and their parents statements concerning the extent to which the schools are disappointing or lack meaning for them. Pupils, particularly those in lower grades and those who are low achievers, rarely possess the fluency and insight to state their cases in terms that are readily comprehensible to those who make decisions about school organization, curriculum changes, and procedures. Social workers, by virtue of their special training, know, at least to some significant degree, how to elicit and interpret pupil responses in order to be useful in a formative fashion. Social workers in schools have an excellent opportunity to be not a remediator (though the function is essential at times) but rather a prime agent in the continuous reconstruction of the school as a social system, with a value climate, rules, and sanctions.

When schools are examined as microcosmic cultures, they frequently are found to operate as social structures that limit the capacity of some pupils to adjust. Hoback (1976) reminds educators that the solution to their attendance headaches lies in finding answers to some very crucial questions rather than in trying to regain authoritarian power—to return to the "good old days" of paternalism. One of the questions he asks may indeed be better answered by the social worker than by the school principal:

> Can we build an educational program (and therefore an attendance policy and practice) on positive reinforcements, or are we hopelessly trapped in the negative "truant officer" syndrome? This implies a curriculum in which the student is an active participant, not a passive observer (p. 24).

We have also tried in this chapter to identify the myriad factors—social, economic, religious, and philosophical—that affect regular attendance among pupils. We have tried to show how society has responded to these factors, particularly through the courts. A review of selected court actions reveals that although compulsory education is viewed as essential for an informed citizenry, rules governing compulsory education vary among the states.

Generally, however, state courts have held that the state may not require all children to attend public school; that the state may require children to attend a public, private, or parochial school; that compulsory attendance laws must be reasonably administered; that parents may use as a legal defense the argument that they had good reason for not sending their child to school; and that a married girl of school age cannot be compelled to attend school. The state courts are in disagreement as to whether parents, in order to meet the requirements of the law, may teach their children at home or may employ a tutor to teach them; however, the courts have held that in order to do so, parents must be able to show that the children are receiving substantially the same educational opportunity they would receive in a public school. Some state courts have explicitly stated that such statutes require the attendance of a child in a public or private school and that education by a parent is not the equivalent of education at a private school. In general, parents have not been permitted to use the defense that a compulsory school attendance law is in violation of their religious principles.

Pupil absenteeism seems to grow more serious each year. Educators and other experts offer varying explanations and solutions, and despite the active participation of the courts in this matter, all solutions seem ineffective. Social workers in schools have much to contribute to an insightful solution. For example. the ecological perspective informs us that the solution to poor attendance in schools may be found in the way in which schools operate. It might sound trite, but the solution is to make the education provided by the school more relevant to the needs of pupils.

Social workers know, perhaps better than other school personnel, that the key to controlling and guiding pupil behavior is the understanding of needs, motives, and interests. An essential role of the social worker in schools, then, is to assist the teacher in (1) relating school work to the pupil's needs, motives, and interests, and (2) appraising the results of teaching and learning in terms of their effect upon the needs, interests, and motivation of pupils.

Social workers can be instrumental in helping school personnel to understand that the pupil's motivation must be considered in a holistic context—that they must analyze the relationship between the child and his or her total environment. The social workers' knowledge of human behavior in the social environment helps them to understand that all human behavior is goal-oriented. Pupils have goals. When there are barriers to their learning goals, they release tension either by withdrawing (absenteeism) or by being aggressive, or both.

The task of the social worker can be viewed as finding ways to break down the barriers. The first step may be to assess the learning environment and aspects of it that encourage children to withdraw. Some factors of assessment are: instructional materials, quantity and quality of support personnel, how subject matter is presented, types of activities students are involved in, classroom management techniques, students' learning styles, level of social interaction, physical structure and design of the environment, and flexibility to meet the unique needs of different pupil groups, such as minorities and pregnant girls.

FOR STUDY AND DISCUSSION

1. You are the chairperson of a committee of your state association of school social workers. Your association has been asked to prepare a policy statement on compulsory school attendance in your state.

a. What issues would you consider in preparing the statement?

b. What would be the likely position of the committee?

2. Do you believe that states' compulsory school attendance requirements are obsolete and are another example of too much government interference in personal lives?

3. From a social work perspective, what are the real dangers of instruction at home rather than at school?

4. What are the pros and cons of grade reduction as a strategy for dealing with chronic truants?

5. If your principal decided to implement a grade reduction program as a means of controlling attendance, what specific guidelines would you recommend? (Use the cases cited in this chapter.)

6. If you were a school board member, what would be your practical concerns with high absenteeism in your district?

ADDITIONAL READING

Bodden, A. (1997). Perceptions of bullying in relation to positions within a school system. *School Social Work Journal, 22*(1).

Dailey, M. B. (1999). Home school children gaining limited access to public schools. *Journal of Law and Education, 28,* 25.

Edelman, M. W. (1996). *The state of America's children yearbook.* Washington DC: Children's Defense Fund.

Fossey, R. (1996). School dropout rates: Are we sure they are going down? *Phi Delta Kappan, 78*(2), 140–144.

Grob, W. (2000). Access denied: Prohibiting home-schooled students from participating in public-school athletics and activities. *Georgia State University Law Review, 16,* 823.

Hicks-Coolick. A. (1996). Decreasing school non-attendance in a special education high school for students with learning disabilities, *School Social Work Journal, 21* (Fall).

Lamdin, D. J. (1995). Evidence of student attendance as an independent variance in education production functions. *Journal of Education Research, 98*(3).

Prather, J. (2000). Part-time public school attendance and the freedom of religion: *Yoder's* impact upon *Thompson. Journal of Law and Education, 29,* 553.

Russo, C. J. (1997). *The yearbook of education law.* Dayton, OH: Education Law Association.

Thompson, T. (2000). Home schooling and "shared" enrollment: Do Nebraska public schools have an obligation to provide part-time instruction? *Nebraska Law Review, 78,* 840.

REFERENCES

Alexander, K., & Alexander, D. M. (1992). *American public school law.* St. Paul, MN: West Publishing Co.

Alexander K., & Alexander, D. M. (1995). *The law of school, students and teachers in a nutshell.* St. Paul, MN: West Publishing Co.

Battles v. *Anne Arundel County Board of Education,* 904 F.Supp. 471, 105 Educ.L.Rep. 93 (D. Md. 1995).

Biernat, L., & Jax, C. (1999). Limiting mobility and improving student achievement. *Hamline Law Review, 23,* 1.

Birst v. *Sanstead,* 493 N.W.2d 690, 79 Ed. Law Rep. 1026 (N.D. 1992)

Blagg, N. R. (1981). *A behavioral approach to school refusal. Behavior modification in education, perspectives (5).* University of Exeter, UK: School of Education.

Blount v. *Department of Educational and Cultural Services.* 551 A.2d 1377 (Ma. 1988).

Brown v. *Board of Education,* 347 U.S. 483, 74 S. Ct. 686, 98 L. Ed. 873 (1954).

Church of God v. *Amarillo Independent School District,* 511 F.Supp. 613 (N.D. Tex. 1981).

DeKalb, J. (1999). Student truancy. *ERIC Digest, Number 125.*

Dorsey v. *Bale,* 521 S.W. 2d 76, Ky. App. (1975)

ECS Selected State Policies (2002). Recent state legislation. *Attendance.*

ECS State Notes (2001). Attendance. *Habitual truancy: Examples of state definitions.*

Eukers v. State, 728 N.E. 2d 219, Md. App. (2000).

Francis v. Barnes, 69 F. Supp. 2d 801 (E.D. Va. 1999).

Goodman, P. (1964). *Compulsory mis-education.* New York: Horizon Press.

Goss v. Lopez. 419 U.S. 565. 95 S.Ct. 729 (1975).

Griffin v. *County School Board of Prince County,* 377, U.S. 218, 84 S.Ct. 1226 (1964).

Gutierrez v. *School District,* 585 P.2d 935 (E. Colo. App. 1978).

Hamer v. *Board of Education,* 383 N.E.2d 23 (Ill. App. 1978).

Hamilton v. *Regents,* 293 U.S. 245, 55 S.Ct. 197 (1934).

Hardy, L. (2001). Learning without school. *American School Board Journal, 188,* 14.

Heller, K., Price, R. H., & Hogg, I. R. (1991). The role of social support in community and clinical intervention. In I. G. Sarason, B. R. Sarason, & G. R. Pierce (Eds.), *Social support: An interactional view: issues in social support research.* New York: Wiley.

Hoback, J. R. (1976). The problem of attendance. *National Association of Secondary School Principals,* (Bulletin 60). No. 4.

Howard, M. A., & Anderson. R. J. (1978). Early identification of potential school dropouts: A literature review. *Child Welfare, 57*(4), 221–231.

Jacobs v. *Benedict,* 301 N.E.2d 723 (Ohio Ct. C.P. 1973).

In re Jeanette L, 71 Md. App. 70, 523 A.2d 1048 (Md. App. 1987).

Knight v. *Board of Education,* 345 N.E.2d 299 (Ill. Supp. Ct. 1976).

Martinez v. *Bynum.* 461 U.S. 321, 103 S.Ct. 1838, 75 L.Ed.2d. 579 (1983).

McCarthy, M., McCabe, N., & Thomas, S. (1998). *Public School Law* (4th ed.). Needham Heights, MA: Allyn & Bacon.

Mervilde, J. (1981). *Student absenteeism. Causes, effects, and possible solutions.* South Bend, IN: Indiana University of South Bend.

Murphy v. *State of Arkansas,* 852 F2d 1039 (1988).

National Home Education Research Institute. (2002). *Facts on home schooling.* Retrieved from http://www.nheri.org/ July 23, 2002.

Nolte, C. M. (1982). Home instruction in lieu of public school attendance. In M.A. McGhehey (Ed.), *School law in changing times.* Topeka, KS: National Organization on Legal Problems in Education.

Note. (1999). The hazards of making public schooling a private business. *Harvard Law Review, 112,* 695.

Opinion of the Attorney General (1978). OAG Number 5414.

People v. *DeJonge,* 442 Mich 266, 501 N.W. 2d 127 (1993).

Pierce v. *Society of Sisters,* 268 U.S. 510 (1925).

Plyler v. *Doe,* 475 U.S. 202, 102 S.Ct. 2382 (1982).

In the Matter of Proios, 111 Misc.2d 252, 443 N.Y.S.2d 828 (N.Y. Sur. 1981).

Raymon v. *Alvord Independent School District,* 639 F.2d 257 (5th Cir. 1981)

Rice v. *Commonwealth,* 49 S.E.2d 342, 3 A.L.R.3d 1392 (1948).

Reid v. *Kenowa Hills Public Schools,* Case No. 99-10536 CZ (Decided January 22, 2002); Court of Appeals No. CA 239473.

Seid, R. et al. (2001). Colloquium, 75 years after *Pierce* v. *Society of Sisters.* 78 *University of Detroit Mercy Law Review* 373.

Snyder v. *Charlotte Public Schools,* 421 Mich 517 (1985).

Sprague v. *Harrison Community Schools,* Case No. 60-005300 (Decided Sept. 10, 1980).

State v. *Anderson,* 427 N.W.2d 316, 48 Ed. Law Rep. 649 (N.D. 1988).

State v. *Garber,* 197 Kan. 567, 479 P.2d. 896 (1966).

State v. *Melin.* 428 N.W.2d 227. 48 Ed.LawRep. 977 (N.D. 1988).

State v. *Patzer,* 382 N.W.2d 631, 30 Ed.LawRep. 1265 (N.D. 1986).

Strangway v. *Allen.* 194 Ky. 681. 240 S.W. 384 (Ky. 1922).

Talluto, R. (2001). Accountability for home-schoolers. *American School Board Journal, 188,* 20.

Texas Education Agency v. *Leeper,* 843 S.W.2d 41 (Texas App. Ft. Worth 1991).

Toby, J. (1999). Obsessive compulsion. (High school attendance should not be mandatory). *National Review.*

Ventura v. *Hardge,* 2000 WL 112362 (N.D. Tex 2000).

In the Matter of Welfare of L. Z, 380 N.W.2d 898, 30 Ed. Law Rep. 518 (Minn. App. 1986)

In the Matter of Welfare of T. K. and W. K, 475 N.W.2d 88, 70 Ed. Law Rep, 194 (Minn. App. 1991).

Wisconsin Legislative Audit Bureau. (2000, August). Truancy reduction efforts. *Best Practices Review.* Madison, WI: Author.

Wisconsin v. *Yoder,* 406 U.S. 205 (1972).

Wright. (1978). Student attendance: What relates where? *National Association of School Principals Bulletin, 62*(415).

Wynn, J., Richman, R. A., Rubinstein, J., Littdll. Britt B., & Yoken, C. (1988). *Communities and adolescents: An exploration of reciprocal supports.* Paper prepared for Youth and America's Future: The William T. Grant Foundation Commission on Work, Family and Citizenship.

Zirkel, P. A., & Gluckman, I. B. (1982, January). Academic penalties for absences. *National Assoc. of Secondary School Principals Bulletin, 66*(450), 102–104.

CHAPTER 6

STUDENT RIGHTS AND CONTROL OF BEHAVIOR

SANDRA KOPELS, UNIVERSITY OF ILLINOIS, URBANA-CHAMPAIGN

In our system, state-operated schools may not be enclaves of totalitarianism. School officials do not possess absolute authority over their students. Students in school as well as out of school are "persons" under our Constitution. They are possessed of fundamental rights which the State must respect, just as they themselves must respect their obligations to the States.
—U.S. Supreme Court in *Tinker* v. *Des Moines*

"Teacher don't you fill me up with your rules
Everybody knows that smokin' ain't allowed in school"
—Mötley Crue, *Smokin' in the Boys Room*

INTRODUCTION

In this chapter, we explore the broad issues that pertain to student rights and the problems associated with student control as a requirement for carrying out the goals and functions of the school. As we pointed out in Chapter 3, schools as social systems have certain boundary maintenance functions that must be reconciled with the guarantees of the First, Fourth, and Fourteenth Amendments. Achieving this balance often presents a dilemma because school officials have the right to control what occurs within the schools although their control needs to be balanced against students' rights to be treated fairly.

The Supreme Court first acknowledged this dilemma in *West Virginia State Board of Education* v. *Barnette* (1943). It affirmed school officials' right to prescribe and control conduct but said that school officials do not have total authority over pupils. The Court upheld the notion that freedom of expression must be protected, but that pupils must understand the principles on which the government stands. It also noted that schools as microcosms of society must also be a "marketplace of ideas" where truth can be discussed through the "robust exchange of ideas and not by enclaves of totalitarianism."

In *Stanley* v. *Northeast Independent School District* (1972), the Court observed: "One of the great concerns of our time, is that our young people, disillusioned by our political processes, are disengaging from political participation. It is most important that our young people become convinced that our Constitution is a living reality, not parchment preserved under glass."

While the courts have expressed concerns regarding the need for children to develop into politically aware citizens, during the late 1980s and 1990s, societal problems such as drugs, weapons, and violence became almost commonplace in the schools. Incidents such as school shootings, wherein children bring weapons into the schools and cause grave injuries and death to other students and teachers, have impacted the philosophies behind decisions about control of student behavior and the maintenance of school safety. Even the terrorist attacks on the United States on September 11, 2001, have impacted certain educational provisions regarding safe school environments.

These issues have impacted the courts as well. As society has passed new laws targeted to reduce drugs, weapons, and violent incidents within the schools, court decisions over the past half-century regarding the control of student conduct have vacillated in their attempts to balance the rights of school officials to control the conduct of students and safety for all with the rights of students to behave in ways that express themselves as individuals. As you will see, the decisions reflect the tenor of the times.

The primary aim of this chapter is to impress upon social workers in schools that democracy and the values which social workers hold inviolable must be preserved and that the role of social workers is to assist society in balancing the rights of children, the interests of parents in raising their children, and the duty of the schools to maintain an orderly learning environment.

The chapter begins with an overview of the principles that provide the legal authority to maintain control over children within the school. Next, we discuss rights students have as persons under the Constitution. We then turn to issues related to the punishment or discipline of students when they challenge the control of school officials. Throughout this discussion, we present leading cases that reflect the balance of the competing interests. Finally, we offer some suggestions and imperatives for school social workers to bridge the gap between student rights and the responsibilities of school districts.

SOURCES OF SCHOOL DISTRICTS' AUTHORITY

In this section, we discuss the sources of the authority that school officials have to maintain a learning environment that is both orderly and safe. These sources include the *in loco parentis* doctrine, the common law of the schools, and the legal authority of the state.

The *In Loco Parentis* Doctrine

The legal concept of *in loco parentis* is a Latin phrase that means "in place of the parents." It describes a relationship similar to that of a parent to a child, in which an individual assumes the status of a parent and the rights and responsibilities of a parent for an individual, usually a child, without formally adopting the child. While *in loco parentis* can be applied to other contexts such as the relationship between a guardian and a ward, the most common usage of the *in loco parentis* doctrine relates to teachers and their students.

The classroom teacher has a closer association with and understanding of the pupil than other school personnel and thereby enters into a special legal relationship. In fact, one of the basic legal principles regarding student control is that the teacher, by virtue of his or her position, has legal authority over a pupil, analogous to a parent's authority over a child, at least for purposes of necessary control and correction.

Initially, this doctrine gave power to school officials to exercise the same control over students at school (or even when students were going to and from schools) that parents could exercise at home. Technically, however, this principle still left open the question of just what powers parents have over children, although generally such power has been interpreted as being extensive, almost unlimited, short of obvious, gross abuse. Thus, when *in loco parentis* was applied to the schools, the result was to give teachers, principals, and other administrators enormous control over students. This control extended not only to formal studies but also to clothing, hairstyle, speech, manners, morals, organizational membership, and even behavior away from school. For example, from the late 1800s to the late 1950s, courts upheld the authority of public school officials to expel pupils for joining a social fraternity (*Smith* v. *Board of Education,* 1913), going home for lunch (*Bishop* v. *Houston School District,* 1931), having a venereal disease (*Kenny* v. *Gurley,* 1923), smoking off campus (*Tanton* v. *McKenney,* 1924), and violating a school rule against going to the movies on weeknights (*Mangum* v. *Keith,* 1918). Courts have also held that pupils can be expelled for speaking against school policy at a student body meeting (*Wooster* v. *Sunderland,* 1915), wearing a fraternity insignia to school (*Antell* v. *Stokes,* 1934), expressing offensive sexual views (*Morris* v. *Nowotny,* 1959), arranging for a communist speaker to speak off campus (*Zarichney* v. *State Board of Agriculture,* 1949), and even for refusing to tell who wrote "dirty words" on the school wall (*Board of Education* v. *Helston,* 1889). As we will see later in this chapter, some of these decisions would no longer be decided in the same way.

The protest movements of the 1960s and the growing tide of civil rights advocacy gave impetus to the decline in the use of the *in loco parentis* doctrine. Despite the shift in the application of the *in loco parentis* doctrine, school officials still have broad powers in exercising discipline in schools. However, a lot depends upon the circumstances in individual cases. For example, courts have given schools wide discretion in punishing pupils so long as their actions are reasonable and connect with the educational process (*Neuhaus* v. *Federico,* 1973). Courts have sanctioned punishments for using tobacco, alcohol, and drugs on the grounds that "an effort to maintain and inculcate habits designed to preserve good health among pupils is a legitimate element of an educational system" (*Rando* v. *Newberg Public School Board,* 1975).

In general, over the last 30 years, the courts have placed limits on the type of behavior that schools can punish. The most important is that pupils may *not* be punished for asserting their First Amendment rights (of free speech, press, or association) unless they disrupt substantially the existing conditions for learning.

Common Law of the Schools

Another closely related concept to *in loco parentis* is the common law of the schools. This concept derived from the colonists as they developed the colonial American schools. The colonists borrowed the English ideal that schools not only have an educational but also a moral responsibility for students. Accordingly, both the teachers and the pupils have mutual responsibilities and obligations. The mutuality of the relationship is predicated on society's expectations of the school in the advancement of the common good of the community (Alexander & Alexander, 1998).

Thus, the common law of the school, as prescribed by extensive judicial precedent, reflects a synthesis, characterized by the school, wherein the highest interest of the individual and the preeminent interest of the community coincide. The individual, in pursuing his or her own interest pursues that of the community, and in promoting the interest of the community, promotes his or her own. This harmony of interests is defined and furthered by the common law of the public school. Therefore, the reasoning of the common law, which conveys to the teacher the authority to maintain an orderly atmosphere of learning, a benefit to both the student and the community, may be understood in the context of both law and philosophy (Alexander & Alexander, 1998).

The Legal Authority of the State

Within constitutional limits, state legislatures have plenary (i.e., complete, absolute, and unqualified) authority with respect to school policy and control. However, the language of statutes dealing with the control of pupils is usually rather general. Much of the legislation concerning student control is permissive in nature, thereby delegating to school districts the authority and responsibility to determine the specifics of such control. Experts consider this proper because a school district is a territorial subdivision of the state, and school board members are thus state officials overseeing the state function of education. Moreover, most authorities argue that the school may be thought of as a legislative body enacting rules and regulations that govern student control within the boundaries of the school district.

While legislatures are given general authority to govern schools and may go beyond the minimal constitutional mandates, they cannot violate the pupils' basic constitutional rights. Where legislators fail to fulfill the constitutional requirements, the courts may invalidate their acts. The fact that education is specifically set out in state constitutions as a required state function gives education a "preferential position" relative to other state governmental functions that are not specified (Alexander & Alexander, 1998).

Because of the very broad authority that schools have under any of these principles, within the last decade "zero-tolerance" policies have developed. Under zero tolerance, a school district will enact a policy that allows for no deviations from the rule. In other words, the school will not tolerate any breach of a school rule, regardless of how minor. As we will discuss later in this chapter, newspaper articles are replete with stories about children being suspended or expelled from school for violating their schools' zero-tolerance policy. The authority of the school is not without limits, however.

BASIC CONSTITUTIONAL RIGHTS

Before we begin to talk about balancing the rights of schools to maintain order and provide a safe learning environment for students, against the constitutional rights of students, it is necessary to have a basic understanding of certain constitutional principles and constitutional rights.

Due Process

According to the Fifth and Fourteenth Amendments to the United States Constitution, before there can be any governmental deprivation of life, liberty, or property, due process must be afforded. Under the concept of substantive due process, the idea is that there are limitations on the substance of what governments may do. Therefore, if the government wants to place restrictions on certain rights of individuals that are considered to be fundamental (i.e., derived from the Constitution), then the government has to have compelling reasons to abridge these rights, and the reasons must be tailored narrowly to accomplish the governmental objectives (Kopels, 1998). For example, if a school district wants all of its students, no matter how young, to have body cavity searches every day to prevent drugs coming into the school, school officials would have to justify how its interest in drug-free schools outweigh students' privacy rights. The schools would also have the burden of proving that there would be no less intrusive way to reach their goal.

Under the concept of procedural due process, the idea is that there are procedural rights that must be afforded to individuals before their rights to life, liberty, or property are taken away. If the governmental purpose is proper, then procedural due process requires that before there is a deprivation of rights, the individual is to be given whatever procedures are required constitutionally before the deprivation occurs. Using the same example, if the schools were to conduct body cavity searches, they would be required, at a minimum, to let parents and students know that the searches were going to occur and how objections could be mounted.

The right to an education, while incredibly important to individuals and the nation, has been determined not to qualify as a fundamental right under the Constitution (*San Antonio Ind. Sch. Dist.* v. *Rodriguez,* 1973). However, education has been determined to implicate liberty and property rights under the Constitution (*Goss* v. *Lopez,* 1975). Courts have determined that liberty or property rights are involved in short-term suspensions, corporal punishment, transfers from one school to another for disciplinary reasons, grade reductions, and expulsion from school or extracurricular activities (Eisenman & Fischer, 1994).

Other Constitutional Rights

Many of the protections of the Bill of Rights to the United States Constitution have been applied to the school context. Among the rights that we will discuss are ones that derive from the First, Fourth, and Eighth Amendments to the Constitution. The First Amendment places prohibitions on the government from making laws that restrict individuals' freedom of speech, freedom of the press, the right to assemble, or the right to the free exercise of their religion. The Fourth Amendment places prohibitions on the government against unreasonable searches and seizures, and the Eighth Amendment prohibits the government from inflicting cruel and unusual punishment on its people. The issues that we will discuss below all find their basis in the constitutional principles of due process and implicate at least one of the above-mentioned constitutional rights.

Freedom of Speech and Expression

The First Amendment states that the government shall make no law abridging the freedom of speech. Until 1969, there had been no determination by the Supreme Court as to the application of this constitutional principle to the public schools.

The Tinker Case

The landmark decision in *Tinker* v. *Des Moines Independent Community School District* (1969) established three general principles regarding freedom of expression in schools: (1) the First Amendment protects the freedom of speech of students in public schools; (2) symbolic speech, such as the wearing of armbands, buttons, or other symbols, is protected as well as actual

speech; and (3) no right, not even the right to speak, is absolute, and this and other student rights may be limited under certain circumstances.

In December 1965, a group of adults and students in Des Moines held a meeting at the Eckhardt home. The members of the group decided to publicize their objections to the hostilities in Vietnam and their support for a truce by wearing black armbands during the holiday season and by fasting on December 16 and on New Year's Eve. The petitioners in the case were John F. Tinker, 15 years old, and Christopher Eckhardt, 16 years old, who attended high schools in Des Moines, Iowa, and Mary Beth Tinker, John's sister, a 13-year-old student in junior high school. The children had engaged in similar activities with their parents previously and decided to participate in this protest.

The principals of the Des Moines schools became aware of the plan to wear armbands. On December 14, 1965, they met and adopted a policy that pupils wearing armbands to school would be asked to remove them; if they refused to do so, they would be suspended until they returned without the armbands. Aware of the regulation that the school authorities had adopted, Mary Beth Tinker and Christopher Eckhardt wore black armbands to their schools on December 16; John Tinker wore his armband the next day. They were all sent home and suspended from school until they returned without their armbands. They did not return to school until after New Year's Day, 1966.

A complaint was filed in the United States District Court by the petitioners, through their fathers, under Section 1983 of Title 42 of the United States Code. It asked for an injunction restraining the school officials and the members of the board of directors of the school district from disciplining the petitioners, and it sought nominal damages. After an evidentiary hearing, the court dismissed the complaint, upholding the constitutionality of the school authorities' action on the grounds that it was reasonable in order to prevent disturbance of school discipline.

The case was later brought to the U.S. Supreme Court. On behalf of the Court, Justice Abe Fortas reviewed the history of the case, including the decision by the district court and the legal principles on which the district court judge had relied. The Court ruled that in the absence of any facts that may have led school officials to forecast a substantial disruption of or material interference with school activities, or any showing that disturbances on school premises, in fact, occurred when students wore black armbands on their sleeves, prohibiting students from wearing armbands to schools and suspending them for failing to remove the armbands, was an unconstitutional denial of students' rights to expression of opinion. In his ruling, Justice Fortas made his oft-quoted statement, "It can hardly be argued that either students or teachers shed their constitutional rights to freedom of speech or expression at the schoolhouse gate" (*Tinker* at 736).

The decision in *Tinker* made it clear that restricting a student's right to freedom of expression, for example, is unconstitutional unless there is evidence to show that the forbidden conduct would "materially and substantially interfere" with the smooth running of the school. The decision left to other courts the determination of what circumstances posed "the potentiality and imminence of disruption."

Almost 15 years later, the Supreme Court again faced an issue of freedom of speech. In *Bethel School District No. 403* v. *Fraser* (1986), a high school student made a nomination speech at a school assembly and referred to his candidate using explicit and graphic terms, full of sexual innuendos. The school suspended him and he appealed. The United States Supreme Court upheld the discipline and concluded that this student's speech was not constitutionally protected. The court wrote that the fundamental values that are essential to a democratic society must include tolerance of divergent political and religious views, even when the views are unpopular. However, the court stated that these values

must also take into account consideration of the sensibilities of others, and, in the case of a school, the sensibilities of fellow students. The undoubted freedom to advocate unpopular and controversial views in schools and classrooms must be balanced against the society's countervailing interest in teaching students the boundaries of socially appropriate behavior *(Fraser* at 683).

The court found that a highly appropriate function of public school education is to prohibit the use of vulgar and offensive terms in public discourse.

Soon after, in *Hazelwood School District* v. *Kuhlmeier* (1988), the Supreme Court upheld the decision of a high school principal to omit two pages from a student newspaper on stories about three students' experiences with teenage pregnancies and about the impact of divorce on students. Student members of the school newspaper's editorial staff had sued the school on the grounds that withholding the speech violated their First Amendment rights. The Supreme Court focused on school-sponsored publications that might be considered to bear the imprimatur of the school. The Court held that a school did not have to tolerate students' speech that is inconsistent with its basic educational mission. Accordingly, the Court stated that educators do not offend the First Amendment by exercising editorial control over style and content of student speech in school-sponsored expressive activities so long as the actions are reasonably related to legitimate pedagogical concerns. Therefore, a school may control speech that is biased or prejudiced, vulgar or profane, unsuitable for immature audiences, or seems to be sanctioned by the school.

The important points in *Tinker* are that (1) in order for the state to prohibit such an expression of speech, it must be able to show that the forbidden conduct will interfere with the discipline required to operate the school; and (2) the test to determine whether a child has gone beyond protected speech is whether she or he materially or substantially interferes with the requirements of appropriate discipline in the operation of the school.

The important points made by *Fraser* and *Hazelwood* show that not all student speech is protected. Taken together, the holdings in *Tinker, Fraser,* and *Hazelwood* establish that while students do not shed their Constitutional rights to freedom of speech and expression at the schoolhouse gate, students' offensive expression in school, or inappropriate student expression identified with a school will not violate the First Amendment, whereas limitations on political expression may violate the First Amendment. School officials can regulate expressions of opinions which materially and substantially interfere with the requirements of appropriate discipline in the operation of the school or that collide with the rights of others. It may be appropriate to impose disciplinary sanctions to make the point to students that vulgar speech and lewd conduct is wholly inconsistent with the fundamental values of public school education (Simpson, 2001).

School social workers promote cultural diversity and respect for the values and beliefs of others. One interesting case that may have implications for school social work practice concerns a Pennsylvania school district that enacted an anti-harassment policy in which students were required to treat members of the school community with mutual respect. The policy defined harassment as verbal or physical conduct based on actual or perceived race, religion, color, national origin, gender, sexual orientation, or disability. The policy prohibited conduct that offends, denigrates, or belittles an individual because of any of the above-mentioned characteristics and further prohibited harassment based on things such as clothing, social skills, intellect, educational program, hobbies, or values. Students who violated the policy were subject to punishment including warnings, counseling, suspension, expulsion, and transfer. Students who were worried that their views on morality, including the harmful effects of homosexuality, would subject them to reprisals under this policy challenged the policy. The

Third Circuit Court of Appeals struck down the school district's anti-harassment policy, ruling that it violated the students' rights to free speech (*Saxe* v. *State College Area School District,* 2001). McCarthy (2002) notes that the appellate court lost sight of the mission of the public school to instill civil behavior, citizenship values, and respect for others as well as the need to prohibit harassing and disrespectful behavior in the light of school violence. Sexual harassment issues are addressed in Chapter 10.

As should be clear, not all issues will be resolved ultimately by the Supreme Court. There are a variety of factors in different cases that change the situation and the balance between the competing interests of schools and students. For example, if a student says, "I understand how being bullied can cause one to snap under the pressure like those kids at Columbine did," can this student be disciplined for his or her speech? Is this a threat? Does it materially and substantially interfere with school discipline? How does Internet usage, at home and at school, impact on free speech? Clearly, if a student uses the school library to look at pornographic websites banned by the school and is punished for his usage, this will not be presumed to violate his free speech. What if a student creates a website, at her home, which is critical of teachers and demeaning to other students and she shares the website address with students from her school? Is this an issue of freedom of speech? It appears that student speech in any location, from any source, in any form, that is considered to cause material disruption in school is not constitutionally protected and may subject the student to discipline (Simpson, 2001). Determining the answers to all of these factors poses a challenge to school personnel.

Freedom of Dress and Appearance

Freedom of expression includes more than the freedom to speak as one wishes. Freedom of expression includes speech, both political and expressive, and has been extended to govern one's personal appearance.

Questions regarding the school's authority to control students' dress and appearance have led to a variety of cases and court opinions. For example, in 1921, Pearl Pugsley was suspended from a public school in Clay County, Arkansas, because she broke a rule prohibiting the use of talcum powder on a student's face. Her teacher told her to wash it off and not to return with it on. Defiant, Pearl later returned to school with powder on her face and was denied admission until she obeyed the rule. Pearl refused to return to school and begged the court to set aside the restriction *(Pugsley* v. *Sellmeyer,* 1923). The court dismissed her case. She then appealed, and the Arkansas Supreme Court, in a split decision, ruled in favor of the school board. One of the court's reasons was that although schools are not without limits, they have a wide range of discretion in matters of school policy and administration.

Almost a half-century later, Chelsey Karr, a 16-year-old pupil, petitioned the courts for a decision against an El Paso high school that refused to enroll him because his long hair violated the school's dress code. After a four-day trial, the U.S. District Court ruled that the denial of a public education to Karr on the basis of the school regulation violated the due process and equal protection guarantees of the U.S. Constitution. The court ruled that "one's choice of hair style is constitutionally practiced" and that the burden was on school authorities to demonstrate that long hair disrupted the educational process *(Karr* v. *Schmidt,* 1972).

However, the El Paso School Board appealed the decision, and the higher court concluded that since the case did not raise issues of fundamental liberty, the regulations would be presumed valid. Judge Morgan, writing on behalf of the court, rejected arguments based on the First and Fourteenth Amendments and the equal protection clause. He emphasized that the court's ruling did not indicate an indifference to the personal rights

of Chelsey Karr, but rather reflected the "inescapable fact" that neither the Constitution nor the federal judiciary had been conceived to be a keeper of the national conscience in every matter "great and small."

Circuit and appellate courts have been divided with regard to grooming issues. The Supreme Court has refused on several occasions to review the constitutionality question.

Why do schools feel the need to govern students' appearance? In *Phoenix Elem. Sch. Dist. No. 1* v. *Green* (1997), the Arizona appellate court, in upholding a school district's dress code policy which was challenged by students who felt it violated their First Amendment rights, cited with approval the following reasons given by the district: 1) the promotion of a more effective climate for learning; 2) creates opportunity for self-expression; 3) increases campus safety and security; 4) fosters school unity and pride; 5) eliminates "label" competition; 6) ensures modest dress; 7) simplifies dressing; and 8) minimizes cost to parents.

Other school districts enact dress code policies to attempt to deal with the rising problems of gangs. Because gang members are often identified with certain clothing or items of clothing, such as hats worn backward, schools create dress code policies to eliminate the wearing of certain clothing for all students. Other schools have created school uniform policies that require all students to wear the same type of clothing. In these schools, for example, all children wear certain school-sanctioned clothing such as blue jeans and a white shirt. Still other schools may ban clothing that the officials consider immodest, overly sexual, or inappropriate to the school environment. In these cases, the school officials believe that the presence of the clothing may lead to an unhealthy school atmosphere.

Despite the fact that these policies may be well intentioned and, more importantly, designed with school safety in mind, dress code policies are not without challenges. For example, in *Chalifoux* v. *New Carey Indep. Sch. Dist.* (1997), school district police officers told two students that they could not wear white plastic rosaries on the outside of their clothing. The students explained that they wore these rosaries as an expression of their Catholic faith. The school district policy prohibited the wearing of "gang-related apparel" in school or in school-related functions and the school police officers had information that members of the "United Homies," a gang present in that school, also wore rosaries as a means of identifying themselves. Pursuant to the analysis in *Tinker,* the court ruled that the students' expression of religious expression did not materially or substantially disrupt the school environment so they were allowed to wear their rosaries.

School social workers may be asked to participate in the development of school dress codes for their school districts. While schools appear to have the authority under *Fraser* and *Kuhlmeier* to prohibit speech that is lewd, vulgar, or could be perceived to be sanctioned by the school, it is also clear that *Tinker* allows speech that is an expression of someone's religious beliefs, so long as those beliefs do not cause material disruption to the school. Gilbert (1999) offers nine principles for drafting a dress code that will take into account factors considered by the courts. He argues that the keys to a successful dress code policy are common sense, the ability to compromise, and the desire of all parties involved to work through their differences.

Freedom of Religion

The questions related to freedom of religion in the public school context are especially complicated because the First Amendment has two clauses related to religion. One clause prohibits the government from interfering with the individuals' rights to worship as they choose, and the other clause prohibits the government from taking action that could be considered the establishment of a religion. Both of these clauses often overlap in their application to specific facts. The underlying idea is that the government should be neutral towards religion by neither advancing religious causes nor inhibiting their private exercise. Because public schools are part of government, schools must be careful not to take actions that violate the First Amendment's religious prohibitions.

Some parents, who believe the public schools promote an environment that is inconsistent with their own religious beliefs, send their children to private religious schools or home-school their children. In this way, the parents feel they can keep their children safe from what the parents see as harmful or immoral situations or keep them from learning ideas that are inconsistent with their religious beliefs. Home schooling is regulated by the laws of the states and is considered to be an appropriate form of education so long as it meets curriculum and other standards set by the state.

One of the first cases to reach the Supreme Court regarding the exercise of religion in the public schools was *Minersville* v. *Gobitis* (1940). In this case, the petitioners, who were Jehovah's Witnesses, sought an injunction to alter the requirement that participation in the salute to the flag was a condition for attending school in the Minersville, Pennsylvania, school district on the grounds that it violated their freedom of religion.

The Supreme Court, by an eight-to-one vote, upheld the compulsory flag salute but did acknowledge freedom of religion as a "precious right." This thought was expressed eloquently in the dissenting opinion of Justice Harlan F. Stone:

The Constitution may well elicit expressions of loyalty to it and to the government which it created, but it does not command such expression or otherwise give any indication that compulsory expressions of loyalty play any such part in our scheme of government as to override the constitutional protection of freedom of speech and religion. And while such expressions of loyalty, when voluntarily given, may promote national unity, it is quite another matter to say that their compulsory expression by children in violation of their own and their parents' religious convictions can be regarded as playing so important a part in our national unity as to leave school boards free to exact it despite the constitutional guarantee of freedom of religion (*Minersville* at 605).

The issue of school prayer in the public schools first reached the Supreme Court in *Engle v. Vitale* (1962). In *Engle,* parents of ten students challenged the constitutionality of a new practice within the New York school system for students to recite a short daily prayer created by school officials. The parents contended that the official prayer was contrary to their beliefs, religions, and religious practices and those of their children. In ruling that the prescribed prayer was in violation of the establishment clause, the Supreme Court focused on the fact that even if a prayer is denominationally neutral or its observance on the part of students is voluntary, the prayer could not be freed from violation of the Constitution. The following year the court struck down provisions of laws from Maryland and Pennsylvania that required daily reading of Bible passages or the recitation of the Lord's Prayer as unconstitutional violations of the establishment clause (*Sch. Dist. of Abington Twp., Pa. v. Schempp*, 1963).

During the 1970s and 1980s, the courts consistently held that prayer, whether at football games or at graduation, violates the establishment clause. However, the trends of the 1990s show that the courts are wavering on this issue more frequently than in the past.

In *Lee* v. *Weisman* (1992), the Supreme Court struck down a Rhode Island school district's policy that allowed principals to invite clergy members to deliver invocations and benedictions at middle and high school graduation ceremonies. School officials had attempted to avoid the church-state conflict by providing clergy with a pamphlet that provided guidelines that were considered appropriate for non-denominational prayer. The Court found that the policy had a coercive effect. Even though the school district

argued that graduation ceremony attendance was voluntary, the Court believed that students would feel pressured to participate in the prayers if they were part of the graduation ceremonies. Because the principal chose the clergy and decided that an invocation and a benediction would be given, the Court found that the involvement of the school system created a state-sponsored and state-directed religious exercise in the public school.

The Supreme Court's decision in *Lee* created a backlash. Certain school authorities and students have identified creative ways to include prayers in graduation ceremonies (McCarthy, 2000). For example, in two cases decided after *Lee,* the issue before the courts was whether prayer is permissible if students freely vote to choose a nonsectarian, nonproselytizing prayer at graduation. When school officials include a prayer, that is an unacceptable violation of the establishment clause. On the other hand, if students have the choice and vote to include a prayer, that may be acceptable because it is protected by the free speech and free exercise clauses of the First Amendment (Condon & Wolff, 1996).

For example, in *Harris v. Joint Sch. Dist. No. 241* (1993), a case originating from Idaho, the school district allowed its senior class to vote on whether it wanted prayer at graduation and to decide who would say the prayer. A group of pupils challenged the ceremonial prayer as a violation of the separation of church and state. The court found that since the senior high school students in School District No. 241 are free to choose whether any prayer will or will not be included in their graduation programs, the mere fact that graduation ceremonies in the district are supervised by faculty and administrators does not begin to constitute the kind of state involvement present in *Lee.*

In another case that upheld student initiated and voted upon prayer, *Jones v. Clear Creek Indep. Sch. Dist.* (1992), the court questioned why so many people attach importance to graduation ceremonies. The court stated:

If they only seek government's recognition of student achievement, diplomas suffice. If they only seek God's recognition, a privately-sponsored baccalaureate will do. But to experience the community's recognition of student achievement, they must attend the public ceremony that other interested community members also hold so dear. By attending graduation to experience and participate in the community's display of support for the graduates, people should not be surprised to find the event affected by community standards. The Constitution requires nothing different (*Jones* at 973).

The court ruled that student-initiated prayer at a public school graduation is allowable because the students made the prayer decision. The court recognized that a majority of students could do what the state acting on its own cannot do to incorporate prayer in public high school graduation ceremonies.

In addition to issues related to prayer in the classroom and at graduation ceremonies, the courts have grappled with many other issues related to the establishment clause in the public schools. These have included 1) distributing Gideon Bibles to fifth-grade public school students (*Berger* v. *Rensselaer Cent. School Corp.,* 1993); 2) posting the Ten Commandments in every classroom (*Stone* v. *Graham,* 1980); 3) requiring the teaching of evolution science with creation science or not at all (*Edwards* v. *Aguillard,* 1987); 4) beginning school assemblies with prayer (*Collins* v. *Chandler Unified School District,* 1981); 5) teaching a transcendental meditation course that includes a ceremony involving making an offering to a deity (*Malnak* v. *Yogi,* 1979); 6) refusal to allow the formation of a Christian Club at the school *(Board of Educ. of Westside Comm. Sch.* v. *Mergens,* 1990); 7) limiting the officers of a Bible Study Club to Christians only (*Hsu by and through Hsu v. Rosyln Free School Dist.,* 1996); and 8) student-initiated, student-led invocation or message before varsity football games (*Santa Fe Independent School District* v. *Doe,* 2000).

One of the newest and more controversial issues that relate to the freedom of religion and public schools concerns school vouchers. The concept of school vouchers is that the government gives parents a voucher, stipend, or credit that can be used to pay for tuition at the schools of the parents' choosing. In some circumstances, the vouchers can be used at private, religious schools. Although the implementation of school vouchers takes on a variety of forms in different locales, its proponents argue that it will bring greater choice and accountability to the schools, while its opponents believe that vouchers, if used for religious schools, violate the establishment clause.

The United States Supreme Court has recently upheld the constitutionality of a case that concerned school vouchers in the Cleveland, Ohio, public school system (*Zelman v. Simmons-Harris,* 2002). As recounted in the U.S. Supreme Court's decision, more than 75,000 children were enrolled in the Cleveland City School District. The majority of these children were from low-income and minority families and were unable to send their children to any school other than an inner-city public school. Cleveland's public schools were among the worst performing public schools in the United States. The district had failed to meet any of the 18 state standards for minimal acceptable performance. Only one in 10 ninth graders could pass a basic proficiency examination, and students at all levels performed at a dismal rate compared with students in other Ohio public schools. Because of this, Ohio enacted, among other initiatives, its Pilot Project Scholarship Program to provide financial assistance to families in any Ohio school district that was under federal court order requiring supervision and operational management of the district.

The pilot program provided two basic kinds of assistance to parents of children in a covered district. First, the program provided tuition aid for students in kindergarten through third grade, expanding each year through eighth grade, to attend a participating public or private school of their parent's choosing. Second, the program provided tutorial aid for students who choose to remain enrolled in public school. Because parents could use the vouchers at private religious schools, the voucher system was attacked as being a violation of the establishment clause of the Constitution.

The United States Supreme Court ruled that the program passed constitutional muster because it was neutral and did not advance religion. The court stated that:

> We believe that the program challenged here is a program of true private choice . . . and thus constitutional . . . [t]he Ohio program is neutral in all respects toward religion. It is part of a general and multifaceted undertaking by the State of Ohio to provide educational opportunities to the children of a failed school district. It confers educational assistance directly to a broad class of individuals defined without reference to religion, i.e., any parent of a school-age child who resides in the Cleveland City School District. The program permits the participation of all schools within the district, religious or nonreligious. Adjacent public schools also may participate and have a financial incentive to do so. Program benefits are available to participating families on neutral terms, with no reference to religion. The only preference stated anywhere in the program is a preference for low-income families, who receive greater assistance and are given priority for admission at participating schools (*Zelman* at 2470).

Because the Supreme Court has ruled that the use of vouchers does not offend the establishment clause, proponents of religious education may advocate for other school districts to adopt a voucher program. If parents can use vouchers to pay for private or religious schools, there is concern about how this will affect the public school system in the United States.

Other Privacy Issues

Although not based on the First Amendment, the protections of privacy guaranteed by the First

Amendment contributed to the passage of a student records law. Congress gave students and their parents new rights when it passed the Family Educational Rights and Privacy Act of 1974 (FERPA), also known informally as the Buckley Amendment.

The Family Educational Rights and Privacy Act of 1974

Congress passed The Family Educational Rights and Privacy Act (FERPA) as a rider to the 1974 education amendments. This act denied federal funds to any school system that refused to show the contents of students' records to their parents or, if the students were 18 years of age or older, to the students themselves. This legislation was significant because it established two principles: 1) Parents (until the student reaches 18 years of age) have the right to see their children's records; and 2) parents may not examine the records of any other pupil. This amendment, combined with the Department of Health and Human Services implementing regulations issued in 1976, have forced significant changes in record-keeping policies and procedures at virtually all institutions that receive federal financial assistance. This includes public elementary, secondary, and post-secondary education.

At least six points contained in FERPA and the implementing regulations are important for school social workers: 1) Parents of a pupil (or of the 18-year-old) must be shown the records no more than 45 days after requesting to see them; 2) any item in the records may be subject to a validity challenge; 3) items inserted before January 1, 1975, need not be shown; 4) a pupil may waive his or her right to see confidential letters such as letters of recommendation; 5) the right of a school to release personal information about a pupil to a third party is restricted; and 6) pupils and parents are to be notified annually of their rights with regard to access to records.

The law specifies that any educational institution receiving federal funds will lose those funds unless it provides parents with access to and the right to challenge their child's full educational records, the right to have inaccurate or misleading records changed, and the right to give their consent before any records can be shown to outside parties. Students who are 18 years old or over, or any person attending a post-secondary institution, must be given the same rights with regard to their records. In addition, all affected school agencies and institutions must notify parents and pupils 18 years old and over of these rights, must establish hearing procedures in the event of disagreements, and must keep on file all requests for school records from outsiders.

Parents and authorized individuals can "inspect and review" at will the "official records, files and data, including all material that is incorporated into each pupil's cumulative record folder and intended for school use" (FERPA, 1974). Educational records, which include information directly related to a student and that are maintained by or for an educational agency, may be shared with parents, their representatives, and other authorized persons. These records include academic work completed, grades, standardized achievement test scores, attendance data, aptitude and psychological tests, health and family background information, and verified reports of serious behavior patterns. The act also puts a near-absolute clamp on distribution of individual records without written consent from a parent or the student, depending upon the pupil's age.

Sharing Student Information

Recent changes to FERPA and its companion regulations shed new light on just how far schools can go to cooperate with local agencies or other persons that share a common interest in serving children. As we have already noted, FERPA protects the privacy of a student's educational record primarily by requiring that educators obtain written consent before disclosing information contained in the record to agencies or personnel outside of the school district. However, not all releases of information between schools and other agencies require prior written consent.

In fact, the increased violence in schools and the USA Patriot Act of 2001, enacted after the September 11 terrorist attacks, have increased the number of situations that student records can be released without prior consent. There are now 16 exceptions to the requirement of prior written consent. We will discuss a few points that are important for school social workers to know.

— Schools can share information with other school officials including teachers and administrators within the school if these persons have legitimate educational interests.

— FERPA does not distinguish between custodial or non-custodial parents. Accordingly, no matter who has custody of a child, either parent has the right to access their child's records and consent to their disclosure. However, if a valid court order concerning divorce or custody of a child has a provision related to access to the child's records, the court order will control.

— Schools can share directory information with other agencies. Directory information is information "which would not generally be considered harmful or an invasion of privacy if disclosed." It includes, but is not limited to, the student's name, address, telephone listing, date and place of birth, major field of study, participation in officially recognized activities and sports, weight and height of athletic team members, dates of attendance, degrees and awards received, and the most recent previous educational agency or institution attended. Parents must be given prior notice when schools adopt a policy of releasing directory information. Parents who object to directory information disclosures may prohibit them by requesting so in writing.

— Educators can communicate orally with other agencies based on their personal knowledge and observations of a juvenile that do not derive from the educational record. Communications based on independent knowledge of students are outside the reach of FERPA.

— A school may communicate without prior written parental consent when it shares the content of records of its law enforcement unit. A law enforcement unit is an individual, division, department, or other component of a school district that is officially authorized to enforce any federal, state, or local law, or to maintain the physical security and safety of the school. Under the regulations, a law enforcement unit "does not lose its status as a law enforcement unit if it also performs other, non-law-enforcement functions for the agency or institution, including investigation of incidents or conduct that might lead to disciplinary action or proceedings against a student." The exempt records include only those that are created and maintained by the unit for the purpose of law enforcement. Internal disciplinary records are not included in this category.

— FERPA permits educational agencies to disclose, without the consent or knowledge of the parent or student, personally identifiable information from the student's record in response to an *ex parte* order from the U.S. Attorney General or designee in connection with the investigation or prosecution of terrorism crimes. The school official does not need to record the fact of this disclosure in the student's records.

— Schools are permitted to disclose, without consent, information contained in student records to comply with lawfully issued subpoenas. This includes grand jury subpoenas and law enforcement subpoenas. The courts that issued the subpoena may order the educational institution not to disclose to anyone the existence or contents of the subpoena.

— In contrast to the grand jury and law enforcement subpoenas, schools may share information with other agencies without obtaining prior written consent when acting in compliance with a court order or lawfully issued subpoena. In these cases, the regulations do require that schools make a reasonable effort to notify the parent prior to compliance with the court order.

— Schools may share information with other agencies without obtaining prior written consent when acting "in connection with an emergency if knowledge of the information is necessary to protect the health or safety of the student or other individuals." These situations now specifically include substantial health risks to the general population like in the case of smallpox, anthrax, or other bioterrorism activities.

It is important that social workers be aware of the laws of their own states as well as those provided by the federal law to ensure confidentiality in the schools (Kopels, 1992; NASW, 2001).

Reasonable Search and Seizure

As we have seen, the rights of students to freedom of speech, expression, and religion find their basis in the First Amendment. Students also have certain rights in the educational setting that stem from the Fourth Amendment.

The Fourth Amendment of the U.S. Constitution states that "the right of the people to be secure in their persons, houses, papers, and effects, against unreasonable searches and seizures, shall not be violated." This guarantee has generally been interpreted to mean that an adult or his or her property can be subjected to a police search only after issuance of a warrant and after a finding of probable cause.

Minors, particularly students, have not had these protections. Generally, it has been held that school officials may search a pupil's locker, without the consent of the pupil and without a search warrant, if they have cause to believe the locker contains an item, the possession of which would be a criminal offense or would present harm to another individual (*People* v. *Overton*, 1969). The legal basis for such action is that the school, not the student, owns the locker and that, at best, they share possession of it. The public notion that the school has the responsibility to provide for and protect the welfare of the entire school is so strong that this responsibility has been allowed to overshadow the intent of the Fourth Amendment.

In *New Jersey* v. *T.L.O.* (1985), the Supreme Court attempted to delineate the power of public school officials to conduct searches of a student. In *T.L.O.,* a teacher discovered two girls smoking in the bathroom and took the students to the vice-principal's office. One of the girls admitted to smoking in the bathroom but the other, T.L.O., did not. Because the vice-principal believed that T.L.O. had violated the school's rule against smoking at school, he opened her purse and saw a package of cigarettes. When he reached into the purse to get the cigarettes, he discovered rolling papers that he thought were related to marijuana use. He continued the search, believing there might be marijuana, and he discovered a small quantity of the drug, a pipe, empty plastic bags, money, and an index card that listed names of persons who owed T.L.O. money. T.L.O. was suspended and found to be a delinquent under state law. The issue presented to the Supreme Court was the constitutionality of the search of her purse.

The court ruled that to determine the reasonableness of a search there had to be a two-fold inquiry. First, school officials had to decide whether the search was justified at its inception and second, whether the search that actually took place was reasonably related in scope to the circumstances which justified the search in the first place. In other words, to determine the reasonableness of searches by school officials, courts must consider the suspicion underlying the search and the scope of the search in light of the reasons for the suspicions. In the context of reasonableness of searches in the public school, the court focused on the schools' need to control students and the special relationship between school officials and students and the mission of the school to educate students in a disciplined learning environment. Because of the special needs of the school, the Court pitted the child's legitimate expectations of privacy against the school's legitimate need to maintain a learning environment. Discipline tipped the balance in favor of school officials (Urbonya, 2001). The following recent cases illustrate the courts' attempts to balance these principles.

Junior high school students in Indiana filed a civil rights action claiming that a principal and teachers conducted an illegal strip-search for four dollars and 50 cents that was missing from a locker room after a physical education class. A federal trial court reasoned that because the principal was not the policymaker for the board, the board could not be held liable for his behavior (*Hines ex rel. Oliver* v. *McClung,* 1995). At the same time, the court decided that since the search was not reasonable under the circumstances, the educators were not entitled to qualified immunity from the civil rights action.

In *People* v. *Dilworth* (1996), a police liaison officer at an Illinois alternative high school searched a student and found nothing suspicious. Right after, he saw the student laughing and making mocking gestures with his friend. Believing something was amiss, the police officer noticed the student had a flashlight, and thinking a flashlight was strange in school, searched the flashlight and found five bags of cocaine. In upholding the conviction, the court decided that a reasonable suspicion was all that was necessary for the liaison officer rather than the probable cause standard that would be required for police.

In another Illinois case, school officials or police liaison officers had searched three students from three different high schools in Chicago. The cases were consolidated to decide the issues of the reasonableness of the searches, all of which resulted in the seizure of handguns (*People* v. *Pruitt,* 1996). In the first search, a student passing through a metal detector set off an alarm and was subject to a pat-down search. The appellate court held that the screening was minimally intrusive since no touching occurred unless the metal detector alerted and once it did, the facts were sufficient to justify a pat-down search. The court found that the second search was permissible because it was based on an informant's tip to a police liaison officer who was in the same position as a school official for the purpose of the Fourth Amendment. The final search occurred when an administrator interviewed a pupil for almost an hour before asking him to empty his pockets. The court acknowledged that while there may have been reasonable suspicion when the interview began, the situation had changed such that by its end the administrator was acting on a mere hunch.

A student who was adjudicated a juvenile delinquent and placed on probation for possessing a knife in school claimed that the search that led to the discovery of the weapon was invalid. The pupil charged that the search was inappropriate because it was not based on individualized suspicion. An appellate court in Pennsylvania disagreed (*In re S.S.*, 1996). The court upheld the action as reasonable since officials searched all students in the same minimally intrusive manner upon entering school, and that the search was justified due to the high rate of violence in area schools.

A 16-year-old pupil in Oregon challenged the discovery of drugs in his jacket. The pupil claimed that the drugs were discovered illegally by an assistant principal who searched his jacket after he went to the administrator's office following his involvement in a fight that took place off school property. When the administrator searched the jacket because he thought that the pupil might be carrying a weapon, he discovered a bong and 20 grams of psilocybin mushrooms. An appellate court in Oregon reversed in favor of the student (*State ex rel. Juvenile Department of Lincoln County* v. *Finch*, 1996). The court was of the opinion that the search of the jacket was impermissible because it had not been supported by reasonable suspicion.

Florida sought further review of an order quashing the discovery of a gun during a search for weapons at a high school. After an administrator searched a coat that was being passed through the room, he found a gun. The pupil who owned the coat not only denied that the gun was his but also charged that the search was unlaw-

ful. An appellate court reversed in favor of the state (*State of Florida* v. *J.A.*, 1996). The court upheld the search on the grounds that it was minimally intrusive and involved the legitimate school concern for safety.

After a security guard at a school noticed a bulge in a student's jacket that was shaped like a gun handle, a search led to the discovery of a loaded weapon. The pupil, who was suspended for a year, claimed that the gun was discovered in an illegal search. When a trial court rejected the pupil's petition to dismiss, he sought further review. An appellate court in New York reversed (*Juan G.* v. *Cortines*, 1996). The court reasoned that because the bulge was not remotely suspicious, the delinquency petition should have been dismissed since the discovery of the gun had to be suppressed.

In *Covington County* v. *G. W.* (2000), the principal of a Mississippi school was informed that a student had been drinking in the school's parking lot. The search revealed seven unopened beer cans and several empty ones. The student admitted drinking beer before class. After he was suspended, his parents appealed. However, the court ruled that the search was reasonable under the circumstances.

The cases described above are typical but by no means exhaustive. The growing violence and increase in students' use of weapons and drugs have made reasonable searches and seizures essential to the orderly operation of the schools. The question remains what is a *reasonable* search. Schools have used strip searches, metal detectors, drug and weapon sniffing dogs, Breathalyzers, pat-downs, and other techniques to ensure safety and discipline in the schools. The reasonableness of these searches will always vary based on the scope of the search, its intrusiveness, the age of the child, the seriousness of the items being searched for and other contextual factors. Beckham (2000) provides recommendations that school officials should consider in striking the balance between the maintenance of a safe learning environment and the student's expectation of privacy.

Ten years after the *T.L.O.* decision, the Supreme Court decided the case of *Veronia Sch. Dist.* v. *Acton* (1995), which concerned the legality of a school district's drug testing policy for athletes. After noticing that student athletes were rude and used profane language in class, and because school officials believed that athletes were role models for other students, the Veronia school district in Oregon adopted a policy of drug testing student athletes. The athletes were not allowed to participate in sports unless they first signed a form consenting to weekly urine testing during their sport's season to detect amphetamine, cocaine and marijuana. One seventh grade student, Acton, refused to sign the consent form and was prohibited from playing on the football team. His parents sued the school district, believing the urine testing policy was unreasonable under the Fourth Amendment. In its decision, the court mentioned the common law power of the schools, the *in loco parentis* concept and the special needs doctrine. In order to determine whether the drug testing was within the special needs of the school, the court examined four factors: 1) the nature of the student's privacy interest, 2) the character of the intrusion, 3) the nature and immediacy of the governmental concern, and 4) the efficacy of the selected means for meeting it. After balancing these factors, the court held that drug-testing athletes under the facts of this case was reasonable under the Fourth Amendment.

The Supreme Court recently expanded this ruling to uphold an Oklahoma school district's policy of requiring drug testing for any middle or high school students who participate in any extracurricular activities (*Bd. of Educ.* v. *Earls,* 2002). The Court found that although there was no proven drug problem within the school, the search was not unreasonable given the school district's important interest in detecting and preventing drug use among its students.

T.LO. involved searches directed at the activities of a particular student. *Veronia* involved a group of students, athletes, who were not under suspicion. However, both decisions heavily relied upon the presumption of diminished constitutional protection for students and characterizing schools as places with special needs in determining the reasonableness of searches under the Fourth Amendment (Urbonya, 2001). By allowing random drug testing of students who participate in any extracurricular activities, the Supreme Court made it clear that the school's interest in drug prevention and control outweighs the individual's right to privacy. In the future, whether the Supreme Court will allow random drug testing to be conducted on any student who attends public school is an open question.

DISCIPLINE IN THE SCHOOLS

As we have seen, schools have a legitimate need to maintain order to provide a safe and effective learning environment. School officials have the responsibility to instill into students the desire to be good citizens and productive members of society. Part of being a member of society is following appropriate rules. Students who misbehave or do not follow rules of conduct set by the school or by society can be punished in a number of ways. Among the methods schools use to discipline children are corporal punishment and suspension and expulsion from school.

Corporal Punishment

Corporal punishment is the infliction of physical pain on an individual for misconduct. Corporal punishment in the school is in part an outgrowth of the *in loco parentis* concept and the tradition of early colonial schools, which practiced corporal punishment in conjunction with their religious philosophy focused on character development and morality. Increased litigation and adverse court decisions have led to less frequent use of such punishment as a primary form of student control.

In order for corporal punishment to be legal, it must be reasonable in the eyes of the judiciary. Courts invariably have based their decisions on the reasonableness of the rules, on the one hand,

and the reasonableness of the penalties, on the other hand.

Courts had discussed the idea of reasonableness as early as 1859, in *Lander* v. *Seaver* (1859). An 11-year-old boy was herding his cow past a teacher's house when, in the presence of other pupils, he called the teacher "Old Jack Seaver." The next morning when the boy arrived at school, he was reprimanded and whipped for his use of "insulting language." The father of the boy insisted that the teacher had no authority to punish the child for an act committed out of and away from school, but the court rejected the father's contention. The reasoning was that since the boy was in the presence of other pupils, his "contemptuous language" had "a direct and immediate tendency to injure the school, to subvert the master's authority, and to beget disorder and insubordination."

The application of the *in loco parentis* doctrine in the early 1970s led to two separate court interpretations. In *Baker* v. *Owen* (1975), the Supreme Court affirmed, without comment, a decision of the federal district court in North Carolina that allowed teachers to administer corporal punishment without the approval of the parents. In order for the person who administered corporal punishment to be protected, certain guidelines were to be observed. These guidelines included that children must be warned in advance regarding what behaviors could be punished, that less drastic measures had to be tried first, that a second staff member be present to witness the punishment, and upon request, parents be furnished a written statement of the paddling, the reasons for it, and the names of witnesses who observed it.

In 1977, the Supreme Court decided its only corporal punishment case to date. In *Ingraham* v. *Wright* (1977), two junior high school students sued their school district for damages they received from being struck with a wooden paddle. The school district's policy was that students could be struck for violating school rules, although the teachers were to consult with the school principal before they hit the students.

Both of the students had received large bruises from repeated strikes from a wooden paddle. One student was beaten more than 20 times with a two-foot-long wooden paddle. He suffered a bruise that kept him out of school for 11 days. Another student complained that he was struck twice on the arm, which resulted in the loss of full use for a week. The plaintiffs argued that these punishments violated the Eighth Amendment and represented cruel and unusual punishment, and the denial of due process. The Court ruled that the Eighth Amendment only applies to criminals in custody, and not to children in school. As for due process, the Court said it was impractical to hold a hearing each time a teacher wanted to use corporal punishment. It said that abuses were not common, that schools were open to public scrutiny, and that teachers and other pupils were there to keep a watch on excessive force.

The court did acknowledge that only such corporal punishment that is reasonably necessary for the proper education and discipline of a child would be allowed. Punishments that go beyond what is reasonable may subject the school or teacher to civil or criminal liability. In other words, parents who do not believe that the corporal punishment of their children is within reasonable limits may pursue criminal prosecution or civil lawsuits.

Although parents have the right to sue for injuries inflicted on their children, the problem in many cases is proving that the punishment was not reasonable in light of the situation. For example, in a Georgia case, the parents of a middle school student sued the teacher and school, alleging that the teacher had physically restrained and choked their son, causing him to have physical and emotional injuries. In her response, the teacher stated that the child had been causing problems and when he would not respond to her attempts to get him to behave, she reached up to him, grabbed his face with her fingers splayed across his cheeks, and turned his face toward her to get his attention. The court ruled against the parents, finding that not all physical contact between a teacher and a child is for punishment and that the teacher was simply exercising her responsibilities to regain control and supervise her class (*Daniels* v. *Gordon,* 1998).

In *Saylor* v. *Board of Education* (1997), a 14-year-old boy got into a "wild" fight with another child at the school. As punishment for the fight, both boys received five licks with a wooden paddle. The Kentucky school district had a policy in place in which parents could tell the school that they did not want their children subjected to corporal punishment. The parents claimed that they had told the school district that they did not want the school to use corporal punishment on their child. The schoolteacher and administrators stated that the father had told them at a meeting that they could discipline the child as needed. Despite the factual dispute, the court ruled in favor of the school district. There was no violation of substantive due process because the child was fully clothed when he was hit on his buttocks and the beating was not so severe or disproportionate as to shock the conscience of the court.

Other cases have found the conduct by school personnel to be shocking. For example, in *Neal* v. *Fulton County Bd. of Ed.* (2000), Durante Neal, a 14-year-old freshman and member of a Georgia high school varsity football team got into a fight with another student, Griffin. Neal reported it to the assistant coach who told him to learn to handle his own business. Neal took a metal weight lock from the coaches' office and put it in his gym bag. After practice, Griffin again approached Neal. Neal took the weight lock and hit Griffin in the head. The two boys started fighting. The coach and the principal came running over to Neal and the coach hit Neal with the weight lock in the left eye, knocking the eye out of the socket and destroying it, leaving Neal blind in one eye.

In *Neal,* the Fifth Circuit Court of Appeals, in reviewing principles created by other courts with respect to corporal punishment, found that constitutional principles protect a student from corporal punishment that is excessive, intentional, and creates a foreseeable risk of physical injury.

The court stated that many corporal punishment cases involve what might be called traditional applications of physical force, such as where school officials, subject to an official policy or in a more formal disciplinary setting, mete out spankings or paddlings to a disruptive student. However, the court stated that not all corporal punishment cases arise under those circumstances and may involve less traditional, more informally administered, and more severe punishments. The court cited the cases of *London* v. *Directors of DeWitt Pub. Schs.* (1999), (school official's acts of dragging student across room and banging student's head against metal pole described as corporal punishment); *P.B.* v. *Koch* (1996), (school principal's conduct in hitting student in mouth, grabbing and squeezing student's neck, punching student in chest, and throwing student headfirst into lockers was corporal punishment); *Metzger* v. *Osbeck* (1988), (official's conduct consisting of grabbing student in chokehold, causing student to lose consciousness, fall to the pavement, resulting in student breaking his nose and fracturing teeth analyzed under corporal punishment framework); *Carestio* v. *School Bd. of Broward County* (1999), (school employees' conduct in ganging up on student and beating him described as corporal punishment); and *Gaither* v. *Barron* (1996), (teacher's head-butting of student described as corporal punishment). In *Neal,* the court, in deciding that Neal's eye loss was a severe form of punishment that did constitute corporal punishment, did not delineate what other types of corporal punishment are excessive or serious enough to support a claim. The question remains, however, whether corporal punishment should *ever* be used to discipline children.

Hyman and Rathbone (1993), strong advocates against corporal punishment, set out many of the arguments in favor of and in opposition to the use of corporal punishment in the schools. They state that some educators who are proponents of corporal punishment believe that when a student learns to associate inappropriate behavior with strong negative consequences, the student will learn quickly to modify the undesirable behavior to conform to educational and social norms. For other proponents, corporal punishment is seen as a useful, moral, and acceptable way to teach children proper behaviors, often in line with religious beliefs. Hyman and Rathbone also delineate arguments used by opponents of corporal punishment. Opponents claim that corporal punishment does more harm than good and is psychologically damaging to those that receive it. Opponents also argue that rather than teaching a preference for cooperation and respect for the thoughts and feelings of others, it teaches the value of aggression and force as a means of settling problems. These authors and others are critical that corporal punishment is meted out differently. Studies show that black children are 2 1/2 times more likely to be subject to physical discipline than are white children. While black children comprise only 17% of the school-age population in the U.S., they receive about 39% of the paddlings (U.S. Department of Education, 2000).

It does appear that the use of corporal punishment is becoming less accepted as an educational technique throughout the country. At the time of the *Ingraham* v. *Wright* decision in 1977, of the 23 states that addressed corporal punishment through legislation, 21 of those states authorized the moderate use of corporal punishment in public schools. Only two states, New Jersey and Massachusetts, prohibited its use. Today, however, only two states directly grant school officials the authority to use corporal punishment; 15 states give local school boards discretion to decide whether to authorize corporal punishment as a means of discipline; one state requires parental or guardian consent before their children can be struck; and most significantly, 19 states expressly forbid corporal punishment (Urbonya, 2001). Additionally, the number of reported paddlings of students has decreased from 1.4 million in the 1979 to 1980 school year to 365,000 in 1997–1998, with 90% of these incidents coming from Louisiana, Mississippi, and Texas (Wigoren, 2001). More than 40 organizations oppose the use of corporal punishment, including the National Association of Social Workers (NCACPS, 2002).

Suspensions and Expulsions

As already mentioned, schools possess the broad authority to establish and maintain the learning environment of the school. Accordingly, schools have the authority to discipline a student in a variety of ways. We have explored the topic of corporal punishment, a very harsh form of discipline. In some cases, schools use milder forms of punishment such as taking away privileges, assigning special duties, denying the right to participate in graduation exercises, and lowering students' grades. Schools also possess the authority to remove from school, through suspension and expulsion, any student whose conduct disrupts or defies the operation of the school and its rules, as well as persons whose behavior poses a threat to other students, school personnel, or school property.

A suspension is usually considered to be a removal from the school environment for a short period of time, usually less than 10 days, while an expulsion is a longer-term removal from school. When students are suspended, it is likely that they will return to school. With suspensions, children are usually excluded from school, school activities, or school transportation for a short term.

With expulsion, the student's status is much more questionable. In some cases, students may be expelled from school for up to the remainder of the school year and in other cases, the expulsion may result in the student's permanent exclusion from school. The permanent exclusion would be more likely to occur with a child who is older than the requirement for compulsory school attendance in the state.

Instead of removing the child temporarily from the classroom, some schools use different forms of suspensions. For example, some schools suspend a student until the parent comes into the school to discuss the child's situation. This may be burdensome for some parents who have different work schedules, who have difficulty arranging childcare, or who will never come to the school. In these cases, the school may resort to in-school suspensions, where the pupil remains in school but is not allowed to attend classes for a period of time. In many school districts, state statutes dictate the length of the suspension.

The landmark case involving suspension occurred during the 1970s in Columbus, Ohio. It involved nine pupils who were suspended for 10 days for a variety of infractions. In *Goss* v. *Lopez* (1975), the Supreme Court ruled that students had constitutional interests both to property and liberty related to school attendance. The court held that the students' rights to a free public education cannot be taken away by suspensions, even temporarily, without due process of law. The Court found that for short suspensions, less than 10 days, students must be given informal notice and a hearing including a statement of the charges and evidence against them, as well as an opportunity to tell their side of the story. In *Wood* v. *Strickland* (1975), the Court expanded the *Goss* ruling to state that school officials may be sued for monetary damages if they know or reasonably should have known that their disciplinary actions would violate the constitutional rights of pupils.

While *Goss* protected the child's procedural due process requirement, the court noted that suspensions are "considered not only to be a necessary tool to maintain order but a valuable education device" (*Goss* at 580). Therefore immediate suspension is sometimes appropriate to protect other pupils and to preserve the decorum of the school. Students whose presence imposes a continuing danger to persons or property or constitutes an ongoing threat of disrupting the academic process may be immediately removed from school.

From the limited case law available on the subject, it is not entirely clear whether a pupil can be expelled from a public school permanently. However, there is no doubt that a pupil can be expelled from public school if the board of education then places the student in an alternative school. Generally, however, expulsion of a student by a board of education does not extend past the end of the current school year.

Another area that remains unclear is the types of incidents that can trigger an expulsion. State law varies on the types of infractions and what procedures are required to be given to students before they can be expelled. Some courts treat expulsions and long-term suspensions as equivalent. Most hold that pupils facing expulsion or long-term suspension have the right to additional due process practices including a written statement of the charges, enough time to prepare a defense, and an impartial hearing on the evidence. Many states delineate the procedures for expelling children from school and the rights students have in these procedures in their legislation. The rights may include presenting and cross-examining witnesses, a hearing before a hearing officer, an appeal to the school board, the right to a transcript of the proceedings, and court review.

The concept of removing children from school on a short-term or permanent basis has been further complicated by two recent developments. One of these developments is the passage of the Gun-Free Schools Act and the other is the overwhelming increase in zero-tolerance policies.

In 1994, Congress passed the Gun-Free Schools Act, which was reauthorized and recodified in 2002. The Gun-Free Schools Act mandates that all local educational authorities have a policy in place that requires a one-year expulsion for any child who brings a firearm to school or possesses a firearm on school property. The law, in defining what constitutes a firearm, refers to the federal Criminal Code (20 U.S.C. 921(a) (2002)). Under the criminal law, a firearm is defined as any weapon, including a starter pistol, that is designed or modified to expel a projectile (like a bullet) by the action of explosives. A firearm also includes "destructive devices" like bombs, grenades, rockets, missiles, and mines. As a result of the Gun-Free Schools Act, school districts must have a policy that children can be expelled from school for bringing a firearm, broadly defined, to school. Many school districts or state laws have broadened the concept of firearms to include other weapons, such as knives. Other districts have also expanded upon the punishment for infractions (e.g., requiring an expulsion to last for the remainder of the school year and the entire following year).

The Gun-Free Schools Act also requires that school districts refer a case to the criminal justice or juvenile delinquency systems when a student brings a firearm or weapon to school. The law does allow for some discretion. Congress attempted to give discretion to school officials by allowing that the gun-free expulsion policy can be modified on a case-by-case basis. Additionally, there is nothing in the federal law to prevent a school district from choosing to provide education in an alternative setting to an expelled student.

While the federal law allows for case-by-case discretion, many school districts have passed zero-tolerance policies that allow none. Within the last decade, "zero-tolerance" policies have developed throughout the country. Zero-tolerance policies proscribe behaviors that will not be accepted and mandates predetermined consequences or punishments for specific offenses. As they first developed, zero-tolerance policies focused on truly dangerous and criminal behavior by students that required mandatory expulsion.

Today, zero-tolerance policies not only include weapons but may also govern drugs and alcohol, gang activities, tobacco offenses, fighting and other disruptive activities, sexual harassment, threatening speech, and other prohibited incidents (Ballard, 2002). Proponents of zero-tolerance policies believe that they increase safety in the school and have the support of educators and parents. The critics of zero-tolerance oppose its one-size-fits-all mentality; in other words, no matter whether there are legitimate reasons or justifications why students break policy, they are treated in the same way and punishment is meted out in accordance with a stated policy.

Henault (2001) reports a number of incidents in which students were suspended or expelled from school because of seemingly innocuous violations of their schools' policies. Among her examples, Henault cites situations that occurred in West Virginia and Louisiana. For example, in West Virginia, a seventh grader who shared a zinc cough drop with a classmate was suspended for three days pursuant to the school's anti-drug policy because the cough drop was not cleared with the office. In Louisiana, a second-grader brought his grandfather's watch to school for show and tell; attached to the watch was a one-inch-long pocketknife. Because the school viewed this a violation of its weapons policy, the child was suspended and sent to an alternative school for a month.

The media, seemingly amused by the newsworthiness of these stories, often report instances where children were suspended or expelled pursuant to zero-tolerance policies. For example, in Georgia, an 11-year-old girl was suspended for two weeks for bringing her "Tweety Bird" wallet to school. The school considered it to be a weapon because it had a short chain connecting the wallet to her key ring (*Georgia girl,* 2000). In Ohio, a 13-year-old honor student was suspended for ten days for accepting two Midol pills, given to her by a friend, for menstrual discomfort. After she agreed to go to drug awareness classes, she returned to her classroom and her suspension was reduced to three days in her school records (*Midol suspension,* 1996).

Just recently, parents angry about their children's suspensions and expulsions have successfully challenged their districts' zero-tolerance policies. In a Pennsylvania case (*Lyons* v. *Penn Hills Sch. Dist.,* 1999), a 12-year-old, seventh-grade honor student was seen filing his fingernail with a miniature Swiss army knife he had found in a school hallway. The instructor requested the child to turn over the penknife and the student complied without incident. The knife was ultimately brought to the school's associate principal, who questioned the child about it.

Lyons told the associate principal that he had found the knife and had intended to turn it over to his instructor. The school informed the parents that the child had violated the school's zero-tolerance policy and that there would be an expulsion hearing before a hearing officer. The school board adopted the hearing officer's recommendation that the student be expelled from school for one year. The parents sued the school district and the appellate court affirmed the trial court's ruling against the district. The court found that the school district, in enacting its local zero-tolerance policy, exceeded its authority because it did not give the superintendent case-by-case discretion as provided in Pennsylvania law. In a Tennessee case, a student was expelled for having a knife in his car on school property. He claimed that he was unaware of the knife's presence, due to his transporting some of his friends. The Sixth Circuit ruled that if the student unknowingly possessed the weapon, then suspending or expelling him for weapons possession was irrational (*Seal* v. *Morgan,* 2000). These cases may be the beginning of a trend that will impose a reasonableness standard in zero-tolerance policies.

Whether or not zero-tolerance policies can be drafted to be reasonable, recent studies have shown that zero-tolerance policies not only increase the numbers of students who are suspended and expelled but also are differentially enforced against African-American and Latino students. For example, the U.S. Department of Education (2000) reported that in 1998, more than 3.1 million students were suspended, with another 87,000 students expelled. However, while African-American children represent only 17% of public school enrollment nationally, they make up 32% of out-of-school suspensions. In contrast, white students, who make up 63% of the national enrollment, make up only 50% of the suspensions and 50% of the expulsions. Another recent study that interviewed attorneys who represent children facing disciplinary actions based on zero-tolerance policies found that

those attorneys believed that racial profiling played a large part in determining which students were subject to harsh penalties (Harvard Project, 2000). The attorneys reported that African-American and Latino students were more likely to be disciplined for offenses such as defiance or disrespect of authority. The attorneys believed that the subjectivity of what is considered "disrespect" could lead to a racial bias in student discipline.

Discipline of Children with Disabilities

As you will see in Chapter 8, students with disabilities have the right to a free and appropriate public education that is appropriate to their needs. Prior to the passage of the Education for all Handicapped Children's Act in 1975 (EAHCA, P.L. 94-142), now known as the Individuals with Disabilities Education Act (IDEA) (P.L. 101-476), school officials often used disciplinary measures to purposefully exclude children with disabilities from education. As a result, safeguards were incorporated into the EAHCA, so that expulsions or long-term suspensions would trigger procedural protections from exclusion.

Many children with disabilities exhibit behaviors that put them in conflict with school rules. For example, a child that has difficulty sitting still may disrupt his or her learning environment. A child with behavior problems may defy school rules. A child who has difficulty reading may exhibit frustration and low self-esteem that may trigger attention-getting behaviors. Because children with disabilities are entitled to receive a uniquely designed education to meet their needs, discipline which involves removing the child from the educational environment is considered to be a change of placement and requires a reconvening of the I.E.P. team to look at the child's behavior. If the parents object to any proposed plan, a child with a disability will "stay-put" in the current educational placement, regardless of the seriousness of the child's behavior, while the dispute is pending. In *Honig* v. *Doe* (1988) a California school district attempted to expel children with disabilities from school, because they exhibited behavior that the school considered dangerous. The U.S. Supreme Court found that no exception to the stay-put requirement exists for children exhibiting dangerous behavior. If a school district believes that a child poses a real and serious risk to others, the Supreme Court suggested that the district go to their local court and seek an injunction to remove the child. Otherwise, the child had statutory rights to remain in the school environment, regardless of concerns regarding his or her behavior.

As should be clear by now, changes in society have made the schools less safe learning environments. When the Gun-Free Schools Act was enacted in 1994, an exception to the "stay-put" aspect of IDEA was included so that students with disabilities who brought weapons to school could be removed from the educational environment. However, this was limited to weapons only and not behavioral issues, and the child could not be removed for more than 45 days. The child would still receive educational services in an interim alternative educational setting.

In 1997, the Individuals with Disabilities Education Act Amendments of 1997 (P. L. 105-17), changed many of the provisions of IDEA. In the new law and the 1999 regulations that interpreted it, rules regarding discipline of children with disabilities became part of legislation for the first time.

Under the new law, public schools are authorized to remove a child with a disability for 45 days to an alternative education setting for possession of not only guns but all dangerous weapons or for the use, possession, or sale of illegal drugs or controlled substances on school grounds. Additionally, a child with a disability can be removed for up to 45 days if the child is substantially likely to cause injury by remaining in the current educational environment. Schools are not required to provide any services to a child with a disability for the first 10 days of any removal. If a child is removed for more than 10 consecutive school days, a disciplinary "change of placement" occurs. In that case, the school district must convene an I.E.P. meeting to determine whether the problematic behavior is actually a manifestation of the child's disability. If it is a manifestation, the I.E.P. team must conduct a functional behavioral assessment and implement a "behavioral intervention plan," to create specific interventions designed to address the problematic behaviors. If the child needs to be removed from school on subsequent occasions, the I.E.P. team must review the plan to determine what modifications are necessary. If the behavior is not a manifestation of the child's disability, the child can be disciplined to the same extent as a non-disabled child. However, appropriate educational services still must be provided to enable the child with disabilities to progress appropriately in the general curriculum and appropriately advance toward the goals set out in the child's I.E.P. (Altshuler & Kopels, in press).

Children with disabilities have heightened legal protections with respect to being suspended or expelled from school and at the same time, schools have more limits placed on their powers to discipline them. Therefore, with respect to the discipline issues we have discussed, children with disabilities have a legal advantage over children who do not have disabilities. However, as we have seen, protections for all children seem to be eroding. For any child, being removed from the school environment has very serious consequences.

Some Negative Consequences of Suspensions and Expulsions from School

It should be apparent that removing children from the learning environment of the school by means of short-term suspensions or longer-term expulsions will have serious negative consequences for students. There are also additional negative consequences for the overall community when children do not receive an education.

Suspensions and expulsions have immediate and long-range effects that impact directly and indirectly on students, the school staff, and the larger community. Suspensions also interrupt the pupils' instructional program. Since many suspended students experience academic difficulty, the lost instructional time may determine their academic success for the semester. If the school does not permit the pupils to make up exams and homework, the lost grades may automatically mean that no matter how high their previous or subsequent grades, the students will receive a failing mark. Consequently, they might not attempt to complete course work or attend school for the remainder of the semester. Additionally, those students who are expelled for the remainder of the school year or longer, especially if they are beyond the age of compulsory school attendance may decide to drop out of school permanently. Punitive discipline policies reject the student and these students are often "pushed out" of the school environment (Dupper, 1994).

Another consequence of suspension and expulsion is that other staff members in the school may label students as problems because the suspensions have been recorded in official school records and because knowledge of the suspensions has circulated among the staff. This may have formal as well as informal consequences. Informally, staff members may be quicker to refer pupils who have been suspended previously due to some vague perception that they are discipline problems. In a formal sense, a suspension is almost always considered in subsequent disciplinary incidents and usually influences the school to impose a longer suspension the next time.

In fact, in some states, newer laws pertaining to school records permit the disclosure of prior disciplinary reports when students transfer to a new school district. In this way, a student who has been suspended or expelled cannot escape serving a long-term suspension or expulsion by beginning anew in a different school district. For example, in Illinois, the student temporary record includes information regarding serious disciplinary infractions that resulted in expulsion, suspension, or the imposition of punishment or sanction. Parents cannot challenge the references to expulsions or out-of-school suspensions if the challenge is made at the time the student's school student records are forwarded (Illinois School Student Records Act, 2002). When the new school receives the student's records, they also are likely to perceive that the child is a discipline problem.

Suspensions and expulsions also isolate students from an important, structured environment. For most children, school is their first formal relationship with the government (Losen & Edley, 2001). Although some students may view suspension as a welcome vacation and may consciously manipulate the system to bring about this vacation, to others it represents the equivalent of solitary confinement. For this latter group, school represents a dynamic and important social setting that is a comfortable balance between structured routines and new and exciting experiences. Suspensions separate these pupils from an important part of their lives and isolate them psychologically from their families.

Suspensions and expulsions often lead to high levels of parent and community resentment because of what is perceived as the school's failure to meet the needs of pupils through less intrusive means. This resentment may cause open hostility that results in a refusal of parents to believe in or to support the schools, not only with regard to issues of discipline but also regarding more general issues that affect education.

Perhaps the most important role social workers can play in matters of suspension and expulsion is to help the school, family, and community appreciate that excluding children from schools has very direct economic consequences for the school and community. For schools that receive state aid based on average daily attendance, suspensions and expulsions may result in a significant loss of state funds. Even for districts that receive state aid based on yearly enrollment, there is a loss in the sense that the schools have structured their instructional program and services for a larger number of pupils than will actually receive those services. The personal consequences of expulsions for the students can also make them extremely costly for society. If students are unable to acquire suitable employment because of their school record or because they lack basic skills for entry-level jobs or continuing education, the cost to society is extremely high. Until skills are developed and the record is overcome, society may have to provide public assistance and other unemployment benefits. Another societal cost resulting from expulsions may be increases in juvenile delinquency and, ultimately, criminal activity. The cost of increases in delinquency can be measured in terms of increased fear and suffering as well as in terms of increased financial costs for police, courts, detention facilities, and insurance.

Because of these factors, the uneducated youth in a community remain in their community and influence its development. Most communities want their youth to improve their situations with increased opportunities. Removal from school decreases opportunities for these students. Given the potential consequences and costs of expulsions for the student, the school, and society, it seems clear that schools should find ways to avoid school expulsions as often as possible and to reduce their negative consequences. There are a variety of other disciplinary tools including behavioral modification, rewards, and behavior contracts that can be tried, depending on a student's age group. These positive behavioral interventions have the advantage of allowing students to remain in school.

CONCLUSION

Student rights and the control of behavior in schools have experienced significant changes during the last half-century. Changes in the application of the principle of *in loco parentis* and the ebb and flow of liberal versus conservative public sentiments have influenced court decisions, and in turn, the actions of students, parents, and school administrators.

Fundamentally, what the various courts' decisions have established is that the school has jurisdiction over the child when the child is under the reasonable control of the school. The courts have held, however, that the teacher's right to control a child is not the same general right as that of parents; it is limited because teachers cannot exceed their responsibility. The courts have attempted to balance the constitutional rights of students to demonstrate their individuality—politically, religiously, and expressively, with the growing need of school personnel to control the learning environment and to keep the schools safe.

The courts have become very instrumental in assisting schools to develop common sense approaches to discipline, notwithstanding school officials' broad discretionary power to decide when punishment is appropriate and necessary. Social workers bring broad insights and social science knowledge in assisting administrators on this subject. For example, the social worker's understanding of frustration and aggression offers a theoretical base for helping school officials to mitigate aggressive impulses. Social workers can strongly advocate at I.E.P. meetings for the formulation of behavioral assessment plans that connect behavior problems to the students' disabilities (Altshuler & Kopels, in press). Evidence-based practice, in which social science data that correlates aggression with self-esteem, suggests certain kinds of interventions.

Social workers can help school officials appreciate that students must perceive that the decision to punish them resulted from reflection rather than anger. Social workers can encourage this perception by trying non-punitive techniques until it is clear that they will not work, and holding, at least, an informal hearing-like discussion about the reasons a student is being considered guilty and the nature of the punishment is a useful strategy.

Work by Schimmel and Eiseman (1982) has found that one important consideration in punishing children is that they must believe that whoever is selecting and inflicting punishment does so equitably. In other words, the pupil must believe that the school official would inflict the same punishment on anyone else who committed the same offense or who engaged in a similar pattern of disruptive behavior. Hearings play a central role in promoting fairness, and the more elements of due process are included, the harder it is for the student to maintain a perception that the official is being unjust. However, the increased use of zero-tolerance policies seems to belie this message. Students may believe that the government can take away their rights or privileges for seemingly trivial violations without first listening to their reasons or explanations regarding their actions.

Social workers in schools can play an important role in this area. They can assist in the development of policies and procedures for securing and maintaining records; they can consult with school officials regarding basic human rights; they can provide firm, constructive counsel to students about their responsibilities and remind them to have respect for others; and they can take the leadership in developing and refining student codes of conduct, and the penalties for their violation. Social workers are well-equipped by training and by their value orientation to organize committees composed of school officials, parents, pupils, and community leaders to prepare written guidelines and policy statements governing student behavior, due process, suspensions and expulsions, and other matters related to the orderly operation of schools.

Following are seven specific ways in which school social workers can assist the school and community to resolve problems related to student rights and student control.

1. Work with the local school board and lobby for restrictions on corporal punishment
2. Assist state lobby groups
3. Work with school officials and administrators to develop school code handbooks specifying reasonable expectations for pupils and teachers
4. Assist and act as advocate for students who have been unjustly or improperly punished
5. Provide in-service training to teachers on classroom management and suggest alternatives to corporal punishment and harsh discipline policies.
6. Advocate against zero-tolerance policies
7. Work to ensure alternative educational programs for students who have been expelled.

Goss v. *Lopez* established a legal principle that is useful for social workers in schools who are acting as mediators in matters of control of pupil behavior. The U.S. Constitution requires that government agencies treat all persons fairly. Specifically, the Fourteenth Amendment states that the government may not "deprive any person of life, liberty, or property, without due process of law." Social workers can play an important role in reminding principals, teachers, coaches, security guards, and all other employees of the school that they are employees of the government and, under the Fourteenth Amendment, they have a legal duty to treat all pupils fairly.

Social workers should provide leadership in guaranteeing that both sides of the story are clearly told. Social workers should ensure that the due process requirement is observed. Serious punishment such as suspension or expulsion should not be imposed for a slight breaking of the rules or for the kind of conduct for which pupils have in the past received only mild punishment. Due process requires not only that procedures for disciplining students be fair but also that school rules be fair.

Social workers should insist that the student know exactly what he or she is being accused of. For example, the typical suspension letter from a principal to a pupil's parents that merely states that the pupil is charged with "violating school rules" or "serious misconduct" or "disrespect" does not state adequately what offense is being charged or what rule has been violated. This, according to the principles enunciated in *Goss,* is not sufficient notice of the charges.

FOR STUDY AND DISCUSSION

1. The concept of *in loco parentis* has been practiced for a long time. Discuss its pros and cons in a society that has moved from a rural-agrarian culture to one now characterized as postindustrial and litigious.

2. What is your opinion regarding the adage, "Spare the rod and spoil the child"?

3. How would you assist school officials in discovering options to suspensions and expulsions? What specific roles could you play?

4. What are your opinions about prayer in schools?

5. What factors should you help the school district consider in developing a zero-tolerance policy?

REFERENCES

Alexander, K., & Alexander, M.D. (1998). *American public school law* (4th ed.). St. Paul, MN: West.

Altshuler, S. J., & Kopels, S. (in press). Advocating for children with disabilities: What's the new I.D.E.A.? *Social Work.*

Antell v. *Stokes,* 287 Mass. 103, 191 N.E. 407 (1934).

Baker v. *Owen,* 437 U.S. 907 (1975).

Ballard, M.K. (2002). *Schools social policy analysis: Zero tolerance policy.* Unpublished manuscript.

Beckham, J. (2000). Searches in public schools. In W. E. Camp, M. J. Connelly, K. E. Lane, & J. F. Mead (Eds.), *The Principal's Legal Handbook,* (2nd ed.) (pp. 3–24). Dayton, OH: Education Law Association.

Berger v. *Rensselaer Cent. School Corp.,* 982 F.2d 1160 (7th Cir., 1993).

Bethel School District No. 403 v. *Fraser,* 478 U.S. 675 (1986).

Bishop v. *Houston School District,* 35 S.W.2d 465 (Tex.Civ.App. 1931).

Board of Education v. Earls, _ U.S. _, 122 S. Ct. 2559 (2002).

Board of Education v. *Helston,* 32 Ill. App. 300 (1889).

Board of Education of Westside Community Schools v. *Mergens,* 496 U.S. 226 (1990).

Carestio v. *School Bd. of Broward County,* 79 F. Supp. 2d 1347 (S.D. Fla. 1999).

Chalifoux v. *New Carey Indep. Sch. Dist.,* 976 F. Supp. 659 (S.D. Tex. 1997).

Collins v. *Chandler Unified School District,* 644 F.2d 759 (9th Cir., 1981).

Condon, T., & Wolff, P. (1996). *School rights. A parent's legal handbook and action guide.* New York: Macmillan.

Covington County v. *G. W.,* 767 So. 2d 187 (Miss. 2000).

Daniels v. *Gordon,* 232 Ga. App. 811, 503 S. E. 2d 72 (1998).

Dupper, D.R. (1994). Reducing out-of-school suspensions: A survey of attitudes and barriers. *Social Work in Education, 16,* 115–123.

Education for All Handicapped Children Act, 20 U.S.C.A. § 1400 (1975).

Edwards v. *Aguillard,* 482 U.S. 578 (1987).

Eisenman, J. W., & Fischer, L. (1994). *The rights of students and teachers.* New York: Harper & Row.

Engle v. *Vitale,* 370 U.S. 421 (1962).

Family Educational Rights and Privacy Act, 20 U.S.C. § 1232(g) (1974).

Gaither v. *Barron,* 924 F. Supp. 134 (M.D. Ala., 1996).

Georgia girl's Tweety Bird chain runs afoul of weapons policy. (2000, September 28). Retrieved June 1, 2002, from http://www.cnn.com/2000/US/09/28/wallet.suspension.02/.

Gilbert, C. B. (1999). We are what we wear: Revisiting school dress codes. *1999 B.Y.U. Education & Law Journal, 3.*

Goss v. *Lopez,* 419 U.S. *565* (1975).

Gun-Free Schools Act. 20 U.S.C.§§ 8921-8926 (1994). 20 U.S.C. 7151 (2002).

Harris v. *Joint Sch. Dist. No. 241,* 821 F. Supp. 638 (D. Idaho, 1993).

Harvard Project. (2000). *Opportunities suspended: The devastating consequences of zero tolerance and school discipline policies.* Report by the Advancement Project and The Civil Rights Project. Retrieved June 1, 2002, from http://www.law.harvard.edu/civilrights/conferences/zero/zt_report2.html.

Hazelwood School District v. *Kuhlmeier,* 484 U.S. 260 (1988).

Henault, C. (2001). Zero tolerance in school. *Journal of Law & Education, 30,* 547.

Hines ex rel. Oliver v. *McClung,* 919 F.Supp. 1206, (N.D. Ind. 1995).

Honig v. *Doe,* 484 U.S. 305 (1988).

Hsu by and through Hsu v. *Roslyn Free School District No. 3,* 85 F.3d 839 (2nd Cir. N.Y., 1996).

Hyman, R. T., & Rathbone, C.H. (1993). *Corporal punishment in schools: Reading the law.* Topeka, KS: NOLPE.

Illinois School Student Records Act. 105 I.L.C.S. § 10/1 et. seq. (2002).

Ingraham v. *Wright,* 430 U.S. 651 (1977).

Jones v. *Clear Creek Independent School District,* 977 F. 2d 963 (5th Cir. 1992).

Juan G. v. *Cortines,* 223 A.D.2d 126, 647 N.Y.S.2d 491 (N.Y.A.D. 1996).

Karr v. *Schmidt,* 460 F.2d 609 (5th Cir. 1972).

Kenny v. *Gurley,* 208 Ala. 625, 95 So. 34 (1923).

Kopels, S. (1992). Confidentiality and the school social worker. *Social Work in Education, 14(4),* 203–205.

Kopels, S. (1998). Wedded to the status quo: Same-sex marriage after *Baehr* v. *Lewin. Journal of Gay and Lesbian Social Services, 8*(3), 69–81.

Lander v. *Seaver,* 32 Vt. 114 (1859).

Lee v. *Weisman,* 505 U.S. 577 (1992).

London v. Directors of DeWitt Pub. Schs., 194 F.3d 873 (8th Cir. 1999).

Losen, D. J., & Edley, C. (2001). The role of law in policing abusive disciplinary practices: Why school discipline is a civil rights issue. In *2001: A Legal Odyssey:2001 conference papers, topic outlines* (pp. 82–103). Dayton, OH: Education Law Association.

Lyons v. *Penn Hills Sch. Dist.,* 723 A.2d 1073 (Pa. Comm. Ct. 1999).

Malnak v. *Yogi,* 592 F.2d. 197 (3rd Cir. 1979).

Mangum v. *Keith,* 145 Ga. 603, 95 S.E. 1 (1918).

McCarthy, M. (2000). Devotional activities in public schools. In W. E. Camp, M. J. Connelly, K. E. Lane, & J. F. Mead (Eds.), *The Principal's Legal Handbook* (2nd ed.) (pp. 293–312). Dayton, OH: Education Law Association.

McCarthy, M. (2002). Anti-harassment policies in public schools: How vulnerable are they? *Journal of Law and Education, 31,* 52.

Metzger v. *Osbeck,* 841 F.2d 518 (3d Cir. 1988).

Midol suspension ends: Honor student returns to class (1996, October 3). Retrieved June 1, 2002, from http://www.cnn.com/US/9610/03/midol.suspension/index.html.

Minersville School Dist. v. *Gobitis,* 310 U.S. 586 (1940).

Morris v. *Nowotny,* 323 S.W. 2d 302 (Tex.Civ.App. Austin 1959).

National Association of Social Workers. (October, 2001). *Confidentiality and school social work: A practice perspective.* Retrieved June 1, 2002, from http://www.socialworkers.org/practice.

National Coalition Against Corporal Punishment in Schools. Retrieved June 1, 2002 from http://www.stophitting.com.

Neal v. *Fulton County Bd. of Educ.,* 229 F.3d 1069 (11th Cir. 2000).

Neuhaus v. *Federico,* 12 Or. App. 315, 505 P. 939 (1973).

New Jersey v. *T.L.O.,* 469 U.S. 325 (1985).

P.B. v. *Koch,* 96 F.3d 1298 (9th Cir. 1996).

People v. *Dilworth,* 169 Ill. 2d 195, 661 N.E. 2d 310 (1996).

People v. *Overton,* 24 N.Y. 2d 522, 242 N.E. 2d 366 (1969).

People v. *Pruitt,* 278 Ill. App. 3d 194, 662 N.E. 2d 540 (1996).

Phoenix Elem. Sch. Dist. No. 1 v. Green, 189 Ariz. 476, 943 P. 2d 836 (1997).

Pugsley v. *Sellmeyer,* 158 Ark. 247, 250 S.W. 538 (1923).

Rando v. Newberg Public School Board, 23 Or.App 425, 542 P. 2d 938 (1975).

San Antonio Ind. Sch. Dist. v. *Rodriguez,* 411 U.S. 1 (1973).

Santa Fe Independent School District v. *Doe,* 530 U.S. 290 (2000).

Saxe v. *State College Area School Dist. (SCASD),* 240 F. 3d 200 (3rd Cir. 2001).

Saylor v. *Board of Educ.,* 118 F. 3d 507 (6th Cir. 1997).

Schimmel, D. M., & Eiseman, J. (1982, Fall). *School discipline, round two.* Update on law-related education. Chicago: American Bar Association.

School District of Abington Twp., Pennsylvania v. *Schempp,* 374 U.S. 203 (1965).

Seal v. *Morgan,* 229 F. 3d. 567 (6th Cir., 2000).

Simpson, R. E. Jr. (2001). Limits on students' speech in the Internet Age. *Dickinson Law Review, 105,* 181.

Smith v. *Board of Education,* 182 Ill. App. 342 (1913).

In Re S.S., 452 Pa. Super. 15, 680 A. 2d 1172 (1996).

Stanley v. *Northeast Independent School District,* 462 F. 2d. 960 (5th Cir. 1972).

State ex rel. Juvenile Department of Lincoln County v. *Finch,* 144 Or. App. 42, 925 P. 2d 913 (1996).

State of Florida v. *J.A.,* 679 So. 2d 316 (1996).

Stone v. *Graham,* 449 U.S. 39 (1980).

Tanton v. *McKenney,* 226 Mich. 245, 197 N.W. 510 (1924).

Tinker v. *Des Moines School Board,* 393 U.S. 503 (1969).

Urbonya, K.R. (2001). Determining reasonableness under the Fourth Amendment: Physical force to control and punish students. *Cornell J. L. & Public Policy, 10,* 397.

U.S. Department of Education. (2000). *Fall 1998 elementary and secondary school civil rights compliance report: National and state projections.* Washington, DC: Author.

USA Patriot Act of 2001, "Uniting and Strengthening America Act by Providing Appropriate Tools Required to Intercept and Obstruct Terrorism." P.L. 107-56, 115 Stat. 272 (2001).

Veronia Sch. Dist. v. *Acton,* 515 U.S. 646 (1995).

West Virginia State Board of Education v. *Barnette,* 319 U.S. 624 (1943).

Wigoren, J. (2001, May 3). Lawsuits touch off debate over paddling in the schools. *The New York Times,* pp. Al, A22.

Wood v. *Strickland,* 420 U.S. 308 (1975).

Wooster v. *Sunderland,* 27 Cal. App. 51, 148 P. 959 (1915).

Zarichney v. *State Board of Agriculture,* 338 U.S. 118 (1949).

Zelman v. *Simmons-Harris,* _ U.S. _, 122 S. Ct. 2460 (2002).

CHAPTER 7

VIOLENCE IN SCHOOLS

RON AVI ASTOR, UNIVERSITY OF SOUTHERN CALIFORNIA
RAMI BENBENISHTY, HEBREW UNIVERSITY
ROXANA MARACHI, UNIVERSITY OF MICHIGAN

INTRODUCTION

Violence prevention in schools is becoming a major focus of practice for school social workers (Astor, 1998; Astor, Behre, Fravil, & Wallace, 1997; Astor, Behre, Wallace, & Fravil, 1998; Astor & Meyer, 1999; Astor, Pitner, Meyer, & Vargas, 2000; Klein, 2002). Social work as a profession has contributed to the national and international dialogue concerning violence intervention programs (for examples see Astor, 1995; Astor & Meyer, 2001; Benbenishty, Astor, Zeira, & Vinokur, in press; Benbenishty, Astor, & Zeira, in press; Jenson & Howard, 1999; Zeira, Benbenishty, & Astor, in press; Zeira, Astor, & Benbenishty, 2002) and school social workers play an increasingly important role in shaping and implementing policy, interventions, and procedures that make U.S. schools safer. In order to be effective, school social workers need to be aware of current philosophical, empirical, and practice issues surrounding school violence. Several intervention approaches have demonstrated significant reductions in school violence and overall national trends have indicated declines in school violence rates (U.S. Departments of Education & Justice, 2000). Social workers could be very effective in creating an accurate national awareness regarding the tremendous strides schools have made on this issue over the past ten years. By providing accurate information on school violence, they may help counter some harmful misperceptions that exist in the media

and general public. In this chapter, we review some of the major trends in U.S. school violence and explore potential areas where school social workers could make an impact, at both conceptual and practical levels.

MAJOR TRENDS AND ISSUES

Expanding school violence definitions and behaviors. During the past 30 years, many physically and psychologically harmful behaviors have been subsumed under the term *school violence.* The concept of school violence now spans an array of behaviors that includes physical harm, psychological harm, and property damage. Currently, the term "school violence" could include behaviors that vary in severity and frequency such as bullying, verbal threats, and intimidation (Batsche & Knoff, 1994; Olweus, 1993; Olweus, Limber, & Mihalic, 1999), vandalism (Goldstein, 1996), school fighting (Boulton, 1993; Schafer & Smith, 1996), corporal punishment (Benbenishty, Zeira, & Astor, in press; Benbenishty, Zeira, Astor, & Khoury-Kassabri, in press; Youssef, Attia, & Kamel, 1998), sexual harassment (Stein, 1995), gang violence (Kodluboy, 1997; Parks, 1995), the presence of weapons (Pittel, 1998), violence directed at school staff (Benbenishty, Zeira, & Astor, 2000), rape (Page, 1997), hate crimes geared at students from ethnic/religious groups or at gay, lesbian, bisexual, and transsexual students (Berrill, 1990), dating violence (Burcky, Reuterman, & Kopsky, 1988; Cano, Avery-Leaf, Cascardi, & O'Leary, 1998), and murder (Bragg, 1997; Hays, 1998). Many of these types of behaviors have evolved into separate research and practice literatures. In this chapter, we present an overview of the trends and prevalence rates of select types of school violence in the United States. We have focused mainly on the kinds of violence (e.g., violent crimes, weapon carrying, school fatalities, school fights, etc.) that have nationally representative data. One potentially harmful myth about school violence is that it is currently on the rise in U.S. schools. However, contrary to what most of the U.S. public perceives, empirical data indicate steady declines in the rates of school violence (U.S. Departments of Education & Justice, 2000). In the next section we outline reductions in violence in detail significant.

THE MYTH OF A CONTINUAL RISE IN SCHOOL VIOLENCE RATES

Fatal victimization on school grounds. It is important for school social workers to know that media perceptions and national norms surrounding violent deaths in schools are not entirely accurate. This understanding is especially important because many of the misperceptions center around issues of race, socioeconomic status, and gender. Furthermore, the efforts of school personnel may go unacknowledged by the media and general public due to the perception that violent school deaths and shootings are on the rise.

The intense public attention on school violence is most likely associated with the widespread media coverage given to late 1990s mass homicides on school grounds. This nationwide attention to violent deaths in schools reflects a normative shift in U.S. cultural attitudes regarding violent deaths on school grounds. However, research suggests that violent death on school grounds existed at comparable or higher rates

before the intense media coverage of the late 1990s. For example, Kachur et al. (1996) report that there were 105 violent deaths on school grounds in 1992–1993 (these numbers include suicide, manslaughter, student, and non-student deaths). However, in 1997–1998 (the year of the Columbine shootings) there were 60 violent deaths and in 1998–1999 there were 50 violent deaths on school grounds. If we examine the number of fatal events, government data show that the actual number of events has also decreased in recent years (e.g., 49 events in 1995–1996 compared with 34 events in 1998–1999). One might argue that we now have a greater awareness about school deaths and should not tolerate even 50 deaths (we support such a position). However, empirical evidence suggests that U.S. schools have seen a 50% *reduction* in violent deaths on school grounds since 1992–1993. We emphasize this reduction in order to acknowledge that efforts at violence prevention may be making an impact and that there is reason to hope that violence rates can decline even further.

Due to the intensified media coverage of the school shootings, many in the general public are now under the impression that violent deaths in schools are a relatively new phenomena and that fatalities are increasing on school grounds in the United States. We suspect that many in the general public have distorted perceptions of the frequency of school fatalities, and may not be aware of how rare school fatalities actually are in U.S. society. Government data indicate that violent deaths are not common occurrences on school grounds when compared with other settings (such as neighborhoods and homes). For example, if we examine the act of murder between students as a subset of "violent deaths," in 1997–1998 there were 2,717 murders off school grounds and 35 murders on school grounds (Kaufman et al., 2000; U.S. Departments of Education & Justice, 2000). This evidence suggests that students may be safer from violent crime when they are in school than when they are out of school and further illuminates the stark difference between public perception and actual violence rates in U.S. schools.

In addition to the misperceptions about overall violence rates, many misunderstandings exist around issues of race, religion, and violence. Patterns of fatal student victimization fluctuate over time, vary across areas, and also differ among ethnic groups. These variations occur in our society in general (Ash, Kellermann, Fuqua-Whitley, & Johnson, 1996; Gray, 1991; Hammond & Yung, 1993; Issacs, 1992; Prothrow-Stith & Weissman, 1991) and also on school grounds (Astor, Pitner, & Duncan, 1996; Kachur et al., 1996; Kaufman et al., 1998).

One of the common public myths of the post-Columbine era is that school fatalities are for the first time occurring in suburban areas, whereas prior to Columbine, fatal school deaths were occurring primarily in urban settings. Another contradictory media myth is that recent violent deaths (especially those involving shootings) have not occurred in inner-city/urban schools in the past and that shootings are associated with a new phenomenon of alienated angry white suburban males. These myths are unsubstantiated. The data suggest that a significant proportion of violent deaths occurred in *both* settings before and after the late 1990 shootings. Kachur et al. (1996) reported that in 1992–1993 (prior to the Columbine shootings), 30% of the school fatalities occurred in suburbs, 62% occurred in urban areas, and 8% occurred in rural settings. These statistics raise serious questions as to why the media and public continue to perpetuate unsubstantiated and potentially harmful myths that serve as "proxies" for racial and economic stereotyping. School fatalities occurred in both urban *and* suburban areas during the early 1990s. Urban and suburban media coverage of violent deaths did not receive the same national media attention as those occurring in the late 1990s in the suburbs. Furthermore, the perception that violence in the late 1990s is exclusive to the "angry white males" ignores the actual rates of

school fatalities of other ethnic groups. For example, in 1998 during the peak of the intense media coverage, Hispanic students were five times more likely and African American students nine times more likely than white students to suffer a school-related lethal event (Kaufman et al., 1998).

Weapons on school grounds. The *potential* for lethal violence in schools remains quite high due to the availability of weapons. Nevertheless, the U.S. public and school personnel are not aware generally of the impressive declines in the presence of weapons on school grounds in recent years. This lack of awareness is particularly problematic because many federal, state, and district policies have been focused on the reduction of weapons on school grounds (U.S. Departments of Education & Justice, 2000). It is possible that the policies implemented have had a dramatic effect. For example, between 1993 and 1999, the Department of Education reported that the percentage of students in grades 9–12 who reported bringing a gun on school grounds during the 30 days preceding the survey dropped from 12% to 7%. If accurate, this would be an astonishing 42% reduction in the number of students who report bringing weapons on to school grounds. There are also significant gender differences in rates of weapon carrying, with male students being almost four times more likely to carry a weapon on school property than female students (11% vs. 2.8%, respectively) (Kann et al., 2000; U.S. Departments of Education & Justice, 2000).

Ironically, the most pronounced decline in weapons use has been the most ignored by the media and society. Although it is not widely known, rates of weapon carrying to school for African American students have dropped considerably more than the national average and have dropped more than any other ethnic group in the United States. For example, between 1993 and 1999 the rate of African American students reporting weapons on school campuses dropped by two thirds. Compared with other groups, African

American students went from having the highest reported rates in 1993 to the lowest reported rates of weapons in 1999. This accomplishment should be tempered with the knowledge that the national percentage of students in grades 9–12 who report being threatened and/or injured by someone using a weapon on school grounds has remained very constant (between 7% and 8% from 1993–1997. These injury rates appear slightly higher (9% to 10%) for African American and Hispanic groups (Kann et. al, 2000; Kaufman et al., 2000; U.S. Departments of Education & Justice, 2000). Nevertheless, from a social work perspective, education surrounding these dramatic reductions should be a primary goal because national policy is often influenced by inaccurate stereotypes. One can only wonder why an increase in weapon carrying by students of color is national headline news, while a historic drop in weapon carrying by students of color has gone largely unreported by the national media.

Expulsion for weapons and zero tolerance. Some are crediting the zero tolerance gun laws as the major cause for the decline of overall weapons on school campuses. Due to national and state zero tolerance laws, many students have been expelled for bringing weapons on school grounds in recent years. However, consistent with the other data presented in this chapter, expulsion rates have also gone down. Rates of expulsion for firearms dropped from 5,724 in 1996–1997 to 3,658 in 1998–1999. While it is true that these school expulsions may be reducing the number of students with weapons, there ought to be serious social concern over where these expelled and potentially violent students are going after they are expelled (U.S. Departments of Education & Justice, 2000).

From a social work and public policy perspective, it is unwise to deprive a potentially violent and armed youth of an education. To the detriment of society as well as the lives of these youth, current policy does not 1) provide alternative programs, 2) track the success of these programs, or 3) track the expelled students' whereabouts. According to current U.S. govern-

ment data, 44% of students expelled were referred to alternative programs; however, we do not know how many students actually went or stayed in those programs and how successful those programs were. This problem is a serious public health/safety gap in the current zero tolerance laws that needs to be addressed. School social workers' advocacy and education of the public could play a vital role in this policy issue.

As a corollary to the zero tolerance laws, some advocacy groups and academicians have argued that the zero tolerance laws should be administered more judiciously in order to create a "safe" climate rather than a punitive climate of fear (Noguera, 1995). It has been argued that what has been defined as "security" does not necessarily translate into a safe environment (Noguera, 1995). Hyman and Snook (2000) suggest that these kinds of extreme measures have created an authoritarian and punitive environment that may be inconsistent with the public schools' overall goals of creating democratic citizens.

In a study conducted through the National Center for Education Statistics, Heaviside et al. (1998) examined some of the effects of tough zero tolerance policies. They found that schools relying too heavily on zero tolerance policies continue to be less safe than schools that implemented fewer components of zero tolerance. A study by Mayer and Leone (1999) used structural equation modeling to predict the incidence of school violence. They found that over-reliance on physical security procedures appeared to be associated with an *increased* risk of school disorder. Also qualitative research has suggested that misuse of school security measures such as locker or strip searches may create emotional backlash in students (Hyman & Perone, 1998). In light of these findings, it becomes increasingly important to assess not only the violence that occurs in schools, but also to examine how the school climate may be impacted by procedures that are enacted to curb violence. Oftentimes, measures intended to remedy a problem may inadvertently exacerbate it. School social workers should add their voices to this kind of debate about what "security" means to students.

Physical fights on school grounds. Serious physical school fights are perhaps one of the most familiar forms of school violence. Teachers and administrators could use social workers' guidance in developing response procedures to school fights from an ecological and school community perspective. Annual rates of fights on school grounds for students in 9th to 12th grade from 1993 to 1999 have shown a slight decline from 16% to 14%. Overall, male students were more likely to report that they had been involved in a physical fight on school property in the past 12 months (20% of males vs. 9% of females). Rates of being involved in a physical fight on school property also varied by grade level with students in lower grades reporting that they had been involved in more fights on school property than students in upper grades. More specifically, approximately 21% of ninth graders reported being involved in a physical fight in the past year, compared to only 10% of twelfth graders (Kaufman, et al., 2000). Statistics from the Youth Risk Behavior Surveillance System (Y.R.B.S.S; Kann, et al, 2000) estimate that 14% of students reported that they had been in a physical fight on school grounds in the 12 months preceding the survey. Kann et al. (2000) also reported significant differences by race/ethnicity in students' involvement in fights on school property. Overall, African American students (18.7%) were significantly more likely than white students (12.3%) to report that they had been involved in a physical fight on school grounds during the 12 months prior to the survey.

We caution the reader, however, about the interpretation of the historical school fight statistics. "School grounds" was not defined in these studies and it is unclear whether students included fights that occurred immediately after school just off of school grounds. This issue of school versus community fights is important because Department of Justice statistics indicate that the highest rates of student/youth fights and assaults occur mainly on school days between 3

p.m. and 4 p.m. (much closer to 3 than 4) near school grounds. We believe that many of these kinds of fights emanate from school social dynamics (i.e., are potentially controllable by the school) and should be categorized as school fights (rather than community or elsewhere). Currently, fights occurring after 3 p.m. are most likely not counted as school fights. Hence, the number of school-related fights is probably much higher than the percentages listed above.

Given this caveat, and as a way of understanding the possible total amount of fights, according to the Centers for Disease Control and Prevention (CDC) in 1997, 37% of secondary-aged students were involved in serious fights (all contexts) during that year (46% of males and 26% of females). Again, the vast majority of these occurred just after 3 p.m. and only on school days. If school social dynamics were *not* a key component, we would see much higher rates on non-school days and more variation in the after school hours. In fact, the rate of fights on non-school days is very low and does not include the afternoon spike in events that accounts for most fights (Snyder & Sickmund, 1999). These overall fight percentages have also slightly declined since 1993.

Other nonfatal forms of violence. If the total number of student victimization events are examined (including nonfatal crimes such as rape, sexual assault, robbery, aggravated assault, and simple assault), there were significant declines in victimization between 1992 (144 crimes per 1,000 students) and 1998 (101 per 1,000 students). That translates into 700,000 fewer crimes committed against students in 1998 than in 1992. Some of the declines for specific crimes are notable. For example in 1992 there were 95 thefts per 1,000 students (ages 12 to 18) whereas in 1998 there were 58 per 1,000 thefts. In 1992 more students reported being victims to serious violent crimes and assault (48 per 1,000) than in 1998 (43 per 1,000). This data adds more evidence that we are in the midst of a profound decline in student victimization rates (Kann et al., 1998; Kaufman et al., 2000; U.S. Departments of Education & Justice, 2000).

Gang activity at school. Between 1995 and 1999, there have been extraordinary reductions in reported gang activity in schools. With all the media hype of the late 1980s and early 1990s on the influence of gangs on school violence, these reductions have gone virtually unnoticed in the national media and public awareness. The percentage of students who reported gangs present in their school dropped significantly from 1995 to 1999 (from 29% to 17%). The reductions of gang activity in school have been strong across all settings. Urban, suburban, and rural schools have reported reductions of 16%, 10%, and 9%, respectively. The reduction in gang activity on school grounds has also been pronounced across different ethnic groups with 10%, 22%, and 10% reductions reported for African American, Hispanic, and white youth, respectively (Kaufman et al., 2000; U.S Departments of Education & Justice, 2000). This is yet another area where the media and general public have not acknowledged positive societal change and dramatic improvements in historically oppressed groups of students.

Student perceptions of safety at school/on the way to and from school. The U.S. Departments of Education and Justice report indicated declines in the percentages of students who reported that they avoided places due to fear of attack at school from 1995 to 1999 (9% to 5% respectively) (Kaufman et al., 2000). The reductions of fear were greater in urban settings (12% vs. 6 % in 1995 and 1999 respectively) and for Hispanic students (13% vs. 6% for 1995 and 1999, respectively). In 1995, students in urban settings were more likely to be fearful at school, whereas in 1999 fear amongst urban students dropped so significantly that urban and suburban students were equally likely to be fearful of violence at schools. Students were also less likely to fear that they would be attacked while traveling to and from school from 1995 to 1999 (7% to 4%, respectively). Across all years, trends suggest that younger students (grades 9 and 10) were more likely than older students (grades 11 and 12) to fear being attacked while traveling to

and from school (Kann et al., 1998; Kaufman et al., 2000; U.S. Departments of Education & Justice, 2000).

Bully/victim rates. Recently, the United States participated in a cross-national research project coordinated by the World Health Organization on the prevalence of bullying and victims on school grounds. This first U.S. representative sample consisted of students in grades 6 to 10. Nansel and colleagues (2001) found that 10.6% of the sample reported bullying others sometimes (moderate), and 8.8% admitted to bullying others frequently (once a week or more). Reports on victimization were slightly lower—8.5% of students reported being bullied sometimes and 8.4% once a week or more. About 30% of the sample reported being involved in school bullying either moderately or frequently, as bullies (13.0%), victims (10.6%), or both as victims and bullies (6.3%).

Teacher and School Social Worker Victimization. According to the National Crime Victimization Survey (see Kaufman et al., 1998, p. 25, Figure 9.1), teachers are also the victims of both theft and violent crimes. Many school violence interventions ignore the fact that teachers and school staff also need support. Between 1992 and 1996, the annual average rate of victimization (combining theft and physical violence) for teachers was 76 incidents per 1,000 teachers (Kaufman et al., p. 71, Table 9.1). However, middle and junior high school teachers were more vulnerable to violent victimization than teachers in elementary and senior high schools. Also, male teachers were more likely to report being the victim of serious violent acts than women teachers (41 vs. 26 crimes per 1,000 teachers for men and women, respectively). Teachers in urban schools were much more likely than in suburban and rural schools to report being the victim of violent acts (Kaufman et al., p. 71, Table 9.1). Within a 12-month period, national data suggest that approximately 15.8% of teachers are either threatened physically with injury or physically attacked by a student (18.6% vs. 14.7% for male and female teachers, respectively). The community setting of the schools appears to influence teachers' victimization as well. Inner-city teachers report being threatened or attacked more often (20.7%) than suburban (14.7%) and rural (12.9%) teachers. We do not have national data indicating how many teachers are threatened or attacked by other adults such as parents, teachers, or school outsiders such as gang members in the community. However, we do have such data on school social workers.

In a national study, 35% of school social workers in the United States reported being physically assaulted or physically threatened during the past year (Astor et al., 1997; Astor et al., 1998; Astor et al., 2000). Of those who reported being threatened or assaulted, 77% identified the assailant as a student, 49% identified the attacker as a parent, and 11% identified the perpetrator as a student gang member (some social workers were attacked more than once and by more than one type of perpetrator therefore the total percentages are higher than 100%). Not surprisingly, many school social workers feared for their personal safety. In fact, one-third of school social workers reported that they feared for their personal safety about once a month or more. However, there were differences in the proportion of social workers in each community setting who reported fear. Compared with social workers in urban (36%), suburban (37%), and rural (31%) schools, more social workers in inner-city schools (71%) reported that they feared for their personal safety. The Astor et al. studies suggest that their fear may be related to a lack of training on how to handle or prevent violent situations. In the Astor et al. studies, few school social workers received formal university training to deal with school violence. The vast majority stated that they wished they had more training to deal with school violence (Astor et al., 1998). School social workers also expressed strong beliefs that school violence needed to be dealt with from an ecological point of view (Astor et al., 1998; 2000).

Is School Violence Still a Problem? Based on the declining overall frequencies regarding school violence, some might conclude that school violence is no longer a problem (or only a small problem). We believe this conclusion, if based only on frequencies, would be a mistake. Clearly, school violence rates have declined across multiple forms of victimization but these rate reductions do not address how society *should* determine when school violence is a problem. When does a specific school cross the threshold from having an average level of school violence to having a "high" level of violence? Conversely, how do we know when a school is considered a "model" safe school? These are not abstract, moral, or academic issues alone. Several state and national politicians, organizations, and task forces have declared publicly that punitive measures should be taken against schools that are "unsafe" (shut them down, hire new staff, etc.). Despite these movements, no one yet has put forth a clear set of criteria on what would constitute an unsafe school district or school. Social work participation in these philosophical discussions could add to the national dialogue because as a society, as practitioners, and as researchers we must have agreed upon ways to understand what is a safe or unsafe school. Without a clear sense of what is considered safe or unsafe it will be difficult to assess the success or failure of prevention/intervention programs.

TYPES OF INTERVENTIONS

Characteristics of Ineffective Interventions

A singular focus on the source of the problem. Most practitioners and researchers would agree that school violence is associated with a wide array of individual, family, community, and societal variables. Figure 7.1 presents select examples of correlates commonly mentioned in the school violence practice and research literatures; these correlates are presented at different ecological levels. The outside circles represent many of the variables outside the school that influence behaviors in the school, such as the family, culture, and peer group. It also presents

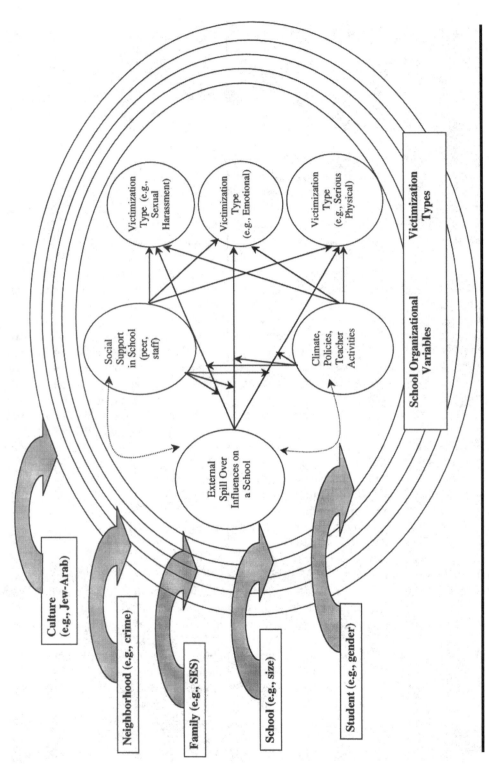

FIGURE 7.1   A Model of Social-Ecological Influences on Student Victimization

factors within the school that can either increase violence or help prevent it, such as the school climate and student/teacher relationships. Given the number of variables associated with school violence, one would expect school violence interventions to target multiple factors both inside and outside the school. Instead, most school violence interventions focus only on one or two variables or ecological levels (e.g., the child, the family, or the classroom) and tend to ignore the complex interplay of multiple variables. Consequently, it is not surprising that most programs that address only one variable tend not to be effective in reducing levels of school violence. Figure 7.1 also represents our theoretical conceptualization of how, with the help of programs or self initiated interventions, the school could buffer or exacerbate outside influences that come from factors external to the school environment. As shown in Figure 7.1, the school policies/procedures and social supports could impact various forms of student victimization differently. Based on our assessment of the research, we believe that successful programs are strengthening the school infrastructure/social environment to buffer students from many risk factors external to the school and ultimately reduce overall rates of victimization in the schools (see Lorion, 1998, for a discussion on community/school influences). We suspect that less successful programs tend not to focus on the *school social environment* at the core of the interventions.

A psychological/behavioral focus. The most popular school violence interventions are psychological and behavioral interventions (e.g., anger management, conflict mediation, peer counseling, curriculum-based programs). Historically, psychology has focused on identifying cognitive, emotional, and social-relational reasons why individual children become violent (American Psychological Association, 1993). Consequently, school-based psychological interventions have focused mainly on psychological variables. These types of interventions have been geared primarily towards individual children (or their families) with very little focus on the inter-

play between social dynamics of normative contexts such as schools and violence in the school setting (Hudley, Britsch, Wakefield, Demorat, & Cho, 1998). Unfortunately, with few exceptions, research suggests that narrowly focused social skills interventions, peer counseling/mediation, and other kinds of psychological interventions have been ineffective in reducing levels of school violence and in some cases (e.g., peer mediation groups and programs like DARE) may even increase aggression and violence levels in schools (see Gottfredson, 1997, for a detailed empirical review of these types of programs). Overall, psychological programs have been effective only when used conjointly with other interventions that target the organizational or social system of the school (Gottfredson; Olweus, 1993).

Conceptual underdevelopment and under-use of the school context. Generally, many "packaged" programs tend to be "add on" programs (Larson, 1998). Often, these types of programs are unrelated to the academic curriculum and social goals of the school. This situation is due, in part, to the fact that the social variables associated with the context of schools and school violence have not been conceptualized clearly (see Astor & Meyer, 2001, for a discussion of these issues). For example, researchers have conducted very few studies regarding the social dynamics surrounding a hallway fist fight or sexual harassment on school grounds. Moreover, until very recently, researchers or practitioners have not distinguished carefully between the concepts of school violence and youth violence (Astor & Meyer; Astor, 1998). Instead, many articles and analyses of youth violence are presented with a strong assumption that the youth is the "carrier" of violent behavior and that dynamics within settings play a small or tangential role in violent behavior.

Focus on "deficits" in children. Many school violence interventions are based on either formal or implicit theoretical assumptions of deficits surrounding what is causing violent behavior in individual children or sub-populations of children. For example, most social skills programs are based on the theoretical assumption that due to a lack of social exposure and practice, aggressive children are lacking in either social-cognitive or behavioral skills needed to deal with conflict appropriately. Without these more complex skills, it is believed that children naturally gravitate towards using aggression as a solution to social conflict. Consequently, these types of programs systematically target specific deficits in cognitive and behavioral skills within specific children or entire schools. What these deficit perspectives ignore is the powerful influence of contextual factors in the school environment that may influence student behavior.

Characteristics of Successful Programs

Based on our review of programs, it appears that successful school-wide intervention programs have the following core implementation characteristics:

— They raise the awareness and responsibility of students, teachers, and parents regarding the types of violence in their schools (e.g., sexual harassment, fighting, weapon use)
— They create clear guidelines and rules for the entire school
— They target the various social systems in the school and clearly communicate to the entire school community what procedures should be followed before, during, and after violent events
— They focus on getting the school staff, students, and parents involved in the program
— The interventions often fit easily into the normal flow and mission of the school setting
— They utilize faculty, staff, and parents in the school setting in order to plan, implement, and sustain the program
— They increase monitoring and supervision in non-classroom areas

Common Types of Interventions That Schools and School Social Workers Are Using

The scope of programs. Nationwide, approximately 78% of principals report that they have programs addressing violence in their schools (Kaufman et al., 1998). Eleven percent of the schools had programs that lasted only one day or less, 24% reported that they had only ongoing violence programs, and 43% indicated that they had both ongoing and one-day programs designed to address school violence. It is unclear what types of programs principals consider to be violence interventions. However, school social workers report that there is a wide array of violence intervention programs and services, which include counseling services, crisis intervention, skill training, peer programs for students, community programs, teacher-based programs, and security measures.

Table 7.1 presents the percentage of social workers who reported in Astor et al. (1998) that their school has such a program or service and the percentage of social workers who are involved with various programs. The vast majority of services, methods-based interventions (e.g., counseling, crisis intervention, and home visits), and programs implemented have not been evaluated extensively as violence reduction strategies. For example, in Astor et al. (1998), 91% of social workers endorsed home visits as an effective intervention for violent children and 82% of the social workers said that they conducted home visits personally to help reduce aggressive behaviors. Nevertheless, there is a paucity of data on the effectiveness of home visits or types of interventions commonly used by social workers.

Common interventions. Few evaluations have been conducted assessing the effectiveness of interventions normally used by schools (such as expulsion, suspension, referral to special education, sending the child to the principal's office, during- and after-school detention, parent conferences, and counseling). However, interventions such as expulsion, suspension, and school transfer are common responses to acts of school violence. During the 1996–1997 school year, 39% of school principals said they expelled, suspended, or transferred a student because of fighting. Twenty-seven percent of the nation's principals reported that they used suspension, expulsions,

TABLE 7.1   Percentage of School Social Workers (N=576) Reporting Specific Violence Programs and Services in Their Schools

TYPE OF PROGRAM OR SERVICE	% OF SCHOOLS WITH PROGRAM	% OF SOCIAL WORKERS INVOLVED IN PROGRAM
Counseling services		
Violence crisis intervention	50	40
Victim assistance and support services	30	24
Individual or family counseling	53	46
Posttraumatic stress groups for observers or victims	15	12
Services targeting ethnic, religious or racial conflicts	24	13
Child abuse education	58	41
Skills training		
Conflict management	63	43
Social skills training	66	53
Pro-social behavior curriculum	53	35
Skill streaming	35	25
Groups for aggressive children	54	43
Leadership training	41	19
Peer programs for students		
Positive peer culture	39	24
Friendship clubs	31	15
After school sports or clubs	75	15
Community programs		
Anti-gang program	22	8
Services that address community violence	15	6
Police anti-violence program	38	7
Parent support group	21	14
Church group or youth group	15	3
Teacher-based programs		
Teacher support groups or training on violence	26	14
Classroom management	60	34
Anti-bully campaign	14	9
Academic programs aimed at aggressors, victims or witnesses	8	3
Physical plant changes		
Metal detectors	14	3
Security guards	37	6

Note: This table was adapted from Astor et al., 1998.

or transfers for students who had a weapon on school grounds (U.S. Department of Education, 1998, p. 81, Table 18). Similarly, there are other common interventions such as contacting parents, parent school meetings about aggressive behaviors, or school-based consequences such as staying after school, better adult supervision in the school yard, better monitoring of the routes to and from school and violence prone school areas that should be researched further. Data from Europe and Australia suggest that these types of interventions are easier to implement and may be highly effective in reducing some types of school violence such as bullying (Olweus, 1993; Sharp & Smith, 1994; Smith & Sharp, 1994).

Special education and violence. Another response schools commonly have to persistent and chronic aggression in individual children is special education referral, assessment, and placement. Unfortunately, the school violence literature has not examined closely the relationships between special education and violence reduction in schools. Nevertheless, it is likely that many children receive services for aggressive behavior through special education. These interventions often include services such as counseling, parent training, contained classrooms, specialized curriculum, and day treatment facilities. This area of research should be developed further because it is possible that social workers, psychologists, counselors, and teachers view the special education process as an important strategy with some aggressive children.

PROGRAM INTERVENTIONS

In the next section we will discuss various types of interventions that are used to address school violence. Some of the interventions discussed are used commonly but have very little research documenting their effectiveness. Other interventions have undergone evaluation procedures and have research studies that support their effectiveness. Had this chapter been written ten years ago, we would most likely conclude that very few interventions show any positive results. Within the past ten years, many new programs and curricula are emerging with multiple studies to support their effectiveness.

Promising Prevention and Intervention Programs

In this section, we present some examples of prevention and intervention programs available to schools and practitioners. The programs discussed here do not represent an exhaustive list of programs available. Table 7.2 includes a longer listing of programs that have been evaluated or are widely used. In this chapter, we highlight a handful of programs that either show promise or have demonstrated a degree of effectiveness in at least one study.

High quality early childhood education. From a primary prevention perspective, high quality preschools may help in reducing violence rates. Data from the Perry Preschool High/Scope study suggest that a high quality preschool education can be highly effective in reducing violence throughout the life span (Schweinhart, Barnes, & Weikart, 1993). In this longitudinal study, researchers found that children who were randomly assigned to participate in a high quality preschool environment were far less likely to have been involved in criminal and violent activity through development than those who were assigned to a lower quality preschool program. These longitudinal data are important because they suggest that the effects carry through early development into adulthood (age 27 was the latest follow-up). Furthermore, the effects are wide-ranging and pronounced. By age 27, students who were assigned to low quality preschool programs were five times more likely than the high quality preschool students to have been arrested five or more times (many for violent acts). In addition, children in the high quality classes were significantly more likely than children in low quality classes to earn more money, own a house, and graduate from high school. Alternatively, they were significantly less likely to have used social services. A cost-benefit analysis suggested that participation in a high quality preschool saved the general public $57,585 per child on issues related to crime and victimization alone (in 1992 dollars). Researchers (Schweinhart et al.) believe that the preschools' focus on social responsibility, empowerment, decision-making, and conflict resolution are important contributors to the reductions in violence. Also, the Perry Preschool High/Scope program emphasized parent education and involvement around parenting issues, and in-depth teacher training regarding issues of conflict and discipline. Schwienhart and col-

TABLE 7.2 Examples of Universal and Targeted Violence Prevention Programs

UNIVERSAL VIOLENCE PREVENTION PROGRAMS

Program (Authors)	Grade	Participants	Program Components	Outcome Measures	Results
Peace Builders (Embry & Flannery, 1999; Embry, Flannery, Vazsonyi, Powell & Atha, 1996; Krug, Brener, Dahlberg, Ryan, & Powell, 1997)	K–5th grades	375 schools have program in place across AZ, CA, UT, OR, OH. Evaluation on 7 schools N= 3899 students.	Aim of program is to change school climate. Goals are to promote pro-social behavior, reduce child aggression, improve social competence. Five universal principles taught: 1) Praise people, 2) Avoid put-downs, 3) Seek wise people as advisers and friends, 4) Notice and correct hurts we cause, and 5) Right wrongs. Adults are to reinforce and model behaviors.	■ Social competence ■ Aggressive behaviors ■ Teacher and self-reports of aggressive behaviors ■ Fight-related visits to nurse	Used growth curve analyses. Teachers rate significant increases in social competence for K–2nd grade and 3rd–5th grade students in initial intervention schools. Teacher and student self-reports show significant decline in males aggression over two years of intervention. Intervention schools experienced fewer student visits to nurse's office for treatment of injuries (compared to control schools) (Krug et al. (1997).
Second Step (Grossman et al., 1997)	2nd–3rd grades	12 schools (49 classrooms) 790 students. Random assignment & matched control group for comparison	Curriculum based program (30 lessons) consisting of activities to teach empathy, impulse control, problem solving, and anger management.	Observer ratings of student behavior in classroom, lunchroom, and playground. Parent and teacher reports of student behavior (physical aggression, verbal hostility, pro-social and neutral behaviors)	Intervention group students rated (by observers) as less physically aggressive than control group. Differences more pronounced in lunchroom/playground settings. Change still significant after 6 months. No significant changes reported by teachers or parents.
Richmond Youth Against Violence: Responding in Peaceful and Positive Ways (Farrell & Meyer, 1997; Farrell, Meyer & Dahlberg, 1996)	6th grade students	6 out of 8 middle schools in one district N=1274 students participating in the program. 65% attrition by time of 2nd follow up. Final sample=452 participants. 90% Afr. Amer.	Lecture-based curriculum focusing on imparting knowledge about ways in which the host, agent, and environment contribute to youth violence. Sessions focus on: 1) Building trust, 2) Respect for individual differences, 3) Nature of violence and risk factors, 4) Anger management, 5) Personal values, 6) Precipitants and consequences of	Self-report data from Violent Behavior Survey. Assesses frequencies of 1) Student being in a fight, 2) Bringing weapon to school, 3) Being threatened, 4) Skipping school from feeling school unsafe (previous 30 days), and 5) Also examined frequency of other risk behaviors such as drug	For boys, participation resulted in significant differences in frequencies of violence and other problem behaviors (post intervention). Overall there was an increase in violent behaviors but intervention group showed less of an increase. Girls did not report benefits. Large attrition (65%) calls into question validity of findings. Students who did not participate in

(continued)

TABLE 7.2 (Continued)

UNIVERSAL VIOLENCE PREVENTION PROGRAMS

Program (Authors)	Grade	Participants	Program Components	Outcome Measures	Results
			fighting, and 7) Non-violent alternatives to fighting	use, vandalism, shoplifting, etc.	follow up had higher pre-test scores of violent behaviors than those who remained under study.
Students for Peace Project (Orpinas, Kelder, Frankowski, Murray, Zhang, & McAlister, 2000)	6th graders followed through 7th and 8th grades	(Student N=2246) 8 middle schools in large, low SES, urban setting, divided into matched pairs. Random assignment of one school in pair to control or intervention.	School Health Promotion Council (paid school coordinator, 3–10 teachers, and nurse or counselor) coordinated curriculum implementation & organized 'peace-related activities': Writing contest about peace, anti-gang plays, 'peace week,' etc. (Curriculum from Second Step) ■ Peer mediation—trained students to mediate conflicts, formally and informally, among peers. ■ Peers Helping Peers—trained students to meet one-on-one who request help w/personal problems (alcohol or drug use, attendance, conflicts, etc.) ■ Parent-education newsletters sent to parents in the 'intervention' schools.	Aggressive behaviors Self-report (teasing, pushing, name-calling, hitting, encouraging students to fight, kicking, threatening to hurt or hit, getting angry easily) ■ Frequency of fights at school ■ Frequency of injuries due to fighting ■ Perceptions of school safety (Ginsberg, 1993) ■ # of days of school absences due to feeling unsafe (0–6 in prior mo.) ■ Frequency of threats received at school (0–6 or more times in the prior yr.)	Controlled for baseline scores, race/ethnicity, and academic performance. No intervention effect in reducing aggressive behaviors, fights at school, injuries due to fighting, missing classes due to feeling unsafe, or being threatened to be hurt. For all variables, strongest predictors of violence in eighth grade were violence in sixth grade and low academic performance. 27% of students read newsletters.
Community Service Program (O'Donnell et al., 1999)	7th and 8th grades	2 large, urban public middle schools surveyed at baseline and 6-month follow up. N=972 students. Mostly low SES, African American, and Hispanic students.	Reach for Health classroom curriculum (10-lesson unit for violence component) Covered interpersonal violence risk and protective factors, practice strategies for dealing with anger in positive ways, avoiding fighting in violent situations, resolving con-	Student self-report measures of threatening others, fighting, weapon carrying, weapon use. Also controlled for Social desirability using Marlowe-Crowne social desirability scale for adults.	Eighth grade intervention students reported significantly less violence at follow-up than control students, controlling for baseline risk behavior, gender, ethnicity, and social desirability. No significant differences between controls and "curriculum-only" condition.

162

TABLE 7.2 (Continued)

UNIVERSAL VIOLENCE PREVENTION PROGRAMS

Program (Authors)	Grade	Participants	Program Components	Outcome Measures	Results
		One school intervention, other control. Schools matched by student demographics, size, high-risk health profile, high risk academic profile, limited access to resources	flicts without fighting or weapon use.

Half of students randomly assigned by classroom to participate in Reach for Health Community Youth Service Program. These students spent several hours/week providing service in local health care agencies. | | Comparing students in community service program compared to curriculum-only condition, there was a significant grade by intervention interaction. Eighth grade students who engaged in community service reported less violence at follow-up than curriculum only peers. |
| (Cirillo, Pruitt, Colwell, Kingery, Hurley, & Ballard, 1998) | High School (9–12 grades) | N=50 students at risk based on low SES, educational failure, evidence of alcohol and drug use, parent drug use, disciplinary actions at school, or poor attendance

Random assignment to control or experimental conditions. 44% white 30% black 23% hispanic, and 2% other. | 10 weekly 2-hour sessions where participants engaged in social-cognitive group intervention. Sessions conducted by licensed counselor who developed program. 10 adult leaders from business community served as mentors.

Focus was on enhancing: 1) Coping and problem solving, 2) Relationships with peers, parent and other adults, 3) Conflict resolution and communication skills, 4) Methods for resisting peer pressure for drug use/violence, 5) Consequential thinking and decision-making abilities, 6) Pro-social behaviors, cooperation with others, self-responsibility, respecting others, and 7) Awareness of feelings of others (empathy) | "Violence avoidance beliefs" as measured by a questionnaire derived from the Student Health Survey (Pruitt, Kingery, & Heuberger, 1992).

Questions pertain to violence education and involvement, ways to avoid fighting, and reasons for fighting. | No significant differences between experimental and control groups in mean scores on violence avoidance beliefs. Both groups had slight decrease in violence avoidance beliefs from pre-to post-test, and slight increase from post-test to follow up.

Students who used drugs/alcohol had significantly lower violence avoidance beliefs than those who did not use drugs/alcohol.

Students who physically fought in school had lower violence avoidance beliefs than students who never fought.

Anecdotal information reveals positive effects, but survey analysis did not tap this. Teachers/counselors commented on positive changes and prosocial behav- |

(continued)

TABLE 7.2 *(Continued)*

UNIVERSAL VIOLENCE PREVENTION PROGRAMS

Program (Authors)	Grade	Participants	Program Components	Outcome Measures	Results
					iors exhibited by participants after intervention. Perhaps outcomes not adequately measured by evaluation instrument used in this study.
FAST Track—Families and Schools Together—Conduct Problems Prevention Research Group "Unified" Prevention program with both Targeted and Universal design. *Targeted component is presented in this table.*	Long term program. Three cohorts of students. Grades 1–10 (Still ongoing)	At-risk kindergartners identified based on combined teacher and parent ratings of behavior (CBCL). Highest 10% recruited for study. N=445 intervention children N=446 control group children	Multiple program components. Weekly enrichment program for high-risk children and their parents. Students placed in "friendship groups" of 5–6 students each. Discussions, modeling stories and films, role plays. Sessions focused on reviewing and practicing skills in emotional understanding and communication, friendship building, self-control, and social problem solving. Parents met in groups led by Family Coordinators to discuss 30 parenting strategies, then 30 minute parent-child cooperative activity time. Biweekly home visits Academic tutoring provided by trained tutors in 30 min sessions 3X/week	■ Externalizing Scale of CBCL—Measures extent to which child exhibited oppositional, aggressive, and delinquent behaviors reported by parents. ■ Parent Daily Report—Degree to which child engaged in aggressive and oppositional behaviors during previous 24 hrs (Administered 3 times overall) ■ Parent Ratings of Child Behavior Change ■ Teacher assessment of acting out behaviors in school (Teacher Report Form, Achenbach 1991) ■ Scale from the TOCA-R (Teacher Observation of Classroom Adaptation-Revised) ■ Authority Acceptance Scale ■ Peer nominations of aggressive and	Intervention group had higher scores on emotion recognition, emotion coping, and social problem solving and lower rates of aggressive retaliation compared to control group. Direct observation results—Intervention group spent more time in positive peer interaction than did the control group. Intervention group received higher peer social preference scores than did control group. Intervention group had higher language arts grades than control group.

TABLE 7.2 (Continued)

UNIVERSAL VIOLENCE PREVENTION PROGRAMS

Program (Authors)	Grade	Participants	Program Components	Outcome Measures	Results
				hyperactive-disruptive behaviors	
BrainPower Program (Hudley, Britsch, Wakefield, Smith, Demorat, & Cho, 1998)	3rd–6th grades	384 male African-American (85%) and Latino (15%) 3rd–6th graders.	Hostile attributions are thought to determine subsequent aggression among boys. Attribution retraining was focus for intervention. Twelve lessons w/ three training components: 1) Designed to strengthen aggressive boys' ability to accurately detect others' intentions. 2) Increase likelihood that aggressive boys would first attribute negative outcomes to accidental causes. 3) Link appropriate, non-aggressive behavioral responses to ambiguously caused negative social outcomes. Groups of 6 students met 2 times weekly in 60 min sessions over 6 weeks. Each group had 4 aggressive boys, and 2 non-aggressive boys.	Teacher ratings of students behavior Student attributions: Each student presented with a hypothetical scenario of destruction of property, physical harm, or social rejection with ambiguous intent. Students' judgment of intent was outcome. "Do you think he did this on purpose?"	Selected participants were classified as aggressive or non-aggressive based on teacher ratings and peer nominations of aggressive behavior. Random assignment to one of three groups: a) Attribution retraining, b) Attention in nonsocial problem solving skills, or c) No-attention control group At baseline, no differences in teacher reports of behavior or suspension rates across schools. Improvements in behavior were related to changes in subjects' attributions. Intervention effects are moderate to strong for many students. Not evident for some. Treatment effects diminished over time.
Young Ladies/Young Gentlemen Clubs (YLYG) Cleveland, OH (Flannery & Williams, 1997)	Youth in grades 1–6 targeted as 'at-risk' for school failure and dropout.	School children in high-risk elementary schools identified and referred by classroom teachers for problem behaviors and/or poor attachment to school	Students participated in group sessions several times per week during course of school year. Group leaders employ series of activities aimed at improving: a) Self-concept, b) Peer relationship skills, and c) Attachment to school	Child social competence Positive classroom behaviors Self-control Peer relationship skills Aggression Delinquency	One year-longitudinal evaluation. Statistically significant improvements in positive classroom behaviors, self-control, general attachment to school. Group leaders reported significant gains in child prosocial behavior and de-

(continued)

TABLE 7.2 *(Continued)*

UNIVERSAL VIOLENCE PREVENTION PROGRAMS

Program (Authors)	Grade	Participants	Program Components	Outcome Measures	Results
		tendance/low academic performance	Home visits also included. Groups focused on developing problem-solving and social skills, character education, and discipline.	Behavior at home. Multi informant—Children, teachers, group leaders, and parents.	creases in aggressive behavior. Parent reports: 96% said club helped children's performance at school, 92% improved behavior at home, and 97% felt important part of child's education.
Youth Action Strategies in Violence Prevention (Carroll, Hebert, & Roy, 1999)	High School	N=384 students responded to evaluation questionnaires 91% response rate	Noon-hour discussions were held in each school, co-facilitated by a professional and adolescent member of Youth Action Committee. 2nd component of program was production of a television talk show. Topics of discussions and talk show focused on violence, rejection, racism, drugs, suicide, assault, emotional abuse and family relationships.	Survey questionnaires assessing perceived effectiveness in increasing awareness about violence prevention.	86% of participants believed noon-hour discussions were effective in increasing their awareness about violence prevention. 84% reported that information provided was useful. 64% of students stated that attending sessions changed their understanding of violence. No data collected on behavioral outcomes. High levels of racism were also identified as a source of violence.
FAST Track—Families and Schools Together Conduct Problems (Prevention Research Group) "Unified" Prevention program with both Targeted and Universal design. *Universal component is presented in this table.*	1st–5th Grades over three cohorts (Results from Grade 1 findings only are reviewed here)	198 Intervention Classrooms 180 Control Classrooms matched by school size, achievement levels, poverty and ethnic diversity. 7,560 total students 845 student were in high risk intervention or control conditions. (6,715 students non-high risk children.)	PATHS curriculum (Promoting Alternative Thinking Strategies). Administered to intervention schools (classrooms). 57 lessons (1/2 hr sessions, 2–3X/week) with focus on: ■ skills related to understanding & communicating emotions ■ skills related to increase of positive social behavior (prosocial behavior, participation, etc.) ■ self-control and steps to social problem solving	1) Teachers interviewed about behavior of each child in class. (Fall/Spring of 1st Gr.) 2) Socio-metric assessments (peer nominations made by students) collected to assess Peer aggression Peer hyperactivity/disruptiveness Peer social status	Hierarchical Linear Modeling (Accounting for gender, site, cohort & intervention) Intervention classrooms had lower ratings of hyperactivity/disruptive behavior, aggression, and more favorable observer ratings of classroom atmosphere. Three cohorts of intervention, so teachers administered curriculum, 1, 2, or 3 times. When 'teacher experience' included in analyses, teachers who taught more cohorts

TABLE 7.2 *(Continued)*

UNIVERSAL VIOLENCE PREVENTION PROGRAMS

Program (Authors)	Grade	Participants	Program Components	Outcome Measures	Results
			Presented through direct instruction, discussion, modeling stories, or video presentation. Intervention teachers also attended 2.5 day training & received weekly consultation from FAST Track staff. Teachers reported on intensity of 'dosage' by reporting weekly # of lessons taught. Quality of implementation was assessed by observer rating of teacher's: 1) Skill in teaching PATHS concepts, 2) Managing the classroom, 3) Modeling and generalizing PATHS throughout day, and 4) Openness to consultation	3) Quality of classroom atmosphere was assessed by Observer ratings assessing the following: ■ Level of disruption during academic time ■ Ability to handle classroom transitions ■ Ability to follow rules ■ Level of cooperation ■ Use of problem solving during conflict/need ■ Ability to express feelings appropriately ■ Ability to stay focused on task ■ Responsiveness to Ind. Student's needs/feelings ■ Level of criticism vs. supportiveness	had higher classroom atmosphere ratings (by neutral observer). Quality of implementation Teacher skill in program implementation was also related to positive outcomes.

leagues believe that the tripartite focus on students, parents, and teachers account for the lower levels of violence throughout development.

School-based bully and victim intervention programs. During the 1970s, surveys in Norway found that bullying was a considerable problem for students in Norwegian schools. In an effort to reduce bully and victim problems, Dan Olweus, a Norwegian professor, developed a comprehensive nationwide anti-bullying program for children in grades one through nine in Norway. The program has many simple interventions and is aimed at students, teachers, and parents in schools, classrooms, and individual settings. Strategies that were offered to reduce bullying included the establishment of clear class rules against bullying, contingent responses (praise and sanctions), regular class meetings to clarify norms against bullying, improved supervision of the playground, and teacher involvement in the development of a positive school climate. Also, a booklet defining and listing ways to counteract bullying was distributed to school personnel, a video illustrating the problem was made available, and parents were sent a booklet with information and advice. Findings from 42 schools that participated in the program showed a 50% reduction in rates of bullying and victimization. Furthermore, the positive effects of the program appeared to increase over time and there was an increase in student satisfaction with school life (Olweus, 1993). Similar anti-bullying programs have been developed in Great Britain (see Sharp & Smith, 1994; and Smith & Sharp, 1994, for empirical evaluations and detailed practical procedures for educators) and Australia (Rigby, 1996). Evaluations of those programs also show significant reductions in aggressive behaviors and increases in student satisfaction with school life.

Second Step. Based on the "habit of thought" model that posits that violence can be unlearned, the Second Step program targets children in preschool through kindergarten, grades one through three, and grades four and five. Second Step is a curriculum-based approach that attempts to prevent aggressive behavior by increasing prosocial behavior through competence in peer interactions and in interpersonal conflict resolution skills. The curriculum is administered twice a week with an average of 50 to 60 lessons. The specific lessons include activities to help youth acquire empathy, impulse control, problem-solving, and anger management skills. An evaluation of the program found it to have some level of impact on participants (Grossman et al., 1997). After taking the 30-lesson curriculum, an evaluation of participants illustrated that Second Step decreased the amount of physical aggression of youth and increased positive and prosocial behaviors both on the playground and in the lunchroom (Grossman et al.). Another study that trained elementary and middle school teachers with the curriculum also suggested that teachers and administrators reported considerable respect for the capacity of the curriculum (Milwaukee Board of School Directors, 1993).

Practitioners should be aware that other similar curriculum-based conflict resolution programs have not performed well when evaluated intensively (Webster, 1993). For example, the popular Violence Prevention Curriculum for Adolescents (Prothrow-Stith, 1987) has little empirical support suggesting that it actually reduces violence (Larson, 1998; Tolan & Guerra, 1994).

Peace Builders. The Peace Builders program (Embry, Flannery, Vazsonyi, Powell, & Atha, 1996) is a school-wide violence prevention program for students in grades kindergarten through five which is operating currently in almost 400 schools in Arizona, California, Ohio, and Utah. Implemented by both staff and students, the program incorporates strategies to change the school climate by promoting prosocial behavior among students and staff, enhancing social competence, and reducing aggressive behavior. Children learn five principles: 1) praise people, 2) avoid put-downs, 3) seek wise people as advisors and friends, 4) notice and correct the hurts they cause, and 5) right wrongs. Teachers, administrators, and parents reinforce and model these behaviors. Peace Builders is different from most school-based programs because it is not curriculum based. Instead, it is described as "a way of life" (Flaxman, Schwartz, Weiler, & Lahey, 1998). The initial evaluation results were positive and demonstrated a significant decrease in aggressive behavior and a significant increase in social competence (Flannery & Vazsonyi, 1996). Also, Krug et al. (1997) have found that intervention schools with the Peace Builders program experienced fewer student visits to the nurse's office for treatment of injuries compared to control schools.

Positive Adolescents Choices Training. The Positive Adolescents Choices Training (PACT) program was "designed to teach African-American youth social skills to aid in prevention of violence" (Hammond & Yung, 1991, 1993; Yung & Hammond, 1998). A unique aspect of PACT is that it is culturally relevant and aimed at reducing aggression and victimization in high-risk youth. The program components include anger management, prosocial skills training, and violence risk education. The sessions are built around videotapes that demonstrate culturally sensitive social situations. Participants learn specific skills needed to solve the situation peacefully. Participants in the program increased an average of 33.5% in the areas of giving feedback, problem-solving, and resisting peer pressure. Teachers also observed a significant improvement in the targeted skills of trained youth (30.4%) compared to untrained youth (–1.1%). In addition, while students perceived their greatest improvement in their ability to provide negative feedback, they felt they had the least gain in problem-solving. Most importantly, students demonstrated a significant reduction of physical aggression at school, and their overall aggressive behavior was improved during the training and maintained when they graduated the program (Yung & Hammond, 1998).

How to Select the Right Program for a Specific School or Document the Success of Grassroots Programs

We believe that school social workers can make a significant impact nationally and locally if they

demonstrated with data how they adapted programs (like the ones listed above) or created "grassroots" interventions. Most practitioners are aware that each school is unique, and may have different kinds of problems, thus necessitating different kinds of approaches. For example, one school may have a problem with sexual harassment among the younger male students, whereas another school in the same district may have a problem with weapons on school grounds primarily with older students. These two types of problems may necessitate very different kinds of programs. Instituting a singular "anti-violence" program across schools with different needs is unlikely to address effectively the specific problems that might exist in each school. As obvious as this may seem, some schools select a "promising program" (such as the ones listed in the earlier section) and never collect data to assess if they initially had a problem in that area or if the intervention program the school adopted actually worked.

Furthermore, from a social work and intervention perspective it is philosophically problematic that most current "school violence interventions" and "programs" *are moving away from developing grass roots and community generated interventions.* How can school violence interventions reflect social work values of community, parent participation, and student/teacher voice? Can school interventions reflect a social work belief in democracy and participation in the definition of the problem and the creation/implementation of the interventions? How do social workers empower school communities to deal with their own specific kinds of school violence problems? How do school social workers know when programs work or fail? The following sections on "monitoring" and "school mapping" are presented as potential responses to these challenges.

MONITORING AND MAPPING AS METHODS AND A PROCESS

This monitoring and data-based approach assumes that successful programs stem out of the following: 1) the belief that the efforts to "fit" a program to a school involves *grassroots* participation, 2) a belief that students and teachers in the school need to be *empowered* to deal with the problem, 3) a belief that *democracy* is at the core of a good violence program, and 4) a belief that schools should demonstrate a *proactive vision* surrounding the violence problem in their school. The implementation of interventions could be slightly different for each school site because it is assumed that the social dynamics of each school site are unique. Each school is expected to adapt the program to their unique demographic, philosophical, and organizational needs.

We believe that *data are necessary* for the successful adaptation of safety programs to schools. Hence, an important element of successful violence prevention programs is the use of data in an ongoing and interactive manner. Figure 7.2 represents our interpretation of the cycle of monitoring and how data should be used to maintain successful programs. This perspective proposes that the ongoing analysis and interpretation of data is an essential part of the intervention process. Data are used to create awareness, mobilize different school constituents, assess the extent of the problem, plan interventions, implementation programs, and evaluation effectiveness. Information is provided continually to different groups in each step of the intervention process.

We argue that the *process of introducing school specific data* to each of the school groups allows each school to identify its specific needs, limitations, strengths, and resources so that the school community can choose and debate which program fits their needs best. Moreover, this approach assumes that the process of building and implementing programs is continuous and cyclical, always changing to respond to new circumstances and emerging needs. The following sections on monitoring and school mapping are presented as quantitative and qualitative processes that a) help create a "whole-school response," and b) help the school identify, create, and/or adapt programs to the site.

Quantitative Monitoring of Violence Prone Locations: Example of School A. School A was a secondary school with about 1,500 students. The vast majority of students came from immigrant and low-income families. The school was slowly turning itself into a "high technology" school setting with courses focusing on computer programming, the sciences, and a business incubator philosophy. Still, there was a sense amongst the administrators and teachers that more could be done to address the issue of violence in their school. The school decided to adopt a monitoring system method as outlined by Benbenishty, Astor, and Zeira (in press).

The students, teachers, and administrators participated in developing and administering a questionnaire about school violence, school climate, and what could be done to address the violence. The entire student body filled the anonymous questionnaire as a form of "voice" and "democracy." The school wanted to raise awareness and involvement of the teachers, students, and parents. In this particular school, they worked out a system where the students and staff were scanning surveys and distributing their own data. Much of this was done through class work under the direction of teachers and administrators. This allowed the school to add their own questions and to carry out analyses to explore specific questions.

These data were shared systematically with the student body in their classrooms, with the teachers in teachers' meetings, and with the PTO. The data were used to create an awareness and generate collaborative solutions, but more importantly (at the first stage) they were used to anchor the dialogue between staff, students, administration, and parents. The process of continual dialogue about the data between the students and teachers created a sense of personal and school-wide investment in the interventions adopted.

As one example, the school chose to use this monitoring system to identify *where* the violence problem exists in their school. They wanted to know where violence is occurring most. Figure 7.3 shows the percentage of students in this

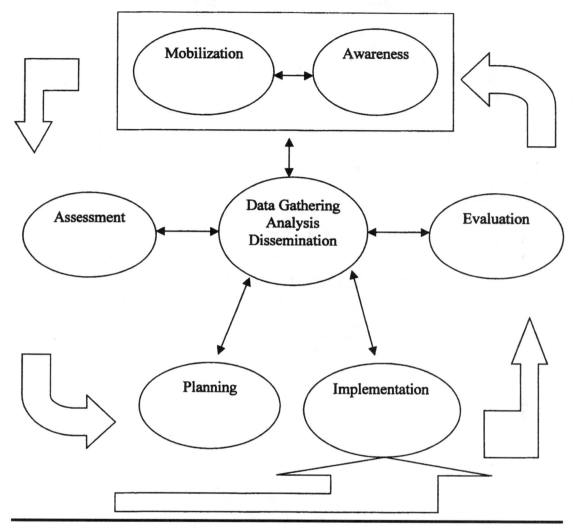

FIGURE 7.2   The Role of Data in the Development and Implementation of Interventions

school rating areas in their school as dangerous. The findings indicate that the school gate at the end of school, the locker room, and the school yard were areas about which students were most concerned. Girls in the school were twice as likely to be fearful of the school gate after school and the locker room. Boys, on the other hand, were more likely to rate the school gate before school and the school yard as more dangerous. The student surveys showed that the school gate after school, the locker room, and the school yard were particular problems for the 10th and 11th graders and not as severe as the 12th graders. These kinds of reports and site-specific data were distributed to all the students, teachers, and parents. Dialogue groups were also formed in classes to talk about the problem and to generate possible student, teacher, and principal solutions to this particular issue.

The staff and students made extraordinary efforts to target violence-prone locations. They even moved the vice principal's offices closer to

FIGURE 7.3   Examples of Actual Tables Given to Principals Regarding Dangerous Times and Places in School

HOW DANGEROUS ARE TIMES AND PLACES IN SCHOOL

	Not at all	A little	Quite dangerous	Dangerous	Mean
	1	2	3	4	
	%	%	%	%	
Class	70	20	7	3	1.43
School yard	35	30	25	10	2.10
School gate, when school starts	70	15	12	3	1.48
School gate, when school ends	30	24	26	20	2.36
Locker room	32	22	25	21	2.35

HOW DANGEROUS ARE TIMES AND PLACES IN SCHOOL—BY GENDER

	Boys	Girls
	%	%
Class	8	12
School yard	42	28
School gate, when school starts	20	10
School gate, when school ends	30	62
Locker room	33	59

Entries are percentages of students saying the place is either "quite dangerous" or "dangerous."

HOW DANGEROUS ARE TIMES AND PLACES IN SCHOOL—BY GRADE

	10th	11th	12th
	%	%	%
Class	11	11	8
School yard	42	40	23
School gate, when school starts	12	17	16
School gate when school ends	53	58	27
Locker room	55	57	26

Entries are percentages of students saying the place is either "quite dangerous" or "dangerous."

Note: The original figures provided to staff were translated, shortened, and modified to be presented in this figure.

the bathrooms and reorganized the physical structure of the school to improve social interaction and staff monitoring of student behaviors. The school implemented school beautification projects, multiple student-led mural projects, and created a website devoted to peace and school discipline where students could voice concerns to the administration and peers. The follow-up monitoring survey showed improvement with school morale/school spirit and subjective feelings about school. Monitoring surveys conducted by the students and staff a year later (see Figure 7.4) showed that the school was successful in reducing a sense of danger in certain locations. However, the data suggested that more work needed to be done to make those locations even safer. Although this feedback was disappointing initially to the staff and students (even though it was their own self-reported data) it prompted them to focus more on reductions of violence rates and new approaches. The staff and students in this school had data suggesting what was working and not working. The data did not always coincide with their subjective feelings of "total success." Therefore the monitoring surveys served as an anchor whereby the students and teachers could talk about ways to make those locations even safer. This approach fit well within a social work, democratic, grassroots, empowerment perspective without compromising the role of comprehensive school wide data.

Qualitative Mapping of Violence Prone Locations: Example of School B

The second school was a high school with approximately 1,000 students from mainly middle- and upper-middle income families. This school was not interested in conducting school-wide surveys but wanted to involve staff and students in the process of violence prevention. They also wanted to adapt the interventions to their specific school. Like the quantitative survey monitoring process, this qualitative mapping process was designed to document 1) the locations and times within each school where violence oc-

curred for that term, and 2) the perspectives of students, teachers, staff, and administrators regarding the school's organizational response (or non-response) to violent events in these locations. The main goal was to use qualitative data to generate clarity about the nature of the problem and diverse perspectives on possible causes and solutions to the problem.

Students, teachers, and staff (e.g., administrators, hall monitors, cafeteria workers) were interviewed in four to five separate *focus groups* about the physical spaces where violence had been committed, and what time of day the violence had occurred. Each group was given an empty map of their school and asked to identify events where they occurred and areas of the school that felt unsafe for them (see Astor, Meyer, & Pitner, 1999; Astor, Vargas, Pitner, & Meyer, 1999, for an in-depth description of the mapping process). After students and teachers individually identified these places, they were interviewed in focus groups as to why they thought it occurred where it did and what could be done to improve the situation.

All the individual maps were consolidated into one large school map. Transferring all of the reported events onto one large map of the school enabled students and staff to locate specific "hot spots" for violence and dangerous time periods within each individual school. For example, events tended to be clustered by time, age, gender, and location. In the case of older students (11th and 12th graders), events were clustered in the parking lot outside of the auxiliary gym immediately after school, whereas for younger students (9th and 10th graders) events were reported in the lunchroom and hallways during transition periods. For this school, the map suggested that interventions be geared specifically towards older students, directly after school, by the main entrance, and in the school parking lot. Students and teachers agreed that increasing the visible presence of school staff in and around the parking lot for the 20 minutes after school had great potential for reducing many violent events. Younger students were experiencing violence

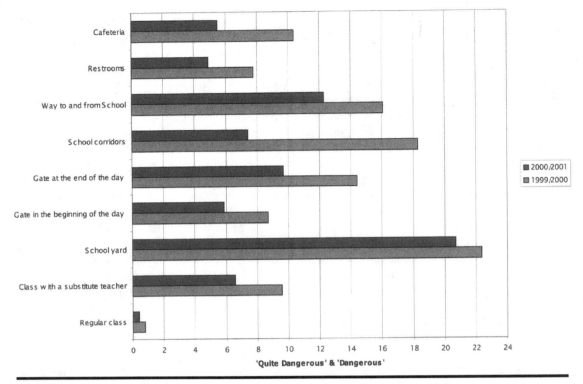

FIGURE 7.4   Specific Places Perceived by Students to Be Dangerous in a School

mainly before, during, and after lunch, near the cafeteria. Many students expressed feelings of being unsafe between classes in the hallways.

Teachers suggested interventions such as all the teachers and support staff standing in hallway during transitions and positively greeting "by name" as many students as possible. Many staff felt this was a different and more positive message to students than "security guards" yet provided a high level of supervision. Students also suggested a role in monitoring the hallways. Some student leaders suggested that they could do more in their student groups to prevent fights. They especially felt they could do more to discourage their peers from forming the large circles that often formed when a fight occurs.

The focus groups also identified organizational issues that could improve the violence situation in the school. Themes from teachers included a sense of "being caught in the middle."

Some teachers expressed a personal desire to prevent violence but did not possess the skills or knowledge of how to intervene. Many staff members were unclear about their professional role in non-classroom locations (see Astor, Meyer, & Behre, 1999, for a detailed description of what types of themes can be anticipated from each group). Tables 7.3 and 7.4 show examples of the kinds of issues that were the focus of discussions about organizational issues and potential interventions.

Non-teaching staff also revealed important information in the focus groups, including very specific interventions associated with their areas of the school. For example, cafeteria workers revealed that only two or three adults were expected to supervise nearly 1,000 children during the lunch period. Additionally, secretaries had very clear suggestions for interventions regarding children who were sent to the office for

TABLE 7.3   Core Student, Teacher, and Administrator Comments Related to Organizational Response

DOMAIN	STUDENTS	TEACHERS	ADMINISTRATORS
Organizational Response	"I wouldn't actually jump in there either because these, like, goons up here they don't care about a teacher and they fight and they not concerned about the teacher. If the teacher gets hit, most likely they going to say they shouldn't be in the way. So it's not they job to break to break up fights."	"Two young ladies were going at it outside of my door, and I went to pull one off. She started punching me . . . and she was swearing. We ended up on the floor. I'll never forget. I looked up and two male teachers were standing there, not doing anything."	"We've told the teachers they can take any level of activity they feel comfortable taking. They can intervene physically if they feel they have to. And I've had some teachers do that."
	"Because I've seen a lot of people who get suspended and, you know, you see them a few weeks later getting in-school suspension. I mean what's the difference?"	"I have a call button . . . they don't answer, they don't respond. I have to run next door and tell my department head. She would pick up the phone and try to locate security . . . the kid would be back in my class in three days."	"If you're in the immediate area, you've got to break that fight up. You're to do what you can . . . state law requires teachers to be responsible in that situation."
	"[A]nd she told me to go to the hallway. We went to the hall. The girl came out into the hall. . . . Then you know the teacher is still in the classroom, but she knows all this time that we are arguing and it is going to be a conflict. Why didn't she stop when we were having words?"	"I can remember a few years back, we had a convicted rapist who was in classes at this school. The teachers were not told that this student was convicted of rape . . . he was scheduled with a number of young women teachers . . . and the principal never said a word. . . ."	"There's a liability issue here. It's something that a lot of teacher's don't seem to understand . . . it means that they must at least give a verbal command to stop."
	"That's like when the tuition office got held up. Don't you know, I was walking down the hall and I didn't even know what happened. Can you imagine how I felt? I could have got shot for no reason. . . . I think they should let us leave at least when the police came. Evacuated out one of these doors."	"I think that some teachers probably would not like to get involved. In fact, I saw one (a fight) about nine months ago where the teacher walked away from it and didn't want to get involved."	"And, many times we would just transfer a student who had one fight. You could say anyone who fights in this building is gone."

Note: Table is adapted from Astor et al., 1999.

TABLE 7.4 Student Reported Violent Events and Suggested Interventions

LOCATION OF EVENT	NATURE OF VIOLENT EVENT	SUGGESTED INTERVENTIONS BY STUDENTS
Hallway	- pushing - fighting - gun pulled - gang fights - assault	"There's so many people that you can understand that the hallways are crowded. That's our number one problem—the hallways are too crowded." "Have a rule that if you surround a fight you're helping . . . so you would get the same punishment as the people fighting, because you're helping people fight." ". . . they (security) should know what is going on in their hallway instead of like two or three of them going down the same way."
Parking Lot	- physical fights - weapons - shooting - stabbing - physical threats - racially motivated fights	"Well where there's not supervision (parking lot) there's always going to be trouble . . . the principal. He should be out there."
Abandoned or Unmonitored Spaces	- physical fights or assault - sexual assault or rape - strangers entering - weapons - robbery	"Maybe if we had regular security guards, like they had a 70-year-old man security guard, and like that guy can't even move." "People walk in at like 7 o'clock. No guards anywhere. It's just quiet—nobody anywhere." "When we have a weapon search, they supposed to check you. There's some people they don't check." "More lights . . . or have a monitor. Have somebody down there." "I mean lock the school doors . . . the back door is always open and people come in." "I think we need to have IDs to show . . . and then like a speaker at the door."
Cafeteria	- physical fights - food fights - throwing chairs - gang scuffles	"They should have at least five teachers in there . . . a minimum of five teachers. Because now there's only two teachers." "It's too crowded . . . our lunch hour is only 25 minutes." "I think you should go basically anywhere during lunch, as long as you clean up after yourself, because keeping a lot of people together kind of generates fights."

Note: Table is adapted from Astor et al., 1999.

fighting during less supervised periods (such as recess, lunch, or transitions between classes).

CONCLUSION

We believe that school social workers can play an important role in school violence interventions at the local, state, and national levels. One important role they could play is educating the public, students, and staff and providing accurate data on school violence. Currently there are many myths surrounding gangs, students of color, suburban white students, and specific forms of violence. These stereotypes about the rates of violence and groups associated with violence are potentially harmful to students *and our society*. These inaccurate perceptions may also be harmful because they do not reflect the possible efforts schools have invested in reducing school violence. School social workers could initiate important conceptual dialogue in their schools and school districts regarding the categorization of a violence problem in schools. We strongly encourage school social workers to adopt the approach that the entire school setting be the focus of violence prevention strategies. School data should serve as the basis for interventions and their subsequent evaluations. One method we endorse is creating a comprehensive survey based *dialogue group* monitoring system that could help generate grassroots interventions and adapt existing program. Furthermore, we suggest an alternative school violence procedure that integrates school maps (to locate violent "hot spots" in the school) and focus groups with students, teachers, school staff and administrators (to identify reasons why violence is occurring in certain places and potential solutions). Information obtained through either the monitoring or the mapping process could 1) increase the dialogue between students, teachers and school staff on issues of school violence, 2) serve as an evaluation of school violence interventions already used in a school setting, and 3) increase school involvement in violence interventions.

FOR STUDY AND DISCUSSION

1. This chapter documents dramatic reductions in various forms of school violence. What social variables do you believe account for these reductions? Discuss specific variables at the cultural "macro" level, but also at the family and individual levels. What kinds of school-related policies and practices could account for these reductions in school violence?

2. Currently, there is a national attempt to create safe schools. Discuss which variables you would focus on or measure to determine if a school was safe or unsafe. Is the safety of a school related to the number of violent events per year in that school? If so, how many violent events would it take in a high school of 1,000 students for you to call it an "unsafe school?" What types of violent behaviors would you consider qualitatively more salient? How many of these kinds of behaviors would constitute an unsafe school during a one year period? What measures or outcomes would you use as a school social worker to determine whether a school has a school violence problem?

3. Discuss several ways that school social workers could educate their school community about the reality of school violence. Generate three types of processes that could involve students, teachers, and parents to own school violence as a problem.

4. What types of empowerment activities should students be responsible for in an effort to reduce school fights?

5. Discuss the specific social dynamics in discrete school contexts such as the school restroom, school yard, hallways, lunchrooms, and routes to and from school (including buses). Are there dynamics unique to each setting that would make grassroots interventions work better than packaged programs? If so, what are they? As an example, discuss the routes to and from school and ways the school/families can define responsibility for monitoring the safety of those routes more effectively.

6. Do you believe there are cultures/countries where school violence is low? If so, which cultures/countries do you think have low school violence

rates? Why do you think they are low in those countries? Could the United States learn from programs in those countries? Explain why or why not. As a follow-up, explore cross cultural articles/chapters (e.g., Smith, Morita, Junger-Tas, Olweus, Catalano, & Slee, 1999. *The nature of school bullying: A cross-national perspective*. Routledge: London & New York) to see if your assumptions of those countries were correct or not correct.

7. What kinds of steps would a school social worker take to prepare their school to respond to crisis? [for comprehensive guides and best practices see Brock, Lazarus, & Jimerson (Eds., 2002) *Best practices in school crisis prevention and intervention*. NASP Publications].

ADDITIONAL READING

American Association of University Women. (2001). *Hostile hallways: Bullying, teasing, and sexual harassment*. Washington, DC: Author.

Arnette, J., & Walsleben, M. (1998). *Combating fear and restoring safety in schools* (NCJ-167888). Washington, DC: Office of Juvenile Justice and Delinquency Prevention.

Artz, S. (1998a). *Sex, power and the violent school girl*. New York: Teachers' College Press.

Artz, S. (1998b). Where have all the school girls gone? Violent girls in the school yard. *Child and Youth Care Forum, 27*, 77–109.

Astor, R. A., & Meyer, H. (2001). The conceptualization of violence prone school sub-contexts: Is the sum of the parts greater than the whole? *Urban Education, 36*, 374–399.

Astor, R. Meyer, H., & Pitner, R. (2001). Elementary and middle school students' perceptions of violence-prone school subcontexts. *The Elementary School Journal, 101*, 511–528.

Baker, J. A. (1998). Are we missing the forest for the trees? Considering the social context of school violence. *Journal of School Psychology, 36*, 29–44.

Benbenishty, R., & Astor, R. A. (in press). Cultural specific and cross-cultural bully/victim patterns. In P. K. Smith, (Ed.), *Violence in schools: The response in Europe*. Routledge Falmer, London.

Bosworth, K., Espelage, D., & Simon, T. (1999). Factors associated with bullying behavior in middle school students, *Journal of Early Adolescence, 19*, 341–362.

Cano, A., Avery-Leaf, S., Cascardi, M., & O'Leary, K. (1998). Dating violence in two high school samples: Discriminating variables. *Journal of Primary Prevention, 18*, 431–446.

Errante, A. (1997). Close to home: Comparative perspectives on childhood and community violence. *American Journal of Education, 105*, 355–400.

Everett, S. A., & Price, J. H. (1995). Students' perceptions of violence in the public schools: The MetLife Survey. *Journal of Adolescent Health, 17*, 345–352.

Finkelhor, D. (1995). The victimization of children: A developmental perspective. *American Journal of Orthopsychiatry, 65*, 177–193.

Hyman I. A., & Snook P. A. (2000). Dangerous schools and what you can do about them. *Phi Delta Kappan, 81*, 7, 488–501.

Kaufman, P., Chen, X., Choy, S., Ruddy, S., Miller, A., Fleury, J., Chandler, K., Rand., M., Klause, P., & Planty, M. (2000). *Indicators of school crime and safety, 2000*. U.S. Departments of Education and Justice. NCES 2001-017/NCJ-184176.

Klipp, G. (2001). *Resalling quids: Resilience of queer youth in school*. Unpublished doctoral dissertation, University of Michigan, Ann Arbor.

Kodluboy, D. (1997). Gang-oriented interventions. In A. Goldstein (Ed.), *School violence intervention: A practical handbook* (pp. 189–214). New York: The Guilford Press.

Meyer, H. A., & Astor, R. A. (in press). Child and parent perspectives on routes to and from school in high crime neighborhoods. *Journal of School Violence*.

Pellegrini, A., & Bartini, M. (2000). A longitudinal study of bullying, victimization, and peer affiliation during the transition from primary school to middle school. *American Educational Research Journal, 37*, 699–725.

Price, J. H., & Everett, S. A. (1997). Teacher's perceptions of violence in the public schools: The MetLife survey. *American Journal of Health Behavior, 21*, 178–186.

Rose, L., & Gallup, A. (2000). The 32nd annual Phi Delta Kappa/Gallup poll of the public's attitudes toward the public schools. *Phi Delta Kappan, 82*, 41–66.

Stein, N. (1999). *Classrooms and courtrooms: Facing sexual harassment in K–12 schools*. New York: Teachers College Press.

Sullivan, K. (2000). *The anti-bullying handbook.* Auckland, NY: Oxford University Press.

Vossekuil, B., Reddy, M., Fein, R., Borum, R., & Modzeleski, W. (2000). *U.S.S.S. Safe School Initiative: An interim report on the prevention of targeted violence in schools.* Washington, DC: U.S. Secret Service, National Threat Assessment Center.

WEBSITES WITH BULLYING INFORMATION AND LINKS TO MANY OTHER USEFUL SITES

http://www.nasponline.org/index2.html
http://www.luckyduck.co.uk
Australian bullying site:
http://www.education.unisa.edu.au/bullying/
Canadian bullying site:
http://www.crime-prevention.org/ncpc

U.S sites with bullying pages/links:
Colorado Center for the Prevention of Violence
http://www.Colorado.edu/cspv

National School Safety Center
http://www.NSSC1.org/
National Center for Educational Statistics
http://nces.ed.gov
Department of Justice
http://www.ojp.usdoj.gov/bjs/
National Resource Center for Safe Schools
http://www.safetyzone.org

REFERENCES

American Psychological Association. (1993). *Violence and youth: Psychology's response (Vol. 1).* Washington, DC: Author.

Ash, P., Kellermann, A., Fuqua-Whitley, D., & Johnson, A. (1996). Gun acquisition and use by juvenile offenders. *Journal of the American Medical Association, 275,* 1754–1758.

Astor, R.A. (1995). School violence: A blueprint for elementary school interventions. *Social Work in Education, 17,* 101–115.

Astor, R. (1998). Moral reasoning about school violence: Informational assumptions about harm within school sub-contexts. *Educational Psychologist, 33,* 207–221.

Astor, R. A., Behre, W. J., Fravil, K. A., & Wallace, J. M. (1997). Perceptions of school violence as a problem and reports of violent events: A national survey of school social workers. *Social Work, 42,* 55–68.

Astor, R., Behre, W., Wallace, J., & Fravil, K. (1998). School social workers and school violence: Personal safety, violence programs and training. *Social Work, 43,* 223–232.

Astor, R., & Meyer, H. (1998). *Making schools safe: A first prerequisite for learning.* Paper presented at the annual meeting of the American Educational Research Association, San Diego, CA.

Astor, R., & Meyer, H. (1999). Where girls and women won't go: Female students', teachers', and school social workers' views of school safety. *Social Work in Education, 21,* 201–219.

Astor, R. A., & Meyer, H. (2001). The conceptualization of violence prone school sub-contexts: Is the sum of the parts greater than the whole? *Urban Education, 36,* 374–399.

Astor, R., Meyer, H., & Behre, W. (1999). Unowned space and time in high schools: Mapping violence with students and teachers. *American Educational Research Journal, 36,* 3–42.

Astor, R., Meyer, H., & Pitner, R. (2001). Elementary and middle school students' perceptions of violence-prone school sub-contexts. *The Elementary School Journal, 101,* 511–528.

Astor, R., Pitner, R., & Duncan, B. (1996). Ecological approaches to mental health consultation with teachers on issues related to youth and school violence. *Journal of Negro Education, 65,* 336–355.

Astor, R. A., Pitner, R. O., Meyer, H. A., & Vargas, L. A. (2000). The most violent event at school: A ripple in the pond. *Children & Schools, 22,* 199–116.

Astor, R. A., Vargas, L. A., Pitner, R. O., & Meyer, H. A., (1999). School violence: Research, theory, & practice. In J. M. Jenson & M. O. Howard (Eds.), *Youth violence: Current research and recent practice innovations* (pp. 139–172). Washington, DC: NASW Press.

Batsche, G., & Knoff, A. (1994). Bullies and their victims: Understanding a pervasive problem in the schools. *School Psychology Review, 23,* 165–174.

Benbenishty, R., Astor, R. A., & Zeira, A. (in press). Monitoring school violence at the site level: Linking national, district, and school-level data. *Journal of School Violence.*

Benbenishty, R., Astor, R. A., Zeira, A., & Vinokur, A. (in press). Jr. High school students' assessments of fear and violence as a problem: A structural equation model. *Social Work Research.*

Benbenishty, R., Zeira, A., Astor, R.A., & Khoury-Kassabri, M. (in press). Victimization of primary school students by educational staff in Israel. *Child Abuse and Neglect.*

Berrill, K. (1990). Anti-gay violence and victimization in the U.S.: An overview. *Journal of Interpersonal Violence: Special Issue: Violence against lesbians and gay men: Issues for research, practice, and policy, 5,* 274–294.

Boulton, M. (1993). Aggressive fighting in British middle school children. *Educational Studies, 19,* 19–39.

Bragg, R. (1997, December 3). Forgiveness, after 3 die in Kentucky shooting; M. Carneal opens fire on fellow students at Heath High School in West Paducah. *The New York Times,* p. A16.

Burcky, W., Reuterman, N., & Kopsky, S. (1988). Dating violence among high school students. *School Counselor, 35,* 353–358.

Cano, A., Avery-Leaf, S., Cascardi, M., & O'Leary, K. (1998). Dating violence in two high school samples: Discriminating variables. *Journal of Primary Prevention, 18,* 431–446.

Carroll, G. B., Hebert, D. M., & Roy, J. M. (1999). Youth action strategies in violence prevention. *Journal of Adolescent Health, 25,* 7–13.

Centers for Disease Control and Prevention. (1998). Youth risk behavior surveillance—United States, 1997. *Morbidity and Mortality Weekly Report, 47.* SS-3. U.S. Department of Health and Human Services: Washington, DC: Author.

Cirillo, K. J., Pruitt, B. E., Colwell, B., Kingery, P. M., Hurley, R. S., & Ballard, D. (1998). School violence: Prevalence and intervention strategies for at-risk adolescents. *Adolescence, 33,* 319–330.

Conduct Problems Prevention Research Group. (1992). Initial impact of the Fast Track Prevention Trial for conduct problems: I. The high-risk sample. *Journal of Consulting and Clinical Psychology, 67,* 631–647.

Conduct Problems Prevention Research Group. (1992). Initial impact of the Fast Track Prevention Trial for conduct problems: II. Classroom effects. *Journal of Consulting and Clinical Psychology, 67,* 648–657.

Embry, D. D., & Flannery, D. J. (1999). Two sides of the coin: Multilevel prevention and intervention to reduce youth violent behavior. In D. J. Flannery & C. R. Huff (Eds.), *Youth violence: prevention, intervention, and social policy.* Washington, DC: American Psychiatric Press.

Embry, D., Flannery, D., Vazsonyi, A., Powell, K., & Atha, H. (1996). Peace Builders: A theoretically driven, school-based model for early violence prevention. *American Journal of Prevention Medicine, 12,* 91–100.

Farrell, A. D., & Meyer, A. L. (1997). The effectiveness of a school-based curriculum for reducing violence among urban sixth-grade students. *American Journal of Public Health, 87,* 979–984.

Farrell, A. D., Meyer, A. L., & Dahlberg, L. L. (1996). Richmond Youth Against Violence: A school-based program for urban adolescents. *American Journal of Preventive Medicine, 12,* 13–21.

Flannery, D., & Vazsonyi, A. (1996). *Peace Builders: A school-based model for early violence prevention.* Chicago, IL: American Society of Criminology.

Flannery, D. J., & Williams, L. L. (1997). *Final report: Evaluation of the Young Ladies, Young Gentlemen Clubs, Partnership for a Safer Cleveland.* (Available from Institute for the Study and Prevention of Violence, 1305 Terrace Hall, Kent State University, Kent, OH 44242.)

Flaxman, E. Schwartz, W. Weiler, J. & Lahey, M. (1998). Trends and Issues in Urban Education, 1998. [Online]. Available: http://eric-web.tc.columbia.edu/monographs/ti20 [1999, January 20].

Goldstein, A. (1996). *The psychology of vandalism.* New York, NY: Plenum Press.

Gottfredson, D. (1997). School based crime prevention. In L. Sherman, D. Gottfredson, D. MacKenzie, J. Eck, P. Reuter, & S. Bushway (Eds.), *Preventing crime: What works, what doesn't, what's promising: A report to the United States Congress.* Washington, DC: Department of Justice.

Gray, D. (1991). *The plight of the African American male: An executive summary of a legislative hearing.* Detroit, MI: Council President Pro Tem Gil, the Detroit City Council Youth Advisory Commission.

Grossman, D. C., Neckerman, H. J., Koepsell, T. D., Liu, P. Y, Asher, K. N., Beland, K., Frey, K., &

Rivara, F. P. (1997). Effectiveness of a violence prevention curriculum among children in elementary school: A randomized controlled trial. *Journal of the American Medical Association, 277,* 1605–1611.

Hammond, W., & Yung, B. (1991). Preventing violence in at-risk African American youth. *Journal of Heath Care for the Poor and Underserved, 2,* 358–372.

Hammond, R., & Yung, B. (1993). Psychology's role in the public health response to assaultive violence among young African-American men. *American Psychologist, 48,* 142–154.

Hays, K. (1998, April 26). Boy held in teacher's killing. *The Detroit News & Free Press,* p. 5A.

Heaviside, S., Rowand, C., Williams, C., & Farris, E. (1998). *Violence and discipline problems in U.S. Public Schools: 1996-1997* (NCES 98-030). Washington, DC: U.S. Department of Education, National Center for Education Statistics (ERIC Document Reproduction Service No. 417 257).

Hudley, C., Britsch, B., Wakefield, T., Demorat, M., & Cho, S. (1998). An attribution retraining program to reduce aggression in elementary school students. *Psychology in the Schools, 35,* 271–282.

Hyman I. A., & Perone, D. C. (1998). The other side of school violence: Educator policies and practices that may contribute to student misbehavior. *Journal of School Psychology, 36,* 7–27.

Hyman I. A., & Snook P. A. (2000). Dangerous schools and what you can do about them. *Phi Delta Kappan, 81,* 488–501.

Issacs, M. (1992). *Violence: The impact of community violence on African-American children and families: Collaborative approaches to prevention and intervention.* Arlington, VA: National Center for Education in Maternal and Child Health.

Jensen, J. M., & Howard, M. O. (1999). *Youth violence: Current research and recent practice innovations.* Washington, DC: NASW Press.

Kachur, P., Stennies, G., Powell, K., Modzeleski, W., Stephens, R., Murphy, R., Kresnow, M., Sleet, D., & Lowry, R. (1996). School-associated violent deaths in the United States, 1992 to 1994. *Journal of the American Medical Association, 275,* 1729–1733.

Kann, L., Kinchen, S., Williams, B., Ross, J., Lowry, R., Hill, C., Grunbaum, J., Blumson, P., Collins, J., & Kolbe, L. (1998). Youth risk behavior surveillance—1997. *Morbidity and Mortality Weekly Report Surveillance Summary, 48*(SS-3), 1–89.

Kann, L., Kinchen, S., Williams, B., Ross, J., Lowry, R., Grunbaum, J., Blumson, P., Collins, J., & Kolbe, L. (2000). Youth risk behavior surveillance—1999. *Morbidity and Mortality Weekly Report Surveillance Summary, 49*(SS-5), 1–32.

Kaufman, P., Chen, X., Choy, S., Chandler, K., Chapman, C., Rand, M., & Ringel, C. (1998). *Indicators of school crime and safety, 1998.* U.S. Departments of Education and Justice. NCES 98-251/NCJ-172215. Washington, DC.

Kaufman, P., Chen, X., Choy, S., Ruddy, S., Miller, A., Fleury, J., Chandler, K., Rand., M., Klause, P., & Planty, M. (2000). *Indicators of school crime and safety, 2000.* U.S. Departments of Education and Justice. NCES 2001-017/NCJ-184176.

Klein, J. (2002, March). School violence: Public and professional policies. *NASW News,* p. 6.

Kodluboy, D. (1997). Gang-oriented interventions. In A. Goldstein (Ed.), *School violence intervention: A practical handbook* (pp. 189–214). New York: Guilford Press.

Krug, E. G., Brener, N. D., Dahlberg, L. L., Ryan, G. W., & Powell, K. E. (1997). A pilot evaluation of a school-based violence prevention program. *American Journal of Preventive Medicine, 13,* 459–463.

Larson, J. (1998). Managing student aggression in high schools: Implications for practice. *Psychology in the Schools, 35,* 283–295.

Lorion, R. (1998). Exposure to urban violence: Contamination of the school environment. In D. Elliott, B. Hamburg, & K. Williams (Eds.), *Violence in American schools: A new perspective* (pp. 293–311). New York: Cambridge University Press.

Mayer, M. J., & Leone, P. E. (1999). A structural analysis of school violence and disruption: Implications for creating safer schools. *Education and the Treatment of Children, 22,* 333–356.

Milwaukee Board of School Directors. (1993). *An evaluation of the Second Step Violence Prevention Curriculum for elementary students.* Milwaukee, WI: Author.

Nansel, T., Overpeck, M., Pilla, R., Ruan, W., Simons-Morton, B., & Scheidt, P. (2001). Bullying behaviors among U.S. youth: Prevalence and association with psychosocial adjustment. *Journal of the American Medical Association, 285,* 2094–2100.

Noguera, P.A. (1995). Preventing and producing violence: A critical analysis of responses to school violence. *Harvard Educational Review, 51,* 546–564.

O'Donnell, L., Stueve, A., San Doval, A., Duran, R., Atnafou, R., Haber, D., Johnson, N., Murray, H., Grant, U., Juhn, G., Tang, J., Bass, J., & Pressens, P. (1999). Violence prevention and young adolescents' participation in community youth service. *Journal of Adolescent Health, 24,* 28–37.

Olweus, D. (1993). *Bullying at school.* Oxford, UK: Blackwell.

Olweus, D., Limber, S. & Mihalic, S.F. (1999). *Blueprints for violence prevention, book nine: Bullying prevention program.* Boulder, CO: Center for the Study and Prevention of Violence.

Orpinas, P., Kelder, S., Frankowski, R., Murray, N., Zhang, Q., & McAlister, A. (2000). Outcome evaluation of a multi-component violence-prevention program for middle schools: The Students for Peace project. *Health Education Research, 15,* 45–58.

Page, R. (1997). Helping adolescents avoid date rape: The role of secondary education. *High School Journal, 80,* 75–80.

Parks, C. (1995). Gang behavior in the schools: Reality or myth? *Educational Psychology Review, 7,* 41–68.

Pittel, E. (1998). How to take a weapons history: Interviewing children at risk for violence at school. *Journal of the American Academy of Child & Adolescent Psychiatry, 37,* 1100–1102.

Prothrow-Stith, D. (1987). *Violence prevention curriculum for adolescents.* Newton, MA: Education development Center, Inc.

Prothrow-Stith, D., & Weissman, M. (1991). *Deadly consequences.* New York: Harper Collins.

Rigby, K. (1996). *Bullying in schools: And what to do about it.* Melbourne, Vic: Australian Council for Educational Research.

Schafer, M., & Smith, P. (1996). Teacher's perceptions of play fighting and real fighting in primary school. *Educational Research, 38,* 173–181.

Schweinhart, L., Barnes, H., & Weikart, D. (1993). Significant benefits of the High/Scope Perry preschool study through age 27. *Monographs of the High/Scope Educational Research Foundation* (No. 10).

Sharp, S., & Smith, P. (1994). *Tackling bullying in your school: A practical handbook for teachers.* London: Routledge.

Smith, P., & Sharp, S. (1994). *School bullying.* London: Routledge.

Snyder, H. N., & Sickmund, M. (1999). *Juvenile offenders and victims: 1999 national report.* Washington, DC: Office of Juvenile Justice and Delinquency Prevention.

Stein, N. (1995). Sexual harassment in the school: The public performance of gendered violence. *Harvard Educational Review, 65,* 145–162.

Tolan, P., & Guerra, N. (1994). Prevention of delinquency: Current status and issues. *Applied and Preventive Psychology, 3,* 251–273.

U.S. Department of Education. National Center for Educational Statistics. (1998). *Violence and discipline problems in U.S. public schools: 1996–1997,* NCES 98-030, by Heaviside, S., Rowand, C., Williams, C., & Farris, E. Project officers: Shelley Burns and Edith MacArthur. Washington, DC, 1998.

U.S. Departments of Education and Justice. (2000). *2000 Annual Report on School Safety.* Washington, DC.

U.S. Department of Justice. Bureau of Justice Statistics. (1998). *National Crime Victimization Survey: School Crime Supplement, 1995 to 1996* [Electronic data file]. Conducted by U.S. Department of Commerce, Bureau of the Census, ICPSR ed. Ann Arbor, MI: Inter-university Consortium for Political and Social Research [Producer and Distributor].

Wahler, Fetsch, & Silliman (1997, January, 8). Research-based, empirically-effective violence prevention curricula: A review of resources. Retrieved January 25, 2000, from the World Wide Web: http://www.nnfr.org/violence/yvp_litrev.html

Webster, D. (1993). The unconvincing case for school based conflict resolution programs for adolescents. *Health Affairs, 4,* 126–141.

Yung, B., & Hammond, R. (1998). Breaking the cycle: A culturally sensitive violence prevention program for African-American children. In L. Lutzker (Ed.), *Handbook of child abuse research and treatments.* New York: Plenum Press.

Youssef, R., Attia, M., & Kamel, M. (1998). Children experiencing violence II: Prevalence and determinants of corporal punishment in schools. *Child Abuse & Neglect, 22,* 975–985.

Zeira, A., Benbenishty, R., & Astor, R. A. (in press). Preliminary results of a national survey on school violence in Israel: Student findings. *Social Work: Child Abuse & Neglect.*

Zeira, A., Astor, R. A, & Benbenishty, R. (2002). Sexual harassment in Jewish and Arab public schools in Israel. *Child Abuse & Neglect, 26,* 149–166.

CHAPTER 8

CHILDREN WITH DISABILITIES

SALLY ATKINS-BURNETT, UNIVERSITY OF TOLEDO

INTRODUCTION

The final decades of the twentieth century were marked by continual change and refinement in the services for children with disabilities. The year 2000 marked not only the change of a century, but also the 25th anniversary of the passage of landmark legislation mandating the rights of children with disabilities to a free and appropriate education in the least restrictive environment. Originally known as Education for All Handicapped Children Act (P.L. 94-142), the law has been refined continually over the years and was later renamed Individuals with Disabilities Education Act (IDEA). This legislation recognizes the role that social workers play in facilitating the education of children. IDEA lists social work among the related services that should be available to children with disabilities.

Multiple pieces of legislation and litigation influenced current practice. Special education services continue to evolve amidst a more contentious atmosphere. This chapter summarizes the major influences and the ongoing debates surrounding the provision of a free and appropriate education to infants and children with special needs. Key provisions of legislation are described briefly and issues surrounding discipline procedures, assessment and evaluation, inclusion, labeling, and how best to provide a free and appropriate education in a standards-based environment are explored. Ongoing longitudinal research efforts are described. The different roles enacted by social workers in the provision of services to children with special needs are discussed.

BACKGROUND AND EARLY INFLUENCES

The confluence of civil rights and education litigation and legislation have shaped special education policy and practices since the 1960s (see Figures 8.1A and 8.1B). Prior to 1970, it is estimated that millions of children with disabilities were excluded from schools or educated inappropriately (U.S. Department of Education, 2000). The 1954 Supreme Court decision in the civil rights case *Brown* v. *Board of Education* ruled to end racial segregation in U.S. schools. Advocates for children with disabilities purported that the court's ruling on the unconstitutionality of segregation and exclusion should be extended to children with disabilities. However, as late as 1969, a North Carolina statute allowed children to be labeled as "uneducable" and made it a crime for parents to challenge the school's designation (Palmaffy, 2001). Civil rights advocates feared that minority children would be labeled "uneducable" or mentally retarded in an effort to exclude them from schools and worked to challenge laws that excluded children.

Two pieces of litigation in 1972 set the stage for later legislation establishing three guiding principles (Palmaffy, 2001). The *PARC* v. *Commonwealth of Pennsylvania* and *Mills* v. *Board of Education of District of Columbia* decisions

FIGURE 8.1A   Summary of Important Special Education Litigation

---

1971   *PENNSYLVANIA ASSOCIATION FOR RETARDED CHILDREN (PARC)* V. *COMMONWEALTH OF PENNSYLVANIA*

On behalf of 13 mentally retarded children, PARC contested a state law that allowed public schools to deny services to children whose mental age was determined to be below 5 years. State agreed to provide full access to a free public education; established standard of appropriateness—each child to be offered education appropriate to his/her learning capacities; established a clear preference for least restrictive placement.

1972   *MILLS* V. *BOARD OF EDUCATION, DISTRICT OF COLUMBIA*

Class action suit on behalf of children who were refused enrollment, suspended, or expelled on the basis of their disability; school district admitted an estimated 12,340 children with disabilities would not be served in 1971–72 school year due to budgetary constraints; court ruled the problem of finance could not be allowed to bear more heavily on handicapped children than on other children. Prohibited schools from budgeting special services in advance and offering only on a "space available" basis. Based primarily on the Equal Protection Clause and Due Process Clause of the U.S. Constitution (Fifth and Fourteenth Amendments), this case granted children with disabilities full procedural protections when a change in status (e.g., suspensions, expulsions, transfers out of regular classrooms, or reassignment) is considered including notice of proposed changes, right to be heard and legal counsel at hearings to determine changes in program access to school records, and regularly scheduled status reviews.

1972   *DIANA* V. *STATE BOARD OF EDUCATION*

Charged that Mexican-American children whose primary language was Spanish had been assessed improperly. Intelligence tests administered in English qualified them for placement in an educable mentally retarded classroom. Retest results indicated seven of nine children involved were not mentally impaired. Court ordered all Mexican-American and Chinese-American students reevaluated in their native language and inappropriate placements rectified. The misuse of tests had been raised initially in *Hobson* v. *Hansen* (1967).

1972   *LARRY P.* V. *RILES*

Questioned the assignment of black students to EMR classes based on psychometric testing. Although only 28.5% of district's students were black, 66% of the students in district EMR classrooms were black. Court prohibited district from using IQ scores as primary criteria for EMR placement.

1982   *BOARD OF EDUCATION* V. *ROWLEY*, 458 U. S. AT 203, 1028. CT. AT 3049

Supreme court interpreted "appropriate" education; a state satisfies the requirement to provide a free and appropriate public education (FAPE) by provision of services and instruction, at public expense, that meet the State's educational standards and are consistent with the child's IEP.

1988   *HONIG* V. *DOE*

Supreme Court ruled schools could discipline students with disabilities using traditional procedures as long as it did not result in a change in placement. In cases of immediate threat to the well-being of students, a child with a disability could be suspended for up to 10 days. A pattern of suspensions (totaling more than 10 days during a single school year) constitutes a change in placement.

1989   *DANIEL R R* V. *STATE BOARD OF EDUCATION*, 874 F.20 1036 (5TH CIR.)

Spelled out two-part inquiry in determining child's placement. First, could regular placement be satisfactorily achieved with supplementary services? Has school taken steps to modify regular education? Can child benefit

FIGURE 8.1A *(Continued)*

from modifications? Will detriment to child result from placement in regular education? What effect will child have on the regular classroom environment? Second, if the decision is made to remove the child for any portion of the day, has the child been mainstreamed to the maximum extent possible? It is not an all or nothing proposition.

1994 *SACRAMENTO CITY UNIFIED SCHOOL DISTRICT, BOARD OF EDUCATION* V. *RACHEL H.,* 12 F.3D 1398 (9TH CIR.)

The Ninth Circuit Court offers a slightly different standard for determining placement using four factors:

(1) educational benefits available in the regular classroom to this child, (2) the nonacademic benefits of interaction with children who are typically developing, (3) effect of the presence of the child with disability on the teacher and other children in the classroom, and (4) the cost of mainstreaming. (IDEA does not allow cost to be considered in placement—where a service is necessary, cost considerations would not excuse a school district from providing the service. However, when more than one service or program is appropriate, school district may be allowed to consider costs.)

1999 *BOARD OF EDUCATION OF LAGRANGE SCHOOL DISTRICT NO. 105* V. *ILLINOIS STATE BOARD OF EDUCATION AND RYAN B,* 184 F. 3D 912 (7TH CIR).

The U.S. Court of Appeals ruled in favor of the family of a preschool child with Down Syndrome. The parents wanted the child educated in a preschool for typically developing children, but the district did not have a preschool and refused to pay for private tuition offering instead a placement in a Head Start or in a special education classroom. The court awarded the parents reimbursement of tuition at the private preschool and held that the LRE decision needed to take into account the special needs of the child.

ruled that 1) the exclusion of students from schools based solely on disability is a violation of the Constitution's guarantees of equal protection and due process; 2) parents of children with disabilities should have available a range of legal remedies (including impartial hearing and access to the courts) for challenging schools regarding the educational programming, and 3) cost is not an acceptable excuse for excluding children from the public school system. These principles have continued to guide later legislation.

Ambiguity regarding what constitutes a free and appropriate education and what the least restrictive environment is for a given child has led to numerous court cases. Is lack of progress in school adequate evidence that a student is not receiving a free and appropriate education? Can a district consider other students' needs when determining programming, some of which may be costly? Case law continues to provide a broad set

of protections for children and youth with disabilities (Palmaffy, 2001). (See Figure 8.1A for a brief description of some of the major court decisions affecting special education.) The court decisions support the education of children with disabilities alongside their peers in the regular classroom to the maximum extent possible. Students may be excluded only if the school demonstrates that they have attempted a range of interventions and the student's behavior continues to seriously disrupt the learning or endanger the students in the classroom. Cost considerations are not acceptable reasons for removing a child to an alternative placement (Palmaffy). The IEP must be "reasonably calculated to enable the child to receive educational benefits" (458 U.S. 176 at 207).

The first federal legislation regarding children with disabilities focused on provision of funding. The 1966 Elementary and Secondary Education

FIGURE 8.1B   Summary of Important Educational Legislation

Trying to broaden the base of support and for all types of disabled people, two groups organized in the early 1950s:
- The National Association for Retarded Citizens (NARC)
- The Council for Exceptional Children (CEC)

1965   ELEMENTARY AND SECONDARY EDUCATION ACT (ESEA) P.L. 9-10
- Provided limited federal support in organizing and maintaining special education in public schools but no support services to make it possible.

1970   EDUCATION OF THE HANDICAPPED ACT (EHA), P.L. 91 -230
- Repealed Title VI of the ESEA.
- Authorized funding but no criteria.
- Did not dictate which, if any, social services could participate in the education of handicapped children.

1973   REHABILITATION ACT SECTION 504, P.L. 93-112
Any agency receiving federal money must end discrimination in offering services to individuals with disabilities. Children with attention deficit disorder are often served under a 504 Plan since A.D.D. is not a category under IDEA. The most recent amendments to IDEA allow attention problems to be included in "other health impairments." Section 504 and ADA offer more remedies to parents and have been a main vehicle for special education litigation in the past few years (Martin, Martin, & Terman, 1996)

1975   EDUCATION OF ALL HANDICAPPED CHILDREN ACT (EAHO), P.L. 94-142.1
- Kept in place as the allocation formula for FY1976–77. Was the allocation formula used in FY 1975 which granted states $8.75 for each child in the state to be used specifically to educate handicapped children.
- Established a new grant formula, to take effect permanently in 1978, authorizing grants equal to the number of handicapped children aged 3 through 21 who received a special education multiplied by:
- 5% of the national per-pupil expenditure in FY78, 10% in FY79, 20% in FY80, 30% in FY81, 40% in FY82 and each succeeding year.
- Stipulated that no state could count more than 12% of its children aged 5 to 17 as handicapped.
- Required each state to provide a free and appropriate education to all its handicapped children, ages 3 to 18, by Sept. 1,1978, and to all its handicapped children, ages 18 to 21, by Sept. 1, 1980. The requirements for ages 3 to 5 and 18 to 21 would not apply to those states where the federal law would be contrary to state law or court order.
- Encouraged status to provide education for handicapped children ages 3 to 5 by authorizing incentive grants of an additional $300 for each child receiving educational services.
- Required that federal funds supplement, not supplant, state and local funds. States and LEAs must pay as much for each handicapped child as they do for normal children.
- Required the LEA, in consultation with the teacher, the parents, "if appropriate," to establish an IEP for each handicapped child.
- Required, where appropriate, the education of handicapped children in the least restrictive environment.
- Strengthened existing due process procedures to guarantee the rights of handicapped children, including due process, in all matters regarding identification, evaluation, and placement of the child, assurance that testing materials and procedures would not discriminate racially or culturally, and assurance that information gathered by the state would be kept confidential.

1977   AMENDMENTS TO EAHC, P.L. 95-49

1983   AMENDMENTS TO EAHC, P.L. 98-199

1986   EDUCATION OF THE HANDICAPPED ACT (EHA), P.L. 99-4572
- Amends EHA to authorize an early intervention program for handicapped infants and toddlers and their families mandated by 1991.
- Establishes a new grant program for state development and operation of early intervention services for handicapped infants and toddlers from birth to age 2 by the fifth year of participation.

FIGURE 8.1B   *(Continued)*

- Requires preparation and review of individualized family plans by local service providers.
- Repeals state exception for children aged 3 to 5 from state special education requirements.
- Mandates free public education for all handicapped children beginning at age 3.
- Authorized appropriations for Dept. of Ed. grants to state, local, and private sector agencies for handicapped education programs, including:
- Handicapped education services at preschool, elementary, secondary, and post-secondary levels; and vocational training.
- Services at handicapped education regional resource centers.
- Development of demonstration programs for extended school year services to severely handicapped children and youth.
- Special education research, teacher training, and support personnel recruitment and training program.

1988   AMENDMENTS TO EHA, P.L. 100-630

1990   INDIVIDUALS WITH DISABILITIES EDUCATION ACT (IDEA), P.L. 101-4763

- Revises and extends through FY94 Dept. of Education discretionary special education programs.
- Includes grants to states for research, demonstration projects, personnel training, and information dissemination on special education and related services to disabled children and youth.
- Denies states immunity from lawsuits for violations of the act.
- Authorizes a new discretionary grant program for the education and related needs of emotionally disturbed children and youth.

1991   AMENDMENTS TO IDEA, P.L. 102-1194

- Amends IDEA to authorize appropriations for FY92–FY94 Dept. of Ed. grants to states for early educational services for disabled infants and toddlers.
- Improves services to disabled children on Indian reservations.
- Expands training programs for paraprofessionals, special education teachers and parents of disabled children.

1996   AMENDMENTS TO ESEA, P.L. 89-750

- Added Title VI. This was the first time federal money had been allocated for support services for handicapped children, but no specific guidelines.
- Established the Bureau of Education for the Handicapped and the National Advisory Committee on the Handicapped.

1997   Amendments to IDEA, P.L. 105-17

- Added categories of disability: developmental delay, autism
- Greater emphasis on access to general curriculum and accountability
- Related services added to transition services
- Required the provision of services to children who have been suspended or expelled from the public school
- Reduced the requirement for testing every three years

No Child Left Behind Act of 2001

- This reauthorization of ESEA emphasized need for more preventative services and research based practices
- Allowed states to use funds for prekindergarten programs

[1]Congressional Quarterly Almanac, 94th Congress, 1st Session, 1975, Vol. XXXI, 1976, pp. 651-652.

[2]Congressional Information Service Annual Legislative Histories for U.S. Public Laws, 1986. Congressional Information Service, Inc.: Washington, DC: 1987.

[3]Congressional Information Service Annual Legislative Histories for U.S. Public Laws, 1990. Congressional Information Service, Inc.: Washington, DC: 1991.

[4]Congressional Information Service Annual Legislative Histories for U.S. Public Laws, 1991. Congressional Information Service, Inc.: Washington, DC: 1992.

Act amendments included funding for students with disabilities and created the Bureau of Education for the Handicapped. In 1970 the Education for the Handicapped Act (EHA), the first legislation devoted to students with disabilities, consolidated several grant programs. In 1973 Section 504 of the Rehabilitation Act of 1973 extended the protections implied in the PARC and Mills decisions to individuals in any institution that receives federal funds (Palmaffy, 2001). It affirmed the principle that students with disabilities have a right to be educated in regular classrooms to the maximum extent possible.

LANDMARK LEGISLATION: THE EDUCATION FOR ALL HANDICAPPED CHILDREN ACT OF 1975 (P.L. 94-142)

In 1975 Congress passed P.L. 94-142, which historians consider the most important and far-reaching piece of federal legislation in the area of special education (The Education for All Handicapped Children Act, 1975). This law can be considered the "bill of rights" for handicapped children. For the first time Congress authorized federal money to be spent by state educational agencies so that local school districts could provide education to disabled children who needed it.

P.L. 94-142 was intended to 1) ensure that all disabled children, aged 3 through 21, have available free, appropriate public education, which includes special education and related services to meet their unique needs; 2) ensure that the rights of disabled children and their parents are protected; 3) assist states and localities in providing for the education of all disabled children; and 4) ensure the effectiveness of efforts to educate these children. At the time of its passage, there were over eight million disabled children in the United States; of this group about 1.75 million were receiving no formal education, and 2.5 million were estimated to be receiving inadequate education.

P.L. 94-142 significantly expanded children's rights and placed substantial responsibility on the educational agencies that serve disabled children. It provided financial support and an opportunity to widen the scope of support services in schools. It also specified assurances of parental involvement in establishing educational programs for their children. It renewed public attention and reinforced the concept of an individualized approach to learning.

At the same time, P.L. 94-142, like much other federal legislation, had funding problems, aroused great expectations, and stimulated controversy. At the time he signed the bill, President Gerald Ford warned that the proposed funding levels would not be possible under the current fiscal constraints.

The promise of federal funding for 40% of the costs of special education has never been realized. By the year 2000, federal funds were supporting approximately 12% of the costs of educating children with disabilities. At the same time, amendments to the law and increased identification of children with disabilities have expanded the scope of special education and the costs have mushroomed. The IDEA has been reauthorized every five to seven years and has expanded educational opportunities to infants and preschoolers with disabilities, and to students with autism, traumatic brain injury, deaf-blindness, or attention deficit disorders. It is estimated that educating children with disabilities costs approximately twice what it costs to educate a typically developing student (Palmaffy, 2001). In addition, the number of identified children has continued to rise. In 1976–77, a little over 8% of all enrolled children were identified as disabled. At the turn of the century, more than 13% of the students were identified as disabled (U.S. Department of Education, 2000).

The passage of P.L. 94-142 impacted social work services in schools profoundly. Social workers were named specifically as one of the related services required to help handicapped children benefit from special education. For the first time, social workers were given legislative recognition for their contribution to the educational process.

The Individuals with Disabilities Education Act (IDEA): P.L. 101-416

This act replaces P.L. 94-142. Its major objectives are:

1. To provide assistance to states to develop early intervention services for infants and toddlers with disabilities and their families, and to assure a free appropriate public education to all children and youth with disabilities;
2. To assure that the rights of children and youth with disabilities from birth to age 21 and their families are protected;
3. To assist states and localities to provide for early intervention services and the education of all children with disabilities;
4. To assess and assure the effectiveness of efforts to provide early intervention services and educate children with disabilities.

THE 1997 AMENDMENTS

On June 4, 1997, President Clinton signed Public Law 105-17, thus enacting into law the reauthorization of the IDEA and its latest set of amendments. As stated previously, this law originated in 1975 as P.L. 94-142, the amendments to what was then known as the Education of the Handicapped Act. It has been refined and expanded during subsequent reauthorizations (see Figure 8.1A for a summary of legislation). IDEA has brought about many positive changes. Every state in the nation now has laws ensuring the provision of a FAPE to all children with disabilities. More than 20 years of experience in implementing this law have demonstrated that effective services to children with disabilities include 1) strong involvement of parents and partnerships between parents and schools; 2) high expectations for children and access to mainstream curriculum to the maximum extent possible; 3) alignment of special education efforts with state and local improvement efforts so that children with disabilities can benefit from the improvements; 4) provision of incentives for prereferral interventions to reduce the need to label children

disabled in order to meet their learning needs; 5) a focus on provision of resources for teaching and learning; and 6) support for high-quality intensive professional development for everyone (e.g., paraprofessionals, teachers, adjunct staff) who works with disabled children to ensure that the knowledge and skills necessary to effectively assist children are attained by all pertinent personnel.

Almost twice as many individuals with disabilities are employed as young adults, and the quality of life has improved for many. Unfortunately, for others the promise of IDEA has not been fulfilled. The number of students with disabilities who drop out of school is twice that of those without disabilities; more of these students do not return to school, and they are more likely than their nondisabled counterparts to have legal difficulties (U.S. Department of Education, 1997b; U.S. Office of Special Education Programs, 1999; Wagner & Backorby, 1996). Students who are minorities are over-represented in separate special education settings, marking special education as a new form of racial/ethnic segregation.

The 1997 legislation restructures IDEA into four parts:

— Part A General provisions including definitions
— Part B Assistance for education of all children with disabilities
— Part C (formerly Part H—Early Intervention) Infants and toddlers with disabilities
— Part D National activities to improve education of children with disabilities

The 1997 amendments to IDEA are focused on improving results for children with disabilities by increasing early identification and early provision of services while ensuring access to the general curriculum and general education reforms. The amendments call for higher expectations for students with disabilities and more accountability of schools. The amendments also attempt to reduce unnecessary paperwork. In

Part C, if a young child is not receiving services in the natural environment, the IFSP needs to justify the reasons why this is the case. Public Law 105-17 makes several important changes to definitions (Council for Exceptional Children, 1997; U.S. Department of Education, 1997a):

— *Developmental delay.* At the discretion of states and local education agencies, a child aged three to nine years who is experiencing developmental delays may be considered a child with a disability. The intent of this change is to increase early provision of services. Research on school-aged children who experience significant reading or behavior problems has demonstrated that waiting until third or fourth grade to refer and begin serving these children only increases the problems. Appropriate interventions are more beneficial when delivered as early as possible. The amendments also allow for more flexible use of IDEA-funded staff in general education classrooms. A state's definition of *developmental delay* under Part B (services for children 3 to 21) may differ from the definition used in Part C (services for children from birth to two). Even if a state adopts the developmental delay definition, local education agencies may not be obligated to use this category.

— *Serious emotional disturbance.* In order to reduce pejorative connotation of the term "serious emotional disturbance," the legislation notes that this category will be "hereinafter referred to as emotional disturbance."

— *Autism* means a "developmental disability significantly affecting verbal and nonverbal communication and social interaction, generally evident before age three, that adversely affects a child's educational performance." Additional characteristics mentioned include repetitive and stereotypical movements, strict adherence to routines and unusual sensory responses.

— *Related services.* The new legislation adds "orientation and mobility services" to the federal definition of related service.

— *Supplemental aids and supports.* This includes aids, services, and other supports provided in regular education settings and other education-related settings that enable students with disabilities to be educated with nondisabled peers to the maximum extent appropriate.

— *Transition services.* Related services are added to the list of services included under the definition of transition services. This is an area in which social workers have a strong role to play.

In addition to these definitions, the U.S. Department of Education (1997b) is proposing that the new regulations (written to implement the changes enacted in IDEA Amendments of 1997) include a definition of "general curriculum" clarifying that this refers to the single curriculum that applies to all children, both nondisabled and disabled, within the jurisdiction of the public agency. This definition was added in response to concerns that districts might interpret "general curriculum" as a general curriculum for specific disabling conditions rather than the curriculum utilized by typically developing children.

Of particular interest to social workers, the currently proposed regulations would amend the definitions of psychological services and social work services to include reference to "assisting in developing positive behavioral intervention strategies" (U.S. Department of Education, 1997b). The department recognizes that psychologists and social workers will be helpful in ensuring the implementation of the new statutory provision (Section 614(d)(3)(b)) requiring that, in the case of a child whose behavior impedes his or her own learning or that of others, the IEP team should consider strategies including, when appropriate, positive behavioral interventions (see Discipline section).

Discipline. The 1997 IDEA legislation contains several provisions that address the discipline of children with disabilities. These provisions were the focus of much debate in the negotiation of this legislation and continue to be sources of contention.

The law allows school personnel to order a change in the placement of a child with a disability to an appropriate interim alternative education setting (IAES), a change to another setting, or suspension for up to ten days in any school year (to the extent such an alternative might be applied to children without disabilities). A child who carries a weapon to school or a school function, or who is involved in possession, use, or solicitation or sale of a controlled substance at school or a school function can be assigned to an IAES for the same amount of time a child without a disability would be subject to discipline, up to 45 days. The legislation further requires that, either before or within ten days of disciplinary action, an IEP meeting be convened to develop an assessment plan to address the problem behavior (if a functional behavior assessment has not already taken place and a behavior intervention plan implemented); or if the student already has a behavior implementation plan, the IEP team will review the plan and modify it as necessary to address the behavior. The IEP team will review the relationship between the child's disability and the behavior subject to disciplinary action (manifestation determination review). If the behavior was not a manifestation of the child's disability, the same disciplinary procedures that would be applied to a child without a disability may be utilized, with the exception that the child will continue (in whatever setting) to receive a free and appropriate public education. In order to determine that the misbehavior is not a manifestation of the disability, the team must decide 1) whether the child's IEP and placement were appropriate, 2) that supplementary aids, services, and behavior intervention strategies were provided according to the IEP, and 3) that the child's disability did not impair the ability of the child to understand the impact and consequences of the behavior or to control the behavior. The law provides new provision for parents who disagree about the determination that the misbehavior was not a

manifestation of the disability to request a hearing that the educational agency is required to expedite. During an appeal, the child would remain in the IAES pending the outcome of the hearing or the expiration of the time limit, unless the parent and educational agency decide otherwise. If the school proposes a placement change after expiration of the IAES, the child will remain in the current placement pending any proceeding challenging the proposed change in placement, unless school personnel maintain that it is dangerous for the current placement to continue, in which case the hearing officer will issue a decision. An educational agency may report a crime committed by a child with a disability but must ensure that copies of special education and disciplinary records of the child are sent for consideration by the authorities.

Placement may be changed to an IAES for not more than 45 days by order of a hearing officer if the officer determines that the public agency has substantial evidence to support an argument that current placement will likely result in harm to the child or others and the agency has already made reasonable efforts to minimize risk of harm in the current placement (including the use of supplementary aids and services). The officer must also consider the appropriateness of the current placement and determine whether the IAES meets the requirements. The IAES must be determined by the IEP team and selected to enable the child to continue to participate in the general curriculum and to receive services and modifications that assist the child in meeting the goals of the IEP, and it must include services and modifications designed to address the problem behavior.

The changes in the legislation are consistent with prior interpretations by the U.S. Department of Education that FAPE continue to be offered to children with disabilities who have been suspended or expelled from schools, but represent a change in the law in the Fourth and Seventh Circuit Court districts affecting the states of Virginia, Maryland, North Carolina, South Carolina,

West Virginia, Illinois, Indiana, and Wisconsin. In these areas, the judicial rulings offered a different interpretation of the law. With the passage of 105-17, these states will now need to serve children in alternative placements.

Functional Behavioral Assessment.   The 1997 IDEA regulations require that when a student's behavior impedes learning—his or her own or that of other students—the IEP team should consider positive behavioral strategies to address the negative behaviors before they re-occur. Many districts address this requirement by developing Functional Behavioral Assessments. These assessments attempt to understand why a student behaves in a certain way by examining both the antecedents to the behavior and the consequences that may be reinforcing the behavior. The steps in completing a functional behavioral assessment include 1) identifying the behavior(s) most in need of change; 2) identifying the context in which the behavior occurs and what contexts may contribute to the behavior; 3) collecting data on student's behavior from a variety of sources to determine the function of the behavior and any contributing factors; 4) developing a hypothesis about the function of the behavior and where and why it is most likely to occur; 5) identifying alternative behaviors that can serve the same function more appropriately and can be taught to the student; 6) trying out the behavioral intervention plan; and 7) evaluating the success of the behavioral intervention (Jordan, 2001). The intervention plan may include teaching the student appropriate social skills, changing the environment to support positive behaviors (e.g., reducing clutter or noise, redirecting traffic patterns), providing a means for students to meet their needs in a more positive manner, and providing reinforcement and support for the student to utilize the appropriate behaviors (e.g., preventive cueing reminding a child to use appropriate behaviors) (Jordan, 2001). Social workers may be called upon to help develop the functional behavioral plan, to help collect data on the student's behaviors, to recommend behavioral intervention

strategies, to teach social skills and strategies to the student, and/or to provide support for the student as part of the behavior intervention plan.

New Evaluation Provisions.   Student evaluations must include a variety of assessment tools and strategies to gather functional and developmental information that may help in determining the presence of a disability and the content of the child's IEP. The assessment should include information provided by the parent. A single procedure is insufficient for determining whether the child has a disability or the appropriate educational program. The education agency must use technically sound instruments that assess cognitive and behavioral factors in addition to physical or developmental factors. The education agency must also assess the child in all areas of suspected disability and utilize assessment tools and strategies that provide information to assist in determining the educational needs. The education agency must ensure that tests are nondiscriminatory and are administered in the child's native language or mode of communication (unless infeasible), and the tests must be valid, administered by trained personnel, and in accordance with the test instructions.

The IDEA amendments of 1997 reduce unnecessary testing costs by relieving districts of the requirement to conduct a reevaluation testing every three years. Section 614 (c) allows the evaluation team to decide to dispense with tests to determine the need for continued eligibility, if the team determines that such testing is unnecessary and the parent agrees with this decision. The team must notify the parent if they decide that testing is unnecessary and explicate their decision. The team must still review existing evaluation data and identify additional data that may be necessary to determine eligibility and current level of functioning and any data needed to recommend any modifications to services and appropriate educational plans. Prior legislation required that every three years a child be reevaluated to determine the existence of a disability, even when the child has a permanent disabling condition (e.g., a child with congenital blindness still needed an optometric examination every three years to determine eligibility).

Race Disproportionality. African-American students are disproportionately over-represented and Hispanic students under-represented in special education. More black students than white students are labeled as having mild mental retardation (Janesick, 1995; Reschly, 1996). While some contend that special education has been used as a dumping ground for minority students (Artiles & Trent, 1994), others attribute over-representation to the effects of poverty (Reschly, 1995; Wagner, 1995b).

Provisions in the 1997 reauthorization of the IDEA require that each state examine data to determine if there is significant disproportionality of race in the identification of children with disabilities or in the placement of children. When such disproportionality occurs, the state must provide for review and, as necessary, revision of policy and practices (Council for Exceptional Children, 1997).

Early Intervention. Beginning with the amendments in Public Law 99-457, IDEA is the most important legislation enacted for young children who are developmentally vulnerable (Richmond & Ayoub, 1993). This legislation calls for statewide, multidisciplinary, comprehensive, coordinated, interagency programs of early intervention for all infants and toddlers with disabilities and their families. Although these services are not mandated by law, all states have elected to participate in this program, initially referred to as Part H and now Part C. Initially, services were required to be delivered by the highest level professional, but the recent legislation allows for use of paraprofessionals in service delivery. In order to coordinate among agencies, each state appoints a lead agency. The lead agency for early intervention differs according to the state. Most states assigned either education (15 states) or health departments (20 states) as lead agencies (Trohanis, 1994).

Public Law 99-457 operationalized the central role of the family through the use of Individualized Family Service Plans (IFSP) in place of IEPs for this age group. Although programs have struggled with how to develop and implement IFSPs that are responsive to families, the lessons learned from the process itself have been helpful in increasing our understanding of how to provide comprehensive, coordinated, interagency services to families. The focus of intervention in the early years has shifted from child to family. A recent volume reviewing research about the effectiveness of early intervention (Guralnick, 1997a, 1997c) offers convincing evidence that early intervention produces important positive effect for children when programs identify and address the many stressors affecting families. Although services that are primarily child focused continue to exist, they are one component of a more comprehensive intervention system. This shift to family-centered care has been so successful in the early years that more and more professionals are advocating its implementation in the preschool years and beyond. In reflecting upon the chapters presented in his book, Guralnick asserts that the most important theme identified is that "the field of early intervention appears to be coalescing in a *systems* and *developmental* sense" (Guralnick, 1997b, p. v).

When a child has a disability or is at significant biological risk of developing a disability, families experience a variety of additional stressors, including interpersonal or family distress (e.g., redefinition of roles, realignment of family resources, possible changes in family support system particularly when a stigma is attached to the disability, reassessment of long-term expectations and goals), increased need for information (e.g., about expected progress, medical and therapeutic interventions, identification of sources of information about disability or intervention approaches, about how to access and navigate the different community resources, advice on behavior management or assistance with parent-child interaction), need for additional resources (e.g., respite care, financial or insurance needs, sources for therapeutic interventions and equipment), and parental concerns about their ability to fulfill primary caregiving roles. Family patterns of interactions including parent-child transactions (e.g., reciprocity, non-intrusive scaffolding), family-community interactions (shopping, visiting friends, child-care arrangements). and family sense of control of child's experiences (developmentally appropriate toys and materials, level of structure in home environment, increased intrusion of professionals into family life) can be altered by the added stress. With more than 30% of the families with children with special needs falling below the threshold for low income (Bowe, 1995), limited financial resources add to the stress of many of the families. In addition, some children are at additional risk due to environmental stressors such as parental mental illness, unrealistic childrearing attitudes or beliefs, strained marital relationships, or lack of social supports. Although we have much to learn about the complex interactions of stressors, family characteristics, services, and developmental outcomes, we have already learned about the importance of attending to the stressors affecting families if we wish to effectively serve them. (See Guralnick, 1997c, for further discussion of what we now know about the connections among stressors, patterns of interaction, and child developmental outcomes.)

No Child Left Behind Act of 2001

The 2001 bill reauthorizing Elementary and Secondary Education Act was signed into law on January 8, 2002. Named the No Child Left Behind Act (NCLB), it included changes that were intended to prevent reading problems. Children identified as having learning disabilities represent approximately half of children with disabilities. The majority of these students are identified due to a failure in learning to read. Provisions were made in NCLB to allow states to use some of the funding for pre-kindergarten programs and for additional paraprofessionals in the classroom. It relies on four principles to bring about the an-

ticipated results: emphasis on proven teaching methods, stronger accountability focused on results, increased flexibility and local control, and more options for parents.

While Congress negotiated the final version of NCLB, President Bush (October 3, 2001) commissioned a committee to make recommendations regarding the next reauthorization of IDEA. The committee was charged with examining current research and trends in special education. Some concern was expressed by advocates that the composition of the committee was not representative of the stakeholders involved. Only two parents of disabled children were included on the committee. In 2002, hearings were held nationwide, accepting testimony on how to rethink special education.

CRITICAL ELEMENTS OF THE IDEA

The IDEA is founded on the provision of a FAPE to children with disabilities. No child may be excluded on the basis of a disability. Even when a district decides that a child is ineducable or disruptive, the district must provide services if the child is covered under Part B of the IDEA (for children younger than age three, states decide which infants and toddlers to serve). Part B is the section of the law that pertains to the delivery of services to children with disabilities from age 3 to 21. The zero-reject principle has been challenged and upheld in court (Turnbull, Turnbull, Shank, & Leal, 1995).

This section will describe the critical elements of the Individuals with Disabilities Education Act (Martin, Martin, & Terman, 1996; Turnbull, Turnbull, Shank, & Leal, 1995) and explore some of the ways in which social workers contribute to the enactment of the principles embodied in this legislation.

Child Find.   States must ensure that all disabled children, regardless of severity of disability, who are in need of special education and related services be identified, located, and evaluated. Children who are eligible for services (see

Figure 8.2 for eligibility definitions) must be offered appropriate educational and related services.

The school social worker can assist in the development of community-based referral procedures that can be utilized by parents, agencies, and doctors, among others, to locate children needing services. He or she can explain the school's programs and the referral procedure to important groups in the community. A part of this role is maintaining open communication between the school and the various community groups. The social worker can also provide in-service training to classroom teachers and relevant groups concerning the identification of children with special needs. A school social worker with an early intervention program may screen the child in the home.

Evaluation and Eligibility—Use of Valid, Reliable, Nondiscriminatory Procedures.

Students who are being considered for specialized services must be evaluated by a multidisciplinary team that is knowledgeable about the specific disability. Tests or assessment instruments must be administered in the child's native language or other mode of communication. In order to prevent inappropriate referrals, Garcia and Ortiz (1988) recommend that factors in the child's culture, language proficiency, learning style, and experiential background be considered when evaluating. The evaluation should include an assessment of the child's adaptive behavior in his or her natural environments (home, community, and playground). No single test can be used as the sole criterion for determining placement into special programs (see Appendix III).

The first three steps are screening, prereferral, and referral. Although prereferral is not required, it is recommended. Students who go through a prereferral process may never need to be referred because appropriate accommodations can be recommended.

The school social worker can provide observational data, a social developmental study, an adaptive behavior assessment, and an eco-

behavioral assessment. This information is essential for a total picture of the child's functioning in significant environments both in and out of the school. When this information is combined with other data (such as psychological testing), a comprehensive profile can be formed.

Social workers can also help other professionals on the team to understand the role of culture in development. Very few teachers have received training in understanding cultural influences on learning and development. Some children may be inappropriately referred to special education due to their use of nonstandard English or behaviors that are inconsistent with the mainstream culture (e.g., avoiding eye contact with adults or those in authority).

Parental Input. Parents are entitled to participate in placement and programming decisions. The most recent IDEA legislation attempts to strengthen parental involvement in the placement decisions. Parents have the right to an impartial hearing if they disagree with the final placement decision. The school district must obtain parental consent in writing prior to the formal evaluation of the child. Parents must also be informed about the multidisciplinary staff conference, which should be held at a time and place that allows their participation. If necessary, school districts should assist parents to utilize the hearing process if they are not in agreement with their child's placement.

The social worker can be instrumental in ensuring parental participation. The worker can make home visits to explain and clarify the nature of parental participation and its benefits. He or she can help foster collaboration among parents and school personnel. The social worker may also explain parental concerns to the educational staff before such concerns develop into problems. This liaison function is important in that it facilitates parental involvement in the education of their child and enables educators to be aware of family stressors that may compromise the success of some interventions, as well as alert the team to strategies that the family has

FIGURE 8.2 Federal Definitions of Eligibility Categories

Mentally retarded means a child who is significantly "subaverage in general intellectual functioning existing concurrently with deficits in adaptive behavior, and manifested during the developmental period which adversely affects the child's educational performance."

Hard of hearing means a child who suffers "from a hearing impairment, with a permanent or fluxuation in his/her hearing [which] adversely affects the child's educational performance, but which is not included under the definition of deaf."

Deaf means a child "with a 'hearing impairment' so severe that his/her hearing is nonfunctional for the purposes of educational performance."

Speech impaired means a child who experiences a "communication disorder, such as stuttering, impaired articulation, a language impairment, which adversely affects educational performance."

Visually handicapped means a child who has a "visual impairment which, after correction, adversely affects educational performance. The term includes partially seeing and blind children."

Severely emotionally disturbed means a child who exhibits "one or more of the following characteristics over a long period of time and to a marked degree:

- an inability to learn which cannot be explained by intellectual, sensory, or health factors;
- an inability to build or maintain satisfactory interpersonal relationships with peers or teachers;
- inappropriate types of behaviors or feelings and a tendency to develop physical symptoms or fears associated with personal or school problems. The term includes autistic, schizophrenic, and emotionally disturbed, but not the socially maladjusted."

Orthopedically impaired means a child with "severe orthopedic impairment which adversely affects educational performance. The term includes impairment caused by congenital anomaly (for example, clubfoot, cerebral palsy, and polomyositis)."

Health impaired means a child who "suffers from limited strength, vitality, or alertness due to chronic or acute health problems, i.e., heart conditions, tuberculosis, rheumatic fever, nephritis, sickle cell anemia, and lead poisoning."

Learning disability means a child who has "disorder in one or more of the basic psychological processes involved in understanding or in using language spoken or written, which may manifest itself in an imperfect ability to listen, think, speak, read, write, spell, or do mathematical calculations. The term includes such conditions as perceptual handicaps, brain injury, minimal brain dysfunction, dyslexia, and developmental aphasia. The term does not include children with learning problems, primarily the result of these visual, hearing, or motor handicaps, of mental retardation, or of environmental, cultural, or economic disadvantages."

Multiple handicaps means "a child who exhibits two or more impairments, severe either in nature or total impact, which significantly affect ability to benefit from the educational program."

Traumatic brain injured (TBI) means an acquired injury to the brain caused by an external physical force, resulting in partial or total functional disability or psychosocial impairment, or both, that adversely affects the child's educational performance. TBI applies to both open and closed head injuries that result in impairments in one or more areas: language, memory, cognition, attention, reasoning, problem solving, perceptual and motor abilities, psychosocial behavior, physical functions, information processing, and speech. The term does not apply to congenital or degenerative brain injuries, or to those induced by birth trauma.

Deaf-blindness means hearing and visual impairments, the combination of which causes such severe communication, developmental, and educational problems that they cannot be accommodated for solely in programs for children who are deaf or in programs for children who are blind.

Developmentally disabled means a child experiencing developmental delays, as defined by the State and as measured by appropriate diagnostic instruments and procedures, in one or more of the following areas: physical development, cognitive development, communication development, social or emotional development, or adaptive development; and who, by reason thereof, needs special education and related services.

Autism means a "developmental disability significantly affecting verbal and nonverbal communication and social interaction, generally evident before age 3, that adversely affects a child's educational performance." Additional characteristics mentioned include repetitive and stereotypical movements, strict adherence to routines, and unusual sensory responses.

found useful. Home and school are the major microsystems for the child. If both are working in synergy, everyone will benefit. Input from the social worker is particularly critical for the involvement of families who are not from the mainstream culture and who are marginalized in society (Harry, 1992a; Harry, 1998; Harry, Allen, & McLaughlin, 1995).

Due Process. Parents of handicapped children must be given prior notice, in their native language, of preplacement evaluations. This notice must include an explanation of the procedural safeguards available to parents, a description of the proposed action and reasons for it, and a description of the evaluation procedures. Written consent from parents is also required before an evaluation can be made and before children can be placed in special education programs. Parents who disagree with the individual education plan can request a hearing. Due to the high cost involved in litigation, the most recent amendments to IDEA encourage the use of mediation in cases of disagreement.

The social worker can inform the parents of their rights and prepare them for the process. He or she can act as a mediator when there are misunderstandings between parents and school officials. The worker can arrange meetings between parents and the educational staff to facilitate further clarification. The social worker can also help locate informal supports (e.g., other parents who have struggled with similar challenges, parent advocates) who may assist and support the parent in problem solving and in their quest for appropriate services.

Individualized Education Program (IEP)

Every student identified as needing education services must have a written statement concerning his or her education that includes the present level of educational performance; annual goals, including short-term instructional objectives; and specific educational and related services to be provided to the student and the extent to which the student will be able to participate in

regular curriculum and classroom (see Appendix III).

The appropriate education principle further requires that the education services benefit the student. Nonmedical related services that are necessary for the provision of FAPE must be provided.

For children younger than age three, an IFSP describes the goals and services to be provided to the family. In recognition of the critical importance of the family to the child's development, the IFSP targets the provision of services that facilitate the family's ability to encourage further development of their child. Part C (formerly known as Part H) includes a wider range of services and more collaboration with other agencies. Unlike Part B, in some states parents may be asked to pay for some service on a sliding fee scale.

At the multidisciplinary staff conference with the parents, the social worker can specify his or her goals and assist in the formulation of overall ⚹ instructional goals. The worker can provide summaries of the child's cultural, family, and community life resources and identify additional resources for the family. The worker may specify the nature of the work with the student (casework, group work, family intervention, behavioral intervention) and how the outcome will be evaluated. The worker may also facilitate parental involvement in the IEP by explaining the process to the parents prior to the conference, helping them to identify their goals and concerns about their child, and actively seeking their input during the conference.

Teachers may need assistance with developing social skills and adaptive behavior skills, particularly for learning disabled and emotionally impaired children. The social worker may utilize a Circle of Friends or a similar program in facilitating social relationships for included children. (See Case Example.)

The social worker may assist in the development of behavioral contracts with children, do an eco-behavioral evaluation and plan, or identify other means of assisting with prevention and management of problem behaviors. The social worker may also help the team to take a more solution-focused approach to designing an IEP, eliciting input from the teachers, parents, and students themselves in designing a program that utilizes the strengths and resources in the students' personal repertoire and ecosystem.

Least Restrictive Environment.   To the maximum extent possible, children should have their educational needs met in natural environments (for infants and toddlers) and/or regular education programs. This will be discussed in more detail in the next section. The social worker may assist with the transenvironmental transition plan, assist regular education teachers in classroom behavior management, help with teaching social skills, and support the collaboration process among administrators, teachers, paraprofessionals, and parents.

Case Example

Mr. Kamin came to the Child Study Team to discuss the problems he was having with George, a fourth grader. By the time classes started each day, George had already been involved in several fights—pushing or hitting other children as he came down the hall to the classroom. The students who had lockers next to George's locker tended to leave the area when they saw George arriving. Mr. Kamin said that he had changed lockers around so that the children on either side of George's locker were some of his most compliant students. Mr. Kamin commented that George "seemed to have so much anger" and "always has a bad attitude." He said that he had tried talking with George and disciplining him by keeping George's desk separated from the other students. None of the other students wanted to work with George anyway.

Mrs. Burke, the social worker, scheduled a morning to observe George's behavior. She watched George get off the bus. As the children approached the doorway, they began to crowd closer together. Whenever someone bumped into George, he would turn and shove them away or hit them. Before things escalated further, Mrs. Burke intervened and asked George to stand with her for a few minutes. George began defending his behavior, "He pushed me." George interpreted the jostling that occurred in narrow spaces as aggressive

moves by his peers. Mrs. Burke asked George to watch with her for awhile. She pointed out that other students were also getting bumped when an area became crowded. When the number of students was dwindling, Mrs. Burke directed George to walk to his locker and said that she would meet him there in a minute. She watched him walk calmly down the hall to his locker without being bumped and without hitting or pushing anyone himself. She joined George at his locker and complimented him on walking so nicely to his locker keeping his hands to himself. George smiled at the compliment, but said that the other children in the hall were nice to him today "probably 'cause you were watching."

Mrs. Burke responded that she thought it was because there were not as many people in the hall and so they were not bumping into him. She made a plan to meet him when he got off the bus the next day and they would watch the other students going in. Mrs. Burke again pointed out to George that other students were bumped. When the number of students dwindled enough, she again suggested to George that it was time to walk to his locker, but she would not be able to stay and watch. She said she would see him at lunchtime and she turned and walked to her car. When she went to meet George for lunch, Mr. Kamin said that George had had the best morning ever. There had been no fighting at all that morning. Mrs. Burke shared that news with George and complimented him on his self-control. During lunch together, they talked about how he managed to walk calmly to his locker and planned how he could do this every day. After school Mrs. Burke met with Mr. Kamin and explained that George attributed aggressive intentions to students who bumped against him in crowded places. George would need help in attributing different intentions to peer actions. Mrs. Burke asked Mr. Kamin if he could recommend some children in the class who might provide a circle of friends for George. She would have lunch with the group of them in her counseling room once a week and help George to form positive relationships with some of his peers.

Services to Infants, Toddlers, and Preschoolers

These services include statewide, multidisciplinary, comprehensive, coordinated, interagency programs of early intervention for all infants and toddlers with disabilities and their families. Some states elected to also serve high-risk populations. The IFSP epitomizes the increased emphasis placed on family involvement.

Social workers may be case managers, primary interventionists, or they may provide supportive and consultative services. In some states, mental health, public health, or social services are the lead agency rather than education.

Transition Planning

Transition planning involves a coordinated set of activities designed to promote movement from school to postschool activities, including postsecondary education, vocational training, supported employment, integrated employment, independent living, community participation, leisure and recreational involvement, and continuing adult education.

The IDEA now mentions social work as one of the services available for transition planning. Social workers can be helpful in coordinating person-centered planning meetings, as well as helping students with learning self-advocacy and socially responsible and adaptive behavior (Kaiser & Abell, 1997; Miner & Bates, 1997).

Related Services

Related services include transportation and developmental, corrective, and other supportive services required to assist a child in benefiting from special education, including audiology, speech therapy, physical therapy, occupational therapy, rehabilitative counseling, assertive technology, school health services, psychological services, and social work services. Under IDEA, social work services in the schools include:

1. Preparing a social or developmental history on a child with a disability;
2. Group and individual counseling with the child and family;
3. Working with those problems in a child's living situation (home, school, and community)

that affect the child's adjustment in school; and
4. Mobilizing school and community resources to enable the child to learn as effectively as possible in his or her educational program (34 C.F.R. Sec. 300.16).

Group and individualized counseling by qualified social workers is one of the related services mentioned in IDEA. In addition, the social worker may be helpful in locating resources, for example, community recreation, financial resources for instructional technology, and home adaptations that will support school efforts,

BEGINNING THE SECOND 25 YEARS

Policy analysts reviewed the many successes wrought during the first 25 years of this legislation and outlined some of the work yet to be done (American Youth Policy Forum and Center on Education Policy, 2001). By the turn of the century, 46% of all school-age students spent greater than 80% of their time in general education classrooms (U.S. Department of Education, 2000), but post-secondary outcomes were still disappointing and the costs associated with implementing IDEA were being questioned. Some policy makers urge caution in too quickly legislating additional changes to special education (Gloeckler, 2002; Hehir, 2002). The regulatory changes made in response to the 1997 reauthorization of IDEA were not promulgated until 1999. A 2002 reauthorization would not allow time to evaluate the changes made in the previous statute (Gloeckler; Hehir). In addition, over-legislation might only increase difficulty in implementation. For example, the 1997 reauthorization attempted to reduce paperwork demands, yet districts reported an increase rather than a decrease in paperwork resulted from the changes (Gloeckler).

Paperwork. Although praise was offered for the great strides made in earlier identification and provision of services to children and youth with disabilities, the success of these efforts was questioned. The monitoring process focused on compliance with procedures rather than positive outcomes for children. The National Council on Disability reported that even compliance with procedures among states and districts was poor. States and districts complained about the mountains of paperwork that IDEA created. Special education teachers spend more time on administrative paperwork than on most of their other teaching duties including communicating with parents and colleagues. The Study of Personnel Needs in Special Education cited burdensome paperwork as one of the major reasons teachers give for considering leaving special education (Billingsley, 2002; Study of Personnel Needs in Special Education, 2002).

Continued Fiscal Concern. Fiscal concerns represent one of the largest areas of contention around special education. Who should be responsible for funding the costs of education and support services that are increasingly specialized given the number of children with physical and health care needs who are surviving beyond the preschool years and attending schools? Despite the commitment by Congress in 1975 to fund 40% of the cost of special education, less than 12% of the costs were provided prior to 2000 and Congress has yet to come close to fulfilling its promise (Palmaffy, 2002). The costs of special education have continued to increase. Districts are burdened with the costs of additional services as well as the litigation that results when parents and districts disagree. Horn and Tynan (2002) contend that IDEA created incentives to identify an ever increasing percentage of children as disabled thus redirecting financial resources from general education to special education. The largest percentage of students receiving special education services are identified as having mild or lesser disabilities" (Horn & Tynan). Policy analysts question whether money might better be allocated in the general fund for more prevention activities. Hence, the provision of prekindergarten funds in the Leave No Child Behind Act of 2001.

The Move Toward More Inclusion

The combination of the curriculum for excellence movement, the school restructuring movement, and the comprehensive schools movement combined to create an atmosphere open to inclusion and collaboration. Inclusion involves the openness of the school system to include *all* students, even those severely impaired, in general education by making accommodations, adaptations to curriculum, and changes within the regular classroom. At the extreme end of the argument, some advocates called for the elimination of the continuum of services, placing all students in the general classrooms with supports. In order for this to occur, strong collaboration must take place between special and general educators. The movement to inclusion gained considerable momentum when the National Association of State Boards of Education (NASBE) issued the report *Winners All: A Call for Inclusive Schools* (1992). This report urges a shift in emphasis away from sorting and labeling children and toward improving instruction for all students. Individualized educational plans should be about programs and instructional strategies, not about places. Advocates of inclusion argue for more cooperative learning, peer tutoring, individual and small-group instruction, and varied teaching strategies (Turnbull & Turnbull, 1996).

The meaning of "all" differs according to where people stand in their agreement with the inclusive education movement. Most parents, teachers, and major organizations (Council for Exceptional Children, Council for Learning Disabilities, The American Council of the Blind and seven additional organizations in the area of blindness in the United States and Canada, and Council for Children with Behavior Disorders) agree with a move toward more inclusion, but continue to support individualization and the maintenance of the continuum of services. General educators are anxious about the scarcity of training they have received in individualizing curriculum. Special educators were trained to work with children and are unsure about collaborating with other adults. Parents are concerned that inclusion will become a new form of "dumping" and their child will lose necessary services. Without training in social skills, cooperative learning techniques will fall short of their intended purposes.

The Standards Movement and Accountability Thrust

The standards movement in education and the move to high stakes testing for schools have affected the delivery and evaluation of special education. McLaughlin (2002) argued that, until recent years, most special education legislation developed relatively independent of the general education and called for a more cohesive policy. Until the turn of the century, students with special education needs were excluded from program evaluation testing. This resulted in schools being evaluated only on children who did not struggle to learn. It encouraged over-identification of low performing students. The momentum from the standards and accountability movements changed the focus of parents, advocates and legislators from the identification of special needs and provision of programs to evaluation of educational results. The measurement of students' progress in special education towards defined standards became an issue. States were urged to include all students in state-wide assessment programs. For those students who experienced moderate to severe impairments or who were unable to participate in the regular assessment program due to sensory impairments, alternative assessments were developed in many states. The 1997 amendments to IDEA changed the focus to results and parents and advocates assert that this entails a shift to a higher standard than the "educational benefit" standard endorsed in the Rowley decision (Palmaffy, 2001). However, the results highlighted in the 1997 Amendments focus on the general education curriculum. Some (Lieberman, 2001) consider the application of the general curriculum to all students (rather than the individualized curricula encouraged by the original legislation) a death knell for special education.

The accountability efforts surrounding higher standards also represent a cause for concern to some (McDonnell, McLaughlin, Morison, et al., 1997; Lieberman). With the application of high stakes to the performance of individual students and more states requiring the participation of children with disabilities in the state assessments (American Youth Policy Forum and Center on Education Policy, 2001), assurances are needed that those students are given the opportunity to acquire the skills and knowledge that is expected. The current testing and measurement system addresses the higher end of the continuum, but does not assess well the progress of children who struggle (McDonnell et al., 1997).

The National Research Council cautions that unintended consequences may occur from the implementation of high standards and accountability procedures. They advise that parents of students with disabilities be given information that allows them to make informed choices about their child's participation in standards-based reform and the potential consequences (McDonnell et al., 1997). Parents are again encouraged to be the primary regulators. This is problematic for many economically disadvantaged and minority families (McDonnell et al.). Advocacy takes time, energy, knowledge of the law and regulations, and assertion in communication. For some families, just meeting the demands of daily life is already burdensome. The addition of an advocacy role is not feasible.

Minority Representation in Special Education

Representation of minority students among those identified with physical or sensory impairments is consistent with minority representation in the general population (Donovan, Cross, & Committee on Minority Representation in Special Education, 2002). However, minority students are overrepresented in the special education categories most directly related to school performance: mental retardation, emotional impairment, and to a lesser extent, learning disabilities. Some of this overrepresentation can be explained by the effects of poverty. Minority children are disproportionately poor and poverty is associated with lower birth weight, greater exposure to harmful toxins early in development, and fewer environmental supports for learning (Donovan et al.). More persistent poverty increases the number of risk factors for child development. In addition, schools in areas of high poverty are less likely to have experienced, well-educated teachers (Westat, 2002).

As noted earlier, despite the higher risks associated with poverty, minority children are not over-represented in the low incidence disability categories (e.g., physical and sensory impairments). Is the higher incidence of identified disability due to child traits or school failures? In addition to increased risk of learning problems due to more limited access to highly experienced, well-educated teachers, minority children are also more apt to be identified as having a disability due to biases in the instruments used to assess them. As early as 1974, Mercer identified biases in the psychometric tests used to evaluate children.

An extensive and rigorous investigation undertaken by Mercer confirmed that psychometric tests are culturally biased and do label a disproportionately large number of minority children as intellectually subnormal (Mercer, 1974). She argues that the schools' sole reliance on psychometric tests in placement decisions violates the right of children to be evaluated within a culturally appropriate normative framework, to be assessed as multidimensional persons, to be fully educated and free of stigmatizing labels, and to be culturally different. Mercer recommends that:

1. IQ tests and/or psychometric tests be supplemented with evaluations of a child's competencies and adaptive behavior outside of school. Adaptive behavior is the child's "ability to perform the social roles appropriate for persons of his/her age and sex in a manner which meets the expectations of the social system in which he/she participates" (see Appendix III).

2. Sociocultural factors be systematically considered in interpreting clinical scores. Psychometric tests are anglocentric and tend to measure an individual's background. Minority children frequently have not had the anglocentric experiences required to score successfully on such tests.

3. Only children scoring in the lowest 3% on the IQ test be classified as educable mentally retarded. Pupils with borderline scores should be regarded as low normal rather than retarded.

Although many improvements have been made in psychometric assessment, continued attention to potential biases in and interpretation of nationally standardized tests is needed, particularly on instruments that measure language (Suzuki, Short, Pierterse, & Kugler, 2001; Valencia & Suzuki, 2001; Washington & Craig, 1992).

The higher proportion of identified children among minority populations would be less troubling if identification of a disability brought adequate supports to enable the children to be successful in school. Unfortunately, no evidence is available to support such a statement. Schools in areas that are likely to serve large percentages of minority children are usually in poor urban areas. The Study of Personnel Needs in Special Education (SPeNSE) documented a greater shortage of trained special educators in schools that were urban or in higher poverty areas (SPeNSE, 2002). As noted in the section on standards, the monitoring of IDEA has examined procedures rather than outcomes. Several longitudinal studies currently underway should contribute to our knowledge of the success of different types of interventions with diverse groups of children and help determine which children will benefit from special education services. We should not assign potentially stigmatizing labels to students who would benefit more by remaining in the regular education classroom.

As much as possible, attention should be paid to supporting the general education program to meet the needs of all children, rather than sort and label children to provide specialized services outside the mainstream.

Longitudinal Research

In an effort to gain more information about the outcomes of special education, the Office of Special Education Programs has funded longitudinal studies designed to document the services provided to children with disabilities and the academic and social performance of children receiving these services. The studies are designed to capture information from birth through postsecondary outcomes. The National Early Intervention Study (NEILS) collects information on more than 3,300 children receiving services through Part C of IDEA. The study began in September 1997 and concludes with the collection of follow-up data when the children are five to seven years old in 2006. The Pre-Elementary Education Longitudinal Study (PEELS) is a seven-year study that follows children from preschool through early elementary school. Data collection began in 2002. The Special Education Elementary Longitudinal Study (SEELS) began collecting data in 1999 on approximately 13,000 elementary and early middle school students and will follow them until 2008. The National Longitudinal Transition Study-2 (NLTS2) is a ten-year study of approximately 13,000 students as they transition from secondary schools into adulthood. It will describe the characteristics of the students and their families, their school programs, related services, extracurricular activities, post-secondary services received, and the outcomes of all these experiences including academic, social, and vocational accomplishments.

ADVANCES IN EARLY INTERVENTION

Services to children from birth to five years old have evidenced the most change in the last de-cade. Early intervention services are more consistent with the tenets of social work than many of the other services offered through special education. As special education continues to evolve, it is hoped that these changes in early intervention and preschool services affect the delivery of services in elementary and secondary schools.

Special Education Philosophy and Intervention

The developmental domains have been the organizing principle *for* determining ability/disability. The entire labeling system attempts to classify students into homogenous groups so services can be efficiently delivered. Typically, however, educational interventions for different categories of students have been more alike than different. Most "effective programming utilizes the same principles and often the same procedures (intensive individual instruction, along with close monitoring and feedback) regardless of whether the student is classified as learning disabled, mildly mentally retarded, seriously emotionally disturbed, a slow learner, or educationally disadvantaged" (Reschly, 1996, p. 47). Research examining aptitude by treatment approaches has little empirical support. This includes approaches using disability categories, modality preferences, cognitive processing, learning styles, and neuropsychologically intact areas (Reschly, 1996).

Our placement of children into categories of disability assumes an underlying attribution of the problem as something inherent in the individual child. Research has attempted to find the cause of different disabilities (in order to prevent recurrence) and to develop appropriate remediations or compensatory strategies when remediation was not possible. This view of disability has been helpful in identifying and preventing further incidences of a number of disabilities, for example, identifying the effects of alcohol on the fetus, identifying the connection between folic acid deficiencies in early pregnancy and spina bifida. However, it is not a helpful paradigm for increasing our understanding of how to help children with the challenges they have.

In early intervention, there has been a shift from a child-focused, educational, deficit-based approach to an approach that embraces family-generated goals and needs, includes recognition of the child and family strengths, views parents as planners and participants, and evaluates family outcomes as well as developmental skills and milestones. Some theorists in early intervention note that the current approach is an add-on to the deficit-based developmental model, and they propose a new paradigm that moves from development to the centrality of relationship as the organizing principle. Under this new paradigm, relationship is viewed as the organizer of development, and family-provider relationships form the medium for the intervention process. Intervention involves a flexible blending of discipline-specific (e.g., education, occupational therapy, physical therapy, audiology) and nondiscipline-specific relationship and process issues. Outcomes focus on parent-child interaction, family functioning, child adaptive capacities, and parent understanding, confidence, and satisfaction (Weston, Ivins, Heffron, & Sweet, 1997). Relationship as the organizer in development is gaining increasing support in research examining brain development, resilience, and infant mental health (Greenspan, 1997; Seligman, 1988; Shore, 1997; Sroufe, 1996). Social workers are uniquely suited to helping early intervention teams and educators to focus more on relationship.

Parent-Professional Relationships

Researchers focusing on parent-professional relationships have emphasized family-centered principles and the development of partnerships that enable or empower parents. Partnerships between parents and professionals that are empowering are purported to reduce stress and increase functioning of families (Dunst, Trivette, & Deal, 1994b). Good partnerships are most often characterized as involving trust and open, honest communication among partners, active listening, reciprocity, mutually agreed goals, flexibility, openness, caring, understanding, shared responsibility, and mutual support and respect, strengths base, proactive, solution-focused stance, future orientation, and enabling competence (Dinnebeil, Hale, & Rule, 1996; Dunst, Trivette, & Deal, 1994a, 1994b; Turnbull & Turnbull, 1996). Respect for cultural diversity is implicit in these partnerships.

Empowering partnerships with parents are guided by a philosophy that emphasizes:

a. Recognizing and strengthening of child and family capabilities using a proactive rather than a deficit approach;

b. Enabling and empowering parents with the necessary knowledge, skills, and resources needed to perform family and parenting functions in a competent manner, by

c. Using partnerships between parents and professionals as the means to strengthen, enable, and empower families (Dunst, Trivette, & Thompson, 1994, p. 209).

Turnbull and Turnbull (1996; Turnbull, 1994) advocate a partnership based on a vision shared by professionals and families. Drawing on four theories (ecological systems theory, attachment theory, Maslow's theory of motivation, and exchange and resource theory [i.e., the need for reciprocity and interdependence to be met]), Turnbull and colleagues (1994) developed group action planning. This approach involves reflective, creative processes with divergent problem solving; a relational fun and affirming atmosphere; regular meetings; visions and relationships guiding the process; equal portions of participants from each ecological level; and reliable alliances with every member assuming responsibility for transforming visions to reality (Turnbull et al., 1994). Great expectations—how people prefer to live their lives guided by synergistic group vision (the whole is greater than the parts)—evolve. The group articulates great expectations with a clear understanding of the reality that needs to be changed for great expectation to occur. The group conceptualizes the contributions and reciprocity of the child in the inclusive relationships. Group action planning emphasizes adding supports so that activities that occurred before the child was born (or identified with a disability) may be continued, rather than directing the child and family to alternative restricted styles of living. The group distributes tasks evenly and is accountable to the whole. Progress is celebrated by the entire group; the synergy is self-renewing.

Drawbacks to this plan include the time commitment required as well as the participation of all ecological levels. Most agencies do not allot the necessary time for professionals to coordinate and regularly attend meetings for individual children. A shared vision may be a challenge for some families and communities.

Zeanah and McDonough (1989) outline practice principles for forming a working alliance with families: 1) sensitivity to family's unique situation; 2) assigning a positive connotation to parent and infant behavior; 3) sensitivity and responsivity to family's needs (information content is less important than the sharing process and how intervention is delivered, e.g., physical accessibility, emotional availability); 4) nonjudgmental attitude (accept and show respect for the parents' current adaptation "even as we entertain the possibility that the parents can acquire new ways of thinking, behaving, feeling, and coping in the future" (p. 520); and 5) willingness to monitor intense feeling aroused by the family (impatience, aversion, rescue, burden—may mean over involvement, i.e., working too hard to impose your agenda on the family or an inappropriate role with the family).

Waters and Lawrence (1993) advocate a competence approach to family intervention. Their framework is useful to collaboration as well. They define competence as encompassing an inborn striving for mastery and growth. In congruence with the Turnbulls, they advocate developing visions, which they distinguish as a mindset moving toward mastery and belonging, rather than some "castle in the air" (p. 107). Less focus is placed on a single vision and more focus is placed on the envisioning process. To proceed toward a vision, one needs courage. Waters and Lawrence are clear about stating that the "road to courage is paved with competence, not just challenge" (p. 107). The professional's role involves encouraging the individual by helping him or her to identify and develop competencies.

Preschool Inclusion

Americans with Disabilities Act (ADA) bars discrimination against individuals on the basis of disability. Title III of ADA requires child care facilities and nursery schools to be accessible to children with disabilities unless "undue burden" or "direct threat to health/safety" can be substantiated (Americans with Disabilities Act, 1991). The issues of "undue burden" and "threat to health/safety" have begun to be tested in the courts. If the struggles to include children with special needs in public schools are mirrored in the preschool population, then medically fragile children and children with behavioral problems will encounter more difficulty in inclusion than other children (Craig & Haggart, 1994). Helping families in advocating for their children by increasing community awareness of the benefits of inclusion, and by helping with transitions and offering ongoing support for placements, are roles that may be assumed by social workers, particularly for children with social-emotional and behavioral difficulties or environmental challenges.

Many young children are now being served in child care in addition to whatever other services they require. Hartley, White, and Yogman (1989) made a conservative estimate of over 600,000 families with infants and toddlers with disabilities requiring child care in order to meet work and financial needs. With the new welfare law, there are more families in need of child care. Child needs surveys and interviews of families of children with special needs consistently note respite and/or child care as one of the greatest needs (Bailey & Simeonsson, 1988; Burrell,

Thompson, & Sexton, 1992). Some potential advantages of community child care for children with special needs include:

— Relief from caregiving responsibilities.

— Possibility of increased social support through contact with other families with young children. Community child care represents one of the social support networks for families of young children.

— Redefinition of child behaviors. If the parents have not had much experience with young children, they may not be aware of the spectrum of behaviors that fall within the range of normal development. Observation of other children in care may help them to recognize that many behaviors exhibited by their child are typical behaviors for young children and help them to focus on the child rather than the disability. Alternatively, if the child's abilities are markedly delayed, observation of other children in care might lead parents to experience increased grief and sorrow.

— Development of cognitive and language skills. Interaction with other children could increase the child's abilities in areas important to the parent. Children are often great imitators of other children.

— Opportunity for the child to develop social and peer-interaction skills. This may be dependent on the skills of the child care provider. Research with preschoolers has demonstrated that when teachers/caregivers scaffold social skills, children increase their use of social strategies. However, it has also been noted that many early childhood teachers devote the majority of their attention to cognitive and academic areas of development, neglecting the social aspects (File & Kontos, 1992).

— Relief of financial stress. When child care is available, parents can maintain their employment, increasing their ability to meet financial needs.

— Providing an outlet for mastery for parent. If a child is not making progress developmentally, some parents cope by seeking mastery in other areas. Child care would allot parents time to develop such mastery.

These advantages depend upon the availability of high-quality care for these young children. As noted in Chapters 1 and 9, quality of care is a problem for even typically developing infants and toddlers receiving care in centers. Poor child care represents a risk factor for children—one that children already identified with special needs can ill afford.

Ecological perspectives of child development emphasize the importance of the interplay among the different systems surrounding the child (see Chapter 4). Those systems closest to the child (microsystems) and the relationship among these systems (mesosystems) have the strongest direct effect on development (Garbarino, 1990). "The quality of a microsystem depends upon its ability to sustain and enhance development and to provide a context that is emotionally validating and developmentally challenging" (Garbarino, p. 81). The home environment, especially parent-child interactions, the child care environment, and the early intervention interactions constitute major microsystems in the lives of young children with disabilities who receive child care.

For infants and toddlers, three states (Connecticut, Delaware, and Massachusetts) are developing integration models of early intervention and community child care. Delaware and Connecticut utilize the ECERs and the Family Day Care Rating Scale to screen potential sites. Delaware reported a wide range of care found among one- and two-year-old center classrooms. All three states have experienced a high staff turnover, which is not peculiar to these states. Given the importance of continuity of relationships to infants and toddlers, it is critical that we find ways to support caregivers so that they will continue to serve these young children.

Bruder and Bologna (1993) assert that integration is an attractive option because it involves families in community-based support systems, the child is receiving early intervention services in a normative environment, and child care providers and early interventionists can learn from one another in collaborations that will benefit all children. One of the difficulties in the provision of early intervention in integrated settings is the different philosophical approaches of early childhood special educators (ECSE) and early childhood educators (ECE). ECE advocates developmentally appropriate practices that support child-initiated activities, emphasize play and active child involvement, and value child interest. ECE is grounded in constructivist theories. ECSE is more didactic in nature, with far more teacher direction and a greater reliance on behavioral theories. ECSE assumes that the child's disability prevents him or her from taking advantage of the typical environmental experiences. ECE and ECSE "have contrasting views regarding the process of development, promote conflicting values with regard to the education of young children, and require teachers to engage in different types of interactions with children" (Mahoney, O'Sullivan, & Robinson, 1992, p. 107). Mahoney et al. (1992) contend that support for building on children's interests and the benefits of nondirective interactions argue for the adoption of ECE philosophy. Early intervention personnel need to find ways to adapt developmentally appropriate practices to the needs and abilities of young children with disabilities.

Professional Collaboration. IDEA (Part C) requires professionals to work collaboratively with families of infants and toddlers who have disabling conditions and with other agencies serving these families. Collaborative relationships with ongoing technical assistance by early intervention specialists has been a successful means of improving program quality for integrated programs serving infants and toddlers (Wesley, 1994).

A study of 67 early intervention professionals in Colorado identified collaborative approaches with directive style in sharing strategies to be the stated preference of the majority of these profes-sionals, followed closely by mental health models (Buysse, Schulte, Pierce, & Terry, 1994). The expert/behavioral method of consultation was least preferred. Babcock and Pryzwansky (1983) characterize collaborative consultation as involving mutual identification of problem and interventions, shared implementation, and ongoing follow-up of intervention with modifications as necessary.

CONCLUSION

Figure 8.1A summarizes the special education legislation of the past three decades. An overall evaluation of current special education services recognizes that large gains have been made in the provision of services to children with disabilities and in the availability of services to a broader group of children. The government is attempting to encourage more preventative programming. Awareness of the inequities of services is heightened. However, threats to special education services abound. The rising cost of delivering special education services is causing grave concerns. The application of general education curriculum standards is questioned by some. Current sentiment regarding students who become discipline problems may threaten access to free and appropriate education for students, particularly those who experience social and emotional disabilities. The number of special education teachers graduating each year is insufficient to meet the needs of schools and children. Vacancies are filled with teachers who are not trained to work with the students whom they serve. General education teachers are asked to provide instruction to students with disabilities, often with no supports and with no training in how to meet these students' needs. Special education teachers are asked to provide consultative support for students when they have never been taught about consultation models or how best to approach the task of consultation. Families are burdened with the job of monitoring their child's educational programming. For families already burdened by multiple stressors, this task is more than they can handle. More and more children with health problems are surviving and being served in special or general education, but need the support of health and medical profession to enable participation. Strong collaboration and interdisciplinary educational preparation would enhance the provision of services to children and families.

Implications for Social Workers

The social work literature reveals that since the passage of P.L. 94-142, the roles and tasks of school social workers have expanded to assist disabled children. For example, besides participation in the multidisciplinary team conferences and consultation, social workers coordinate IEP and IFSP conferences, serve as trained mediators, act as advocates, lead parent education and informational groups, function as core managers, and facilitate the development of relationships that link the services of the school with those found in the community.

However, in order to function in the public school and to serve this target population, a social worker must stay informed about legislation and litigation that impact the school and other service providers' responsibility to this group as well as their roles and those of others.

The school social worker will need specialized knowledge in human development, disabilities, case management, evaluating outcomes, how to link services and build support systems for families—because the number of agencies that could become involved with population continues to grow, how to work across disciplines, and as stated earlier, knowledge of special education litigation and legislation. In the chapter on the history of social work, it is made clear that since our early beginning, we have served as the liaison/link between school and home/community.

The social work profession is founded on democratic and humanitarian ideals. It is committed to protecting the right of individuality, self-respect, and the opportunity for development, without discrimination. Legislation that grants infants and youths the right to an appropriate education in the least restrictive environment is consistent with these ideals.

FOR STUDY AND DISCUSSION

1. Each month the Center for Effective Collaboration and Practice (CECP) offers an online discussion with an author around a current article addressing the challenges of serving children with special needs. CECP is focused on improving the services to children with emotional and behavioral problems. Review some of the articles and discussions (or participate in a current discussion) by visiting the website http://cecp.air.org/.

2. Read "Eliminating Ableism in Education" by Thomas Hehir. Identify ways in which ableism is manifested and interferes with the education of children with physical, emotional, and mental impairments. Online: http://gseweb.harvard.edu/%TEhepg/hehir.htm.

3. Analyze your state's rules and regulations governing special education programs and services. What are the implications for social work tasks and services? What changes need to be made to enable students with disabilities?

4. Interview the parents of students in a classroom that includes students with moderate to severe disabilities. What are the advantages and disadvantages perceived by parents of typically developing students? What are the advantages and disadvantages perceived by parents of the student with disabilities?

5. Adaptive behavior is an important aspect to be assessed when evaluating students with disabilities. Locate and discuss definitions of adaptive behavior found in the social work and education literature. What are the implications of adaptive behavior for school social work tasks? What scales are widely used to assess adaptive behavior?

6. Visit a program designed to assist infants and toddlers with disabilities. Find out what services

are typically provided to families of children with differing disabilities. Ascertain how these services are incorporated into the Individualized Family Service Plan and what roles, if any, are carried out by the school social worker.

7. Talk with teachers who have children included in their classrooms. From a teacher's perspective, what are the challenges to providing appropriate education for all the children in their class?

8. Programs have been designed to prevent social and emotional problems in schools. Visit the website http://cecp.air.org/preventionstrategies/Default.htm to compare information about the Achieving Behaving Caring (ABC) Program, Behavior Prevention Program, Conflict Resolution/Peer Mediation Program, Improving the Lives of Children, Linkages to Learning Program, and Project Success.

9. Learn more about the various disability categories and ways to assist students with disabilities by visiting the websites for the National Clearinghouse for Children and Youth with Disabilities http://www.nichcy.org/, IDEA Practices, funded by the U.S. Office of Special Education Programs, http://www.ideapractices.org/, or the Educational Resources Information Center (ERIC) digests available on the Department of Education website www.eric.ed.gov

10. Explore the most recent findings of the OSEP funded longitudinal studies of children with disabilities: NEILS http://www.sri.com/neils/, PEELS http://www.sri.com/peels/index.html, SEELS http://www.seels.net/, NLTS-2 http://www.sri.com/policy/cehs/dispolicy/nlts2.html

ADDITIONAL READING

American Youth Policy Forum, and Center on Education Policy (2001). *Twenty-five years of educating children with disabilities: The good news and the work ahead*. Washington, DC: Authors. [Online] Available: www.aypf.org or www.ctredpol.org.

Atkins-Burnett, S., & Allen-Meares, P. (2000). Infants and toddlers with disabilities: Relationship-based approaches. *Social Work, 45*(4), 371–379.

Center for Effective Collaboration and Practice (1998). *Addressing student problem behavior—Part II: Conducting a functional behavioral assessment*. Washington, DC: Authors.

Durrant, J. E. (1994). A decade of research on learning disabilities: A report card on the state of the literature. *Journal of Learning Disabilities, 27*(1), 25–33.

Eder, D. (1981, July). Ability grouping as a self-fulfilling prophecy: A microanalysis of teacher-student interaction. *Sociology of Education, 54*(3), 151–162.

Ensign, J. (1998). *Homeschooling gifted students: An introductory guide for parents*. ERIC EC Digest #E543. Reston, VA: The ERIC Clearinghouse on Disabilities and Gifted Education.

Fecser, F. A., & Long, N. J. (1998). *Life space crisis intervention*. Retrieved January 31, 2003 from http://cecp.air.org/interact/authoronline/april98/1.htm

Ford, D. (1994). Nurturing resilience in gifted black youth. *Roeper Review, 17*(2), 80–85.

Fuchs, D., Fuchs, L. S., Fernstrom, P., & Hahn, M. (1991). Toward a responsible reintegration of behaviorally disordered. *Behavioral Disorders, 16*(2), 133–147.

Glennon, T. (1993, Winter). Disabling ambiguities: Confronting barriers to the education of students with emotional disabilities. *Tennessee Law Review, 60*, 295–364.

Gorman, S. (2001). Navigating the special education maze: Experiences of four families. In C. E. Finn, A. J. Rotherham, & C. R. Hokanson, Jr. (Eds.), *Rethinking special education for a new century* (pp. 233–257). Dayton, OH: Thomas B. Fordham Foundation and the Progressive Policy Institute. Retrieved January 31, 2003 from www.edexcellence.net.

Greenblatt, A. P. (1994). Gender and ethnicity bias in the assessment of attention deficit disorder. *Social Work in Education, 16*(2), 89–95.

Krauss, M. W., Upshur, S. C., Shonkoff, J. P., & Hauser-Cram, P. (1993). The impact of parent groups on mothers of infants with disabilities. *Journal of Early Intervention, 17*(1), 8–20.

Wagner, M. (1995a). Outcomes for youths with serious emotional disturbance in secondary school and early adulthood. *The Future of Children, 5*(2), 90–112.

REFERENCES

Americans with Disabilities Act (28 CFR Part 36). *Federal Register.* July 26, 1991.

American Youth Policy Forum, and Center on Education Policy (2001). *Twenty-five years of educating children with disabilities: The good news and the work ahead.* Washington, DC: Authors. Retrieved January 31, 2003 from www.aypf.org/publications/special_ed/Special_Ed.pdf

Artiles, A., & Trent, S. (1994). Overrepresentation of minority students in special education: A continuing debate. *The Journal of Special Education, 27,* 410–437.

Babcock, N. L., & Pryzwansky, W. B. (1983). Models of consultation: Preferences of educational professionals at five stages of service. *Journal of School Psychology, 21,* 359–366.

Bailey, D. B., & Simeonsson, R. J. (1988). Assessing needs of families with handicapped infants. *Journal of Special Education, 22*(1), 117–127.

Billingsley, B. S. (2002). *Beginning special educators: Characteristics, qualifications and experience.* Retrieved January 31, 2003 from www.spense.org/IHEsummaryfinal.pdf

Bowe, F. G. (1995). *Birth to five: Early childhood special education.* Albany, NY: Delmar Publishers.

Bruder, M. B., & Bologna, T. (1993). Collaboration and service coordination for effective early intervention. In W. Brown, S. K. Thurman, & L. F. Pearl (Eds.), *Family-centered early intervention with infants and toddlers: Innovative cross-disciplinary approaches* (pp. 103–428). Baltimore: Paul H. Brookes.

Burrell, B., Thompson, B., & Sexton, D. (1992). The measurement integrity of data collected using the child-abuse potential inventory. *Educational Psychology Measures, 52*(4), 993–1001.

Bush, G. W. (October 3, 2001). Executive order on excellence in special education. Washington, DC: Author. Retrieved January 31, 2003 from www.whitehouse.gov/news/releases/2001/10/20011003-12.html

Buysse, V., Schulte, A. C., Pierce, P. P., & Terry, D. (1994). Models and styles of consultation: Preferences of professionals in early intervention. *Journal of Early Intervention, 18*(3), 302–310.

Council for Exceptional Children (1997). *Summary of the Individuals with Disabilities Education Act amendments of 1997.* Reston, VA: Author.

Craig, S. E., & Haggart, A. G. (1994). Including all children: The ADA's challenge to early intervention. *Infants & Young Children, 7*(2), 15–19.

Daniel R. R. v. *State Board of Education.* (1989). 874 F. 2d 1036 (5th cir.).

Dinnebeil, L. A., Hale, L. M., & Rule, S. (1996). A qualitative analysis of parents' and service coordinators' descriptions of variables that influence collaborative relationships. *Topics in Early Childhood Special Education, 16*(3), 322–347.

Donovan, S., & Cross, C. T. (Eds.). Committee on Minority Representation in Special Education, National Research Council. (2002). *Minority students in special and gifted education.* Washington, DC: National Academies Press.

Dunst, C. J., Trivette, C. M., & Deal, A. G. (1988). *Enabling and empowering families.* Cambridge, MA: Brookline Books.

Dunst, C. J., Trivette, C. M., & Deal, A. G. (1994a). Enabling and empowering families. In C. I. Dunst, C. M. Trivette, & A. G. Deal (Eds.), *Supporting and strengthening families. Volume 1: Methods, strategies and practices* (pp. 2–11). Cambridge, MA: Brookline Books.

Dunst, C. J., Trivette, C. M., & Deal, A.G. (Eds.). (1994b). *Supporting and strengthening families. Volume I: Methods, strategies and practices.* Cambridge, MA: Brookline Books.

Education for All Handicapped Children Act. (1975). *Federal Register* (P.L. 94-142 41:46977).

File, N., & Kontos, S. (1992). Indirect service delivery through consultation: Review and implications for early intervention. *Journal of Early Intervention, 16*(2), 221–223.

Garbarino, J. (1990). The human ecology of early risk. In S. J. Meisels & J. P. Shonkoff (Eds.), *Handbook of early childhood intervention* (pp. 78–96). New York: Cambridge University Press.

Garcia, S., & Ortiz, A. (1988). Preventing inappropriate referrals of language minority students to special education. *New Focus, 5,* 1–3.

Gloeckler, L. C. (2002). IDEA reauthorization: It's time to simplify and focus on performance. In *A timely IDEA: Rethinking Federal Education Programs for Children with Disabilities* (pp. 14–23). Washington, DC: Center on Education Policy. Retrieved January 31, 2003 from www.ctredpol.org/specialeducation/timelyidea.2002.htm

Greenspan, S., with Benderly, B. L. (1997). *The

growth of the mind and the endangered origins of intelligence. Reading, MA: Addison-Wesley Publishing Company, Inc.

Guralnick, M. J. (Ed.). (1997a). *The effectiveness of early intervention.* Baltimore: Paul H. Brookes Publishing.

Guralnick, M. J. (1997b). Organizing themes in early intervention. *Infants & Young Children, 10*(2), v–vii.

Guralnick, M. J. (1997c). Second generation research in the field of early intervention. In M. I. Guralnick (Ed.), *The effectiveness of early intervention* (pp. 3–22). Baltimore: Paul H. Brookes Publishing.

Harry, B. (1992a). *Cultural diversity, families, and the special education system communication and empowerment.* New York: Teachers College Press.

Harry, B. (1992b). Developing cultural self-awareness: The first step in values clarification for early interventionists. *Topics in Early Childhood Special Education, 12*(3), 333–350.

Harry, B. (1998). Leaning forward or bending over backwards: Cultural reciprocity in working with families. *Journal of Early Intervention, 21*(1), 62–72.

Harry, B., Allen, N., & McLaughlin, M. (1995). Communication versus compliance: African-American parents' involvement in special education. *Exceptional Children, 61*(4), 364–377.

Hartley, M., White, C., & Yogman, M. W. (1989). The challenge of providing quality group child care for infants and young children with special needs. *Infants & Young Children, 2*(2), 1–10.

Hehir, T. (2002). IDEA 2002 reauthorization: An opportunity to improve educational results for students with disabilities. *A timely IDEA: Rethinking Federal Education Programs for Children with Disabilities* (pp. 4–13). Washington, DC: Center on Education Policy. Retrieved January 31, 2003 from www.ctredpol.org/specialeducation/timelyidea.2002.htm

Hobson v. *Hansen,* 269 F.Supp. 401. (D.D.C. 1967), cert. Dismissed 393. U.S.80l(1968), *aff'd* in part, rev'd in part sub nom. *Smuck* v. *Hobson* 175 (D.D.C. 1969). 408 F2d.

Horn, W. F., & Tynan, D. (2001). Time to make special education "special" again. In C. E. Finn, A. J. Rotherham, & C. R. Hokanson, Jr. (Eds.), *Rethinking special education for a new century* (pp. 23–52). Dayton, OH: Thomas B. Fordham and the

Progressive Policy Institute. Retrieved January 31, 2003 from www.edexcellence.net/library/special_ed/special_ed_ch2.pdf

Individuals with Disabilities Education Act (IDEA). (1991). *Congressional Information Service Annual Legislative Histories for U.S. Public Laws* (P.L. 101-476).

Janesick, V. J. (1995). Our multicultural society. In Meyen, E. L. & T. M. Skrtic (Eds.), *Special education & student disability: An introduction—Traditional, emerging, and alternative perspectives* (pp. 713–727). Denver: Love Publishing Company.

Jordan, D. (2001). *Functional behavioral assessment and positive interventions: What parents need to know.* Minneapolis, MN: Families and Advocates Partnership for Education. On-line Available: www.fape.org

Kaiser, D., & Abell, M. (1997). Learning life management in the classroom. *Teaching Exceptional Children, 30*(1), 70–75.

Larry P. v. *Riles,* 343 F. Supp. 1306, affd., 502 F. 2d 963, *Further proceedings,* 495 F, Supp. 926 affd., *502* F. 2d 693 (9th Cu. 1984).

Lewit, E. M., & Baker, L. S. (1996). Child indicators: Children in special education. *The Future of Children, 6*(1), 139–151.

Lieberman, L. M. (January 17, 2001). The death of special education. *Education Week, 201*(18), 60, 40. [On-line] Available: www.edweek.org

Mahoney, G., O'Sullivan, P. S., & Robinson, C. (1992). The family environments of children with disabilities: Diverse but not so different. Use of the family environment scale. *Topics in Early Childhood Special Education, 12,* 386–402.

Martin, E. (1995). Case studies on inclusion: Worst fears realized. *Journal of Special Education, 29*(2), 192–199.

Martin, E. W., Martin, R., & Terman, D. L. (1996). The legislative litigation history of special education. *The Future of Children, 6*(1). Retrieved January 31, 2003 from www.futureofchildren.org/information2826/information_show.htm?doc_id=72450.

McDonnell, L. M., McLaughlin, M. J., & Morison, P. (Eds.), and Committee on Goals 2000 and the Inclusion of Students with Disabilities, Board on Testing and Assessment, Commission on Behavioral and Social Sciences and Education National Research Council (1997). *Educating one and all: Students with disabilities and standards-based reform.* Washington, DC: National Academy Press.

McLaughlin, M. J. (2002). Issues for consideration in the reauthorization of Part B of the Individuals with Disabilities Education Act. In *A timely IDEA: Rethinking Federal Education Programs for Children with Disabilities* (pp. 24–42). Washington, DC: Center on Education Policy. Retrieved January 31, 2003 from www.ctredpol.org/specialeducation/timelyidea.2002.htm

Mercer, J. (1974, February). A policy statement on assessment procedures and the rights of children. *Harvard Educational Review, 44*(1), 125–144.

Mills v. *Washington, DC, Board of Education,* 348 F. Supp. 866 (D. DC 1972); *contempt proceedings.* EHLR 551:643 (D.DC 1980).

Miner, C. A., & Bates, P. E. (1997). Person-centered transition planning. *Teaching Exceptional Children. 30*(1), 66–69.

National Association of State Boards of Education (NASBE). (1992). *Winners all: A call for inclusive schools.* The report of the NASBE Study Group on Special Education. Alexandria, VA: NASBE.

National Association of State Directors of Special Education (NASDSE), National Association of School Psychologists (NASP), Office of Special Education Programming (OSEP). (1994). *Assessment and eligibility in special education: An examination of policy and practice with proposals for change.* Alexandria, VA: NASDSE.

National Council on Disability (January 25, 2000). Back to school on civil rights: Letter of transmittal. On-line available: www.ncd.gov/newsroom/Publications/backtoschool.html

Oberti v. *Board of Education.* (1993), 995 F. 2d 1204.

Palmaffy, T. (2001). Special education history and issues. In C. E. Finn, A. J. Rotherham, & C. R. Hokanson, Jr. (Eds.) *Rethinking special education for a new century* (pp. 1–21). Dayton, OH: Thomas B Fordham Foundation and the Progressive Policy Institute. On-line available: www. edexcellence. net

Pennsylvania Association for Retarded Citizens [PARC] v. *Commonwealth of Pennsylvania,* 334 F. Supp. 1257, 343 F. Supp. 279 (B. D. Pa. 1971, 1972).

Reschly, D. J. (1995). *IQ and special education: History, current status, and alternatives.* Washington, DC: National Research Council, Commission on Social Sciences and Education, Board of Testing and Assessment.

Reschly, D. J. (1996). Identification and assessment of students with disabilities. *The Future of Children, 6*(1), 40–53. Reprinted with permission of the Center for the Future of Children of the David and Lucille Packard Foundation.

Richmond, I., & Ayoub, C. C. (1993). Evolution of early intervention philosophy. In D. M. Bryant & M. A. Graham (Eds.), *Implementing early intervention: From research to effective practice* (pp. 1–17). New York: The Guilford Press.

Roncker v. *Walters.* (1983). 700 F. 2d 1058 (6th Circuit 1983), cert. den. 464 U. S.864, 1045. Ct. 196, 78 L. Ed. 2d 171.

Rowley v. *Board of Education.* (1982). *458* U.S. at 203, 102 5. Ct. at 3049.

Sacramento City Unified School District, Board of Education v. *Rachel H.* (1994). 12 F.3d 1398 (9th cir.).

Seligman. S. (1988). Concepts in infant mental health: Implications for work with developmentally disabled infants. *Infants & Young Children, 1*(1), 41–51.

Shore, R. (1997). *Rethinking the brain: New insights into early development.* New York: Families and Work Institute.

Sroufe, A. (1996). *Emotional development: The organization of emotional life in the early years.* New York: Cambridge University Press.

Study of Personnel Needs in Special Education (2002). SPeNSE fact sheet: Paperwork in special education. On-line available: www.spense.org.

Suzuki, L. A., Short, E. L., Pierterse, A., & Kugler, J. (2001). Multicultural issues and the assessment of aptitude. In L. A. Suzuki (Ed.) *Handbook of multicultural assessment: Clinical, psychological, and educational applications* (2nd ed., pp. 359–382). San Francisco: Jossey-Bass.

Trohanis, P. L. (1994). Early intervention—a national overview. *The Exceptional Parent, 24,* 18–20.

Turnbull, A. P. (1994). *Group action planning for families with infants and toddlers.* Richmond, VA: Zero to Three.

Turnbull, A. P., & Turnbull, H. R. (1996). *Families, professionals, and exceptionality.* Columbus, OH: Merrill-Prentice Hall.

Turnbull, A. P., Turnbull, H. R., & Blue-Banning, M. (1994). Enhancing inclusion of infants and toddlers with disabilities and their families: A theoretical and programmatic analysis. *Infants & Young Children, 7*(2), 1–14.

Turnbull, A. P., Turnbull, H. R., Shank, M., & Leal, D. (1995). *Exceptional lives: Special education in today's schools.* Columbus, OH: Merrill-Prentice Hall.

U.S. Department of Education. (1997a, July). The inclusion of students with disabilities and limited English proficient students in large-scale assessments. A summary of recent progress. National Center for Education Statistics, Doc #97-482. Washington, DC: Author.

U.S. Department of Education. (1997b). To assure the free appropriate public education of all children with disabilities: Nineteenth annual report to Congress on the implementation of the Individuals with Disabilities Education Act. Washington, DC: Author.

U.S. Department of Education. (2000). *Twenty-second annual report to Congress on the implementation of the Individuals with Disabilities Education Act.* Washington, DC: Author. On-line www.ed. gov

U.S. Office of Special Education Programs. (1999). Youth with disabilities in the juvenile justice system. Retrieved January 31, 2003 from www. ideapractices.org/resources/files/youthinjjsystem. pdf.

Valencia, R. R., & Suzuki, L. A. (2001). *Intelligence testing and minority students: Foundations, performance factors, and assessment issues.* Thousand Oaks, CA: Sage.

Wagner, M. (1995). *The contributions of poverty and ethnic background to the participation of secondary school students in special education.* Menlo Park, CA: SRI International.

Wagner, M. M., & Backorby, J. (1996). Transition from high school to work or college: How special education students fare. *The Future of Children, 6*(1). Retrieved January 30, 2003, from www. futureofchildren.org/information2826/information _show.htm?doc_id=72487.

Washington, J. A., & Craig, H. K. (1992). Performances of low-income, African American preschool and kindergarten children on the Peabody Picture Vocabulary Test—Revised. *Language, Speech, & Hearing Services in Schools, 23*(4), 329–333.

Waters, D. B., & Lawrence, E. C. (1993). *Competence, courage, and change.* New York: W. W. Norton.

Wesley, P. W. (1994). Providing on-site consultation to promote quality in integrated child care programs. *Journal of Early Intervention, 18,* 391–402.

Westat (2002). Personnel recruitment, retention, and shortage data tables: Table 3.130, Table 3.146, Table 3.147, Table 5.130, Table 5.146, Table 5.147. Retrieved April 30, 2002, from www. spense.org

Weston, D. R., Ivins, B., Heffron, M. C., & Sweet, N. (1997). Formulating the centrality of relationships in early intervention: An organizational perspective. *Infants & Young Children, 9*(3), 1–12.

Zeanah, C. H., Jr., & McDonough, S. (1989). Clinical approaches to families in early intervention. *Seminars in Perinatology, 13*(6), 513–526.

CHAPTER 9

SOME TARGET GROUPS OF CHILDREN

The failure of a person to display competencies is due not to deficits within a person, but to the failure of social systems to provide opportunities for competencies to be acquired or displayed. When new competencies are needed, the optimal way of providing them is through experiences that allow people to make positive self-attributions regarding their ability to influence important life events.
—Rappaport, 1981[1]

What do you love about these people? It is often the key to finding a way in to a level of collaboration that can make a difference. If the answer is nothing, then we are not joined with them. We do not have enough appreciation of how they came by their problems honestly and we do not see past those problems to their strengths. We believe that every problem has a caring side but that side will remain imperceptible until one finds a way to care about the person.
—Waters and Lawrence, 1993, p. 117[2]

INTRODUCTION

School social workers play a variety of roles in relation to different target groups of pupils. First and most important is the identification of pupils who are at risk and experiencing difficulty in learning and meeting school requirements. Their vulnerability may be attributed to numerous factors: their stage of psychosocial development and approaching developmental transition; a unique characteristic (such as their minority status, family background, or poverty); academic ability or the lack thereof; and an inability to behave according to school policies and expectations. A part of the role of identifying these children is assessing the quality of transactions between them, the family, the school, and the community. Are school policies and practices fair? Does the staff provide equal support and assistance to these groups? If not, why? What factors interfere with engaging these children in learning? Are community values in conflict with

[1]Rappaport, J. (1981). In praise of paradox: A social policy of empowerment over prevention. *American Journal of Community Psychology, 9*(1), 1–25.

[2]Waters, D. B., & Lawrence, E. C. (1993). *Competence, courage and change: An approach to family therapy.* New York: W. W. Norton & Company, Inc.

those of the school? Social workers must make referrals, file petitions in the court, assist in the development of policies and programs within the school and community, work with the parents of these children, and advocate changes in unfair institutional policies and practices. In other words, the practitioner should seek changes in the pupil or in the quality of the impinging environment, or both.

In this chapter we discuss several types of vulnerable pupils and call attention to the concept of pupil life tasks. We recognize that there are many more vulnerable pupil groups, but discussion of all of them is beyond the scope of any one text. This chapter will focus on such pupil groups as disadvantaged preschool children, children from low-income areas, migrant children, homeless children, school-age pregnant girls and school-age parents, youth suffering with AIDS, gay and lesbian children, abused and neglected children, and children involved with gang violence and delinquent behavior such as nonattendance and drug and alcohol abuse (see Table 9.1).

ENROLLMENT AND STAFFING

During the 1970s, enrollment in elementary and secondary public institutions was on the decline. In just a few decades this trend has been reversed. Enrollment in public and private institutions is expected to surpass a historic all-time high. Influenced primarily by the rising number of annual births since 1977 (referred to as the "baby-boom echo"), the 5- to 17-year-old population is projected to increase by 17 percent from 1989 to 2004 (see Tables 9.2 and 9.3). In 1979 there were 46.7 million pupils in kindergarten through grade 12; by 2004 there will be 53.4 million, and by 2009 it is projected there will be

TABLE 9.1 21 Key Facts about American Children

3 in 5	preschoolers have their mothers in the labor force.
2 in 5	preschoolers eligible for Head Start do not participate in the program.
1 in 3	is born to unmarried parents.
1 in 3	will be poor at some point in childhood.
1 in 3	is behind a year or more in school.
1 in 4	lives with only one parent.
1 in 5	is born to a mother who did not graduate from high school.
1 in 5	children under 3 is poor now.
1 in 6	is born to a mother who did not receive prenatal care in the first three months of pregnancy.
1 in 7	children eligible for federal child care assistance through the Child Care and Development Block Grant receives it.
1 in 8	has no health insurance.
1 in 8	never graduates from high school.
1 in 8	is born to a teenage mother.
1 in 8	lives in a family receiving food stamps.
1 in 12	has a disability.
1 in 13	is born at low birthweight.
1 in 16	lives in *extreme* poverty.
1 in 24	lives with neither parent.
1 in 60	sees their parent divorce in any year.
1 in 141	will die before their first birthday.
1 in 1,056	will be killed by firearms before age 20.

Source: Children's Defense Fund, *The State of Children in America's Union: A 2002 Action Guide to Leave No Child Behind®*. Washington, DC: Children's Defense Fund, 2002.

TABLE 9.2 Actual Public School Enrollments in Grades K–12 in the United States

	ENROLLMENT (IN THOUSANDS)			
GRADE	**1985**	**1990**	**1995**	**1998**
K	3,041	3,306	3,536	3,443
1	3,239	3,499	3,671	3,727
2	2,941	3,327	3,507	3,682
3	2,895	3,297	3,445	3,696
4	2,771	3,249	3,431	3,592
5	2,776	3,197	3,438	3,520
6	2,789	3,110	3,395	3,497
7	2,938	3,067	3,422	3,530
8	2,982	2,979	3,356	3,480
Elementary Ungraded	511	543	502	450
TOTAL, K–8	**27,034**	**29,878**	**32,341**	**33,344**
9	3,439	3,169	3,704	3,856
10	3,230	2,896	3,237	3,382
11	2,866	2,612	2,826	3,018
12	2,550	2,381	2,487	2,724
Secondary Ungraded	303	282	245	211
TOTAL, 9–12	**12,388**	**11,338**	**12,500**	**13,171**
TOTAL, K–12	**39,422**	**41,217**	**44,840**	**46,535**

Source: National Center for Education Statistics (2000). Digest of Education Statistics 2000: Table 42, Enrollment in Public Elementary and Secondary Schools, by Grade: Fall 1984 to Fall 1998.

53.0 million. According to the National Center for Education Statistics, 2000 enrollment trends differ by region and state. Higher fertility rates and new immigrants will also fuel the increase in enrollment.

The percentage of minority students increased from 24 percent in 1984 to 38 percent in 1999, with increases in Native American, Asian/Pacific Islander, and Hispanic students, while the percentage who were African-American remained somewhat stable.

The teaching staff in our nation's schools is about 74 percent female, while 66 percent of the public school principals are male. Among private schools, only 46 percent of the principals are male. Almost 91 percent of the public school teachers are white—though the racial and ethnic composition of pupil enrollment has shown an increase in minority representation. From the mid-eighties into the nineties there had been an increase in the percentage of minority teachers in our public school. Sadly, this trend has reversed (see Table 9.4).

In 1999, 23.5 percent of students in grades 3–12 attended schools chosen by their families. Less than half of these students (9% of all students) attended a private school (see Figures 9.1 and 9.2). Fourteen percent attended a public school of choice. As the charter school movement continues to grow (discussed in Chapter 1), the number of options is likely to increase.

Family income differences are apparent in options for schooling. Students whose families had incomes exceeding $50,000 were more likely to attend a school of choice than were the students from families with incomes below $15,000,

TABLE 9.3   Actual and Projected School Enrollment in the United States, 1959–2009 (in thousands)

ALL SCHOOLS		PUBLIC			PRIVATE		
YEAR	**K TO 12**	**K TO 8**	**9 TO 12**	**TOTAL**	**K TO 8**	**9 TO 12**	**TOTAL**
1959	40,857	26,911	8,271	35,182	4,640	1,035	5,675
1964	47,718	30,025	11,391	41,416	5,000	1,300	6,300
1969	51,050	32,513	13,037	45,550	4,200	1,300	5,500
1974	50,073	30,971	14,103	45,074	3,700	1,300	5,000
1979	46,651	28,034	13,616	41,650	3,700	1,300	5,000
1984	44,908	26,905	12,304	39,209	4,300	1,400	5,700
1989	45,471	29,152	11,390	40,543	4,035	1,132	5,198
1994	49,609	31,898	12,213	44,111	4,335	1,163	5,498
1999	52,875	33,488	13,369	46,857	4,765	1,254	6,018
2004*	53,356	33,276	14,218	47,494	4,527	1,334	5,862
2009*	53,014	32,913	14,265	47,178	4,509	1,327	5,836

Source: National Center for Education Statistics, 1993 and 2000 Editions. U.S. Department of Education: Office of Education Research and Improvement.

*Projected.

and more of the wealthier students attended private schools (15%). Parents of students in private schools indicate more satisfaction with the school, teachers, academic standards, and discipline policy (National Center for Education, 2001). A comparison of workload and class size of public and private school teachers found that the former taught about 4.9 periods a day with about 24 students in class, while the latter taught 4.6 periods with about 20 students in a class. The average basic salary for public school teachers in 1994 was $36,498, and for private school teachers, it was $24,053.

TABLE 9.4   Racial and Ethnic Representation among Public School Teachers 1976 to 1996 (percent)

	1976	1981	1986	1991	1996
White	90.8	91.6	89.6	86.8	90.7
Black	8.0	7.8	6.9	8.0	7.3
Other	1.2	0.7	3.4	5.2	2.0

Source: National Center for Education Statistics (1997). Digest of Education Statistics 1997: Table 69, Selected Characteristics of Public School Teachers: Spring 1961 to Spring 1996.

In personal conversations with teachers employed in private institutions several themes emerge. Though their salaries are substantially lower in many cases, they maintain that the working conditions are much better. Work conditions were operationalized as smaller class size, fewer students in class, fewer behavioral problems, more constructive parental involvement and support of education, better prepared students who are interested in learning, and more flexibility and support for innovation in instruction. In personal conversations with educators in public institutions, we have determined the following: The public educators believe in the historical mission of the schools to serve as the foundation for democracy; students and parents are too often judged unfairly because they represent the wide spectrum of racial, ethnic, and economic groups; the diversity of creativity among these pupils needs to be recognized and developed; and the isolation of pupils by economic and racial lines is not congruent with the fact that the population of the twenty-first century will be more diverse than ever before. This increasing diversity is seen by public educators as causing "white flight" to private schools in an attempt to

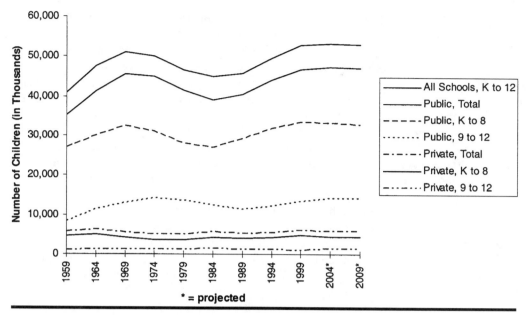

FIGURE 9.1   K–12 Enrollment (1959–2009)

Source: National Center for Education Statistics, 2001 Edition, U.S. Department of Education: Office of Education Research and Improvement.

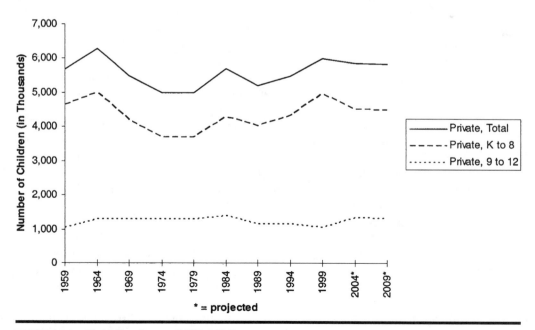

FIGURE 9.2   K–12 Enrollment (1959–2004)

Source: National Center for Education Statistics, 2001 Edition, U.S. Department of Education: Office of Education Research and Improvement.

escape from areas within particular states (inner cities) and from groups of people (African-American and Latino).

Will public education, as we know it, exist in the future? Will public education come to serve only one class of citizens—the lower socioeconomic class and/or those pupils of minority status? Will we have an educational system that encourages class and economic separation? Most urban areas have fewer resources available to support the schools and yet enroll children whose needs for educational support are greater due to lack of resources, overburdened families that are unable to provide experiences that would be supportive of academic achievement, and language barriers. New immigrants to our nation tend to flock to urban areas.

THE CONCEPT OF PUPIL LIFE TASKS

During the 1950s and 1960s, the dominant view as to why some pupils failed and others progressed was believed to be associated with genetics. Today, this controversial position has returned with the publishing of Herrnstein and Murray's *The Bell Curve* (1994). The authors of this book suggest that intelligence is less a function of environment and more a function of genes. Success in life is tied to "good genes" that yield a higher IQ.

According to these authors, low intelligence is a good predictor of poverty, school failure, criminality, high divorce rates, and poor parenting. These authors ignore the critical role environment plays in the prenatal and other developmental stages. They ignore institutional racism, sexism, cultural bias, and other stresses that impact intelligence and influence its development. Recent research demonstrates their error by showing that IQ differences between black and white children are almost completely eliminated when you control for the effects of family poverty, neighborhood economic conditions, mother's education, and prior learning experiences (Brooks-Gunn, Klebanov, & Duncan, 1996).

Furthermore, it has been shown that, contrary to Hernstein and Murray's notion of "inequality of endowments" including intelligence, and other conclusions, the level of inequality and privilege in America is determined by social conditions and national policies, and not by nature (Fisher, Hout, Jankowski, Lucas, Swidler, & Voss, 1996; Jacobs, 1999). Moreover, according to Jencks and Phillips (1998), there is no direct genetic evidence for or against the theory that the so called "race gap" is innate, because we have not yet identified the specific genes to substantiate this conclusion. So, what the Bell Curve offers is merely a set of hypotheses and not scientific truths—essentially, some of the aforementioned authors question the scientific method data and ideology undergirding this book.

All children are vulnerable to stress at various stages of their pupil life cycle (that is, at one or more of the normal points of progression through the education system). Stress can be produced during the initial entry into the education system: the separation of children from their families for extended periods during the day, and/or when children are required to enter a new or different school at any point of their school career. As children pass from preschool to elementary school and then to secondary school, specific biological, maturational, and psychosocial changes occur. As they attempt to respond to their own developmental changes, they must simultaneously respond to the expectations of significant others and to different environmental conditions. However, some degree of stress (a stimulating environment) is essential for human growth and for developing the skills required to cope with life tasks. The adaptability of individual pupils to certain stages of the educational process varies and is in part related to the availability of resources and sources of support that can be drawn upon in making such adjustments (see Table 9.5).

Many children can do what is required of them without experiencing excessive stress, but others cannot, for the following reasons. (1) They lack access to an appropriate remedy. A child who has a special learning need upon entering elementary

TABLE 9.5   Moments in America for All Children

Every 9 seconds	a high school student drops out.*
Every 11 seconds	a child is reported abused or neglected.
Every 20 seconds	a child is arrested.
Every 24 seconds	a baby is born to an unmarried mother.
Every 37 seconds	a baby is born to a mother who is not a high school graduate.
Every 43 seconds	a baby is born into poverty.
Every minute	a baby is born to a teen mother.
Every minute	a baby is born without health insurance.
Every 2 minutes	a baby is born at low birthweight.
Every 4 minutes	a baby is born to a mother who received late or no prenatal care.
Every 4 minutes	a child is arrested for drug abuse.
Every 8 minutes	a child is arrested for violent crimes.
Every 19 minutes	a baby dies.
Every 42 minutes	a child or teen dies in an accident.
Every 3 hours	a child or teen is killed by a firearm.
Every 5 hours	a child or teen commits suicide.
Every day	a young person under 25 dies from HIV infection.

*Based on calculations per school day (180 days of seven hours each).

Source: Children's Defense Fund, *The State of Children in America's Union: A 2002 Action Guide to Leave No Child Behind®.* (Washington, DC: Children's Defense Fund, 2002.)

school might find his or her adjustment problematic if the appropriate educational service is not provided. (2) They experience stress associated with a traumatic event or an unbalanced combination of stressful conditions (for example, the loss of a parent who had been relied upon for emotional support, or a violent episode at school, such as racial conflict), or are physically or emotionally abused by parents. (3) Some children lack adequate skills to cope with pupil life tasks and environmental demands. Their social skills are poorly developed; their self-confidence is low; their exposure to different or strange environmental conditions has been limited; and the interactional patterns within their own family are maladaptive, resulting in maladaptive social interaction with peers, which then becomes exacerbated by the demands placed on them by the school environment and the staff. (4) Other pressures may arise from subtle but powerful community forces, such as the idiosyncratic philosophy of a juvenile court judge; characteristics of the foster care system; health care policy; and sociocultural attitudes regarding delinquency, mental retardation, and poverty.

Such stress in a child's life can lead to a crisis if resources are fragmented or limited. Such crises generally take two forms: situational or developmental. A situational crisis may be the loss of a parent or sibling, or abuse and neglect by a significant other. Frequently, with the appropriate social work intervention, such children can be helped to restore or develop adequate coping mechanisms and experience minimal (if any) long-term harm. Developmental crises may occur as the child moves into adolescence, or when a preschool child is separated from his or her family for the first time. Some children adjust better than others to such changes. When adjustment is problematic, the child often exhibits specific symptomatic behaviors. The school social worker can identify different target groups of pupils that share particular stress-including characteristics and can work with such children individually and in small groups. The social worker should determine whether the stress felt by these pupils can be attributed to another system (school, family, community, or peer group) and whether change or supports for that system are warranted.

PUPILS WHO ARE AT RISK OF SCHOOL FAILURE

The Disadvantaged Preschooler

One in six children in America lives in poverty. Among children under the age of 6, 21 percent are poor (Children's Defense Fund, 2001). As stated in Chapter 1, the child who lives in poverty and whose parents find the fulfillment of basic needs a difficult accomplishment often enters the school system lacking some of the prerequisite skills. Academic handicaps are in large part attributable to overburdened home situations in which acquisition of the basic necessities (food and shelter) takes priority over books, health care, and educational experiences. A developmental lag may begin from birth, and these experiences become more difficult to make up as time passes (see Table 9.6).

With increased demand for more rigorous standards in education, the expectations of the public schools in regard to kindergarten skills have steadily increased. Yet the diversity of skill level found among children entering kindergarten is extensive—ranging from children who do not know their last name to children who are already reading proficiently.

During the early 1960s, concern was expressed about the disadvantaged child and the educational implications of such deprivation. The word "deprived" has come to mean, or is used interchangeably with, "disadvantaged," "educationally deprived," "culturally deprived," and "lower class" (today referred to as "child-at-risk"). Today some refer to these children as "children of promise," indicating that they have strengths that can be nourished given a fertile environment. Alternatively, these talents are wasted if the environment does not provide

even the most basic of needs for food, safety, and relationships.

The Head Start Program, established in 1965, was to provide disadvantaged children with preschool experiences that were not available to them in their home and community environments, in order to develop these children to their maximum potential. Designed as the first comprehensive intervention, the hope was that if these children could be better prepared to enter school, their future educational achievement would be comparable to that of their middle-class peers. Head Start programs (both summer and full-year programs) funded by the federal government sprang up all over the United States—in large, medium, and small urban areas; in suburban and rural communities; in migrant camps; and on Indian reservations. Such programs provided medical, dental, and nutritional services; they involved parents and mobilized social service and community resources.

The goals of the Head Start Program were well accepted until 1969, when the Westinghouse evaluation of the program indicated that the educational gains of those children who participated were not permanent; in fact, the momentum gained was generally lost in a few years (Kean, 1969). Such findings raised considerable doubt that the effects of poverty could be eliminated by large-scale social programs (Pierre, 1979). Though the research methodology of the Westinghouse study was questioned, its findings were well publicized and generally accepted. Advocates of Head Start questioned the narrow measurement used to evaluate the program and argued that one could not expect a single year of even the most comprehensive program to reduce the effects of years of poverty.

One consequence of this debate was "Follow Through," a program aimed at continuing the services provided to disadvantaged children through the third grade and supporting those gains that had been made as a result of their participation in the Head Start programs. Funding problems for "Follow Through" forced a change

TABLE 9.6 Children Under 18 Living Below the Poverty Level in Types of Families, by Race/Ethnicity, 1960–1998

RACE/ETHNICITY	YEAR	NUMBER OF CHILDREN UNDER 18 (IN THOUSANDS)			PERCENTAGE OF CHILDREN UNDER 18 (PERCENT)		
		ALL PERSONS	ALL FAMILIES	SINGLE-MOTHER FAMILIES	ALL PERSONS	ALL FAMILIES	SINGLE-MOTHER FAMILIES
All Races	1960	39,851	17,288	4,095	22.2	26.5	68.4
	1970	25,420	10,235	4,689	12.6	14.9	53.0
	1980	29,272	11,114	5,866	13.0	17.9	50.8
	1990	33,585	12,715	7,363	13.5	19.9	53.4
	1998	34,476	12,845	7,627	12.7	18.3	46.1
White	1960	28,303	11,229	2,357	17.8	20.0	59.9
	1970	17,484	6,138	2,247	9.9	10.5	43.1
	1980	19,699	6,817	4,940	10.2	13.4	41.6
	1990	22,326	7,696	3,597	10.7	15.1	45.9
	1998	23,454	7,935	3,875	10.5	14.4	40.0
Black	1960	9,927	5,022	1,475	55.1	65.5	81.6
	1970	7,548	3,922	2,383	33.5	41.5	67.7
	1980	8,579	3,906	2,944	32.5	42.1	64.8
	1990	9,837	4,412	3,543	31.9	44.2	64.7
	1998	9,091	4,073	3,366	26.1	36.4	54.7
Hispanic Origin	1960	2,991	1,619	694	26.9	33.1	68.4
	1970	3,491	1,718	809	25.7	33.0	65.0
	1980	5,236	2,512	1,247	29.0	39.6	72.4
	1990	6,006	2,750	1,314	28.1	37.7	68.4
	1998	8,070	3,670	1,739	25.6	33.6	59.6

Source: Digest of Education Statistics, 2000, Table 21. Adapted from U.S. Dept. of Commerce, Bureau of the Census, Current Population Reports, series P-60, No. 198.

in emphasis—specifically, a full-scale service program became an experimental program in education in which a variety of specialists implemented an educational model. The areas of focus included skills in reading and arithmetic, cognitive thinking skills, problem-solving skills, creative writing skills, and assisting parents to improve the education and development of their children. An evaluation of "Follow Through" suggested that the effects varied from site to site and from group to group.

In 1995, Head Start began an effort to develop and report on its accountability for services to approximately 800,000 children and their families each year, via an evaluation process. This effort was in response to a specific legislative mandate, strategic-planning for the program, and more emphasis on accountability and results-oriented evaluations. The conceptual framework for these evaluations includes attention to input/process and outcome measures. The framework was driven by the ultimate goal of the program which is to promote the social competence of children by enhancing their health and development; to provide education, health and nutritional services; to link children and families to community resources; and to involve parents in decision-making.

These recent evaluations of the Head Start program's performance have included a wide spectrum of input and outcome measures (i.e., program quality and its link to classroom performance; characteristics of the teachers; cognitive, social, emotional, and physical development of the child; and characteristics, well-being, and accomplishments of the families, etc.). These evaluations have documented the positive benefits of this educational intervention in terms of the development of readiness skills for kindergarten, social skill development, and parental involvement. For example, in one study, program quality was linked to child performance. The more time spent in Head Start correlated positively with better classroom performance (Administration on Children, Youth, Families, DHHS, 2000).

The latest research on brain development has led policy makers to begin Head Start at birth rather than waiting until the child is three or four. The Head Start Act Amendments of 1994 established Early Head Start—services "to reinforce and respond to the strengths and needs of each child and family" (Administration for Children and Families, 1997a). The four cornerstones of Early Head Start programs are child development, family development, community building, and staff development. The program seeks to enhance the child's development and help parents to meet their own goals, while assisting parents to be better caregivers and teachers to their children. In the fiscal year 2000, Early Head Start funds were over 500 million dollars, an increase of over 300 percent from the 1997 allocation of 150 million dollars (Administration for Children and Families, 2000).

A rigorous national evaluation of Early Head Start Programs, which included 3,000 children and families in 17 sites, and began in 1995, found that after a year or more of program services, when compared with a randomly assigned control group, two-year-old Early Head Start children performed significantly better on a range of measures of cognitive, language, and social-emotional development. Their parents scored significantly higher than control group parents on many of the measures of the home environment, parenting behavior, and knowledge of infant-toddler development. Early Head Start families were more likely to attend school or job training and experienced reductions in parenting stress and family conflict. Although these impacts are generally modest in size, the pattern of positive findings across a wide range of key domains important for children's well-being and future development is promising. For example:

— Early Head Start children, at two years of age, scored higher on a standardized assessment of infant cognitive development than the control children and were reported by their parents to have larger vocabularies and to use more grammatically complex sentences. On the assessment of cognitive development, Early Head Start children were less likely to score in the at-risk range of developmental functioning; Early Head Start is moving some children out of the low-functioning group, perhaps reducing their risk of poor cognitive outcomes later on.

— Early Head Start two-year-olds lived in home environments that were more likely to support and stimulate cognitive development, language, and literacy, based on researcher's observations using a standard scale. Their parents were more likely to read to children daily and at bedtime.

Although Head Start's long-term consequences have been debated in the political and scientific arenas, today there are over 46,000 Head Start classrooms in the United States serving more than 850,000 children, with a budget of over 5 billion dollars annually (Administration for Children and Families, 2001). The Administration for Children and Families is collaborating with the National Institutes of Health and the National Academy of Sciences to develop strong research on young children and families over time.

The new welfare legislation proposes new challenges to the benefits of Head Start. Most Head Start programs are half-day programs. With the work requirement, fewer parents will be able to continue to be involved in the parental component of Head Start, and children will either be shifted from one environment to another (child care to Head Start) or they will no longer receive Head Start services. Some areas have begun to provide full-day Head Start, usually for the same time period that the area public schools are in session. Some of the existing day care programs vary widely in terms of goals and the quality of care. Some merely provide custodial care with few, if any, educational or experiential learning activities. Such programs may be full-time or part-time. They are operated under different auspices—public, private nonprofit, and private for profit—and are housed in public facilities, churches, housing units, private homes, and schools. Day care programs can be utilized, particularly if they have an educational component, to prepare economically disadvantaged children for entry into school. Given that it is a necessity for many households in the United States to have both parents employed, quality day care takes on additional importance.

Welfare Reform and Child Care.   The issue of availability of acceptable care for children has become more important as welfare reforms have gone into effect. The Personal Responsibility and Work Opportunity Reconciliation Act of 1994 (PRWORA) ended entitlement (federal guarantee) to assistance for eligible families. Welfare funds are now distributed to the states as a lump sum grant. This block grant, called Temporary Assistance to Needy Families (TANF) will remain at the same level regardless of economic changes. A lifetime five-year limit has been placed on the amount of time that a family

may receive assistance. The law restricts the exemptions from five-year lifetime limit to 20 percent of the caseload. There are many factors that make it difficult for families to meet the five-year limit, such as parents with disabilities, parents of children with disabilities, grandparents who are parenting grandchildren, or residing in areas of high unemployment. Nine states set a lifetime limit shorter than five years, ranging from six months in Arizona's JOBSTART program to 48 months in Florida and Georgia. An additional 16 states have limited the time period for consecutive assistance (Rowe, 2000). States can continue to receive the full block grant after 2002 only if at least half the adults receiving federal assistance work 30 or more hours per week. The law allows states to exempt parents with children under one year of age from the work requirements, and by the end of 1999, all but seven states chose to do so. The law has ended aid to legal immigrants who arrive in the United States after the passage of this legislation, although some state rules allow noncitizens to collect TANF after having lived in the state for five years. The law also reduces income support and food stamps for the disabled (Supplemental Security Income, or SSI). The law increases the stringency of eligibility requirements for children who receive SSI and eliminates the functional assessment previously used to qualify children for assistance. Caseloads have fallen from 5 million in 1996 to 2.18 million in 2000 (Blum & Francis, 2001). The new TANF law gives the states "unprecedented discretion in choosing which families to assist, what services to provide, what requirements to impose, and how to respond to families who cannot find work to support their households within the allotted time" (Larner, Terman, & Behrman, 1997, p. 6).

An underlying assumption of the current welfare bill is that the needs of poor children are best met through education and employment of their parents. If high-quality child care is *not* available to parents, this act has the potential to affect children negatively through both exposure to poor substitute care arrangements and increased stress on parents (Kisker & Ross, 1997; Larner, Terman, & Behrman, 1997). In addition, as California's experience with the JOBS program demonstrated, welfare recipients are more likely to withdraw from welfare to work programs when child care is inadequate or considered by mothers to be unsafe. "Successful completion of job training is contingent on child care that is reliable and of acceptable quality and that matches parents' scheduling needs" (Phillips, 1995, p. 11).

States vary in their child care regulations. While the majority of states require a ratio of one caregiver to every four infants and a one-to-ten ratio for children under the age of four, some states allow ratios of five or six infants per caregiver, and Idaho allows 12 infants per caregiver (Children's Defense Fund, 1997). Only ten states meet national recommendations for child-staff ratios in their licensing requirements and only ten states require all family child care providers to meet any regulations (Children's Defense Fund, 2001).

Although the legislators recognized that child care was a necessary component of the new legislation, estimates by the Congressional Budget Office indicate that the amount allocated (approximately four billion dollars in new child care funds over six years) is 1.4 billion dollars less than will be needed. Although states are required to provide matching funds, this has, in fact, been borne out since state implementations of PRWORA. Nationally, only 12 percent of nearly 15 million children eligible for child care assistance under federal law receive any help. Many states are unable to serve all those who apply for child care slots and have accumulated long waiting lists. For example, there are 14,500 children on the waiting list for child care assistance in North Carolina and over 41,000 children on the waiting list in Texas (Children's Defense Fund, 2001). Other states, including Michigan, indicated that their waiting lists would be longer if all those eligible applied for child care slots

(Seefeldt, Leos-Urbel, McMahon, & Snyder, 2001).

The School Social Workers' Role with At-Risk Preschoolers. With the extension of the Individuals with Disabilities Education Act to include infants, toddlers, and preschoolers with developmental disabilities and those at risk of developing disabilities, there are numerous roles for the school social worker. These include family assessment (e.g., interview the family to assess its strengths, emotional, social, and psychological characteristics, resources available to it, and cultural ways of behaving); case management—linking the family with various services and advocating on their behalf; family support and counseling (an infant or toddler who is developmentally delayed constitutes a crisis in the family and adds stress to its functioning); in-home training (sometimes the social worker must provide home-based instruction to help the family respond to the developmental needs of the child); and program development and evaluation (conducting needs assessment, developing programs, and evaluating their effectiveness) (Clark, 1992). A part of the service plan must be concern for developmental transitions (e.g., from infancy to the toddler stage and from the toddler stage to the preschool stage). The social worker must engage in long-term planning and understand the individualized needs and required interventions. Support groups for parents can be a part of the service planning to facilitate adaptations in their behaviors in accordance with the needs of the child. School social workers can also be instrumental in the development of community-service networks.

Children from Low-Income Areas

The poverty rate of children is higher than for any other age group. Although children represent only 26 percent of the total U.S. population, they make up 40 percent of those in poverty. Since the early 1980s the poverty rate for children has hovered around 20 percent (Federal Interagency Forum on Child and Family Statistics, 2000). Very young and minority children bear the worst burden. Eighteen percent of the children under six in America live in poverty. For minorities, the statistics are even more disheartening (National Center for Children in Poverty): 33 percent of black and 30 percent of Latino families in America live in poverty—and among female households, 52 percent of black families and 52 percent of Hispanic families live in poverty! As our nation has gotten richer, children and especially minority children have become poorer. The parents of many of these children might be considered the "working poor"—they have low earning power. In 1999, 42 percent of all working single mothers with children could not earn enough to pull their families out of poverty (Federal Interagency Forum on Child and Family Statistics, 2000).

The Urban Institute estimates that 1.1 million more children will be pushed into poverty by the new welfare law and more than 4 million already-poor families will be pushed deeper into poverty. Poverty places children at a much greater health and developmental risk. These children are also three times more likely to die in childhood, and are at greater risk of disability, academic failure, and adolescent pregnancy (Children's Defense Fund, 1997). They are more likely to be exposed to environmental hazards such as lead and toxic fumes, high violence, driveby shootings, and substandard housing (Kozol, 1995).

Preschoolers in low-income households have poorer cognitive and verbal skills due in large part to limited exposure to books, toys, and stimulating experiences (Smith, Brooks-Gunn, & Klebanov, 1997). Higher-income families provide richer learning environments for children. However, a study of two large samples of families with young children found that even when the effects of home environment (as measured by the Home Observation of Measurement of the Environment, which examines learning materials, experiences offered to the child, and maternal warmth) are statistically controlled, income in early childhood remains a significant predictor of ability and achievement. The effects of poverty are more pronounced and long-lasting when it occurs in early and middle childhood (Duncan & Brooks-Gunn, 1997).

Effects of hunger in children are often subtle: frequent headaches, fatigue, difficulty concentrating, dizziness, irritability, and frequent illness. Data from both advocacy and government organizations indicate that children and youth experience food insufficiency (sometimes or often do not have enough to eat) at a rate of 5.3 to 6.1 percent (Lewit & Kerrebrock, 1997).

Children from impoverished families are more likely to have poor attendance records and to fall behind in achievement. Children in poverty are at additional risk if the mother's education is also low. Poverty and low maternal education exert independent negative effects on children's development. As one would anticipate, the effect of low maternal educational levels on children's achievement increases as children become older (Smith, Brooks-Gunn, Klebanov, 1997). This places Hispanic children at higher risk of school failure and dropout. In addition to a high incidence of poverty, 43 percent of all Hispanic children live in a home where neither parent is a high school graduate (Children's Defense Fund, 1997).

The Migrant Child

The migrant child, another victim of poverty, moves from place to place as the family searches for work in farming communities. Proof of how isolated these families are is the fact that their exact number is unknown. These migrant families are black, Puerto Rican, Mexican-American, and white. Compensation for their labor is not controlled, and many labor regulations, including workmen's compensation, are not guaranteed to them. These families must often tolerate inhumane living conditions; housing is generally substandard and very crowded.

The Migrant Head Start programs are one attempt to help these families. In addition to the typical Head Start services, Migrant Head Start centers have a unique emphasis on serving infants and toddlers as well as preschool children, so that these children need not be cared for in the field or left in the care of very young siblings. Migrant centers provide extended day services up to 12 hours a day and 7 days a week when harvest season is at its peak. In 2000 Migrant Head Start served over 31,000 children in 33 states.

Since passage of the Elementary and Secondary Education Act of 1965, funds are available to states to assist in developing educational programs for children of migrant workers. The effects of poverty, constant migration, poor health care, and tenuous ties with schools make this population clearly at risk. Children younger than 6 years are taken into the fields to assist with work, making attendance at school virtually impossible. How can these children be alert and ready to learn? How can teachers meet their learning needs and compensate for their developmental lags?

At the very heart of a successful school experience is acceptance and understanding by the school staff. Teachers must be willing to reach out to these children and families. Traditional educational structure and procedure should take a backseat to encouragement of attendance and learning. Development of human potential—appreciating the life experiences of these children and attempting to expand their view of the world and the self—should be the focus of a sound educational program. School social workers, who serve as a link between home, community, and school, can facilitate the communication essential for promoting understanding. Further, they can support these children as they gain self-confidence and engage in learning.

An investigation of the prevalence of mental health problems and the utilization of mental health services by migrant and seasonal worker families in North Carolina found that 64 percent of the children evidenced clinical levels of problem behaviors (Martin, Kupersmidt, & Harter, 1996). The severity of the children's mental health problems was not related to the use of school support services (special education, counseling, remedial education). The only variable related to use of school services was the mother's country of birth. The mother's command of English and ability to negotiate the school culture may be affecting the delivery of services to migrant children.

Under the Improving America's Schools Act of 1994, migrant children are defined as the children of fisherman and farmworkers who move their families in order to seek seasonal work. A new category of migrant youth has been identified—an unschooled migrant population. Non-English-speaking immigrants who suffer continual mobility and interruptions in their schooling, these youth are often illiterate in their primary language and may come from a culture with an oral rather than written tradition (e.g., the Hmong). School itself represents an additional cultural shock for many of these students with its locker assignments, bells, and schedules. Because these youth represent only a small percentage of students, few schools have programs to assist them in adapting to and benefiting from school. Programs that provide appropriate assistance find that these students can make dramatic progress. Successful schools have well-trained staff and create climates that are inviting, flexible, and based on mutual respect. Language instruction is obviously a key component of these programs. Access to additional services and resources for the student and families also contributes to success (Morse, 1997).

Homeless Children

Millions who need low cost housing cannot locate it. In 2001, the National Low-Income Housing Coalition reported that even full-time work at minimum wage is inadequate to afford moderate housing in every state. Families with children represent 38 percent of the homeless population (National Alliance to End Homelessness, 2000). Requests for emergency shelter by homeless families with children increased by 22 percent between 2000 and 2001. The average stay by families in homeless shelters ranged from under two months in Burlington, Vermont and St. Louis, to just over nine months in Boston and Philadelphia (U.S. Conference of Mayors, 2001). The new federal welfare law eliminates the Emergency Assistance Program, which previously provided help for families in crises such as domestic abuse and homelessness.

Approximately 1 million children run away each year and another 300,000 are homeless (Children's Defense Fund, 1996). Some believe government estimates of homelessness to be conservative, as many homeless children find a series of temporary living arrangements (e.g., relatives, special hotels) and thus are not included in these statistics.

A homeless child can be defined "as one who lacks a fixed, regular, adequate nighttime residence, or who resides in a temporary, supervised privately or publicly owned institution, or who sleeps in a place not designed as a regular accommodation for humans (e.g., a car)" (Michigan Department of Education, 1993). This definition also applies to runaway children who have been abandoned or forced by their parents to leave home (throwaway children) and now reside with friends or relatives. Some of these youth live in shelters, abandoned buildings, and the like.

These youth and their families are at risk of psychological, emotional, and health problems. They lack adequate food, clothing, and supportive environments. Many of these children/youth live in an environment in which violence, crime, and prostitution are prevalent. The impact of these conditions on their educational development is devastating. Escalating homelessness in our society has been attributed to industrial changes (downsizing), lack of jobs, decreases in availability of low-income housing, cuts in public assistance, and the erosion of spending

power—for those in entry-level positions earning minimum wage.

The Stewart B. McKinney Homeless Assistance Act (1987) protects the rights of these homeless children to an education. The 1990 amendments to this act extend the mandate beyond access to education to increased efforts to facilitate academic success (Masten et al., 1997). Thanks to the McKinney Act, educational services, school breakfast and lunch programs, and informal educational assessments of homeless children are available. However, homelessness presents a host of challenges for children. It increases child health problems, breaks up families (shelters divided by sex), disrupts schooling (as children move from one district to another), and causes extreme emotional distress. According to Bassuck and Rubin (1987), homeless children suffer developmental delays, severe anxiety, learning difficulties, and multiple impairments that require special interdisciplinary intervention. A recent investigation highlighted the prevalence of both internalizing and externalizing problem behaviors among this population and the relationship of these problems to academic difficulties (Masten et al., 1997). A comparison of the parenting practices of homeless mothers and mothers who were low-income but housed found that the homeless mothers provided less structure, provided less academic stimulation, and offered less warmth and affection (Koblinsky, Morgan, & Anderson, 1997).

Adolescent Parents

The incidence of parenthood among adolescents 13 to 19 years of age increased steadily for some groups in the 1980s. There was an overall 13 percent increase in adolescent childbirth from 1980 to 1990. The age of sexual onset declined in all sectors of the population during the 1970s, and rates of sexual activity among those under age 20 continued to rise in the last decade. Disparities between the sexes and between races are lower now than at any previous time, because recent increases have occurred primarily in the white, nonpoor children (Zabin & Hayward, 1993).

Although the black adolescent birthrate is twice that of white adolescents—a difference attributable to despair and greater poverty—recent figures indicate that the incidence of birth to black adolescents has declined by 26 percent. The number of births to all groups of adolescents has declined significantly in the 1990s: the birthrate for all women under age 20 fell 18 percent between 1991 and 1998, while the birthrate for Hispanic young women fell 12 percent, for white non-Hispanic women the birthrate fell 19 percent, and for Asian, Pacific-Islander, and Native American women under 20, the birthrate fell 15 percent (Ventura, Mathews, & Curtin, 1999).

Initiation of sexual activity is associated with several variables or factors, including the norms of the peer group, early maturation of the young female (some girls reach menarche at age 9), early dating (Biro, 1992), and sexual exploitation by older males. A 1989 study (Luker et al., 1989, reported in Children's Defense Fund, 1997) revealed that 74 percent of girls who had sex before age 14 and 60 percent of those who had sex before age 15 had been coerced. Sexual abuse and exploitation is commonly found among adolescent mothers (Musick, 1993; Smith, 1996).

We know that certain environmental conditions contribute to the other variables that are highly associated with "risk" for becoming pregnant during the adolescent years. Poor, overcrowded, socially deprived rural and urban areas, and environments in which social integration is low, contribute to this problem (Dryfoos, 1990). The research on predictors of adolescent pregnancy has been summarized in two words: disadvantage and discouragement (Luker, 1996, in Children's Defense Fund, 1997).

A recent longitudinal study (Underwood, Kupersmidt, & Coie, 1997) found that fourth-grade peer sociometric measures predicted adolescent pregnancy as well as a variety of other adolescent problem behaviors. Girls who received more peer nominations as aggressive (i.e., says mean things, starts fights, hits or kicks kids)

were twice as likely to bear children in adolescence. The authors noted that peer ratings of aggression are almost as stable as IQ scores and consistently predict other outcomes. This implies that pregnancy prevention should begin in elementary school by providing children with appropriate social and problem-solving skills. Another interesting finding of this study is that controversial girls, those well-liked by some and strongly disliked by others, are at the highest risk of pregnancy. This is the first time that a controversial peer sociometric status has been linked with a negative outcome. The authors hypothesized that these girls, who possess both prosocial and antisocial behaviors, probably become the group that others have referred to as competent adolescent mothers. They may also pose the greatest challenge to pregnancy prevention programs.

We also know that school attendance reduces adolescent sexual risk-taking behaviors. Youth who have dropped out of school "are more likely to initiate sexual activity earlier, fail to use contraception, become pregnant, and give birth" (Satcher, 2001, p. 7). Other protective factors for those in school include involvement in athletics and other school activities, which lead to less sexual risk-taking, later age of initiation of sex and lower frequency of sex, pregnancy, and childbearing. Schools can provide an opportunity for positive peer learning that can influence social norms and create an environment that discourages unhealthy risk-taking (Satcher, 2001).

Though the adolescent male plays a critical role in determining the sexual behavior of the adolescent female, too little research and intervention have specifically targeted him (Allen-Meares & Roberts, 1994). Both adolescent parents are less likely to complete their schooling, increasing their risk for sporadic employment and/or welfare dependency. Premature parenthood preempts the educational, vocational, and social experiences that are required for adulthood. Moreover, the baby is at risk of developmental delays, premature birth, and lower birth weight. However, with adequate support and assistance, these negative consequences can be buffered or minimized. It is essential that we recognize the heterogeneity of this target group. Many young parents who continue their schooling do so with considerable struggle. Arranging child care, coordinating transportation and doctor appointments, playing multiple roles (e.g., mother, student, daughter, and in some cases, wife) contribute to their educational failure and/or underachievement. In 1972, the commissioner of the United States Office of Education stated: "Every girl in the United States has a right and need for the education that will help her prepare herself for a career, for family life, and for citizenship. To be married or pregnant is not sufficient cause to deprive her of an education and the opportunity to become a contributing member of society" (Howard & Eddinger, 1973, p. 29). Title IX of the Education Amendment of 1972 (which became effective July 12, 1975) prohibits schools that receive federal funds from excluding students solely on the basis of pregnancy or a pregnancy-related condition.

Comprehensive Sex Education.

Even with the risk of AIDS, sex education as the primary strategy for the prevention of pregnancy and sexually transmitted diseases remains controversial. In some communities, sex education is seen as the cause of adolescent pregnancy—"It gives our youth ideas."

Nevertheless, a majority of Americans favor some form of sexuality education in public schools and believe that some form of birth control information should be available to adolescents (Smith, 2000, in Satcher, 2001). Solid research shows that abstinence-only sexuality education programs—those that emphasize abstinence as the most appropriate choice for young people—sometimes fail to work. No effect on initiation of sexual activity was found in reviews of abstinence-only programs (Satcher). Providing information about contraception has not been shown to increase adolescent sexual activity, either by hastening the onset of sexual intercourse, increasing the frequency of sexual intercourse, or

increasing the number of sexual partners. Some of the evaluated programs actually increased condom or contraceptive use among adolescents who were sexually active.

Though many youth complain about the content and relevance of sex education, when technical information is augmented with discussions about relationships and responsible sexual behavior, opinions change for the better (Scott-Jones, 1993). Sex education programs should not be limited to school-based health clinics or the health curriculum; churches and community-based agencies should also provide this content.

Career Planning and Personal Development.

Research reports suggest that those youth with career and/or educational plans are more likely to forestall pregnancy (Scott-Jones, 1993; Manlove, 1998; and Moore et al., 1998, cited in Satcher, 2001). Youth need to know that they have a future and that there are opportunities for them. Social workers, coordinating their activities with other school-based staff and external agencies, can assist youth via small groups, career development workshops, and other goal-setting activities. The best way to prevent adolescent pregnancy (and many other risky and antisocial behaviors) is to instill within youth aspirations for the future.

AIDS and Youth

As stated previously, sexual activity among adolescents is often unplanned and sporadic. Report after report documents the spontaneity of the first sexual encounter and the negative consequences for the young parents and their offspring (unplanned pregnancy, baby at risk of developmental delays, sexually transmitted disease, etc.). Now with the human immune deficiency virus (HIV/AIDS) epidemic, another consequence could be death. Pupils need accurate information concerning the consequence of intercourse and the risk for infection. This will require youth to change their sexual behaviors—a very difficult challenge indeed. AIDS prevention needs to be developed, not only in schools, but within different settings as well (e.g., community, churches). Clearly a comprehensive community-based approach is required.

It is estimated that by the year 2000, over 40 million persons worldwide will be infected with the AIDS virus (Shiltz, 1987). By 2000, almost 40,000 AIDS cases and over 13,000 deaths among people age 25 and under have been reported (Children's Defense Fund, 2001). Fifty-nine percent of all pediatric AIDS cases reported through June 2000 were among black children and 23 percent were among Hispanic children. Many infected adults acquired HIV as adolescents (Children's Defense Fund, 1997). It is clear that both educational and behavioral interventions are necessary if we are to prevent the spread of this deadly virus. We know from other research on adolescent sexuality and pregnancy that educational intervention alone has not influenced behavioral change. Many youth believe that it cannot happen to them—that they are invincible or lucky or it cannot happen "this one time." Although an increased proportion of sexually active adolescents (about two-thirds) use condoms, they do not use them all of the time (Children's Defense Fund, 1997). White students (92 percent) were more likely than black (87 percent) or Hispanic (84 percent) students to have received HIV/AIDS education at school.

HIV/AIDS education belongs in the health education curriculum and wherever discussions focus on sexuality, health, and prevention (Fulton, Metress, & Preil, 1987). Schoolwide interventions that begin in the elementary school are essential. School social workers can organize discussions with small groups of parents, teachers, and/or students. The small-group context allows for more intimate sharing and feedback, as well as an opportunity to role-play responses to situations that could lead to the risk of an infection. The school social worker, in consultation with others (school-based health personnel), could be instrumental in planning and organizing inservice training for school staff, parents, and community leaders. If there is a school-based health clinic, it should work with other support staff and the school's administration to formulate guidelines and/or policies to allow infected youth who are physically and emotionally capable to attend school. Instruction on minimizing risk should be a central aspect of the educational intervention (e.g., handwashing, use of gloves when handling any body fluids, etc.). The emphasis should be on promoting safe behavior, and the intent should take into consideration the developmental readiness of the pupils. School social workers are also in a unique position to meet the intervention needs of HIV-affected children (those whose parents died of or are ill with HIV or AIDS) (Gilbert, 2001).

Gay and Lesbian Youth

Youth whose sexual orientation or whose dress or behavior do not conform to gender expectations are at a high risk of victimization. The National School Climate Survey, conducted yearly by the national Gay, Lesbian, and Straight Education Network (GLSEN) reported that "the majority of LGBT students reported feeling unsafe at school . . . [and] transgender students were the least likely to feel their school communities were places of safety (2001). Unfortunately, this is not new. Previous findings in other geographic areas are consistent. Gay, lesbian, and bisexual youth encounter verbal insults, are physically assaulted, beaten, kicked, spat upon, threatened, and raped. Even more tragic, the act of emotional abuse is not limited to other students, but sometimes is perpetrated by staff and teachers—the individuals these students should be able to trust as their advocates. Antiharassment policies and practices ignore sexual orientation. Thirty-one percent of students are so threatened that they feel they cannot attend school (Gay, Lesbian, and Straight Education Network, 2001). Many schools fail to recognize the abuse faced by LGBT students and resources and supportive persons were "rare." Yet, there was a significant increase in the number of LGBT students around the country who reported a greater sense of belonging at school

(GLSEN, 2001). The physical and emotional abuse they receive takes its toll on these youth. Researchers (Hershberger, Pilkington, & D'Augelli, 1997) estimate that up to 40 percent of lesbian, gay, and bisexual youth attempt suicide. These youth are at greater risk if they have disclosed their sexual orientation more completely, been victimized more (verbal abuse and physical assaults), or lost friends due to disclosure. The loss of friends due to disclosure is one of the strongest predictors of suicide attempts. Youths who self-identified as bisexual were at highest risk (five times more likely) of attempting suicide more than once. More discussion of this group takes place in Chapter 11.

Abused and Neglected Children

Another target group of children that comes to the attention of school social workers consists of those who are physically or sexually abused and/or neglected by their parents or significant others. Often, these children come from homes characterized as having multiple problems: The father may be unemployed for an extended period; there may be marital discord; the child may live with several other siblings in a single-parent household; the child may live in a middle-class or upper-middle-class home where more attention is devoted to obtaining material goods and services than to satisfying the needs of the child; the child may have a learning or physical handicap; the child may have been left in the care of a babysitter who was unstable; the child may have been unwanted from birth, or born to a mother who was ill-prepared to provide proper nurturing; and the parent may have a mental health or personal problem.

Abuse and neglect have been increasing in this decade, and unfortunately the outcomes have become more severe as overtaxed social systems are unable to respond with enough services to protect America's children. The number of children seriously injured tripled from 1986 to 1993. The percentage of reported cases that were investigated fell during that same time from 44

percent to 28 percent (Sedlak & Broadhurst, 1996). Although the National Committee to Prevent Child Abuse reported that 996,000 children were abused or neglected in 1995 (almost 25% more than in 1990), a recent study conducted by the U.S. Department of Health and Human Services (National Incidence Study of Child Abuse and Neglect) suggests that this statistic seriously underestimates the incidence rate. Interviews of child-serving professionals (schools, agencies, child care centers, police, and mental health agencies—rather than just protective service workers) place the estimate at 2.8 million for 1993, with younger children and females more likely to be abused or at risk of harm than older children and males (Children's Defense Fund, 1997).

In 1962, California became the first state to require by law the reporting of child abuse. By 1979, 43 states and the District of Columbia had statutes that required medical personnel and educators to report suspected cases of child abuse. In the remaining seven states, the law stated that "any person" should make a report if his or her suspicions are aroused (Fisher & Sorenson, 1991). As of 1991, all but six states had laws stating that those persons mandated to report child abuse and neglect would he held liable for failure to report (Fisher & Sorenson, 1991). All states require the social worker to make such reports.

Physical and Emotional Abuse. Each state is responsible for providing its own definitions of child abuse and neglect within the civil and criminal context of that state (U.S. Department of Health and Human Services, Administration on Children, Youth and Families [DHHS-ACF], 2001a). Federal guidelines from the Child Abuse Prevention and Treatment Act provide that child abuse and neglect are "any recent act or failure to act on the part of a parent or caregiver which results in death, serious physical or emotional harm, sexual abuse, or exploitation . . . or which presents an imminent risk of serious harm" (DHHS-ACF, 2001a, Sec.111 [42U.S.C.

5106g]). Sexual abuse is "the employment, use, persuasion, inducement, enticement, or coercion of any child to engage in, or assist any other person to engage in, any sexually explicit conduct or simulation of such conduct for the purpose of producing a visual depiction of such conduct . . . or the rape, statutory rape, molestation, prostitution, or other form of sexual exploitation of children, or incest with children" (DHHS-ACF, 2001a, Sec.111 [42U.S.C. 5106g]).

All states have included a modified version of this definition in their own statutes. In general, child abuse statutes include the following types of maltreatment: physical abuse, emotional injury, sexual abuse, neglect, and abandonment (applies to a child under the age of eighteen or the age specified by the child protection law of the state). Unfortunately, many cases of child abuse go unreported, and too many children die each year as a result. Professionals, including doctors, may be reluctant to report such abuse; the NIS study did not explain why so few cases of child abuse and neglect were investigated. Some may have been screened out, and some may never have been reported. In many areas, child protection workers are overburdened by the number and complexity of the cases to be investigated. The number of children entering foster care continues to exceed the number of children leaving foster care. From 1990 to 1999, the number of children in foster care increased from 400,000 to 568,000 (DHHS-ACF, 2001b). The 1996 reauthorization of the Child Abuse Prevention and Treatment Act includes grant money for demonstration projects to promote innovative interagency responses to abuse and neglect that enlist and involve public and private partnerships including schools, religious organizations, and private agencies.

Cities in seven states have programs modeled after New Zealand's Family Group Decision Making. The goal of this program is to assist families in altering their behaviors as they maintain responsibility for their children. Families who agree to this program participate in family conferences that include extended family workers, clergy, nurses, teachers, and others whom the family and child designate as helpful. The group determines how the child can be kept safe and presents a plan to the child protection agency. If the agency disagrees with the plan, the court makes the decision.

The number of children in nonparental relative care increased by 59 percent from 1990 to 1996. A large part of this increase represents more grandparents serving as primary caregivers for their grandchildren. Grandparent care increased from 935,000 in 1990 to 1,431,000 in 1996 (Children's Defense Fund, 1998). This presents an additional challenge to the schools in trying to involve parents, in this case grandparents, in the child's education.

As stated earlier, the etiology of child abuse is multiple and interactional. Some researchers argue that the forces are sociological. For example, poverty and social change place considerable stress on a family: When the family has no one to turn to, a crisis can result with which they are unable to cope. The parents' substance abuse (drugs and/or alcohol), depression, and poor nurturing during their own childhood can also contribute to child abuse. There are also contributing environmental conditions, such as the lack of social services and other community-based services required to help high-risk parents, lack of parental knowledge of normal child development and appropriate expectations of children, the escalating cost of medical services, high unemployment, inflation, and complicated bureaucratic procedures as well as cultural values that prevent people from seeking help.

The Neglected.   It is much easier to identify and to prove the physical abuse of children than it is to prove neglect. A child who comes to school dirty, ill-fed, lacking adequate rest, dressed in soiled clothing, and who otherwise shows signs of the absence of parental care can be considered neglected. With the cutbacks in government aid and the low buying power of minimum wage, families can be overwhelmed with trying to provide even the most basic care. The private sector struggles to try to help provide safety nets, but private sources also are overburdened by the numbers seeking care. In addition, substance abuse by parents or mental illness may prevent parents from providing adequate care for their children.

Parents who do not take an interest in the child's academic progress, fail to support the child's efforts in school, and fail to work cooperatively with the school administration may be considered neglectful; however, sometimes this is the result of an ignorant or neglectful school system. Most teachers do not receive training in how to involve families in school or in important cultural differences and good communication skills with parents. The Harvard Family Research Project (Shartrand, Weiss, Kreider, & Lopez, 1997) reports that the majority of states do not even mention family involvement in their teacher certification requirements, and most teacher education programs do not offer substantial training in family involvement. Shartrand et al. describe the overall picture of teacher preparation for involving families as dismal. Unfortunately, the lack of home and school collaboration frequently results in a child who fails to develop and to achieve.

Social workers can help teachers to develop skills in working with families as well as assist in identifying necessary resources for families. Inservice workshops and ongoing consultation can help teachers to learn important skills in working with families. Drawing on the theorists Joyce Epstein, Moncrieff Cochran, Luis Moll, and James Coleman, the Harvard Family Research Project proposes four philosophical approaches to training teachers for family involvement: functional, cultural competence, parent empowerment, and social capital. Table 9.7 offers examples of attitudes, knowledge, and skills that would be addressed by each of these models (Shartrand, Weiss, Kreider, & Lopez, 1997).

The Sexually Abused. The 1993 annual data from the National Center on Child Abuse and Neglect indicate that 140,000 children were sexually abused (Sedlak & Broadhurst, 1996). The majority were females. Victims of sexual abuse exhibit a wide range of behaviors (e.g., sexual play, excessive masturbation, seductive sexual behavior, poor performance in school, and involvement in delinquency and substance abuse). These children can find themselves in court offering testimony about the perpetrator and the actual incident or events. Today, the courts consider these victims to be competent witnesses. Social workers in the child and family service and the court system may work with school social workers to prepare a child to give testimony. Identification, reporting, and preventive intervention are the tasks of the school social worker in such cases. These children also need emotional support, guidance, and an advocate. The social worker can work with the police department, the child protection agency, and community agencies to assist the family and the child. Inservice training for teachers should include such topics as how to identify these children, teachers' legal responsibility to report abuse, and the kind of assistance the child will need to meet the educational expectations of the school. The school environment may need to be assessed for areas that need additional supervision in order for children to be safe. Establishing schedules for monitoring hallways, bathrooms and any identified areas of risk will help in preventing victimization of students by others, that is, older or stronger students. Social workers may be helpful in developing or implementing programs to teach children to safely assert their rights and protect themselves from all kinds of abuse. The establishment of parent education classes to teach appropriate techniques of discipline and the provision of parent effectiveness training can be considered as both preventive and remedial strategies. On the community level, the establishment of preventive programs and the development of community awareness

TABLE 9.7   Models for Teacher Training in Family Involvement

FUNCTIONAL APPROACH

Knowledge about benefits and goals of family involvement

Skills in involving parents of all backgrounds in school

Respect for different family structures, lifestyles, and cultural beliefs

Knowledge of family functions

Communication skills that are effective in dealing with frustrated, angry parents, defensive behaviors, distrust, and hostility

Skills in parental involvement of children's learning outside of the classroom and in sharing teaching skills with parents

Skills in ways to involve parents in school

Knowledge about consultation, interprofessional collaboration, referral procedures, and ways in which schools can support families

Skills in sharing and transferring leadership to parents; sharing information that aids parents in making decisions; interacting with parents on an equal basis

CULTURAL COMPETENCE

Skills in developing culturally appropriate themes in the curriculum

Awareness of personal assumptions, value systems, and prejudices that may affect interactions with families

Knowledge of cultural differences and influences on childrearing, expectations, and development, communication

Skills in incorporating family "funds of knowledge" into curricular projects involving families and communities in actively contributing to learning

Understanding of the constraints (e.g., time, financial) that may prevent more active involvement in the school program

Skills in discovering potential contributions and creating opportunities for involvement

Sensitivity toward different families' perceptions of help and reciprocity

Incorporation of parental preferences into family and school involvement activities

PARENT EMPOWERMENT

Respect for the family's role in nurturance and education of children and faith that all parents want what is best for their children

Attitude that parents are first and most important teachers and that the most useful knowledge about raising children is found within the community; teachers seek to understand parents' views and needs rather than control them

Knowledge of power differences and the historical influences on disenfranchised groups

Focus on strengths rather than deficits and support rather than blame

Skills in developing activities that build parental skill and confidence in home learning activities; provide helpful constructive feedback to families

Skills in effective communication and developing partnerships with parents, incorporating parents' self-identified needs and goals into the programs and activities offered

Empower parents through adult education and parent education courses; including parents in governance roles and allowing their voices to be heard in meetings

Invitations to parents to share their expertise in the school and classroom as well as at home

SOCIAL CAPITAL

Understanding of the concept of social capital

Knowledge of differences and similarities in values and norms

Skills in conflict negotiation, consensus building, trust building, home visiting

Skills in motivating families and communities to become involved in home learning and educational activities

Skills in fostering parental and family investment in their child's program through attendance at school events, volunteering, fundraising

Skills in utilization of community resources

Reciprocal exchanges between schools and families

Adapted from a model in Shartrand, A. M., Weiss, H. B., Kreider, H. M., & Lopez, M. E. (1997). *New skills for new schools: Preparing teachers in family involvement.* Cambridge, MA: Harvard Family Research Project. Developed with contractual support from U.S. Department of Education. (Reprinted with permission.)

are also appropriate roles for the school social worker.

Gang Violence and Delinquent Behaviors

Gang violence is a complicated and multifaceted social problem (see Chapter 7). According to the National Center for Health Statistics, over 30 years, death rates decreased in every age group except among 15- to 24-year-olds (Cohen & Wilson-Brewer, 1991). Increased mortality rates for this group were caused by violence and were gang-related. Assault (homicide) is the second leading cause of death for individuals age 15–24. Adolescents who are members of minority groups and live in high-poverty areas are often the victims or perpetrators. More male adolescents die from gunshots than any other cause.

The school is no longer a safe haven for learning and growing—in fact, it, too, has become one of the battlegrounds for gang warfare and violence. The Carnegie Council on Adolescent Development has taken an active role in identifying risk factors of violence (e.g., being male, unemployed, poor, minority, residing in an urban environment, having poor conflict-management skills, and with ready access to weapons) as well as preventive interventions. But in recent years gangs have expanded beyond low-income urban neighborhoods to working- and middle-class suburban areas (Virgil, 1997). Media coverage of gangs has compounded the problem.

Interventions must address the individual, interpersonal, and social and systems levels if we are going to reduce and prevent violence (Cohen & Wilson-Brewer, 1991). Social workers employed in schools should lead in the development of peer mediation programs and skills; family and community groups should be engaged in the formulation of solutions; and since churches play a critical role in many minority groups, they, too, should be considered partners in this effort. The efficacy of these suggestions still needs to be proven. However, we do know that family and behavior interventions have shown efficacy and effectiveness for reducing such behaviors. Suppression strategies dominated early attempts at intervention (Vigil, 1997). A more comprehensive approach is needed (see Chapter 7, on violence in schools).

Nonattenders

The first compulsory attendance laws were enacted in Massachusetts in 1852, and by 1918 every state had such laws. However, many children who enter schools never complete the twelve years of academic preparation. Education is a basic requirement for survival in a society that is growing more and more technical. Also, education teaches character and the duties of citizenship, two other requirements essential for survival in society. Yet, every day, large numbers of pupils fail to report to school. For example, on any given day, roughly 30,000 of the 450,000 pupils are absent without excuses that are acceptable to schools. Dropouts and truant children often have a disorganized home life and parents who may not value education and have poor academic skills. Other problems of this population are low grades, reading failure, a history of behavioral problems (including suspension and/or expulsion from school), emotional and financial inability to participate in extracurricular activities, and negative relations with teachers and other authority figures. Some children experience so much failure at school, both academically and socially, that it is amazing that they are able to attend as often as they do. School and teacher attitudes that place the locus of the problem in the student rather than recognizing structural inequalities and social disadvantage may further impede both motivation and achievement (Hudley, 1997). In addition, for some children schools are not safe environments. It is estimated that as many as 7 percent of eighth graders in America stay home at least once a month in order to avoid bullies (Banks, 1997). As mentioned earlier, gay, lesbian, and bisexual youth are at particular risk of victimization.

Table 9.8 identifies some typical problem areas that are of concern to teachers in public

TABLE 9.8   Teachers' Perceptions about Serious Problems in Their Schools: 1990–91 and 1993–94

	Percent of Teachers Indicating Item Is a Serious Problem				
	Public School Teachers				
Problem Area	1990–91	1993–94			
	Total	Total	Elementary Schools	Secondary Schools	Combined Schools
1	2	3	4	5	6
Student tardiness	11.2	10.5	6.3	18.3	7.8
Student absenteeism	14.1	14.4	7.2	27.1	15.0
Teacher absenteeism	1.6	1.5	1.3	1.9	2.0
Students cutting class	4.6	5.1	1.3	11.9	4.6
Physical conflicts among students	6.5	8.2	7.8	8.6	8.1
Robbery or theft	3.4	4.1	3.0	5.8	3.6
Vandalism of school property	5.4	6.7	5.2	9.0	5.9
Student pregnancy	6.4	7.3	1.1	18.4	10.1
Student use of alcohol	8.2	9.3	1.6	23.1	14.2
Student drug use	4.2	5.7	1.0	14.2	7.1
Student possession of weapons	1.2	2.8	1.2	5.6	2.7
Verbal abuse of teachers	7.5	11.1	8.6	14.8	14.3
Student disrespect for teachers	13.0	18.5	15.3	23.6	20.3
Students dropping out	6.3	5.8	1.2	14.1	7.7
Student apathy	20.6	23.6	15.6	38.0	28.9
Lack of academic challenge	5.7	6.5	4.2	10.4	9.9
Lack of parental involvement	25.4	27.6	23.0	34.5	35.5
Parental alcoholism/drug abuse	12.0	13.1	12.9	12.3	18.7
Poverty	17.1	19.5	20.8	15.9	26.8
Racial tension	3.8	5.1	4.0	6.7	5.5
Students coming unprepared to learn	_____	28.8	24.3	36.0	30.9

_____ Data not available.

Source: U.S. Department of Education, National Center for Education Statistics, "Schools and Staffing Survey," 1990–91 and 1993–94.

schools. When student tardiness, student absenteeism, and cutting class are combined for public secondary schools, nonattendance becomes a major problem. These problems are not as prevalent in the private secondary institutions, where family involvement is stronger and where schools foster a sense of community.

For children, the consequences of truancy are devastating. They are unable to compete in the labor market and, embittered by their school experience, have difficulty functioning in society. Social workers, particularly those who work at the elementary level, can identify early patterns of nonattendance that suggest which pupils are at risk of becoming chronic attendance problems. They should also act as liaison with home, school, and community agencies to help these children and their families. They can help the school to develop communities of learners who are supportive of one another and provide relationships that facilitate active positive involvement in schools. Programs on social problem solving and creating school climates in which bullying and aggressive behavior are not tolerated may also be needed. Further, social workers may help teachers in understanding the societal, cultural, and social influences on a child's learning. Appropriate tutoring that allows them to build on and track their successes is necessary for many of these children. The establishment of alternative schools or innovative in-school programs for pupils who find learning in the "traditional" school difficult can be another course of action. Evaluation of the educational environment, including the staff's attitude toward different pupil groups and its willingness to modify learning materials and expectations, should be a target of intervention. Development of extracurricular activities that are appealing to potential dropouts is one means of facilitating identification between them and the school.

The School of Social Work at the University of North Carolina worked with Communities-in-Schools (CIS) representatives (CIS is the nation's largest dropout prevention program) to develop an instrument for planning and monitoring success (Richman & Bowen, 1997). They provide a framework for thinking about and developing multifaceted interventions. Stability, load balance and participation are examined at the family, school, peer group and community level. Stability refers to the availability of stable supportive relationships. Load balance involves an understanding of how well the capabilities of the child match the demands of the environment, e.g., if a child's home is noisy and chaotic, how capable is the child at filtering stimuli when attempting to attend to homework. Participation refers to the meaningful involvement in the environments that constitute the child's microsystems. Developing social relationships and involvement decreases anomie and gives life meaning and the student reasons for caring (Richman & Bowen, 1997). The goal of interventions in these areas is to increase the student's social competence, sense of purpose, autonomy, and problem-solving abilities.

Drug and Alcohol Users

Substance abuse is becoming an increasingly serious problem for adolescents. A study conducted in 2000 indicated that 80 percent of high school seniors had experimented with alcohol; 52 percent of these youth had experimented with alcohol before the eighth grade (Johnston, O'Malley, & Bachman, 2001). This high school survey, conducted by the University of Michigan, with a sample of 13,000 high school seniors, found that a variety of chemical substances was used. In fact, one of five high school seniors had used marijuana in the month prior to the survey, three of ten had used cigarettes, and about half had consumed alcoholic beverages.

Some attribute the growth of this problem to the acceptability of alcohol by the adult culture and the widespread use of drugs in society. The reasons why youths and adults become dependent upon alcohol and drugs are complicated. Like other problem behaviors, the risk factors for alcohol and drug abuse occur at a number of levels. It is important to note that while societal attitudes toward alcohol and drug use have fluctuated, the risk factors for substance abuse have remained stable for the past 20 years (Jenson, 1997). Residential mobility, school transitions, low neighborhood attachment, and neighborhood disorganization (i.e., high population density, high crime areas) are neighborhood variables associated with substance abuse. Family factors include parental substance abuse, poor family management practices (lax supervision or very severe or inconsistent discipline), poor family communication, and weak parent-child relationships. School-level risk factors include lack of attachment to school and lack of commitment to education. Adolescent substance abusers are more likely to be truant and to perform poorly. Involvement with peers who use drugs or participate in other deviant activities is one of the strongest predictors of adolescent substance abuse. Attention deficit disorders and poor impulse control are predictors of age of onset of drinking and drug use. Children who are aggressive at age five have an increased likelihood of deviant behaviors, including substance abuse, as adolescents. Early onset of drug use increases the likelihood of subsequent drug use and involvement in deviant behaviors. Sensation-seeking orientation—love of risk-taking—is also associated with substance abuse (Jenson, 1997). Thus, youths may drink or use drugs to emulate the adult figures in their lives, to defy their parents and society, to be accepted by peer groups, to avoid dealing with reality, and to escape emotional problems.

Warning signals that one should be alert to include impulsive behavior, lack of perseverance, not caring about other people, nervous tremors, sudden changes in mood, inability to cope with frustrations, irritability with family members and friends, rebelliousness (McDermott, 1984), and a decrease in short-term memory skills.

Adolescent substance abusers encounter numerous difficulties in attempting to satisfy the expectations of their families and school. When confronted, their response is generally denial. Because the school is the one institution that almost every youth has some contact with, it must play an important role in identifying adolescent substance abusers, educating youths concerning the harmful effects of drugs and alcohol, and helping to provide protective conditions for youth—such as developing social bonds with teachers, parents, and prosocial peers, participation in prosocial activities, and increased commitment to school. The involvement of school social workers can include referring abusers to appropriate treatment centers, providing inservice training to school staff members and parents

on how to identify these youths, and developing a preventive substance abuse curriculum that can be used in health education classes.

Gifted and Talented Youth

Programs for gifted and talented youth have been affected by decreased use of categorical funds, concerns about equity, and the belief of some that gifted and talented programs represent a form of tracking. Some contend that the challenge offered to gifted and talented youth should be available to all. Indeed, many enrichment programs and thinking skills curricula developed for gifted and talented youth are now being utilized in regular classrooms. However, the national struggle between equity and excellence fails to recognize that we achieve equity when we strive for personal excellence for each student in programs that are more inclusive.

Minorities have been underrepresented in gifted and talented programs due, in part, to the narrow admissions policies of some school districts. Heavy reliance on nationally standardized tests as admissions criteria deters the inclusion of many minority children in these programs. These tests are often biased toward a majority middle-class culture. Increased recognition of multiple intelligence has helped to decrease the narrow definition of giftedness.

The federal definition of gifted and talented recognizes the potential for many areas of talent:

- Children and youth with outstanding talent perform or show the potential for performing at remarkably high levels of accomplishment when compared with others of their age, experience, or environment.
- These children and youth exhibit high performance capability in intellectual, creative, and/ or artistic areas, possess an unusual leadership capacity, or excel in specific academic fields, and they require services or activities not ordinarily provided by the schools.
- Outstanding talents are present in children and youth from all cultural groups, across all economic strata, and in all areas of human en-

deavor. (Office of Educational Research and Improvement, 1993, p. 26)

Current best practices with gifted and talented youth emphasize use of appropriately differentiated instruction within classrooms that use flexible grouping, offer student choice in classes, and utilize gifted and talented resource specialists. Advocates for gifted and talented youth warn against heavy use of cooperative learning strategies, contending that these heterogeneous learning groups result in gifted and talented children performing as assistant teachers and limit the challenge to these students (Robinson, 1990; Tomlinson, 1995a). In order to provide adequate intellectual challenge and the opportunity to learn together with other exceptionally bright students, while not creating separate classrooms for them, experts recommend cluster grouping. Cluster grouping involves placing talented children in groups of less than ten together in classrooms. This arrangement allows the teacher to more easily attend to the special needs of this group of children (need for increasing challenge) and offers children the opportunity to understand their learning differences as they explore them with others of similar ability, but avoids some of the dangers of tracking by avoidance of permanent grouping arrangements for students of more limited ability levels (Winnebrenner & Devlin, 1996).

Best practices in regular and gifted education highlight many similar beliefs and values: theme based, integrated curriculum; student choice and interest; self-understanding; student involvement in assessment; critical thinking development; group interaction; establishing communities of learners; family involvement; school-community connections; curriculum built upon student interest and relevance to the learner, including inquiry- or problem-based approaches that utilize the study of significant problems in the child's realm of experience (Tomlinson, 1995a). Differentiated instruction in mixed-ability classrooms allows children to exhibit what they know in a variety of ways and is principle- or concept-focused, with advanced learners offered the opportunity to apply key concepts and explore some areas in greater depth or breadth. Learning contracts, learning centers, computer programs, multiple sources of information, complex instruction, multiple intelligence orientation, and negotiated criteria may all be a part of a differentiated instruction classroom that meets children at their own level and challenges them in growth-producing ways (Tomlinson, 1995b).

Children with exceptional talents may need assistance in understanding their feelings and developing social networks. They may experience increased sensitivity and be frustrated when others are unable to perceive what, to them, seems so obvious. Perfectionism in themselves is another concern for very bright children. Tomlinson (1995a) contends that for the middle-school gifted and talented population, belonging is particularly problematic among females and culturally diverse students who experience peer pressure to conform in a somewhat different context.

Teachers may refer gifted and talented children for psychological assessment, expressing concern that they have attention deficit hyperactivity disorder (ADHD). Most of the behaviors listed in the diagnostic criteria for ADHD may also be exhibited by children with exceptional abilities (e.g., blurts out answers to questions, fidgets, talks excessively) (American Psychiatric Association, 1987, in Webb & Latimer, 1993). As stated previously, although a gifted child may also have an attention deficit, not every gifted child has ADHD. A key determinant is the context in which the behaviors occur. For gifted and talented children, the presence of problematic behaviors fluctuates greatly from one setting to another, according to the amount of structure and challenge. Although the activity level of some gifted children is often quite high (about 25% require less sleep), their activity is more focused and directed than that of children with ADHD. Unlike the inconsistent performance of ADHD children, when appropriately challenged and interested, children who are gifted maintain high performance and effort, and may be intensely focused (Webb & Latimer, 1993). If the tasks assigned are repetitive or below the level of intellectual challenge, the gifted and talented child may appear to have ADHD. It is important to evaluate all the possible causes of behavior including consideration of a mismatch between the child's abilities and the classroom curriculum and instruction. Evaluations that include assessment of intelligence, emotional problems (e.g., anxiety and depression), and appropriateness of curriculum and instruction, and that collect information from a variety of contexts and significant individuals in the child's life (i.e., teachers, parents), are most apt to provide adequate information to determine whether a child's exceptional talents are a contributor to the observed behaviors or if ADHD is present (Webb & Latimer, 1993).

CONCLUSION

The goal of social work that cuts across these different pupil groups is to increase equal educational opportunity for all children and youth by introducing and facilitating change in the systems in which they function—the school, the community, the home, and the pupil group itself. The earlier the intervention, the more likely positive outcomes (see Figure 9.3).

A national study of 18 schools that were effective in serving at-risk youth identified two broad conditions typically present in these successful schools: (1) a strong sense of community and (2) characteristics similar to high-reliability organizations that provide whatever level of support is necessary to attain success 100 percent of the time (Irmsher, 1997). Elements involved in the creation of community included shared vision and purpose: shared values; participation by families; an ethos of caring; trust; incorporation of diversity–inclusiveness; teamwork; good communication among staff, students, and families; recognition; extended roles for staff; and respect for all (Irmsher, 1997; Royal & Rossi, 1997). High-reliability organizations are also

characterized by a shared mission and maintain the belief that failure to achieve core tasks represents disaster. High-reliability organizations incorporate flexible hierarchies with clearly defined roles and responsibilities that utilize collegial decision making when appropriate, and empower all staff members to cross traditional boundaries in responding to emergencies in order to avoid failure. Reliance on, and continuing development of, the professional judgment of all staff members contributes to the success of the organization.

Mike Rose (1998) traveled around the United States for three and a half years visiting public schools that had promising practices. He visited urban, rural, and suburban schools. His account concentrates largely on the promising practices found in schools that served high-risk populations. He summarized the commonalties across these successful schools: (1) Sense of safety—a climate of physical and emotional safety including the safety to take risks; (2) Respect—fair treatment, respect for the culture, language, and history of people; (3) Teacher's authority came from multiple sources—knowledge, respectful consideration of others, caring—rather than solely from role or age, and authority was distributed even in traditional classrooms; (4) Classrooms were places of expectation and responsibility supported by mechanisms to aid in involvement and achievement; and (5) Creation of a vital public space—children learning, doing, making contributions, generating knowledge; places of challenge and reflection, quiet work, and public presentation. Teachers created collaborative relationships among themselves that served to nourish each other so that they in turn could nourish their students. These teachers believed in the value of their work and were able "to affirm in a deep and comprehensive way the capability of the students in their classrooms" (Rose, 1995, p. 422).

Research on resilience, the ability to succeed even in very negative environmental circumstances, indicates that three major areas of protective factors enable children to circumvent negative life experiences. These areas are (1) caring and supportive relationships—at least one—who was often a teacher when the family was highly dysfunctional; (2) positive and high expectations, with the belief that success is attainable; and (3) opportunities for meaningful participation—education, employment, growth, and achievement (Bernard, 1995; Kirby & Fraser, 1997; Werner & Smith, 1992).

The National Association of Secondary School Principals (1997) called for personalization of the high school as a key challenge for re-

form. Research supports the premise that a strong sense of community among staff enhances instructional efforts and a sense of personal well-being, as well as fostering a collaborative climate and student cooperation (Royal & Rossi, 1997). Social workers have the knowledge and skills to assist in the development of community, particularly in encouraging the involvement of families in the school community, but also in helping staff to develop a shared vision and collaborative relationships, and to recognize and use resources flexibly to achieve their goals.

FOR STUDY AND DISCUSSION

1. Review the characteristics of each target group of pupils discussed in this chapter. Identify additional characteristics and discuss intervention strategies.

2. Identify other target groups of pupils in the school who might come to the attention of the school social worker. Specify what might be the nature of the intervention. What aspects of the school environment could cause these children difficulty?

3. Numerous demands are made on the time of social workers in schools; they must serve many different pupil groups. Discuss how you as a professional would respond to these demands. What roles would take on more importance and how would you define "practice"?

4. Obtain a copy of your state's child abuse reporting act. Analyze it for clarity, weaknesses, and implications for reporting abuse found in the schools. How would a school district implement it?

5. Interview school social workers, teachers, and school administrators. Ask them to identify the

pupil groups in their schools who are most vulnerable. Ask them to elaborate on their intervention and the type of assistance they provide these pupils and their families. What insights do they have regarding the etiology of pupils' situations?

6. Devise a strategy for identifying vulnerable pupil groups who are at risk.

7. Review the Identified Pupil Situation Complex chart (Figure 9.3). Then discuss the specific goals (i.e., B. Behavioral Objectives; C. Measurable Outcomes) that you would want to accomplish for the remaining four pupil groups identified in the chart.

8. Visit the ERIC EC website on gifted and talented <www.ericec.org/gifted/gt-menu.html> and explore resources there or join the TAGFAM (Families of talented and gifted) listserve. Find out what issues are important for families of gifted and talented children.

ADDITIONAL READING

Costin, L., Karger, H., & Stolz, D. (1996). *The politics of child abuse in America.* New York: Oxford Press.

Goldstein, A. P., Sprafkin, R. P., Gershaw, N. J., & Klein, P. (1980). *Skillstreaming the adolescent: A structured learning approach to teaching prosocial skills.* Champaign, IL: Research Press Company.

Markward, M. (1994). Compliance with the McKinney Act: Providing homeless children with educational opportunity. *Social Work in Education, 16,* 31–38.

Morrow, D. F. (1992). Social work with gay and lesbian adolescents. *Social Work, 28,* 655–660.

Rogers, K., Segal, E., & Graham, M. (1994). The relationship between academic factors and running

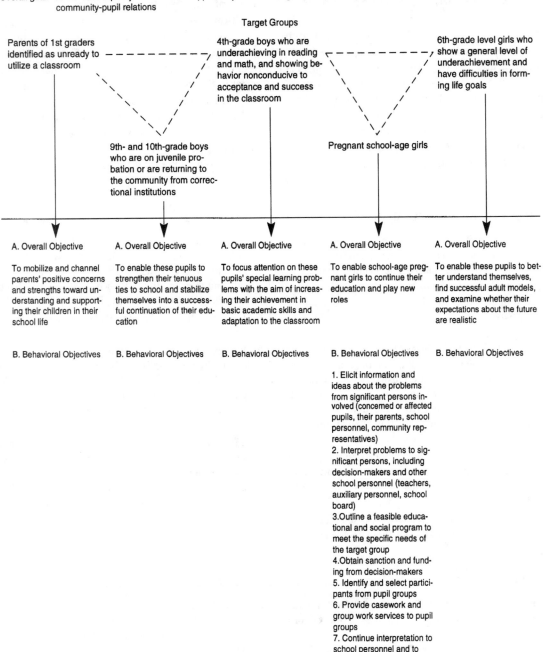

Overall goal: To increase equality of educational opportunity for selected groups of pupils by introducing change into the system of school-community-pupil relations

Target Groups

Parents of 1st graders identified as unready to utilize a classroom

4th-grade boys who are underachieving in reading and math, and showing behavior nonconducive to acceptance and success in the classroom

6th-grade level girls who show a general level of underachievement and have difficulties in forming life goals

9th- and 10th-grade boys who are on juvenile probation or are returning to the community from correctional institutions

Pregnant school-age girls

A. Overall Objective

To mobilize and channel parents' positive concerns and strengths toward understanding and supporting their children in their school life

A. Overall Objective

To enable these pupils to strengthen their tenuous ties to school and stabilize themselves into a successful continuation of their education

A. Overall Objective

To focus attention on these pupils' special learning problems with the aim of increasing their achievement in basic academic skills and adaptation to the classroom

A. Overall Objective

To enable school-age pregnant girls to continue their education and play new roles

A. Overall Objective

To enable these pupils to better understand themselves, find successful adult models, and examine whether their expectations about the future are realistic

B. Behavioral Objectives

B. Behavioral Objectives

B. Behavioral Objectives

B. Behavioral Objectives

1. Elicit information and ideas about the problems from significant persons involved (concerned or affected pupils, their parents, school personnel, community representatives)
2. Interpret problems to significant persons, including decision-makers and other school personnel (teachers, auxiliary personnel, school board)
3. Outline a feasible educational and social program to meet the specific needs of the target group
4. Obtain sanction and funding from decision-makers
5. Identify and select participants from pupil groups
6. Provide casework and group work services to pupil groups
7. Continue interpretation to school personnel and to other pupils to modify their attitudes and behaviors toward pupil groups
8. Set up mechanisms for continuing referrals and determination of the best individual plan

B. Behavioral Objectives

9. Work with community groups to develop supportive out-of-school programs and services
10. Institute systematic recordkeeping for interpreting outcome

C. Measurable Outcomes	C. Measurable Outcomes	C. Measurable Outcomes	C. Measurable Outcomes	C. Measurable Outcomes
			1. Extent of sanction and support 2. Amount of funding and its adequacy 3. Number of girls who continued in school 4. Number of girls who made adequate plans for care of the baby 5. If baby was kept, number of girls who were able to play traditional maternal role 6. Number of girls who completed education 7. Number of girls who moved into labor market or higher education 8. Decrease in recidivism	

FIGURE 9.3 An Identified Pupil Situation Complex

Source: Printed with permission of Lela B. Costin, Professor Emeritus, School of Social Work, University of Illinois, Urbana-Champaign.

away among adolescents. *Social Work in Education, 16,* 46–54.

Rose, M. (1995). *Possible lives: The promise of public education in America.* New York: Penguin Books.

Sjostrom, L., & Stein, N. (1996). *Bullyproof: A teacher's guide on teasing and bullying for use with fourth and fifth grade students.* Boston: Wellesley College Center for Research on Women and National Education Association Professional Library.

Stevens, B. A., & Ellerbrock, L. S. (1995). *Crisis intervention: An opportunity to change.* Greensboro, NC: ERIC Clearinghouse on Counseling and Student Services. (ERIC Document Reproduction Service No. ED 405 535)

REFERENCES

Aber, J. L., Brooks-Gunn, J., & Maynard, R. A. (1995). Effects of welfare reform on teenage parents and their children. *The Future of Children, 5*(2), 53–71.

Administration for Children and Families. (2000, December). *Leading the way: Characteristics and early experiences of selected Early Head Start programs.* Washington, DC: Department of Health and Human Services.

Administration for Children and Families. (2001, March). *Head Start fact sheet.* Washington, DC: Department of Health and Human Services.

American Psychiatric Association. (1987). *Diagnostic and statistical manual of mental disorders* (3rd ed., rev.). Washington, DC: Author.

Allen-Meares, P., & Roberts, E. (1994). Associations of social integration variables with prenatal care use by adolescents and young adults. *Journal of Social Service Research, 19,* 23–47.

Banks, R. (1997). *Bullying in schools.* Champaign, IL: ERIC Clearinghouse on Elementary and Early Childhood Education (ERIC Document Reproduction Service No. ED 407 154).

Bassuck B., & Rubin, L. (1987). Homeless children: A neglected population. *American Journal of Orthopsychiatry, 57,* 279–286.

Bernard, B. (1995). *Fostering resilience in children.* Urbana, IL: ERIC Clearinghouse on Early Childhood Education (ERIC Document Reproduction Service No. EDO-PS-95-9).

Biro, F. (1992, August). Adolescents and sexually transmitted diseases. *Maternal and Child Health Technical Information Bulletin.* Washington, DC: Department of Health and Human Services.

Blum, B. B., & Francis, J. F. (2001, August). *Welfare Research Perspectives: Past, Present, and Future, 2001 Edition.* Washington, DC: National Center for Children in Poverty.

Brooks-Gunn, J., Klebanov, P. K., & Duncan, G. J. (1996). Ethnic differences in children's intelligence test scores: Roles of economic deprivation, home environment, and maternal characteristics. *Child Development, 67,* 396–408.

Capps, R., Pindus, N., Snyder, K., & Leos-Urbel, J. (2001, June). Recent changes in Texas Welfare and Work, Child Care, and Child Welfare Systems. *Assessing the New Federalism* State Update No. 1. Washington, DC: Urban Institute.

Children's Defense Fund. (1997). *The state of America's children yearbook, 1997.* Washington, DC: Author.

Children's Defense Fund. (1998). *The state of America's children yearbook, 1998.* Washington, DC: Author.

Children's Defense Fund. (2001). *The state of America's children yearbook, 2001.* Washington, DC: Author.

Clark, J. (1992). School social work with infants and toddlers with disabilities and their families: Major roles and key competencies. *School Social Work Journal, 16,* 40–43.

Cohen, S., & Wilson-Brewer, R. (1991). *Violence prevention for young adolescents: The state of the art of program evaluation.* New York: Carnegie Council on Adolescent Development.

Dryfoos, J. (1990). *Adolescents at risk: Prevalence and prevention.* New York: Oxford University Press.

Duncan, G. J., & Brooks-Gunn, J. (1997). Income effects across the life span: Integration and interpretation. In G. J. Duncan & J. Brooks-Gunn (Eds.), *Consequences of growing up poor* (pp. 596–610). New York: Russell Sage Foundation.

Federal Interagency Forum on Child and Family Statistics. (2000). *America's Children: Key National Indicators of Well-Being.* Washington, DC: Federal Interagency Forum on Child and Family Statistics.

Fischer, C. S., Hout, M., Jankowski, M., Lucas, S., Swidler, A., & Voss, K. (1996). *Inequality by design: Cracking the bell curve myth.* Princeton, NJ: Princeton University Press.

Fisher, L., & Sorenson, G. (1991). *School law for counselors, psychologists, and social workers* (2nd ed.). White Plains, NY: Longman Press.

Fulton, G., Metress, E., & Preil, J. (1987). AIDS: Resource materials for school personnel. *Journal of School Health, 57,* 14–18.

Gay, Lesbian and Straight Education Network. (2001). *The national school climate survey: Lesbian, gay, bisexual, and transgender students and their experiences in schools.* New York: Author.

Gilbert, D. J. (2001). HIV-Affected Children and Adolescents: What School Social Workers Should Know. *Children and Schools, 23*(3), 135–142.

Hare, I. (1980). Legal rights of children: Child abuse and neglect and the school social worker. In *Conference Proceeding: School social work and the law.* Washington, DC: National Association of Social Work.

Herrnstein, R., & Murray, C. (1994*). The bell curve: Intelligence and class structure in American life.* New York: Free Press.

Hershberger, S. L., Pilkington, N. W., & D'Augelli, A. R. (1997). Predictors of suicide attempts among gay, lesbian, and bisexual youth. *Journal of Adolescent Research, 12*(4), 477–497.

Howard, M., & Eddinger, L. (1973). *School-age parents.* Syracuse, NY: National Alliance Concerned with School-Age Parents.

Hudley, C. A. (1997). Teacher practices and student motivation in a middle school program for African-American males. *Urban Education, 32,* 304–319.

Irmsher, K. (1997). *Education reform and students at risk.* Eugene, OR: ERIC Clearinghouse on Educational Management (ERIC Document Reproduction Service No. ED 405 642).

Jacobs, L. A. (1999). Equal opportunity, natural inequalities, and racial disadvantage: The Bell Curve and its critics. *Philosophy of the Social Sciences, 29*(1), 121–145.

Jencks, C., & Phillips, M. (1998). The black-white test score gap. *Brookings Review, 16,* 24–27.

Jenson, J. M. (1997). Risk and protective factors for alcohol and other drug use in childhood and adolescence. In M. W. Fraser (Ed.), *Risk and resilience in childhood: An ecological perspective* (pp.

117–139). Washington, DC: National Association for Social Workers.

Johnston, L. D., O'Malley, P. M., & Bachman, J. G. (2001). *Monitoring the future: National survey results on drug use, 1975–2000. Volume I: Secondary school students.* (NIH Publication No. 01-4924). Bethesda, MD: National Institute for Drug Abuse.

Kean, J. M. (1969). The impact of Head Start: An evaluation of the effects of Head Start on children's cognitive and affective development by Victor G. Cicirelli. The Westinghouse Learning Corporation and Ohio University. *Childhood Education, 46*(8), 449–452.

Kirby, L. D., & Fraser, M. W. (1997). Risk and resilience in childhood. In M. W. Fraser (Ed.), *Risk and resilience in childhood: An ecological perspective* (pp. 117–139). Washington, DC: National Association of Social Workers.

Koblinsky, S. A., Morgan, K. M., & Anderson, E. A. (1997). African-American homeless and low-income housed mothers: Comparison of parenting practices. *American Journal of Orthopsychiatry, 57*(1), 37–47.

Kozol, J. (1995). *Amazing grace: The lives of children and the conscience of a nation.* New York: Crown Publishers.

Larner, M. B., Terman, D. L., & Behrman, R. E. (1997). Welfare to work: Analysis and recommendations. *The Future of Children, 7*(1), 4–19.

Martin, S. L., Kupersmidt, J. B., & Harter, K. S. M. (1996). Children of farm laborers: Utilization of services for mental health problems. *Community Mental Health Journal, 32*(4), 327–340.

Masten, A. S., Sesma, Jr., A., Si-Asar, R., Lawrence, C., Miliotis, D., & Dionne, J. A. (1997). Educational risks for children experiencing homelessness. *Journal of School Psychology, 35*(1), 27–46.

McDermott, D. (1984, Spring). The relationship of parental drug use and parents' attitude concerning adolescent drug use. *Adolescence, 19*(84), 77–88.

Musick, J. S. (1993). *Young, poor, and pregnant: The psychology of teenage motherhood.* New Haven: Yale University Press.

National Alliance to End Homelessness. (2000). *A plan, not a dream: How to end homelessness in ten years.* Washington, DC: Author.

National Association of Secondary School Principals. (1997). *Breaking ranks.* Washington, DC: Author.

National Center for Children in Poverty. (2001, June).

Child Poverty Fact Sheet. Washington, DC: NCCP.

National Center for Education Statistics. (1993). The Condition of Education 1993. Washington, DC: Department of Education.

National Center for Education Statistics. (1997). The Condition of Education 1997, Supplemental Table 44-2. Washington, DC: Department of Education.

National Center for Education Statistics. (2000a). Digest of Education Statistics 2000: Tables, 21, 42, 65. Washington, DC: Department of Education.

National Center for Education Statistics. (2000b). The Condition of Education 2000. Washington, DC: Department of Education.

National Center for Education Statistics. (2001). The Condition of Education 2001. Washington, DC: Department of Education.

National Low Income Housing Coalition. (2001). *Out of Reach 2001: America's Growing Wage-Rent Disparity.* Washington, DC: Author.

Phillips, D. A. (Ed.). (1995). *Child care for low-income families: Summary of two workshops.* Washington, DC: National Academy Press.

Pierce, W. D. (1979). *Deciphering the learning domains: A second generation classification model for educational objectives.* Washington, DC: University Press of America.

Richman, J. M., & Bowen, G. L. (1997). School failure: An ecological-interactional-develomental perspective. In M. W. Fraser (Ed.), *Risk and resilience in childhood: An ecological perspective* (pp. 95–116). Washington, DC: National Association of Social Workers.

Robinson, A. (1990). Cooperation or exploitation: The argument against cooperative learning groups for talented students. *Journal for the Education of the Gifted, 14*(1), 9027.

Rose, M. (1998). Taking control of teacher quality. *American Teacher, 83,* 6–10.

Rowe, G. (2000, November). *Welfare Rules Databook: State TANF Policies as of July 1999.* Washington, DC: Urban Institute.

Royal, M. A., & Rossi, R. J. (1997). *Schools as communities.* Eugene, OR: ERIC Clearinghouse on Educational Management (ERIC Document Reproduction Service No. ED 405 157).

Satcher, D. (2001, July). *The Surgeon General's Call to Action to Promote Sexual Health and Responsible Sexual Behavior.* Washington, DC: Office of the Surgeon General, U.S. Department of Health and Human Services.

Scott-Jones, D. (1993, November). Adolescent child-bearing: Whose problem? What can we do? *Phi Delta Kappan, 75,* 1–12.

Sedlack, A. J., & Broadhurst, D. D. (1996, September). *Third national incidence study of child abuse and neglect.* Washington, DC: U.S. Department of Health and Human Services—Administration for Children and Families, National Center on Child Abuse and Neglect.

Seefeldt, K. S., Leon-Urbel, J., McMahon, P., & Snyder, K. (2001, July). Recent changes in Michigan Welfare and Work, Child Care, and Child Welfare Systems. *Assessing the New Federalism* State Update No. 4. Washington, DC: Urban Institute.

Shartrand, A. M., Weiss, H. B., Kreider, H. M., & Lopez, M. E. (1997). *New skills for new schools: Preparing teachers in family involvement.* Cambridge, MA: Harvard Family Research Project.

Shiltz, R. (1987). *And the band played on.* New York: Mountain Press.

Smith, C. (1996). The link between childhood maltreatment and teenage pregnancy. *Social Work Research, 20*(3), 131–141.

Smith, J. R., Brooks-Gunn, J., & Klebanov, P. K. (1997). Consequences of living in poverty for young children's cognitive and verbal ability and early school achievement. In G. J. Duncan & J. Brooks-Gunn (Eds.), *Consequences of growing up poor* (pp. 132–189). New York: Russell Sage Foundation.

Tomlinson, C. A. (1995a). Gifted learners and the middle school: Problem or promise? ERIC EC Digest #E535. Reston, VA: The ERIC Clearinghouse on Disabilities and Gifted Education. Available online: <http://www.cec.sped.org/ericec.htm>

Tomlinson, C. A. (1995b). Differentiating instruction for advanced learners in the mixed-ability middle school classroom. ERIC EC Digest #E536. Reston, VA: The ERIC Clearinghouse on Disabilities and Gifted Education.

Tout, K., Martinson, K., Koralek, R., & Ehrle, J. (2001, July). Recent changes in Minnesota Welfare and Work, Child Care, and Child Welfare Systems. *Assessing the New Federalism* State Update No. 3. Washingotn, DC: Urban Institute.

Underwood, M., Kupersmidt, J. B., & Coie, J. D. (1996). Childhood peer sociometric status and aggression as predictors of adolescent childbearing. *Journal of Research on Adolescence, 6,* 2–15.

U.S. Department of Health and Human Services, Administration on Children, Youth and Families. (2001a). *Child maltreatment 1999.* Washington, DC: U.S. Government Printing Office.

U.S. Department of Health and Human Services, Administration on Children, Youth and Families. (2001b, April). *Foster care national statistics.* Washington, DC: U.S. Government Printing Office.

United States Conference of Mayors. (2001, December). A status report on hunger and homelessness in America's cities 2001: A 27-city survey. Washington, DC: Author.

Ventura, S. J., Mathews, T. J., & Curtin, S. C. (1999, October). Declines in teenage birth rates, 1991–98: Update of national and state trends, *National Vital Statistics Report, 47*(26). Washington, DC: U.S. Department of Health and Human Services, Centers for Disease Control and Prevention, National Center for Health Statistics.

Vigil, J. D. (1997). Learning from gangs: The Mexican American experience. Charleston, WV: ERIC Clearinghouse on Rural Education and Small Schools (ERIC Document Reproduction Service No. ED 405 157).

Webb, J. T., & Latimer, D. (1993). ADHD and children who are gifted. ERIC EC Digest #E522. Reston, VA: The ERIC Clearinghouse on Disabilities and Gifted Education. Available online: <http://www.cec.sped.org/ericec.htm>

Weinberg, D. H. (1997). Income and poverty 1996: Press briefing on 1996 income, poverty, and health insurance estimates (September 29, 1997). Washington, DC: U.S. Census Bureau.

Werner, E., & Smith, R. (1992*). Overcoming the odds: High risk children from birth to adulthood.* New York: Cornell University Press.

Whitebook, M., Howes, C., & Phillips, D. (1989). Research report: Who cares? Child care teachers and the quality of care in America. *Young Children, 45,* 41–44.

Winebrenner, S., & Devlin, B. (1996). Cluster grouping of gifted students: How to provide full-time services on a part-time budget. ERIC EC Digest #E538. Reston, VA: The ERIC Clearinghouse on Disabilities and Gifted Education. Available online: <http://www.cec.sped.org/ericec.htm>.

Zabin, L., & Hayward, S. (1993). Adolescent sexual behavior and child bearing. *Developmental clinical psychology and psychiatry.* Newbury Park, CA: Sage.

CHAPTER 10

SECURING EQUAL EDUCATIONAL OPPORTUNITY: LANGUAGE, RACE, AND GENDER

SANDRA KOPELS, UNIVERSITY OF ILLINOIS AT URBANA-CHAMPAIGN

All children living in our democracy have certain inalienable rights. One is the opportunity to experience and to use to their fullest capacity the educational program offered by our American schools.[*]
—Alma Laabs

INTRODUCTION

Court orders and legislation have greatly impacted educational policies and practices. Chapter 8, on special education, describes how children with disabilities have been denied their fair share of "public education." The Education of All Handicapped Children Act of 1974—commonly known as the "bill of rights for the handicapped"—drastically altered school policies and practices, thus opening up educational opportunities for students who previously had been excluded from education.

Children with disabilities are not the only students who have been denied equal educational opportunities. Children whose primary language is not English, children who are ethnic and racial minorities, and female students have been denied access to certain programs offered by schools.

Discrimination and other unfair policies either covert or overt, have focused these student groups into educational tracks that deny them equal educational opportunities. In this chapter, I examine the unique status of non-English speaking children and members of ethnic and racial minorities, and explore the role of sexism and gender discrimination in education.

BILINGUAL AND BICULTURAL EDUCATION

The ethnic composition of the United States will continue to change greatly over the next few decades. The early immigrants to the United States were primarily of European descent. Today, data from 2000 Census indicates that there are 28.4 million people in the United States who were not U.S. citizens at birth, about 10% of the population. Among the foreign-born, persons from Latin America, composed of Central America, South America, and the Caribbean, constituted 51% of the population, 25.5% were born in Asia, 15.3% were born in Europe, and 8% came from other regions of the world. The population from Central America, including Mexico, constitutes about one third of the total persons born outside of the United States who reside in the United States (Lollack, 2001). These new immigrant groups are less familiar racially, culturally, and linguistically than previous immigrant groups (McMullen & Lynde, 1997).

No matter what country they originate from, many people immigrate to the United States because they see it as a land of opportunity and freedom. However, the United States has become more exclusionary. For example, the United States federal government passed welfare reform legislation known as "The Personal Responsibility and Work Reconciliation Act of 1996." This legislation may affect immigration to the United States because of the ineligibility of immigrants to receive food stamps and SSI benefits for the first five years after entry into the country.

Other restrictions exist. For example, there are limitations on the numbers of persons that can immigrate from different countries. Additionally, after the terrorist attacks of September 11, 2001, persons from certain countries, especially those who are Arabic, are finding increased scrutiny of their backgrounds. University students will have to account for their whereabouts once they enter the country. Independent of these events, there has been a movement in certain states that have large non-English speaking populations, such as California and Arizona, to draft official state policies that reflect English as the official language of the state.

While many immigrants enter the United States legally, a significant number enter the country illegally. States such as California, Florida, and Texas have opted to increase the amount of money they spend on keeping illegal immigrants out of their states. Some states claim that illegal immigrants are costing taxpayers billions of dollars in health and educational services. As a result, California voters approved Proposition 187, which denied most public services to illegal immigrants. This proposition prohibits undocumented immigrants from receiving education, social services, and nonemergency medical care and would require public officials, including social workers, to report persons who entered the U.S. illegally (Hiratsuka, 1995). Numerous court challenges have been filed against the measure. Opponents warn that California could lose $1 billion in federal funds for education and health care.

The 1990 census reported 6.3 million children between the ages of 5 and 17 who speak languages other than English at home; this was a 38% increase over the previous decade (Crawford, 1997). Anstrom (as cited in Crawford, 1997) uses a more expansive definition of language minority to estimate that 9.9 million children, or 22% of the school-age population, live in a home where a language other than English is spoken. The estimates of the numbers of children who speak languages other than English varies. Borden (2001) extrapolates from 1990 Census data to estimate that presently more than 14 million people in the United States live in homes where English is not the primary language. Of the children who have limited proficiency in English, 73% speak Spanish.

Persons born outside the United States are more geographically concentrated and more likely to live in central cities of metropolitan areas than those born in the United States. For example, immigrants from Mexico and Central America have settled primarily in the western and southern United States, those from South America and the Caribbean have settled in the Northeast and South, and almost half of the persons from Asia have settled in the West (Lollack, 2001). Nearly half of limited English proficient children live in either California, Texas, or New York which has significant implications on the educational system (Borden, 2001).

The schools are ill prepared to respond: A shortage of bilingual educators and programs; an unclear understanding as to how special educational services might assist those students who need services; and distance between the home/community and school all interact to undermine educational success for Hispanic and other linguistically different students. Chapter 8 discusses issues concerning the assessment of students needing special education assistance. The assessment and development of intervention strategies for language minority students presents still another challenge.

Children of racial minorities and non-English speaking children tend to come from families occupying a lower socioeconomic position. Socioeconomic status is one of the single largest determinants of a student's school performance (Borden, 2001). Their parents are often poorly educated and somewhat mystified by the educational process and all of its special programs. Moreover, their parents also may not have a command of the English language and may lack the financial resources to be able to afford money for books, tutoring, or extracurricular activities. These children generally find entry into the public school difficult because they lack the family resources and experiential background that usually lead to successful achievement in what has been called a middle-class institution.

Antecedent Movements in the United States

In the eighteenth and nineteenth centuries, non-English and bilingual instruction was typical in many parts of the United States. During the early 1700s, school instruction throughout Pennsylvania, Maryland, Virginia, and the Carolinas gave importance to German, often to the exclusion of English. In a school district in Wisconsin, funds were specified for German texts, and in other school districts in the state, the school board could hire only German-speaking teachers. In California, private schools were composed mainly of descendants of Spaniards, and thus study of the Spanish language was required. As late as

1884, a law was passed in New Mexico requiring that reading and writing be taught in either Spanish or English or both. During that same period, the Cherokee Indians had an educational system that produced a population that was 90% literate in its native language and could use bilingual materials.

What happened to this early commitment to recognize a child's heritage and his or her specific language needs? The mandatory school attendance laws, elimination of public funding for church-related schools, and the movement toward an isolationist policy in the United States led the way toward English as the only instructional language. Some states outlawed the use of languages other than English, except in foreign-language classes.

The Move to Americanize Immigrant Children

The trend toward making the United States a one-language nation continued in the early 1900s. Theodore Roosevelt, who was committed to this notion, took the position that any person entering the United States must adopt the institutions of the United States, and therefore must adopt the language that is the native tongue of the people. He felt that it would be not merely a misfortune but a crime to perpetuate differences of language in this country (Roosevelt, 1919). Roosevelt added that the United States should provide for every immigrant to learn English in schools, for the young during the day and night schools for adults, and if five years passed without English being learned, the immigrant should be sent back to the land from where he or she came (Roosevelt). From a governmental perspective and considering the age of the nation and the desire for national unity, cultural and linguistic homogeneity was a priority. It was assumed that different languages would further divide the nation and make it difficult to develop a national philosophy and a unified government.

Leibowitz (1983) suggested that the reason for this restriction might have its roots far deeper in the foundation of the nation's ideology, and that it may be a manifestation of the social and institutional racism that is now known to operate throughout the society. Further, he maintained that an analysis of the historical records during this period indicates that official acceptance or rejection of bilingualism in U.S. schools was dependent on whether the group involved was considered politically and socially acceptable. The decision to impose English as the exclusive language of instruction in the schools has reflected the popular attitudes toward the particular ethnic group and the degree of hostility evidenced toward that group's development. One study indicated that, after World War I, 23 states passed laws restricting the teaching of foreign languages, especially German, in response to postwar anti-German sentiment (Wexler, 1996). If the group was viewed as different in some way (color, religion) or alien, the United States imposed harsher restrictions on its language practices. Today, the attitudes and hostilities are directed toward other groups. Adults and children who practice the Muslim religion or originate from Arabic speaking countries face increased suspicion and hostility after the terroristic attacks on the World Trade Center and the Pentagon in September 2001.

The Emergence of a New Philosophy

The cry for assimilation has dominated the way of thinking for so long in the United States that educators have lost sight of the child's right to his or her cultural identity, and that richness has been lost in a nation founded on the right of all to liberty and freedom. The belief that a child is entitled to the preservation of his or her cultural and linguistic identity gained popularity in the mid-twentieth century. A movement toward bilingual and bicultural education emerged.

Definition and Intent of Bilingual and Bicultural Education

Before we discuss the legal framework of bilingual and bicultural education, it is essential to understand what is meant by these and related terms.

The intent of bilingual and bicultural education is to develop an educational system that will develop the intellectual abilities of each child adequately by utilizing the child's native language to enable him or her to acquire proficiency in English. Another aim of this type of education is to attend to the cultural needs of the child and his or her community by using English and the languages that reflect the makeup of the community in instruction. Not only do bilingual and bicultural education programs promote mastery of the English language, but they also foster native language proficiency and preserve the child's cultural heritage (Moran, 1988).

The instructional form of bilingual and bicultural education programs has varied. Several types have been identified: transitional programs, bilingual maintenance programs, culturally pluralistic programs, and bicultural and bilingual restorationist programs. These programs differ in their emphasis on such factors as involvement of families and parents, focus on history of language, inclusion of students of different languages and cultural identities, and how the staff is trained.

Some specific terms used to define teaching approaches or program models of bilingual and bicultural education are defined by Crawford (1997) as follows:

— Transitional bilingual education (TBE) is a model in which the primary goal is to mainstream students to all-English classrooms; it uses native language instruction to help students keep up in their other subjects, phasing in English instruction as soon as possible.
— Developmental bilingual education (DBE) is a model in which the goals include fluent bilingualism as well as academic excellence; English is typically phased in more gradually than in TBE and continues to develop students' skills in the native language after they have become fully English-proficient.
— Two-way bilingual education or bilingual immersion is a model that combines DBE for lan-

guage-minority students and foreign language immersion for students who are English proficient; it includes peer tutoring and seeks to enable each group to learn the other's language while also meeting high academic standards.

Unfortunately, to differ culturally, linguistically, or racially can mean that one is treated differentially. Students who are "different" can encounter negative attitudes and expectations that are rooted in a racist ideology that denies them their right to have self-respect and to be culturally different. Civil rights advocates have documented the extent of miseducation of minorities and other children who were different linguistically. Legislation and court decisions have forced a reevaluation of such attitudes and practices, and some positive institutional change has resulted, although there is still room for improvement.

The Legal Framework of Bilingual and Bicultural Education

Before 1968, no federal legislation existed regarding the need for children with limited English proficiency to be able to speak English. By 2002, under the No Child Left Behind Act, it is apparent there has been serious retrenchment in the federal government's interest in teaching students whose primary language is not English. By examining the history of bilingual education legislation and its goals carefully, we will see the beginnings of a return to more isolated policies regarding teaching non-English speaking students.

Passed in 1968, the addition of Title VII to the Elementary and Secondary Education Act (ESEA) can be considered the first legislation aimed at linguistically different children. In fact, Title VII, known as the Bilingual Education Act, can be considered a major breakthrough for this group of children. The act provided grants to school districts that implemented programs aimed at increasing English proficiency but allowed school districts to retain discretion in developing bilingual programs and in applying for

funds (McMullen & Lynde, 1997). While the act did not mandate districts to provide bilingual education, it did improve state and local bilingual education policy. Prior to 1968, no state had enacted bilingual educational provisions. By 1973, at least 6 states had created such provisions while a number of other states repealed their statutes making English the exclusive language of instruction (McMullen & Lynde).

Because the Bilingual Education Act authorized funding only until 1973, hearings were held before Congress for the act's reauthorization. These hearings noted studies that had shown that schools were still failing to meet the needs of limited English-proficient children. The Bilingual Education Act of 1974 provided stronger support for bilingualism and biculturalism than the 1968 act. The policy declaration of the act recognized that these children had distinctive cultural heritages and that their native languages and heritages were primary means for instruction. Congress recognized that schools could meet the needs of these children through bilingual education programs that used multiple languages and cultural resources. The 1974 amendments authorized higher levels of funding from 1974 to 1978 than did the 1968 act, but also put more limits on the types of bilingual education programs that could qualify for funding (Moran, 1988).

As amended in 1978, the Bilingual Education Act's definition of acceptable programs emphasized that a child's native language was to be used "to the extent necessary to allow a child to achieve competence in the English language" (P.L. 95-561). However, the act made far clearer that the primary goal of bilingual instruction was for English acquisition.

Importantly, the amendments addressed concerns about segregation. In order to promote these children's acquisition of English and to prevent segregation, the act explicitly permitted English-speaking children to participate in bilingual education classes, not to exceed 40% of the class. Elective classes, such as music, physical education, and art, could not be segregated (Moran, 1988).

In 1984, the Bilingual Education Act expanded the definition of acceptable instructional techniques and enlarged the state's role in the grant and policy-making processes. The act recognized the usefulness of programs that rely heavily on native-language instruction but also began to place increased importance on "special alternative instructional programs," that is, programs that use structured English language instruction and other special services to allow a child to achieve competence in the English language rapidly and to meet grade-promotion and graduation standards.

In 1988, Congress again reauthorized the Bilingual Education Act. Studies presented to Congress concluded that the federal government's own research had understated consistently the benefits of programs that rely heavily on native-language instruction, and overstated the potential benefits of alternative techniques that use more English-language instruction. Despite these findings, Congress gave greater discretion to educators in their choice of instructional methods by raising the cap on funds for special alternative instructional techniques to 25% of total program grant appropriations. To justify the increase in funding for special alternative instruction programs, legislators cited reports indicating that a significant number of school districts served a broad array of small language groups rather than a large number of children from a single language group. Because local school districts did not have sufficient ability to handle large numbers of limited English-proficient students of many diverse languages, no one teaching approach could fit all situations; therefore, Congress felt it was necessary to give discretion to each district (Moran, 1988).

In 1994, Congress reauthorized the Bilingual Education Act for the fifth time as Title VII of the Improving America's Schools Act (P.L. 103-382). Section 7102 of the law contained the findings, policy, and purposes underlying the passage of the act. This comprehensive statement, incorporated into the law, helped explain the federal government's commitment to bilingual education (Crawford, 1997).

Among the 16 enumerated findings in the Improving America's Schools Act, Congress found that limited English-proficient children face a number of problems in receiving an education that include:

- segregated education programs;
- disproportionate and improper placement in special education and other special programs due to the use of inappropriate evaluation procedures;
- the limited English proficiency of parents, which hinders the parents' ability to fully participate in the education of their children; and
- a shortage of teachers and other staff who are professionally trained and qualified to serve such children.

In the Improving America's Schools Act, Congress also found that the use of a child's native language and culture in classroom instruction can promote self-esteem and contribute to academic achievement and learning English by limited English-proficient children and youth; benefit English-proficient children and youth who also participate in such programs; and develop the nation's national language resources, promoting the nation's competitiveness in the global economy. Other important Congressional findings included that language-minority Americans speak virtually all world languages plus many that are indigenous to the United States, and that there are a growing number of children who have a cultural heritage that differs from that of their English-proficient peers.

Court Challenges and Bilingual Education

Lau v. *Nichols* (1974) was a class action lawsuit brought by non-English-speaking Chinese students against the officials responsible for the operation of the San Francisco, California, public schools. The United States District Court found that there were 2,856 students of Chinese ancestry who spoke little or no English. While 1,000 of these students were given supplemental courses in the English language, at least 1,800 students did not receive any such instruction. The plaintiffs claimed that the absence of bilingual programs designed to meet the needs of Chinese students violated both Title VI and the Equal Protection Clause of the Fourteenth Amendment to the Constitution. They argued that equality in education goes beyond providing the same building and books to all students and includes intangible factors. Because these students had not mastered standard English and could not understand the instruction provided, they were denied or deprived of their right to even a minimally adequate education; consequently, they received an education inferior to that of other children. Both the United States District Court and the 9th Circuit Court of Appeals denied relief to the plaintiff class.

These courts ruled that the students' rights to an equal educational opportunity had been satisfied because the same education was made available on the same terms and conditions to the other students in their school district. In 1970, the Department of Health, Education and Welfare (HEW) had determined that Title VI of the Civil Rights Act of 1964 required schools to provide special educational assistance to students not proficient in English. HEW had issued an official memorandum mandating that school districts receiving federal funds rectify the language deficiencies of non-English-speaking students and that to ignore the needs of these students was a form of national origin discrimination (Moran, 1988). The Department of Health, Education and Welfare, concerned about the impact of the lower court's decision on bilingual policies, was granted permission to argue in support of the petitioners as *amicus curiae.*

The department's interpretation was upheld by the U.S. Supreme Court. The Court noted that California law required English as the basic language of instruction in California schools and that school districts had the discretion to deter-

mine the circumstances when instruction could be provided bilingually. The Court further noted that no student could receive a diploma of graduation from grade 12 if he or she were not proficient in English as well as other subjects. The Supreme Court ruled that under these "state-imposed standards there is no equality of treatment merely by providing students with the same facilities, textbooks, teachers, and curriculum; for students who do not understand English are effectively foreclosed from any meaningful education" (*Lau* at 566). Because the Court reasoned that basic English skills are at the core of what the public schools teach, requiring that before a child could meaningfully participate in the educational program, the child must have already acquired those basic skills would make a mockery of public education.

Unfortunately, this decision did not specify the types of educational programs to be provided to the Chinese students. The Court stated that teaching English to the students of Chinese ancestry who do not speak the language, giving instruction to them in Chinese, or using other methodological options were among the choices of instruction. The Court only ordered appropriate relief to be granted. In his concurrence, Justice Blackmun emphasized that his agreement with the result in the case was based only on the large number of Chinese students who were being deprived of meaningful schooling. He stated that if another case concerned only a very few youngsters or a single child who spoke a language other than English, he would not find the Court's interpretation of the HEW guidelines or the *Lau* case to require the same outcome. His concurrence demonstrated his belief that other ethnic groups in America have had to overcome language barriers with their own efforts and not rely on governmental help.

Congress codified the *Lau* decision by enacting the Equal Educational Opportunities Act (EEOA) of 1974. Section 1703(f) of this act states that "No State shall deny equal educational opportunity to an individual on account of his or her race, color, sex or national origin, by . . . the failure by an educational agency to take appropriate action to overcome language barriers that impede equal participation by its students in the instructional program." While state and local school districts maintain a great deal of discretion in the area of bilingual education, federal statutes and case law impose an affirmative obligation on schools to provide some special language instruction to non-English speaking students (McMullen & Lynde, 1997).

The Equal Educational Opportunities Act mandates that districts take appropriate action to overcome the language barriers of limited English-proficient children. Courts have taken a variety of approaches when considering whether school districts have taken "appropriate action" to overcome the language barriers of children. For example, in an earlier case interpreting the EEOA, a federal district court ruled that black children who spoke "Black English" were impeded from equally partaking in the educational system and that "Black English" could be considered a language barrier entitling them to English language instruction *(Martin Luther King, Jr., Elementary School Children* v. *Ann Arbor School District Board,* 1978).

More recent cases, however, seem to uphold school districts' choice of methodologies as being "appropriate action." In *Teresa P.* v. *Berkeley* (1989), the Berkeley, California, school district had 571 limited English-proficient children who spoke 38 languages other than English. Some of these languages were spoken by only one to three of the district's children. The plaintiffs filed a class action against the school district. They alleged that the school district's testing and procedures for identification and assessment of the district's limited English-proficient students was inadequate and that the district employed inappropriate criteria and procedures to determine when special language services for individual students were no longer necessary and appropriate. They also claimed that the district failed to allocate adequate resources to the district's special language services

for limited English-proficient students and failed to assure that teachers and other instructional personnel had enough qualifications and skills to provide effective services. The students also argued that the district had not provided them with adequate English language development instruction and adequate native tongue instruction and support.

The court concluded that the plaintiffs had failed to establish a violation of the EEOC and agreed with prior court decisions that courts should not substitute their educational values and theories for the educational and political decisions properly reserved to local school authorities and the expert knowledge of educators, since courts are ill-equipped to do so. The court applied the three-pronged test established in *Castaneda* v. *Picard* (1981) to determine whether districts have taken appropriate action to overcome language barriers. According to *Castaneda,* the court must determine that the school district has selected a program based on sound educational theory. Next, the court examines whether the district has implemented the theory effectively through its choice of programs and practices. Finally, the court must evaluate whether the district has carefully monitored the program's results and modified it as necessary. The *Teresa P.* court noted that this same, three-pronged test was used in cases in Illinois and Colorado and denied the plaintiffs' claims, finding that the school district had a sound educational program.

A Serious Threat to Bilingual Education

As we have discussed, Title VII's inclusion in the Improving America's Schools Act (1994) indicated the expectations of high standards for limited English-speaking children as part of a broader goal of school reform. Despite its reauthorization, the 104th Congress also considered legislation to repeal the law, to eliminate its funding, and to outlaw most federal government operations in other languages (Crawford, 1997). The English-only or Official English movement has been gaining momentum since the early 1980s. In 1980, only two states had enacted legislation declaring English as the official language of the state; currently, 22 states have enacted such legislation (McMullen & Lynde, 1997). This legislation varies from simply declaring English as the official language of the state to more restrictive provisions that prohibit any state agency or political subdivision from providing any documents, information, literature or other writings in a language other than English (McMullen & Lynde). In 1996, the federal government considered, but did not pass, legislation to declare English as the official language of the government. Recently, the U.S. Supreme Court decided a case challenging the constitutionality of the Arizona "official English" constitutional amendment. Because the plaintiff in the case no longer worked for the State of Arizona, the case was dismissed without the Court reaching the fundamental question regarding "English only." Even though the constitutional challenge was dismissed, in 2000, voters in Arizona passed a legislative referendum to make English the official language of the state.

The No Child Left Behind Act

In January 2002, President George W. Bush signed the No Child Left Behind Act (the NCLB) which had bipartisan Congressional support. The NCLB is touted as the most sweeping reform of the Elementary and Secondary Education Act (ESEA) since it was enacted in 1965. The NCLB redefines the federal role in kindergarten through high school education and is hoped to help close the achievement gap between disadvantaged and minority students and their peers. It is based on four basic principles: stronger accountability for results, increased flexibility and local control, expanded options for parents, and an emphasis on teaching methods that have been proven to work.

Overall, the NCLB is expected to be a broad-based educational reform. As it relates to bilin-

gual education, the NCLB consolidates the 13 current bilingual and immigrant education programs into a state formula program and significantly increases flexibility and accountability. The act is designed to maintain the current focus on assisting school districts in teaching English to limited English proficient students and in helping these students meet the same challenging state standards required of all other students. The new act will focus on helping limited English proficient students learn English through scientifically based teaching methods, although the term is undefined. As part of its accountability provisions, children will be limited to three years of bilingual education and schools will be assessed in the English fluency of its students each year.

The act is not without its critics. Crawford (2002) wrote an obituary for the Bilingual Education Act and its quiet expiration, at age 34, with the passage of the NCLB Act. Ramirez (2001) calls the new act "single-minded" in that limited English proficient students will receive English-only instruction rather than two-way bilingual immersion education programs. Ramirez also notes that by consolidating the funding of different programs for the immigrant, foreign language, and Title VII children into one block grant to address the needs of limited English proficient students, it would profoundly negatively affect all three populations. Krashen (2001) criticizes the three-year time limitation for attaining English fluency, stating that there is no evidence that children languish for excessive periods of time in bilingual education, that English immersion is faster, or that continued instruction in the primary language hurts English development.

While the effect of the new legislation is unknown, it does indicate the trend to erode the statutory protections for bilingual and bicultural education. Borden (2001) argues that zealous advocacy is needed to protect the plight of minorities that have limited English proficiency. In order for them to have a meaningful chance to succeed in society, students need to have a substantially equal education (Borden). To do so, they need the chance to acquire English language skills according to their needs.

BACKGROUND OF DESEGREGATION— INTEGRATION EFFORTS

Whereas non-English-speaking children tend to be unfairly handicapped by their inability to speak structured English, black children bear color as a characteristic that sets them apart from the majority. Desegregation of the public schools in the United States, which has primarily involved this group of pupils, has a long and bitter history. In the United States, education is fundamental to accessing other economic and social opportunities. Public education was perceived by early immigrants as a way to enter the mainstream. In the middle of the nineteenth century, Horace Mann (1848) defined education as the great equalizer—the balance wheel of the social machinery.

Blacks are most often identified as the victims of segregation in the United States. In 1998, however, Latinos comprised a greater percentage of the national school-age population than did African-Americans and this trend is expected to continue (Bowman, 2001). Typically, school segregation and desegregation efforts have been viewed as a black vs. white issue. Bowman argues that the Latino history of educational segregation is often overlooked—desegregation efforts include Latinos as if they have the same history and oppression as blacks, in other words, as if they were blacks.

Before 1954, states could establish policies regarding which public schools students could attend. In *Plessy* v. *Ferguson* (1896), the Supreme Court enunciated the "separate, but equal" doctrine in a case that involved separate transportation systems for blacks and whites. So long as the facilities were equal, there was no violation of constitutional law. Relying on this decision, states argued that if they provided separate but equal educational facilities for blacks, they were fulfilling their constitutional obligations.

Unfortunately, the facilities provided blacks were often of basically inferior quality.

The Challenge: *Brown* v. *Board of Education of Topeka*

Brown v. *Board of Education of Topeka* (1954) was the consolidation of a number of cases that asked the United States Supreme Court to determine the meaning of equality in the public schools. In this landmark decision, the Court recognized that education is perhaps the most important function of state and local governments. Four separate cases had originated in Kansas, South Carolina, Virginia, and Delaware, all of which denied black elementary and high school students admission to public schools attended by white children under laws requiring or permitting segregation by race. In all four cases, evidence was presented to show that black and white schools had been or were being equalized with respect to buildings, curricula, and qualifications and salaries of teachers. In a unanimous decision, the U.S. Supreme Court ruled in *Brown* v. *Board of Education* that by reason of segregation, these individuals (blacks) were being deprived of the equal protection of the laws guaranteed by the Fourteenth Amendment. The Court stated that "in the field of public education, the doctrine of separate but equal has no place. Separate educational facilities are inherently unequal" (*Brown* at 495). Opportunity for an education, where the state has undertaken to provide it, must be made available to all on equal terms. Thus, the Court ruled that state-mandated public school segregation on the basis of race is inherently unequal and therefore unconstitutional.

The ruling was especially notable because it pointed out the negative effects of segregation on public education and, specifically, the detrimental effects of segregation on minority children. Segregation that has the sanction of law usually denotes inferiority of the minority group; a sense of inferiority affects the motivation of a child to learn. To be educated in a separate facility, to be different physically from the majority, and to interact daily with persons who view minority children as not being a part of the mainstream must affect children's self-worth. This momentous decision not only outlawed school segregation but also provided a legal basis for attacking racial segregation in virtually every aspect of society.

Because this decision was expected to have an enormous effect on schools and on the whole of society, the Court did not hand down its implementation decree until a year later. *Brown* v. *Board of Education of Topeka* (1955), popularly known as "Brown II," called for good-faith compliance. In another unanimous opinion, the Court gave local school districts the major responsibility for desegregation. The only relief afforded by the Court was for desegregation of schools to take place "with all deliberate speed."

Implementation of the *Brown* Decision

The lower courts interpreted the phrase "with all deliberate speed" to mean that school boards be allowed time to consider the problems involved in desegregating so that they could develop appropriate plans. Unfortunately, this interpretation only intensified delays. At the time of the *Brown II* decision, southern educators were aware that the location of public schools was an important factor in maintaining segregated school attendance patterns.

Throughout the 1950s, southern cities made considerable investments in new school facilities, and almost every school constructed was located in a racially homogeneous residential area. In some areas where the black population was growing, more schools were added to keep that population isolated rather than allowing the races to mix.

Also, the districting of a state or local area—where both blacks and whites lived—in some cases made it impossible to have totally integrated schools. In the ten years after *Brown,* the southern segregated school system remained largely intact. By 1964, only one out of fifty southern black children attended integrated schools (Orfield, 1996b). The major problem was the outright rejection of any type of school integration policy throughout the South. Many states passed laws to thwart school integration by closing public schools or setting up rigid eligibility requirements for blacks who wanted to attend white schools (Armor, 1995). In Prince Edward County, Virginia, the county board of supervisors did not levy taxes or appropriate funds for desegregated schools, resulting in the exclusion of black children from public schools. Another attempt to circumvent the law was the selective assignment of black students within a school—black children were separated from white students in segregated classrooms so there was segregation within an otherwise desegregated school. Such practices were challenged eventually in court and forbidden.

This manipulation and the delay in achieving integration of public schools led to further court and congressional involvement. In 1969, in *Alexander* v. *Holmes County Board of Education,* the U.S. Supreme Court declared that "all deliberate speed no longer is constitutionally permissible" and "the obligation of every school district is to terminate dual school systems at once and to operate now and henceforth only unitary schools" (*Alexander* at 320).

The Neighborhood School

Another important issue that emerged during the struggle to integrate the public schools was how to desegregate schools in areas where persons of certain economic, racial, and ethnic groups had clustered to form neighborhoods. The neighborhood school can be defined as a school (particularly an elementary school) located in the center of a population cluster that was often the one institution binding together most of the area residents. The courts' response to the legitimacy of neighborhood schools composed of persons of only one race was reluctance. The neighborhood school was generally held to be a product of segregated housing and/or the gerrymandering of school districts (the division of geographical areas and political units to give special advantages to one group). In the case of school desegregation, gerrymandering meant maintaining white schools as "white" and redefining community and district boundaries to maintain black schools as "black."

Busing Students and Racial Balance: A Legal and Political Issue

The fact that blacks and whites were segregated as a result of community living patterns led to the idea of busing children to achieve racial balance. This, in turn, aroused considerable controversy, which escalated following the U.S. Supreme Court decision in *Swann* v. *Charlotte-Mecklenburg Board of Education* (1971)—the first "busing" case.

In the particular school district involved in the *Swann* case, assignment of children to the school nearest their grade would not have resulted in an effective dismantling of the dual educational system. Accordingly, the Court approved the busing order and held that desegregation could not be limited to walk-in schools. In a companion case, *North Carolina Board of Education* v. *Swann* (1971), the Court affirmed an order declaring unconstitutional a North Carolina statute prohibiting racial assignment of students and busing based on racial assignment. The Court held that a ban on racial assignment would deprive school authorities of the one tool absolutely essential to fulfillment of their constitutional obligation to eliminate existing dual school systems. The Court also concluded that the ban on busing was invalid because bus transportation has long been an integral part of all public educational systems. Thus, it was unlikely that an effective remedy could be devised without continued reliance on busing. Further, the Court suggested the use of mathematical ratios as a starting point in devising remedies and the assignment of students according to race to promote integration.

An extremely important part of the *Swann* decision was the Court's distinction between *de jure* and *de facto* segregation, holding that only *de jure* segregation is unconstitutional. *De jure* segregation concerns actions that are officially intended or mandated by law. *De facto* segregation is inadvertent and caused not by actions of the state, but rather by social, economic, or other factors. As we will see, the distinction between these types of segregation is crucial in later cases in which resegregation is at issue.

Before a court mandates desegregation in a school district, the court must make a finding of *de jure* segregation. After the court makes this finding, a federal court will require the school board to propose a plan to desegregate. If the court does not find the district's plan acceptable, it will create and implement its own plan to remedy the segregation. Once the plan is entered by a district court, the school district is bound by the provisions of the plan until the district has achieved unitary status, that is, until it removes the vestiges of state-sanctioned segregation and creates a district that is not segregated by race, or is, in other words, dual (Teitlebaum, 1995).

In 1974, Congress passed the Equal Educational Opportunities Act of 1974 (P.L. 93-380), which declared the policy of the United States to be "that all children enrolled in public schools are entitled to equal educational opportunity without regard to race, color, sex, or national origin and that the neighborhood is the appropriate basis for determining public school assignment." Transportation of students—busing—was considered to be harmful to students as demonstrated by the Congressional findings in the Equal Educational Opportunities Act:

— The maintenance of dual school systems in which students are assigned to schools solely on the basis of race, color, sex, or national origin denies to those students the equal protection of the laws guaranteed by the 14th amendment.
— For the purpose of abolishing dual school systems and eliminating the vestiges thereof, many local educational agencies have been required to

reorganize their school systems, to reassign students, and to engage in the extensive transportation of students.

— The implementation of desegregation plans that require extensive student transportation has, in many cases, required local educational agencies to expend large amounts of funds, thereby depleting their financial resources available for the maintenance or improvement of the quality of educational facilities and instruction provided.

— Transportation of students which creates serious risks to their health and safety, disrupts the educational process carried out with respect to such students, and impinges significantly on their educational opportunity is excessive.

— The risks and harms created by excessive transportation are particularly great for children enrolled in the first six grades.

— The guidelines provided by the courts for fashioning remedies to dismantle dual school systems have been, the Supreme Court of the United States has said, "incomplete and imperfect," and have not established a clear, rational and uniform standard for determining the extent to which a local educational agency is required to reassign and transport its students in order to eliminate the vestiges of a dual school system. (20 U.S.C. § 1702)

Congress set out a priority of remedies for courts to use when a court determined that a denial of equal educational opportunity had taken place and that court-ordered desegregation should occur. These included assigning students to the schools closest to their places of residence that provided the appropriate grade level and type of education for such students; taking into account school capacities and/or natural barriers; permitting students to transfer from a school in which a majority of the students are of their race, color, or national origin to a school in which a minority were; creation or revision of attendance zones or grade structures without requiring transportation; construction of new schools or the closing of inferior schools; and the construction or establishment of magnet schools. Busing of students was just one of many remedies courts could take in fashioning court orders to desegregate school districts.

The Major Question Raised by the Busing Controversy

Central to the issue of whether busing should be used to achieve equal educational opportunity is this question: To what extent are pupils' aspirations and achievements related to the educational backgrounds and performance of other pupils in the same schools? Coleman's 1964 study of the status of school desegregation resulted in a report entitled *Equality of Educational Opportunity,* popularly known as the Coleman Report (Coleman et al., 1966). This report has been the topic of considerable controversy.

Coleman's aim was to investigate the effects of a mandate (desegregation) that suddenly had changed the entire complexion of a school district. His findings were used as a basis for the recommendations of the U.S. Commission on Civil Rights, contained in *Racial Isolation in the Public Schools* (1967), and for paving the way to critical litigation to bring about a desegregation of schools. The main findings of the Coleman Report were that blacks were by far the most segregated group in the United States and that this segregation was extensive not only in the South but in the urban North, Midwest, and West. The report also noted that inadequate educational facilities and resources seemed related to low academic achievement; that schools provided no opportunity at all for most blacks to overcome initial deficiencies; that the quality of teachers showed a strong relationship to pupil achievement; and that black children tended to have less access to the physical facilities that seemed to he related to high academic achievement.

The Coleman Report supported the notion that busing was the only available remedy for dismantling segregated educational systems in large cities. Proponents of busing argued that integrating the nation's schools was crucial to the effort to create an integrated society in which social interaction could overcome racism; thus, educational benefits or losses were incidental to the ongoing attempts to integrate schools. Opponents argued that if children's achievement (particularly reading achievement) was not improved clearly by racial integration, busing should be ended, and there should be a return to neighborhood schools along natural residential boundaries. While the Coleman Report may seem outdated because it was written in the 1960s, these same arguments continue today.

Does School Desegregation Accelerate "White Flight"?

The Court in *Swann* did not address the issue of community opinion and possible flight from the public schools, nor did it consider the possibility that opposition to the Court's policies could undermine their effectiveness and create resegregation between a city and its suburbs or between public and private schools (Armor, 1995).

Coleman's research in the decade following the 1966 study led him to renounce his earlier conclusion that massive busing programs would improve the quality of education (1975). In analyzing the stability of racial and white groups in the largest central-city districts from 1968 to 1973, Coleman found that as cities became more integrated, whites either abandoned these areas for the suburbs or transferred their children to private schools. He concluded that urban school desegregation leads to "white flight," the consequences of which are disastrous for the long-term integration of society because they exacerbate the black city/white suburb racial separation.

According to Armor (1995), for the first five or six years after *Swann,* nearly all desegregation plans emerging from federal courts or federal government actions involved the mandatory reassignment of students through busing to attain a fairly high degree of racial balance. In smaller school districts, racial balance was attained by redrawing school attendance boundaries, some-

times accompanied by carefully chosen school closures. In larger school districts, however, racial balance usually requires cross-district busing of both white and black students, known as *mandatory busing plans.* Armor claims that mandatory busing frequently led to significant white flight, and in some cases to resegregation. He reviewed the research on white flight and the effectiveness of court-ordered remedies for desegregation and concluded that the most important causal link between a desegregation plan and changes in school enrollment are the opinions, attitudes, and behaviors of the parents and students involved. He argues that the relationship between desegregation plans and enrollment trends in schools is determined by the responses to a desegregation program by parents, who must decide whether to support, oppose, participate in, or withdraw from the plan. If community and parental support are lacking, this leads to loss of public support for school funding, loss of white and middle-class students, long-term enrollment instability, and resegregation.

In contrast, Orfield (1996a) argues that the huge changes in the racial composition of American public schools are a consequence of basic changes in birth rates and immigration patterns, rather than a consequence of white flight from the public to private schools. He examined data from the National Center for Education Statistics and the U.S. Census Bureau and found no significant redistribution between public and private school enrollment. Between 1984–1991, public school enrollment increased by 7%, while private school enrollment dropped 9%. This was the reverse of falling public and rising private school enrollment from 1970 until 1984. During this same time period, the number of black students in public schools in the United States increased 3% from 1972 to 1992, which were the first two decades of widespread busing plans. In contrast, Latino enrollments soared 89% and white enrollments fell 14%. Orfield argues that these trends led to incorrect claims that whites were abandoning public education because of resistance to integration. The decline was not the result of whites leaving public schools but, instead, was due to a dramatic drop in the white birth rate. Whites have not abandoned the public schools; in 1992, approximately 90% of the white children attended public elementary and high schools.

A Return to Racial Isolation

During the 1970s, the Supreme Court dealt with a number of complex legal issues involving the definition of desegregation, the nature of remedies, the obligations of school districts, and the remedial powers of the lower court (Armor, 1995). As the South began to dismantle its dual system in the aftermath of the *Swann* decision, there was increased movement to desegregate schools in large northern systems in the face of segregated housing patterns.

Keyes v. *Denver School District No. 1* (1973) was the first United States Supreme Court ruling concerning a case that arose from outside the South, where there was no *de jure* segregation—that is, no state laws requiring segregation. The school district argued that the segregation was *de facto,* because of housing patterns and economic conditions. In *Keyes,* the federal court judge found that the Denver school board used rezoning tactics and constructed schools in racially isolated neighborhoods to intentionally segregate one part of the Denver schools. The Supreme Court ruled that if the school district intentionally segregated one part of its district, the entire district was presumed to be segregated illegally.

Milliken v. *Bradley* (1974) was the first major Supreme Court decision since *Brown* to limit the scope of desegregation remedies (Armor, 1995). In *Milliken,* the lower court had decided that it was impossible to desegregate the Detroit school system without involving the predominately white suburbs around it. The U.S. Supreme Court ruled that cross-district remedies were prohibited unless it could be shown that the discriminatory action by the state or suburban communities created the pattern of all white suburbs and heavily black city schools. Detroit would have to desegregate by mixing its own small

white enrollment with its huge and rapidly growing black enrollment. The ruling in *Milliken* prevented city school districts with large minority populations from drawing students from the heavily white surrounding suburbs to overcome segregation.

During the 1980s, the U.S. Supreme Court did not issue any significant decisions concerning school desegregation. However, the 1990s demonstrated the Court's departure from the desegregation of the *Brown* case and a radical return toward resegregation. Whereas *Milliken* blocked desegregation efforts in the North and Midwest, three significant Supreme Court cases have led to the *de facto* segregation even in the South (Orfield, 1996b).

In *Board of Education* v. *Dowell* (1991), desegregation litigation began in 1961. A desegregation plan was implemented in 1972 and resulted in a substantially integrated school system. Upon finding that the school board had successfully eliminated all vestiges of *de jure* segregation, the district court granted the school board's request for unitary status and ordered the case terminated. Later, the plaintiffs wanted to reopen the case for a new desegregation plan because of demographic changes that had taken place in the school district, but the lower court refused (LaVine, 1995). When the case reached the Supreme Court, the Court stated that judicial supervision ends when the school board complies in good faith with the desegregation decree and vestiges of past discrimination have been eliminated to the extent practicable. A court-supervised district that has never been declared unitary is obligated under the law to avoid actions that create segregated and unequal schools. After a declaration of unitary status, the courts presume any government action creating racially segregated schools to be innocent, unless a plaintiff proves that the school officials intentionally decided to discriminate (Orfield, 1996b).

In *Freeman* v. *Pitts* (1992), the question before the Supreme Court was whether a district court could relinquish its supervision over those aspects of a school system that comply with a desegregation order if other aspects of the system remain in noncompliance. *Freeman* reaffirmed a district court's ability to exercise broad discretion over cases, and listed a number of factors that courts should consider when contemplating a partial withdrawal.

In 1995, the Supreme Court decided the case of *Missouri* v. *Jenkins*. In 1977, Kansas City, Missouri, implemented a desegregation plan that reassigned students within the school district and attempted to effect a minimum of 30% minority enrollment in every Kansas City school. The plan changed school boundary lines, created attendance zones, and transferred minority students from schools with large minority enrollments to schools with low minority enrollments and vice versa. By 1985, the plan had failed because of white flight to private and suburban Kansas City schools. The federal district court ordered a court-imposed remedial desegregation plan that consisted of multiple components that strove to integrate schools and improve student achievement. The focal point of the court's plan involved magnet schools and massive capital improvement programs to attract students from outside the district and from private schools. These remedies provided Kansas City with facilities and opportunities not available anywhere in the country. In 1992, the school district presented the court with its proposed budget for the eighth year of the plan. The State of Missouri objected to the budget and asked for a finding that the school district deserved unitary status (LaVine, 1995).

The Supreme Court began its analysis of the desegregation plan by defining the limits on a district court's power to fashion a desegregation remedy. The nature and scope of a remedy must directly address the relevant constitutional violation. The trial and appellate courts in *Jenkins* had consistently promoted a remedy focused on "desegregative attractiveness" coupled with "suburban comparability," rather than focusing on eliminating desegregation to the extent practicable. The Supreme Court noted that numerous external factors independent of *de jure* segrega-

tion can potentially affect both racial composition of schools and minority students' academic achievement. According to the Court, factors that do not stem from school segregation should not guide judicial remedies; the district court's plan extended beyond constitutional limitations.

The Supreme Court's recent rulings are considered to be a profound step backward in the effort to desegregate the nation's schools (Orfield, 1996b). Since the decision in the *Jenkins* case, courts have used the Supreme Court's holding to sharply curtail broad desegregation remedies. It appears that as long as school districts temporarily maintain some aspects of desegregation for several years and do not express the intention to discriminate, the Court will approve state plans. Rather than upholding the *Brown* decision to eliminate desegregation and the damage that racial segregation causes, these cases demonstrate the Court's goals of minimizing judicial involvement in education and restoring power to local and state governments (Orfield, 1996b).

Conditions for Successful Desegregation

Little data exist regarding the nation's engagement with school desegregation. Heise (1996) provides information on a recent survey that reports that 960 school districts attempted to desegregate between 1968 and 1986. In 1990, the Department of Education's Office of Civil Rights reported that 256 school districts, with a total combined student enrollment exceeding two million, operated under court supervision in school desegregation cases brought by the Justice Department (Heise, 1996). Parker (2000) conducted studies that covered 192 school districts. She concluded that while a large proportion of very large school districts have been released from judicial oversight of their desegregation efforts, a greater number of school desegregation lawsuits continue.

In addition to court-ordered remedies, parents and communities play a large part in desegregation efforts. Certain school districts have attempted to provide racial balance in their schools by using race-conscious measures such as transferring children to other schools in the district and by using magnet schools. In some cases, African-American, Asian-American, and white parents have worked together to challenge these race-conscious student assignment practices as not being in their children's best interest (Parker, 2000). Some parents have challenged the use of these policies after their children were excluded from programs that used quotas or other devices to achieve ethnic and racial balance (Parker). However, sometimes these parental efforts have limited ways in which schools attempt to achieve integrated student bodies.

The primary goal of any desegregation remedy should be the advancement of high-quality education for all students, especially where past segregation obstructed the achievement of such an education (LaVine, 1995). According to Orfield (1996a), national data show that most segregated African-American and Latino schools are dominated by poor children. However, 96% of white schools have middle-class majorities. This extremely strong relationship between racial segregation and concentrated poverty in the nation's schools is a key reason for the educational differences between segregated and integrated schools. Orfield argues that one of the most consistent findings in research on education has been the powerful relationship between concentrated poverty and virtually every measure of school-level academic results. For example, segregated schools that have large numbers of impoverished students tend to have much lower test scores, higher dropout rates, fewer students in demanding classes, less well prepared teachers, and a low percentage of students who will eventually finish college. In Chapter 9, we discuss these and other effects of impoverishment on the school performance of school-aged children.

In a Harvard project on school desegregation, Orfield, Bachmeier, James, and Eide (1997) suggest policies they believe will move the country toward less polarization and more integration. These include:

— resumption of serious enforcement of desegregation by the Justice Department and serious investigation by the Department of Education of the degree to which districts have complied with all Supreme Court requirements;

— creation of a new federal education program to train students, teachers, and administrators in human relations, conflict resolution, and multiethnic education techniques and to help districts devise appropriate plans and curricula for successful multi-racial schools;

— serious federal research on multiracial schools and the comparative success of segregated and desegregated schools;

— a major campaign to increase non-white teachers and administrators through a combination of employment discrimination enforcement and resources for recruitment and education of potential teachers;

— incorporation of successful desegregation into the national educational goals;

— federal and state efforts to expand the use of integrated two-way bilingual programs as a major technique for improving both second language acquisition for both English speakers and other language speakers and successful ethnic relationships.

Is the Country Desegregated?

Unlike studies that show that schools are resegregating, and despite very real evidence that schools remain segregated, the federal government in the No Child Left Behind Act (2002) claims that the United States schools are now desegregated. The NCLB notes that the achievement gap between races has been caused by public education's failure to deliver the promise of quality education to African-Americans, Hispanics, and Native Americans. In the fact sheets put out by the government at its No Child Left Behind Act website, the act is considered to be the solution to the problem. Their simple solution to provide a quality education is to attack the "soft bigotry of low expectations and demand that schools close the achievement gap" for African-Americans, Hispanics and Native Americans. Whether the No Child Left Behind Act can accomplish equality of education for racial minorities remains to be seen.

SEX-ROLE DEVELOPMENT AND EDUCATIONAL OPPORTUNITY

So far in this chapter, we have talked about the attempt to have equitable education for all children in the areas of language acquisition and by the elimination of racial segregation. The plight of women in Afghanistan, including their lack of any rights to receive an education, was among the issues receiving attention after the terroristic attacks of September 2001. Americans were horrified by the treatment that women received at the hands of a governing authority that seemed to value them less than men. In the United States, historically, girls have received a lesser education than have boys, although not nearly as restrictive as girls in some other countries have received. More recently, with an increase in feminism and the passage of legislation, the playing field has been much more equalized, although it may still be argued that girls are not receiving an equal education to boys. The fairness of educational opportunities between the sexes is often referred to as gender equity.

According to the landmark study of the American Association of University Women Education Foundation, sex and gender make a difference in the nation's schools, and the needs of girls are not being met (AAUW, 1992). While research suggests boys are over-represented in special education classes, girls face challenges by not being offered encouragement or gaining equal access to educational opportunities.

According to one report, girls are of equal ability to boys when they enter school but fall behind boys in academic areas such as math and science and suffer greater loss of self-esteem (Gender Equity in America's Schools, 1992). The school as a primary institution has much to contribute to the sex-role development of its students, particularly since interpretations of sex roles drastically change over time. However, the learning of these behaviors occurs long before formal entry into school. At the child's birth, parents assign a gender label and respond differently to the labels "boy" and "girl" in accordance with their own sex-role ideal. In addition, by their own words and actions, parents provide the child with models of sex-typed behavior (beliefs and behaviors defined by one's culture as being appropriate for a given sex). Also, peers as early as three years of age play a role in social learning through modeling expectations and selective reinforcement. Children contribute to their own acculturation. They selectively assimilate in accordance with their own label, and they generally consolidate sex-role identity as part of their self-concept. By the time most children enter school, they are well acculturated but still open to new influences.

Throughout the 1970s, feminists defined gender equity in terms of formal equality (Salomone, 2000). Since girls and boys were identical in intelligence and abilities, any differences in interests must therefore be the result of social conditioning. They fought to make schools gender-neutral. But in the 1980s, some educational theorists began to view sex differences through a new lens. The discussion turned to the different experiences of women and men, which have resulted in different moral and intellectual perspectives about education and gender (Salomone).

THE SYSTEMATIC RELATIONSHIP BETWEEN SEX-ROLE DEVELOPMENT AND EDUCATIONAL PRACTICES

A primary task of the school is to serve the educational needs of both girls and boys without favoring either group. Teachers may have well-defined sex-role expectations and preferences and may communicate them to their pupils. Levitin and Chananie (1972) found that student teachers and first- and second-grade teachers have well-defined sex-role expectations; they defined their preferred student as being orderly, conforming, and dependent. Further, they found that teachers tend to distinguish rather sharply between their preferred student role and their perception of the male sex role.

Sadker and Sadker (1994) reported that boys dominate classroom discussion and were more likely to be praised, corrected, helped, and criticized by teachers, all of which may foster student achievement. Salomone (2002) reports that during the 1990s, the American Association of University Women (AAUW) issued a series of reports on how schools unintentionally shortchanged girls, noting that girls disproportionately lost self-esteem and interest in math and science as they approached adolescence; that women were underrepresented in the school curriculum; that teacher behavior and tests tended to favor boys; that girls lagged seriously behind boys in math and science; that girls experienced widespread sexual harassment in public schools, and that they faced social and institutional challenges as they formed identities and negotiated the middle school environment (Salomone).

In its newest study on gender differences (AAUW, 1998), the AAUW reviewed over 1,000 articles and studies about girls in kindergarten through twelfth grade. While the study confirms that public schools are making progress providing equitable treatment of boys and girls, serious concerns remain. Some of the problems are ongoing, such as academic tracking in which girls are encouraged to take fewer science and math courses than do boys. The study found that while the gap has diminished between the numbers of boys and girls taking math and science classes, boys tend to take more advanced courses and take all three core science courses (biology, chemistry, and physics) by the time they graduate. On the other hand, girls outnumber boys in

subjects like sociology, psychology, foreign languages, and fine arts, and enroll in fewer computer science and computer design classes. The AAUW believes the impact of technology in the schools is significant because computer access may eventually bridge the educational gap between rich and poor students.

Some of the other problems reported in the Gender Gaps study (AAUW, 1998) are of more recent origin. Girls have serious threats to their health and education including being at risk of depression, delinquency, substance abuse, and pregnancy. Girls are more vulnerable than boys because they confront widespread sexual violence and harassment, within the family and within the schools, that interferes with their ability to learn. They also report that while boys repeat grades and drop out of school more often than girls, girls who repeat grades are more likely than boys to drop out of school and that girls who drop out are less likely to return and complete school. The study also reports that Hispanic girls have especially high dropout rates; in 1995, 30% of the Hispanic females over 16 had dropped out of school and had not yet passed a high school equivalency examination. At the same time, dropout rates for Hispanic males and African-American females had declined.

The report (AAUW, 1998) makes more than 20 recommendations for change in the areas of math and science, technology, the classroom, risks, the work force, and future research. Among the recommendations that are important for social workers in the schools are:

— the development of specific programs for Hispanic girls to reduce their dropout rate;
— the development of extracurricular activities that address the socioeconomic and other factors that limit girls participation in these activities;
— the development of programs that reduce students' vulnerability to risks such as violence and teen pregnancy by drawing on their cultural strengths and resources;

— the development, implementation, and enforcement of sexual harassment policies.

Legal Provisions: Sex Discrimination in Public Schools

Educational practices, such as the restriction of girls from woodworking or auto mechanics class and boys' athletics on the basis of sex rather than on the basis of individual capability, have been challenged successfully since 1972. Title IX of the 1972 Education Amendments is a clear statement of federal policy against sex discrimination in areas previously untouched by legislation. This legislation is significant in that it provides support at the national level for abolishing the sexist practices that permeate educational institutions in the United States.

Title IX is the first comprehensive federal law to prohibit sex discrimination in the admission and treatment of students by educational institutions receiving federal assistance. Sex discrimination in the employment policies and practices of educational institutions is also prohibited. The law reads in part:

> No person in the United States shall . . . on the basis of sex be excluded from participation in, be denied the benefits of, or be subjected to discrimination under any education program or activity receiving federal assistance (20 U.S.C.§ 1961(a).

The implementing regulations for the legislation were issued by the Department of Health, Education, and Welfare in June 1975. Their provisions can be grouped into five major sections: (1) general provisions, which outline procedures for ensuring nondiscrimination and compliance with the regulation; (2) coverage provisions, which identify the educational institutions, programs, and activities covered by the regulations; (3) admissions provisions, which prohibit discrimination in the recruitment and admission of students; (4) provisions pertaining to the standards of nondiscrimination in student educational programs; and (5) employment provisions, which establish the requirements for nondiscrimination in employment (U.S. Department of Health, Education, and Welfare, 1975).

Violations of Title IX.   Some rules, regulations, and policies that are violations of Title IX are:

> requiring different courses for males and females; allowing boys but not girls to be crossing guards; sponsoring special school programs for male students only; awarding academic credit to males, but not to females who participate in interscholastic athletics; providing an after-school bus for boys who participate in after-school athletics but making girls walk; and requiring higher grades for admission from girls than from boys (U.S. Department of Health, Education, and Welfare, 1978).

According to Representative Dick Swett, in 1990, 37% of school district administrators had not complied with Title IX, and some saw no need to address the issue of equity between the sexes (Gender Equity in America's Schools, 1992). He recommended that school districts report their compliance with Title IX on a regular basis to the Office of Civil Rights (OCR) in the Department of Education. He also recommended that OCR receive full funding so that it can monitor race and gender discrimination in our nation's schools.

Sex Discrimination and Pregnancy

Title IX also prohibits schools that receive federal funds from discriminating against females who are pregnant teens and teen mothers. While outright exclusion of pregnant students from regular classrooms no longer occurs, pregnant students are likely to face more subtle forms of discrimination (Brake, 1994). This may include coercive counseling to attend separate education programs and the withholding of information about educational options. Moreover, pregnant teens and teen mothers often face a number of other requirements that are not directed against others with medical conditions. These actions include requiring pregnant students to submit a doctor's certificate in order to stay in school and continue to participate in activities; revoking membership in the National Honor Society after the girl becomes pregnant; requiring a medical clearance to return to school after having given birth; requiring a pregnant student to sign a waiver of liability; not providing accommodations that are provided for students with medical conditions, such as unlimited use of the bathroom, access to an elevator, extra time between classes to travel; failing to provide make-up work for a student who misses school to give birth; not giving credit for the work done before leaving school to give birth; and failing to provide home instruction for those who need to stay home for pregnancy-related reasons (Brake).

Adolescent pregnancy and parenting are correlated negatively with educational achievement. The economic and social costs of dropping out of school for pregnant teens and teen mothers include higher rates of poverty and welfare dependence and higher rates of academic failure for the children of unwed teen mothers. Pregnancy is the most common reason for young women to drop out of school (U.S. Department of Education, 1991). The benefits of pregnant teens continuing their education is substantial. Teen mothers who are enrolled in school during pregnancy and immediately after childbirth are more likely to complete high school and delay subsequent pregnancies (Brake, 1994). In order to break the cycle of poverty associated with teen parenthood, young mothers must obtain the educational skills necessary to become financially self-sufficient. Pregnant students have the right to remain in their regular education program and activities throughout their pregnancy, and that right can be limited only in the same manner that other students with medical conditions are prohibited from engaging in such activities. The demands of pregnancy and raising a child, coupled with the demands of being a full-time student, can be extremely difficult. The most subtle forms of discrimination may be enough to preclude pregnant and parenting students from the classroom. School social workers must be aware of the Title IX protections afforded to these students.

Title IX was designed to protect individuals from sex discrimination by denying federal financial assistance to educational institutions that had sexually discriminatory practices. Lawsuits based on Title IX have primarily challenged discriminatory practices in admission policies and athletic programs; the only remedy available to those who successfully challenged the practices would be the denial of federal financial assistance to the offending educational institutions. The very fact that public schools now have women's and girls' sports teams, like soccer or basketball, owes its origins to Title IX legislation and the lawsuits that have successfully challenged certain practices.

Most recently, Title IX challenges have been directed against single-sex schools and classrooms for teaching girls only. The philosophy behind this movement already has been discussed in this chapter. In other words, because the public schools are failing at addressing the special needs of girls, certain programs that contain only one gender in the classroom will better address the self-esteem, sexual harassment, high pregnancy rates and gender inequities in the public classroom. The Supreme Court has addressed this situation with respect to military institutes that only admit men and found the policy unconstitutional (*United States* v. *Virginia,* 1996). However, there have been no single-sex public school challenges that have reached the high court. The No Child Left Behind Act (2002) specifically allows local educational agencies to support same-gender schools and classrooms, if they so choose.

Sexual Harassment

Sexual harassment is considered to be a form of sex discrimination. The Equal Employment Opportunity Commission (EEOC) defines sexual harassment as "unwelcome sexual advances, requests for sexual favors, and other verbal or physical conduct of a sexual nature . . . when (1) submission to or rejection of such conduct by an individual is made either explicitly a term or condition of an individual's employment, (2) submission to or rejection of such conduct by an individual is used as the basis for employment decisions affecting such individual, or (3) such conduct has the purpose or effect of unreasonably interfering with an individual's work performance or creating an intimidating, hostile, or offensive working environment" (29 C.F.R. §1604.11). Although much of the law on sexual harassment derives from the workplace situation under Title VII of the Civil Rights Act of 1964, recent cases have looked at sexual harassment in the school setting as being a form of sex discrimination under Title IX. Since 1992, Title IX has been used in an altogether different manner, serving as a basis to financially compensate victims of sexual harassment in the school setting (Kopels & Dupper, 1999).

In 1992, the U.S. Supreme Court decided the case of *Franklin* v. *Gwinnett Co. Public Schools* (1992). In *Franklin,* a high school student alleged that she had been sexually assaulted and harassed by her teacher. She claimed that not only was the school district aware of the teacher's conduct, but it took no action to stop the harassment and discouraged the student from pressing charges. The student also alleged that the school district dropped its own investigation of the matter when the teacher agreed to resign from school. The student claimed that she had been subjected to sex discrimination and was entitled to monetary recovery under Title IX. The U.S. Supreme Court ruled that Title IX places on the schools the duty not to discriminate on the basis of sex. The Supreme Court drew an analogy to sexual harassment in the workplace, which is covered by Title VII of the Civil Rights Act of 1964. The Court reasoned that when a supervisor sexually harasses a subordinate worker because of the subordinate's sex, then the supervisor is discriminating on the basis of sex. The Court believed that the same rules should apply when a teacher sexually harasses and abuses a student. The Supreme Court ruled that because Congress had enacted Title IX to prohibit sex

discrimination in schools, Congress would not intend to financially support schools that engaged in such discriminatory actions. Therefore, the Court ruled that the student was entitled to recover monetarily under Title IX for the school district's intentional conduct in failing to stop the teachers' known sexual harassment of the student. Because of the ruling in this case, school districts that have knowledge or should have knowledge of their employees' sexual harassment of their students must take action to stop the conduct or they may incur financial liability (Kopels & Dupper, 1999).

While the *Franklin* case concerned teacher-student harassment, lawsuits have been filed against school districts for their failure to stop sexual harassment of students by other students. Sexual harassment between students, also called peer sexual harassment, has been experienced in a large number of instances. A study by the American Association of University Women (1993) found that 85% of girls and 76% of boys experience some form of sexual harassment in schools. The most common form of harassment, reported by 65% of girls and 42% of boys, was being the target of sexual comments, jokes, gestures, or looks. The second most common form of harassment was being touched, pinched, or grabbed in a sexual manner (AAUW, 1993). Another survey reported that for 39% of respondents, sexual harassment occurred on a daily basis; other results indicated that two-thirds of harassing incidents occur with other persons present (Stein, 1993). Peer sexual harassment affects the school performance of a number of victims, especially girls; repeated sexual harassment may lead to high rates of truancy and have a detrimental impact on school achievement (AAUW, 1993). After the *Franklin* decision in 1992, lawsuits were filed throughout the country attempting to obtain monetary compensation for children who were harassed by their peers. By 1996, several of these peer sexual harassment cases had reached the federal appellate level (Kopels & Dupper, 1999).

One of these cases, *Davis v. Monroe County Board of Education* (1996), imposed liability on a school board under Title IX for its knowing failure to respond to peer sexual harassment. A fifth-grade student alleged that another fifth-grade student fondled her breasts and vaginal area; directed offensive, explicit remarks to her; and rubbed against her sexually. After each incident the student told her mother and reported the harassing student to her teachers. Her mother repeatedly called school officials to see what actions could be taken to protect her daughter from these behaviors. The school district never disciplined the offending student. The 11th Circuit Court of Appeals ruled that when an educational institution knowingly fails to take action to remedy a hostile environment caused by one student's sexual harassment of another, the harassed student has been denied the benefits of, or has been subjected to, discrimination under that education program in violation of Title IX (*Davis v. Monroe,* 1996).

In another case, in a factually analogous situation, the 5th Circuit Court of Appeals reached a contrary result. In *Rowinsky v. Bryan Independent School District* (1996), the court disagreed with the analogy to the workplace situation, believing that unwelcome sexual advances of one student to another did not carry the same coercive effect or abuse of power as that made by a teacher, employer, or coworker. In *Rowinsky,* the court ruled that to hold a school district liable for peer sexual harassment, a student must show that the school district responded differently to sexual harassment claims based on the sex of the complainant. If a student could demonstrate that school officials treated claims of sexual harassment of boys more seriously than claims that affect girls, then the school would have impermissibly discriminated under Title IX.

To resolve the differences between the *Davis* and *Rowinsky* cases, as well as other federal appellate cases that had ruled on peer sexual harassment, the United States Supreme Court agreed to hear the appeal of the *Davis* case. In a

5–4 decision, the Court ruled that Title IX could be used to sue school districts for monetary damages for peer sexual harassment. The Court stated that school districts may be held liable only when "they are deliberately indifferent to sexual harassment, of which they have actual knowledge, that is so severe, pervasive, and objectively offensive that it can be said to deprive the victims of the access to the educational opportunities or benefits provided by the schools" (*Davis v. Monroe County Board of Education,* 1999). While the Supreme Court did not define the kinds of behaviors it was limiting, it stated that sexual harassment claims will depend on a variety of factors that include the ages of the harasser and the victim, and the number of individuals involved. The court recognized the need for school officials to have flexibility in how they want to respond to peer sexual harassment. The Court stated that all that is necessary is that school officials respond to known peer harassment in a reasonable manner in light of the known circumstances. Clearly, this standard will invite future lawsuits to delineate its terms.

Courts have begun to respond to cases that relate to peer harassment of students who are harassed because they are not heterosexual. According to the National School Climate Survey (2001), lesbian, gay, bisexual, and transgender (LGBT) students in 48 states and the District of Columbia completed a survey regarding their experiences in high school. Of the respondents, 84% reported hearing homophobic remarks like "faggot" or "dyke"; 23% reported that these kinds of comments came from faculty or school staff; 81.8% stated that even when staff are present when homophobic remarks are made that staff failed to intervene; and that 41.9% of LGBT students reported being shoved, pushed, punched, kicked or subject to other physical assaults.

In a peer sexual harassment case involving a gay high school student, he alleged that from seventh grade when he realized he was gay until he dropped out of school in eleventh grade, he was subjected to ongoing harassment and abuse from other students. He was called names, struck, spat upon, and subjected to a mock rape while 20 students watched and laughed. When he complained to the school principal in charge of discipline, she replied that "boys will be boys" and that, if he were going to be so openly gay, he should expect such behavior. In ninth grade, he was assaulted and urinated on; no actions were taken against the offending students. Instead, the official responses throughout his school career were to ignore his complaints, make false promises of aggressive action, and to tell him that he deserved the treatment because he was gay. Although his sexual harassment claim was based on an alternative legal theory to Title IX, in *Nabozny* v. *Podlesny* (1996), the 7th Circuit Court of Appeals ruled in his favor, believing he was denied the equal protection of the law in his claim of sex and sexual orientation discrimination. The court found it impossible to believe that school personnel would have responded in such a cavalier fashion if a female student had complained about a mock rape; the court ruled that he was entitled to the equivalent level of protection as given to female students. The court also found no justification for the school's allowing one of its students to assault another based on the victim's sexual orientation. The case was settled in the student's favor for $900,000 (Kopels & Dupper, 1999).

Kopels and Dupper (1999) suggest that the use of lawsuits as a primary intervention strategy in peer sexual harassment cases is inadequate, providing a remedy for students only after they have been harmed. They suggest actions that school social workers and other personnel can take to prevent or minimize peer sexual harassment. These include prevention efforts beginning in middle schools, ensuring that school districts have policies that define and prohibit peer sexual harassment, sensitizing school personnel and students to peer sexual harassment, establishing a grievance procedure, and familiarizing themselves with the Office of Civil Rights Title IX guidelines on peer sexual harassment.

EQUAL EDUCATIONAL OPPORTUNITY: SOCIAL WORK VALUES AND PRACTICES

Much needs to be done to secure equal educational opportunities for the groups of children discussed in this chapter. The values of social work are founded on such principles as encouraging persons to develop to their maximum potential and acting as advocate on behalf of groups that are not receiving their fair share of society's wealth, opportunities, and resources. Even though the goal for equal educational opportunity is supported by the values held by the social work profession, the profession's commitment to its achievement and record of accomplishment are not what they should be. In their work to advance equity, it is essential that social workers attempt to influence change in educational institutions as well as in those systems that support them. It is their professional obligation to create new policies, programs, attitudes, and approaches that promote equal educational opportunity.

To bring about these changes, I advocate a broad perspective of the practice—one that allows social workers to intervene in large-scale, complex social systems at several levels (governmental agencies and legislative policymaking bodies at the local, state, and national levels), as well as in small groups and in the social systems within the school and the community.

The larger perspective, which serves as an umbrella for intervention, is ecological. Social work roles that may emerge as workers attempt to promote equal educational opportunity for all groups of pupils are:

1. Consciousness training of teachers via in-service programs that focus on such issues as how they interact with certain groups of pupils, their hidden expectations, selection of nonbiased curriculum material, and enhancement of pupil self-esteem

2. Analyzing the curriculum to remove culturally biased, racist, and homophobic materials; serving on a school or district-wide committee established for that purpose

3. Working with parent groups to enable them to help remove language, race, and sex barriers to equal educational opportunity

4. Interpreting the requirements of laws such as Title IX, and where indicated, acting as advocate for an individual pupil or for groups of pupils

5. Serving as the Title IX grievance officer for a school district

6. Testifying at public hearings on equal educational opportunity

7. Supporting legislation that promotes equal educational opportunity through membership in professional associations and other appropriate groups

8. Providing direct services (casework and/or group work) to children who are experiencing difficulty

9. Developing human relations activities and programs that bring children and the educational staff together for the purpose of promoting amicable relationships and better understanding

10. Working with the administration to establish and implement policies that promote equal educational opportunity

11. Mediating between the school and community when it is appropriate

12. Reducing barriers to students' receipt of equal educational opportunities.

CONCLUSION

Equal educational opportunity is guaranteed by law to every pupil regardless of language, race, or gender. Legislation and court decisions have played a major role in bringing issues of equality of educational opportunity to the forefront. Though the law has had significant impact at several levels, such as providing direction for states and protecting the individual rights of each student, there is still much to be done to achieve equality. The goal of eliminating barriers to equal education has yet to be achieved. Social workers in schools are in a strategic position to identify such barriers and can work to remove them. Inequality in educational opportunity and educational resources reinforces and promotes a caste system, organized on the basis of language, race, and gender. Inequality in education can lead to poverty, underachievement, and impaired intellectual growth.

FOR STUDY AND DISCUSSION

1. Identify several reasons why some educators and parents would be against bilingual programs.

2. Obtain a copy of your state's position on bilingual educational programs. Then discuss the strengths and weaknesses of the document as well as potential roles for social workers in such programs.

3. Identify the roles social workers can potentially play in securing equal educational opportunities for racial/ethnic and bilingual children. Use an ecological perspective in identifying at least three roles for each component.

4. Obtain copies of the most recent state and/or federal legislation regarding bilingual education, desegregation, and Title IX. Analyze it in terms of its implications for education and social work.

REFERENCES

Alexander v. *Holmes County Board of Education,* 396 U.S. 19 (1969).

American Association of University Women (AAUW). (1992). *How schools shortchange girls.* Washington, DC: Author.

American Association of University Women (AAUW). (1993). *Hostile hallways: The AAUW survey on sexual harassment in America's schools.* Washington, DC: Author.

American Association of University Women. (1998). *Gender gaps: Where schools still fail our children.* Washington, DC: Author.

Armor, D. J. (1995). *Forced justice: School desegregation and the law.* New York: Oxford University Press.

Board of Education v. *Dowell,* 498 U.S. 237 (1991).

Borden, G. (2001). Creating an underclass through benign neglect: The plight of minorities with limited English proficiency. *Geo. Journal of Poverty Law & Policy, 8,* 395.

Bowman, K. L. (2001). The new face of school desegregation. *Duke Law Journal, 50,* 1751.

Brake, D. (1994). Legal challenges to the educational barriers facing pregnant and parenting adolescents. *Clearinghouse Review, 28,* 141.

Brown v. *Board of Education of Topeka (I),* 347 U.S. 483 (1954).

Brown v. *Board of Education of Topeka (II),* 349 U.S. 294 (1955).

Castaneda v. *Picard,* 648 F.2d 989 (5th Cir. 1981).

Coleman, J. (1975). Has forced busing failed? James Coleman offers new insights from recent research. *Phi Delta Kappan, 2,* 75–78.

Coleman, J. S., Campbell, E. Q., et al. (1966). *Equality of educational opportunity.* Washington, DC: U.S. Government Printing Office.

Crawford, J. (1997). *Best evidence: Research foundations of the Bilingual Education Act.* Washington, DC: National Center for Bilingual Education.

Crawford, J. (2002). Obituary, the bilingual ed act, 1968–2002. [Electronic version]. *Rethinking schools online.* Retrieved June 1, 2002, from http://www.rethinkingschools.org/Archives/16_04/Bi1164.htm.

Davis v. *Monroe County Board of Education,* 526 U.S. 629 (1999).

Davis v. *Monroe County Board of Education,* 74 F. 3d 1186 (11th Cir. 1996).

Equal Employment Opportunity Commission, 29 C.F. R. § 1604.11 (a) (1992).

Franklin v. *Gwinnett County Public Schools,* 503 U.S. 60 (1992).

Freeman v. *Pitts,* 503 U.S. 467 (1992).

Gender equity in America's schools. 101st Cong., 2d Sess. (1992) (testimony of Dick Swett).

Heise, M. (1996). Assessing the efficacy of school desegregation. *Syracuse Law Review, 46,* 1093.

Hiratsuka, J. (1995, January). Immigration cost, compassion collide. *NASW News,* 5.

Keyes v. *Denver School District No. 1,* 413 U.S. 189 (1973).

Kopels, S., & Dupper, D. R. (1999). Peer sexual harassment in schools. *Child Welfare, 78*(4), 435–460.

Krashen, S. (2001). Bush's bad idea for bilingual ed [Electronic version]. *Rethinking schools online.* Retrieved June 1, 2002, from http://www.rethinkingschools.OrgArchives/l5_04/Bied154.htm.

Lau v. *Nichols,* 414 U.S. 563 (1974).

LaVine, J. A. (1995). The Supreme Court's latest rendition of equality in education: Examining the traditional components of success in *Missouri* v. *Jenkins. Villanova Law Review, 40,* 1395.

Leibowitz, A. (1983). Immigration law and refugee policy. New York: Matthew Bender.

Levitin, T. E., & Chananie, J. D. (1972). Response of female primary school teachers to sex-typed behaviors in male and female children. *Child Development, 43,* 1309–1316.

Lollack, L. (2001). *The foreign-born population in the United States. Population characteristics.* March 2000, Current Population Reports, P20-534. U.S. Census Bureau, Washington, DC: Author.

Mann, H. (1848/1958). Twelfth annual report—Secretary of Massachusetts State Board of Education. In H. S. Commanger (Ed.), *Documents of American history* (6th ed.). New York: Appleton-Century-Crofts.

Martin Luther King, Jr., Elementary School Children v. *Ann Arbor School District Board,* 451 F. Supp. 1324 (E.D. Mich. 1978).

McMullen, L. A., & Lynde, C. R. (1997). The "Official English" movement and the demise of diversity: The elimination of Federal judicial and statutory minority language rights. *Land and Water Law Review, 32,* 789.

Milliken v. *Bradley,* 418 U.S. 717 (1974).

Missouri v. *Jenkins,* 515 U.S.70 (1995).

Moran, R. F. (1988). The politics of discretion: Federal intervention in bilingual education. *California Law Review, 76,* 1249.

Nabozny v. *Podlesny,* 92 F. 3d 446 (7th Cir. 1996).

National School Climate Survey (2001). The GLSEN 2000 National Climate Survey: The school related experiences of our nation's lesbian, gay, bisexual and transgender youth. [Electronic version]. Retrieved June 1, 2002, from http://www.glsen.org/templates/news/record html.

No Child Left Behind Act of 2001, P.L. 107-110, 115 Stat. 1425.

North Carolina Board of Education v. *Swann,* 402 U.S. 43 (1971).

Orfield, C. (1996a). The growth of segregation. In G. Orfield & S. E. Eaton (Eds.), *Dismantling desegregation: The quiet reversal of Brown* v. *Board of Education* (pp. 53–71). New York: The New Press.

Orfield, C. (1996b). Turning back to segregation. In G. Orfield & S. E. Eaton (Eds.), *Dismantling desegregation: The quiet reversal of Brown* v. *Board of Education* (pp. 1–22). New York: The New Press.

Orfield, G., Bachmeier, M. D., James, D. R., & Eide, T. (1997). Deepening segregation in American public schools. [Electronic version]. Harvard Project on School Desegregation. Retrieved June 1, 2002, from http://www.bamn.com/resources/97-deeping-seg.htm.

Parker, W. (2000). The future of school desegregation, *94 N. W U. L. Rev. 1157.*

Personal Responsibility and Work Opportunity Reconciliation Act of 1996. P.L. 104-193, 110 Stat. 2105 (1996).

Plessy v. *Ferguson,* 163 U.S. 537 (1896).

Ramirez, D. (2001). No child left behind: A blueprint for education reform. Testimony given to the United States Commission on Civil Rights. Retrieved June 1, 2002, from http://www.clmer.csulb.edu/ramirez_testimony.html.

Roosevelt, T. (1919). *The foes of our household.* New York: George Doran.

Rowinsky v. *Bryan Independent School Dist.*, 80 F. 3d 1006 (5th Cir. 1996).

Sadker, M., & Sadker, D. (1994). *Failing at fairness: How schools shortchange girls.* New York: C. Scribner's Sons.

Salomone, R. (2000). Education and the Constitution: Shaping each other and the next century: Rich kids, poor kids, and the single-sex education debate. *Akron L. Rev., 34,* 209.

Stein, N. D. (1993). Secrets in public: Sexual harassment in our schools. Wellesley, MA: Wellesley College Center for Research on Women.

Swann v. *Charlotte-Mecklenburg Board of Education*, 402 U.S. 1 (1971).

Teitlebaum, J. (1995). Issues in school desegregation: The dissolution of a well-intended mandate. *Marquette Law Review, 79,* 347.

Teresa P. v. *Berkeley Unified School Dist.* 724 F. Supp. 698 (N.D. Cal. 1989).

United States Bureau of the Census. (1990). *Statistical abstract of the United States.* Washington, DC: U.S. Department of Commerce.

United States Commission on Civil Rights. (1967). *Racial isolation in public schools: A report.* Washington, DC: Author.

United States Department of Education. (1991). *Teenage pregnancy and parenthood issues under Title IX of the Education Amendments of 1972.* Washington, DC: U.S. Government Printing Office.

United States Department of Health, Education, and Welfare. (1975). *Title IX of the Education Act of 1972: A summary of the implementing regulation.* Washington, DC: U.S. Government Printing Office.

United States Department of Health, Education, and Welfare. (1978). *Taking sexism out of education: A national project on women in education.* Washington, DC: U.S. Government Printing Office.

United States v. *Virginia*, 518 U.S. 515 (1996).

Wexler, L. S. (1996). Official English, nationalism and linguistic terror: A French lesson. *Washington Law Review, 71,* 285.

CHAPTER 11

THE DESIGN OF SOCIAL WORK SERVICES

MARY BETH HARRIS, NEW MEXICO HIGHLANDS UNIVERSITY
CYNTHIA FRANKLIN, THE UNIVERSITY OF TEXAS AT AUSTIN

INTRODUCTION

For the past two decades, education reform and an increasing emphasis on educational achievement have produced an expansion of social and mental health services in schools. Now mandated to develop systems that address barriers to learning for all students, not only those in special education (Flaherty, Weist, & Warner, 1996), schools are relying more on social workers. Currently, social workers provide services in 45% of the public schools across the country (Brener, Martindale, & Weist, 2001). Chapter 12 provides a more detailed analysis of these trends.

Although social work plays an essential role in public school education, important differences between the two professions in a context of growing sociopolitical complexities remain as challenges for social workers in schools. How well the school and the social worker are able to find a fit between their diversity of professional values, outcome goals, and sociopolitical positions determines the quality of benefits received by students and their families (Osborne & Collison, 1998). This chapter explores organizational and community contexts, professional priorities and needs, and political considerations important for social workers in planning and carrying out their function in schools. The chapter provides guidance for assessing one's own fit for school social work, the school as a practice environment, student and family contexts, and school/community resources and needs.

CONTEXTS FOR PLANNING IN SCHOOL PRACTICE

Sociopolitical and Multicultural Context

Public schools are responsible for educating an increasingly diverse and troubled student population. Important social phenomena over the past few decades have contributed to diversity as well as a wider spectrum of social issues and needs. Today's school social worker must be prepared to work in a multicultural context and to be competent with people from widely diverse cultural and economic backgrounds.

Dimensions of race and culture are shifting among school populations. An important cultural shift resulting from a new surge of immigration beginning in the 1970s from South and Central America, Cuba, the Middle East, Vietnam, and other Asian countries (Rosenberg, 1991), has brought challenges of language and acculturation to urban schools. Language and cultural barriers are cited as the main obstacles when children of minority cultures do not achieve in school. Wright, Taylor, and Ruggiero (cited in Franklin & Soto, 2002) studied the problems encountered when the cultures of the student and of the system vary. They found that minority language offered the most robust explanation for why students could not obtain the information needed to do well in school. This is vital information for public education when it is predicted that nearly one in four school-aged children will be of Hispanic origin by 2030 (Archer, 1996). According to the National Center for Education Statistics (1999), Hispanic youths are the most at-risk group for dropout. While the dropout rate is 7.3% for white youth and 12.6% for African-American youth, the rate for Hispanic youth is 28.6%. For those Hispanic youth born outside the United States it is an astounding 44.2%.

Advocacy roles may become more important as schools struggle to equalize education for all children. Franklin and Soto (2002) cite an example of how a teacher got involved in advocating for a group of Hispanic youths who were not allowed to participate in advanced math classes due to their language proficiency:

Ms. Mellor, a middle-aged Pennsylvania Quaker, relocated to a farmworker town in the central valley of California. She taught advanced math. She was amazed to find that in a school of 51% Latino students, her advanced math class was entirely white, like her. She asked the administration why there were no Hispanic students in her class and was told that they didn't speak English well enough to take her class. The Latino students explained to her that they were not allowed to enroll in honors English class, either, because Latinos were not college-bound. One student explained that, "as a Mexican you're supposed to be humble."

Mellor refused to accept the situation. She plucked promising Latino children from her other classes and installed them with the other advanced students. She pushed the students to work hard and told them they could succeed (p. 5).

In this example, the teacher's efforts resulted in academic and career success for numerous students. School social workers need to be prepared to adopt advocacy roles and to work with educators such as Mellor to assure that cultural competencies are a part of every school program.

The rise in poverty for women and children since the early 1980s has consistently placed 20% to 25% of the country's children under age 18 in poverty (Annie E. Casey Foundation, 1997), giving the United States the highest poverty rate for children of all industrialized countries (Jozefowicz-Simbeni & Allen-Meares, 2002). High-poverty schools and their neighborhoods must be linked with resources and interventions aimed at building school and community resources if schools are going to be successful with poor children (Jozefowicz-Simbeni & Allen-Meares).

A profusion of social and health issues face children and youth of all races and cultures. Every year one in five children and adolescents experiences the signs and symptoms of a DSM-IV disorder (Mental health: A report of the Surgeon General, Chapter 3, 1999). In the past decade the juvenile arrest rate for violent crimes such as homicide, rape, and aggravated assault has continued to rise. Suicide is the third leading cause of death for adolescents, and AIDS is the sixth leading cause of death among youth ages 15 to 24 (Natasi, 1998).

A dramatic withdrawal of economic and social resources from urban and rural communities over the past few decades has changed the context of community for families and the school. Disengagement from the urban neighborhood out of fear has become a norm (Bowen & Van Dorn, 2002; Taylor, Zuckerman, Harik, & Groves, 1994). Violent crime and juvenile access to guns has increased in both urban and rural communities to the point that witnessing violence, identified as *covictimization*, is now associated with a sense of hopelessness and a vendetta mentality in children and youth (Fick & Thomas, 1995; Garbarino, 1993; Sparks, 1994).

These problems all point to more students entering school with basic physical, social, and emotional needs that must be met if they are to be able to learn. The scope of problems demands social and mental health services ranging from prevention to treatment. They stretch public education resources in a time when other interests are competing for Federal dollars in a struggling economy and a conservative political environment. It is obvious that school social workers cannot meet every need and offer all the important services. School social workers must be prepared to work with many other professionals, paraprofessionals, and parents in interdisciplinary teams in order to best serve the needs of schools and their students.

Preparing Oneself

Not every social worker will find school social work satisfying. Taking stock of our interests and fit with school practice is important in making an informed and conscious choice about entering this field. Exploring issues such as our childhood school experiences, cultural and racial sensitivities, and abilities for working in a multidisciplinary milieu very different from social work in many respects is helpful for any social worker considering a career in school social work.

Assessing Transference and Countertransference Issues.
An awareness of unresolved personal issues from years as a student is important when we reenter the school environment as a professional. Looking at past experiences for feelings and attitudes that may be triggered easily in the present can help us to perceive the teachers and administrators with whom we will work in a clearer, more current light. For example, what did you like about school? What was painful or frightening? What feelings arise when you remember these things?

The following example illustrates these issues:

> "I had waited all week to discuss my concerns about a particular student with this teacher. She was a veteran educator at the school and was already teaching when I was born. She was friendly and warm when I entered her classroom for our appointment, but when I sat down in a student desk facing her behind her own desk I felt like a high-school kid again. It was hard for me to pull

myself out of that and confer with her as a colleague."

Assessing Issues of Culture, Ethnicity, and Race.
From our training as social workers, we are fundamentally aware of cultural diversity and the importance of accepting differences. Yet this does not ensure that we are free of biases regarding people not of our own race and culture. Nor does it guarantee the knowledge and competence to be effective with culturally diverse children and families. Assessing our fitness and practice competence for the cultural, ethnic, and racial diversity in school social work requires that we examine at least three areas:

— Our values and beliefs from our own cultural and racial context
— Our attitudes and expectations about persons from other cultures and races
— Our knowledge and practice competence with other cultures and races

Examining our own values and beliefs involves a close look at the cultural and racial context in which they are embedded. Are our life experiences laced with racial or cultural discrimination and alienation, or with power and privilege? When do we find ourselves judging, patronizing, or resenting the lifestyles, beliefs, and values of people racially and culturally different from ourselves? These are difficult questions, essential for us in developing the self-awareness and insight that we need for working in a diverse school environment.

No social worker can claim to be aware of all nuances of cultures that differ from their own. Even so, it is important to gain knowledge and familiarity with culturally based values, world views, and systems of students and families in the local school and community. As social workers, we develop our practice positions using knowledge and beliefs about particular characteristics of clients and their problems as well as the environments in which they live. In building our perspectives for working with culturally diverse children and families, we draw on specific cultural knowledge and familiarity as well as our own values and beliefs. Without cultural knowledge, using only generic social work and personal values and beliefs, our perspectives can become value-based and biased (Caple, Salcido, & di Cecco, 1995).

The following case vignette illustrates this practice principle:

> Eileen had been a school social worker on the East Coast for six years when she moved to a southwestern city on the Mexican border. She began working in the teen parent program of a local school district, where she provided services to students and their families. Eileen became discouraged after several home visits with Mexican American families, where she felt her time in the home was more social than problem-solving. She perceived the families as interested in small talk and refreshments rather than in dealing with the issues at hand. These behaviors were puzzling to Eileen, who saw them as time-consuming and a form of resistance. Eileen's supervisor, herself a Mexican American social worker, explained to Eileen that she was being received into these homes with great respect, indicated by the families treating her as a potential friend rather than strictly as a professional. Allowing time for customary social rituals and for families to become familiar with her on a more personal level was a culturally linked key to establishing the relationships that Eileen and the families needed for their work together.

Assessing Professional Values and Ethics.

The school is a host setting where education values, above social work values, are the norm. As "owner" of its mental health and social services, the school district endorses services which support its priorities and policy mandates and may restrict services which appear to conflict with its policy position. For example, in an article describing six school-based teen pregnancy programs, Moraga (1997) stated that four of the schools allowed students to attend parenting classes during regular class periods, while only one school allowed students to receive more con-

troversial family planning services during regular class hours.

Differences between social work and education priorities can present ethical dilemmas related to client rights and service needs. The size of client load and constraints on time, frequency, and facilities for program interventions, for example, can affect quality of service. In order to deal effectively with such priority conflicts, social workers must have clear personal understanding of social work values and perspectives as well as the ways in which social work and education are different and alike in their priorities.

The philosophy of intervention is a major difference between education and social work that affects the climate of school social work. Schools relate to children and adolescents as students, while social workers see them as client consumers. In the hierarchy of school organization, student stakeholders have the least power and participation of anyone in determining their own outcomes. As social work client consumers, the same children and adolescents have more input into their own intervention and significant options in decision-making and responses.

In the education culture, the "student at risk" model, generally seen as a deficits model by education and other social sciences (e.g., Frymier & Gansneder, 1989), has been dominant in explaining school failure (Richardson, Casanova, Placier, & Guilfoile, 1989; Ronda & Valencia, 1994). The model assumes that poor school performance is rooted in students' personal cognitive and motivational deficits and in pathologies in their social environments. With these assumptions, it contains descriptive, explanatory, and predictive elements that have shaped educational policy and practice. This model is contrary to the strengths perspective used by social workers, which posits that the strengths and resources of people and their environment, rather than their problems and pathologies, should be the central focus of the helping process (Saleeby, 1997). Unlike the at-risk model, the strengths perspective places the client in the role of partner with the worker to achieve desired goals. Partnering with students and families as social services clients in an environment where the dominant theory and philosophy minimizes their personal and environmental/cultural strengths requires clear vision and strong skills.

Assessing Professional Competency. The breadth of knowledge and skills needed to work effectively in schools is more than any one individual may possess. While social work education provides a sound conceptual foundation for practice, the increase in problems such as school violence, substance abuse, homelessness, child abuse, and school dropout, makes it important for school social workers to be current in these specific areas. An important professional task is to acquire expertise in one or more of these areas through professional reading and specialized training.

It is beneficial to examine our skills and interests periodically in light of these expectations and issues confronting school social workers. This allows us an ongoing awareness of whether this field of practice continues to be a good match for our professional growth and satisfaction.

The School Organization

A school is a complex organizational structure with multiple processes and entities. Arum (2000; cited in Bowen & Richman, 2002) discusses a neoinstitutional perspective of school-community relationships. From this viewpoint both schools and communities are "situated in larger, nonlocal, institutional contexts" known as organizational fields (p. 68). These organizational fields influence school policy and practice through policies at the state and national levels and mechanisms for financing programs. Some organizational fields that influence schools are federal and state welfare policy, health and social services programs, the court system, education agencies, and state boards (Bowen & Richman).

Organizational skills are as important to social workers as clinical practice skills. Most school organizational structures are hierarchical in nature, and learning how the social worker fits into the organizational hierarchy is important. To be accepted and accommodated, the social worker must gain some understanding of the school's organizational culture and neoinstitutional context, and assume a role protocol that supports organizational norms (Austin, 1999).

Needs and Sociopolitical Demands of Multiple Stakeholders. Unlike many social work arenas, the education system is continually at the center of public attention, reflected by political, religious, and media activity. In addition to constituency groups within the institution, community and societal stakeholders with diverse agendas continually interact with public education, looking to influence policy and programs according to their own priorities.

Perhaps the most obvious reflection of the public's investment in education is the school board, an elected body from the community. As such, the school board is expected to reflect the general values and concerns of the community in the policies and function that drive school programs and operations. In some communities this may mean that the school board takes a leadership role in expanding services and responses to diverse student needs. For others it can mean that the board upholds traditional values in the schools. It is useful for school social workers to understand the political climate of the community as well as demographics such as age, cultural identity, and professional background of board members.

As a constituency group, parents may be perceived as a consumer group with an important voice in the discourse about school programs and priorities. On the other hand, parents, especially those outside the mainstream culture, may be an underrepresented constituency group whose value to student learning and well-being is under-utilized. As discussed in Chapter 6, parents have rights under the Family Educational Rights and Privacy Act of 1974, as well as a history of successful court cases regarding their children's education. However, parents receive varying degrees of sanction across the country regarding safety and quality of education for their children (e.g., Parents' rights as defined in Chapter 864, Statutes of 1998, Education Code, 1998).

Some community groups not involved directly with the school have an influence on program and policy. Among the most visible are religious groups versus community health constituencies, both concerned with issues like sex education and abortion (Kelley, 1996). Although these and other groups may not have direct connections to the schools, their issues often stir the interest of the media, which can have important consequences for social services.

The stakeholder importance of school staff and school administrators must not be underestimated. It is discussed at length in a later section.

Administrative Style. As an organization every school has its own personality, the climate dominated by the administrative style of the school principal. The *open system* principal is one who is more responsive to external and internal pressures and more readily responds and adapts to these pressures by making adjustments to the organization of the system (Moriarty & McDonald, 1991). The *closed system* administrator places value on formalization, centralization of power, and a clearly defined hierarchy of authority (Center for Study of Social Policy, 1993). The *laissez faire* style is characterized by largely passive leadership, resulting in lack of coordination of both goals and performance duties. (See Table 11.1, Analysis of School Dynamics and Political Environment.)

Political Dimensions in the Organization. Knowledge of political dimensions is implicit in understanding school organizational culture. For example, school social workers need to understand who has formal and informal power within a school and how they use their power. Following the principle that influencing the right people

is the key to achieving results, social workers can learn who the key players are through knowing who influences school policy (Streeter & Franklin, 1993). They should also determine who may help or hinder work with officials, teachers, students, or families (Pawlak & Cousins, 1999). This knowledge of formal and informal power allows school social workers to understand why certain people have a lot more influence than others in the local school or school district, and learn how to use informal power. School social workers must be able to "sell" themselves and their services in a setting that may not know or appreciate social work practice, which requires that they be visible, accountable, and perceived by the organization as effective and supportive of school agendas.

Obtaining Sanction for Social Work Services. A number of state and national bodies provide legitimacy and sanction for school social work services. Awareness of social work's contribution to schools is reinforced through the efforts of the National Alliance of Pupil Services Organizations (NAPSO), the National Association of Social Workers (NASW), the School Social Work Association of America (SSWA), and state school social work associations. Mental health services including social work are written into federal education programs such as Head Start and federal laws such as the Americans with Disabilities Act of 1990 and Goals 2000: Educate America Act (P.L. 103-227, 1994). Additionally, a number of states have regulations that mandate school social work service.

At the local school level, decisions for selecting personnel are based on accountability and effectiveness that is closely tied to performance objectives (Streeter & Franklin, 1993). Without hard data to support the effectiveness of social services, administrators and school board members do not always make a direct association between school effectiveness and social work services. Data that substantiates the volume and results of social work services should be re-

TABLE 11.1   Analysis of School Dynamics and Political Environment

1. What kind of leadership exists in the school, both formal and informal? Who are the key leaders? Is the leadership widely recognized and accepted? How does school decision-making take place? What opportunities exist for the development of leadership among staff?

2. What values are typical of the school staff? The administrator? Are values congruent or dissonant between staff and student body?

3. What is the school climate?
    a. Degree of warmth? Is there a friendly atmosphere?
    b. Do rules and regulations provide comfortable boundaries?
    c. What is the reward system? Is there respect and recognition of professional ability of staff and fairness in evaluation? Are students reinforced for competent behavior?
    d. Risk? Is the school open to change or afraid to risk new ideas and programs?
    e. Responsibility? What degree of freedom is available to work without continually checking with the administrator?
    f. Support? What is the perceived degree of helpfulness from others in the school? Are students and staff exposed to enough diversity in roles and relationships?
    g. Standards? What is the perceived level of required performance standards?
    h. Identity? What is the perceived degree of belonging or pride in being a member of the faculty at this school?
    i. To what degree are individual differences of students and staff in relation to gender, handicaps, race, ethnic orientation, abilities respected?
    j. Conflict? Identify nature of conflicts and means used to resolve them. Safety? To what degree do students and faculty feel physically safe?
    k. Are school discipline policies and practices overly punitive? Are students of color disproportionately suspended and expelled in the school?

4. What are the external pressures which affect relationships within the school?

5. What are the significant types of groupings or social categories that characterize the school staff? The student body? What are the special problems or orientations of these groupings? Race, ethnic orientation, gender, career orientation?

6. What is the nature of school support services and personnel in the school? How effective are they? What are the gaps in services?

7. What is the level of participation by faculty in school affairs?

8. What are the key power influences in the school?

9. What forces in the school make for cooperation or conflict among, or insulation of, groups?

Source: Based on material prepared by Betty Deshler, Associate Professor, Western Michigan University, Kalamazoo, Michigan, 1983. Revised 1998.

ported regularly to administrators and other stakeholders in the local school, school district, and community.

Developing a Relationship of Trust with School Personnel.   Good interpersonal skills as well as awareness and respect for the concerns and priorities of other staff are essential to developing relationships with other school personnel. An understanding of potential barriers to good relationships is important. Some relationship barriers are as unique as the local school culture and personalities involved, while others are universal. Four potentially conflictual issues that appear common between social work services and other school personnel are job security, overlap in jobs and roles, competition for resources, and work overload.

Programs and services staffed by social workers are being established with greater frequency. In a random sampling of public schools in a western state, for example, 80% of the schools reported the presence of one to five social service providers at the school site (Melaville & Blank, 1991). With this growing trend, school counselors, for example, voice concerns about being replaced by social workers and are plagued with a sense of competition for limited resources (Osborne & Collison, 1998).

Related to social work services, teachers may be concerned about workloads associated with record-keeping and additional responsibilities consequent to social and health services programs (Kelly, 1998). Since teachers have more contact with students than other staff and control a large part of students' daily schedules, their support for social work activities is vital. As well, the relationship between teachers and students impacts students' academic performance and behavior profoundly. It has been shown that a teacher's expectations about a child's academic ability influence the teacher's behavior toward that child, and that a teacher is more effective with students they believe are able academically (Rosenthal, 1987). Some studies have found that teachers often have lower expectations for the academic performance of poor and minority children, and this lower expectations of student performance can be a self-fulfilling prophecy (Aguilar, 1995).

The following is an example of the importance of teacher support for school-based services:

Ellie was six months pregnant and a sophomore in high school. At the beginning of the semester, Ellie was invited by the school social worker to participate in a weekly lunch-time group for pregnant and parenting young women in her school. The social worker told Ellie that the group would help her with skills to pass in school and be able to graduate. Lately she had missed several days of school for medical and social service appointments and was falling behind. Although a memo had circulated asking teachers to excuse group participants for the first minutes of their class after group, Ellie's teacher stopped the class after her first group meeting to ask why she was late. When she told him she had been in a group, he replied that she needed to be in class more than in some group. When the teacher responded similarly after the second group session, Ellie told the social worker that she was going to drop out of the group. She feared failing the class due to her teacher's irritation with her being late each week. When the social worker spoke personally with Ellie's teacher about the value of the group for Ellie, the teacher reluctantly agreed to allow Ellie's participation without penalty. Near the end of the group two months later, the teacher sent a note with Ellie to the social worker saying, "Ellie's performance in my class has improved tremendously this semester in carrying out assignments from her group. Give us more like this!"

Involving and informing teachers and other staff in the planning phase of social services diminishes conflicts of priorities and enhances the possibility of much-needed support. Conferring with other staff personally shows respect for their priorities and reduces the possibility of misunderstandings and oversights. A relationship of trust can develop when the social worker demonstrates competence and a willingness to be an active team player in addressing the concerns of the school.

Interprofessional Practice.   In planning for school social work services, we must recognize the inevitability of the interprofessional team as well as the power of a collective voice advocating for the needs of children and youth. A collaborative system that evolved from the 1970s multidisciplinary approach in the health field, the interprofessional team "involves the interaction of various disciplines around an agreed-upon goal to be achieved only through a complex integration or synthesis of various disciplinary perspectives" (Schmitt, 1982, p. 183, cited in Casto et al., 1994, p. 36). Interprofessional practice in the schools is a collaboration expanded beyond traditional "teaching," to recognize and address issues that affect the student's whole ecology. In this context, the school social worker is required not only to collaborate on services with other professionals, but to understand the perspectives and priorities of other professions in negotiating common goals and objectives for the school.

Streeter and Franklin (2002) suggest that school social workers adopt transdisciplinary team models to enhance their work with diverse professionals. Transdisciplinary team models are consistent with the philosophy guiding interprofessional practice described above. Professionals commit to teaching-learning-working with other service providers across traditional disciplinary boundaries. As a team comprised of different professional disciplines, transdisciplinary teams seek to expand the common core of knowledge and competency of each team member systematically through a focused attempt to pool and exchange information, knowledge, and skills across disciplines. This type of boundary spanning requires a number of strategies including planned individual study, one-to-one instruction among team members, and a planned and systematic team teaching-learning process.

A System of Integrated Services.

Osborne and Collison (1998) offer a team model from the perspective of the school counselor. This model, as well as others (e.g., Casto et al., 1994), recognizes that although most human service professionals are prepared in academic programs that emphasize separateness rather than collaboration, the concepts and assumptions in consultation theory and group theory contain the needed framework for developing collaborative work relationships across professional boundaries.

Osborne and Collison (1998) present five processes in the model: (1) a school counselor convenes the group, the rationale being that the counselor is the person specifically prepared and licensed to work in the schools; (2) the group articulates its reason for working cooperatively in serving its mutual clients more effectively; (3) the group begins by providing a goal and rationale statement to the school administrator containing recommendations for organizational structure and operational procedures that lead to client services; (4) the group identifies shared goals and makes those goals public throughout the school; and (5) leadership is on a rotating basis, and the group identifies the strengths and contributions that each individual or agency brings to the team.

Although parts of this model reflect issues of ownership of the program by traditional school personnel, it shows respect for the diversity of strengths and perspectives represented by different disciplines. It also gives social workers an integrated networking system for interpreting program priorities and values with other school staff. The possible barriers to effective working relationships discussed earlier would have a considerable chance for resolution within this sanctioned collaborative structure.

An Ecosystems Model.

A frame for interprofessional collaboration developed by Brandis and Philliber (1998), though similar to the system of integrated services model, recommends a broader system which involves service professionals in the school as well as those who provide services for students and their families in the community outside the school. The ecosystems approach upon which this model relies heavily, advocates for enlarging the system of community resources and investment in the initial planning phase as well as in ongoing collaboration.

The roles of professionals and organizations in the community, since they are not involved directly in school-based services, are to serve as mediators and contributors to a broader perspective and program concept without the motivation of self-gain. Although it may be optimistic to expect that programs and agencies not involved directly in school programs would make such a commitment, it may be worth the effort to recruit those who would agree to participate.

Community Context

The school social worker has clear and compelling reasons for maintaining good working relationships in the community. The simple truth is that the school cannot do all that needs to be done for the community's youth. This is a job that the community must be equipped and willing to share. The community must be informed continually and developed, since the spirit of willingness may not come easily, especially in this time of fewer resources and competing political priorities. Prevention education programs and active community coalitions concerned with specific problems confronting children and youth can be powerful sources of change and support for children and adolescents in the school.

When problems and distressed students are identified, the school social worker can take the lead in getting the needed services. Accessing resources for students and families in distress is often complex and requires sophisticated knowledge of community systems. The continual change in eligibility requirements and alliances among service systems can make this process like detective work, time-consuming and tedious. "Any commitment to vulnerable children places the school in the difficult and unwanted position of having to interact with community agencies in complex planning efforts" (Kordesk & Constable, 1999). The role of learning and engaging with community service systems on behalf of students or their families is most often filled by the school social worker.

"Wrap-around" services, the result of recent community collaboration trends and managed care, may be of considerable benefit for getting services for children who need them. "Wrap-around services emphasize the development of comprehensive, interagency community based systems of care in which professionals and parents work together collaboratively to serve children. . ." (Duchnowski, Kutash, & Friedman, 2002, p. 21).

Essential elements of the wrap-around process include community-based services, team leadership involving natural supports, child agencies, and families working together to develop and implement individual service plans. Services are strengths based and promote the continuance of children in a community setting as contrasted to being sent to a residential or more institutional setting. Wrap-around has flexible ways of operating, including using monies to buy needed services. It uses both formal and informal support systems, implementing all plans through a collaborative process. Established outcomes track services to assure effectiveness (Burchard, Bruns, & Burchard, 2002).

In communities where wrap-around services exist, it is important for school social workers to establish the school as a team member of the wrap-around process. Being a part of the wrap-around services will assure quicker and better services for children in need.

Assessing Sociopolitical Dynamics of School and Community. The need for effective collaboration and integration of school with other community resources has clearly intensified in response to the increasing number of children and youth vulnerable to school failure and future employment limitations. Since collaboration is a planned process that creates opportunities for people to work together, gaining knowledge of the demographics and sociopolitical dynamics of the community is valuable.

Demographic data about the community can be obtained readily from sources such as census tracts, city and county records, and national data. Meaningful knowledge of the culture and dynamics of the community is gained through interactions and observations over time. One way that social workers enhance their familiarity with the sociopolitical dynamics of the community is by attending city council and school board meetings and tracking members' positions and activities. Another way is by participating in community organizations where they become familiar with community needs, conflicts, and alliances. Table 11.2 gives questions that are helpful in assessing community dynamics.

TABLE 11.2   Analysis of Community Dynamics

A. What are some significant types of groupings or social categories in the community (religious, political, nationality, racial, economic, social class)? What are the special problems or community orientations of these groupings?

B. What are the key institutions in the community—those with the greatest power, influence, or social utility (schools, churches, hospitals, banks, libraries, welfare agencies)?

C. What is the status of human service agencies and personnel in the community? What are the gaps in services, and how effective are these agencies?

D. Does there seem to be a relatively high level of participation by citizens in community life? Or passivity? Or apathy?

E. Is there an operating power structure in the community? Of what groups or individuals is it comprised? What is significant about it?

F. What kind of leadership exists in the community? Who are the key leaders? Who are the unofficial leaders? Is the leadership widely recognized and accepted? How does community decision-making take place?

G. What means of communication exist in the community—formal and informal, written and oral, ongoing and ad hoc, sub rosa)?

H. What forces in the community make for cooperation or conflict among, or insulation of, groups?

I. What values are typical of this community?

J. What are the major social problems or issues in the community? What are the positions of various groups and individuals on them? Are community feelings about these issues strong or subdued? Which groups seem to be central to resolving each issue? To intensifying it? Does conflict serve a particular social function in the community?

K. What are some major external or environmental forces acting on this community that affect interrelationships and general community development?

L. From a community-welfare standpoint, what are the forces for change, resistant forces, and interference forces?

M. What is the nature of community commitment/support for education?

Source: Based on material prepared by Betty Deshler, Associate Professor, Western Michigan University, Kalamazoo, Michigan, 1983. Revised 1998.

These are some good sources of data for such an assessment:

— Interviews or conversations with people in the community about needs and problems, which should include a diversity of citizens ranging from children to the elderly, varied professionals and business owners, and service providers;

— Current census records provide demographic data, such as education level, races and cultures, income, and other useful facts about the population;

— The chamber of commerce has information about social and health resources such as clinics, hospitals, and mental health services, churches and synagogues, social service agencies, recre-ational facilities and services, and civic organizations;

— The chamber of commerce or the United Way have information about foundations and other public or private funds designated for use in the community.

Family and Parents Context

Socioeconomic Family Trends.   Family trends indicate that children entering school today come from diverse family compositions, including intact, single parent, blended families, cohabitating families, and gay and lesbian families. There is also a family trend toward grandparents raising their grandchildren. The American Association of Retired Persons (AARP) (AARP Webplace, 1999, cited by Franklin, 1999, p. 132) reports, for example, that "6% of U.S. children under the age of 18 (3.9 million) live in grandparent-headed households."

Poverty and economic and social stresses impact the quality of family life for many children. Poverty, for example, impedes the availability of family resources to support academic achievement of children. Families without adequate financial resources often lack food, appropriate housing, health care, and stimulating in-home materials to promote the cognitive and developmental growth of children (Jozefowicz-Simbeni & Allen-Meares, 2002). Gay and lesbian families face many social stresses including stigma, homophobia, and out-right discrimination (Elia, 1993).

Working with Parents and the School. Parents are the experts on their children, and family resources and needs are of crucial consideration in the child's school achievement. The need is clear for families and schools to work in partnership around their children, although too often this is not the case. As Constable and Walberg (1999) discuss:

> The family and school, two critical institutions in the ecology of childhood, have long maintained a studied disregard for each other, paying cautious inattention to the extent of their real interdependence. Such cautious and strategic inattention works well when the family and school are in implicit agreement, when the pupil is succeeding in school and when the family is in control of the socialization processes outside of school hours.
>
> However, assumptions that such an ideal picture of family life is usual are no longer valid for a great many pupils. Changes in the structure of families and fragmentation and atomization of communities have increased the incidence of vulnerable children and pupils at risk in the educational process (p. 226).

Assessing and intervening between school and family as separate entities with different,

often conflicting, needs and demands can be confusing and challenging for the social worker. An ecosystems approach may be helpful, where families and the school are viewed as vital systems linked together around the child's growth, development, and learning. The guiding assumption from this perspective is that when parent systems and school systems find ways to be involved together in children's education, children are more likely to be successful in school and in life. A clear goal becomes helping families and the school to develop skills and motivation for involving and participating with one another. Toward this goal, the school social worker can identify at least three objectives:

1. Educating school personnel toward understanding the psychosocial strengths and needs of families and supporting school staff relationships with vulnerable families.

2. Offering relevant program interventions for parents and families based on an ongoing and current needs assessment.

3. Helping the interprofessional team, the PTA, and school staff to develop avenues for parent involvement in the operations and programs of the school.

Given the goal of creating a stronger family and school partnership, program interventions should take place in the school and involve other school personnel whenever possible. Programs may include parenting classes and support groups, literacy programs, acculturation classes, Parents Anonymous groups, and others that respond directly to the needs of parents and families. Curricula for many such interventions are available from community family agencies and national organizations such as the Child Welfare League and Family Services of America.

Designing Empirically Supported Interventions Around Needs of the School

Matching Interventions to Diverse Client Groups and School Needs. Statistics show us that children of color and children living in poverty (National Center for Education Statistics, 1999) are more vulnerable to school failure than white children and children of middle- or high-income families. It is logical to conclude from this that all children do not have an equal opportunity to succeed in school. We can assume that most school organizations fit with the needs and abilities of white, middle- and upper-income students more than lower-income students and/or children of color (Baker, Terry, & Bridger, 1997; Tapia, 1998). While education institutions across the country are in the midst of an enormous shift toward multiculturalism in education, the needs are many, and social workers can play an important role.

Although diversity is reflected in schools in numerous ways, the lack of fit between the school and children who are not white and/or middle-to-upper-income may be the school social worker's greatest challenge in program design and service delivery. Social workers know that multicultural education goes beyond the inclusion of curricular content about various cultures. It includes instructional methods and interpersonal relationships in the classroom as well as approaches to discipline, family interactions, and outcome goals throughout the school. In an organizational environment that has been based traditionally on white, mainstream cultural skills and expectations, the school social worker can model cultural awareness and competence to school staff, students, and families. We can continue to inform ourselves of the specific cultural values and traditions of families and children in our schools and stress the meaning and importance of this to our colleagues in the school. We can develop culturally sensitive services for students and families and interpret the basis for these with administrators and staff. We can help bridge the gap between school and family by engaging with families in culturally informed, culturally responsive ways.

Reconciling School and Social Work Outcome Priorities.
Austin (1999) describes social work as interested in *private outcomes* for students such as healthy support systems and a good sense of self, while education is interested in *public outcomes* such as passing grades and high-school graduation. Outcomes that concern social work and education mutually are problems such as school violence and teen pregnancy, which social workers view as barriers to life quality and schools perceive as barriers to educational outcomes. It is in this arena of mutual concerns that school social workers have more flexibility to address immediate needs of students and their families with the sanction and support of the school. Clarifying connections between private and public outcomes in funding proposals and including public outcome measures in social service evaluations are two effective ways to bridge different priorities.

Prevention and Crisis Intervention.
Substance abuse and violence in schools have escalated in recent years—these are only two examples of many social problems that increasingly affect the well-being of children and adolescents. Over the past several decades, our knowledge of "what works" in school-based prevention programs has increased dramatically (Sloboda & David, 1997). Programs which have been tested and demonstrated successful include the Resolving Conflicts Creatively Program (Aber, Brown, Chaudry, Jones, & Samples, 1996); Second Step (Grossman et al., 1997); Life Skills Training Program (Botvin, Baker, Filazzola, & Botvin, 1990) and the Safe Harbor Program (Nadel, Spellman, Alvarez-Canino, Lausell-Bryant, & Landsberg, 1996). These school-based prevention programs incorporate individual and school change strategies that reflect a social work perspective and utilize social work skills. This creates a logical lead for the school social worker to advocate and implement such programs that show promise for the needs of the local schools.

School social workers and other student service professionals may be called upon at any time to assist in a school crisis. Social workers must be prepared to intervene in various situations, including physical attacks on students and teachers, use of weapons, child and adolescent suicide, child physical and sexual abuse, bomb threats, and natural disasters. In response to school violence in several states, many school districts across the country have developed district-wide comprehensive crisis management teams with action plans for any emergency. School social workers receive training along with other student service professionals, for various crisis situations. In the event that such a team has not been established in the school district, it may become the social worker's responsibility to coordinate its development in the local school.

Services Evaluation and Reporting

Standards and Accountability.   Accountability in public education is here to stay. With the enactment and subsequent amendment of the Goals 2000: Educate America Act, schools are being evaluated on eight national goals for education, at least four of which relate to aspects of the school in which social workers are directly involved. Schools are bound to account for every public tax dollar they receive, and their Goals 2000-related accomplishments often determine the extent of public funding support that they receive. In this time of fiscal conservatism, schools also compete for private grants and foundation money to provide for programs that traditional funds no longer support. School social workers must demonstrate that social work interventions lead to improved educational achievement and that public and private funds supporting school social work are well spent.

Social workers not only must describe what they do but also show the impact of their interventions using specific *outcome measures*. Evaluation should be built into the design of social work services, defined by up-front goals and objectives for every service. Outcome measures should include issues that both social work and education consider important, such as attendance, grades, behavior, and retention. "The credibility of pupil services professionals' roles within the school partly depends on the ability to

document that services make a difference to students and their families and to the achievement of the school system's goals" (Gibelman, 1993, p. 48). Developing service goals and objectives and using outcome measures and other observations to evaluate services is discussed fully in Chapter 13.

Social Work Services Plan.   A plan for social work services is the primary tool for organizing, monitoring, and evaluating our services. The plan should be guided by the results of community and school assessments and remain sensitive to the dynamics operating within both entities. The plan should be clearly presented and easy to read and understand. It should include every social work service in the school, both those which are identified formally and those that are done spontaneously or by immediate request. Service priorities identified in the plan can draw upon a number of school social work roles and tasks, including facilitator, consultant, collaborator, mediator, advocate, broker, home-school-community liaison, educator, program director, clinician, community organizer, and cultural diversity specialist. These roles are discussed more fully in Chapter 12.

Reporting School Social Work Services. Periodic progress reports for stakeholder groups during the year are vital to local sanction and support. Administrators are responsible for what happens in their schools and need to be kept informed of activities and progress with students and families. Additionally, school district personnel as well as private and public funding sources expect regular feedback on the volume of services and the extent of impact. Yet informing diverse constituencies in ways that reflect their own interests and accessibility requires careful thought. For example, while periodic reports containing detailed data on outcome objectives are essential for informing school administrators, teachers may be more receptive to a brief verbal report and fact sheet during a faculty meeting or in-service. The school board may respond positively to successful case vignettes and other client-specific examples, as well as hard data. The media, its own powerful constituency, can also be employed effectively to inform outside community groups with periodic (school-approved) stories about positive results from social work services. Stakeholders such as parents, community service providers, and potential or current funding sources should be identified and provided with reports or information using the same individualized approach.

CONCLUSION

In planning and designing services, the school social worker needs a broad understanding of the organizational and political context of public education, as well as the diverse cultural contexts and needs of students and families. As a partner with educators, the social worker designs services that will enhance, maintain, or restore the educational performance of students. Such a task requires assessments of the needs and resources among students, families, schools, the school district, and the community.

The emphasis on interdisciplinary teamwork means that social workers share responsibilities with professional colleagues and collaborate with team members on the development of service designs. As services that are especially scrutinized in public schools, social services require careful assessments and evaluation planning, with emphasis on outcomes that are valuable for both social work and the school.

FOR STUDY AND DISCUSSION

1. Identify barriers that may deter social workers from developing a program for social work services in your community.

2. What activities might social workers undertake to overcome these barriers?

3. Large caseloads and restrictions on time and facilities are identified as challenges to service quality in schools. Discuss some ways that social workers can maintain service integrity with these conditions.

4 Create and discuss a specific school practice situation in which the at-risk model and the strengths perspective would conflict for intervention planning.

5. A group of Haitian refugees has been relocated in the local community, bringing a number of newly-immigrated Haitian students into the school district over the past months. Assess your readiness for working with these students and their families. What are some ways that you can go about gaining knowledge that you may need?

6. As a school social worker, your practice expertise is in drugs and alcohol. You have recently moved to a school district challenged with school violence and gang involvement. Design a plan for preparing yourself to work with these new problems.

7. You are proposing a group intervention for pregnant and parenting adolescent mothers. Identify three outcome objectives that will satisfy both a social work focus on private outcomes and the school's focus on public outcomes.

ADDITIONAL READING

Briggs, M. H. (1997). *Building early intervention teams: Working together for children and families.* Gaithersburg, MD: Aspen Publishers.

Burford, G., & Hudson, J. (2000). *Family group conferencing: New directions in community-centered child and family practice.* New York: Aldine de Gruyter.

Cohen, J. J., & Fish, M. C. (Eds.). (1993). *Handbook of school-based interventions: Resolving student problems and promoting healthy educational environments.* San Francisco: Jossey-Bass.

Gorski, J. D., & Pilotto, L. (1993). Interpersonal violence among youth: A challenge for school personnel. *Educational Psychology Review, 5,* 35–61.

Horton, C. B., & Cruise, T. K. (2001). *Child abuse and neglect: The school's response*. New York: Guilford Press.

Keyes, P. (Ed.). (1994). *School social workers in the multicultural environment: New roles, responsibilities, and educational enrichment*. New York: Haworth Press.

Knowles, C. R. (2001). *Prevention that works: A guide for developing school-based drug and violence prevention programs*. Thousand Oaks, CA: Corwin Press.

Lin, Q. (2001). Toward a caring-centered multicultural education within the social justice context. *Education, 122*(1), 107–114.

Nolin, M. J., & Davies, E. (1995, October). Student victimization at school (NCES 95-204). Rockville, MD: Westat.

Schonfeld, D. J., & Kline, M. (1996). School-based crisis intervention: An organizational model. *Crisis Intervention, 1*, 155–166.

Schwartz, W. (1994). *Improving the school experience for gay, lesbian, and bisexual students*. ERIC Digest No. 101 (ED377257).

Tower, K. (2000). Image crisis: A study of attitudes about school social workers. *Social Work in Education, 22*(2), 83–107.

Woebrle, K. L. (2000). Interprofessional practice in school-based programs: Lessons learned from the Safe and Drug-Free Schools program in Ohio. *Social Work in Education, 22*(1), 1–64.

REFERENCES

Aber, J. L., Brown, J. L., Chaudry, N., Jones, S. M., & Samples, F. (1996). The evaluation of the Resolving Conflict Creatively Program: An overview. In K. E. Powell & D. F. Hawkins, *Youth violence prevention: Descriptions and baseline data from 13 evaluation projects* (pp. 82–90). Supplement to *American Journal of Preventive Medicine, 12*(5).

Aguilar, M. A. (1995). Promoting the educational achievement of Mexican American young women. *Social Work, 18*(3), 145–156.

Annie E. Casey Foundation (1997). *Kids count databook: State profiles of child well-being 1997*. Baltimore: Author.

Archer, J. (1996, March 27). Surge in Hispanic student enrollment predicted. *Education Week*, p. 3.

Austin, D. (1999). *Human services management: Organizational leadership in social work practice*. Unpublished manuscript, The University of Texas at Austin.

Baker, J. A., Terry, T., & Bridger, R. (1997). Schools as caring communities: A relational approach to school reform. *The School Psychology Review, 26*(4), 586–602.

Boes, M., & Van Wormer, K. (2002). In A. R. Roberts, & G. J. Greene (Eds.), *Social workers desk reference* (pp. 619–623). New York: Oxford University Press.

Botvin, G. J., Baker, E., Filazzola, D. D., & Botvin, E. M. (1990). A cognitive-behavioral approach to substance abuse prevention: A one-year follow-up. *Addictive Behaviors, 15*, 47–63.

Bowen, G., & Richman, J. (2002). Schools in the context of communities. *Children & Schools, 24*, 67–71.

Brandis, C., & Philliber, S. (1998). Room to grow: Improving services for pregnant and parenting teenagers in school settings. *Education and Urban Society, 30*(5), 242–261.

Brener, N. D., Martindale, J., & Weist, M. D. (2001). Mental health and social services: Results from the school health policies and programs study 2000. *The Journal of School Health, 71*(7), 305–312.

Burchard, J. D., Bruns, E. J., & Burchard, S. N. (2002). The wrap-around approach. In B. J. Burns & K. Hoagwood (Eds.), *Community treatment for youth* (pp. 69–90). New York: Oxford University Press.

Caple, F. S., Salcido, R. M., & di Cecco, J., (1995). Engaging effectively with culturally diverse families and children. *Social Work in Education,, 17*(3), 159–170.

Casto, R. M., Julia, M. C., Platt, L. J., Harbaugh, G. L., Waugaman, W. R., Thompson, A., Jost, T. S., Bope, E. T., Williams, T., & Lee, D. B. (1994). *Interprofessional care and collaborative practice* (pp. 35–58). Belmont, CA: Brooks/Cole.

Center for the Study of Social Policy. (1993). *Kids count data books 1993: State profiles of child well-being*. Washington, DC: Author.

Constable, R., & Walberg, H. (1999). Working with families. In R. Constable, S. McDonald, & J. P. Flynn (Eds.), *School social work: Practice, Policy, and research perspectives* (4th ed., pp. 226–247). Chicago: Lyceum Books.

Duchnowski, A. J., Kutash, K., & Friedman, R.M. (2002). Community-based intervention in a system of care and outcome framework. In B. J. Burns & K. Hoagwood (Eds.), *Community treatment for youth* (pp. 16–38). New York: Oxford University Press.

Elia, J. P. (1993). Homophobia in the high school: A problem in need of a resolution. *The High School Journal, 77,* 177–185.

Fick, A. C., & Thomas, S. M. (1995). Growing up in a violent environment: Relationship to health-related beliefs and behaviors. *Youth and Society, 27*(2), 136–147.

Flaherty, L. T., Weist, M. D., & Warner, B. S. (1996). School-based mental health services in the United States: history, current models and needs. *Community Mental Health Journal, 32,* 341–352.

Franklin, C. (1999). Grandparents as parents. Editorial, *Children & Schools, 21*(3), 131–135.

Franklin, C., & Soto, I. (2002). Keeping Hispanic students in school. *Children & Schools, 25,* 4–7.

Frymier, J., & Gansneder, B. (1989). The Phi Delta Kappan study of students at risk. *Phi Delta Kappan, 71,* 142–151.

Garbarino, J. (1993). Children's response to community violence: What do we know? *Infant Mental Health Journal, 14*(2), 103–115.

Gibelman, M. (1993). School social workers, counselors, and psychologists in collaboration: A shared agenda. *Social Work in Education, 15,* 45–53.

Grandparents raising grandchildren (1999). Retrieved January 15, 1999, from http://www.aarp.org/getans/consumer/grandparents/html

Grossman, D. C., Neckerman, H. J., Koepsell, T. D., Liu, P., Asher, K. N., Beland, K., Frey, K., & Rivara, F. P. (1997). Effectiveness of a violence prevention curriculum among children in elementary school. *Journal of the American Medical Association, 277,* 1605–1611.

Jozefowicz-Simbeni, D. M. H., & Allen-Meares, P. (2002). Poverty and schools: Intervention and resource building through school-linked services. *Children & Schools, 24,* 123–136.

Kelly, D. M. (1996). Stigma stories: Four discourses about teen mothers, welfare, and poverty. *Youth and Society, 27*(4), 421–449.

Kelly, D. M. (1998). Teacher discourses about a young parents program: The many meanings of "good choices." *Education and Urban Society, 30*(2), 224–241.

Kordesk, R. S., & Constable, R. (1999). Policies, programs, and mandates for developing social services in the schools. In R. Constable, S. McDonald, & J. P. Flynn (Eds.), *School social work: Practice, policy, and research perspectives* (4th ed.). Chicago: Lyceum Books.

Melaville, A. I., & Blank, M. J. (1991). *What it takes: Structuring interagency partnerships to connect children and families with comprehensive services.* Washington, DC: Education and Human Services Consortium.

Mental health: A report of the Surgeon General—chapter 3. Retrieved April 15, 2002, from http://www.Surgeongeneral.gov/library/mentalhealth/chapter3/sec1.html

Moraga, A. (1997, July 9). Mary's shelter provides pregnant teens a place to finish school and learn skills. *The Orange County Register,* p. 4.

Moriarty, A., & McDonald, S. (1991). Theoretical dimensions of school-based mediation. *Social Work in Education, 13,* 176–184.

Nadel, H., Spellman, M., Alvarez-Canino, T., Lausell-Bryant, L., & Landsberg, G. (1996). The cycle of violence and victimization: A study of the school-based interventions of a multidisciplinary youth violence prevention program (pp. 109–119). In K. E. Powell & D. F. Haskins, *Youth violence prevention: Descriptions and baseline data from 13 evaluation projects.* Supplement to *American Journal of Preventive Medicine, 12* (5).

Natasi, B. K. (1998). A model for mental health programming in schools and communities: Introduction to the mini-series. *The School Psychology Review, 27*(2), 165–174.

National Center for Educational Statistics (1999). *Dropout statistics.* Washington, DC: Author.

Osborne, J., & Collison, B. (1998). School counselors and external providers: Conflict or complement. *Professional School Counseling, 1*(4), 7–11.

Parents' rights as defined in chapter 864, Statutes of 1998, Education Code. Retrieved May 23, 2002, from http://www.cde.ca.gov/iasa/parntrts.html

Pawlak, E. J., & Cousins, L., (1999). School social work: Organizational Perspectives. In R. Constable, S. McDonald, & J. P. Flynn (Eds.), *School social work: Practice, policy, and research perspectives* (4th ed.) (pp. 150–165). Chicago: Lyceum Books.

Richardson, V., Casanova, U., Placier, P., & Guilfoyle, K. (1989). *School children at risk: Schools as communities of support.* Philadelphia: Falmer Publishers.

Ronda, M. A., & Valencia, R. R. (1994). "At risk" Chicano students: The institutional and communicative life of a category. *Hispanic Journal of Behavioral Sciences, 16*(4), 363–395.

Rosenberg, D. E. (1991). Serving America's newcomers: States and localities taking the lead in the absence of a comprehensive national policy. *Public Welfare,* Winter, 28–37.

Rosenthal, R. (1987). Pygmalion effects: Existence, magnitude, and social importance. *Educational Researcher, 16,* 37–41.

Saleeby, D. (Ed.). (1997). *The strengths perspective in social work practice.* New York: Longman.

Sloboda, Z., & David, S. L. (1997). *Preventing drug use among children and adolescents: A research-based guide.* National Institute on Drug Abuse. NIH Publication No. 97-4212.

Sparks, E. (1994). Human rights violations in the inner city: Implications for moral educators. *Journal of Moral Education, 23*(3), 315–332.

Streeter, C. L., & Franklin, C. (1993). Site-based management in public opportunities and challenges for school social workers. *Social Work in Education, 15,* 71–81.

Streeter, C. L., & Franklin, C. (2002). Standards for school social work in the 21st century. In A. R. Roberts & G. J. Greene (Eds.), *Social workers desk reference* (pp. 612–618). New York: Oxford University Press.

Tapia, J. (1998). The schooling of Puerto Ricans: Philadelphia's most impoverished community. *Education Quarterly, 29*(3), 297–323.

Taylor, L., Zuckerman, B., Harik, V., & Groves, B. M. (1994). Witnessing violence by young children and their mothers. *Developmental and Behavioral Pediatrics, 15*(2), 120–123.

CHAPTER 12

THE DELIVERY OF SCHOOL SOCIAL WORK SERVICES

CYNTHIA FRANKLIN, THE UNIVERSITY OF TEXAS AT AUSTIN

INTRODUCTION

Using an ecological framework, this chapter provides an overview of social work interventions in schools. Gitterman (1996) states that the focus of practice strategies from an ecological perspective is to improve the fit between a person and their environment through 1) "improving a person's (collectivity's) ability to manage stressor(s) through more effective personal and situational appraisals and behavioral skills; 2) influencing the social and physical environments to be more responsive to a person's (collectivity's) needs; and 3) improving the quality of person-environment exchanges" (p. 395). This chapter presents practice roles and intervention skills for school social workers which are compatible with this perspective. The new roles of school social workers in school-linked services are reviewed. The effects of managed behavioral health care on school social workers is highlighted. Intervention roles of school social workers are also summarized. Finally, specialized intervention skills, such as those necessary to work with individual students, families, groups, classrooms, and school systems, are discussed. Since space limitations do not permit the presentation of detailed information about practice interventions, an annotated bibliography of books and materials is provided at the end of the chapter.

The School as a Human Service Delivery System

One way to look at a school system is as a human service organization created for the purpose of providing education to America's children. In the legacy of Dewey, education may be viewed in the broad spectrum of knowledge and skills acquisition and socialization. The optimal goal of any educational system is the output of capable and competent students who have both knowledge and skills and are able to participate fully as good citizens in the broader communities of family, work, and civic life. Schools, however, reflect the diversity and challenges of public life and display the character of communities of which they are integral parts. The ecological perspective provides a useful framework for understanding this systems view of schools as human service organizations.

To meet the demands of schooling diverse children with social, mental health, and health needs, schools have increasingly employed and integrated into their repertoire of services to meet those needs. School social workers are specialized human service professionals who deliver social work services in schools instead of social agencies or mental health clinics. Social workers employed by school districts work in a host setting; that is, school social workers are not the primary personnel or operators of the organization. A host setting is not an unusual work situation for social workers in that host settings are common for other fields of practice as well, such as, for example, social workers employed by hospitals.

School social workers work as team members with other specialized helping professionals (referred to as a *pupil services team*) who serve the mental health, social, and health needs of students and families in schools. Other professionals serving on the pupil services team include but are not limited to school psychologists, guidance counselors, and nurses. School social workers have distinct but sometimes overlapping roles with these other helping professionals (see Figure 12.1). The overlap between the roles of helping professions in the schools sometimes creates confusion and competition among the helpers. School social workers have to be prepared to educate others about the unique aspects of their roles and to mediate the sociopolitical conflict inherent in the role confusion.

Social workers have many options regarding service delivery in the school setting. Unlike clinic or social agency personnel, the social worker observes the child or adolescent in the context of everyday life in the school. Therefore, interventions that improve the functioning of family members, teachers, administrators, classroom members, and peers may be as important as, or more important than, those that focus on the student.

MANAGED CARE, SCHOOL-LINKED, MENTAL HEALTH SERVICES MODELS

Managed Behavioral Health Care and School Social Workers

School services programs are becoming increasingly intertwined with managed behavioral health care. Managed care is a way of financing health, mental health, and social services in which the major focus is on cost containment and increasing the quality of services delivered (Strom-Gottfried, 1997). Various human ser-

vices contractors (both public and private) are gaining access to public funds to provide services to children and families, and many of these services take place on or near the school campus. For example, Medicaid funding is becoming increasingly available to fund human services on school campuses. Armbruster and colleagues (1999) offer an excellent example of how Connecticut achieved partnerships between managed care organizations and school-based mental health services. Because education is so important to the long-term outcomes of children, managed care funding is including contingencies for school improvement as part of designated outcomes for contracts, which will likely lead to a greater investment in schools by human services providers and advance further the need for partnerships with schools (Franklin & Allen-Meares, 1997; Franklin & Johnson, 1996).

Managed care systems are encompassing all public and private services and are changing the way that social workers and other professionals conduct their practices. As noted by Franklin and Johnson (1996), the current practice context of managed care is blurring the boundaries in a manner that the former public versus private distinction no longer applies. The current trend in managed behavioral health care is to finance brief and effective service delivery models (Corcoran & Vandiver, 1996; Franklin & Johnson; Strom-Gottfried, 1997; Winegar, 1993). These systems of care mandate the development of "best practices," the use of accurate assessment, and diagnosis to see that clients are referred to the most effective, cost-efficient interventions, with an emphasis on being able to measure the outcomes of cases. Schools are not exempt from the need to develop efficient and effective intervention models. The new breed of practitioners who will be able to compete in the current market-driven social services and mental health care delivery systems needs to be equipped with a variety of diverse skills in empirically based assessment and an ability to monitor the effectiveness of their practices (Blackwell & Schmidt, 1992; Corcoran & Gin-

NURSE		**COUNSELOR**
▬ Apply clinical nursing Knowledge and assessment skills to determine student health needs, interventions and expected outcomes. ▬ Educate school community to the nature and educational relevance of disabling health conditions. ▬ Develop individual health care plans that focus on restoring health, promoting wellness, and minimizing/removing health barriers to learning. ▬ Create, disseminate, and monitor school health practices and protocols.		▬ Serve as school-based coordinator of comprehensive developmental guidance and integrated counseling services. ▬ Coordinate post-secondary education and school-to-work training programs. ▬ Broker resources for educational/academic curricula and program information. ▬ Provide initial access point to on-site individual and group counseling in academic, personal, social/ emotional, and career areas for entire school population.
	Education reform **Team Building** **Program planning** **Crisis intervention/counseling** **Whole child development** **Community support building** **Assessment and referral** **School community wellness**	
PSYCHOLOGIST		**SOCIAL WORKER**
▬ Apply learning theory for individuals and groups to improve instruction. ▬ Coordinate and evaluate plans for needs unique to individuals with special learning/behavior problems. ▬ Promote the use of psychology theory/practice in curriculum development, including sports and athletics. ▬ Design, implement, and analyze research studies/school programs. ▬ Provide psychotherapeutic interventions, including crisis interventions.	←——HEALTH EDUCATORS——→	▬ Apply an ecological perspective to psychosocial assessments that link home, school, and community factors affecting learning. ▬ Provide case management services to mobilize and coordinate resources for students and families. ▬ Takes social action to create comprehensive community resources for students and families. ▬ Use dynamics of family systems to develop effective strategies for families of high-risk students.

FIGURE 12.1

gerich, 1994; Giles, 1991; Lazarus, 1995; Sabin, 1991).

School social workers can equip themselves for the demands of managed care by learning empirically based assessment methods and outcome measures. There are many measures available for assessing and monitoring the effectiveness of practice interventions.

In order for school social workers to work successfully with managed care, it is also important to learn new and briefer models of intervention such as those associated with cognitive-behavioral, brief, solution-focused, and brief consultation models. Hoyt (1995) summarizes the elements of brief practice as follows.

1. Concrete and well-defined goals that are set quickly, usually in the first session.

2. Focus on prevention and crisis intervention.

3. Development of a therapeutic contract that specifies exactly what is expected of the therapist and client. Time limitedness of the therapy is also specified.

4. Flexible scheduling of sessions to meet client need (e.g., spacing sessions, shortening sessions, etc.).

5. Interdisciplinary cooperation including the use of psychopharmacology and allied professionals to help client obtain rapid improvement.

6. Use of multiple formats for treatment simultaneously including individual and group sessions. Strong use of self-help approaches encouraged. Bibliotherapy and psychoeducation will be offered in most cases.

7. Frequent use of intermittent treatment model where clients are seen on a periodic basis instead of every week format.

8. Strong emphasis on accountability and results orientation.

Table 12.1 presents a list of questions derived from the cognitive-behavioral practice model known as multi-modal therapy. These assessment questions work very well with the use of brief, consultant models in that they help the school social worker find out quickly what the main issues are for change and to move toward a collaborative solution. A consultant model is a brief practice model frequently used by social workers in schools to help teachers and other school personnel work with the behavioral problems of youths in their classes. See below for further description of this role.

TABLE 12.1 Twelve Essential Questions to Ask in a Brief Assessment Interview

1. Why is the client entering services now?
2. Are there any signs of psychosis, delusions, or thought disorders that would indicate that the client needed immediate medical/psychiatric treatment?
3. Are there signs of organicity indicating the need for neurological or other medical treatment?
4. Is there evidence of depression or suicidal or homicidal ideations?
5. What are the presenting complaints?
6. What are the important antecedent factors that preceded the client's problem and seeking help?
7. Who or what is maintaining the problem?
8. What does the client wish to derive from this service?
9. What are the client's preferences for style of service? How can you match that style? Or, the customer is always right.
10. Are there clear indications for a specific modality or method that will work with this client? OR what has worked before?
11. Can the school maintain a relationship and provide the services, or should the client be referred?
12. What are the client's positive attributes and strengths?

Managed Behavioral Health Care and School Social Workers

School social workers can equip themselves for the demands of managed care by giving attention to learning evidenced-based assessment methods and outcome measures. There are many measures available for performing assessment and monitoring the effectiveness of practice interventions. Sauter and Franklin (1998), for example, discuss some of the best assessment measures to use when working with children experiencing trauma who may also develop Posttraumatic Stress Disorder. Corcoran and Fischer (2000), Corcoran (2000), and Jordan and Franklin (2003) review and illustrate several assessment measures that can be used with children and families.

Further, Bowen and colleagues have developed *The School Success Profile* (SSP) (Bowen, Richman, & Bowen, 2002), a comprehensive

tool for evaluating and monitoring the effects of interventions in school settings. The SSP assesses youth in the social environment and considers both risk and protective factors in the social environment and the individual that can lead to school success and failure. (See Box 12.1 for a list of areas assessed by the measure.) The SSP is available on-line and can be administered in both English and Spanish. Chapman and Richman (1998) illustrate how to evaluate school practice and point out some of the positives and negatives that a school social worker can encounter when taking on such an approach as the use of the SSP.

In order for school social workers to work successfully with managed care, it is also important to learn new and briefer models of intervention such as those associated with cognitive-behavioral, solution-focused, and consultant models. Table 12.1 presents a list of questions derived from the cognitive-behavioral practice

---

BOX 12.1   Measurement Dimensions of the School Success Profile

ABOUT YOU—REFERENCE INFORMATION (9 ITEMS)
Basic Demographics

SOCIAL ENVIRONMENT PROFILE
Neighborhood (35 items)
Neighborhood Support
Neighborhood Youth behavior
Neighborhood Safety
School (55 items)
School Satisfaction
Teacher Support
School Safety
Friends (26 items)
Friend Support
Peer Group Acceptance
Friend Behavior
Family (47 items)
Family Togetherness

Parent Support
Home Academic Achievement
Parent Education Support
School Behavior Expectations

INDIVIDUAL ADAPATATION PROFILE
Personal Beliefs and Well-Being (48 Items)
Social Support Use
Physical Health
Happiness
Personal Adjustment
Self-Esteem

SCHOOL ATTITUDES AND BEHAVIOR
School Engagement
Trouble Avoidance

ACADEMIC PERFORMANCE
Grades

model known as multi-modal therapy. These questions focus practitioners on brief assessment and problem solving for the purpose of reaching goals of the client. These assessment questions work very well with the use of brief, consultant models in that they help social workers find out quickly what the main issues are for change and move toward collaborative solutions. A consultant model is a brief practice model frequently used by social workers in schools to help teachers and other school personnel work with the behavioral problems of youths in their classes. See below for further description of this role.

School-Linked, Mental Health Services Models

The emphasis in the 1990s on funding collaborative-based services in the human services, and school-linked services programs in particular, has added to a plethora of clinical professionals working in schools including clinical social workers. Larson and colleagues (1992) define school-linked services as:

> part of a larger movement for more integration of education, health and social services for children. In the school-linked approach to integrating services for children, a) services are provided to children and their families through a collaboration among schools, health care providers, and social services agencies; b) the schools are among the central participants in the planning and governing of the collaborative effort; and c) the services are provided at, or are coordinated by personnel located at, the school or a site near the school (p. 7).

Proponents of school-linked services exist across services systems and often refer to the school as a central "hub for the delivery of human services" because it is a place where the services can converge that also has the maximum access for children.

A recent national survey the School Health Policies and Programs Study (SHPPS), conducted by the Centers for Disease Control and Prevention (CDC) has confirmed the expansion of school mental health and social services

(Brener, Martindale, & Weist, 2001). Interestingly, the survey describes the essential functions of school mental health and social services as including the provision of "direct services, and instruction, developing systems, programs and resources, and connecting school and community resources" (Brener, Martindale, & Weist, p. 305) and these roles are very similar to those performed by school social workers. The survey indicates that a large number of school mental health and social services are being offered from outside of the school by mental health providers working in school-linked health centers, or who have contractual arrangements or memorandums of agreements with school districts. "More than one-fourth (28.6%) of states require districts or schools to provide mental health or social services to students through these types of arrangements, and 59% of districts have such arrangements" (Brener, Martindale, & Weist, 2001, p. 308). The SHPPS indicates that 91% of schools have agreements for services to be provided through local mental health or social services centers, 56.8% through local departments of health, and 44.1% through hospitals. In addition, the survey suggests that there are several other outside providers of mental health and social services in the schools: private psychologists (35.8%), private counselors (29.8%), private psychiatrists (26.7%), school-linked health centers (23%), private social workers (22.5%), managed care organizations (13.4%), and university or medical schools (12.9%) (Brener, Martindale, & Weist, 2001).

As a part of the expansion of mental health services a number of community and national resources have developed to support the school-based health and mental health service centers (Brener, Martindale, & Weist, 2001; Franklin & Allen-Meares, 1997; Franklin & Streeter, 1995; Streeter & Franklin, 2002; Taylor, 2000). For example, there are two national training and technical assistance centers for school-based mental health services. Both centers are housed in universities and have been operating since 1995. The UCLA School Mental Health Project, Center for Mental Health in the Schools is operated by the UCLA Department of Psychology (smhp.psych.ucla.edu/), and the Center for School Mental Health Assistance is operated by The University of Maryland Department of Psychiatry (www.nasbhc.org/) (Streeter & Franklin, 2002). These centers have been funded in response to a national mental health crisis with children and adolescents. They provide tremendous support to mental health professionals who are coming from outside agencies to provide services on the school campuses. The technical centers have also provided literature, training, and support aimed at helping outside and inside mental health professionals such as school social workers collaborate together.

Roles of School Social Workers in School-Linked Services

Franklin (1999, 2000, 2001) discusses the possibility that the changes in mental health delivery ushered in by the increasing use of school-linked services and school-based mental health services are redefining the roles and practices of school social workers. Increasing competition in services delivery is requiring school social workers to find better ways to work with outside mental health professionals who are delivering services on school campuses. In some cases it has also become important for school social workers to define the importance of their job roles more explicitly and even compete against outside professionals for their jobs.

As Franklin and Allen-Meares (1997) state, the specific effects of school-linked services on the roles of school social workers are not completely known. The Center for Disease Control (CDC) survey mentioned above (Brener, Martindale, & Weist, 2001), however, offers some insights concerning the changes in the school-based practice. According to the CDC survey, there are many different renditions for how school mental health and social services are provided. Several models exist, including student assistance programs, school-based health cen-

ters, and comprehensive expanded school mental health programs designed to reach all students. Anecdotal experience points to the complex relationships that these types of services are bringing to the school campuses and the need for better collaboration between the different services providers (Franklin, 2001). It is important to note, also, that the increases in mental health service delivery is not always viewed as an effective means of educating children from the viewpoint of educators. Fast (1999) reports, for example, a satirical cartoon that appeared in the educational journal *Phi Delta Kappan* which communicates skepticism about the expanding services approach in education. The cartoon's heading was "The School of the Future" and depicted a building with many wings labeled Detox Center, Day Care Center, Child Development Center, etc. One small addition in the back was labeled "Education Wing" (p. 100). It is important for school social workers to identify strongly with public school interests and to focus on the mission of the school, which is education. It is equally important to assure that the diverse services delivery does not detract from children's learning and to assure that each and every child receives a quality education.

One of the important contributions that school social workers may make to school-linked mental health services is to take more active roles in balancing the educational needs of the child with their mental health services needs. School social workers who work in schools that participate in many school-linked mental health services may find it necessary to expand their roles in case management, resource management and coordination, community liaison, and community organization. If the school becomes a hub for the delivery of human services, then it becomes necessary for school social workers to take an active role in coordinating those services in the best interest of the students and the school.

Another role emerging in the context of school-linked services is that of diversity specialist. Schools are encountering a range of parents, family, and community members from diverse socioeconomic and cultural backgrounds. The school needs more expertise, education, and support in areas of cultural diversity. To some extent these are traditional administrative and community roles and tasks carried on by school social workers (Allen-Meares, 1994). Franklin and Streeter (1995) discuss additional roles for social workers working with school-linked and integrative services programs.

Intervention Roles

Consultant.   Research provides convincing evidence that consultation services are effective at the client, consultee, and system levels (Sabatino, 1991). Consultation is a method of intervention which takes place between a professional consultant and a consultee who has responsibility for direct service to another person in a voluntary relationship aimed at solving a job-related problem through a shared problem-solving process (Mannino & Shore, 1975; Medway & Updyke, 1985). It is important for the consultee to feel comfortable, accepted, and respected. Social work consultation may occur with teachers, principals, other school personnel, or community members. School social workers provide information, education, and support and help consultees develop a plan of action. The plan may focus on an individual child, a family, or the classroom; policies or procedures; or services and programs. Teachers frequently want advice and education on working with a student with classroom behavior problems. The consultant makes short-term educational and supportive interventions aimed at helping teachers feel competent in making changes. A strengths perspective is assumed. Most social work consultants use a collaborative model, which is discussed and illustrated below.

Practice Example. A school social worker in a high school often served in the role of consultant to administrators and teachers on social functioning and mental health issues. The principal wanted the school social worker to provide di-

rection for how to set up a group of peer counselors for working with students returning from psychiatric hospitalization. The principal wanted to know whether this type of peer counseling approach was advisable. Instead of answering yes or no to the question, the social worker took an exploratory approach, asking questions aimed at examining the pros and cons of the idea and helping the principal formulate a clear idea of what he thought. Thus, he was able to come to a decision about pursuing this approach.

Clinical Interventionist.   In a study of social work services, Markward (1993) found that traditional clinical services were the focal point of school social workers in a school district. Over the years the meaning of the term "clinical" has expanded from a narrow definition of social workers involved in psychiatric social work or providing long-term therapeutic services to mean any type of direct services intervention delivered to individuals, families, and small groups (Dorfman, 1996). According to Dorfman, this includes services to elementary and secondary schools. School social workers provide a number of clinical and counseling services to children and their parents. Clinical services are often delivered in the role of home-school-community liaison where a school social worker is trying to fix a child's difficulties in school and finds it necessary to involve parents and other social agencies. Social workers in clinical interventionist roles work to bring forth both psychosocial change and to change social systems. They may conduct counseling sessions with students and parents or run small, clinically oriented support groups to help students and families change.

Practice Example. A 15-year-old adolescent girl who was being truant from school was referred to a school social worker. In an individual counseling session it was discovered that the child was clinically depressed. In addition, there were extreme family circumstances involved with the case. The mother left town two months ago with her boyfriend. The girl did not know the whereabouts of her mother since that time.

The father was a man with Obsessive Compulsive Disorder and a drinking problem. The social worker used clinical interventions to help the girl. She made a referral and helped her get on medication for her depression. The social worker saw both the girl and father in counseling sessions in the school that focused on resolution of their mental health problems. The school social worker also helped the father get into further treatment at a mental health agency. The girl joined the social worker's weekly support group that focused on grief issues to help her cope with the loss of her mother.

Enabler and Facilitator.

Central to the role of facilitator is assisting the student, parent, or staff member in the use of various techniques to accomplish a defined change (Radin, 1988). This empowerment function establishes an inner locus of control to meet present and future challenges. An old adage of practice wisdom in social casework practice demonstrates the role of the enabler or the facilitator: "Never do anything for clients that they can do for themselves." The facilitator works within the capacities of clients and enables them to help themselves.

Practice Example. A school social worker served as the parents' group coordinator and assisted the elementary-school principal in the development of curriculum work groups. Within this role the social worker encouraged one of the parents who emerged as a internal leader to assume the leadership of this group. The social worker directed the parent leader toward resources that the parent sought out on her own. Each time the parent made strides in moving the group forward the social worker praised and reinforced this self-initiative. When the parent leader tried to defer to the social worker, the social worker was quick to give the parent leader the credit for the progress of the group, pointing out all the group's achievements. The social worker also denied that she had done anything to help but abdicated responsibility for the success of the program to the parent leader and the group members.

Collaborator.

This role differs from that of consultant in that it signifies that participants have different but equally valuable contributions to make at various times and under various circumstances (Germain, 1991). Although the roles of collaborator and consultant often compliment each other, "collaborator" denotes an exchange of information that results in joint problem-solving efforts. The ability of team members to link their unique contributions to those of other professionals is essential to interdisciplinary practice (Pugach & Allen-Meares, 1985). Collaboration allows for personal development while working with other persons toward the attainment of a common goal. It helps to build relationships by recognizing and encouraging the strengths and contributions made by others. A collaborative relationship allows for stimulation of more ideas, approaches, and solutions than any one person can generate independently. In the continuous process of feedback and support, successes are reinforced and the team is strengthened. The higher the level of collaboration, the greater the strength the group will have for collective action and commitment to the goals that have been developed. Finally, a collaborative relationship encourages the many talents available in the professional staff, thus multiplying resources in an organization. In today's school environment building collaborative relationships with many other services providers is absolutely necessary to effective school practice. Waxman (cited in Streeter & Franklin, 2002) offers the following suggestions for ways that school social workers and other mental health professionals can enhance collaborations among diverse professional groups.

1. Being positive, affirming and receptive to collaborations.
2. Setting up school teams and assuming leadership and coordination of roles on inter-agency teams.
3. Working with agencies and collaborators to overcome barriers that prevent them from getting along.

4. Serving as mediators in resource conflicts and disputes.
5. Taking the initiative in leading efforts at mapping and coordinating resources.
6. Working with the school and agency to develop formal agreements and formal mechanisms for maintaining programs and relationships.
7. Working to help other mental health professionals achieve outcomes that are academic as well as behavioral in nature.
8. Adelman and Taylor provide other papers on effective practices, and practice guidelines for working with diverse professionals in school settings at the website of The Center for Mental Health in the Schools (UCLA School Mental Health Project, 2002).

Practice Example. Social workers often set up collaborative meetings between teachers and students for helping students with behavior problems. Ms. Johnson was at her wit's end in dealing with John, who was a class clown and a constant disruption in her classroom. Sending him to the principal, Mr. Peterson, had not worked, and John quickly returned to her classroom. The school social worker was asked to collaborate on the case. The school social worker called a collaborative meeting between John, Ms. Johnson, John's parents and his outside therapist to come up with solutions. In that meeting the worker focuses on John's strengths and times that he does better in the classroom. Other participants gave similar input about times when John is mature and goal directed. The teacher and John worked out a special cue for settling down and a reward system that would motivate John.

Metcalf (1995) provides a helpful format for running a collaborative meeting, and the school social worker followed this format in her work (see Table 12.2). The strengths-based orientation of the meeting focuses teachers and others involved in coming up with rapid solutions to difficulties.

TABLE 12.2   An Example of a Teacher–Social Worker–Student Collaborative Meeting

---

To the student:
What reason do you think your teachers and counselor will give for our meeting?

To all involved in the meeting:
What do each hope happens in the meeting?

To teacher and student:
How will each of you know when things are better for _____? What will you see him or her doing that will tell you things are better?

To teachers and student:
In what classes does this goal already exist? or When have you ever seen this goal exist?

To student:
How have you managed that? What does the teacher do that helps this happen?

To teacher:
How have you seen _____ do this? What have you done that helps this happen?

Source: L. Metcalf. (1995). *Counseling toward solutions: A practical solution-focused program for working with students, teachers, and parents.* Englewood Cliffs, NJ: Simon & Schuster. This material is used by permission of John Wiley & Sons, Inc.

Educator. In the role of educator, the social worker provides specific information, imparts knowledge, and deepens comprehension in work with pupils, teachers, and families. The teaching role is a way of sharing knowledge that others need to fulfill their responsibilities. Social workers provide workshops for parents and teachers in areas such as parenting, values clarification, and communication skills. Skills training interventions, like parenting training and social skills training, are some of the most popular approaches in which school social workers fulfill their role as "educator." Skills training is based on psychoeducational, social learning, and behavioral models of change which assume that clients lack certain behavioral skills for performing pro-social or competent behaviors. Social skills training, problem solving training, anger control training, parent training, and life skills training are a few examples of the types of skills training programs that are useful in schools. Goldstein (1980, 1984; Goldstein & McGinnis, 1984) has developed several curricula for social skills training that are useful. These teaching methods may be used in skills training regardless of the content the school social worker is delivering.

1. Present the information the client needs to know didactically (e.g., steps of problem solving).

2. Model for the skills presented (e.g., have the student come up with a problem and the social worker demonstrates how to go about problem solving while the client watches).

3. Practice the skills being taught through role play (e.g., have the student role play solving a problem with the social worker).

4. Provide feedback to the client about their performance in practicing the skills. Be sure and provide both positive and corrective feedback (e.g., student role plays problem solving process about Johnny bullying at his locker in the hall. The social worker notes he did a good job in generating different options for how to handle the situation but had difficulty evaluating the op-

tions and selecting one. The social worker shows him how to correct his actions.).

5. Practice in the real world (social worker asks student to practice with problem situations).

6. Evaluate (social worker schedules time with student to evaluate the real world outcomes and the steps start over to enhance learning).

Practice Example. One practitioner developed an Annual Parent University day. The program is sponsored jointly by the local community college and the school district's community education department. Parents pay no fee for a choice of two classes from among the 15 offered. Transportation, refreshments, and lunch are provided, and child care is available. The social workers are responsible for several workshops on such topics as, "How to Talk So Your Kids Will Listen," "How to Listen So Your Kids Will Talk," and "What's Normal and What's Not—Children's Ages and Stages." A skills training approach is used in the workshop presentations.

Mediator. The role of mediator places the social worker in a position between clients and their environment, providing a problem-solving service to both parties. Because of school violence, models for conflict resolution have been developed as a preventive measure to deter violence. Social workers are active in teaching this skill to others and use it themselves to mediate conflict between peers, between and among student and teacher/administration, and between parent and teacher. The severity of situations ranges from children fighting on the playground to random or planned violence that results in physical injuries or death. Mediation balances concern for the needs of students with the needs of the institution effectively, which provides a format for addressing problems that have a disruptive and negative effect on students' daily lives (Moriarty & McDonald, 1991).

Practice Example. A school social worker found the principal of an elementary school to which he had just been assigned in the process of developing a conflict-resolution program with the teachers in the school. The social worker became a partner in this project, which resulted in fewer violent conflicts among students and taught an alternative means of settling differences, skills which could be used throughout life.

Advocate.   Advocacy differs from mediation in that the goal of the mediator is to achieve dispute resolution through compromise on both sides, whereas the goal of the advocate is to win for the client. The social worker becomes the speaker for the client and will argue, debate, bargain, negotiate, and manipulate the environment on behalf of the client (Compton & Galaway, 1984). This role is particularly important in supporting the rights of vulnerable populations (the developmentally disabled, the unmarried pregnant student, parents with limited resources, and minority students) when it is not possible to empower them to advocate for themselves. Advocacy is particularly important at Individual Educational Planning Committee meetings, when the parents and/or students require support.

Advocacy on behalf of student populations can take place on several different levels. A social worker may use advocacy skills, for example, in school and community committees; at the state and national levels (advocating the rights of high-risk pupil groups); and within the school and community systems (identifying inadequate services and unfair policies and practices).

Practice Example. A child with behavior problems was repeatedly expelled from school and/or put in in-school suspension. The mother (an African American woman of low socioeconomic status) was concerned that there was a learning disorder but due to resource restraints and lack of support from a teacher who said that this is just a "bad kid" and that learning problems were not indicated, the school would not test the child or consider him for special education placement. The social worker's assessment indicated that a learning disorder was a possible.

The social worker sided with the mother and educated her concerning her rights to have her son tested and educated. The social worker also used the policy mandates of the Individuals with Disabilities Act (IDEA) to educate the school district on their legal obligations to act and to provide an appropriate educational placement for this child. Through these advocacy efforts the child was tested and found to have a learning disorder as well as another psychiatric disorder that qualified him for special education placement.

Diversity Specialist.   Schools work with an extremely culturally diverse and heterogeneous group of students (see Chapter 11 for a discussion). Many cultural conflicts turn into problems between schools, parents, and students. A new role that the school social worker might assume in the twenty-first century is that of cultural specialist or specialist in diverse lifestyles. The key to being effective in this role is helping others develop knowledge and skills for effectively interacting with others. Learning about diverse cultures is a must and the school social worker might arrange in-service trainings and panel groups to discuss various cultural preferences and lifestyles. Mediating cultural differences and conflicts is another way that the school social worker might serve in this role.

Practice Example. The Mexican celebration of the Mayan festival starts well before Christmas and ends days into the New Year. In Mexico, the festival serves to unite the people and to reestablish ties. Hispanic children, however, are taken out of school by their parents so that the family can travel home to Mexico to join in the celebrations and feel rejuvenated in the Mexican traditions. The time missed at school was creating a problematic situation for the school (Franklin & Soto, 2002). Only about half of the Mexican children, for example, were returning in time for class and some were one to two weeks late. A school committee on which the social worker served wanted to pass a policy that required parents to sign an agreement stating that they will return from Mexico in time for students to attend classes. The school social worker knew, however, that this policy would further alienate the parents who were very invested in the participation in the cultural tradition with their families. The school social worker was able to help the committee to think about the cultural conflict and implications of this policy resulting in an alternate plan. A group of Mexican parents was asked to join the committee to discuss the issue and they came up with the following resolution. The parents would make sure that no child was more than one week late for their classes and they would get the school work before the holidays so that their children could complete the work before returning to the school. Each child would also be asked to give a report on their experiences in Mexico to their classes so that the missed class time could become an enriched learning experience for all.

Manager. Every social worker in a school is a manager. The design and delivery of social work service in a school require management skills: planning, negotiating, implementing, and evaluating a service. A management role, however, may become more formalized, and social workers may even assume administrative duties, such as being the lead social worker in charge of a unit of school social workers in a school district. Management may also include the role of coordinator, which requires the ability to comprehend and conceptualize relationships between a client and multiple services and among various school, community, and agency resources (Germain, 1991). Today, many school social workers coordinate the work of the Individualized Educational Planning Committee or act as case managers of pre-referral intervention teams. School-linked service programs provide additional opportunities for management and coordination of social and mental health services on the school campus.

Practice Example. In a school district fostering school-linked programs, the roles involving management increased for the school social worker as the service providers moved onto cam-

pus. For example, the presence of several social and mental health agency personnel required the full-time attention of the pupil services team, who were being bombarded with a diversity of programs and professionals. This required some adjustment in job functions for the school social worker in that the clinical and counseling services she was offering were also being offered by social workers and other therapists working as a part of mental health teams. The school social worker found a new administrative role in coordinating the clinically oriented school-linked programs, and the principal supported her in this new role.

Case Manager and Broker. The case management and broker role provides a link between the problem situation and the resources that are support sources. Community agencies have been the most common resource used, but many other resources are available in the community and school, sometimes in the most unlikely places. Case management will be needed, for example, to track students involved in the myriad services being received on campus. School-linked services programs foster the need for more complex case management and new roles needed such as social services coordinator.

Practice Example. A mid-sized school district began to solicit help from the community and recruited a number of youth-serving agencies. Several mental health and social service providers offered services as diverse as substance abuse counseling, self-esteem groups, and anger control training. Unfortunately, the "right hand did not know what the left hand was doing." Someone needed to coordinate the efforts between the diverse services and track the progress of students in those services. Under direction of the assistant principal, the school social worker became a case manager and assumed this function.

Community Intervention. Social workers have long been valued by schools for their extensive knowledge of community resources and their skill in helping pupils and their families use those resources. Their participation on agency boards and councils has enhanced this knowledge and has resulted in pupils receiving agency services that match their individual needs. In some instances, the social worker in the school has been responsible for identifying a social need and taking steps to mobilize forces within the community to establish a new service, such as a shelter for runaways, crisis-line service, or a quiet supervised place to study in a noisy apartment building.

Communities that have a low income and that place a low value on education require interventions that will increase positive attitudes about education and encourage the school to reach into the community and provide services responsive to community need. The development of bilingual education programs, preschool child care programs that are part of the high school curriculum, and after-school care programs that involve school personnel are of mutual benefit to the school and community.

Practice Example. There are times when the community requires the school's assistance. One city was condemning property while expanding its cultural center, which threatened the existence of the school. The low-income families had established roots in the community and had a compatible relationship with the school. Under the leadership of the school social worker, the faculty joined the community members in establishing a school-community collaborative that developed enough power to engage the city in negotiations for a compromise of the demolition plan. Through the joint efforts of the school and community, the community was saved, with only minor property loss.

Policy Initiator and Developer.   School social workers influence, initiate, and develop policy, which affects the social and emotional development of children and youth within the school and community. Through participating in policy-making committees, writing grants, and as members of professional organizations, they are active in creating programs that benefit the edu-

cational process. The knowledge of when and how to use political "know-how" is an essential skill for this role.

Practice Example. A state agency wrote in their policies on hiring school social workers that other professionals could be hired in those roles. A school social worker wrote a letter to the NASW and the state licensing board for social work practice, bringing this to their attention. The practice was clearly illegal, since "social worker" is a protected title. The school social worker worked with these social work agencies to have the practice changed, which protected the integrity of the social work services and assured that clients would receive quality services.

Specialized Intervention Skills

Schools provide a natural environment in which to use the full range of practice methods. In ecological practice, an intervention is one component of a larger plan requiring intervention techniques that join and link systems in the change process (Freeman & Pennekamp, 1988).

Intervention with Individual Students.   Skills in assessment of individual dynamics, interviewing and counseling techniques, consultation, and linking and joining with other systems are required to intervene effectively with individual students. Counseling services range from individual counseling, providing temporary support, crisis intervention, and operating specific intervention programs such as grief support programs, transition programs and violence prevention, to preparation of the client for referral to outside resources. This includes assistance to students returning to their home school following hospitalization or confinement in a juvenile facility or special education program. Sometimes a student's need for individual counseling and support can be met by a well-trained volunteer such as a senior citizen or peer counselor (Pryor, 1992).

Interventions that empower individual pupils to cope with life situations should occur simultaneously in all systems affected by or exacerbating the presenting concern. For example, consider situations involving sensitive counseling of gay or lesbian students. Individual counseling may be helpful to the gay or lesbian student, but he or she still faces a hostile environment. Initiatives directed toward acceptance of different sexual orientations by the school and community are necessary for the healthy development of all adolescents in the future (Marks, 1987; Morrow, 1993).

Crisis Intervention. Even though a nationwide survey of school social workers' job tasks and skills indicates that school social workers prefer doing preventative work, school social workers provide most interventions in the context of crisis intervention (Allen-Meares, 1994). Crisis situations occur throughout the normal life span of individuals, families, groups, communities, and nations. A crisis demands immediate short-term help. Crisis situations frequently addressed by school social workers may be created by a suspension, a failing grade, the divorce or death of parents, the death or injury of a friend, attempted suicide, drug use, a change to a physically disabling state, or an unwanted pregnancy.

Child abuse is a situation that requires immediate attention. Service is required for both the child and the abuser and requires the involvement of a child protection agency. Because of violence in neighborhoods and schools, social work services have been made available to the victim, as well as to other students and staff who have been traumatized by the incidents (NASW, 2002; Dwyer, Osher, & Warger, 1998). Each school district has developed a plan for crisis intervention, and social workers need to be prepared to respond appropriately at the time of a crisis. For example, hypothetically, a first-grade teacher was shot and killed by her estranged husband in front of her class. A crisis team of social workers was immediately formed to assist the parents, students, and teachers to come to terms with the trauma and grief they experienced.

Working with Emotionally and Behaviorally Disturbed Students. Although most severely emotionally disturbed students requiring medication and/or specialized care are referred to outside agencies or to special education programs designed to serve them, schools can find themselves providing the needed service when a family or student refuses outside service, or when an agency cannot accept the referral because either the service needed does not fall within its guidelines of any agency or there is a long waiting list. Lack of medical coverage also limits referral options. Social workers who provide service to severely emotionally disturbed students in general education or who work in special education classrooms or day treatment programs for emotionally disturbed children should seek supervision, consultation, or collaboration with mental health professionals with expertise in these areas. Often such support is available within the program, but may have to be obtained from an outside source. (Sources of support may come from both inside and outside the program; it varies from school to school.)

School social workers often get involved in working with children with special needs and require expert skills to manage the behavioral difficulties of these youths. Youths who have severe behavior problems and conduct disorder may commit violent acts against others and violate others' rights. Work with such youth requires considerable expertise in order to develop effective practice skills and programs. To move beyond the generalist level to offer in-school intervention, even more expertise and advanced training is required. It is unlikely that every school social worker can become an expert in helping aggressive youth with a conduct disorder. School social workers refer many students to other school professionals and experts in the community. Aggressive, disruptive, and antisocial behaviors, are responsible for most of the referrals to clinic and agency settings (Kazdin, 1996). Also, one of the most worrisome behaviors for schools today is the aggressive acts committed by these children in school, including fighting, assaults, and even murder (NASW, 2002; Dwyer, Osher, & Warger, 1998). An example of the types of the specialized knowledge and skills needed for working with children with severe behavior problems and conduct disorder is described below.

Severe Behavior Problems and Conduct Disorder. Kazdin (1996) describes the characteristics of children with conduct disorder. Children exhibit behaviors such as aggressive acts, theft, vandalism, firesetting, lying, truancy, and running away. The prevalence rate of conduct disorder is between 2% and 6%. In the United States, this translates to approximately 1.3 million to 3.8 million cases.

According to Kazdin (1996), children with conduct disorder also are likely to have academic problems, poor grades, and learning disorders in reading. They are a constant challenge to the school, which often does not know how to manage children with such severe learning and behavior problems. Thus, schools desperately need the help of school social workers in their work with these children.

Helping Individual Students with Conduct Disorder. Helping students with conduct disorder has also been a constant challenge to school social workers and other helping professionals. Children with conduct disorder show a variety of cognitive errors related to their cognitive processes (perceptions, self-statements, attributions, and problem solving skills) concerning themselves and others. Examples of the errors in cognitive processing include social cognitive skills such as cognitive problem-solving skills and misattributions of hostile intent to others (Kazdin, 1996). Kazdin explains that the aggression exhibited by conduct disordered youth is not triggered exclusively by environmental events, but depends upon how events are perceived. School social workers working with these youth may intervene with cognitive models designed to help youth with their cognitive deficits such as the cognitive processing models. See Table 12.3 for an example of the steps used in this model.

The pervasiveness and intensity of conduct disorder demands a multi-modal response from school practitioners. To manage the behavior of conduct disordered children, school social workers must intervene with parents, teachers, and students. Several parent and teacher training models have been developed to help children with conduct disorder. Webster-Stratton (1996), for example, has developed parent and teacher training programs for use in schools, as well as curricula and programs for students. These multi-modal programs include curricula, videotapes, and teaching modules. See Table 12.4 for an example of these programs. They have also been empirically tested and found to be moderately effective.

Because conduct disorder is associated with a variety of contextual conditions such as large

---

TABLE 12.3   Cognitive Processing Model

1. **Encoding deficits:** The child conducts an incomplete search of social cues before evaluating another person's intentions.
2. **Interpretation deficits:** Presumably based on a history of actual victimization, parental psychopathology, or neuropsychiatric vulnerabilities, the youngster is biased toward perceiving hostile intent in others.
3. **Response search deficits:** The child generates too few—and often less-appropriate—alternative solutions.
4. **Response decision deficits:** The child awards more value to aggressive responses and evaluates them more favorably.
5. **Enactment deficits:** The child lacks prosocial negotiation skills.

Source: S. I. Pfeiffer. (1995). New directions in research. In G. P. Sholevar (Ed.), *Conduct disorders in children and adolescents.* Washington, DC: APA.

TABLE 12.4 Overview of Videotape Interventions

INTERVENTIONS	SKILLS TARGETED	PERSON TRAINED	SETTING TARGETED
Parenting skills (BASIC)	Parenting skills ■ Play, involvement ■ Praise, rewards ■ Limit setting ■ Discipline	Parent	Home
Interpersonal skills training (ADVANCE)	Interpersonal skills ■ Problem solving ■ Anger management ■ Communication ■ Depression control ■ Giving and receiving support	Parent	Home, work, community
Academic skills training (PARTNERS 1)	Academic skills ■ Academic stimulation ■ Learning routine after school ■ Homework support ■ Reading ■ Limit setting ■ Involvement at school ■ Teacher conferences	Parent	Home-school connection
Child skills training (KIDVID)	Social skills ■ Friendship ■ Teamwork ■ Cooperation, helping ■ Communication Problem solving ■ Anger management ■ Steps 1–7 Classroom behavior ■ Quiet hand up ■ Compliance ■ Listening ■ Stop-look-think-check ■ Concentrating	Child	Home and school
Teacher training (PARTNERS 2)	Classroom management skills Promoting parent involvement	Teacher	School

Source: C. Webster-Stratton. (1996). Early intervention with videotape modeling: Programs for families of children with oppositional defiant disorder or conduct disorder. In E. D. Hibbs & P. S. Jensen (Eds.), *Psychosocial treatments for child and adolescent disorders: Empirically based strategies for clinical practice* (pp. 435–474). Washington, DC: APA.

family size, overcrowding, poor housing, and disadvantaged school settings, it is also important to intervene into the mezzo and macro conditions that develop and maintain these problems (Kazdin, 1996). The ecological model explains how stressful living conditions produce situations where parents and children may get locked into a never-ending spiral of coercive interactions that lead to the escalation of aggressive behaviors.

Interventions with Bullying and Aggressive Behaviors.   In recent years, there has been an outbreak of school violence and school social workers have taken on leadership roles in the prevention of violence (NASW, 2002; Klein, 2002). One of the behavior problems that puts children at-risk for violent behaviors is bullying. Bullying is the type of aggressive responding that occurs over time and is threatening and intimidating, and is meant to disturb or harm others. There is also an imbalance of power that exists between bully and victim such that the bully is larger and has more power than those being bullied (Garret, 2001). Like other children who propose a threat of school violence, bullies often come from family and community situations where they have witnessed or been victims of violence themselves. As individuals they possess aggressive and impulsive characteristics and tend to lack inhibitions about using physical hitting or intimidation as a means of solving problems or controlling others. They also tend to be poor students and to have difficulty in their relationships with others. School social workers help schools stop bullying by identifying bully behaviors and developing policies of non-tolerance on school grounds.

It is also important to educate all school staff, including bus drivers and other school personnel, so that they have the skills to monitor children closely to make sure that aggressive behaviors are not tolerated. Schools have to have firm policies that assure careful monitoring and supervision of children on playgrounds, bathrooms, and halls to stop bullying (Astor, Behre, Wallace, & Fravil, 1998). Teachers can also use classroom time to help children learn conflict management and appropriate social skills. Role plays to teach children how to respond to bullies and psychoeducation materials that send a strong message that bullying is inappropriate behavior may also be used in the classroom. For other sources of in-

formation on stopping bullying, see Garrett, 2001, or the National Association of Social Workers' practice guidelines on bullying in youths (NASW, 2002).

Violence Prevention.   Even though children are statistically more likely to be murdered in their own home or neighborhood, there has been increasing concern over incidences of school violence (Dwyer, Osher, & Warger, 1998). The highly publicized school shootings that occurred in the late twentieth century and early part of the current century have pointed to the need for schools to have violence prevention and crisis intervention policies and plans. Policies and interventions for the prevention of acts of violence is most important, in particular, the identification of at-risk youths (Klein, 2002). The identification of at-risk youths, however, is a difficult task for schools because there are so many risk factors, and violence-prone youths often have overlapping characteristics with other troubled youths who may not be violence prone (Klein, 2002). The United States Department of Education (1998) released information on how to identify youths at-risk for violent acts. The following early warning signs are to serve as "red flags" to school personnel.

1. Social withdrawal
2. Excessive feelings of isolation or being alone
3. Excessive feelings of rejection
4. Being a victim of violence
5. Feelings of being picked on and persecuted
6. Low school interest and academic performance
7. Expression of violence in writings or drawings
8. Uncontrolled anger
9. Patterns of impulsive and chronic hitting, intimidating and bullying behaviors
10. History of discipline problems
11. Past history of violent or aggressive behaviors

12. Drug use and alcohol use
13. Affiliation with gangs
14. Inappropriate access to, possession of, and use of firearms
15. Serious threats of violence (Dwyer, Osher, & Warger, 1998, pp. 8–11).

One of the roles of school social workers is to help educators respond to risk factors such as those named above and to help assess and intervene with youths before a violent act is committed. School social workers can also help schools not stereotype and jump to the wrong conclusions about youths. They can focus schools on violence prevention policies and interventions that both protect and preserve the rights of individual students and families. Some of the effective school programs that can be put into place are comprehensive mental health services, special education programs, day treatment and alternative school programs with intensive clinical services instead of punitive alternatives or simple removal programs (Klein, 2002).

Practice Example. A 16-year-old Euro-American ninth grader, Julian was referred to the school social worker because he wrote a letter about wanting to kill a classmate (Joey) who had been picking on him in the halls. Julian was withdrawn and had few friends. He wore a unusual black coat with red markings but did not belong to any particular gang or cult. He was mostly known as a loner and a "real quiet boy." He had been sent to the principal's office two times the previous school year for fighting and conflicts with other students but had not been in fights this year. He had been known in younger years to bully some of the younger kids during middle school and to have a younger peer group than his age. He was a marginal student and had failed fifth grade because his mother was getting a divorce and moving around with her new boyfriend. Consequently, he missed too much school and could not catch up in time to be promoted. Further, family history indicated that Julian has observed violent incidents between his mother

and stepfather and that there was much history of family conflict.

Julian currently lived with his father in a rural setting, and visited his mother, who lived about 30 minutes away in the next town. When the school social worker asked him about the letter he said that he was mad at the student for picking on him and had written the letter to scare the student so that he would stop calling him names in the hall. The school social worker worked with the pupil services team to do a more thorough mental health evaluation of Julian. He was found to be a depressed and anxious boy with much anger toward his parents because of the divorce and the hardships it had caused. His father was called in for family work and the school social worker discussed the risk factors and the importance of keeping guns away from Julian. His father agreed to keep his hunting guns under lock and key and to work with the school on getting Julian help. Julian's mother was called but failed show up at the school for a meeting. Julian was referred to mental health services and a support group for children who had witnessed violence. It was also agreed that Julian would limit his visits with his mother to times that his stepfather was not present and that these meetings would not take place in her home. The school social worker also alerted hall monitors to keep Joey away from Julian. Joey was also reprimanded for his behavior by the assistant principal and his parents were called.

Intervention with Families. Families and schools are a part of the ecological context—subsystems of the child's world. They are interdependent systems that can support the maturation and productivity of the child when the family and the school are in agreement (Constable & Wallberg, 1991). There are many ways of developing parent partnerships with the school, including being invited to participate in activities such as general meetings, social events, report card conferences, and potluck suppers, serving as a parent aid in the classroom, or participating in policy determination (Winters & Easton, 1983). In a study by Kurtz and Barth (1989), the degree of social work involvement with parents was rated by 54% of the respondents as "very much," by 26% as "much," and the remaining 20% indicated "some"; the involvement included parent conferences, referrals, crisis work, family assessment, advocacy, parent groups, program development, and parent associations.

Many families function under oppressive conditions. Substance abuse, violence, economic instability, homelessness, and fear for safety drain energy from child-nurturing tasks. School social workers involve themselves in providing ongoing support to families in need and help them with their oppressive conditions.

Fortunately, in recent years several evidenced-based family treatments have emerged that help school social workers with youths who are violence prone, delinquent, and who may also have substance abuse problems. Two of these programs are the Multisystemic family therapy (Henggeler et al., 1998) and the family-based preventative program developed by Hogue and Liddle (1999). The Multisystemic family therapy is a home-based intervention that targets the risk factors that contribute to youth violence, substance abuse, and delinquent behaviors. Interventions focus on all the systems in the ecological context of the student including schools, peer groups, and family relations. Hogue and Liddle's program also targets risk factors and provides family-based treatment alternatives for youths who might otherwise be incarcerated.

Practice Example. Mrs. Erickson, her two young daughters, and her 15-year-old son, John, a developmentally disabled student in a wheelchair, were evicted from their rented home and were living in a shelter for the homeless. The mother and part-time father had been substance abusers over the years and had worn out their families with their constant demands for help. John not only suffered from the loss of home, car, and attention, he was afraid of losing his classmates' friendship if they learned of his homeless status. His grief and embarrassment became a focus in counseling with the social worker. Based on an ongoing relationship with Mrs. Erickson, the social worker responded to the immediate crisis by mobilizing her resources to assist the family in locating suitable housing. They would need to be on the first floor to accommodate John's wheelchair. Since little support or assistance was available from the shelter, the social worker contacted the county housing authority and, with the mother, combed newspaper ads for leads. Although an afternoon of following up on some of the ads with the mother was not immediately successful, it did mobilize John's mother to continue the search on her own. Support and continued contact with John eased some of the pain he was experiencing until the family was able to move from the shelter.

Immigrant Families. Immigrant families often find themselves in culturally conflicting situations with schools that can require interpretation and mediation. Adjustment problems, misunderstandings of a cultural nature, and lack of follow-through on medical care for the handicapped child may require interpretation of customs of Western culture to the immigrant family and the culture of the family to school personnel or health care providers.

Adjustment for immigrant families is often stressful. Many children of immigrants, especially adolescents, experience pressure for conformity by their peers and friction in their relationships with their parents on adherence to traditional gender roles and values as defined in their cultures. At the same time, parents have a strong need for their children to maintain their heritage and often find it difficult themselves to accept American culture. Differences in dress, foods, recreation, social expectations, gender roles, and language all create stress.

Practice Example. Ray, an 11-year-old sixth grader of mixed ethnicity (Hispanic/Anglo), was referred to a school social worker, due to his inability to make decisions for himself and his passive behavior in class, such as not turning in his work. Ray was initially assessed to determine the need for special education services when he was in the fifth grade, which was the most recent evaluation. At that time, he was found to demonstrate a significant academic deficit in math calculation and a significant behavioral deficit in peer relationships. It was determined that he met the eligibility criteria for the handicapping condition of Other Health Impaired. He had been placed in regular classrooms and had been performing well until the last six weeks. The school social worker visited the parents for a consultation on Ray's behavior. Ray lived with his multiethnic parents. His father was a Mexican who had immigrated to the U.S. three months ago. The family had been going through a tremendous amount of transition with the father looking for work. He currently worked as a sharecropper, and it was feared that unless he got another job, that he might have to leave the family to follow the crops, and the family may have to go with him. The mother did not want to leave her job, and she did not want to work in the fields like the father. The situation had created discord in the family. In speaking to Ray, the social worker determined that he was not getting much sleep due to the parental arguments. He also was worried about his father leaving. The school social worker held two problem-solving sessions with the family and referred the father to an employment agency that helped him obtain a different job. Ray's passive and indecisive behavior began to improve.

Interventions with Groups. The school is an organization composed of many groups: teacher, parent, classroom, and students (Johnson, 1991). Most activities take place within a group context: classroom, committee meetings, assemblies, lunchroom, sports, and other activities. Groups are particularly useful when development of socialization skills is indicated, when activity is desirable, and when natural groups can reinforce change (Johnson, 1983). The objectives also include exchanging information, clarifying value orientations, and diverting antisocial behaviors into productive channels.

With the advent of managed behavioral health care, groups are becoming a preferred method of treatment in different practice settings. Groups are believed to be an efficient and cost-effective method for intervention. Groups may be used for treatment and education, but there are also groups in which students and teachers work together to accomplish various tasks and goals. A differentiation can be made between a task group and an intervention group. An example of a task group is a committee formed to study a problem in a school and come up with a set of solutions. An intervention group is aimed at resolving the social problems and difficulties of students, parents, or teachers. For example, social workers may form parent groups to help parents learn how to respond to the drug problems of their children or a parenting skills group to help parents learn to be better parents. Groups may also be formed to help students with various problems such as grief, death of a friend, ADHD, family problems, etc.

Volumes have been written about group dynamics, the uses of groups, and the skills needed to lead them. One type of group structure and process that appears to be helpful to for schools is the task-centered group which was originally developed by Reid (Reid, 1992; 2000). Task-centered group work is a behaviorally-focused group that is usually formed to help youths solve various problem issues. Reid and Bailey-Dempsey (1995), for example, used the task approach and monetary incentives to help youths increase their school performance. Harris and Franklin (under review) recently found the task group process to be helpful when helping pregnant and parenting adolescents stay in school and improve their grades. Table 12.5 describes the group structure and process for task-centered groups.

School social workers are involved in a tremendous amount of school and community committee work. As members of or consultants to curriculum committees, social workers are in a position to influence thoughtful consideration of cultural and mental health content.

TABLE 12.5   Task Group Model Process

1. *Problem Specification:* The focus is on determining the problems the client wishes to work on. This is expected to take place in the first one to three sessions. During this phase a contract is developed, written or verbal, which delineates the problems, goals, and duration of treatment. Focus is on what the client wants and not on what the practitioner thinks the client may need. The practitioner may engage with the client in a mutual process of deliberation in which the practitioner contributes her/his own knowledge and perception, arriving at an explicit agreement on the identified problems.

2. *Task Planning and Implementation:* The focus is on formulating, planning, and evaluating tasks to resolve target problems. A task is an action that the participant agrees to take toward resolving the problem. Group leaders and participants define the task in a highly structured way, thus increasing chances that the task will be accom-

plished. This process usually happens over 6 to 10 sessions. The model offers specific strategies to assist the participant during this phase of intervention. One of these is assessing whether the group member has the knowledge and skills to perform as she desires, and if not, how to develop them. Another strategy, especially if the problem involves a formal organization, is for the practitioner to act as an advocate on behalf of the client to the organization. Leader activities as a strategy has evolved, as preferred over clinical techniques such as encouragement, direction, and explanation, and express the collaborative spirit of the model—what the practitioner and client do together to achieve common ends.

3. *Termination:* Progress is reviewed and summarized, and plans are made to increase lasting results from intervention gains. The last one to two sessions are assigned to this phase.

Social workers also lead many different types of prevention groups to accomplish goals and objectives of helping students. Examples of prevention groups include those focused on preventing HIV infection and pregnancy, values education, and substance abuse prevention.

Practice Example. A school social worker employed in a high school was asked to develop groups that focused on the prevention of HIV infection and pregnancy. Sex education curricula are often used in these types of groups in schools, and thousands of curricula have been developed by school districts. The school social worker was concerned about finding out what were the best curricula in use, and she read the professional literature to identify an effective curriculum. Four curricula in particular have demonstrated effectiveness with impacting sexual behavior (Kirby, 1992). The first is "Postponing Sexual Involvement," a curriculum given in conjunction with instruction on human sexuality and contraception. It was developed at Emory University School of Medicine and Grady Memorial Hospital (Howard & McCabe, 1990). The second curriculum

discussed is "Reducing the Risk," developed by Barth, a social work professor at the School of Social Welfare at the University of California at Berkeley (1989; Kirby, Barth, Leland, & Fetro, 1991). "Reducing the Risk" is used in California school districts.

Schinke, Blythe, and Gilchrist's (1981) cognitive-behavioral curriculum, developed in Seattle at the University of Washington School of Social Work, is a forerunner to "Reducing the Risk" curriculum. The final curriculum discussed is "AIDS Prevention for Adolescents in School," developed by Walter at Columbia University (Walter & Vaughan, 1993) in collaboration with participating high schools and the New York City Board of Education. Table 12.6 presents a summary of the components of these four curricula. Equipped with this knowledge, the school social worker chose to use the "Reducing the Risk" curriculum.

Intervention with Classrooms.   School social workers often work with classrooms of students and their teachers. Teachers may become col-

TABLE 12.6 Four Effective Sex Education Curriculums

CURRICULUM	FOCUS OF INTERVENTION	IMPLEMENTATION	THEORETICAL ORIENTATION
Reducing the risk—Barth (1989)	Avoiding sexual intercourse and improved contraceptive use through gains in knowledge and skill.	Trained school teachers deliver the 15-session curriculum over a 3-week period to 9th through 12th graders.	Social learning, social inoculation, and cognitive-behavioral
Postponing sexual involvement—Howard & McCabe (1990, 1992)	Avoiding sexual intercourse by increased knowledge and skill.	Trained, slightly older teens deliver the curriculum through 10 classes over a 3-month period to 8th graders.	Social influence model
Schinke, Blythe, & Gilchrist (1981)	Improving decision-making skills related to sexual behavior and contraceptive use.	Two MSW facilitators lead mixed-sex groups of 10th graders in 14 one-hour sessions.	Cognitive-behavioral
AIDS preventive curriculum—Walter & Vaughan (1993)	Building knowledge about AIDS and the skills to prevent unwanted pregnancy.	Trained school teachers deliver the curriculum through 6 one-class period sessions on consecutive days to 9th and 11th graders.	Health belief model, social cognitive theory, and social influence model

Source: C. Franklin & J. Corcoran. (1999). *Adolescent pregnancy prevention: A review of programs and practices.* Social Work.

laborators or co-facilitators in this process. One area of concern for classrooms is the integration of new students. New students change the group dynamics of the classroom. It takes time and often assistance before a new classroom equilibrium is established. Equilibrium is also disturbed when a class member leaves to attend another school or program or dies; or when a class member or members are suspended or expelled. Each circumstance may require different approaches by the teacher and others. The social worker can play a major role in this process by identifying the need to pay attention to these issues and by providing consultation and support as requested.

The transition of a new student entering the classroom may be made easier, for example, if the social worker and the teacher work together to prepare the class to accept the new student. The new student may not speak English, may be

suspended from another school, might be a former special education student who is now being included in the general education program, or is possibly a homeless child or a child from a military family or from another state due to company reassignments or job changes (Bloomfield & Holzman, 1988).

Practice Example. In an elementary school, a school social worker co-facilitated a classroom group with the teacher on setting rules for conduct and respect for each other in the classroom. The class was broken into smaller groups and exercises were provided to help identify who liked whom, and what was the general consensus on setting rules for treatment of classmates and the teacher. New rules for behavior and social skills were practiced through role plays, and the concepts learned were reinforced throughout the day by the teacher who remained with the class.

Intervention with the School. The school is the second most important influence (after the family) on the behavior and accomplishments of the children (Allen-Meares, 1985), and Allen-Meares lists some of the important qualities schools model for children:

> Its atmosphere and academic expectations; quality and consistence of the teacher interaction; resourcefulness of the teacher and the educational program; its responsiveness to children of different ethnic, socio-economic, and status backgrounds; its willingness to reach out to parents and work together to resolve conflicting points of view and/or support each other; and the degree of humanness and flexibility that exists in policies and educational programs (p. 103).

Facilitating a nurturing climate in the school may include recognizing efforts and achievements of teachers, staff, and volunteers. Some schools have an annual teacher appreciation day. In one school, the social workers developed a list of ways in which students and classes could show their appreciation.

Practice Example. Middle school students were moved from a new urban middle school to an old elementary school building that still contained furniture and fixtures used by its previous tenants. During the first month, students broke windows, hurled furniture down the stairs, and scrawled graffiti on walls. Teachers found that little energy was being spent on learning and that the students were restless. The school administrators viewed the students' behavior as deviant. With each escalation in disciplinary measures, the situation became worse. After talking with students, teachers, and parents, the social worker concluded that the students were expressing a strong resentment toward the change in school buildings. She sat down with the principal and engaged him in an assessment of the situation, resulting in a plan of action that involved the pupils in creating a school environment that was more appropriate for their age group. The word "elementary" was removed from the sign on the front of the building, appropriately sized furniture was ordered from the supply department, and members of the art department worked with students to paint attractive murals on the walls. In addition, programs were developed in the school to build school spirit, and teachers, through in-service training, learned alternative ways of allowing the students to vent their anger about school conditions. Within a few weeks, the vandalism ceased and the students were back to work.

CONCLUSION

Using an ecological framework, this chapter provided an overview of social work interventions in schools. The new roles of school social workers in school-linked services are overviewed. The effects of managed behavioral health care on school social workers was highlighted. Intervention roles of school social workers were also summarized. The clinical role of counselor or therapist is one of the main functions of the school social workers, but the roles of broker, teacher, advocate, facilitator, manager, mediator, consultant, collaborator, community organizer, and policy initiator and developer are equally important. In school-linked services programs community organization roles are increasingly important. Finally, specialized intervention skills such as those necessary to work with individual students, families, groups, classrooms and school systems were overviewed.

FOR STUDY AND DISCUSSION

1. Camille is a Hispanic student who is failing Language Arts and social studies. As a school social worker you have been asked to contact her parents about the problem. The parents do not speak English and do not have a telephone. What types of intervention skills would you use in working with this family and helping Camille with her school problems?

2. Five-year-old Kendra Beal was referred to a school social worker by her kindergarten teacher because of destructive behavior in the classroom and for acts of self-mutilation. During the first interview, Mrs. Beal revealed that she had a terminal illness and wanted to find a good home for her three daughters. She was receiving help from other social workers representing three different agencies (health facility, family agency, and DSS); each gave conflicting advice. She was confused. What steps would you take to assist Mrs. Beal and Kendra?

3. An African American student's parents show up at the school frantic because their 14-year-old daughter, Lynda, has been skipping school and leaving with an 18-year-old boy. The last incident of leaving school, which occurred two days before, resulted in her staying out all night in a hotel and being returned by the police. The parents are in a crisis and are asking for help. They are especially worried that their daughter may become pregnant or contract HIV. As a school social worker, how would you proceed with this family?

4. The population of the school is multicultural. What role can or should the social worker assume to maintain harmonious cultural relationships?

5. A 12-year-old boy is committing violent acts such as fighting and destroying school property. He has been expelled or served time in in-school suspension several times. Other students say he brags about torturing animals and owning guns. One student expresses to a school counselor that she is afraid of him because "he gives her the creeps" when he repeatedly asks her to come to his house even though she has declined his offer on several occasions. The teachers are worried about his violent tendencies. As a school social worker what roles and intervention skills would you use to help this student?

ADDITIONAL READING

Allen-Meares, P. (1996). School social work services in the schools: A look at yesteryear and the future. *Social Work in Education, 18,* 202–209.

Amanto, P. R., & Keith, B. (1991). Parental divorce and the wellbeing of children: A meta-analysis. *Psychological Bulletin, 110,* 26–46.

Ashman, K. K., & Hull, G. H. (2001). *Generalist practice with organizations and communities* (2nd ed.). Pacific Grove, CA: Brooks/Cole.

Ayasse, R. H. (1995). Addressing the of foster children: The foster youth services program. *Social Work in Education, 17,* 207–216.

Bowen, N. K. (1999). A role for school social workers in promoting student success through school-family partnerships. *Children & Schools, 21,* 34–48.

Burns, B. J., & Hoagwood, K. (2002). *Community treatment for youth.* New York: Oxford University Press.

Chapman, C., & Kleiner, B. (2000). Youth service learning and community service among 6th through 12th grade students in the United States: 1996 and 1999. *Education Statistics Quarterly, 2*(1).

Ciffone, J. (1993). Suicide prevention: A classroom presentation to adolescents. *Social Work, 38,* 197–203.

Corcoran, J. (2000). *Evidence-based social work practice with families: A lifespan approach.* New York: Springer.

Corcoran, K., & Fischer, J. (2000). *Measures for clinical practice.* New York: Free Press.

Delva-Tauili'ili, J. (1995). Assessment and prevention of aggressive behavior among youths of color: Integrating cultural and social factors. *Social Work in Education, 17,* 83–91.

Duke, D. L., & Griesdorn, J. (1999). Considerations in the design of alternative schools. *The Clearing House, 73*(2), 89–92.

Dupper, D. R., & Bosch, L. A. (1996). Reasons for school suspensions. An examination of data from one school district and recommendations for reducing suspensions. *Journal of Just and Caring Education, 2,* 140–150.

Dupper, D. R., & Evans, S. (1996). From Band-Aids and putting out fires to prevention: School social work practice approaches for the new century. *Social Work in Education, 18,* 187–192.

Eddy, M., Reid, J., & Fetrow, B. (2000). An elementary school-based prevention program targeting modifiable antecedents of youth delinquency and violence: Linking the Interests of Family and Teachers (LIFT). *Journal of Emotional and Behavioral Disorders, 8,* 165–176.

Early, T. J., & Vonk, M. E. (2001). Effectiveness of school social work from a risk and resilience perspective. *Children & Schools, 23,* 9–31.

Felner, R., Brand, S., Adan, A., Mulhall, P., Flowers, N., Sartain, B., & Dubois, D. (1993). Restructuring the ecology of the schools as an approach to prevention during school transitions: Longitudinal follow-ups and extensions of the School Transitional Environment Project (STEP). In L. Jason, K. Danner, & K. Kurasaki (Eds.), *Prevention and school transitions* (pp. 103–136). New York: Haworth Press.

Franklin, C., Biever, J. L., Moore, K., Clemons, D., & Scamardo, M. (2001). The effectiveness of solution-focused therapy with children in a school setting. *Research on Social Work Practice, 11*(4), 411–434.

Fraser, M. (Ed.). (2002). *Risk and resiliency in childhood: An ecological perspective* (2nd ed.). Washington, DC: NASW Press.

Fraser, M., Nash, J. K., Galinsky, M. J., & Darwin, K. M. (2000*). Making choices: Social problem solving skills for children.* Washington, DC: NASW Press.

Franklin, C. (1992). Alternative school programs for at-risk youths. *Social Work in Education, 14,* 239–251.

Freeman, E. (1992). *The addiction process: Effective social work approaches.* New York: Longman.

Freeman, E., Franklin, C., Fong, R., Shaffer, G., & Timberlake, E. (Eds.). (1998). *School social work practice: Multisystem skills and interventions.* Washington, DC: NASW Press.

Garrett, K. J. (2001). Reducing school-based bullying. *Journal of School Social Work, 12,* 74–90.

Gingerich, W. J., & Wabeke, T. (2001). A solution-focused approach to mental health intervention in schools. *Children & Schools, 23,* 33–48.

Goldhaber, D. D. (1999). School choice: An examination of the empirical evidence on achievement, parental decision making, and equity. *Educational Researcher, 28*(9), 16–25.

Hare, I. (1996). Regulating school social work practice into the 21st century. *Social Work in Education, 18,* 250–258.

Henggeler, S. W., Schoenwald, S. K., Borduin, C. M., Rowland, M. D., & Cunningham, P. B. (1998). *Multisystemic treatment of antisocial behavior in children and adolescents.* New York: Guilford Press.

Hogue, A., & Liddle, H. A. (1999). Family-based preventive intervention: An approach to preventing substance abuse and antisocial behavior. *The American Journal of Orthopsychiatry, 69,* 278–290.

Jordan, C., & Franklin, C. (1995; 2003). *Clinical assessment for social workers. Quantitative and qualitative methods.* Chicago: Lyceum Books/ Nelson Hall Books.

Karoly, J. C., & Franklin, C. (1996). Using portfolios to assess students' academic strengths: A case study. *Social Work in Education, 18*(3), 179–185.

Raines, J. C. (1996). Appropriate verses least restrictive: Educational policies and students with disabilities. *Social Work in Education, 18,* 113–127.

Roberts, A. L., & Greene, G. J. (2002). *Social workers desk reference.* New York: Oxford University Press.

Rotheram-Borus, M. J., Miller, S., Murphy, D. A., & Draimin, B. H. (1997). An intervention for adolescents whose parents are living with AIDS. *Clinical Child Psychology and Psychiatry, 2,* 201–219.

Schargel, F. P., & Smink, J. (2001). *Strategies to help solve our school dropout problem.* Larchmont, NY: Eye on Education.

The Center for Mental Health in Schools. (1999, winter). *Addressing barriers to learning: New ways to think, Better ways to link.* Los Angeles: Author.

Wall, J. C. (1996). Homeless children and their families: Delivery of education and social services through school systems. *Social Work in Education, 18,* 135–144.

Ward, B. R. (1995). The school's role in the prevention of youth suicide. *Social Work in Education, 17,* 92–100.

Weisz, J. R., & Jenson, P. S. (1999). Efficacy and effectiveness of child and adolescent psychotherapy and pharmacotherapy. *Mental Health Services Research, 1,* 125–157.

Williams, E. G., & Sadler, L. S. (2001). Effects of an urban high school-based child care center on self-selected adolescent parents and their children. *Journal of School Health, 71*(2), 47–52.

Williamson, D., Warner, D. E., Sanders, P., & Knepper, P. (1999). We can work it out: Teaching conflict management through peer mediation. *Children & Schools, 21,* 89–99.

**ANNOTATED BIBLIOGRAPHY FOR SOCIAL WORK
INTERVENTION WITH PUPILS, SMALL GROUPS,
CLASSROOMS, SCHOOLS, FAMILIES, AND COMMUNITIES**_____

Alexander, R., & Curtis, C. M. (1995). A critical review of strategies to reduce school violence. *Social Work in Education, 17,* 73–82. Reviews literature and reports interventions being used to reduce school violence.

Astor, R. A., Behre, W. J. , Wallace, J. M., & Fravil, K. A. (1998). School social workers and school violence: Personal safety, training and violence programs. *Social Work, 43,* 223–232. Reports finding from a national survey that questioned school social workers on violence.

Chavkin, N. F. (Ed.). (1993). *Families and schools in a pluralistic society.* New York: SUNY Press. Presents information on working with multi-cultural families in a school context.

Dupper, D. R., & Poertner, J. (1997). Public schools and the revitalization center of impoverished communities: School-linked family resource centers. *Social Work, 42,* 415–422. Discusses how school-linked family resources can be used to make community interventions. Provides helpful guidelines for developing such centers.

Dupper, D. R. (1994). Preventing school dropouts: Guidelines for school social work practice. *Social Work in Education, 15,* 141–149. Provides information on the problems facing schools concerning dropouts and provided practice guidelines for how to reduce the dropout problem in schools.

Dwight, L. (1992). *We can do it.* New York: Checkerboard Press. A positive support book for upper elementary children with Spina Bifida, Down's Syndrome, Cerebral Palsy, Visual Impairments. Excellent photographs of children engaging in many activities.

Ewalt, P. L., Freeman, E. M., Kirk, S. A., & Poole, D. L. (1996). *Multicultural issues in social work.* Washington, DC: NASW Press. A large book of case readings and intervention strategies on working with multicultural clients.

Flick, G. L. (1998). *ADD/ADHD Behavior-change resource kit.* West Nyack, New York: The Center for Applied Research in Education. A comprehensive resource guide and intervention manual for work in schools with children with ADHD. Provides step-by-step directions and resources for classroom and other behavioral management issues. Also, discusses work with parents and how to collaborate with other professionals for behavior change.

Franklin, C. (2001). Establishing successful relationships with expanded mental health services. *Children in Schools, 23*(4), 194–197. Points to the need for school social workers to find ways to collaborate with expanded mental health services.

Franklin, C., Grant, D., Corcoran, J., Mill, P. O., & Bultman, L. (1997). Effectiveness or prevention programs for adolescent pregnancy: A meta-analysis. *Journal of Marriage and the Family, 59,* 551–567. Synthesizes the studies on the primary prevention of adolescent pregnancy for community-based and school-based programs. Discusses the state-of-the-art in effective interventions.

Franklin, C., & Jordan, C. (1999). *Family practice: Brief systems methods for social work.* Pacific Grove: CA. Provides overviews of several different brief practice models for families. Includes transcripts of cases and case studies illustrating different methods for family practice.

Friedrich, M. J. (1999). Twenty-five years of school-based health centers. *Journal of the American Medical Association, 28,* 781–881. Speaks to statistics and experiences in establishing health clinics in the schools. Offers information on funding issues.

Gibelman, M. (1993). School social workers, counselors and psychologists: A shared agenda. *Social Work in Education, 15,* 45–54. Reviews the roles of related services professionals and highlights similarities and collaboration.

Henggeler, S. W., Schoenwald, S. K., Borduin, C. M., Rowland, M. D., & Cunningham, P. B. (1998*). Multisystemic treatment of antisocial behavior in children and adolescents.* New York: Guilford Press. Treatment manual that teaches practitioners how to do multisystemic therapy. A step-by-step guide with case studies.

Hogue, A., & Liddle, H. A. (1999). Family-based preventive intervention: An approach to preventing substance abuse and antisocial behavior. *The American Journal of Orthopsychiatry, 69,* 278–290. Journal article illustrating an evidenced-based, family-based, intervention program.

Jordan, C., & Franklin, C. (1995; 2003). *Clinical assessment for social workers. Quantitative and qualitative methods.* Chicago: Lyceum Books/ Nelson Hall Books. Provides information on for different methods for assessing children and families and provides measurement tools for assessment.

McNeece, C. A., & DiNitto, D. M. (2002). *Chemical dependency: A systems approach* (3rd ed.). Boston: Allyn and Bacon. Introduces students to the broad range of topics necessary for a basic understanding of professional practice with alcohol and other drug abusers.

McWhirter, I. J., McWhirter, B. T., McWhirter, A. M., & McWhirter, E. H. (1993). *At-risk youth: A comprehensive response.* Pacific Grove, CA: Brooks/Cole. Presents information on how to intervene with youth across several areas of concern including youth suicide, adolescent pregnancy, family problems, and academic problems.

Moe, J., & Ways, P. (1991). *Conducting support groups for elementary children K–6.* Minneapolis: Johnson Institute. This book provides the professional with an educational strategy that engages students in the affective. Support groups provide a way for many hurting children to get help.

Morgan, G. "Finding your 15%: The art of mobilizing small changes to produce large effects." Imaginization Website, http://www.imaginiz.com/ provocative/concept/find.html. Provides information on setting up collaborations and interprofessional teams.

National Assembly on School-Based Health Care, http://www.nasbhc.org/. Website for school based health clinics statistics and information

National Crisis Prevention Institute, 3315-K North 124th Street, Brookfield, Wisconsin 53005. CPI has developed a number of products and services to train staff in nonviolent crisis intervention.

Pryor, C. B. (1996). Techniques for assessing family-school connections. *Social Work in Education, 18,* 85–94. Reviews eight techniques for assessing family-school connections.

Reinecke, M. A., Dattilio, F. M., & Freeman, A. (1996). Cognitive therapy with children and adolescents. New York: Guilford. Presents a casebook of information on how to help children with diverse problems using cognitive therapy.

Taylor, L. (2000). Achieving coordinated mental health programs in schools. *Journal of School Health, 70*(5), 169. Provides information on how to work well with outside mental health professionals.

Taylor, L., & Adelman, H. (2000). Toward the end of marginalization and fragmentation of mental health in schools. *Journal of School Health, 70*(5), 210. Advocates a comprehensive and collaborative approach to school mental health services.

Waxman, R. P., Weist, M., & Benson, D. M. (1999). Toward collaboration in the growing education-mental health interface. *Clinical Psychology Review, 19,* 239–253. Sets forth important principles for working with diverse professionals in a school setting.

Weist, M. D., Myers, C. P., Hastings, E., Ghuman, H., & Han, Y. (1999). Psychosocial functioning of youth receiving mental health services in the school vs. community mental health centers. *Community Mental Health Journal, 35*(1), 69–81. Study that compares mental health services offered in school-based clinics with community mental health clinics. Schools were just as effective and offered greater access to the services.

CATALOGUES

Following are a few catalogues which address mental health needs through games and books and professional literature:

ABC School Supply, P.O. Box 4750, Norcross, GA 30171.

AGS Early Childhood Catalog, American Guidance Service, 4201 Woodland Road, Circle Pines, MN 55014. AGS provides a wide variety of toys and games for preschool and elementary students.

Childwork/Childplay, Center for Applied Psychology, Inc. P.O Box 1586, King of Prussia, PA 19406.

CPPC, 4 Conant Square, Brandon, VT 05733. Offers professional books, monographs, tests, and software.

Childcraft, P.O. Box 3081, Edison, NJ 08818-3081 Lexington Books, 125 Spring Street, Lexington, MA 02173. They publish professional books on topics of sociopsychological concern to school social workers.

Research Press, *Publications/Medical Catalog,* Box 3177 Dept. H, Champaign, IL 61821.

REFERENCES

Allen-Meares, P. (1985). Children with behavioral disorders: An eclectic approach for social workers. *Social Work in Education, 7,* 100–114.

Allen-Meares, P. (1994). Social work services in schools: A national study of entry-level tasks. *Social Work, 39,* 560–565.

Armbruster, P., Andrews, E., Couenhoven, J., & Blau, G. (1999). Collision or collaboration? School-based health services meet managed care. *Clinical Psychology Review 19*(2), 221–237.

Barth, R. A. (1989). *Reducing the risk.* Santa Cruz, CA: Network Publications/ETR Associates.

Blackwell, B., & Schmidt, G. L. (1992). The educational implications of managed mental health care. *Hospital and Community Psychiatry, 43,* 962–964.

Bloomfield, K. M., & Holzman, R. (1988). Helping today's nomads: A collaborative program to assist mobile children and their families. *Social Work in Education, 10,* 183–189.

Bowen, G. L., Richman, J., & Bowen, N. K. (2002). The School Success Profile: A results management approach to assessment and intervention planning. In A. R. Roberts & G. J. Greene (Eds.), *The Social Workers Desk Reference* (pp. 787–793). New York: Oxford University Press.

Brener, N. D., Martindale, J., & Weist, M. D. (2001). Mental health and social services: Results from the school health policies and programs study 2000. *Journal of School Health, 71,* 305–312.

Chapman, M. V., & Richman, J. (1998). Promoting research and evaluation of practice in school-based programs: Lesson learned. *Social Work in Education, 20,* 203–208.

Compton, B., & Galaway, B. (1984). *Social work processes* (3rd ed.). Homewood, IL: Dorsey Press.

Constable, R., & Wallberg, H. (1991). School social work: Facilitating home-school partnerships in the 1990s. In R. T. Constable, J. P., Flynn, & S. McDonald (Eds.), *School social work: Practice and research perspectives* (2nd ed., pp. 189–204). Chicago: Lyceum.

Corcoran, J. (2000). *Evidenced-based social work practice with families: A life span approach.* New York: Springer.

Corcoran, K., & Fisher, J. (2000). *Measures for clinical practice.* New York: Free Press.

Corcoran, K., & Gingerich, W. J. (1994). Practice evaluation in the context of managed care: Case recording methods of quality of assurance reviews. *Research on Social Work Practice, 4,* 326–337.

Corcoran, K., & Vandiver, V. (1996). *Maneuvering the maze of managed care.* New York: Free Press.

Dorfman, R. A. (1996). *Clinical social work: Definition, practice and vision.* New York: Brunner/Mazel.

Dwyer, K., Osher, D., & Warger, C. (1998). Early warning, timely response: A guide to safe schools. Washington, DC: U.S. Department of Education. Retrieved June 27, 2002 from http://cecp.air.org/guide/guide.pdf

Fast, J. (1999). Where were you fifth period? Five strategies for high school group formation in the 1990s. *Social Work in Education, 21,* 99–107.

Franklin, C. (1999). Preparing for managed behavioral health care in children's services. *Children & Schools, 21,* 67–71.

Franklin, C. (2000). Predicting the future of school social work practice in the new millennium. *Social Work in Education, 22*(1), 3–7.

Franklin, C. (2001). Establishing successful relationships with expanded mental health services. *Children in Schools, 23*(4), 194–197.

Franklin, C. (2002). The changing landscape of school mental health and social services. *NASW Section Connection, 8,* 1–3.

Franklin, C., & Allen-Meares, P. (1997). School social workers are a critical part of the link. *Social Work in Education, 19,* 131–135.

Franklin, C., & Johnson, C. (1996). Family social work practice: Onward to therapy and policy. *Journal of Family Social Work, 1*(3), 33–47.

Franklin, C., & Soto, I. (in press). Keeping Hispanic youths in school. *Children & Schools, 24.*

Franklin, C., & Streeter, C. L. (1995). School reform: Linking public schools with human services. *Social Work, 40,* 773–782.

Freeman, E., & Pennekamp, M. (1988). *Social work practice: Toward a child, family, school, community perspective.* Springfield, IL: Charles C. Thomas.

Gallant, C. B. (1982). Marketable social work skills. In *Professional issues for social workers in schools: Conference proceedings.* Silver Spring, MD: NASW Press.

Garrett, K. J. (2001). Reducing school-based bullying. *Journal of School Social Work, 12,* 74–90.

Germain, C. B. (1991). An ecological perspective on

social work in the schools. In R. T. Constable, J. P., Flynn, & S. McDonald (Eds.), *School social work: Practice and research perspectives* (2nd ed., pp. 17–30). Chicago: Lyceum.

Giles, T. R. (1991). Managed mental health care and effective psychotherapy: A step in the right direction? *Journal of Behavior Therapy and Experimental Psychiatry, 22,* 83–86.

Gitterman, A. (1996). Life model theory and social work treatment. In F. J. Turner (Ed.), *Social work treatment* (4th ed., pp. 389–408). New York: Free Press.

Goldstein, A. P. (1980). *Skill streaming for adolescents.* Champaign, IL: Research Press.

Goldstein, A. P. (1984). *The prepared curriculum.* Champaign, IL: Research Press.

Goldstein, A. P., & McGinnis, E. (1984). *Skill streaming for elementary school children.* Champaign, IL: Research Press.

Harris, M. B., & Franklin, C. (under review). Effects of a cognitive-behavioral, school-based, group intervention with Mexican-American pregnant and parenting mothers.

Henggeler, S. W., Schoenwald, S. K., Borduin, C. M., Rowland, M. D., & Cunningham, P. B. (1998). *Multisystemic treatment of antisocial behavior in children and adolescents.* New York: Guilford Press.

Hogue, A., & Liddle, H. A. (1999). Family-based preventive intervention: An approach to preventing substance abuse and antisocial behavior. *The American Journal of Orthopsychiatry, 69,* 278–290.

Howard, M., & McCabe, J. A. (1990). Helping teenagers postpone sexual involvement. *Family Planning Perspectives, 22,* 21–26.

Howard, M., & McCabe, J. A. (1992). An information and skills approach for younger teens: Postponing sexual involvement program. In B. C. Miller, J. J. Card, R. L. Paikoff, & J. L. Peterson (Eds.), *Preventing adolescent pregnancy* (pp. 83–109). Newbury Park, CA: Sage.

Hoyt, M. F. (1995). Brief therapy and managed care: Readings for contemporary practice. San Francisco: Jossey-Bass.

Johnson, L. (1983). *Social work practice: A generalist approach.* Boston: Allyn and Bacon.

Johnson, J. (1991). The no-fault school: Understanding groups—understanding schools. In R. T. Constable, J. P., Flynn, & S. McDonald (Eds.), *School*

social work: Practice and research perspectives (2nd ed., pp. 290–310). Chicago: Lyceum.

Jordan, C., & Franklin, C. (2003). *Clinical assessment for social workers.* Chicago: Lyceum.

Kazdin, A. E. (1996). Problem solving and parent management in treating aggressive and antisocial behavior. In E. D. Hibbs & P. S. Jensen (Eds.), *Psychosocial treatments for child and adolescent disorders.* Washington, DC: APA.

Kirby, D. (1992). School-based programs to reduce sexual risk-taking behaviors. *Journal of School Health, 62,* 281–286.

Kirby, D., Barth, R. P., Leland, N., & Fetro, J. V. (1991). Reducing the risk: Impact of a new curriculum on sexual risk taking. *Family Planning Perspectives, 23,* 253–263.

Klein, J. (2002). *NASW policy statement on school violence.* Washington, DC: NASW.

Kurtz, P. D., & Barth, R. P. (1989). Parent involvement: Cornerstone of school social work practice. *Social Work, 34,* 407–417.

Larson, C. S., Gomby, D. S., Shiono, S., Lewit, E. M., & Behrman, R. E. (1992). School-linked services. *Analysis. Future of Children, 2,* 6–18.

Lazarus, A. (1995). Preparing for practice in an era of managed competition. *Psychiatric Services, 46,* 184–185.

Mannino, F., & Shore, M. (1975). The effects of consultation: A review of empirical studies. *American Journal of Community Psychology, 3,* 1–21.

Marks, J. A. (1987). Stresses on gay and lesbian adolescents. *Social Work in Education, 9*(3), 169–180.

Markward, M. J. (1993). Assessing the effectiveness of social work practice in a school-community partnership: An illuminative approach. *Early Child Development and Care, 86,* 105–121.

Medway, F. J., & Updyke, J. F. (1985). Meta-analysis of consultation outcome studies. *American Journal of Community Psychology, 13,* 389–405.

Metcalf, L. (1995). *Counseling toward solutions: A practical solution-focused program for working with students, teachers, and parents.* Englewood Cliffs, NJ: Simon & Schuster.

Moriarty, A., & McDonald, S. (1991). Mediation as a form of peer-based conflict resolution. In R. T. Constable, J. P. Flynn, & S. McDonald (Eds.), *School social work: Practice and research perspectives* (2nd ed., pp. 281–289). Chicago: Lyceum.

Morrow, D. F. (1993). Social work with gay and

lesbian adolescents. *Social Work, 38*(6), 655–660.

National Association of Social Workers (2002). *Bullying among school-age youths.* Washington, DC: Author.

Pryor, C. B. (1992). Peer helping programs in school settings: Social workers report. *School Social Work Journal, 16*(2), 16–25.

Pugach, M., & Allen-Meares, P. (1985). Collaboration at the preservice level: Instructional and evaluational activities. *Journal of Teacher Education and Special Education, 8*(1), 3–11.

Radin, N. (1988). Alternatives to suspension and corporal punishment. *Urban Education, 22*(4), 24.

Reid, W. J. (1992). *Task strategies: An empirical approach to social work practice.* New York: Columbia University Press.

Reid, W. J. (2000). *The task planner.* New York: Columbia University Press.

Reid, W. J., & Bailey-Dempsey, C. (1995). The effects of monetary incentives on school performance. *Families in Society, 76,* 331–340.

Sabatino, C. A. (1991). School social work consultation: Theory, practice, and research. In R. T. Constable, J. P. Flynn, & S. McDonald (Eds.), *School social work: Practice and research perspectives* (2nd ed., pp. 257–272). Chicago: Lyceum.

Sabin, J. E. (1991). Clinical skills for the 1990s: Six lessons from HMO practice. *Hospital and Community Psychiatry, 42,* 605–608.

Sauter, J., & Franklin, C. (1998). Assessing post-traumatic stress disorder in children: Diagnostic and measurement strategies. *Research on Social Work Practice, 8,* 251–270.

Schinke, S. P., Blythe, B., & Gilchrist, L. (1981). Cognitive behavioral prevention of adolescent pregnancy. *Journal of Counseling Psychology, 28,* 451–454.

Streeter, C., & Franklin, C. (2002). Standards for school social work in the 21st century. In A. L. Roberts & G. J. Greene (Eds.), *Social work desk reference* (pp. 612–617). New York: Oxford University Press.

Strom-Gottfried, K. (1997). The implications of managed care for social work education. *Journal of Social Work Education, 33,* 7–18.

Taylor, L. (2000). Achieving coordinated mental health programs in schools. *Journal of School Health, 70*(5), 169.

UCLA School Mental Health Project, Center for Mental Health in Schools. (n.d.). Homepage. Retrieved June 27, 2002, from http://smhp.psych.ucla.edu/temphome.htm

Walter, H. J., & Vaughan, R. D. (1993). AIDS risk reduction among a multiethnic sample of urban high school students. *Journal of the American Medical Association, 270,* 725–730.

Webster-Stratton, C. (1996). Early intervention with videotape modeling: Programs for families of children with oppositional defiant disorder or conduct disorder. In E. D. Hibbs, & P. S. Jensen (Eds.), *Psychosocial treatments with children and adolescents* (pp. 435–474). Washington, DC: APA.

Winegar, N. (1993). Managed mental health care: Implications for administrators and managers of community-based agencies. *Families in Society, 74,* 171–177.

Winters, W. G., & Easton, F. (1983). *The practice of social work in schools: An ecological perspective.* New York: Free Press.

CHAPTER 13

EVALUATING PRACTICE AND PROGRAMS

SRINIKA D. JAYARATNE, UNIVERSITY OF MICHIGAN

The need for systematic evaluation of practice and programs and accountability are not academic questions but a service delivery and management reality. The conduct of systematic evaluation, however, is part politics, part knowledge, and part skill. An evaluator must be able to design and implement a study which can withstand the criticism of detractors. This chapter will address key concepts, principles and practices related to the development, design, implementation and write-up of evaluation studies. Attention will be paid to the value and utility of understanding context and the ethical responsibilities of the evaluator.

INTRODUCTION

Organizations and practitioners engage in some form of evaluation explicitly or implicitly at virtually all levels of functioning. Evaluating social work programs and practices in schools is no different. The efficacy of a school and its programs are judged by the school board and administrators, parents, students, and indirectly by the community. Social work services within the larger milieu of a school system may constitute a unit or department, albeit small in many instances. In other instances, social workers may be contract workers external to the school system. Its centrality to the overall functioning of the school lies in its ability to demonstrate the need for and the effectiveness of services provided, just as a corporate manager must demonstrate the value and utility of products and product lines. Thus, the onus of responsibility for demonstrating the functional value of social work practice lies with the practitioners. In the absence of evidence, it may not be too cynical to say that a school system may eliminate school social workers just as corporations eliminate low performing product lines. It is in this context that school social workers must brace themselves for systematic evaluations of their practice and programs.

PROGRAM AND PRACTICE EVALUATION: MEANING AND CONTEXT

The object or target of an evaluation effort can be an individual, group, family, program, or an organization. The textbooks on evaluation research are generally dichotomous, in that those that reference the evaluation of programs and organizations generally use the term "program evaluation" (see, for example, Berk & Rossi, 1999; Rossi & Williams, 1972; Royse et al., 2001; Weiss, 1972). In contrast, evaluation texts which focus on individuals, groups, and families typically identify themselves as "practice evaluation" (see, for example, Alter & Evens, 1999; Bloom et al., 1999; Shaw & Lishman, 1999). In effect, the former emphasize "macro" assessments while the latter focus on the individual practitioner and practice interventions. This distinction aside, both utilize similar research concepts, principles, methods and strategies.

I. Why Evaluate Programs?   This is perhaps a rhetorical question in that societal expectations, budget allocation models, and consumers, all expect some information or evidence to justify the existence of programs and services. Formal evaluation of programs is seen as a vehicle to move from a reactive or crisis-oriented approach in the delivery of services to a more guided and disciplined strategy to provide needed services. The logic being that certain programs, if evaluated, would turn out to be more "effective" and "efficient" than other programs. Once we identify these "effective and efficient" programs, then indeed one could justify their existence and continuation, and the elimination of others. As simplistic as this logic may appear, this is the political reality of many funded programs. In fact, some have argued that evaluation is useful only to the extent that it produces timely results that would help decision-makers in their deliberations (see, for example, Patton, 1978; Smith & Glass, 1987). Tripodi (1983) states that "evaluative research should not be conducted if its results cannot be utilized" (p. 14).

As will become apparent later, what is considered effective and efficient may depend on the eyes of the beholder. "Stakeholders," individuals and groups who have a vested interest in a program and presumably its evaluation, will influence decisions as well as the methods of evaluation. Thus, the relative simplicity of program evaluation is, by default, encumbered by ideology, values, and political gainsay. The potential objectivity of an evaluation is subjected to goals and objectives of stakeholders. Everything from theory, to design, to analysis, to interpretation and dissemination, may all be prone to conjuncture debate. Thus, not only the characteristics of the program but also the context of practice become relevant and critical to the evaluation of a program.

II. Why Evaluate Practice?   In contrast to the evaluation of programs, the evaluation of practice has somewhat of a different history, one that is more deeply rooted in the profession of social work. The question is perhaps all too simple: How do we know that we are doing what we think we are doing, and how do we know what we are doing has a demonstrable effect?

The first part of this question asks the practitioner to specify the process, nature, and character of the interventions being utilized in a given situation. For a practitioner to say "I am doing group work" is meaningless from the perspective of process evaluation. On the other hand, to say that in session one of a fourteen session program, we engaged in an assertiveness training exercise designed to help the group members feel comfortable in expressing their opinions freely, is more informative. But, to also say that the exercise consisted of the following activities would provide far more specification about the intervention. Such details provide information on planned activities that are purposefully designed to bring about change in a situation or to reach some goal. However, to truly answer the question, a practitioner must be able to demonstrate that s/he did in fact carry out the program as described.

The second part of the question addresses the issue of outcome. Were the goals of intervention achieved? As with the specification desired of intervention, clarity and specificity in the definition of problems and goals would enhance the likelihood of demonstrating the effects of intervention. To say that the student is more assertive in communicating with peers would be considered a weak measure of outcome. If, on the other hand, the practitioner is able to demonstrate that the student has engaged in certain assertive behaviors in defined situations, and furthermore, the frequency with which such behaviors occur has increased compared to pre-intervention levels, then we may have a demonstrable effect. If, in addition to the behavioral measure, the practitioner had administered an "assertiveness scale" before intervention and again at termination, and the scale score shows a higher level of assertiveness, then we have even more evidence to demonstrate a positive outcome.

These questions hearken back to the very beginnings of professional social work practice, and re-gained momentum in the '70s and '80s under the rubrics of "empirical practice" or "practitioner-researcher" (see, for example, Briar, 1980; Bloom & Fischer, 1982; Jayaratne & Levy, 1979; Thomas, 1975). This is not merely an exercise in professional growth and development, but something fundamental to good practice. As Alter & Evens (1990) point out, "today's need for accountability to clients, organizations and communities requires that we be able to evaluate our practice; the push for legitimacy and full professional status requires that social work services be effective; and competition for scarce resources requires that social work services be efficient" (p. 1). It is important to note, in this regard, that the *Social Work Code of Ethics* states that "social workers should monitor and evaluate policies, the implementation of programs, and practice interventions" 5.02(a) (NASW, 1999).

III. Politics of Context.

It should be clear by now, that evaluation is rarely free of politics. Regardless of the form of evaluation, the purposes will always be defined by some as having a political motive. We have discussed the why of program and practice evaluation, and in so doing, have emphasized the importance of specificity and definition so that those in decision making roles can then use the data appropriately. But sometimes, as Cohen (1970) points out, "decision-making, of course, is a euphemism for the allocation of resources—money, position, authority, etc." (p. 214). Thus, perceived or real, the very act of evaluation may begin with presuppositions of bias and fear of change.

What makes the context of evaluation politicized are the potentially disparate goals of stakeholders. Regardless of the outcome, some will favor the continuation of a program and others may be more skeptical. School districts and boards may ask for information on whether or not a program should be continued. Principals and program heads may be tuned in to relative effectiveness and cost/benefits of different types of

services within a program. The direct service social workers may be more concerned with how best to deliver services. Teachers may want to know how the services provided will result in better learning or less disruptive behavior on the part of a child. And, parents and community advocates may want to have a greater say in the types of services and how services are provided. It will be difficult if not impossible for a single evaluation study to address all of these dimensions. Thus, an effective evaluator must be someone who is sensitive to the vagaries of politics and multiple constituencies, and at the same time, have the knowledge and stature to ensure the implementation of the best evaluation design possible under the circumstances.

In this context, the political demands on program evaluation will presumably be more contentious than in practice evaluation. At least in theory, practice evaluation should be more idiosyncratic and driven by the particulars of the given situation. However, to the extent that a program is being judged by the sum of its components, success of a program may be viewed as the sum of successful cases. Under this scenario, the definition of "success" may become critical to the various stakeholders since that becomes synonymous with the program outcome. At this juncture, the distinction between program evaluation and practice evaluation becomes blurred and artificial. As Tripodi, Fellin, and Epstein (1978) note, "naïve evaluators without political sophistication may draw up evaluation plans that are irrelevant and unrealistic" (p. 19).

IV. Role of the Evaluator.

Given political and fiscal necessities, evaluation has now become big business. Unfortunately, however, many evaluators are hired or brought in to the picture only after program activities have gone on for some time, typically, when someone sees an opportunity for a grant or questions are being asked about the efficacy of the program. The net result is that the evaluator is usually faced with assessing unclear programmatic practices, ill-defined outcomes, and systemic problems that make evaluation difficult at best. Regardless, evaluation is increasingly a way of organizational life, and as a result perhaps, private entities with the defined purpose of hiring themselves out as "external evaluators" are now quite common place. Several large for-profit and non-profit organizations are now almost synonymous with evaluation, for example, *Research Triangle Institute, RAND Corporation,* and *National Opinion Research Center.* In addition, more and more larger human service agencies are developing the capacity to conduct evaluations of their programs by employing "internal evaluators," individuals trained in the art and science of evaluation, who are a part of an evaluation unit within the agency. The reality, however, is that quite often, the political and policy debates dictate whether or not the evaluation will be conducted by an internal or external evaluator.

An external evaluator, someone who is not a part of the organization being evaluated, is hired to go in to an organization and conduct an evaluation of a part of or the entire organization. For example, a teacher's union may hire an evaluator to examine the effectiveness of substitute teachers, or a school district might hire an evaluator to determine whether social workers are providing needed services in a school system. Such evaluators are perceived as being more independent, and thereby, more objective and less prone to influence by organizational politics. They typically report findings to a funding body, committee, or some entity that has oversight over the organization. By definition then, what the external evaluator will study will be determined to a large extent by the expectations of this group. Thus, an evaluator hired by a school board to determine whether needed services are being provided by social workers, will take their cue from the board, with goals being specified in the form of a contract. The extent to which the study includes various stakeholders (families, teachers, social workers, etc.) may truly depend on the predilections and goals of the school board.

However, it is the responsibility of the evaluator to present to the board an evaluation design that can withstand controversy and criticism. If the evaluator fails to include relevant stakeholders, resistance and skepticism is likely—after all, it is possible that the evaluator is merely helping the school board meet its agenda. If an evaluator is viewed as independent, they may be provided with unsolicited and unedited information, because they are perceived as independent. But, if you don't *know* the program, you cannot evaluate it well, and the only way to learn it, is to meet with the program participants. Thus, the time taken to learn must be built in to the time of an external evaluator. The fact of the matter is that an external evaluator must first learn the organization and its culture. In general, an evaluation conducted by an external evaluator is likely to cost more than one conducted by an internal evaluator on the payroll.

"Internal evaluators" are employees of the organization with reporting responsibility to management. They are far more likely than external evaluators to *know* program details. But knowing the program could be a double-edged sword in this instance. The very fact of knowing may result in bias and an unwillingness to ask the hard questions, since there is the potential of having to deal with issues such as collegiality and possible job losses of co-workers. However, they are also more likely to have access to less obvious information and possibly a higher level of trust from the participants. To the extent that an individual has a defined title and office, as opposed to an ad-hoc role as an appointed evaluator, there may be greater legitimacy attached to actions and findings. Thus, on balance, it may appear that using an outside evaluator is more compelling. But, as you will see, the practice of good evaluation requires commitment and effort on the part of the whole program. "Good" programs will build in evaluation such that it is a part of organization culture, just as the "good" practitioner systematically assesses their practice.

In a school setting, a program evaluation may likely involve the school board, administrators, teachers, social workers, counselors, parents, and possibly students depending on the nature of the questions being addressed. It is incumbent upon the evaluator to seek input from all identified stakeholders prior to embarking on the evaluation. Such input will not only help address the appropriate questions, but it will also help develop a design, measures and outcomes that will maximize the acceptance of findings after the fact.

V. Evaluability Assessment. Just because someone says a program *needs* to be evaluated does not mean the program *can* be evaluated at that time. For example, a program designed to increase social work services to adolescents by increasing the number of hours spent by social workers in a school is not evaluatable without further specification on what kinds of services or a better understanding of the need for services. As such, evaluability assessment is viewed as a process for determining the goals and objectives of the program, the components of the program itself, the extent to which appropriate measures of the goals and objectives are in place, and the potential utility of evaluation data (see, for example, Berk & Rossi, 1999; Rossi & Freeman, 1993; Smith, 1989; Wholey, 1987).

Evaluability assessment is an oft overlooked but well worthwhile procedure. Berk & Rossi (1999) have identified several criteria for establishing evaluability. First, is it possible to clarify program goals? This is a time-consuming process that typically requires interviews with stakeholders and an analysis of written documents. Second, is it possible to specify the content of the program, that is, what is the intended intervention? This again is a task that may require interviews with direct service providers, administrators, consumers, and others who may be in a position to specify the nature and character of interventions intended, interventions delivered, and interventions received. Third, is it possible to measure the impact of the program? This may require inquiry in to the availability of pre-post measures, comparison groups, time-series data and so forth. And finally, is there evidence of resource commitment and stakeholder

buy-in? If the resources are limited, or if there is inadequate time to develop stakeholder ownership, the utility of an evaluation may be questioned. In effect, this is time and money well spent lest we end up with a study which is open to a wide range of criticism.

PROCESS AND OUTCOME EVALUATION: COMPATIBILITY AND PURPOSE

The purpose of process evaluation, also referred to as formative evaluation, is primarily to generate information that would be useful for revising and refining practice or a program. In contrast, the purpose of outcome evaluation, also referred to as summative evaluation, is to generate information about the relative success or failure of a program. In theory, process and outcome evaluations could be conducted independently, and they often are. In practice, the conduct of a formative evaluation is usually viewed as a strategy to increase program efficacy, and usually supported by practitioners and program administrators. The conduct of a summative evaluation, in contrast, is often considered when there is a question of program continuation, and typically requested by funders and sponsors. This is an unfortunate dichotomy in evaluation research, since both are essential elements of good practice.

I. Process Evaluation. Process evaluation and treatment monitoring are intended to operationally define and establish the fact that the specifics of a particular intervention are in fact being delivered. In other words, this is a method for confirming the nature of the independent variable. If the purpose of an evaluation is to find out whether X (independent variable) had an effect on Y (dependent variable), the more we know about X, the greater the likelihood we can in fact establish a relationship between X and Y, everything else held constant.

In general, program monitoring is important for several reasons. First, it allows us to establish whether or not the program is being delivered as intended. Such information would allow administrators to modify the program, establish ways to ensure the delivery of all components of the program, and even determine which aspects of the program are essential to keep and which may be harmful or ineffective. Second, in the absence of process evaluation, we have a much weaker case in establishing cause and effect as noted above. Finally, monitoring will allow for replication and diffusion. If program components can be described with a high degree of specificity, then it is much more transferable. By knowing the "elements" of intervention in the program, an evaluation plan could be put in place that actually determines the extent to which the planned activities occurred. The relationship between the intended activities of an intervention and the activities actually delivered is referred to as "treatment integrity" or "treatment fidelity." As McGrew et al. (1994) note, treatment fidelity means not only conforming to the prescribed elements of a program but also ensuring the absence of non-prescribed elements. The greater the integrity or fidelity of the program, the greater its "testability," as well as transferability and potential utility. Consider the following study:

Peer-led, school-based nutrition education for young adolescents: Feasibility and process evaluation of the TEENS study (Story et al., 2002).

Peer education has become a popular strategy for health promotion interventions with adolescents, but it has not been used widely in school-based nutrition education. This paper describes and reports on the feasibility of the peer leader component of a school-based nutrition intervention for young adolescents designed to increase fruit and vegetable intake and lower fat foods. About 1,000 seventh grade students in eight schools received the intervention. Of these, 272 were trained as peer leaders to assist the teacher in implementing the activities. Results . . . based on peer leader and classroom student feedback, direct classroom observation, and teacher ratings and interviews are presented. Results show that peer-led nutrition education approaches in schools are feasible and have high acceptability among peer leaders, classroom students, and teachers" (edited abstract, p. 121).

This study reports on the feasibility of one component of the *Teens Eating for Energy and Nutrition at School* (TEENS) intervention program using peer leaders to deliver a structured curriculum across ten 40–45-minute classroom sessions. The peer leaders were trained, and each session was reviewed and rehearsed. In addition, each received a manual detailing session activities. The interventions are described in detail. For example, a specific knowledge development exercise is described as a "race for labels, a relay-race type activity where students divide into teams and compete to count fat grams in food packages" with the goal being to "teach students how to use food labels to make healthy changes" (p. 122).

The authors then delineate a set of process evaluation measures:

a. Attendance at training sessions to assess knowledge of training.
b. Peer leader and student feedback to assess self-perception and helpfulness as peer leaders.
c. Classroom observation to assess fidelity to intervention protocols.
d. Teacher ratings on how well the peer leaders conducted the tasks.
e. Teacher interviews to assess the effectiveness of the peer leaders.

A systematic effort was made by the authors to assess the extent to which the defined interventions were being delivered as planned. One could certainly argue about the adequacy and/or appropriateness of the measures, for example, does an attendance log provide information about knowledge acquired? Yet, the variety of measures and different sources of information contributes to the strength of this process evaluation. Both the details provided on the intervention program, and the multiple evaluation measures allow for a reasonable assessment of the extent to which the intervention as designed was being implemented.

II. Outcome Evaluation.

II. Outcome Evaluation. Outcome evaluation is intended to operationally define and measure the impact of an intervention, that is, the extent to which a program is meeting its stated goals. In conducting an outcome evaluation, one must specify what changes are expected, devise methods of assessing change, and design methods for the collection of data. Typically, one measures several outcomes, gathers data from more than one source, and attempts to get more than one type of data. The greater the specificity in the definitions of intended outcomes, the higher the probability of obtaining "good" indicators of outcome. Consider the following example:

> *Does mentoring work? An impact study of the Big Brothers Big Sisters program* (Grossman & Tierny, 1998).

> "Our random assignment evaluation found that this type of mentoring had a significant positive effect on youth ages 10 to 16. Over the 18-month follow-up period, youths participating in Big Brothers Big Sisters Programs were significantly less likely to have started using illegal drugs or alcohol, hit someone, or skipped school. They were also more confident about their school performance and got along better with their families. Mentors were carefully screened, trained, and matched with a youth whom they met, on average, three or four times a month for approximately a year" (edited abstract, p. 403).

The authors hypothesized that this program, which pairs unrelated adult volunteers with youths from single-parent families, would lead to a reduction in antisocial behaviors, show positive changes in academic attitudes, behavior, and performance, would carryover to other peer relationships as well as family, and positively impact self-concept. They operationalized "antisocial behavior," for example, as alcohol or drug use and delinquent behavior. Similarly, they measured "self-concept" by administering instruments measuring global self-worth, social acceptance, and self-confidence. By identifying a set of outcome variables, and systematically measuring them before and after the Big Brother/Big Sister matching, they were able to assess whether or not change occurred on each of the expected dimensions. By gathering pre-post data as well as relatively discrete measures, the authors were in a position to establish with some degree of accuracy the nature and quantity of change as hypothesized. Thus, from the perspective of evaluability assessment, one may conclude that this meets the standard as far as outcome criteria are concerned. However, from the perspective of process measurement, there is little information about the actual activities that occurred in the Big Brother Big Sister relationships.

Therefore, this study may meet the criteria for outcome evaluation, but it essentially fails in meeting the criteria for process evaluation. While the specified outcomes may have been achieved, we are in no real position to say why. Since each BBBS pair did whatever they did, we have no sense of critical components, and as such, there is no way to test or monitor the fidelity of intervention.

III. Process and Outcome: One without the Other.

III. Process and Outcome: One without the Other. It is an accurate and unfortunate representation of evaluation to say that outcome evaluation holds sway when it comes to program evaluation. Most funders of programs, as well as administrators and consumers, are comforted by data indicating the effectiveness of a program, however ill-defined. The bottom-line, so to speak, is whether problems are being ameliorated and goals being met. If they are, little attention will be paid to the specifics of the interventions that constitute the program. As a result, program evaluation studies tend to use broad indicators of service such as number of interviews, time spent, reported delivery of services, etc. For example, the BBBS study imputes positive outcomes to the mentoring relationships, but we know very little about the nature of the activities. But, as Grinnell (2001) has pointed out, "we cannot be certain, however, that any change was caused by the program's activities unless we know precisely what these activities were" (p. 498).

Interestingly, the conduct of process evaluation is often confined to practice effectiveness studies because of a narrow definition of practice. This is mostly a result of increasing pressure placed on practitioners to demonstrate the effectiveness of their interventions. The scientist-practitioner and evidence-based practice movements reflect the degree of attention being paid to the dimensions of intervention. The TEENS study clearly addresses the issue of whether or not a particular part of a program is being implemented as planned. However, we do not know whether the overall program was successful, a situation perfectly amenable to practice evaluation but somewhat at odds with the expectations of program evaluation.

What should be abundantly clear by now, is that an evaluation effort must pay close attention to *both* process and outcome. Failure to address one and not the other merely results in partial answers and, usually, more questions. Thus, an evaluability assessment must address the evaluation potential of both the intervention and the outcome. It is, of course, important to note that the utility of any evaluation study will be only as good as its design and methodology.

IV. Needs Assessment. Needs assessment studies which are conducted to determine whether a program or components of a program are needed are usually categorized under the rubric of evaluation research. The questions addressed by a needs assessment vary from determining the existence of a problem, to determining the nature of desired services, to identifying sources of resistance, to determining the character of available resources. Practically, this means finding out whether or not particular services are needed, and if they are, how best to deliver them. In theory, a needs assessment is something that should be done well before a program is implemented. On the other hand, a needs assessment is also justified if existing program services are being underutilized, and there are realistic questions about the need to continue a given program.

Strategies for conducting a needs assessment can be complex (see, for example, Krueger, 1993; Warheit, Bell, & Schwab, 1977). The cardinal rule, however, is to identify stakeholders. It should also be kept in mind, that stakeholders for needs assessment may not necessarily include the primary beneficiaries of service, as would be the case with services for children. Here, the gamut could run from teachers and parents to professional organizations and advocacy groups. Sensitivity to the perceptions of these various parties is critical to the conduct of a useful needs assessment.

We will simply identify some of the principle strategies employed in needs assessment studies, and urge the reader to go to primary sources for more detailed practices.

Stakeholder survey—a simple survey could be done among identified stakeholder groups to gather preliminary information about program needs. For example, it may be useful to conduct a survey among students, teachers and parents in order to obtain a sense of the need for an after-school math tutoring program.

Key informant study—key informants are individuals in the community, who by virtue of their job, training or experience, are viewed as experts. Once identified, these individuals could be interviewed to gather information on the question under consideration. For example, math teachers could provide critical information about the need for an after school tutoring program. University faculty in a School of Education may provide good information about programs that worked and relevant research.

Focus groups—by getting together a small number of individuals in a group representing different attributes (student, teacher, parent), a facilitator can conduct a session where questions are posed in a structured manner. The dialog that emanates from these structured discussions could help define the needs and elements of a program. For example, parents might prefer that the program be immediately after school and students may prefer one later in the evening.

A "best practice" for a needs assessment study would be to incorporate a variety of methods in one study. If conducted properly, needs assessment will increase the likelihood of stakeholder buy-in, and thereby, increase the probability of program success. Consider the following example:

Parent involvement: A needs assessment (Neely-Barnes, 1999).

"A needs assessment of parent involvement was conducted at two elementary schools. There are many reasons why parent involvement is important to children's education. . . . Parents' level of involvement, barriers to involvement, and values concerning their children's education were measures at two elementary schools in a large Midwestern city. . . . Parents who said that work or other conflicts made it difficult for them to come to school were less likely to communicate with their children's teachers and less likely to participate in school activities. Findings suggest that staff at these two elementary schools should be sensitive to parents' work schedules when planning activities" (edited abstract, p. 29).

This straightforward study illustrates the practical utility of a needs assessment. The author defined "parent involvement" as "talking to children about their school experience, helping with homework, attending school events, and talking to teachers" (p. 32). In one elementary school, 15 children were chosen randomly from each grade, while at the other school, "the principal chose one classroom at each grade, and the entire classroom was surveyed." They then proceeded to survey parents to determine the extent to which parent involvement occurred, was valued by the parents, and the barriers to such involvement. The survey instrument contained 17 questions. The survey was distributed by teachers to the students to take home, and resulted in a 24% response rate.

While the study design has numerous weaknesses (different selection strategies in the two schools, low response rate, etc.), it provides potentially useful information and direction to decision makers.

DESIGNING AND IMPLEMENTING EVALUATION STUDIES

As with any good research, the design of an evaluation should be guided by the research questions. At some level, implicitly or explicitly, every program is being evaluated and every practitioner is assessing the impact of their work. Such information, however, may be gathered quite informally and unsystematically. By formalizing the evaluation, we systematize the process and presumably bring it consistency and legitimacy. Presented below are implementation steps with illustrative examples from three different types of evaluation studies to elucidate the meaning of each step (see, for example, Thomas, 1984; Tripodi, 1983).

Validating school social work: An evaluation of a cognitive behavioral approach to reduce school violence (Whitfield, 1999).

"This study evaluated the effectiveness of anger control training with conduct-disordered male adolescents at a day treatment program. A multiple baseline single-subject design . . . combined with visual analyses and groups comparison methods were used in the assessment. The experimental students significantly improved in their weekly self-reports of using better anger control and experiencing more positive management and expression of anger. The experimental students also significantly improved in their use of self-control as shown by a pretest through six-month follow-up assessment" (edited abstract, p. 399).

Evaluating a sexual assault and dating violence prevention program for urban youth (Weisz & Black, 2001).

"A sexual assault and dating violence program presented in an urban middle school was evaluated to assess its influence on the knowledge and attitudes of an intervention group of 46 and a comparison group of 20 African American seventh graders. A quasi-experimental pretest, posttest, follow-up groups design was used to evaluate the program's effectiveness. . . . Results support the need for early prevention programming among youths in the inner-city schools" (edited abstract, p. 89).

Evaluation of an alternative discipline program (Andrews, et al., 1998).

"Students who misbehave tend to perform poorly in school and tend to be absent frequently from school. . . . This has led researchers to examine the relationship of school suspension to attendance and achievement, and further the relative impact of suspensions in school (ISS) and out of school (OSS). One stated purpose of this study was to compare the effects of a lunch detention versus an out of school suspension program for secondary school students. Students were assigned to one of the two conditions and the frequency of suspensions were monitored. Results showed that lunch detention was associated with a statistically significant and meaningfully lower frequency of suspension than after school detention" (edited summary of article).

Now, let us consider the evaluation implementation steps for each of the above studies:

a. The Purpose of the Evaluation Must Be Established.

Whitefield: Identifies the study purpose as "evaluating the effectiveness of a cognitive-behavioral intervention (i.e., anger control training) with explosive and conduct-disordered male adolescents in reducing school violence" (p. 400).

Weisz & Black: Identify the study purpose as an evaluation of "a sexual assault and dating violence prevention program...The study sought to evaluate both the short-term and intermediate effects on the knowledge and attitudes of participants" (p. 91).

Andrews et al.: "The purposes of this study were threefold: (1) What is the effect of a school

lunch detention versus an out of school suspension program on the suspension frequencies of secondary school students? (2) How do school policies affect the suspension frequencies of secondary school students? And (3) what is the perception by the school community of the effectiveness of alternative discipline programs?" (p. 210).

By reading these statements we know the overall purpose of the evaluations. All three studies purport to evaluate the effectiveness of a particular intervention program. We also know that Whitfield and Andrews hope to change behavior while Weisz and Black hope to impact knowledge and attitudes. All three could be construed as focusing on outcome, but we do not know the specifics about outcome in two—what is meant by "violence" in the Whitefield study or "knowledge and attitudes" in the Weisz and Black study. These are questions that must be answered as we move forward with implementation.

b. The Goals Must Be Made Clear, Specific, and Measurable.

Whitefield: ". . . the student receiving Anger Control Training would have higher Anger Control scale scores and lower anger expression scale scores relative to control students' self-reports for these two measures" (p. 406).

Weisz & Black: "Program goals included increasing knowledge about the extent and causes of teenage sexual assault and dating violence, including knowledge of community resources; increasing intolerance for sexual assault and teenage dating violence . . . (p. 92).

Andrews et al.: These authors essentially stated their goals for the study in presenting the purpose above. However, one could say their goal is to compare the effects of school lunch detention versus an out of school suspension on the suspension frequencies of secondary school students, and in addition, to gather information on the perception of these alternative discipline programs from the larger school community.

These statements tell us specifically what it is that the authors intended to evaluate. Whitefield specifies the goals in terms of expected changes in scale scores, a hypothesis. Weisz and Black want to examine changes in knowledge and attitude, and further want to see whether these changes will be maintained over time. Andrews et al. not only want to look at a change in behavior within one population (students), but are also interested in what one group of stakeholders may think about the program.

The second step in the process further clarifies program objectives. These statements help us understand the specific purpose of the evaluations. What we don't know up to now, is how the attainment of these objectives will be monitored or measured, a question that must be answered in the next step of the process.

c. Valid and Reliable Goal Attainment Measures Must Be Identified.

Whitefield: employed "two self-report measures and a behavioral count or measure of acting-out behaviors" (p. 404). The self-report measures are *The State-Trait Anger Expression Inventory* and the *Self-Control Rating Scale*. A behavioral count was obtained through *The Staff Daily Report*.

Weisz & Black: the authors developed four instruments to measure knowledge, attitudes, behavior or anticipated behavior and incidence. The authors note that they "adapted questions from instruments developed for older youth . . ." (p. 93).

Andrews et al.: "the dependent variable under investigation was the frequency of suspension. For each student in the study, school files and system computer records were used as the source of information regarding the discipline infraction and subsequent punishments" (p. 211).

Both Whitfield and Weisz and Black rely on measures of self-report, although Whitfield also employed an observational measure completed by a designated staff member. In contrast, Andrews uses the frequency of occurrence data from the school's administrative date base.

We have now reached a point in the evaluation design and implementation process when the study design has to be considered. Given the purpose of the study and the goals, and given the "best" measures of goal attainment, what would be the best design to use? This question is addressed in the next step of the process.

d. Choose and Implement an Appropriate Research Design.

Whitefield: "I used a single-subject, multiple baseline design across subjects as the main research design" (p. 403).

Weisz & Black: although the authors don't state it as such, they employed a "non-equivalent control group design." For the treatment group, seventh grade "students voluntarily chose to participate in the program. . . . The comparison group consisted of seventh grade students from the same charter school who were not enrolled in the program" (p. 91).

Andrews et al.: ". . . a quasi-experimental design was used to evaluate the effectiveness of the alternative discipline program." The students suspended during the first and second six weeks of school were in out-of-school detention, while the students suspended during the fourth and fifth six-week periods were placed in lunch detention. . . . The qualitative research design included surveys of . . . administrators and selected teachers (as well as student volunteers)" (p. 211).

Along with the choice of design comes the decision on data collection. Since the decisions have already been made about instrumentation in the previous step, the implementation phase requires a decision when and how the data are to be gathered. More often than not, these decisions are made concurrently, but we have separated them because they are important decisions in of themselves.

Whitefield: The *State-Trait Anger Expression Inventory* was completed weekly by the students, while *The Staff Daily Report* was also completed weekly by program staff. In contrast, the *Self-Control Rating Scale* was administered at pretest, at posttest, and six months after the program.

Weisz & Black: utilized a pre-post strategy in their evaluation of the violence prevention program. They "administered pretest and posttest questionnaires during the sessions on the initial and final day of the program and again six months later" (p. 92).

Andrews et al.: "Specifically, the numbers of students referred to detention during the time periods of the study and the numbers of students suspended for failure to serve detention during those time periods were tabulated from the computer data." To address the question regarding community perception, "open-ended survey questions related to the two forms of detention under investigation were completed by school personnel and students" (p. 211).

The design and the measures together constitute the methodology of the study in conjunction with the study subjects. As should be self-evident, methodology is dictated by the study questions and constrained by the context of practice. In examining the steps of design and implementation, it is important to note that more often than not, compromises have to be made. Realistically, perfect designs with ideal measures are rarely within the realm of possibility in evaluation research. This is due to a lack of control over the context of evaluation, the demands of stakeholders, the ethics of providing human services, and the very real fact that there are no "perfect measures" for the complex problems encountered in the service arena. As Rossi & Freeman (1993) note, "evaluations may be justifiably undertaken that are 'good enough' for answering relevant policy and program questions even though from a scientific standpoint they are not the best possible designs" (p. 30). However, it is the obligation of the evaluator to come as close to the ideal as possible.

e. Analyzing, Interpreting, and Reporting Data.

Analysis and interpretation is necessarily guided by the methodology and the level of measurement. Thus, time-series data from single-case studies are unlikely to be analyzed statistically, but rather, they are more likely to be visually

examined for trend and direction. In contrast, evaluations which compare groups of subjects should undergo statistical analyses, and the resulting statistics would help interpret the impact of interventions.

Whitfield: "In summary, patterns of improvement with this self-report data were evident with four anger control training clients. One student displayed a negative pattern of change from baseline to intervention phase and three students' data patterns were ambiguous or unchanged" (p. 407). No statistical analyses were conducted.

Weisz & Black: compared the "students' pretest and posttest scores to determine any immediate effects" and compared the "intervention and comparison group students at follow-up six months after the program ended" (p. 95). The authors used t-tests and ANOVA statistics for these analyses across groups.

Andrews et al.: in order to compare the frequency of suspensions under the two conditions, the authors conducted a Chi-Square analysis. No statistical analyses were conducted with the survey data. The authors simply presented percentage distributions across the various questions.

In sum, these studies illustrate the tremendous variations that exist in evaluation studies. What we wish to emphasize is the importance of the step-wise process in that it will guide the evaluator through the questions that need to be answered prior to implementation of an evaluation study.

I. Designs for Evaluation.

Fitz-Gibbon & Morris (1987) defined an evaluation design as "a plan which dictates when and from whom measurements will be gathered during the course of an evaluation" (p. 9). Presumably, if you go through the step-wise procedures stated above, you should have a good sense of when and how data should be gathered. While there are many designs to choose from, and many that are desirable given the questions you want answered, only two or three will probably work in a particular situation. There are numerous books which describe the different designs and their relative strengths and weaknesses (see, for example, Alter & Evens, 1990; Bloom et al., 1999; Campbell & Stanley, 1963; Cook & Campbell, 1979; Royse et al., 2001; Weiss, 1998; Yegidis et al., 1999). Readers are strongly advised to look at these and other resources prior to designing and implementing an evaluation study, since issues around validity of designs, generalizability of information, selecting subjects and so on will be addressed in most of these texts on evaluation research. As such, this chapter will not go into the details of these designs and will introduce only those that are considered to be of pragmatic value within the general context of evaluation. Table 13.1 presents a summary of selected designs based on their perceived utility. The designs have been organized in terms of rigor or their ability to control for threats to validity. In general, if it is possible to randomly select subjects to go in to the different group designs where intervention/no-intervention comparisons are to be made, the validity of the findings will be enhanced. In reality, random assignment is difficult, but it is a worthy goal to strive for in the context of evaluation research.

II. Measurement Issues.

"Measurement is controversial" (Smith & Glass, 1987, p. 82). Yet, along with selecting a study design, no other evaluation question is as important as determining the appropriate outcome measures. Although measurement has been defined as "nothing more than a systematic procedure to assign numbers to objects" (Berk & Rossi, 1999, p.16), the practical questions of selection are far less elegant. Measurement is not an end to itself, it must serve a purpose helping the decision process in an evaluation. As with research design, there is a rich literature on measurement and related issues including some excellent volumes on collections of instruments (see, for example, Fischer & Corcoran, 2000; Lake et al., 1973; Miller, 1991; Nugent, Sieppert & Hudson, 2001; Robinson et al., 1991; Sederer & Dickey, 1996).

Berk & Rossi (1999) suggest that a "'good' measure is, in common sense terms, one that is likely to measure accurately what it is supposed to measure" (p. 16). We will add to that a good measure will be even better if it will accurately measure what it is supposed to measure over and over again. In other words, the better the validity and reliability of a measure, the greater the probability of a better evaluation. With this caveat in mind, and reminding the reader to go to the various resources on measurement, we will highlight some critical issues related to the selection of a measurement strategy.

In deciding upon a measure or measurement strategy, four basic questions need to be answered (see Jayaratne & Levy, 1979):

What do you measure—typically references variables (outcome, process or both), that need to be monitored.

When do you measure—a decision needs to be made about the points at which measurement should occur.

Who does the measuring—refers to the fact that a determination has to be made about the sources of information.

With what do you measure—once a decision has been made about what to measure, another decision has to be made about the selection of appropriate instrumentation.

Radin (1988) identified nine "modalities" of measurement (Table 13.2). Any given evaluation may utilize one or a number of these modalities as measurement strategies.

Hard data—references objective reports of events such as attendance, grades, police reports, dropout rates, etc. Such measures are indirect and unobtrusive, and the data may be collected for reasons other than the study in question. However, it is possible that the nature of the problem being evaluated allows for the use of such indicators. The proliferation of management information systems and centralized data bases have resulted in literally volumes of data at the individual, family, organization, community, state and federal levels, much of which are ready

TABLE 13.1   Selected Designs for Practice and Program Evaluation

SINGLE-SYSTEM DESIGNS A= BASELINE B=INTERVENTION	WHAT DO YOU MEASURE	WHEN DO YOU MEASURE	WHO DOES THE MEASURING	WITH WHAT DO YOU MEASURE
B-design *No pre-post intervention or a comparison with those who did not receive the intervention is possible.*	Target problems or identified goals. Typically specific observable or self-reported behaviors. Most often used in clinical situations but can be used in macro practice.	No baseline or intervention phase. Data gathering occurs during the course of intervention. Typically time series data are collected.	Any relevant party involved in the intervention and/or other suitable stakeholders. Typically, the client and/or worker.	Usually identified behaviors. Questionnaires and administrative data may also be used.
AB-design *Pre-post comparison possible, but no comparison with those who did not receive intervention.*	Target problems or identified goals. Typically specific observable or self-reported behaviors. Most often used in clinical situations but can be used in macro practice.	Baseline or pre-intervention data must be gathered. In addition, the same data are gathered during the course of intervention. Typically time series data are collected.	Any relevant party involved in the intervention and/or other suitable stakeholders. Typically, the client and/or worker.	Usually identified behaviors. Questionnaires and administrative data may also be used.
ABAB-design *Pre-post comparison possible, but no comparison with those who did not receive intervention.*	Target problems or identified goals. Typically specific observable or self-reported behaviors. Most often used in clinical situations but can be used in macro practice.	Baseline or pre-intervention data must be gathered. A reversal phase is present during which time data are gathered but no intervention occurs. Typically time series data are collected.	Any relevant party involved in the intervention and/or other suitable stakeholders. Typically, the client and/or worker.	Usually identified behaviors. Questionnaires and administrative data may also be used.
AB **AAB** **AAAB** **Multiple baseline design** *Pre-post comparison possible, and limited comparison with those who did not receive the intervention. The same interventions are applied sequentially.*	Target problems or identified goals. Typically specific observable or self-reported behaviors. However, these could be monitored across individuals, situations, or problems/goals. Most often used in clinical situations but can be used in macro practice.	Baseline or pre-intervention data must be gathered. Typically time series data are collected.	Any relevant party involved in the intervention and/or other suitable stakeholders. Typically, the client and/or worker.	Usually identified behaviors. Questionnaires and administrative data may also be used.

Design	Measures	Timing	Source	Data type
X O—one group posttest only design. *No pre-post comparison or a comparison with those who did not receive the intervention is possible.*	Target problems or identified goals. Typically, attitudes, beliefs, presence of problems, etc.	After the intervention has ended. Typically data collected at one point in time.	Any relevant party involved in the intervention and/or other suitable stakeholders.	Usually questionnaires, but behaviors and administrative data may also be used.
X O / **O** / **Non-equivalent posttest only group design.** *No pre-post intervention is possible. But, comparison with those who did not receive the intervention is possible, although groups are not randomly selected. If randomized, we have a true experimental design: **Posttest only control group design.***	Target problems or identified goals. The same measures are administered to both groups. Typically, attitudes, beliefs, presence of problems, etc.	After the intervention has ended. Both groups are administered the tests at the same time. Typically data collected at one point in time after intervention.	Any relevant party involved in the intervention and/or other suitable stakeholders.	Usually questionnaires, but behaviors and administrative data may also be used.
X1 O / **X2 O** / **Posttest only comparison group design.** *X1 represents one type of intervention and X2 a different intervention. No pre-post comparison or comparison with those who did not receive an intervention is possible. Can compare different types of intervention, although groups are not randomly selected.*	Target problems or identified goals. The same measures are administered to both groups. Typically, attitudes, beliefs, presence of problems, etc.	After the intervention has ended. Both groups are administered the tests at the same time. Typically data collected at one point in time after intervention.	Any relevant party involved in the intervention and/or other suitable stakeholders.	Usually questionnaires, but behaviors and administrative data may also be used.
O1 X O2 / **One group pretest-posttest design.** *O1 represents the first time of measurement and O2 the second. Comparison at pre-*	Target problems or identified goals. Typically, attitudes, beliefs, presence of problems, etc.	Before and after intervention has ended. Typically data collected at one point in time.	Any relevant party involved in the intervention and/or other suitable stakeholders.	Usually questionnaires, but behaviors and administrative data may also be used.

(continued)

TABLE 13.1 (Continued)

GROUP DESIGNS O=MEASUREMENT X=INTERVENTION	WHAT DO YOU MEASURE	WHEN DO YOU MEASURE	WHO DOES THE MEASURING	WITH WHAT DO YOU MEASURE
post intervention is possible. But no comparison is possible with those who did not receive the intervention.				
O1 X O2 *O1 O2* **Non-equivalent control group design.** *Comparison at pre-post and with a group who did not receive intervention possible, although groups not randomly selected. If randomized, we have a true experimental design:* **Pretest-posttest control group design.**	Target problems or identified goals. The same measures are administered to both groups. Typically, attitudes, beliefs, presence of problems, etc.	Before and after intervention has ended. Typically data collected at one point in time.	Any relevant party involved in the intervention and/or other suitable stakeholders.	Usually questionnaires, but behaviors and administrative data may also be used.
O1 X O2 *O1 O2 X O3* **Non-equivalent crossover design.** *Comparison at pre-post and with a group who did not receive intervention possible, although groups not randomly selected. Both groups receive the intervention, the second group receiving it after the completion of intervention with the first group. If randomized, we have a true experimental design:* **Crossover control group design.**	Target problems or identified goals. The same measures are administered to both groups. Typically, attitudes, beliefs, presence of problems, etc.	Before and after intervention has ended. Typically data collected at one point in time. Note that the data are collected again a third time after the second group receives the intervention.	Any relevant party involved in the intervention and/or other suitable stakeholders.	Usually questionnaires, but behaviors and administrative data may also be used.

for analyses. However, since these data were not necessarily gathered for the primary purpose of evaluating the specific problem or goal under consideration, they may be more indirect in their measurement of attributes. In the realm of research, such data sets are referred to as "secondary data," but within the context of evaluation, they could indeed play a much more direct role. Consider the following examples:

"Implementation was considered a series of stochastic steps. Measures included (a) number of schools (of seven) to enlist a school staff person to serve as the student ASB group staff advisor; (b) number of schools that organized a drug-abuse focused ASB; (c) number of schools that established a student chair, co-chair, publicity chair, videotape person, and events organizers . . ." (Sussman, et al., 1997, p. 100).

"For each student in the study, school files and system computer records were used as the source of information regarding the discipline infraction and subsequent punishments. Specifically, the numbers of students referred to detention during time periods of the study and the number of students suspended for failure to serve detention during those time periods were tabulated from the computer data" (Andrews, et al., 1998, p. 211).

Tests—usually refer to standardized measures such as the SAT, Beck Depression Inventory, final examination score, IQ, etc. There is a presumption of objectivity and fairness that is attributed to such tests, but this has been brought in to question by researchers. Within the practice arena, however, psychological testing is commonplace, and frequently employed as an assessment device for purposes of diagnosis or problem presence. Consider the following examples:

"Data on self-esteem, empathy, communication skills . . . were collected using paper and pencil tests. . . . Self-esteem . . . was measured by the 25 item Short Form of the Coopersmith Self-Esteem Inventory, and . . . Empathy was measured by the 10 item empathy subscale of the Social Skills Rating System" (Westhues, et al., 2001, p. 483).

"At the beginning of the 1998–00 school year, the principal of the Carmen School announced that the school would be re-engineered if standardized test scores did not improve. In order to avoid dismissal of the teaching and administration staff, 25 percent of the student population must perform at grade level on the ITBS (Iowa Test of Basic Skills)" (Terzian, 2002, p. 282).

Observations—requires identifying a specific behavior or group of behaviors, training someone to identify these behaviors, designating the location or locations for the observation, and defining time periods for observation. This process, therefore, is sometimes referred to as *structured observation*. In theory, this strategy could lead to relatively objective information if the behaviors are sufficiently well defined and the behaviors are being observed unobtrusively by more than one person. In practice, however, observational data are gathered from parents about their children and teachers about students in class, for example. In addition, participant observation is also a common practice where participants in a group session, for example, may provide information on other group members. These types of measurement tactics are more likely to result in biased data, although they have the potential to be validated. Consider the following examples:

"The Staff Daily Report was another weekly repeated measure. . . . Essentially, the SDR was a behavioral count of the aggressive episodes and the specific instances of rules violations. In calculating these scores, the severity of the offense was not being rated but whether a specific problem occurred or not" (Whitfield, 1999, p. 405).

"The direct observations were conducted using the Student Teacher Interaction Profile (STIP). . . . The STIP requires the observer to code the student's behavior for 15 seconds and then code the teaching staff's behavior for the next 15 seconds. Student behaviors were coded in to categories including appropriate behavior, off-task behavior, mildly disruptive behavior, severely disruptive behavior, and other behaviors" (Gerdtz, 2000, p. 101).

Rating scales—refer to self-reports or reports by others on the intensity, frequency, or magni-

TABLE 13.2 Techniques of Assessing School Social Work Practice: An Update

MODALITY	OUTCOME CRITERIA		
	IMPROVED FEELINGS AND ATTITUDES OF CLIENTS	**IMPROVED VIEWS OF SIGNIFICANT OTHERS ABOUT CLIENTS (TEACHERS, PARENTS, PEERS)**	**INDICES OF COMPETENT SOCIAL FUNCTIONING**
Hard data (Objective reports of events)	Suicide rates and attempts; acts of vandalism	Number of negative teacher reports to principals about child; verbatim reports of statements by parents during parent-teacher conferences	Attendance records; dropout rates; placement in or out of special education classes; pregnancy rates; employment records
Tests	n.a.	n.a.	Standardized tests; project or teacher-designed tests (of factors such as academic achievement, adaptive behavior, and knowledge in special areas)
Observations (Recordings of behaviors that were seen)	Minutes spent crying as reflections of feelings	Counts of verbalizations or behaviors of significant others regarding child or directed at child	Systematic observations in the classroom, playground, or at home of parent-child, teacher-child, and child-child interactions; counts of number of times peers approached client during given amount of time at recess
Rating scales (Ratings of data on some dimension such as frequency or intensity)	Ratings completed by clients regarding their own feelings; Q-sorts	Teacher or parent ratings of specific behaviors of client; peer ratings of attractiveness or liking of classmates including client	Tape recordings of dyadic interactions or group discussions rated in blind judging for evidence of competence of participants
Questionnaires (Instruments with questions that do not have right	Structured and semistructured assessment of attitudes and	Structured and semistructured assessment of views of parents and teachers	n.a.

TABLE 13.2   *(Continued)*

and wrong an-swers)	feelings of cli-ents, preferably with standardized instruments	about clients; peer nominations of chil-dren in class espec-ially liked; peer checking of names of classmates having specified traits	
Simulations (Hypothetical problematic situations)	n.a.	Task of selecting several classmates to help plan a hypo-thetical class party is given to peers of client	Clients are asked what they could do when other chil-dren try to take their toys away
Graphics (Use of pictures or models to express feelings)	An 8-inch circle is presented to cli-ent who is then asked to divide it into wedges to reflect import-ance of different roles s/he plays	Line drawings of faces with a smile, frown, or neutral expression are pre-sented to peers of client along with names of students in class and peers are asked to mark the face showing their liking of each child	n.a.
Interviews (Open-ended inquiries)	Semistructured or open interviews with client eval-uated by blind judging as to feel-ings revealed	Semistructured or open interviews with teachers evaluated by blind judging as to feelings and at-titudes toward client revealed	n.a.
Self-Reports (Descriptions by clients or signi-ficant others regarding their feelings and attitudes)	Diaries of feelings and attitudes, evaluated by blind judging	Diaries of feelings toward, or evalua-tions of client's behaviors evaluated by blind judging	Clients' records of their specific behav-iors performed under specific circum-stances which can be corroborated (e.g., completed homework assignments)

Note: n.a. = not applicable

Source: Norma Radin, "Assessing the Effectiveness of School Social Workers: An Update Focused on Simulations, Graphics, and Peers," in James G. McCullagh and Paula Allen-Meares, eds., *Conducting Research: A Handbook for School Social Workers* (Des Moines, IA: Iowa Department of Education, 1988), pp. 77–78.

tude of specific behaviors and feelings. These types of indicators are widely used, for example, indicating level of anxiety on a 1–10 scale or peer ratings of classmates attractiveness. Often, these are not standardized and validated measures, but rather, serve the function of providing self-reported, observed or perceived changes in some client characteristic in a systematic manner. Consider the following:

> "Parent involvement was measured through the use of a survey. . . . There were four questions measuring the parents' level of involvement. These questions asked how often parents communicated with teachers, participated in school activities, talked to their children about school, and helped their children with homework. Responses were on a six-point scale ranging from 'every day' to 'a few times a year'" (Neely-Barnes, 1999, p. 33).

> "The extent to which . . . school-related behaviors and attitudes had changed as a result of being mentored was measured by the administration of the Child Behavior Checklist . . . completed by foster parents, and the School Attitude Measure . . . and a mentee satisfaction questionnaire completed by the mentees" (Altshuler, 2001, p. 19).

Questionnaires—typically, respondents answer a series of questions about a variety of topics in questionnaires, which may be self-administered or administered by another. In general, survey questions have no right or wrong answers, but hope to obtain information about the respondents feelings, beliefs, values, etc., in given areas. This is perhaps the most commonplace of all data collection strategies used in research, but, unless done carefully, could provide misleading and erroneous information. Consider the following examples:

> "A survey instrument was used to obtain students' perceptions of various prevention strategies. Students gave each strategy letter grades (consistent with the grading system used in their schools and quantified on a Likert-type scale for statistical analyses" (Lisnov, et al., 1998, p. 303).

> "After project implementation, 15 of 16 health educators evaluated their role as linking agent by completing an open-ended questionnaire that addressed three main evaluation questions. The first question assessed support activities provided by the researchers. The second question evaluated time spent on the project and the advantages and disadvantages of participation" (Dijkstra, de Vries, & Parcel, 1993, p. 340).

Interviews—personal interviews may be conducted with students, teachers, parents, and others to examine observed changes, feelings, and perceptions. These interviews may be *open-ended,* where the individual is free to express their feelings and opinions about the questions asked, or they may be more *structured* where the response options are generally guided. In either case, the clients have an opportunity to express their views, and the evaluators have an opportunity to design the questions and obtain information directly from the relevant parties. Consider the following examples:

> "Within two weeks after the curriculum was completed, classroom teachers who taught the curriculum were interviewed at school by a trained TEENS evaluation staff member to assess their perceptions of the curriculum, including effectiveness of peer leaders and responsiveness of the students" (Story et al., 2002, p. 124).

> "To obtain mentees' perspectives with respect to their expectations regarding the program and their relationship with their mentors, individual audio-taped interviews employing a standardized set of open-ended questions were conducted in a community meeting room" (De Anda, 2001, p. 99).

Self-reports—once a problem or goal is defined, changes may be monitored and measured through daily logs, behavior checklists, questionnaires, and even self-monitored by physiological measures. The particular measures may be individualized or validated instruments. By definition, self-report requires the individual to report about him or herself or report their observations or perceptions of others, and therefore, have the distinct advantage of being able to gather data in the natural environment. While it is indeed possible to collect such information systematically, they are susceptible to bias, subjectivity and idiosyncratic judgment. However, such strategies are widely used in single system evaluations and increasingly employed in evaluation studies as one type of measure in a given study. Consider the following examples:

"At the end of the TEENS curriculum, peer leaders completed an evaluation form to assess their perception of being a peer leader. The form listed 16 attitudinal and behavioral statements (with which the students expressed the degree of agreement or disagreemnt)" (Story, et al., 2002, p. 123).

"In focus groups and interviews, stakeholder perceptions about four topics of interest were investigated. (1) Positive aspects of the program, (2) suggestions for improving services, (3) how to reach youth in need of mental health services (e.g., the 'hard to reach student'), and (4) ideas for measuring treatment outcomes" (Nabors, Reynolds, & Weist, 2000, p. 4).

Simulations and graphics—are the two additional assessment techniques identified by Radin (1988). Simulations present hypothetical situations to a client and solicit responses to these situations. For example, a student may be asked how she would respond to a situation where there is a physical attack by one student on another in the playground, and there is no adult present. Graphics use a model or picture to generate information about feelings about a person or situation. Graphics as assessment devices are typically employed with younger children. For example, a child may be presented with a picture of scene in a family, and asked to describe his feelings about the picture. His responses are recorded by him on a line drawn face as either a smile, frown, or neutral expression. These types of assessment devices are less common and are more prone to alternative interpretations.

III. Selection of Instruments.

Within the categories of measurement noted above, the utility of a particular instrument or strategy will depend on (a) its relevance and appropriateness to target group or situation, (b) ease of administration, (c) ease of interpretation, (d) reliability and validity, (e) sensitivity to change, and (f) cost (see, for example, Royse et al., 2001). The "golden rule" is to measure the same concept (problem or goal) in more than one way using valid and reliable measures as much as possible. By employing a multiple measurement strategy, one can increase the likelihood of obtaining better quality and more accurate data. For example, Gerdtz (2000) describes the following multiple measurement strategy he used in evaluating an autistic child: "The descriptive analysis had the following components: direct observations of RS in a number of different classrooms during the school day, interviews with RS, interviews with teachers and other teaching staff, and review of school records" (p. 101). This type of assessment is likely to result in a more complete and better report on how the child is doing than any one of these reports alone would have achieved.

As a social worker assesses a client and evaluates practice, he or she must integrate a subjective intimate knowledge of the client and his or her environment with an objective grasp of the critical variables. For example, the social worker first can use qualitative methods to achieve a grounded, subjective understanding of the client's situation and then determine which aspects must be measured quantitatively. . . . Then, the social worker can draw on quantitative methods to provide the data baseline necessary to gain an understanding of the frequency and occurrence of selected variables. These data help shape and guide the intervention. Finally the social worker may return to either qualitative or quantitative data-collection techniques to asses the effects of intervention. Each step of the social work process requires specific knowledge and data requirements that could fall into either or both of the paradigms (Allen-Meares & Lane, 1990).

One of the key tasks to be considered when one is conducting an evaluation is selecting the most appropriate instrument. "It is measurement of the client's problem that allows feedback on the success or failure of treatment efforts. . . . It helps standardize and objectify both research and practice. . . . Because formal measurement procedures provide some of the best bases for evaluating what we do, they are essential components of responsible, accountable practice" (Fischer & Corcoran, 1987, pp. 8–9).

Several principles underlie sound measurements. According to Fischer and Corcoran (1987), a good measurement/instrument is one that is reliable—meaning that it consistently measures the same entity in the same way, over time. It is valid, meaning that it accurately assesses the phenomenon that it is designed to assess. For example, a self-concept scale should measure self-concept and not depression or another phenomenon. Many of the instruments used to evaluate clinical practice, in particular, are not completely reliable or valid; therefore, it is prudent for the practitioner to review the data and/or information on the development of the measurement/instrument to ascertain its degree of validity and reliability, and any unique aspect that would bear on its use in his or her practice.

Goal Attainment Scale (GAS).

The Goal Attainment Scale (GAS) is an efficient evaluation and recording device. GAS measures the degree of attainment over time. It differs, however, in that measures can be taken on more than one desired outcome. With this scale it is possible to see at a glance the changes that have taken place as shown in Figure 13.1. GAS can provide a foundation for the more formal evaluations of service outcomes (Harris, 1981).

By examining Figure 13.1, components of the scale become clearer. The first step is to place specific goals (ones which can be measured) at the head of each column. The left vertical column identifies the Predicted Levels of Attainment. The vertical rows identify the possible levels of functioning such as MUCH LESS THAN EXPECTED, SOMEWHAT LESS THAN EXPECTED, EXPECTED LEVEL, SOMEWHAT MORE THAN EXPECTED, and MUCH MORE THAN EXPECTED. A statement in each row and under the column for each goal describes the status expected to be achieved for each one. The LESS-THAN-EXPECTED and MORE-THAN-EXPECTED levels are filled

in last. The handwritten dates on each scale indicate the student's level of behavior for a designated period. In Figure 13.1 dates are recorded for the week as reported during Friday scoring. The handwritten word "final" indicates the scorer's judgment of the level of achievement on the follow-up date.

Staudt and Alter encourage the practitioner to create his or her own scale when:

> you cannot locate a scale that measures the indicator you wish to observe, or when the goal is so idiosyncratic or specific that you know better than to spend time looking. . . . With practice, social work practitioners have written scales that are innovative and useful, and that are adopted across their organizations as a way of routinely monitoring client change (Staudt & Alter, 1992).

It is easy to see the difference between the chart-type graph depicted in Figure 13.1 and the multivariable graph depicted in Figure 13.2. Examination of each type indicates goal achievement but at the same time raises questions to be answered; questions from Figure 13.2 such as, "What is the meaning of the decline in school performance and what is the relationship to success in the other two gains?" and in each graph "What are the implications for future service?"

As an effective treatment tool, GAS can provide an opportunity for the client to be responsible for recording change. Being in charge of mapping progress, GAS serves as a motivator. It can also provide a communication link among students, parents, and teachers. What it doesn't do is to specify how to measure change, nor does it offer options for techniques of measuring change. Although Figure 13.2 focuses on an individual, the concept can be effectively used with any situation requiring intervention. Detailed background information is not necessary in order to write down the first set of goals; as goals are discussed, background information begins to emerge. This measure of goal attainment indicates the effectiveness of the change in the client system, since it determines the extent to which goals were achieved.

GOAL ATTAINMENT SCALE

STUDENT'S NAME <u>SALLY</u>
GOAL-SETTING DATE <u>JANUARY 12</u>
FOLLOW-UP DATE <u>MARCH 6</u>

GOAL SETTERS <u>LINDA AND SALLY</u>
NUMBER OF GOALS WRITTEN <u>4</u>
GOALS ACHIEVED <u>3</u>

Predicted Levels of Attainment	Goal 1 Making Efforts to Overcome "Bad Moods"	Goal 2 Reducing Frequency of "Bad Moods"	Goal 3 Arranging for College Career	Goal 4 Terminating Relationship with Daughter
Much less than expected	Does nothing to try to stop depression *1/16 2/20*	Feels bad 5 days *1/16 2/20*	Does nothing	*3/6* Begins but does not complete letter to daughter or daughter's adoptive parents **Final**
Somewhat less than expected		Feels bad 4 days *1/23*	Visits college but does not apply	Begins letters to daughter and to daughter's adoptive parents
Expected level	*1/23* Initiates any of the following activities: plays violin, jogs, cooks, goes out with a friend *1/30* **Final**	*2/6* Reports feeling bad, or "bummed out," 3 days during week *2/13* **Final**	*3/6* Visits and applies to at least 1 college by March 6 **Final**	Completes letter to daughter or to daughter's adoptive parents by March 6; is satisfied with contents
Somewhat more than expected	*2/6* Takes action 2 times per week *2/27* *2/13*		Visits and applies to 1 college; visits but does not apply to another	Completes letter to daughter and to daughter's adoptive parents; is satisfied with contents; mails both letters
Much more than expected	Takes actions whenever depressed *3/6*	*2/27* Feels bad 2 days *3/6 1/30*	Applies to at least 2 colleges	Completes letters to daughter and to daughter's adoptive parents; tells therapist and own parents about contents; mails both letters

FIGURE 13.1   Sample Goal Attainment Guide for Use in Evaluating Individual Students' Attempts to Improve Functioning in School

Source: Linda Hall Harris, "Goal Attainment Scaling in the Treatment of Adolescents," *Social Work in Education 5,* no. 1 (October 1981): 10–11. Copyright 1981, National Association of Social Workers Inc. Reprinted with permission. Modified.

Note: The handwritten dates on each scale indicate the student's behavior for the week as reported during Friday scoring. The handwritten word "final" indicates the scorer's judgment of the level of achievement on the follow-up date.

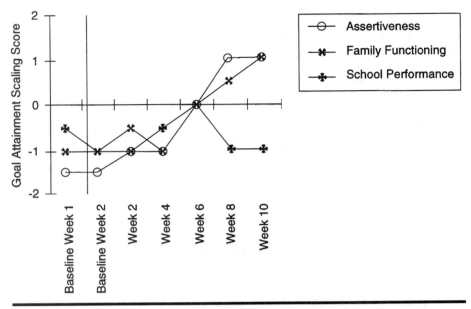

FIGURE 13.2 Concurrent Graphing of Multiple Variables on a Goal Attainment Scale
Source: Mark A. Mattaini, *More Than a Thousand Words: Graphics for Clinical Practice*
(Washington, DC: NASW Press, 1993), p. 70. Reprinted with permission.

When Goals or Outcomes Are Not Achieved.
Examination of the process employed is one avenue to follow in identifying why the outcome was not achieved. Some of the following possibilities may also be involved.

1. A common error in writing the goals and outcomes is to describe the intervention to be used instead of identifying the change desired. For example, if the social worker wants to increase parenting skills and the parent's knowledge of available resources, the objective is correctly stated if written "To increase parenting skills and knowledge of available resources," rather than wording the objective "To provide programs to parents for their education," which reflects the intervention to be used.

2. Is the objective realistic and attainable? For example, Johnny was referred for social work services by his third-grade teacher because his reading level remained low despite the use of various teaching techniques. Social work assessment of Johnny showed ability to achieve academically, but identified low self-esteem as a major barrier. The social worker believed that once Johnny felt better about himself, his reading would improve and designed interventions accordingly. Responding to the teacher's referral, the social worker wrote the following: "To increase Johnny's reading score to grade level by the end of the semester." At the end of the semester, not only his reading ability had not changed, but self-reports from Johnny, and tests and observation of the teacher indicated that Johnny was depressed. Specifying the *goal* to increase reading level by the next school year with the *outcome* stated "To reduce depression" would provide an achievable step toward the larger goal.

3. Would a different intervention or combination of interventions be more appropriate? There are times when the objective is clear,

but the intervention chosen is just not the right one to do the job.

Preparing an End-of-the-Year Report. An end-of-the-year report can serve several purposes by "assessing effectiveness of one's interventions" and "interpreting the effectiveness of social work service to administrators of the local education agency and other appropriate persons" (*NASW Standards for Social Work Services in Schools,* 1992). Such a report provides valuable data about client characteristics and changes achieved, all of which lays the groundwork for the development of a plan of work for the next year. In addition, when a summative report is submitted to administration, the contribution of social work service is substantiated. In times of financial retrenchment, when jobs are on the line, social workers often scramble to defend their worth. An article in the city newspaper about the success of the apartment homework study room developed by the Epsilon school social worker increased visibility of social work in the school and community (see Appendix II). It also provided positive support for the students who benefited from the program and for the efforts of the apartment manager and parent volunteers. When the Epsilon program, designed to ease the move of students from one program or school to another, was evaluated and presented to the school board, requests were made to introduce the program in other schools. Evaluating outcomes of social work interventions and presenting them to administration or the public cannot only increase the understanding of social work services, but also enhance the image of the school.

The social worker evaluates the plan of service developed at the beginning of the year, which includes IEP, end-of-the-year, and service reports that map the progress of special education clients. A summary report of the data and information regarding individual clients can provide the administrator with information about reasons for referrals, patterns of service requests, effective interventions, and any other types of in-formation which may be relevant. Outcome Evaluation of Individual Referrals in Table 13.3 illustrates this work. The same recording system used in developing IEPs also provides an appropriate format for recording the progress of both special and general education students and any changes in program or home situation. Outcome evaluations of these services are determined by the use of the various evaluation frameworks discussed previously. As mentioned earlier, gathering data and writing these reports are less tedious and time-consuming with the aid of computer technology to record data and analyze results.

Each school social worker or administrative unit develops its own format for an end-of-the-year report. The social worker in Appendix II organized her summary in five parts: (1) Introduction, (2) Report of outcome evaluation of the service plan developed at the beginning of the year, (3) Indirect outcome summary, (4) Outcome of evaluation of individual referrals, and (5) Recommendations for the next school year.

Although the sample service report in Table 13.3 sounds glowing, the social worker reported many discouraging times during the school year. The five crisis situations that occurred during the school year interrupted several of the programs. The university fraternity, at the last minute, hesitated following through on developing the program, and there were times when some members failed to show and there was a scramble to rearrange activities. There were, as is common, those students who did not respond to interventions, and all parent contacts weren't positive, especially in several of the child abuse and neglect situations.

ETHICAL AND HUMAN SUBJECTS ISSUES IN EVALUATION

As Babbie (1998) has noted, "ethics and evaluation are intertwined in many ways" (p. 360). In fact, it is fair to say that evaluation research in the human service arena by its very nature is ripe with ethical dilemmas and issues of human sub-

TABLE 13.3   200_ School Social Work Service Report Epsilon School[*]

Introduction: By the fourth week of the school year a social work service plan was prepared based on recommendations from the previous year. The plan, which was designed to contribute to the accomplishment of goals of Epsilon school, was developed by the social worker and principal and accepted by the School-Based Management Team. The following report shows the outcome of this work with recommendations for next year. Social work services were provided by the building school social worker (2 days a week) and two graduate social work interns (2 days a week each).

REPORT OF OUTCOMES OF EPSILON SCHOOL SOCIAL WORK SERVICE PLAN

Objective	*Interventions*	*Data Collection Methods*	*Outcome*
1. To increase coping ability of students moving from one school or educational program to another by facilitating the transition process.	1. Developed, trained, and monitored a welcoming committee of student volunteers who also served as "buddies" throughout the semester. 2. Discussed the program at three faculty meetings. 3. Conducted four class meetings in the receiving school. 4. Consultation with teachers. 5. Prepared pamphlet for parents on ways to support child at the time of a move.	Observation reports of teachers. Self reports of students. Rating scale upon entrance to school or program and at end of first marking period completed by current teacher.	Only 5% of students in transition program required continued support. Fewer referrals of students due to inability to cope with change in program.
2. To increase student afternoon "on task" behavior of students referred for disruptive behavior by 75%.	1. Recruited university fraternity to provide activities during lunch time. 2. Monitored the program with the principal.	Reports of teachers re: behaviors of students in P.M. Overall program evaluation: (See program evaluation report.)	There was a significant change in behavior of 85% of the referred disruptive students. The remaining 15% required additional service.
3. To increase completion of homework by referred students living in X apartment house by 75%.	1. Arranged with the apartment manager to provide a room for students to do homework. 2. Recruited five parents to supervise. 3. Met with parents and teachers to discuss ways to help students with homework.	Teacher's records of completed homework of participating students.	Objective was surpassed. All students turned in homework 80% of the time with half exceeding that amount.

[*]Sample of an End-of-the-Year Report of school social work services.

4. To increase positive relationships among teachers, students, and parents.	1. Developed in-service program for teachers on interviewing skills. 2. Arranged for a graduate credit university course on classroom management. 3. Acted as member of planning committee for the week at camp for 4th and 5th grades.	Questionnaires completed by teachers, parents, and students and informal interviews. Evaluation of camp program by the school.	Increased parent participation at open house in spring and attendance at parent-teacher conferences. Principal reported an increase in home visits by teachers. Pupil school attendance increased 10%.
5. To increase age appropriate verbal communication skills among six siblings of the Johnson family.	1. Twice a week meetings with sibling group for 12 weeks. 2. Collaboration with classroom teachers of the siblings to discuss ways in which they could increase positive verbal interaction and decrease physical interaction. 3. Conferences with Mrs. Johnson to support her to encourage verbal interaction. 4. At termination time, the siblings invited their parents to a lunch they had prepared for them.	Time-series design of each sibling in classroom and on playground every four weeks. Interview with mother and father re: any changed behaviors. Periodic diagrams of verbal interactions during group sessions.	One of the twins refused to participate saying she did not have a problem. Other siblings showed marked change in communication skills. The teacher of the kindergarten student felt she was well prepared to succeed in 1st grade.

INDIRECT OUTCOMES

Secondary benefits emerged from the evaluations:

1. Student volunteer mentors (Objective 1) reported increased ability to provide leadership, and the four mentors who were clients achieved objectives previously set with the social worker. Both teachers and student mentors reported more positive relationships with each other.
2. By increasing student afternoon "on task" behavior (Objective 2) not only did the students benefit, but teachers and the lunchroom aides reported less stress. In addition to providing lunchtime activities, the university students served as role models for the students and some friendships developed.
3. More homework was completed through the study room in the apartment house (Objective 3), and the program also provided opportunity for building a closer working relationship with some of the parents.
4. As positive relationships among teachers, students, and parents increased (Objective 4), there was evidence of some increase in parents and teachers volunteering in both school and community projects.
5. Not only did verbal communication skills increase for members of the sibling group (Objective 5), but four of the six siblings increased a grade in at least one subject.

(continued)

TABLE 13.3 *(Continued)*

6. As the social worker, I feel better accepted in the school and community.
7. The planning, implementation of the plan, and evaluation of outcomes provided a valuable practice experience for the two graduate social work interns.

OUTCOME EVALUATION OF INDIVIDUAL REFERRALS

During the year 75 individual students were referred for social work service; some were identified as requiring additional service through the lunchtime program and the transition program. Assessments of each referred student were processed and recorded utilizing the same format as the Individual Educational Plan requires for special education students. Following the initial assessment process, fifteen students were referred to the Special Education Department and twenty students were referred to child welfare and community agencies. Of the remaining forty students, the presenting problems focused mainly on underachievement, aggressive behavior, poor social skills, and low self-esteem. As reported above, many of these clients benefited from programs in the service plan. Additionally, interventions designed to meet the objectives of each individual included consultation and collaboration with parents and teachers and individual and group counseling. Outcome evaluations showed that 75% of the 150 objectives identified for forty students had been met within the agreed time limits.

RECOMMENDATIONS FOR NEXT SCHOOL YEAR

1. Based on the outcome evaluation of the transition program, it is recommended that a student mentor group composed of "experienced" and new mentors be used again next year. Training material is already developed and the school faculty is familiar with the plan. Social work services would be used to support the mentors and continue as a coordinator of the program. The parent booklets received a favorable response and changes recommended by teachers and parents will be incorporated.
2. The evaluation of the lunchtime program indicated sufficient benefits to both students and faculty that the faculty requested continuation of the program. There is uncertainty that the same fraternity will be able to provide the service next year. There is a need to explore alternative sources. What about the active Senior Citizen club in the neighborhood? A parent group? In any case recruitment, planning, and monitoring are important tasks for this project to continue.
3. Teachers have identified a number of students with homework problems other than those benefiting from the X apartment house study room. The program was brought before the last meeting of the school-community collaborative seeking additional study room resources. The Boys Club is interested and will be explored as a potential resource by the school social worker and the principal.
4. Continue to support any effort which builds on work accomplished to date to encourage positive, trusting relationships among teachers, students, and parents.
5. Maintain supportive contact with members of the Johnson family.
6. Review of the objectives not accomplished will be made in the fall and incorporated in services provided in the new school year.

A design for service for the next school year will be presented to the School Site-Based Management Team by the fourth week in September. It will be based on the above recommendations and additional service needs identified in initial weeks of the fall semester.

jects. In order for services to be evaluated, ethical guidelines must be followed, both by virtue of law and professional standards. The moment data are collected about an individual and that individual has the potential to be identified, we have encountered a situation where that individual has now become the "subject" of inquiry. *Before* that moment occurs, protocols for the protection of human subjects must be put in place. Broadly speaking, such protocols must include procedures for: (a) obtaining voluntary informed consent; (b) protecting subjects from physical or mental harm; (c) ensuring confidentiality; and (d) the provision of information about the nature of interventions, purpose of the study, what will happen to the data, and any known risks and benefits.

Some evaluation strategies are more likely to engender ethical concerns than others. For example, the use of control groups or the withholding of intervention may be viewed by some as ethically unjustifiable, even if the intervention itself has questionable efficacy. After all, is it not better to provide some service than none at all? On the other hand, a B-design where behavior monitoring using self-report procedure is employed, may draw little or no attention, and in fact, will be viewed as an example of good practice. If an unobtrusive measurement (an objectively "good" measurement strategy less prone to reactivity on the part of the subject) were to be used in this situation, it may be frowned upon as "big brother" research. Needless to say, it is the responsibility of the evaluator to carefully assess the pros and cons of all procedures, and to receive the necessary human subjects approval prior to embarking on the evaluation study.

By definition, evaluation in schools is particularly sensitive given the participation of minors. The implementation of the *Family Privacy Act* requires explicit written consent from parents or guardians before children can participate in studies where sensitive information (e.g., sexual behavior, psychological problems, etc.) is requested. This requirement, in turn, may impact the quality and accuracy of information collected from children. There are, of course, other issues about the very notion of children as subjects, with concerns being raised about labeling and fear of parental reprisals (Gensheimer, Ayers, & Roosa, 1997).

It is an ethical responsibility of the evaluator to present findings to relevant stakeholders in a manner that is comprehensive and comprehensible. As has been noted earlier, evaluation efforts are usually employed because someone wants information for decision-making. However, it is not uncommon for evaluation results to be downplayed and not have an impact on practice. First, the findings may not always be presented in an understandable manner. The typical consumer will not be a researcher, therefore, to present "path models" and "t-tests" may impress some, but may have little practical impact until these findings are "translated in to English." Second, the evaluation findings may contradict or bring in to question some fundamental beliefs and attitudes. If someone believes that sex education in school results in greater promiscuity, data to the contrary may have little impact on this individual. To the extent that this individual holds sway over the situation, questions will emerge about "quality of the evaluation" or the "adequacy of the measures." In other words, values will rule the day. Third, the degree of vested interest in a program will make any contrary information unpalatable. It would be very difficult for someone who has invested the time to develop and implement a program and, perhaps, has been told by some participants that is successful, to deal with contrary evidence from a more systematic and comprehensive evaluation. Fourth, the entire evaluation, including its defined purpose and methodology may be brought in to question by those with a different agenda. This is most likely to occur in situations where the evaluators did not do their homework and failed to involve relevant stakeholders in the process. Thus, an evaluator must present data as objectively as possible. Decisions will be made and programs may be changed either as a result or in spite of the evaluation data.

FOR STUDY AND DISCUSSION

1. Identify a client system. Using one or more of the assessment and measurement strategies identified in Table 13.2, develop a plan (design) to evaluate the effectiveness of services provided.

2. Identify a client system. Conduct a process evaluation such that a) you are able to identify interventions you are using and b) you are able to specify and measure the impact of the interventions.

3. Interview a school social worker and a school administrator, and identify any concerns they have about social work services in the school. How would you go about confirming these concerns and remedying the conditions?

ANNOTATED BIBLIOGRAPHY OF EVALUATION RESOURCES

Altschuld, J. W., & Witkin, B. R. (2000). *From needs assessment to action: Transforming needs into solution strategies.* Thousand Oaks, CA: Sage Publications. An introduction to needs assessment strategies is followed by a straightforward discussion on tactics, analysis, and most important, application. This book offers the reader numerous examples of how to conduct needs assessments using mixed methods. The variety of illustrative examples provided offer good ideas in to how needs assessments may be conducted in complex settings.

Bloom, M., Fischer, J., & Orme, J. G. (1999). *Evaluating practice: Guidelines for the accountable professional* (3rd ed.). Boston, MA: Allyn & Bacon. This is perhaps the most comprehensive book currently available on how to evaluate practice. It walks the reader through the various steps in practice evaluation from formulating goals, to developing measures, to the application of a design and evaluating results. The book provides both breadth and depth, and would be of singular importance to both administrators and practitioners who wish to evaluate programs as well as practice.

Fischer, J., & Corcoran, K. (2000). *Measures for Clinical Practice* (3rd ed.). New York: Free Press. This two volume compendium contains a wide array of measures that could be used in research and evaluation. The authors present relevant data on reliability and validity when available, and also comment on other attributes of scales. As a single source of information on available scales, these two volumes stand out.

Nugent, W. R., Sieppert, J. D., & Hudson, W. W. (2001). *Practice evaluation for the 21st century.* Belmont, CA: Brooks/Cole-Thomson Learning. The authors provide an introduction to the single-case methodology, but spend most of the time introducing and discussing issues related to case aggregation. A major emphasis is on measurement tools and relevant statistical procedures. This book will serve as a good reference for time series measures that can be used in practice evaluation.

Royse, D., Thyer, B. A., Padgett, D., & Logan, T. K. (2001). *Program evaluation: An introduction* (3rd ed.). Belmont, CA: Brooks/Cole. This is basic introductory text to program evaluation. It provides basic definitions and a good overview of evaluation methodology, instrumentation, and relevant issues. This is an excellent text for anyone interested in the rudiments of evaluation, but it is not particularly helpful in providing the details of implementation.

REFERENCES

Allen-Meares, P., & Lane, B. (1990). Social work practice: Integrating qualitative and quantitative data collection techniques. *Social Work, 35,* 453–454.

Alter, C., & Wayne E. (1990). *Evaluating your practice: A guide to self-assessment.* New York: Springer Publishing Company.

Altshuler, S. J. (2001). When is mentoring not helpful for students living in foster care? *School Social Work Journal, 26,* 15–29.

Andrews, S. P., Taylor, P. B., Martin, E. P., & Slate, J. R. (1998). Evaluation of an alternative discipline program. *The High School Journal, 81*(4), 209–217.

Babbie, E. (1998). The Practice of Social Research (7th ed.). Belmont, CA: Wadsworth Publishing Company.

Berk, R. A., & Rossi, P. H. (1999). *Thinking about Program Evaluation.* Thousand Oaks, CA: Sage Publishers.

Bloom, M., Fischer, J., & Orme, J. G. (1999). *Evaluating practice: Guidelines for the accountable professional* (3rd ed.). Boston, MA: Allyn & Bacon.

Briar, S. (1980*)*. Toward the integration of practice and research. In C. Fanshel (Ed.). *Future of social work research*. Washington, DC: NASW Press.

Campbell, D. T., & Stanley, S. J. (1963). *Experimental and quasi-experimental designs for research*. Chicago: Rand McNally.

Cook, T. D., & Campbell, D. T. (1979). *Quasi-experimentation: Design and analysis issues for field settings*. Chicago: Rand McNally.

Cohen, D. K. (1970). Politics and research: Evaluation of social action programs in education. *Review of Educational Research, 40*(2), 213–238.

De Anda, D. (2001). A qualitative evaluation of a mentor program for at-risk youth: The participants perspective. *Child and Adolescent Social Work Journal, 18,* 97–117.

Dijkstra, M., de Vries, H., & Parcel, G. S. (1993). The linkage approach to a school-based smoking prevention program in the Netherlands. *Journal of School Health, 63,* 339–342.

Fischer, J., & Corcoran, K. (2000). *Measures for clinical practice* (3rd ed.). New York: Free Press.

Fitz-Gibbon, C. T., & Morris, L. L. (1987). *How to design a program evaluation*. Beverly Hills, CA: Sage.

Gensheimer, L. K., Ayers, T. S., & Roosa, M. W. (1993). School-based prevention interventions for at-risk populations. *Evaluation and Program Planning, 16,* 159–167.

Gerdtz, J. (2000). Evaluating behavioral treatment of disruptive classroom behaviors of an adolescent with autism. *Research on Social Work Practice, 10*(1), 98–110.

Grossman, J. B., & Tierney, J. P. (1998). Does mentoring work? An impact of the Big Brothers Big Sisters program. *Evaluation Review, 22*(3), 403–426.

Jayaratne, S. D., & Levy, R. (1979). *Empirical clinical practice*. New York: Columbia University Press.

Krueger, R. A. (1993). *Focus groups: A practice guide for applied research*. Newbury Park, CA: Sage.

Lake, D. G., Miles, M. B., & Earler, R. B. (1973). *Measuring human behavior*. New York: Columbia University Press.

McGrew, J. H., Bond, G. R., Dietzen, L., & Salyers, M. (1994). Measuring the fidelity of implementation of a mental health program model. *Journal of Consulting and Clinical Psychology, 62*(4), 670–678.

Miller, D. (1991). *Handbook of research design and social measurement* (5th ed.). Newbury Park, CA: Sage.

Nabors, L. A., Reynolds, M. W., & Weist, M. D. (2000). Qualitative evaluation of a high school mental health program. *Journal of Youth and Adolescence, 29*(1), 1–13.

National Association of Social Work. (1992). *Standards for social work services in the schools*. Washington, DC: NASW Press.

National Association of Social Work. (1999). *Code of ethics*. Washington, DC: NASW Press.

Neely-Barnes, S. L. (1999). Parent involvement: A needs assessment. *School Social Work Journal, 24*(1), 29–43.

Nugent, W. R., Sieppert, J. D., & Hudson, W. W. (2001). *Practice Evaluation for the 21st Century*. Belmont, CA: Brooks/Cole-Thomson Learning.

Patton, M. Q. (1978). *Utilization-focused evaluation*. Beverly Hills, CA: Sage.

Radin, N. (1988). Assessing the effectiveness of school social workers: An update focused on simulations, graphics, and peers. In J. G. McCullaugh & P. Allen-Meares (Eds.), *Conducting research: A handbook for school social workers* (pp. 77–78). Des Moines, IA: Iowa Department of Education.

Robinson, J. P., Shaver, P. R., & Wrightsman, L. S. (Eds). (1991). *Measures of personality and social psychological attitudes*. San Diego, CA: Academic Press.

Rossi, P. H., & Freeman, H. E. (1993). *Evaluation: A systematic approach*. Newbury Park, CA: Sage.

Royse, D. D., Thyer, B. A., Padgett, D. K., & Logan, T. K. (2001). *Program evaluation: An introduction*. Belmont, CA: Brooks/Cole Thomson Learning.

Sederer, L. I., & Dickey, B. (Eds.). (1996). *Outcomes assessments in clinical practice*. Baltimore, MD: Williams & Wilkins.

Shaw, I., & Lishman, J. (Eds.). (1999*)*. *Evaluation and social work practice*. Thousand Oaks, CA: Sage.

Smith, M. F. (1989). *Evaluabililty Assessment: A Practical Approach*. Boston: Kluwer Academic.

Smith, M. L., & Glass, G. V. (1987). *Research and evaluation in education and the social sciences.* Englewood Cliffs, NJ: Prentice Hall.

Story, M., Lytle, L. A., Birnbaum, A. S., & Perry C. L. (2002). Peer-led, school-based nutrition education for young adolescents: Feasibility and process evaluation of the TEENS study. *Journal of School health, 72*(3), 121–127.

Sussman, S., Galaif, E. R., Newman, T., Hennessy, M., et al. (1997). Implementation and process evaluation of a student "school-as-community" group. *Evaluation Review, 21*(1), 94–123.

Terzian, S. (2002). On probation and under pressure: How one 4th-grade class managed high-stakes testing. *Childhood Education, 78,* 282–284.

Thomas, E. J. (1975). Uses of research methods in interpersonal practice. In N. A. Polansky (Ed.), *Social work research.* Chicago: University of Chicago Press.

Thomas, E. J. (1984). *Designing interventions for the helping professions.* Beverly Hills, CA: Sage.

Tripodi, T. (1983). *Evaluative research for social workers.* Englewood Cliffs, NJ: Prentice-Hall.

Tripodi, T., Fellin, P., & Epstein, I. (1978). *Differential social program evaluation.* Itasca, IL: F.E. Peacock Publishers Inc.

Warheit, G. J., Bell, R. A., & Schwab, J. J. (1977). *Planning for change: Needs assessment approaches.* Rockville, MD: National Institute of Mental Health.

Weiss, C. H. (1972). *Evaluation research: Methods of assessing program effectiveness.* Englewood Cliffs, NJ: Prentice Hall.

Weiss, C. H. (1998). *Evaluation* (2nd ed.). Upper Saddle River, NJ: Prentice Hall.

Weisz, A. N., & Black, B. M. (2001). Evaluating a sexual assault and dating violence prevention program for urban youth. *Social Work Research, 25*(2), 89–100.

Whitfield, G. W. (1999). Validating school social work: An evaluation of a cognitive behavioral approach to reduce school violence. *Research on Social Work Practice, 9*(4), 399–426.

Wholey, J. S. (1987). Evaluability assessment: Developing program theory. In L. Brickman (Ed.), *Using program theory in evaluation.* San Francisco, CA: Jossey-Bass.

AN EXAMPLE OF RURAL PRACTICE

The following example of practice illustrates the development and implementation of a design for social work service for a rural school district. Due to less density and smaller population, the organization of the school system tends to be less complex than an urban or even many suburban school systems. With fewer levels of administration, there tend to be fewer rules and regulations. It is easier to know upper administration and for them to know you. The same is true in relation to community resources. Drawbacks include scarcity of professional supervision, isolation, and often a paucity of resources.

IDENTIFYING DATA

Alpha is a small school district with a student enrollment of approximately 740 students. There is one elementary school, grades K–6, and one high school, grades 7–12. The two school buildings are located on one campus, with a play area for the elementary school and a medium-sized athletic field with bleachers for spectators at the fall football games and other athletic events. There is a new superintendent who is enthusiastic and a strong proponent of accountability. The elementary-school principal is young and has taught in the school district for the past five years. He is highly respected in the community. This is his first year as principal. The high-school principal is also a young man who was previously a vocational education teacher. He has been principal for five years. Half of the elementary-school teachers are new to the school system due to retirements and an increase in student population. The high-school teachers have taught in the system for an average of five years. The home economics teacher is new to the system. A special education classroom in the elementary school is used as a resource for students with various learning impairments. A new course in the high school, developed by the high-school counselor the previous year, provides achieving students the opportunity to tutor elementary-school students who are having difficulty in reading. A woman from the community was hired as coordinator of the parents program under Chapter 1/ Title I funds. A part-time librarian and full-time school counselor are employed in the high school. Additional services such as the teacher of speech and language impaired, reading consultant, and school psychology and school social work services are provided by the Intermediate School District (ISD). Nursing services are provided by the county health department. The community supports the educational program in millage campaigns.

A small business community of eight stores is within walking distance of the schools. The financial support of the community comes from farming, tourist trade, and a small sawmill. The county seat (where medical, mental health, and social services and the court system are located) is 30 miles away. Thirty percent of the population receives some form of government supplement, either financial assistance or surplus food. The population is approximately 3000 (larger in the summer because of summer residents) and consists largely of white Anglo-Saxon Protestants. There is a small Native American population of 20—all are members of the same family.

All members of the school community have expressed feelings of isolation, especially during the long winter months. Alcoholism is prevalent among adults and teenagers. Child abuse and incest are commonly expressed concerns. These concerns contribute to family dysfunction and were expressed by members of the Chapter 1/ Title I parents' group. The principal and teachers of the elementary school identified concerns about their newness and wondered if they could work together to avoid the effects of isolation. The principal realized that he would lose teachers the next year if they were unable to find satisfaction in their professional lives. He was also concerned about the inexperience of the new teachers and wanted to help them increase their knowledge and skills in working with children. The high-school principal and teachers did not specify any problems with staff relations, but each identified three ninth-grade girls whose behavior was disrupting the whole school. The building administrators and the program coordinator asked for some support from the social worker with the parents' group.

Figure A.1, an ecomap, shows the stress being experienced within the Alpha School District community. There is stress between the girls' group and the high-school teachers, pupils, school administrators, and the business community. The social worker has not yet been able to establish working relationships with any of the systems. There is intermittent tension between the minority population and the business community and between that population and both the elementary school and high school. Intermittent tension is also evident between parents (both Chapter 1/Title I and others) and both schools. There is intermittent tension between the high-school students and the elementary-school students. As shown by the solid lines, there are a number of positive relationships existing within this school district. Reasons for the tensions shown in the figure will become clear later in the discussion.

MAKING A CONTRACT FOR SERVICE

The social worker developed the following goals and objectives for social work service for the year based on the information that she had gathered in the initial phase of her work. The goals were discussed and accepted by the school district administrators and the superintendent of the Intermediate School District, who was also the supervisor of the social worker.

The goal focused on the concern about the effect of isolation on the total community. If the feeling of isolation could be reduced among all members of the school community, the quality of life could be improved. The goal was stated as follows:

> To increase positive social interaction among children, adolescents, their families and school personnel

Objectives, intended to achieve the above goal by the end of the school year, were:

1. To provide a satisfying professional experience for new elementary school teachers
2. To strengthen the coping abilities of Chapter 1/Title I families
3. To increase the social functioning of three high-school girls referred for disruptive behavior in the classroom

The objectives served as the boundaries for service for the school year. If information and circumstances changed, these objectives would be modified.

DESIGN OF SOCIAL WORK SERVICE TO MEET OBJECTIVES

Objective 1. To Provide a Satisfying First Year Professional Experience for the New Elementary School Teachers

Interventions (Activities)

1. Supporting the principal to establish groups of teachers to work on tasks (The principal established teacher groups to write down curriculum learning objectives.)
2. Teaching at the school a university extension course on classroom management for elementary teachers (The course also provided

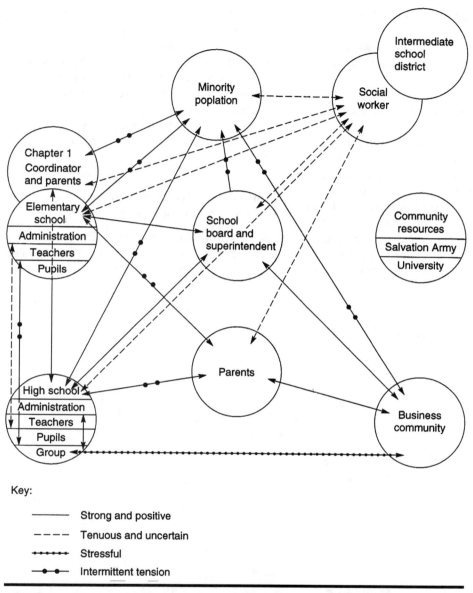

Key:

—————— Strong and positive

– – – – Tenuous and uncertain

••••••• Stressful

—•—•— Intermittent tension

FIGURE A.1 Ecomap of the Assessment of Relationships in the Alpha School District

needed postgraduate credits for teacher certification. Eighty percent of the elementary-school teachers enrolled and 10 percent of elementary-school teachers from nearby school districts enrolled.)

3. Developing two in-service education sessions for all of the teachers on interviewing techniques to use in parent-teacher interviews

4. Participating in the school's open house, during which some of the parent-teacher conferences involved children whom the social worker was serving

5. Collaborating and consulting with teachers and principal about classroom and individual behavior concerns

Outcome. Every elementary-school teacher signed a contract for the next year, indicating a degree of satisfaction with the past year's experience. The staff became a cohesive group. The emphasis on group process in the university course not only developed their awareness of group dynamics in their classrooms but also provided them with some insight into their interactions with each other. During the year, the teachers and principal learned to trust and respect one another, and the social worker was ac-

cepted as a member of the school staff. Communication between parents and teachers was increased as a result of the in-service training sessions on interviewing techniques. The positive relationships that developed between the teachers and the building administrator, the teachers and the social worker, and the building administrator and the social worker are shown in the Alpha school community ecomap (Figure A.2).

Objective 2: To Strengthen the Coping Abilities of Families

Background Information.   The elementary school was receiving Chapter 1 funding. The purpose of the project was to increase the read-

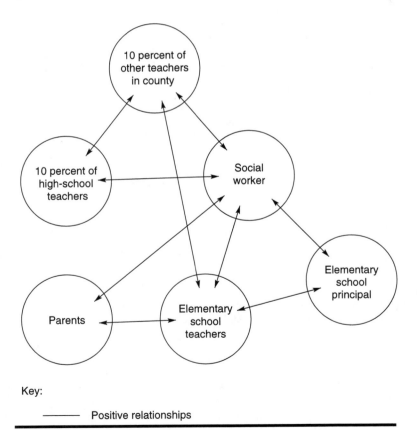

Key:

———— Positive relationships

FIGURE A.2   Ecomap of the Outcome of Work on Objective One

ing level of the elementary-school pupils through the establishment of a commercial reading program and the involvement of parents in the educational process. A mother who had worked as a paraprofessional in another community was hired to coordinate the parent segment of the program. The parents had met several times during the previous year. They were informed about the reading program, saw a demonstration, and were encouraged to read with their children at home. Mrs. Brown, the coordinator, asked the social worker to help her accomplish the program goals. Mrs. Brown and the social worker developed a working relationship by identifying roles and boundaries. The Chapter 1/Title I parents' group consisted of between 30 and 40 mothers and some fathers. The school's goal was to involve the parents in their child's education; the social work goal was to increase positive family interaction. The following interventions and results show how both goals were accomplished.

Interventions (Activities)

1. Making a presentation at the November parent meeting, which focused on toys that educate and encourage family interaction. A booklet of toys for different age-groups was developed and distributed, and samples of toys were demonstrated and passed among the parents. The question raised by one parent was: "Can we make some of these toys for our children?"
2. Establishing Christmas toy workshops (Used toys donated by a service group were repaired, and new toys, such as blocks, puzzles, and games, were made with materials bought with funds from the Salvation Army.)
3. Inviting teachers and administrators to an open house to see the display of toys prepared by the parents (Cookies baked with ingredients from the surplus foods were served.)
4. Focusing meetings on concerns of the parents (In January the program centered on "living within a budget." Mothers said they did not know how to use some of the surplus foods they received. Also, their experience of dressing dolls for Christmas led the mothers to ask for instruction in sewing and other tips related to home management. Sewing machines and kitchen equipment in the Home Economics Department of the high school were made available to the parents.)
5. Involving the minority population (As spring approached, the parents, mostly mothers, wanted to make baskets for their children. Mrs. Simpson, the Native American grandmother in the community who made baskets for sale, was paid a consultant's fee to teach the parents how to weave their own baskets. This project became complicated because black ash trees in the nearby national forest had to be cut down, with permission, and the wood dried, split, and dyed before the baskets could be made.)
6. Encouraging the development of a toy library (Toys could be borrowed just as books are borrowed from the library. The project was begun by teachers who lent classroom games and materials to children to take home for a specified period.)

Outcomes. Providing consultation to Mrs. Brown was a fruitful use of the social worker's time. Mrs. Brown worked directly with the parents, although the social worker also attended meetings and visited projects. The parents' Christmas tea for the teachers provided an opportunity for the teachers to know the parents' strengths and promoted communication between them. Comments in the teachers' lounge indicated that the teachers had a new respect for parents, whom they had previously viewed as inadequate. As the mothers learned new skills and received support from each other, stress in many of the homes lessened. There were fewer reports of abuse, and teachers reported that many of the children seemed more relaxed. Hiring Mrs. Simpson as a consultant and instructor improved the image of the Native American population in the community. It was a beginning. The ecomap (Figure A.3) shows the changes that took place in relationships over the year.

Objective 3. To Increase the Social Functioning of Three High-School Girls Referred for Disruptive Behavior in the Classroom

Background Information.   Sandy, Ellen, and Helen had much in common. They were friends largely because their antisocial behavior had alienated them from their peers. Each girl would turn 16 before the end of the school year. As eighth-graders, they were two years behind grade and did not plan to continue school beyond their sixteenth birthday. Ellen had been born in this community and lived with her mother, step-father, a 14-year-old brother Frank (also in the

eighth grade), and an 18-year-old brother who was a senior in the high school. There was constant conflict among family members. Helen lived with her father in a cabin partially destroyed by fire. Her father entertained a variety of women and Helen was expected to be the housekeeper. Sandy lived with her mother in their summer cottage. She had experienced difficulty in the urban school district where she and her mother formerly lived. Her father was a chauffeur for a company and could not leave that community. Sandy was given the alternative of leaving the community or being sent to a juvenile facility. The mother had taken Sandy to the Alpha Community hoping that the new environment would make a difference. Testing indicated that Sandy and Helen possessed average ability but were underachieving academically. Ellen's tests indicated a learning disability and a need

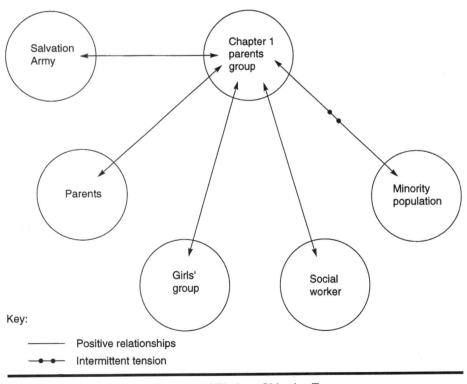

Key:

—————— Positive relationships

—•—•— Intermittent tension

FIGURE A.3 Ecomap of the Outcome of Work on Objective Two

for special education services. All three girls were discouraged about school and said that they would quit when they were 16. In one of the social worker's early meetings with the group, the girls confided that they felt dumb and not valued by anyone. They said they were expected to have deviant behavior and did not know why they should disappoint anyone. Because their families had limited incomes, the girls had little spending money. The result was that they could not participate in some of the community activities with peers, and they were bored. Behaviors of the girls that the teachers reported as offensive included not completing work, making loud noises in class, and swearing at classmates and teachers. Ellen was excluded from her home economics class because she used profane language when her teacher told her that she would have to tear out the stitching in a pair of slacks and start over. The three were restricted to the school grounds during the lunch hour because they had been caught shoplifting from seven of the eight shops on Main Street during lunch hour.

The social worker and the girls identified three objectives to achieve during the school year: (1) to gain status among peers and teachers, (2) to increase spending money, and (3) to decrease isolation and boredom.

Interventions (Activities)

1. Arranging for Ellen to have individual tutoring by the special education resource teacher (This followed her being certified as learning disabled and the development of an Individualized Education Program.)
2. Inviting teachers to meet with the girls individually, so they could discuss their concerns (Some agreements were made between the girls and the teachers. Some issues were raised and some were not, but communication was improved.)
3. Broadening the scope of the tutoring program, which provided high school credit, and had been developed the year before by the counselor and the parents' group coordinator to in-

clude achieving high school pupils as tutors (Each girl received an assignment appropriate to her interests and abilities. The social worker arranged in-service training sessions for all of the tutors and established feedback sessions that included the tutors, Mrs. Brown, the social worker, and the counselor. Each girl received an "A" in the course. This was the first "A" Ellen or any member of her family had ever received.)

4. Helping the parents' groups make gifts for their children (Ellen designed a drawstring purse and made it from a donated deerskin. She did such an excellent job that when she showed her work to her home economics teacher, she was readmitted to the class.)
5. Forming a group patterned after a Junior Achievement Club (Group members decided to make items that could be sold to friends as well as tourists during the tourist season. The owner of the crafts store, the one shop from which the girls had not shoplifted, agreed to sponsor the venture. He not only sold them materials and advised them on profitable items to make, but also placed the items in his shop for sale and gave them the profits. There were ups and downs in this experience, but the girls worked together for a common cause. They gained an awareness of their abilities and limitations, and in the process of displaying and selling their items, they gained some respect from their teachers and peers. There was a small profit—not enough to meet all their financial requirements—but they felt that the effort had been worthwhile.)
6. Holding counseling interviews with the families throughout the year

Outcomes.   At the end of the school year, the three girls evaluated their year's work together. They said that they felt better about themselves and felt that others viewed them differently than before. They decided not to drop out of school although they were now 16 years old. They had some new interests and enjoyed the tutoring and craft projects. They had developed positive relationships with the storekeeper and with some of their teachers. They still felt bored in the evenings and still did not have spending money, but they now knew there were opportunities and they could be rewarded for their efforts. Helen returned to live with her mother in another town as a result of a plan that she and the social worker had developed with her father and the juvenile authorities. There were still some incidents in the school, and the girls' grades, although improved,

were marginal; however, teachers and the principal reported significant changes in the behavior of each girl.

The outcomes are shown in the ecomap (Figure A.4). The areas of intermittent tension remain, but if the girls receive continued support, the tension need not increase. Compare Figure A.5 with Figure A.1 and note the changes in interactions among the various systems following social work intervention.

REFERENCES

Hartman, A. (1978, October). Diagrammic assessment of family relationships. *Social Casework, 59,* 465–476.

Johnson, L. (1983). *Social work practice: A generalist approach.* Boston: Allyn & Bacon.

Lauffer, A. (1982). *Assessment tools for practitioners, managers, and trainers.* Beverly Hills, CA: Sage.

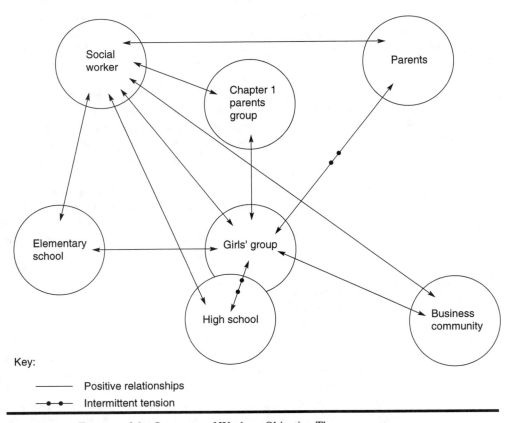

FIGURE A.4 Ecomap of the Outcomes of Work on Objective Three

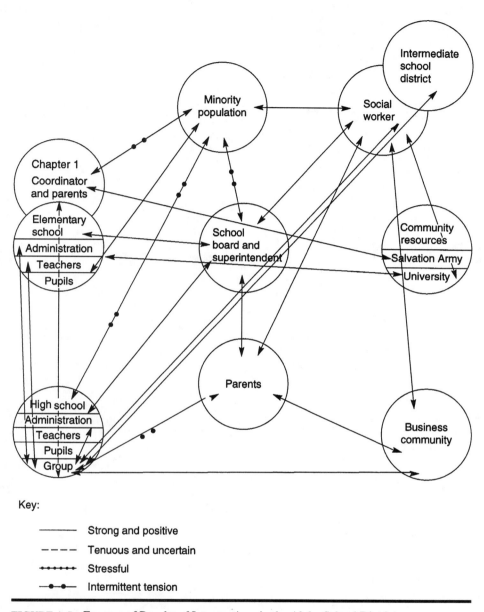

Key:

——————   Strong and positive

– – – –   Tenuous and uncertain

+++++++   Stressful

—•—•—   Intermittent tension

FIGURE A.5   Ecomap of Results of Interventions in the Alpha School District

AN EXAMPLE OF URBAN PRACTICE

The following example of practice illustrates the development and implementation of a design for social work service for an inner-city elementary school in a large metropolitan school district. In this example, the school social worker is a member of the school's newly formed site-based management team.

IDENTIFYING DATA

The School

Located in the center of the city, Epsilon public school serves 500 kindergarten through fifth-grade children. The building and playground fill one city block and overlook an expressway on the east side. Across the street on the south side of the school there is a complex of buildings which once housed TB and mentally ill patients. Utilizing about half of the facility, the complex now provides outpatient physical and mental health services, department of vital statistics, and adult education programs. On the west side, across from the school, there is a fire station. A small fenced-in playground is behind the school. The school was built in the 1920s and has wide hallways and high ceilings. It has been well maintained. The rooms were recently painted, and there are decorative bulletin boards in each room. The art teacher has worked with her fourth- and fifth-grade classes to design and paint murals on the walls in the hall depicting the accomplishments of various Americans. The teaching staff consists of classroom teachers for the kindergarten through third grade. There are English, social studies, science, music, and art classroom teachers for the fourth- and fifth-grade students. Fourth- and fifth-grade classrooms

have scheduled use of a computer laboratory. A staff person is responsible for this curricular area. There is a resource room and teacher for high incidence special education students. She not only instructs students on a scheduled basis, but also provides classroom teachers with appropriate teaching material when special education students are mainstreamed or included in a general education classroom. Support team services are provided to students based on needs of the student and classroom situation.

The school is at full capacity of 500 elementary students, with an average class size of 30 students. There are two kindergartens, each with a morning and afternoon session. The first-through third-grade students are in self-contained classrooms, while the curriculum of fourth and fifth grades are on a platoon system where the students as a class move to music, art, science, and computer classrooms. Classrooms share bathroom facilities. All students stay for lunch and are supervised by two school aides. The cultural composition of the student population is 60 percent African American, 20 percent Hispanic, 5 percent Native American, 10 percent Asian, and 5 percent white.

The teachers have an average of 5 years teaching experience. Most of the teachers take university courses toward continued certification or an advanced degree in education. The principal, an African-American female, is a seasoned educator with a strong commitment to meet the educational and socio-emotional needs of her students. She is open to any programs that will assist her in achieving the goals of the school.

During the previous year, the school district, in its search for new ways to restructure the educational program to achieve more effective educational outcomes, elected to use a site-based management approach. Under this management system, a team of school staff, parents, and students is empowered with the authority to tailor its educational program to the needs of their students. The management team consists of the principal, two teachers, parents, students, and community leaders elected or appointed by their group, plus a member of student support services, which in this school is the school social worker. The site-based management team developed a school mission statement and established goals for the year. Through the efforts of the management team, a crisis plan was revised, and on the recommendation of the school social worker, the services of the district Student Assistant Program (SAP) were requested.

The Epsilon school social worker, who is an African-American female, has an MSW degree and has been a practicing social worker for 10 years. She previously worked with children and youth in a private multiservice agency and has been with this school system for the past 5 years; however, this is her second year in this building. She is assigned to the building Monday and Thursday mornings and Friday afternoons. She has two second-year graduate social work interns, a white male and female, both in their thirties. They are assigned to Epsilon school all day on Thursdays and Fridays. The social worker has a pager which makes her accessible any time when there is a question or concern requiring her attention. The social workers in this school system are under the supervision of a department head, and the social workers' plans for service are reviewed by the department supervisor as well as by the site-based management team.

Other physical and mental health support services include the school psychologist who is available from the psychology department of the school district for testing students referred for special education and a school nurse from the public health department. Although all of the social workers in the district have training in crisis intervention, district teams are available when a crisis of magnitude occurs. There is an extensive preschool program (Head Start, a state program for high-risk preschool children, and a program for pre-primary impaired children) in the school district that employs a staff of social workers, who in addition to their other duties, are responsible for facilitating the transition of preschool children to the kindergarten. The district Student Assistance Program (SAP), staffed by social workers, provides a comprehensive substance abuse prevention and intervention program for students that is available to individual schools on request. A special education districtwide social work staff collaborates with the school psychologist to make decisions about eligibility for and placement in a special education program and inclusion decisions and re-evaluations of students who are in the program.

The Community

Housing in the community consists of small apartment buildings, duplexes, and a few single family dwellings. Although most of the property is adequately maintained, the community is dotted with vacant, deteriorating buildings. City services are minimal. Trash is sometimes not picked up for weeks and street lights are undependable. Unemployment runs 40 percent, with 50 percent of the residents on some form of welfare. There is a homeless shelter in the neighborhood and several group homes for the mentally retarded. Fifteen percent of the residents are retired, supported by Social Security. There is a senior citizens club in the community operated through the department of recreation. A Boys Club is the only recreation facility in the community with the exception of summer programs operated by the department of recreation. As in many inner-city communities where poor economic conditions spawn crime and discontent, the majority of households own some type of weapon. Iron bars are on first-floor windows and doors to provide protection from intruders. Five unattended children died in a fire when the bars prevented them from escaping the building. Three of the children attended Epsilon. Because of the increase in youth violence and substance abuse related crimes, a community collaborative is in the process of development. At this point it is composed of representatives of city departments such as the Youth Division of the Police, Department of Parks and Recreation, Housing Department, Department of Social Services, Health Department, and Department of Public Safety. Representatives of the Boys Club and the Neighborhood Service Organization are active members. The churches and community are represented by their leaders. The three public schools within the boundaries of this collaborative or coalition of services to the community are represented by an administrator and interdisciplinary team member from each school. The collaborative is in the process of assessing social needs of the community and developing an action plan to promote a stronger, healthier, and safer community.

PLAN FOR SOCIAL WORK SERVICES BASED ON A NEEDS ASSESSMENT

The following design for service is the result of program decisions made by the Epsilon site-based management team. The plan is social work's contribution to Epsilon's goals to maintain a safe and nurturing environment and to improve social and academic skills of the students. These two goals are implementation goals of the school district's overall goal: "To Promote Student Success." The activities outlined evolved from an assessment of the Epsilon school and community using outlines detailed in Chapter 11, Tables 2 and 3. Transactions between and among various systems were examined and evaluated with a view to minimizing stress factors and increasing coping abilities of students, utilizing the resources of administration, school staff, support services, families, and community. In addition to implementing the plan, the school social worker carried other responsibilities, such as responding to crisis situations, consultation, coordination with school and the various social work staff members, supervision of the two graduate social work interns, and attention to X number of referrals.

School Social Work Service Plan for Epsilon School for the School Year of 200___

OBJECTIVE	PRESENTING PROBLEM	INTERVENTIONS	WITH WHOM?	EVALUATION CRITERIA
1. To increase coping ability of students moving from one school or educational program to another by facilitating the transition process.	Increase in student turnover during the school year. Last year there were a number of preventable incidents involving teachers and students who were not prepared for new members of the class. At the same time students transferring to other schools because of family moves or returning from mental health or correctional facilities or being mainstreamed from special education programs showed signs of stress due to the absence of preparation for the move.	1. Develop a welcoming committee composed of student volunteers. Provide a training program and monthly progress report meeting. Include a buddy mentor system. 2. Report to teachers at a faculty meeting on progress and discuss ways in which new students can feel welcome and those leaving feel support for the move. 3. Conduct a class meeting to discuss the part classmates play to help the new student succeed when a special education student is integrated into the general education class. 4. Provide support services to assist the teacher when requested. 5. Prepare a small pamphlet for parents on ways in which they can support their child at the time of a transition.	Social worker and one intern will take responsibility for implementing plan in cooperation with teachers and the principal.	Observation report. Self reports of students at the end of a semester.

School Social Work Service Plan for Epsilon School for the School Year of 200___   (Continued)

OBJECTIVE	PRESENTING PROBLEM	INTERVENTIONS	WITH WHOM?	EVALUATION CRITERIA
2. To increase "on task" behavior of 40 students referred for disruptive behavior in afternoon classes.	Many teacher referrals indicated a pattern of behavior problems in the afternoon. Due to recent budget cuts only two aides are available to supervise the 500 students who stay for lunch. To prevent fights and disruption students are not permitted to talk or engage in any physical exercise during the 60 minute lunch hour. For 30 min., 250 students are in gym with hands on head while the other 250 eat lunch. At the end of 30 min. the two groups are reversed. Consequently, pent-up energy is expressed in acting out behavior in afternoon classes.	1. Locate outside resource to organize lunchtime activities. A possibility is the Afro-American fraternity at the nearby university that is looking for a project in the urban school system. If not available identify other possibilities. 2. Monitor the program by providing feedback sessions with those leading activities and make changes if necessary.	Planning committee: Principal, university fraternity leadership, lunchroom aides, and social worker as chairperson. Social worker and principal coordinate and supervise group that provides the lunchroom activity program.	Reports of teachers. Reduction in referrals with same concerns.
3. To increase positive relationships between teachers, students, and parents.	Conversation in teachers' room frequently focuses on desire to increase positive relationship with parents and students. Questionnaires to teachers indicated the same desire.	1. Develop in-service program for teachers focused on interviewing skills with parents at parent-teacher conferences. 2. Arrange for course from university (with credits for teacher certification) on managing a classroom as a group.	Social worker as in-service leader. Social worker as liaison with the university.	Questionnaire and sample interviews with teachers, parents, and students.

(continued)

School Social Work Service Plan for Epsilon School for the School Year of 200___ (Continued)

OBJECTIVE	PRESENTING PROBLEM	INTERVENTIONS	WITH WHOM?	EVALUATION CRITERIA
		3. Suggest to teachers and principal that fifth- and sixth-grade students and teachers spend a week at the city camp together.	Social worker as consultant and social work interns as camp counselors for the week.	
4. To increase completion of homework by referred students living in X apartment house.	Pattern of incomplete homework by the ten students who all live in the same apartment building.	1. Contract with apartment manager to see if space is available to use as a study room. 2. Recruit at least five parents willing to supervise according to a schedule developed by them. 3. Meet with parents and teachers identifying ways to help students with homework. 4. Include students in final planning.	Social worker to take main responsibility for developing the program. Social work interns will take responsibility for periodic meetings with parents and apartment manager, with parents and teachers, and with parents, teachers, and students. Interns will conduct support sessions for the parent tutors.	Teacher records of completed homework of participating students.
5. To increase age appropriate communication skills among six siblings of the Johnson family.	Six of the Johnson's 12 children were in Epsilon school. Each of them was referred by his or her teacher because of a lack of verbal communication skills. Instead of asking another child for something, they hit them. Hitting was not an angry act	1. Develop intervention plan following an assessment of each child and the family. 2. Twice a week lunch time group meetings of a sibling group. Use parallel activities and gradually increase activities which require interaction.	Social worker and both interns.	Three interrupted time series measurements of each sibling in classroom and on playground. Three interviews with parents on change in verbal interactions and physical interactions. Use of an ecogram at every third group meeting.

School Social Work Service Plan for Epsilon School for the School Year of 200___   *(Continued)*

OBJECTIVE	PRESENTING PROBLEM	INTERVENTIONS	WITH WHOM?	EVALUATION CRITERIA
	but in place of the verbal word. They were each able to talk but had developed a pattern in the family that spilled into the school. The children ranged in age from 5 to 12 with one set of twins in the third grade. The father worked two jobs to make expenses meet, and the mother was overwhelmed by her responsibilities. The children did household chores in isolation. For example, 12-year-old Yolanda was responsible for washing dishes for 14 people every night by herself. Testing indicated average ability of each of the children and each had passed each grade, but teachers were worried about their inappropriate communication skills.	3. Collaborate with the classroom teachers of the siblings to discuss ways in which they could increase positive verbal interaction and decrease physical interaction. 4. Conferences with Mrs. Johnson to support her coping abilities. She was eager for assistance. 5. Culminating activity at the end of the school year such as an invitation to parents to lunch prepared by the sibling group.		

ASSESSMENT OF ADAPTIVE BEHAVIOR AND INDIVIDUAL EDUCATION PROGRAM

PRACTICE ILLUSTRATION

The case of Maggie illustrates the process as it is prescribed by the federal law, including the procedural steps and the ways in which social work services can become an integral part of the educational decision-making process.

Background

Maggie, aged 14 years and 7 months, has been in the EMH program for several years. She was assigned to a full-time special education class when she was identified as needing special education services in the fourth grade. She is now a ninth grader, and she has been referred by her special education teacher for a reevaluation, to ascertain whether modifications should be made in her instructional program.

Maggie comes from a large family. There is no father present, and the mother is employed as an unskilled laborer outside the home. No known physical problems or traumatic life experiences account for Maggie's handicap. A recent physical examination revealed that she is developing according to the pattern of other children in her age group. Her mother is very concerned that Maggie should acquire skills to enable her to be self-sufficient and that she have more interaction with nonhandicapped students before entering high school.

Assessment Data

The social worker completed and updated information about Maggie's home situation and conducted an assessment of her adaptive behavior. The American Association of Mental Deficiency Scale, Public School Version, was used to ascertain information about her adaptive behavior. This scale showed Maggie to be above average in independent functioning, economic activity, language development, vocational activity, self-direction, assumption of responsibility, and socialization. The final scores indicated that she exhibited appropriate adaptive behaviors in the environment outside the school. She was responsible and took care of herself and others without a lot of supervision. She initiated tasks and worked until they were completed.

The psychometric tests administered by the psychologist showed that Maggie was performing as follows:

Weschsler Intelligence Scale for Children (Revised):

Verbal IQ	68
Performance IQ	63
Full Scale IQ	63
Median Verbal Test	Age 8–10
Median Performance Test	Age 6–7

Wide Range Achievement Test (1978 Norms):

	Standardized		
	Grade	Score	Percentile
Reading (Level II)	5.7	83	23
Spelling (Level II)	4.8	78	7
Arithmetic (Level I)	4.5	—	—

Note: Level I Arithmetic was administered because of the level of difficulty of Level II. She performed 3-digit addition, 2-digit multiplication, and 2-digit subtraction. No fraction problems were completed.

A projective test (on the subject of "How I Feel about School") was also administered. The results indicated that she was rather reticent in responding; she offered no spontaneous conversation and did not elaborate in giving answers. She found math and reading very difficult but did not know why. Most important, she thought she was liked by others, and most of the time she liked being in school.

The psychologist concluded that Maggie needed help in the following areas:

1. Expressive and receptive vocabulary development
2. Attention to visual information
3. Learning units of measurements
4. Reading comprehension

Multidisciplinary Staff Meeting

A staff meeting was called following the collection of information obtained from parent, student, and teacher interviews; social development study; psychometric testing; and an assessment of adaptive behavior. Participants included the school social worker, psychologist, Maggie's special education teacher, the invited regular education staff, a school administrator, her mother, and Maggie.

Each participant shared the information that he or she had collected and gave a recommendation. Both the mother and Maggie had an opportunity to share information and to participate in the discussion and final recommendation. In other words, a consensus was reached.

The final recommendations were:

1. Maggie is still eligible for special education classes (EMH).
2. More emphasis needs to be placed on vocabulary and reading comprehension.
3. Maggie should be integrated into regular classes (such as home economics, art, physical education, and music) as much as possible.
4. When Maggie enters high school, she and her parent should consider enrollment in a vocational education program.

Individual Educational Program

These recommendations were then translated into instructional goals and included in Maggie's IEP (Individual Education Program), which was latter signed by all who participated in the meeting. Examples of the instructional goals are:

Goal 1: To improve reading comprehension and vocabulary skills in order to be able to answer literal questions after reading a chapter or story.
Criterion of successful performance: Student will achieve a 90 percent correct response rate.

Goal 2: To define a word verbally from a unit.
Criterion of successful performance: She will achieve a score of 85 percent or better on written vocabulary tests.

Goal 3: To match words with their meanings.
Criterion of successful performance: She will achieve an accuracy rate of 75 percent or better on tests.

The school social worker's role will be to support the student during the transition from a specialized classroom to a part-time special class assignment. Further, he or she will consult and collaborate with the special education teacher, regular teacher, and mother, for facilitating the transition. Specifically, the school social worker's major annual goal will be:

Goal 1: For Maggie to increase positive social relations (that is, number of positive interactions) with nondisabled peers through interaction experiences in a group with the social worker. The group will consist of both special education and regular education students.
Criterion of successful performance: Maggie's interaction (the number of times that she speaks) with a nondisabled group member will increase by 50 percent during the life of the group experience.